Lecture Notes in Computer Science 15598

The series Lecture Notes in Computer Science (LNCS), including its subseries Lecture Notes in Artificial Intelligence (LNAI) and Lecture Notes in Bioinformatics (LNBI), has established itself as a medium for the publication of new developments in computer science and information technology research, teaching, and education.

LNCS enjoys close cooperation with the computer science R & D community, the series counts many renowned academics among its volume editors and paper authors, and collaborates with prestigious societies. Its mission is to serve this international community by providing an invaluable service, mainly focused on the publication of conference and workshop proceedings and postproceedings. LNCS commenced publication in 1973.

Arpita Patra
Editor

Topics in Cryptology – CT-RSA 2025

Cryptographers' Track at the RSA Conference 2025
San Francisco, CA, USA, April 28–May 1, 2025
Proceedings

Springer

Editor
Arpita Patra
Indian Institute of Science
Bengaluru, Karnataka, India

ISSN 0302-9743 ISSN 1611-3349 (electronic)
Lecture Notes in Computer Science
ISBN 978-3-031-88660-7 ISBN 978-3-031-88661-4 (eBook)
https://doi.org/10.1007/978-3-031-88661-4

This Springer imprint is published by the registered company Springer Nature Switzerland AG
The registered company address is: Gewerbestrasse 11, 6330 Cham, Switzerland

Preface

The RSA Conference is the premiere trade show for the security industry since 1991, hosting over 40,000 attendees each year from industry, government, and academia. The Cryptographers' Track (CT-RSA) is RSAC's venue for scientific papers on cryptography. This volume represents the proceedings of the 2025 edition of the Cryptographers' Track at the RSA Conference, which took place in San Francisco, California, USA during April 28–May 1, 2025. We received 51 submissions. Two submissions were deemed out of scope and desk rejected by the program chair. The remaining 49 full papers were each assigned three reviewers. Papers that included a program committee member as author were assigned an additional reviewer. The reviewing process was double-blind, and carried out using the HotCRP conference management system. We followed the IACR policy for conflicts of interest.

The review process was concluded by selecting 16 papers for acceptance and 1 paper as conditionally accepted. These 17 papers comprised the final scientific program. The acceptance rate was $17/48 = 35.4\%$. CT-RSA would not have been possible without the valuable contributions of many volunteers. My sincere thanks go out to all program committee members, as well as external reviewers, for their consistently thoughtful, constructive reviews, and for actively participating in the paper selection discussions. Special thanks are due to:

- the committee members who shepherded conditionally accepted papers;
- Mike Rosulek (CT-RSA 2023 program chair) and Elisabeth Oswald (CT-RSA 2024 program chair) for graciously sharing institutional knowledge about the role of program chair
- the RSA Conference team, in particular, Samantha Mello, Christie Ross, Bree LaBollita, Kacy Zurkus, and Britta J. Glade, for their support with scheduling and procedural matters.

February 2025 — Arpita Patra

Organization

Program Committee Chair

Arpita Patra	Indian Institute of Science, Bangalore, India

Program Committee

Riham AlTawy	University of Victoria, Canada
Elena Andreeva	TU Wien, Austria
Shi Bai	Florida Atlantic University, USA
Shivam Basin	NTU Singapore, Singapore
Lejla Batina	Radboud University, The Netherlands
Sarani Bhattacharya	IIT Kharagpur, India
Michele Ciampi	University of Edinburgh, UK
Sofia Celi	Brave, Portugal
Suvradip Chakraborty	Visa Research, USA
Liqun Chen	University of Surrey, UK
Avijit Dutta	TCG Crest, India
Maria Eichlseder	Graz University of Technology, Austria
Patrick Felke	University of Applied Sciences Emden/Leer, Germany
Antonio Flórez-Gutiérrez	NTT Social Informatics Laboratories, Japan
Julius Hermelink	MPI-SP, Germany
Javier Herranz	Universitat Politècnica de Catalunya, Spain
Tetsu Iwata	Nagoya University, Japan
Fuyuki Kitagawa	NTT Social Informatics Laboratories, Japan
Lisa Kohl	CWI Amsterdam, The Netherlands
Péter Kutas	University of Birmingham, UK and Eötvös Loránd University, Hungary
Yi-fu Lai	Ruhr-Universität Bochum, Germany
Fenghao Liu	Washington State University, USA
Chen-Da Liu-Zhang	Lucerne University of Applied Sciences and Arts & Web3 Foundation, Switzerland
Victor Mateu	Technology Innovation Institute, UAE
Brice Minaud	Inria and ENS, France
Amir Moradi	TU Darmstad, Germany
David Naccache	École normale supérieure, France

Khoa Nguyen	University of Wollongong, Australia
Anca Nitulescu	Input Output Global, France
Sikhar Patranabis	IBM Research India, India
Eduardo Persichetti	Florida Atlantic University, USA
Divya Ravi	CCI Amsterdam, The Netherlands
Chester Rebeiro	IIT Madras, India
Amin Sakzad	Monash University, Australia
Patrick Schaumont	Worcester Polytechnic Institute, USA
Dominique Schröder	TU Wien, Austria
Mark Simkin	Ethereum Foundation, Switzerland
Nigel Smart	KU Leuven and Zama, Belgium
Benjamin Smith	Inria, École Polytechnique, France
Fang Song	Portland State University, USA
Yifan Song	Tsinghua University, China
Pante Stanica	Naval Postgrad Institute, USA
Igors Stepanovs	Amazon, USA
Sri AravindaKrishnan Thyagarajan	University of Sydney, Australia
Ni Trieu	Arizona State University, USA
Srinivas Vivek	IIIT-Bangalore, India
Rupeng Yang	University of Wollongong, Australia

Additional Reviewers

Simon Gerhalter
Vincent Hwang
Kelsey Melissaris
Lorenzo Magliocco
Rutvik Patel
Harshal Bhadreshkumar Shah
Yu Shen
Nitin Singh
Yangguang Tian
Bart van Vulpen
Yalan Wang
Tiancheng Xie
Aaram Yun
Dandan Yuan
Yijian Zhang

Contents

Cryptanalysis

The Window Heuristic: Automating Differential Trail Search in ARX Ciphers with Partial Linearization Trade-offs

Emanuele Bellini[1], David Gerault[1], Juan Grados[1](✉), and Thomas Peyrin[2]

[1] Cryptography Research Centre, Technology Innovation Institute, Abu Dhabi, UAE
{emanuele.bellini,david.gerault,juan.grados}@tii.ae
[2] Nanyang Technological University, Singapore, Singapore
thomas.peyrin@ntu.edu.sg

Abstract. The search for optimal differential trails for ARX ciphers is known to be difficult and scale poorly as the word size (and the branching through the carries of modular additions) increases. To overcome this problem, one may approximate the modular addition with the XOR operation, a process called linearization. The immediate drawback of this approach is that many valid and good trails are discarded.

In this work, we explore different partial linearization trade-offs to model the modular addition through the *window heuristic*, which restricts carry propagation to windows of w_s consecutive positions. This strategy enables the exploration of full linearization ($w_s = 0$), normal modelling ($w_s = n$), and all the different trade-offs between completeness and speed in between.

We give the corresponding SAT and MILP model and their parallel versions, and apply them to ChaCha, SPECK, LEA, and HIGHT. Our method greatly outperforms all previous modeling of modular addition. In particular, we find the first differential path for 4 rounds of ChaCha with a probability greater than 2^{-256}, and a corresponding 6 rounds boomerang distinguisher. This indicates that purely differential-based attacks have the potential to become competitive with differential-linear attacks, currently, the best-known attacks against ChaCha and other ARX ciphers.

On SPECK, we find many improvements over the state-of-the-art in terms of speed of the differential trail search in the single-key setting and new upper bound probabilities in the related-key setting.

Finally, we exhibit an improved key recovery attack on reduced LEA.

Keywords: differential cryptanalysis · modular addition · ARX · MILP · SAT

1 Introduction

Addition-Rotation-XOR (ARX) ciphers have become popular primitives in the community for their good performances in software, as they are constructed

A. Patra (Ed.): CT-RSA 2025, LNCS 15598, pp. 3–26, 2025.
https://doi.org/10.1007/978-3-031-88661-4_1

upon CPU-friendly components. Despite their relative simplicity, they can provide good resistance against well-known cryptanalysis. A famous example is the cipher ChaCha20 [8], which is widely used by several protocols such as SSH and in the more recent version of the TLS protocol, TLSv1.3.

Together with linear cryptanalysis [35], differential cryptanalysis [9] is among the most famous and powerful attack techniques against symmetric-key ciphers, including ARX ones. The main preparation of a differential attack is to find a differential path that will occur with a relatively high probability. Such differential paths can, in turn, be used to build a more advanced distinguisher, or a global key-recovery attack (for example, using probabilistic neutral bits against ChaCha [2]).

In the past decade, we have seen a strong push by the community towards the usage of automated solvers, based on Boolean Satisfiability (SAT), its generalization to Modulo Theory (SMT), Mixed Integer Linear Programming (MILP), or Constraint Programming (CP), to look for good differential paths [25,36,42]. The task of building a differential path search algorithm is essentially reduced to the task of efficiently producing accurate modeling of the path search problem, and many recent works have been devoted to improving such modeling [34,40,45,50].

Compared to Substitution-Permutation Network (SPN) ciphers, in ARX ciphers the study of differential properties has been shown to be more complex. This is mainly because of the usage of modular addition. In particular, the number of possible input/output differential pairs, i.e. the number of entries in the Differential Distribution Table (DDT), of a nonlinear vectorial Boolean function (such as an S-Box or a modular addition) is exponential in the input/output bit length. A consequence of this is the exponential explosion of the tree of the possible differential paths. To overcome this explosion, researchers try to discard in advance paths that lead to low probability. This is achieved in essentially two ways: (1) considering entries of the DDT that only have a probability above a certain threshold [10,13,15]; (2) approximating the modular addition with the XOR operation, a process called *linearization* [2,17,24,48,49]. The main drawback of both approaches is that good trails might be discarded. In the first case, this can happen because a globally optimal path (i.e. with optimal probability) might have local probabilities that are not optimal. In the second case, local high probabilities might simply be missed.

In this paper, we focus on the second approach, and explore various levels of linearization of the modular addition through a heuristic termed the *window heuristic*. This heuristic provides a good and adaptable balance between the retention of the non-linearity of the modular addition and the size of the search tree. The idea is to let the modular addition behave non-linearly only for a fixed number of consecutive bits. Throughout this paper, we refer to this limit as the window size, denoted as w_s. Applying our technique to a selection of notable ARX ciphers, we obtain improvements over the state-of-the-art, by rediscovering known differential trails faster and by finding new differential trails.

1.1 Related Works on Automated Differential Path Search Tools for ARX Ciphers

The automation of differential characteristic search in cryptanalysis is crucial, reducing both time and error for crypyanalysts. However, it remains challenging to find efficient differential trails for ARX ciphers with large word sizes, such as ChaCha, which has seen limited analysis against pure differential cryptanalysis [1,7]. Early methods relying on local constraint propagation [19,30] were restricted by engineering limitations, unlike later approaches using solvers like SAT, SMT, MILP, and CP. Biryukov *et al.* [10,13,15] advanced the search by approximating modular addition as a large S-Box and employing a partial difference distribution table (pDDT), significantly enhancing the search process.

Subsequent research further integrated solver-based techniques. Mouha *et al.* [36] used SAT solvers for ARX ciphers such as Salsa20, building on Lipmaa and Moriai's XOR-differential probability model [33]. Fu *et al.* [25] and Song *et al.* [42] used MILP methods to uncover improved differential and linear trails for SPECK, while Monte Carlo Tree Search techniques [6,23] refined differential path discovery for LEA. More recently, Sadeghi *et al.* [41] validated differential trails using MILP, and Liu *et al.* [34] split modular additions into smaller parts to identify differential and linear trails for SPECK and HIGHT. Notably, SAT-based improvements such as sequential encoding for Matsui's bounding condition [16,45] and Laurent *et al.*'s clustering technique [31] further optimized differential cryptanalysis for ciphers like SIMON and Simeck.

Other approaches tried to tackle the modular addition component by linearizing it, essentially by replacing it with an XOR. This strategy was extensively used for the cryptanalysis of the `MD-SHA` family of ARX hash functions [17,48,49]. Specifically, in those works the authors explore differential cryptanalysis methods for MD5, SHA-0, SHA-1 focusing on the linearization of modular addition. They induce modular addition behave as a XOR linear operation under certain conditions. This is achieved by strategically applying perturbations and corrections to the input, ensuring that no carry propagation occurs during modular addition.

In [24], Fischer *et al.* used this technique to improve the search for differential trails in `Salsa20` and `TSC-4`. Similarly, [2] Aumasson *et al.* showed that approximating the modular addition as an XOR improves the time complexity of searching for collisions in `Rumba`. Interestingly, in both papers, the authors remarked that this technique worked well only when applied to the initial rounds. Indeed, the approximation does not remain valuable after a few rounds, after the diffusion property of the modular addition starts to kick in.

1.2 Our Contributions

- **The Window Heuristic** We propose the *window heuristic* to partially linearize modular additions in differential trails search, and the corresponding SAT and MILP models and their parallel versions (https://github.com/Crypto-TII/modadd_window_heuristic). In the window heuristic, the carry

propagation is bounded to w_s consecutive positions, with $w_s = -1$ denoting no heuristic used, $w_s = 0$ corresponding to linearization, $w_s = n$ to regular modular addition modelling, and the values in between being explored for the first time. In other words, if the window heuristic is not used, it is equivalent to the regular modular addition modeling.
- **Differential Cryptanalysis of `ChaCha`** We demonstrate the power of window heuristic by proposing the first 4-round single-key differential trail with probability higher than 2^{-256}, improving the state of the art from 2^{-316} to 2^{-217}; for 3 rounds, we improve the known differential bounds from 2^{-147} to 2^{-120} (Table 4). In addition, we propose a boomerang distinguisher for 6 rounds (Table 7);
- **Single-Key Differential Cryptanalysis of `SPECK`** Using the parallelized version of the window heuristic, we retrieve known results with speedups of up to 5x (and an outlier of 152x), using 5 cores, compared to the state of the art (Table 1);
- **Related-Key Differential Cryptanalysis of `SPECK`** Using the window heuristic, we improve the known bounds for related-key differential trails (Table 3); in particular, we improve by a factor 2^{12} for SPECK-32/64, propose the first 16-round trail for SPECK-48/96, and improve the best 19-round trail for SPECK-128/256 by a factor 2^{19};
- **Single-Key Differential Cryptanalysis of `LEA`** Using the window heuristic, we improve the known bound for 13 rounds of LEA-128 by a factor 2^{11}; this differential trail is used to build a key recovery for 14 rounds, with time and data complexity $2^{111.97}$; these results are summarized in Table 10.
- **Single-key Differential Cryptanalysis of `HIGHT`** Using the window heuristic, we improve the search speed for trails up to 11 rounds. On the other hand, for 12 rounds, our tool with window sizes 0, 1, 2, and 3 do not retrieve the state-of-the-art trails; in fact, the best known 12-round trail for `HIGHT` contains a window size of 5, which is out of the capacities of our tool at the moment.

In the main contributions cited above, our work is improving differential probabilities by utilizing a window size of 0 or 1 in our heuristic approach. We emphasize that this exploration into the value of 1 was previously unconsidered. It enabled us to uncover more efficient differential trails in ARX ciphers, enhancing both the field's understanding and the efficiency benchmarks of differential cryptanalysis on ARX ciphers. For instance, using the window size 1, we improve the best-known differential trail probability for `ChaCha` by an impressive factor 2^{98}. While extending the window size beyond 1, our research observed comparable results to those of previous works, yet notably, our methodology achieved these outcomes faster in most instances. This advancement not only prompts a reassessment of existing differential search models for ARX ciphers but also provides a strong basis for future research.

We would like to highlight that, when possible, the differential trails found in this work were verified using the tool presented in [41].

Finally, we note that an extended version of this paper is available at [5].

1.3 Outline

In Sect. 2, we first provide some preliminaries. We introduce our new strategy, the window heuristic, in Sect. 3 and explain how to encode it in SAT and MILP. We apply this new method to find XOR-differential trails and various attacks on selected ARX ciphers in Sect. 4 and provide our conclusions and future work in Sect. 5.

2 Background

In this section, we provide a brief description of differential and boomerang distinguishers, and of existing SAT and MILP encoding techniques for searching XOR-differential trails on ARX ciphers. The studied ciphers, `ChaCha`, `SPECK`, `LEA` are very well-known, and described in the extended version of this paper [5].

2.1 Differential and Boomerang Distinguishers

Differential cryptanalysis is a well-established cryptanalytic technique introduced by Biham and Shamir in the early 1990s [9]. It examines how differences in pairs of plaintexts propagate through the encryption process to produce differences in ciphertexts. The core concept involves analyzing an input difference, denoted as $\Delta X = X \oplus X'$, where X and X' are two different plaintexts. By observing how this input difference evolves into an output difference $\Delta Y = Y \oplus Y'$, cryptanalysts aim to find high-probability differential characteristics over multiple rounds of the cipher. The probability of a differential characteristic $(\Delta X \rightarrow \Delta Y)$ is defined as:

$$\Pr(\Delta X \rightarrow \Delta Y) = \frac{\#\text{pairs}(X, X') \text{ such that } E(X) \oplus E(X') = \Delta Y}{\#\text{all possible pairs}(X, X')}$$

where E represents the encryption function for the cipher. The goal is to identify differentials with a higher-than-random probability.

In 1999, Wagner *et al.* developed a technique called the boomerang attack [46], for ciphers where the differential probability is very small for long differential trails, but high for shorter ones. The technique considers a cipher E as two parts, the top part and the bottom part, denoted here as E_0 and E_1, with respectively r_0 and r_1 rounds. Given a differential $(\Delta_{in}, \Delta_{out})$ for E_0 with probability p, and another differential $(\nabla_{in}, \nabla_{out})$ for E_1 with probability q, the corresponding boomerang distinguisher for r_0+r_1 rounds has probability of p^2q^2, assuming that E_0 and E_1 are independent.

In 2011, Murphy found that the aforementioned assumption causes some invalid boomerang distinguishers [37]. Many studies have been done to evaluate the interaction between the differential of the top and bottom parts [11,12,22, 29], with the majority of insights being integrated into the so-called sandwich attack framework introduced in [22]. Within this perspective, a cipher is divided into three parts: $E = E_1 \circ E_m \circ E_0$. Here, E_m can be seen as a small boomerang distinguisher of probability p_m. For ciphers based on S-Boxes, and if E_m covers only a single round, the probability can be computed by analyzing each active S-Box.separately

This idea was elucidated in [21], where the switching effect was represented using a table termed the Boomerang Connectivity Table (BCT), with dimensions $2^n \times 2^n$. For components like modular addition, the table's size can grow considerably. If one interprets a modular addition component as an S-Box $M(x_0, x_1) = x_0 + x_1 \parallel x_1$ of dimension m, this table can expand to a size of 2^{128}, as observed in the case of ChaCha. In [47], a suite of methods is presented to tackle this challenge. Specifically, the authors have devised a technique that minimizes the computation of this table by employing another table named the partial boomerang connectivity table, inspired by [14]. Additionally, the authors integrated their techniques into an automated tool designed to identify boomerang distinguishers in ARX ciphers. In this paper, we used these techniques through their automated tool to construct boomerang distinguishers against ChaCha in Subsect. 4.2.

2.2 Finding XOR-Differential Trails with MILP and SAT Solvers

In this section, we review the existing MILP and SAT general modeling techniques we will use to find the differential trails for ARX ciphers: [25] for MILP and [45] for SAT.

MILP-based Automatic Search for Differential Trails. As described in [25], one can build a model for ARX ciphers using linear inequalities. In the following paragraphs, we describe the inequalities used to model each component of the ARX ciphers.

Constraints from a XOR *Operation.* For every n-bit XOR operation with input differences $\mathbf{a} \in \mathbb{F}_2^n$ and $\mathbf{b} \in \mathbb{F}_2^n$ and output difference $\mathbf{c} \in \mathbb{F}_2^n$, the constraints at bit level for j in $\{0, \ldots, n-1\}$ are

$$\begin{aligned} d_\oplus[j] &\geq a[j], & d_\oplus[j] &\geq b[j], & d_\oplus[j] &\geq c[j], \\ a[j]+b[j]+c[j] &\geq 2d_\oplus[j], & a[j]+b[j]+c[j] &\leq 2. \end{aligned} \tag{1}$$

where $d_\oplus[j]$ is a dummy variable used to verify that there are at least two active terms in $a[j] \oplus b[j] = c[j]$, every time that $a[j] \neq 0$, $b[j] \neq 0$, or $c[j] \neq 0$.

Constraints from a Modular Addition. To construct the constraints of the n-bit modular addition, we again follow [25]. We use $13 \times (n-1) + 5$ inequalities to model the modular addition operation modulo 2^n with input differences $\mathbf{a} \in \mathbb{F}_2^n$ and $\mathbf{b} \in \mathbb{F}_2^n$, and output difference $\mathbf{c} \in \mathbb{F}_2^n$. These constraints are derived from the differential propagation rules of modular addition [32]; each output bit is the XOR of two input bit, and a carry difference bit. The carry difference bit at position i can be: (1) 0 with probability 1 if $a[i-1] = b[j-1] = c[j-1] = 0$;

(2) 1 with probability 1 if $a[i-1] = b[j-1] = c[j-1] = 1$; (3) 0 or 1 with probability $\frac{1}{2}$ otherwise. For $j \in \{0, \dots, n-2\}$, the inequalities are detailed in Section A of the appendix in the extended version of this paper [5]. Among these inequalities, some involve a specific variable, $d[j]$, which represents the probability weight variable [25].

Constraints from a Rotation Operation. Assume that $Rot(\cdot, \alpha)$ is the rotation operation whose rotation amount is α. Then, for every rotation operation where the input difference is $\mathbf{a} \in \mathbb{F}_2^n$ and the output difference is $\mathbf{b} \in \mathbb{F}_2^n$, the constraints at bit level are $Rot\,(\mathbf{a}, \alpha)_j = \mathbf{b}[j]$ for j in $\{0, \dots, n-1\}$.

Objective Function. Let R be the number of rounds that we are modeling. Also, let $d[r][j]$ be the variable representing the probability weight price at round r and bit j if there is a difference in the carry bit. Then according to [25], we need to minimize $\sum_{r=1}^{R} \sum_{i=0}^{n-2} d[r][j]$.

Finding XOR-Differential Trails with SAT Solvers. In this section, we recall the methodology to model ARX ciphers with CNF clauses for the search of differential trails from [45].

CNF Clauses for the XOR *Operations.* For every n-bit XOR operation with input differences $\mathbf{a} \in \mathbb{F}_2^n$ and $\mathbf{b} \in \mathbb{F}_2^n$ and output difference $\mathbf{c} \in \mathbb{F}_2^n$, the CNF clauses at bit level for j in $\{0, \dots, n-1\}$ are:

$$\begin{aligned} a[j] \vee b[j] \vee \neg c[j] &= 1, & a[j] \vee \neg b[j] \vee c[j] &= 1, \\ \neg a[j] \vee b[j] \vee c[j] &= 1, & \neg a[j] \vee \neg b[j] \vee \neg c[j] &= 1. \end{aligned} \tag{2}$$

CNF Clauses for the Modular Addition Operations. For every n-bit modular addition operation with input differences $\mathbf{a} \in \mathbb{F}_2^n$ and $\mathbf{b} \in \mathbb{F}_2^n$ and output difference $\mathbf{c} \in \mathbb{F}_2^n$, the CNF clauses at bit level for j in $\{0, \dots, n-2\}$ are described in the extended version of this paper [5]. Specifically, 13 clauses are used to model the differential propagation in the modular addition. From that set of clauses $\sum_i^{n-2} w[i]$ is the exponent of the differential probability multiplied by -1.

In contrast to MILP modeling, SAT modeling lacks a built-in mechanism to identify differential trails with minimal probability weight. An incremental approach is taken instead. This approach involves assessing the satisfiability of a problem representing the search for differential trails, with the probability weight $\sum_i w[i]^{n-2}$ initially set to 0. If the result is satisfiable, the search ends; if not, the search increments the probability weight to 1 and continues iteratively until satisfiability is achieved. Following the method illustrated in [45], we utilize the sequential encoding technique to depict $\sum_i w[i]^{n-2} \leq k$, where k encompasses the potential values from the incremental procedure. This leads to an additional $2 \times k \times n + n - 3 \times k - 1$ clauses.

2.3 Splicing and Extending Heuristics and Linearisation Technique

Within the existing literature, two primary heuristics emerge in the search for differential trails using SAT or MILP solvers on ARX ciphers: the *splicing* heuristic and the *extending* heuristic, as well as their combined approach. These heuristics are elaborated upon in [25] and [42]. The motivation for these heuristics comes from the fact that fixing some differential states reduces the complexity of the search for differential trails. The word heuristic is used because the proposed method in the following section, and others described in this section, only explores part of the search space and may therefore miss optimal solutions.

The splicing heuristic divides the problem of finding a long differential characteristic into the (easier) problem of finding two short matching differential characteristic. In this technique, two differentials $\Delta_a \to \Delta_b$ and $\Delta_b \to \Delta_c$ (where the output difference of the first differential matches the output difference of the second one) are concatenated into $\Delta_a \to \Delta_c$.

The extending heuristic is characterized by the expansion of a known differential trail either m rounds upward or downward. These heuristics are frequently cited in the literature and have proven to be efficient in determining upper-bound probabilities of differential trails. For instance, to the best of our knowledge from the literature, the best bound for the probability of the differential trail of `SPECK-128-128` reduced to a 19-round was identified in [25] using both heuristics.

In addition to these heuristics, the *linearisation technique* provides a powerful method to simplify the analysis of non-linear operations such as modular addition. The core idea of this technique is to transform modular addition, which typically involves complex carry propagation, into a form that behaves similarly to the XOR operation under certain conditions. By introducing restrictions on the input differences (e.g., controlling the Hamming weight of the input differences or ensuring no carry propagation), modular addition can be linearized, allowing it to behave like XOR. This linearization reduces the complexity of modeling modular addition in differential cryptanalysis.

3 The Window Heuristic

In this section, we introduce the window heuristic and describe its benefits. The corresponding SAT and MILP models are derived from [25] for SAT and [45] for MILP, which are described in Subsect. 2.2.

3.1 The Window Heuristic Using MILP and SAT Constraints

We conducted an analysis of the differential trails obtained using the model delineated in Subsect. 2.2. Our observations indicated that, for high-probability differential trails, the carry difference stops propagating beyond a certain point. Specifically, for most of the analyzed differential trails, the number of carry-bit differences involved in the propagation is usually less than or equal to 3. For instance, this pattern is evident in all differential trails outlined in [25], with the exception of SPECK-96-96. A comparable pattern was noted in the trails for LEA-128 from [42]. Notably, the upper-bound probabilities in the trails from [25] have remained unchanged for over six years.

Based on these insights, we propose the window heuristic. This involves creating a few new constraints to control the propagation of differences in the carry. We describe these new constraints below, but first, we formalize the terms *carry difference* and *carry propagation* in Definition 1 and Definition 2, respectively.

Definition 1 (i^{th} carry difference). *Let* $\mathbf{a} \in \mathbb{F}_2^n$ *and* $\mathbf{b} \in \mathbb{F}_2^n$ *be input differences propagating to the output difference* $\mathbf{c} \in \mathbb{F}_2^n$ *of the modular addition* 2^n *with certain probability. Then the* i^{th} *carry of this modular addition is given by* $\mathcal{C}[i] = a[i] \oplus b[i] \oplus c[i]$, *for* $i = 0, \cdots, n-2$.

Definition 2 (m-window carry propagation). *With* $\mathbf{a}, \mathbf{b}, \mathbf{c}$ *as above, we say that the carry difference* $\mathcal{C}[i]$ *propagates to the next* m *bits if* $\mathcal{C}[i+j] = 1$ *for* $j = 1, ..., m$.

Using a window heuristic with smaller window sizes, w_s, prioritizes speed rather than precision. For words of size n, the carry differences can propagates up to $k = \lceil (n/(w_s+1)) \rceil$ times, which reduces the search area exponentially by a factor of k. When it comes to precision, a window of w_s consecutive carries offers, at most, a probability bounded by $2^{-w_s/2}$. Given that the most favorable transitions involve few carries (as outlined in Theorem 4 of [32]), cutting out lengthy sequences of carries is a practical strategy, albeit not the most accurate one for precision.

Let us see an example. Consider a modular addition component with input differences of 0x080000001e4a0848 and 0x08000000000e0808, where the Most Significant Bit (MSB) is on the left. Assume its resulting output difference is 0x00000000f2400040. This leads to carry differences (with background yellow) of 0xec040000=11101100000001000000000000000000 (i.e., the last active carry is at position 31). Observations from this example reveal a 1-window carry propagation at the 18th-bit position, a 2-window carry difference propagation at the 26th-bit position, and a 3-window carry difference propagation at the 29th-bit position.

As we said, based on the observation that a carry difference $\mathcal{C}[i]$ does not propagate to a large number of their subsequent differences, we added constraints in the SAT and MILP models with the aim of fixing the propagation of $\mathcal{C}[i]$ to their m subsequent carry differences.

The Window Heuristic using MILP Techniques. For every modular addition with input differences $\mathbf{a}$ and $\mathbf{b}$ and output difference $\mathbf{c}$, the constraints for the m-window carry propagation are

$$\sum_{i=1}^{m+1} \mathcal{C}[j-i] \leq m \text{ for all } j \text{ in } m+1, \cdots, n-1. \tag{3}$$

In other words, we are adding $n-1-m$ new constraints for every modular addition. Adding the new constraints to those described in Sect. 2.2 gives us a total of $R \times ((14 \times n - 9 - m) \times \mathtt{a}_r + 5 \times n \times \mathtt{x}_r + n \times \mathtt{r}_r)$ constraints. Where $\mathtt{x}_r$ is the number of XOR operations at round r, and $\mathtt{r}_r$ is the number of rotation operations at round r, and $\mathtt{a}_r$ is the number of modular additions at round r.

The Window Heuristic using CNF Formulas. For every modular addition with input differences **a** and **b** and output difference **c**, the clauses for the m-window carry propagation presented in Definition 2 are derived from

$$\bigwedge_{j=m+1}^{n-1} \bigvee_{i=1}^{m+1} \neg(a[j-i] \oplus b[j-i] \oplus c[j-i]) \tag{4}$$

For every j the expression $\bigvee_{i=1}^{m+1} \neg(a[j-i] \oplus b[j-i] \oplus c[j-i])$ generates $2^{2(m+1)}$ clauses. In other words, we are adding $2^{2(m+1)}(n-1-m)$ new clauses for every modular addition. Adding these new clauses to those described in Sect. 2.2 gives us a total of $R(\mathtt{x}_r(4(k-1)n)) + (13(n-1) + 2^{2(m+1)}(n-1-m))R\mathtt{a}_r$ clauses.

A different model for Eq. 4, using the xor-exclusive CNF clauses proposed by Cryptominisat [43], was implemented as well; however, it did not yield a significant advantage, so that we only report the more generic CNF model.

We explored the possibility of constructing more heuristics centered around carry differences with the aim of uncovering novel upper-bound probabilities for the differential trail search of ARX ciphers. Regrettably, these heuristics did not yield the anticipated results. For instance, one of these heuristics was designed by imposing constraints on the number of clusters in the carry difference variables. By "number of clusters," we refer to sequences of consecutive active carry differences. For instance, the binary strings: for example: 10101010111 and 10000011111 have 7 clusters. We noticed that the number of these clusters in high-probability differential trails was relatively small. Consequently, we incorporated constraints into our SAT and MILP models to limit the number of clusters present in the carry difference variables. One other attempt was to devise a heuristic that restricted the total number of active differences within the carry bits. This attempt, too, was unsuccessful.

3.2 Model-Level Parallelism Through the Window Heuristic

Solvers supporting parallel resolution sometimes allow to solve problems significantly faster; for instance, the optimal trail for 10 rounds of SPECK-128-128 was found using the parallel SAT solver ParKissat [4]. However, the speedup obtained by solver-level parallelization techniques is often weaker than that obtained through informed decomposition into sub-problems, as in [26]; such decompositions have however rarely been used for ARX ciphers.

Our window heuristic enables straightforward model-level parallelism, as each window size w_s can be solved as an independent sub-problem: an instance of the solver is started for each window size w_s between zero and an upper bound provided by the user. An instance with a special window size $w_s = -1$, denoting no window heuristic, can be started in parallel. In other words, in this instance, the solver considers the full search space without imposing any restrictions on carry difference propagation.

We combined this model-level parallelism with solver-level, using 16 cores for each window size, from −1 to 3, in the corresponding MILP model, resulting in 80 cores being used in total.

Furthermore, more subproblems can be built by fixing the number of "full windows", *i.e.,* windows that actually contain exactly w_s carries. For instance, in the 9-round differential trail for SPECK-32-64 presented in Table 16 of the extended version of this paper, the carries for every modular addition in each round, represented as binary numbers for each round are as follows: 0, 11000000, 1000001000000110, 1000000000000, 1100000, 0, 0, 0, 0. Thus, there are three "full windows" with $w_s = 2$, which are highlighted in yellow for illustration.

4 Applications of the Window Heuristic

The models were solved on a machine running Ubuntu 20.10 and using 80 parallel Intel(R) Xeon(R) Platinum 8280 CPUs clocked at 2.70 GHz. The MILP models were implemented in MiniZinc [38] and solved with OR-Tools [39][1]; the SAT models were solved with CadiCal. Unless stated otherwise in the text, all our experiments were run with a 24 h timeout, so that the solutions for each instance may not be optimal.

In the following sections, we distinguish between "Timing Results" (the cumulative time it takes to complete a specific experiment across for all considered window sizes) and "Individual Timing Results.", denoting the time our tool requires to solve a particular experiment using a single, specific window size value.

4.1 Application to SPECK

Search for Differential Trails in the Single-key Scenario. In the single-key scenario, optimal (or close to optimal) bounds for many versions of SPECK are already known (*e.g.,* [25,34,42] and Table 10 of [45]).

Our parallel SAT implementation retrieved these results, albeit significantly faster. For instance, compared to [45], our tool is 152 times faster for SPECK-128-128 reduced to 8 rounds (Table 1). Our parallel MILP model achieves similar results, with detailed timings provided in Tables 16, 18, 20, 22, and 24 of Section D in the appendix of the extended version of this paper [5].

[1] The more popular Gurobi did not perform as well on our problems, though we did not run a detailed comparison as it was out of scope.

Table 1. Timing comparison between the tool developed in [45] and a parallelized version of the tool presented in this paper for SPECK-128-128, with a window size ranging from -1 to 3 using SAT techniques. In the parallel version, the search is divided into five parts, each solved by a different core, using distinct window size. Probability is denoted as $-\log_2(\cdot)$. For rounds 1 to 4 and round 7, the results are nearly identical, with no significant timing differences (this pattern is very similar also to the results obtained with MILP techniques, see table 24 of the extended version of this paper.). Thus, the results we obtained with the tool developed in [45] for these rounds, after rounding, were the same to those results found by our tool. For rounds 5, 6, 8, and 9, the timings diverge, especially in rounds 8 and 9.

Number of rounds	[45]	5 cores	Pr
	Time (s)		
1	0.02	0.02	0
2	0.03	0.03	1
3	0.05	0.05	3
4	0.27	0.27	6
5	1.82	0.95	10
6	8.65	1.19	15
7	10.49	10.49	21
8	264.55	1.73	30
9	6685.22	1876.24	39

Window Heuristic and Splicing Heuristic. For more difficult problems, where the known bounds still diverge significantly from the block sizes, the basic parallel tool was not sufficient, even increasing the timeout to over two week. However, by combining it with splicing heuristics, we were able to match known results considerably faster. In particular, to recreate the 19-round differential trail cited in [42], we used the splicing heuristic described in [25] and [42]. Specifically, we set all bits to 0, with the exception of the bit at position 71 in the internal state at round 15. Relying solely on the splicing heuristic, we determined a probability weight of 119 for SPECK-128-128 reduced to 19 rounds, accomplishing this in 45 minutes. When we combined a window size of $w_s = 3$ with the splicing heuristic in the same 15th round and using the parallel SAT version, we achieved the identical probability weight in a mere 300 seconds. While one might argue that we were already privy to the intermediate value at round 15, where the single-bit difference should be placed, the time taken to pinpoint this intermediate value is indeed the same for both methods.

For differential trail searches, utilizing both the window and splicing heuristics, coupled with the parallel MILP version, the timings were comparable.

Window Heuristic Constraining the Number of "Full Windows". Inspection of the obtained trails shows that the length of carry propagations rarely reaches the allowed window size. For instance, the 13 round trail on SPECK-128-128 given in the section C of the extended version of this paper [5] has window size 3, but only one series of consecutive carries reaches this length through the entire trail.

Therefore, the number of *full windows*, *i.e.*, the number of times the maximum allowed length of carry propagation appears, can be used to divide into additional sub-problems, where the number of full windows is set to be lower than, equal to or greater than a fixed value k.

In these additional experiments, we searched for differential trails using four configurations and two SAT solvers: a sequential SAT solver and a parallel SAT solver (16 cores). The configurations were: 1) window size without "full windows"; 2) window size with "full windows" and the "exactly" constraint; 3) window size with "full windows" and the "at least" constraint; and 4) window size with "full windows" and the "at most" constraint. The corresponding timings are given in the section C of the extended version of this paper [5].

Constraining the number of "full windows" significantly helps in the search for trails (see figure 2 in the extended version of this paper); in particular, we successfully find a new 19-round differential trail for `SPECK-128-128`, available in the repository accompanying this paper. Interestingly, we did not use the splicing heuristic to perform this search like in previous papers. This was achieved in approximately six hours using a window size of 3 and constraining the number of "full windows" to be at most 1. This result is notable because our previous attempts using ParKissat or CadiCal and similar window sizes ran for weeks without success.

However, the results using sequential SAT solver, shown in figure 3 of the extended version of this paper, were less consistent. Out of 11 versions of SPECK, the sequential solver was beneficial in only 5 cases. It appears that the sequential solver is effective when there is more than one full window, but less so when there is only one. This phenomenon requires further investigation to fully understand.

Search for Differential Trails in the Related-key Scenario. We conducted several experiments applying the window size heuristic to search for differential trails in the related-key scenario. Given that the key schedule round function of `SPECK` mirrors its permutation round function, the diffusion characteristics of both processes align closely. Consequently, drawing parallels with studies such as [41] and [40], our search for differential trails will lead to differential distinguishers in the weak-key setting. This implies that, in line with earlier research, the differential distinguishers generated from our differential trails are effective for only a subset of the key space.

In Table 3, we present our related-key results compared with the state-of-the-art; the full trails and timing informations are given in https://github.com/Crypto-TII/modadd_window_heuristic. As shown in Table 3, the results were obtained with $w_s = 0$. Similar results can be achieved for other values of w_s, but they are not included here because the time required to discover these trails with larger w_s was greater than for $w_s = 0$. In Table 3, the $\log_2(P_D)$ represents the probability weight for the internal permutation, and $\log_2(P_K)$ represents the probability weight for the key schedule process. Similar to previous works, we set the objective function in the MILP and in the SAT models as the minimum of $\log_2(P_{DK}) = \log_2(P_D) + \log_2(P_K)$; our results improve the upper-bound probabilities for all the versions of SPECK in the related-key scenario.

On Related-key Boomerang Distinguishers and Hash Distinguishers on SPECK. Using our newly found related-key differential trails for SPECK to build related-key (boomerang) distinguishers covering a larger number of rounds might seem promising at first sight. However, as SPECK has a quite strong key schedule compared to many other lightweight block ciphers (basically a repetition of the internal cipher round function), this is not quite the case. One can observe from Tables 16, 18, 20, 22, and 24 in section D of the appendix in the extended version of this paper [5], that for a given number of rounds, a related-key differential path for SPECK is not really always better than a single-key one. It can actually be much worse, especially for SPECK versions for which the key size is the same as the block size, for larger versions of SPECK, and when the number of rounds increases. Therefore, except for small SPECK versions on a small number of rounds, the related-key (boomerang) distinguishers have little chance to improve over single-key (boomerang) distinguishers, while requiring a much less realistic attack setting in practice.

However, another interesting scenario is the chosen-key model, or when SPECK is used as an internal component to building a block-cipher-based compression/hash function, as proposed for example in [44] with the classical Davies-Meyer (DM), Matyas-Meyer-Oseas (MMO), and Miyaguchi-Preneel (MP) configurations. In this setting, the adversary can attack the internal state and the key schedule parts independently, and the cost of a related-key differential trail reduces from $P_D \times P_K$ to $P_D + P_K$. We have conducted experiments to search for differential trails in this setting. Specifically, we looked for related-key differential trails that minimizes $\max\{P_D, P_K\}$ instead of P_{DK} and we get improvements compared to single-key ones.

Table 2 shows the differential trail probabilities found in the related-key scenario for SPECK minimizing $\max\{P_D, P_K\}$ and that can be used to mount distinguishers in the chosen-key model. We started by selecting the lowest probabilities between P_D and P_K for every specific version of SPECK in the related-key scenario, i.e., those presented in Table 3. Using these values as lower bounds, we launch experiments to search for related-key differential trails, but instead of minimizing $P_D \times P_K$, we minimize $P_D + P_K$. This way, we discovered differential trails for SPECK-48/96 and SPECK-64/128. In this setting, different from the results obtained for Table 3, where all trails were found with $w_s = 0$, we manage to find a better differential trail for SPECK-48/96 reduced to 15 rounds only by using $w_s = 1$. In this setting, for other versions SPECK we did not manage to find better trails than those that we already presented in Table 3.

The differential trails obtained in Table 2 can lead to simple distinguishers in the chosen-key model. However, these results can be enhanced using more sophisticated strategies such as the start-from-the-middle technique and the application of truncated differences at the extremities to identify limited-birthday distinguishers [27,28]. Implementing this approach requires a different minimization function for the MILP encoding and a unique counting method for the SAT encoding.

We employ the start-from-the-middle strategy to derive new distinguishers on SPECK. In this strategy, the attacker gains access to certain rounds in the "middle" of the cipher, specifically within the key-schedule process and the permutation process. These rounds are referred to as *controlled* rounds. This strategy is based on the observation that higher probability weights are generally concentrated in a sequence of cipher rounds. By identifying these rounds, the attacker can leverage the degrees of freedom within them, allowing the extremities to be verified probabilistically.

Different configurations of the window heuristic can be applied to each round of ARX ciphers. Using the start-from-the-middle approach, we find distinguishers by enabling the attacker to search for differential trails with the controlled rounds set to $w_s = -1$, permitting higher values in these rounds while restricting the window size to be less than or equal to 0, 1, 2, or 3 for the other rounds. This choice is based on the observation that the best probability weights for differential trails in SPECK occur with window sizes not exceeding 3. We create a window for the controlled rounds and move it across the rounds to determine where the best distinguishers can be found.

As the controlled rounds are manipulated by the attacker, the probability weight of the distinguisher is calculated only from the rounds outside the controlled rounds. To select the number of controlled rounds, we consider the parameter m of the SPECK cipher (refer to Sect. 2). Since the attacker can select m words, each assigned to a different round, we choose a number of controlled rounds close to m. Specifically, we select the following pairs for the key-schedule and permutation controlled rounds: (4, 1), (5, 2), and (6, 3).

We encode all the described constraints and configurations into SAT CNF clauses and apply them to SPECK-48/96. We select this version of SPECK due to its higher m value and because it provides results for constructing distinguishers in the chosen-key model without considering the start-from-the-middle approach (see Table 2). We discovered a distinguisher for 19 rounds with a probability weight of 43, with $w_s = 0$, and 5 controlled rounds in the key-schedule and 2 in the permutation. Namely, we are able to produce a pair of plaintexts/ciphertexts/keys (P, C, K) and (P', C', K') such that the exact differences predicted by the differential path $(P \oplus P', C \oplus C', K \oplus K')$ is present. As described in [27,28], in the generic case the attacker can't use the birthday search strategy (since all differences are fixed) and will require to use 2^{48} cipher calls to achieve the same goal. One can find this distinguisher in the repository accompanying this paper.

Interpretation of some "Timing Jumps" in the Experiments. Throughout our experiments searching for differential trails in SPECK within the single-key scenario, a notable spike in timings can be observed starting around round 6 to round 8. This is evident in Table 1 as well as in Tables 16, 18, 20, 22 and 24 in Section D of the appendix in the extended version of this paper [5]. We attribute this timing anomaly to the diffusion properties inherent to SPECK. Tak-

Table 2. Differential trail probabilities in the related-key scenario for SPECK found minimizing $\max\{P_D, P_K\}$ and that can be used to mount distinguishers in the chosen-key model.

Version	Rounds	$\min\{\log_2(P_D), \log_2(P_K)\}$	$\log_2(P_D)$	$\log_2(P_K)$	w_s
SPECK-48/96	14	−33	−33	−32	0
SPECK-48/96	15	−38	−38	−37	1
SPECK-64/128	15	−40	−40	−37	0

ing SPECK-128-128 as an example, its Avalanche Factor (AF) becomes prominent around rounds 7 and 8, as detailed in Table 1 of [18]. This diffusion characteristic of SPECK likely accounts for the observed jump in the timings. Furthermore, when juxtaposing our timings with those from two other studies, a consistent pattern emerges. This congruent behavior can be seen, for instance, in Tables 18-20 of [45].

4.2 Application to ChaCha

Search for Differential Trails in the Single-key Scenario. Differential cryptanalysis of ChaCha is notoriously difficult; not only is the choice of input difference positions restricted to one row out of four in the single-key scenario, but the high number of modular addition results in a combinatorial explosion that renders the search of long trails difficult. Therefore, ChaCha is a valuable benchmark to assess the strength of our heuristic. The main point of comparison is the single-key trails for ChaCha reduced to 1, 2, 3, and 4 rounds documented [7].

The summarized results are presented in Table 4. We managed to identify differential trails spanning up to four rounds with $w_s = 1$. Remarkably, our 3-round distinguisher outperforms the best known pure differential distinguisher by a factor 2^{27} (see table 26 in the extended version of this paper). Even more remarkably, we outperformed by a factor 2^{98} the 4-round distinguisher presented in [7].

These trails were found with a combination of sequential and parallel SAT and MILP implementations of the heuristic. More specifically, for 1 and 2 rounds, we allocated 16 cores to MILP (with $w_s = 3$) and 1 to SAT. For 3 and 4 rounds, we did could not find new bounds with the MILP model, even though the search used 80 cores (16 for each w_s value, from −1 to 3). The same bounds were found for ChaCha reduced to 3 rounds by using the parallel implementation of our tool for SAT. Surprisingly, the bound 2^{-218} for ChaCha reduced to 4 rounds was found using the parallel MILP implementation of our heuristic, but was not found in either the sequential or the parallel SAT versions of our tool. This might be a sign that our encoding method of the proposed heuristic still has room for improvement. We leave this as future research since exploring deeply how internal algorithms of MILP, or SAT, solvers are not in the scope of this paper. Individual timings and results for MILP and SAT can be found in Table

Table 3. Upper-bound comparison on the differential trails probability in the related-key scenario for SPECK variants. w_s denotes the window size. P_D represents the probability of the differential trail for data encryption. P_K represents the probability of the differential trail for the key-schedule process, while $P_{DK} = P_D \times P_K$.

Version	Rounds	$\log_2(P_{DK})$	$\log_2(P_D)$	$\log_2(P_K)$	Ref.
SPECK-32/64	15	–94.0	–32.0	–62.0	[41]
	15	–85.0	–32.0	–53.0	[40]
	15	–73.0	–31.0	–42.0	$w_s = 0$
SPECK-48/96	14	–68.0	–43.0	–25.0	[41]
	14	–66.6	–43.0	–23.6	[40]
	14	–65.0	–34.0	–31.0	$w_s = 0$
	15	–89.0	–46.0	–43.0	[41]
	15	–83.5	–42.0	–41.5	[40]
	15	–75.0	–41.0	–34.0	$w_s = 0$
	16	–86.0	–43.0	–43.0	$w_s = 0$
SPECK-64/128	14	–88.0	–37.0	–51.0	[41]
	14	–72.0	–35.0	–37.0	[40]
	14	–66.0	–32.0	–34.0	$w_s = 0$
	15	–105.0	–45.0	–60.0	[41]
	15	–89.0	–42.0	–47.0	[40]
	15	–76.0	–33.0	–43.0	$w_s = 0$
	16	–103.0	–60.0	–43.0	[41]
	16	–85.0	–39.0	–46.0	$w_s = 0$
	17	–112.0	–62.0	–50.0	[41]
SPECK-128/256	16	–121.0	–76.0	–45.0	[41]
	16	–96.0	–52.0	–44.0	$w_s = 0$
	19	–190.0	-111.0	–79.0	[41]
	19	–171.0	–102.0	–69.0	$w_s = 0$

Table 4. Comparative results of differential trail weight probabilities with [7] for ChaCha in a single-key scenario. Probability is denoted in $-\log_2(\cdot)$.

Number of rounds	MILP + window heur.		SAT + window heuristic + "full window size"	MILP [7]	S-function [7]
	Pr	w_s	Pr	Pr	Pr
1	3	3	3	3	3
2	37	3	37	37	37
3	120	1	120	147	157
4	218	1	217	316	349

Table 5. Individual timing results for `ChaCha-512-256` using MILP. Probability is denoted in $-\log_2(\cdot)$. Between parenthesis is given the window size for this result.

r	Single-key			
	no-condition		conditions	
	Time	Pr	Time	Pr
1	2.17s	3	1.62s	3
2	13.2s	37	3.30s	37(0)
3	13.6s	147	319s	120(0)
4	36728s	316	48745s	218(1)

Table 6. Individual timing results for `ChaCha-512-256` using SAT. Probability is denoted in $-\log_2(\cdot)$. Between parenthesis is given the window size for this result.

r	Single-key			
	no-condition		conditions	
	Time	Pr	Time	Pr
1	0.62 s	3	0.3 s	3
2	108 s	37	1.81 s	37(0)
3	–	–	95.0 s	120(0)
4	–	–	–	–

5 and Table 6 respectively. In Table 6, the symbol (–) indicates that we were unable to determine the probability weights listed in the fifth column even after one day.

Window Heuristic Constraining the Number of "Full Windows". We conducted experiments similar to those described in Subsect. 4.1, utilizing the window heuristic with constraints on the number of "full window sizes". This time, we constrained the number of "full window sizes" to be at most 7 to search for differential trails on `ChaCha` reduced to four rounds. Using ParKissat (with 16 cores), we found a trail in approximately 4.5 hours with a probability weight of 217 (see table 27 in the extended version of this paper), which is better than the one found using MILP. The details of this trail are available in the repository accompanying this paper.

Boomerang Distinguishers. In order to showcase the potential of the window heuristic, we applied it to the search of *boomerang distinguishers*, as defined in Subsect. 2.1. In particular, we extended the ARX-oriented automatic search tool of [47], which adapts the notion of BCT table and its derivatives to ARX, to include the window heuristic. More specifically, we build boomerang distinguishers for 2 to 6 rounds of `ChaCha`. In the single-key scenario, the input difference is constrained to the last row of the state; in contrast, the difference in intermediate rounds is unconstrained, leaving more freedom in the bottom part of the distinguisher. Therefore, the choice of the middle round is crucial to the quality of the distinguisher.

We wanted to see how the probabilities shifted with different round numbers after cutting the cipher into top and bottom parts. If the probabilities were balanced, it meant a good split point. Our tests showed that the best places to split `ChaCha` are as follows: after the first round for 2 and 3 rounds, and after the second for 4, 5, and 6 rounds distinguishers. To make these distinguishers even better, we applied the BCT methods from [47] to the first modular addition in the bottom part. In Fig. 1, we show an example of where we applied the BCT method for rounds 2, 3.

A summary of our results by using these techniques and the window heuristic is presented in Table 7. The details and differentials used in that table can be found in https://github.com/Crypto-TII/modadd_window_heuristic.

Table 7. New boomerang distinguishers for ChaCha.

Number of rounds	Theoretical probability	Experimental probability
2	2^{-6} ($w_s = -1$, bottom part starting round 2)	$2^{-0.05}$
3	2^{-10} ($w_s = -1$, bottom part starting round 2)	$2^{-1.41}$
4	2^{-90} ($w_s = 0$, bottom part starting round 3)	–
5	2^{-154} ($w_s = 1$, bottom part starting round 3)	–
6	2^{-228} ($w_s = 1$, bottom part starting round 3)	–

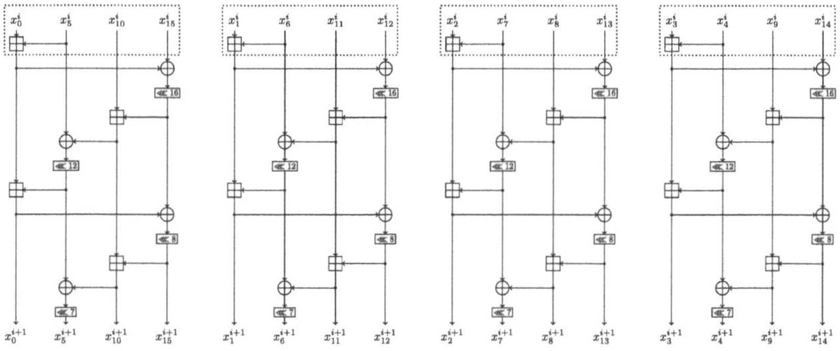

Fig. 1. The dotted lines highlight the BCT utilized to create the boomerang distinguishers in ChaCha for an odd round.

4.3 Application to LEA

We use the window heuristic to search for differential trails on LEA-128, improving the state-of-the-art differential characteristic for LEA-128 reduced to 13 rounds, by a factor of 2^{11} without taking into consideration the differential effect, and by a factor of 2^4 taking into account the differential effect. Individual timings and results for MILP can be found in Table 8

We used the aforementioned trail for LEA-128 and the strategy proposed in [20,42], to mount a key recovery attack against LEA-128 reduced to 14 rounds. Specifically, given a r-round differential characteristic of LEA-128 with probability $p > 2 \times 2^{-128}$, the attack recovers the key LEA-128 reduced to $(r+1)$ rounds

Table 8. Differential trails weight probabilities results and comparisons for LEA-128 (top) and individual timing results using MILP (bottom). Probability is denoted in $-\log_2(\cdot)$. Between parenthesis is given the window size for this result.

r	Window size		Others			
	Pr	w_s	Pr	Ref.	Pr	Ref.
12	107	9	112	[42]	107	[3]
13	123	1	134	[42]	127	[3]

r	Single-key			
	no-condition		conditions	
	Time	Pr	Time	Pr
12	100709s	107/(-1)	73405s	107/(9)
13	609.53s	143/(-1)	7985s	123/(1)

Table 9. Differential effect of the 13-round differential trail of LEA-128. Pr. and Σ_{acc} are denoted in $\log_2(\cdot)$.

weight	#sol.	Pr.	Σ_{acc}
123	22	–118.54	–118.54
124	167	–116.62	–116.28
125	720	–115.51	–114.84
126	2783	–114.56	–113.69
127	5926	–114.47	–113.03
128	30785	–113.09	–112.06
129	79668	–112.72	–111.35
130	124094	–113.08	–110.97

Table 10. Upper-bound probabilities and key-recovery complexities comparison on LEA using pure differentials. w_s denotes the window size.

Distinguisher			Key recovery		
Rounds	Pr	Ref.	Rounds	Complexity	Ref.
13	$2^{-123.79}$	[42]	14	$2^{124.79}$	[42]
13	$2^{-110.97}$	Ours ($w_s = 1$)	14	$2^{111.97}$	Ours ($w_s = 1$)

with $2 \times p^{-1}$ plaintexts, in expected time complexity of $2 \times p^{-1}$ encryptions. Using the probability $p = 2^{-123}$ of our distinguisher and $r = 13$, we have a distinguisher with an expected time complexity of $2^{111.97}$ after taking into account the differential effect similar to how it was done in [42] (see Table 9). This complexity outperforms the previously pure differential known key-recovery attack for LEA-128 reduced to 14 rounds by a factor 2^{11}. A summary, of our distinguishers and key-recovery attack against LEA can be found in Table 10.

4.4 Application to HIGHT

We applied the window heuristic to HIGHT-64-128; the corresponding results are given in Table 11, and the individual timings in Table 12, where (–) denotes no results within 24 h.

A window size of 7 was used to identify the differential trail 11 rounds with the MILP model. Interestingly, this window size significantly deviates from the typical values we have adopted when seeking enhanced trails for other ciphers discussed in this paper. Yet, with a window size of three and through the application of SAT techniques, we the best documented trail in the existing literature.

Table 11. Differential paths probabilities results (denoted in $-\log_2(\cdot)$) and comparisons for HIGHT-64-128. Between parenthesis is given the window size for this result.

Number of rounds	Single-key		
	ours (MILP)	ours (SAT)	heuristic
11	45/(7)	45/(3)	45/([34])
12	54/(7)	–	53/(splicing [3])([34])

Table 12. Individual timing results for HIGHT-64-128 using MILP. Probability is denoted in $-\log_2(\cdot)$. Between parenthesis is given the window size for this result.

Number of rounds	Single-key (MILP)				Single-key (SAT)			
	no-condition		conditions		no-condition		conditions	
	Time	Pr	Time	Pr	Time	Pr	Time	Pr
11	1635 s	46	24408 s	45(7)	703 s	45	374 s	45(3)
12	42 s	55	13 s	54(7)	–	–	–	–

5 Discussions, Conclusions and Future Work

In this work, we proposed a generalization of the linearization technique used to find differential trails in ARX ciphers. Our technique allows us to significantly decrease the space size during a tree-like search for good differential trails, by focusing on those trails that have a small number of consecutive carry-bit differences. As observed in the literature and in our experiments, and with few exceptions, this property seems to be enough to quickly spot trails with the best (often optimal) probability. We demonstrate this claim by showcasing novel results in the case of ChaCha, SPECK, and LEA.

We would like to emphasize that our method is different from [31]. While both use the word "window", this article's strategy is very different and has a different goal from ours. The technique presented in [31], forces the differences to only appear in a small window of the state words of the differential trail to exploit the strong clustering effect in SIMON and SPECK (because of the structure of these ciphers). In our case, the differences in the state can appear anywhere. We are restricting the consecutive carry-bit differences in the modular additions. Our technique is relevant for any ARX cipher (it would actually not apply to SIMON as it is not ARX).

Looking ahead, our techniques open several possibilities for future research in automated cryptanalysis tools. In particular, one could try different heuristics, such as limiting the total number of carries, not necessarily consecutive or by limiting the total number of window heuristic sizes summing to n. Another research direction could be to investigate the effect of the window heuristic on the search for other types of trails, such as linear trails or truncated differential trails. Regarding the applications, interestingly, we could push the boundaries of the basic boomerang distinguishers against ChaCha, now competing with known differential-linear distinguishers. Another application we explore in this work is to use SAT encoding to search for good differential paths on ARX ciphers to be used in the chosen-key scenario. This require taking into account the possibility for the attacker to start from the middle of the path. The window heuristic's flexibility enabled us to discover distinguishers in this setting. A future research in this direction is the usage of truncated differences on both extremities of the differential path (to be used as limited-birthday distinguishers [27,28]). This would basically boil down to building a new and much more involved minimization function in the SAT/MILP encoding.

References

1. Aaraj, N., Caullery, F., Manzano, M.: MILP-aided Cryptanalysis of Round Reduced ChaCha. Cryptology ePrint Archive, Report 2017/1163 (2017). https://ia.cr/2017/1163
2. Aumasson, J.P., Fischer, S., Khazaei, S., Meier, W., Rechberger, C.: New features of latin dances: analysis of salsa, ChaCha, and rumba. In: Nyberg, K. (ed.) Fast Software Encryption, pp. 470–488. Springer (2008)
3. Bagherzadeh, E., Ahmadian, Z.: MILP-Based Automatic Differential Searches for LEA and HIGHT. Cryptology ePrint Archive, Report 2018/948 (2018). https://ia.cr/2018/948
4. Bellini, E., et al.: CLAASP: a cryptographic library for the automated analysis of symmetric primitives. Cryptology ePrint Archive, Paper 2023/622 (2023). https://eprint.iacr.org/2023/622
5. Bellini, E., Gerault, D., Grados, J., Peyrin, T.: The window heuristic: automating differential trail search in ARX ciphers with partial linearization trade-offs. Cryptology ePrint Archive, Paper 2024/1743 (2024). https://eprint.iacr.org/2024/1743
6. Bellini, E., Gérault, D., Protopapa, M., Rossi, M.: Monte Carlo tree search for automatic differential characteristics search: application to SPECK. In: Isobe, T., Sarkar, S. (eds.) INDOCRYPT 2022. LNCS, vol. 13774, pp. 373–397. Springer (2022)
7. Bellini, E., Vasquez, J.D.C.G., Makarim, R., Sanna, C.: Finding differential trails on ChaCha by means of state functions. Int. J. Appl. Cryptogr. (IJACT) (2023)
8. Bernstein, D.J.: ChaCha, a variant of Salsa20. In: Workshop Record of SASC, vol. 8, pp. 3–5 (2008)
9. Biham, E., Shamir, A.: Differential cryptanalysis of DES-like cryptosystems. J. Cryptol. **4**(1), 3–72 (1991)
10. Biryukov, A., Velichkov, V.: Automatic search for differential trails in ARX ciphers. In: CT-RSA 2014, pp. 227–250. Springer (2014)
11. Biryukov, A., Cannière, C.D., Dellkrantz, G.: Cryptanalysis of SAFER++. In: Boneh, D. (ed.) CRYPTO 2003. LNCS, vol. 2729, pp. 195–211. Springer (2003)
12. Biryukov, A., Khovratovich, D.: Related-key cryptanalysis of the full AES-192 and AES-256. In: Matsui, M. (ed.) ASIACRYPT 2009. LNCS, vol. 5912, pp. 1–18. Springer, Heidelberg (2009). https://doi.org/10.1007/978-3-642-10366-7_1
13. Biryukov, A., Roy, A., Velichkov, V.: Differential analysis of block ciphers SIMON and SPECK. In: Cid, C., Rechberger, C. (eds.) FSE 2014. LNCS, vol. 8540, pp. 546–570. Springer, Heidelberg (2015)

14. Biryukov, A., Velichkov, V.: Automatic search for differential trails in ARX ciphers. In: Benaloh, J. (ed.) CT-RSA 2014. LNCS, vol. 8366, pp. 227–250. Springer (2014)
15. Biryukov, A., Velichkov, V., Corre, Y.L.: Automatic search for the best trails in arx: application to block cipher SPECK. Cryptology ePrint Archive, Report 2016/409 (2016). https://ia.cr/2016/409
16. Bittner, P.M., Thüm, T., Schaefer, I.: Sat encodings of the at-most-k constraint: a case study on configuring university courses. In: SEFM 2019, pp. 127–144. Springer (2019)
17. Chabaud, F., Joux, A.: Differential collisions in SHA-0. In: Krawczyk, H. (ed.) CRYPTO 1998. LNCS, vol. 1462, pp. 56–71. Springer, Heidelberg (1998). https://doi.org/10.1007/BFb0055720
18. Coutinho, M., de Sousa Júnior, R.T., Borges, F.: Continuous diffusion analysis. IEEE Access **8**, 123735–123745 (2020). https://doi.org/10.1109/ACCESS.2020.3005504
19. De Cannière, C., Rechberger, C.: Finding SHA-1 characteristics: general results and applications. In: Lai, X., Chen, K. (eds.) ASIACRYPT 2006. LNCS, vol. 4284, pp. 1–20. Springer, Heidelberg (2006)
20. Dinur, I.: Improved differential cryptanalysis of round-reduced speck. IACR Cryptol. ePrint Arch., p. 320 (2014). http://eprint.iacr.org/2014/320
21. Dunkelman, O.: Efficient construction of the boomerang connection table. IACR Cryptol. ePrint Arch., p. 631 (2018). https://eprint.iacr.org/2018/631
22. Dunkelman, O., Keller, N., Shamir, A.: A practical-time related-key attack on the KASUMI cryptosystem used in GSM and 3G telephony. In: Rabin, T. (ed.) CRYPTO 2010. LNCS, vol. 6223, pp. 393–410. Springer (2010)
23. Dwivedi, A.D., Srivastava, G.: Differential cryptanalysis of round-reduced LEA. IEEE Access **6**, 79105–79113 (2018)
24. Fischer, S., Meier, W., Berbain, C., Biasse, J.F., Robshaw, M.J.B.: Non-randomness in eSTREAM candidates Salsa20 and TSC-4. In: Barua, R., Lange, T. (eds.) Progress in Cryptology - INDOCRYPT 2006, pp. 2–16. Springer (2006)
25. Fu, K., Wang, M., Guo, Y., Sun, S., Hu, L.: MILP-based automatic search algorithms for differential and linear trails for speck. In: Peyrin, T. (ed.) FSE 2016. LNCS, vol. 9783, pp. 268–288. Springer, Heidelberg (2016). https://doi.org/10.1007/978-3-662-52993-5_14
26. Gérault, D., Lafourcade, P., Minier, M., Solnon, C.: Revisiting AES related-key differential attacks with constraint programming. Inf. Process. Lett. **139**, 24–29 (2018)
27. Gilbert, H., Peyrin, T.: Super-sbox cryptanalysis: improved attacks for AES-like permutations. In: Hong, S., Iwata, T. (eds.) FSE 2010. LNCS, vol. 6147, pp. 365–383. Springer, Heidelberg (2010)
28. Iwamoto, M., Peyrin, T., Sasaki, Y.: Limited-birthday distinguishers for hash functions - collisions beyond the birthday bound can be meaningful. In: Sako, K., Sarkar, P. (eds.) ASIACRYPT 2013, Part II. LNCS, vol. 8270, pp. 504–523. Springer, Heidelberg (2013)
29. Leurent, G.: Analysis of differential attacks in ARX constructions. In: Wang, X., Sako, K. (eds.) ASIACRYPT 2012. LNCS, vol. 7658, pp. 226–243. Springer (2012)
30. Leurent, G.: Construction of differential characteristics in ARX designs application to Skein. In: Canetti, R., Garay, J.A. (eds.) CRYPTO 2013, Part I. LNCS, vol. 8042, pp. 241–258. Springer, Heidelberg (2013)
31. Leurent, G., Pernot, C., Schrottenloher, A.: Clustering effect in SIMON and SIMECK. In: Tibouchi, M., Wang, H. (eds.) ASIACRYPT 2021. LNCS, vol. 13090, pp. 272–302. Springer, Cham (2021). https://doi.org/10.1007/978-3-030-92062-3_10

32. Lipmaa, H., Moriai, S.: Efficient algorithms for computing differential properties of addition. In: FSE 2001, LNCS. vol. 2355, pp. 336–350. Springer (2001)
33. Lipmaa, H., Moriai, S.: Efficient algorithms for computing differential properties of addition. In: Matsui, M. (ed.) FSE 2001. LNCS, vol. 2355, pp. 336–350. Springer, Heidelberg (2002)
34. Liu, Z., Li, Y., Jiao, L., Mingsheng, W.: A new method for searching optimal differential and linear trails in ARX ciphers. IEEE Trans. Inf. Theory **67**(2), 1054–1068 (2021). https://doi.org/10.1109/TIT.2020.3040543
35. Matsui, M.: Linear cryptanalysis method for DES cipher. In: Helleseth, T. (ed.) EUROCRYPT'93. LNCS, vol. 765, pp. 386–397. Springer (1993)
36. Mouha, N., Preneel, B.: Towards finding optimal differential characteristics for ARX: Application to Salsa20. Cryptology ePrint Archive, Report 2013/328 (2013). https://eprint.iacr.org/2013/328
37. Murphy, S.: The return of the cryptographic boomerang. IEEE Trans. Inf. Theory **57**(4), 2517–2521 (2011). https://doi.org/10.1109/TIT.2011.2111091
38. Nethercote, N., Stuckey, P.J., Becket, R., Brand, S., Duck, G.J., Tack, G.: MiniZinc: towards a standard CP modelling language. In: Bessière, C. (ed.) CP 2007, pp. 529–543. Springer (2007)
39. Perron, L., Furnon, V.: OR-Tools. https://developers.google.com/optimization/
40. Qin, H., Wu, B.: Towards non-independence of modular additions in searching differential trails of ARX ciphers: new automatic methods with application to SPECK and Chaskey. CoRR **abs/2203.09741** (2022). https://doi.org/10.48550/arXiv.2203.09741
41. Sadeghi, S., Rijmen, V., Bagheri, N.: Proposing an MILP-based method for the experimental verification of difference-based trails: application to SPECK. SIMECK. Des. Codes Cryptogr. **89**(9), 2113–2155 (2021)
42. Song, L., Huang, Z., Yang, Q.: Automatic differential analysis of ARX block ciphers with application to SPECK and LEA. In: Liu, J.K., Steinfeld, R. (eds.) ACISP 2016. LNCS, vol. 9723, pp. 379–394. Springer (2016)
43. Soos, M., Nohl, K., Castelluccia, C.: Extending SAT solvers to cryptographic problems. In: Kullmann, O. (ed.) SAT 2009. LNCS, vol. 5584, pp. 244–257. Springer (2009)
44. Su, Y., Gao, Y., Kavehei, O., Ranasinghe, D.C.: Hash functions and benchmarks for resource constrained passive devices: a preliminary study. In: 2019 IEEE PerCom Workshop, pp. 1020–1025 (2019)
45. Sun, L., Wang, W., Wang, M.: Accelerating the search of differential and linear characteristics with the SAT method. IACR Trans. Symmetric Cryptol. **2021**(1), 269-315 (2021). https://tosc.iacr.org/index.php/ToSC/article/view/8840
46. Wagner, D.A.: The boomerang attack. In: Knudsen, L.R. (ed.) FSE '99. LNCS, vol. 1636, pp. 156–170. Springer (1999)
47. Wang, D., Wang, B., Sun, S.: SAT-aided automatic search of boomerang distinguishers for ARX ciphers (Long Paper). IACR Cryptol. ePrint Arch. p. 202 (2023). https://eprint.iacr.org/2023/202
48. Wang, X., Yin, Y.L., Yu, H.: Finding collisions in the full SHA-1. In: Shoup, V. (ed.) CRYPTO 2005. LNCS, vol. 3621, pp. 17–36. Springer, Heidelberg (2005)
49. Wang, X., Yu, H.: How to break MD5 and other hash functions. In: Cramer, R. (ed.) EUROCRYPT 2005. LNCS, vol. 3494, pp. 19–35. Springer, Heidelberg (May 2005)
50. Zhang, Y., Sun, S., Cai, J., Hu, L.: Speeding up milp aided differential characteristic search with matsui's strategy. In: Chen, L., Manulis, M., Schneider, S. (eds.) Information Security, pp. 101–115. Springer International Publishing, Cham (2018)

Quasidifferential Saves Infeasible Differential

Improved Weak-Key Key-Recovery Attacks on Round-Reduced GIFT

Chengcheng Chang[1,2], Meiqin Wang[1,2,3], Wei Wang[1,2,3], and Kai Hu[1,2,3](✉)

[1] School of Cyber Science and Technology, Shandong University, Qingdao 266237, Shandong, China
chengcheng.chang@mail.sdu.edu.cn
[2] Quancheng Laboratory, Jinan 250103, China
[3] Key Laboratory of Cryptologic Technology and Information Security, Ministry of Education, Shandong University, Qingdao 266237, Shandong, China
{mqwang,weiwangsdu,kai.hu}@sdu.edu.cn

Abstract. GIFT, including GIFT-64 and GIFT-128, is a family of lightweight block ciphers with outstanding implementation performance and high security, which is a popular underlying primitive chosen by many AEADs such as SUNDAE-GIFT. Currently, differential cryptanalysis is the best key-recovery attack on both ciphers, but they have stuck at 21 and 27 rounds for GIFT-64 and GIFT-128, respectively. Recently, Beyne and Rijmen proposed the quasidifferential transition matrix for differential cryptanalysis at CRYPTO 2022 and showed that the fixed-key probability of a differential (characteristic) can be expressed as the sum of correlations of all quasidifferential trails corresponding to this differential (characteristic). As pointed out by Beyne and Rijmen in their paper, the quasidifferential methodology is useful in identifying weak-key differential attacks.

In this paper, we apply Beyne and Rijmen's method to GIFT. Some differential characteristics with small (average) probabilities can have much larger probabilities when weak-key conditions hold. Improved weak-key differential attacks on GIFT-64 and GIFT-128 are thus obtained. For GIFT-64, the probability of a 13-round differential is improved from $2^{-62.06}$ to $2^{-57.82}$ with 4 bits of weak-key conditions, then an improved differential key-recovery attack on 21-round GIFT-64 is obtained with $2^{117.42}/2^{64}$ time/data complexities; the probability of a 13-round multiple differential (containing 33 characteristics) is improved from $2^{-58.96}$ to $2^{-55.67}$ with 4 bits of weak-key conditions, then an improved multiple differential key-recovery attack on 21-round GIFT-64 is obtained with $2^{123.27}/2^{64}$ time/data complexities. For GIFT-128, the probability of a 20-round differential is improved from $2^{-121.83}$ to $2^{-114.77}$ with 6 bits of weak-key conditions; the probability of a 21-round multiple differential (containing 2 differentials) is improved from $2^{-128.38}$ to $2^{-122.77}$ with 4 bits of weak-key conditions. Improved (multiple) differential weak-key key-recovery attacks are obtained for 27 and 28 rounds of GIFT-128 with $2^{115.77}/2^{115.77}$ and $2^{123.77}/2^{123.77}$ time/data complexities, respectively.

A. Patra (Ed.): CT-RSA 2025, LNCS 15598, pp. 27–50, 2025.
https://doi.org/10.1007/978-3-031-88661-4_2

As far as we know, this is the first time that a (weak-key) key-recovery attack can reach 28 rounds of GIFT-128.

Additionally, as an independent interest, we perform the first differential attack on SUNDAE-GIFT. The differential used in this attack is checked with quasidifferential trails, thus the probability is reliable. Our attack is nonce-respecting and has significantly better complexities than the currently best attack.

Keywords: Quasidifferential · Differential · Weak-Key · GIFT

1 Introduction

Differential cryptanalysis is one of the most fundamental methods to analyze the security of block ciphers, which was proposed by Biham and Shamir [6] at CRYPTO 1990 to attack the block cipher DES. The core concept of the differential attack is to construct the probabilistic transition from an input difference to an output difference for iterated ciphers. This involves choosing plaintext pairs that satisfy the input difference, tracing the difference transitions of the iterated block cipher throughout the multi-round encryption process, and finding high-probability differentials over a large number of rounds. The differential transition that traces the large number of rounds is usually converted to tracing intermediate differences, the calculation of the differential probability of long rounds can be estimated heuristically as the product of multiple probabilities of intermediate differences, and Lai et al. [13] showed that it yields the correct value of the *key-averaged probability* for *Markov ciphers*. In addition, Lai et al. introduced an additional assumption, which is called the *hypothesis of stochastic equivalence*, to deal with the problem that the actual probability may be different from *key-averaged probability*, which is caused by the fixed-key throughout a differential attack. This assumption states that the probability for each key is close to the average probability.

At CRYPTO 2022, Beyne and Rijmen [5] proposed the quasidifferential transition matrix in differential cryptanalysis, and established the connection between the correlation matrix in linear cryptanalysis [10] and the quasidifferential transition matrix in differential cryptanalysis. The quasidifferential transition matrix satisfies similar properties to the correlation matrix in linear cryptanalysis. One such property is that the fixed-key probability of a differential can be expressed as the sum of the correlations of all its quasidifferential trails, without any assumption. Given one differential (characteristic), correlations of its corresponding quasifferentials are heavily affected by keys. Thus, differential probability in different key spaces can be analyzed relatively more easily now. It is not surprising that in some key spaces, the differential probability would be significantly larger than others.

GIFT [4] is a lightweight block cipher with two versions: GIFT-64 and GIFT-128. The outstanding implementation performance and high security make GIFT be a popular underlying primitive for many Authenticated Encryptions with

Associated Data (AEADs) such as SUNDAE-GIFT [2], GIFT-COFB [3], and HyENA [8]. In the security evaluation of GIFT, differential cryptanalysis is currently the most effective attack compared with other attacks. At CT-RSA 2019, Zhu et al. [23] proposed the first third-party cryptanalysis on GIFT, which includes a 19-round attack on GIFT-64 and a 22-round attack on GIFT-128, respectively. Sasaki et al. [16] improved the meet-in-the-middle (MitM) attack on 15-round GIFT-64. The 20-round and 21-round differential attacks on GIFT-64 were proposed by Chen et al. [9] at ICISC 2019 using the full codebook. Chen et al. [9] also performed the 20-round differential key-recovery attack on GIFT-64 without the full codebook. Li et al. [14] proposed the 26-round differential attack on GIFT-128, and the 26-round attack is improved by Ji et al. [12] at SAC 2021. At FSE 2021, Zong et al. [25] proposed the key-recovery-attack friendly distinguishers, gave a 27-round differential key-recovery attack and a 22-round linear key-recovery attack on GIFT-128, respectively. For the linear cryptanalysis of GIFT, Sun et al. [19] proposed a 19-round linear attack on GIFT-64 at SAC 2021, and a 24-round linear attack on GIFT-128 at FSE 2021 [20]. After that, Sun et al. [21] gave a 25-round linear attack on GIFT-128 at FSE 2022, and improved the 25-round linear attack to increase the success probability by using more data and higher time complexity. Antonio Flórez-Gutiérrez et al. [11] further improved the complexity and success probability of the 25-round linear key-recovery attack on GIFT-128 at EUROCRYPT 2024. In addition, Wang et al. [22] proposed the differential-linear attacks on 18-round GIFT-64 and on 19-round GIFT-128 at CIC 2024. All the above attacks are under the single-key setting. In the relate-key setting, Liu et al. [15] proposed a 21-round boomerang attack on GIFT-128, and Ji et al. [12] proposed a 23-round rectangle attack on GIFT-128 at SAC 2021.

Although extensive cryptanalysis from the community has been applied to GIFT, the security of GIFT is still strong. All attacks stuck at 21 and 27 rounds for GIFT-64 and GIFT-128 in the single-key setting, respectively. Considering the importance of GIFT (as mentioned, GIFT-128 is the underlying primitive of three NIST LWC candidates), a better evaluation on GIFT's security is always warranted, even in the extreme scenarios such as under the weak-key settings.

On the other hand, Beyne and Rijmen's quasidifferential approach has been successfully applied to RECTANGLE, KNOT, SPECK, and SIMON, and new weak-key attacks are presented. However, few works tried to extend their attacks to more ciphers, to the best of our knowledge. In this paper, we aim to bridge the gap by studying how to utilize the quasidifferential method to analyze the security of GIFT.

Our Contributions. This paper applies Beyne and Rijmen's quasidifferential approach [5] to GIFT, studying the differential attacks in the weak-key setting. Some differential characteristics with small probabilities that are infeasible in a normal differential attack can be used now in a weak-key setting, by putting some weak-key conditions. The best attacks on GIFT-64 and GIFT-128 are provided, in terms of the complexity or the number of rounds.

Concretely, by diving deep into the linear key-schedule of GIFT, we extract linear equations for round-key bits, based on the signs of correlations of quasid-

Table 1. Summary of the attack results on GIFT-64, GIFT-128 and SUNDAE-GIFT, respectively. SK stands for single-key setting. RK stands for related-key setting.

Algorithm	Attack Type	Rounds	Scenario	# Keys	Time	Data	Memory	P_S	Reference
GIFT-64	Boomerang	23	RK‡	2^{128}	$2^{126.60}$	$2^{63.30}$	-	-	[15]
	Rectangle	24	RK‡	2^{128}	$2^{106.00}$	$2^{63.78}$	$2^{64.10}$	-	[12]
	Rectangle	25	RK‡	2^{128}	$2^{120.92}$	$2^{63.78}$	$2^{64.10}$	-	[12]
	Differential	26	RK‡	2^{128}	$2^{123.23}$	$2^{60.96}$	$2^{102.86}$	-	[18]
	Differential	26	RK‡	2^{128}	$2^{115.96}$	$2^{60.96}$	$2^{102.86}$	-	[7]
	Differential-Linear	18	SK	2^{128}	$2^{124.61}$	$2^{61.57}$	-	-	[22]
	Linear	19	SK	2^{128}	$2^{127.11}$	$2^{62.96}$	2^{60}	60%	[19]
	Differential	19	SK	2^{128}	2^{112}	2^{63}	2^{80}	-	[23]
	Multiple Differential	20	SK	2^{128}	$2^{112.68}$	2^{62}	2^{112}	-	[9]
	Differential	20	SK	2^{128}	$2^{101.68}$	2^{64}	2^{96}	-	[9]
	Multiple Differential	**21**	**SK**	$\mathbf{2^{124}}$	$\mathbf{2^{123.27}}$	$\mathbf{2^{64}}$	$\mathbf{2^{112}}$	**99.9%**	**Sect. 5.1**
	Differential	21	SK	2^{128}	$2^{121.66\dagger}$	2^{64}	2^{96}	51.60%†	[9]
	Differential	**21**	**SK**	$\mathbf{2^{124}}$	$\mathbf{2^{117.42}}$	$\mathbf{2^{64}}$	$\mathbf{2^{96}}$	**81.06%**	**Sect. 5.1**
	Differential	**21**	**SK**	$\mathbf{2^{124}}$	$\mathbf{2^{120.60}}$	$\mathbf{2^{64}}$	$\mathbf{2^{96}}$	**99.41%**	**Sect. 5.1**
GIFT-128	Boomerang	21	RK‡	2^{128}	$2^{126.6}$	$2^{126.6}$	$2^{126.6}$	-	[15]
	Rectangle	23	RK‡	2^{128}	$2^{126.89}$	$2^{121.31}$	$2^{121.63}$	-	[12]
	Differential-Linear	19	SK	2^{128}	$2^{121.53}$	$2^{122.51}$	-	-	[22]
	Differential	22	SK	2^{128}	2^{120}	2^{120}	2^{86}	-	[24]
	Linear	22	SK	2^{128}	2^{117}	2^{117}	2^{78}	-	[25]
	Linear	24	SK	2^{128}	$2^{124.45}$	$2^{122.55}$	2^{105}	80.01%	[20]
	Linear	25	SK	2^{128}	$2^{126.77}$	$2^{124.75}$	2^{96}	50%	[21]
	Linear	25	SK	2^{128}	$2^{127.77}$	$2^{125.75}$	2^{96}	75%	[21]
	Linear	25	SK	2^{128}	$2^{124.61}$	$2^{123.02}$	2^{112}	80%	[11]
	Differential	26	SK	2^{128}	$2^{124.415}$	2^{109}	$2^{124.415}$	-	[14]
	Differential	26	SK	2^{128}	$2^{123.245}$	$2^{123.245}$	2^{109}	-	[12]
	Differential	27	SK	2^{128}	$2^{124.83}$	$2^{123.53}$	2^{80}	-	[25]
	Differential	**27**	**SK**	$\mathbf{2^{122}}$	$\mathbf{2^{115.77}}$	$\mathbf{2^{115.77}}$	$\mathbf{2^{92}}$	**99.9%**	**Sect. 5.2**
	Multiple Differential	**28**	**SK**	$\mathbf{2^{124}}$	$\mathbf{2^{123.77}}$	$\mathbf{2^{123.77}}$	$\mathbf{2^{96}}$	**86.5%**	**Sect. 5.2**
SUNDAE-GIFT	Linear	16	Nonce-respecting	2^{128}	$2^{91.20}$	$2^{60.00}$	2^{96}	-	[25]
	Linear	17	Nonce-respecting	2^{128}	$2^{123.38}$	$2^{61.51}$	2^{49}	80.01%	[20]
	Differential	**17**	**Nonce-respecting**	$\mathbf{2^{128}}$	$\mathbf{2^{75.37}}$	$\mathbf{2^{62.5}}$	$\mathbf{2^{66}}$	**99.9%**	**Sect. 6**

† The 21-round differential key-recovery attack on GIFT-64 presented by [9] with $2^{107.61}/2^{64}/2^{96}$ time/data/memory complexities, which is the combination of the 1-round attack and the 20-round attack, is not accurate, we reevaluate the complexities and success probability by the successive 21-round attack.

‡ Note that there is no security claim of GIFT under the related-key setting, the results under the related-key setting are shown in grey.

ifferential trails, and convert them to equations for master-key bits. Then the weak-key space of master-key bits is obtained, and the probability of the differential characteristic in this weak-key space is improved. Furthermore, in order to use the *differential* to amplify the probability, we introduce a method to derive the best weak-key conditions from all the characteristics of the differential. These analyses are based on a reasonable assumption that the exact probability of a differential characteristic can be approximated by the sum of correlations of those trails whose absolute correlation is equal to the average probability of the characteristic. We have done experiments on GIFT-64 and GIFT-128 to verify the validity of the assumption, and the experimental results are exactly consistent with our assumption.

After applying the quasidifferential cryptanalysis to GIFT, we present improved (multiple) differential attacks on GIFT-64 and GIFT-128 in the weak-key settings, respectively. For GIFT-64, the probability of a 13-round differential is improved from $2^{-62.06}$ to $2^{-57.82}$ with 4-bit conditions of master-key, which can mount a 21-round differential attack with $2^{117.42}/2^{64}$ time/data complexities. The probability of a 13-round multiple differential of GIFT-64 is improved from

$2^{-58.96}$ to $2^{-55.67}$ with 4-bit conditions of master-key, which can boost the multiple differential attack on GIFT-64 from 20-round to 21-round with $2^{123.27}/2^{64}$ time/data complexities. For GIFT-128, the probability of a 20-round differential is improved from $2^{-121.83}$ to $2^{-114.77}$ with 6-bit conditions of master-key, and the probability of a 21-round multiple differential is improved from $2^{-128.38}$ to $2^{-122.77}$ with 4-bit conditions of master-key. The 27-round and the first 28-round improved (multiple) differential attacks on GIFT-128 are obtained with $2^{115.77}/2^{115.77}$ and $2^{123.77}/2^{123.77}$ time/data complexities, respectively.

Finally, an 11-round differential characteristic whose probability is 2^{-60} without conditions of master-key can be utilized to launch the first differential attack on 17-round SUNDAE-GIFT with $2^{75.37}/2^{62.5}$ time/data complexities. The related results and our attacks are summarized in Table 1.

The source code, the results of this paper, and the full paper are provided at https://github.com/ccc53021/quasidifferential-gift.

Outline. In Sect. 2, we briefly describe the differential cryptanalysis, linear cryptanalysis, and quasidifferential proposed in [5], define some notations, recall the description of GIFT. In Sect. 3, we revisit and discuss the roles of the keys in the exact probability of a characteristic. In Sect. 4, we introduce how to apply the quasidifferential cryptanalysis to GIFT, derive weak-key differential (characteristic) distinguishers, and make some experiments on GIFT. Section 5 presents the weak-key (multiple) differential attacks on GIFT-64 and GIFT-128, respectively, and the attack on SUNDAE-GIFT is given in Sect. 6. Section 7 concludes this paper.

2 Preliminaries and Related Works

In this section, we first recall the differential cryptanalysis and linear cryptanalysis, and introduce the quasidifferential proposed by Beyne and Rijmen [5], which shows that the fixed-key probability of a differential can be expressed as the sum of the correlations of its quasidifferential trails. In addition, we define the notations used in this paper and briefly review the description of GIFT and SUNDAE-GIFT with GIFT-128 as an underlying primitive.

2.1 Review of Differential Cryptanalysis in Fixed-Key Model

Differential Cryptanalysis. Differential cryptanalysis [6] is used to analyze the propagation of differences through the function $\mathsf{F} : \mathbb{F}_2^n \to \mathbb{F}_2^m$, and find a differential with high probability to attack the cipher. The target of the adversary is to find a differential $(a, b) \in \mathbb{F}_2^n \times \mathbb{F}_2^m$ that maximizes the number of solutions x to the difference equation

$$\mathsf{F}(x \oplus a) \oplus \mathsf{F}(x) = b. \tag{1}$$

The difference distribution table of F, denoted as $\mathtt{DDT}^{\mathsf{F}}$, is a $2^n \times 2^m$ table with rows and columns indexed by input and output differences. The corresponding entries are equal to the number of solutions x for a particular differential (a, b):

$$\mathtt{DDT}^{\mathsf{F}}_{(a,b)} = \left|\{x \in \mathbb{F}_2^n | \mathsf{F}(x \oplus a) \oplus \mathsf{F}(x) = b\}\right|. \tag{2}$$

Differential cryptanalysis typically focuses on functions F structured as compositions $\mathsf{F} = \mathsf{F}_r \circ \mathsf{F}_{r-1} \circ \cdots \circ \mathsf{F}_1$, where individual functions F_i exhibit differentials with relatively high probability, making them more suitable for analysis. Thus, it is possible to estimate the probability of differential (a_1, a_{r+1}) based on *characteristics*. A characteristic is a sequence $(a_1, a_2, \ldots, a_{r+1})$ of compatible differences between intermediate inputs and outputs through each F_i. The estimation of characteristic probabilities frequently relies on the assumption of independence among intermediate differentials:

$$\Pr[\wedge_{i=1}^{r} \mathsf{F}_i(x_i \oplus a_i) \oplus \mathsf{F}_i(x_i) = a_{i+1}] \approx \prod_{i=1}^{r} \Pr[\mathsf{F}_i(x_i \oplus a_i) \oplus \mathsf{F}_i(x_i) = a_{i+1}]. \quad (3)$$

When functions $\mathsf{F}_1, \ldots, \mathsf{F}_r$ are dependent on keys $k_1, \ldots, k_r$, the heuristic proposed in Eq. (3) can be justified by applying the *Markov cipher* assumption [13]. Specifically, it has been demonstrated that if all round keys are uniformly random and independent, the *key-averaged probability* of a characteristic aligns with the product of intermediate key-averaged probabilities.

Quasidifferential. Beyne and Rijmen [5] proposed the quasidifferential framework by introducing the quasidifferential transition matrices as a differential analog of correlation matrices [10] to achieve a more complete understanding of differential cryptanalysis.

Definition 1 (Quasidifferential basis [5]**).** *Let n be a positive integer. For any $u, a \in \mathbb{F}_2^n$, the function $\beta_{u,a} : \mathbb{F}_2^n \times \mathbb{F}_2^n \to \mathbb{R}$ is defined by*

$$\beta_{u,a}(x, y) = \chi_u(x)\delta_a(x + y). \quad (4)$$

The set of all $\beta_{u,a}$ is called the quasidifferential basis for $\mathbb{R}[\mathbb{F}_2^n \times \mathbb{F}_2^n]$.

The functions δ_x such that $\delta_x(y) = 1$ if $y = x$ and zero elsewhere, and the functions χ_x such that $\chi_u(x) = (-1)^{u^\top x}$ with $u \in \mathbb{F}_2^n$. The functions $\beta_{u,a}$ are not only linearly independent but also orthogonal. Similar to the Fourier transformation, Beyne and Rijmen define the change-of-basis operator $\mathscr{Q}_n : \mathbb{R}[\mathbb{F}_2^n \times \mathbb{F}_2^n] \to \mathbb{R}[\mathbb{F}_2^n \times \mathbb{F}_2^n]$ by $(\mathscr{Q}_n f)(u, a) = \langle \beta_{u,a}, f \rangle$. The definition of the *quasidifferential transition matrix* using the change-of-basis operator $\mathscr{Q}_n$ and the transition matrix for pairs of values is in Definition 2. The Kronecker (or tensor) product $T^{\mathsf{F}} \otimes T^{\mathsf{F}}$ is defined as a $2^{2m} \times 2^{2n}$ matrix with coordinates

$$(T^{\mathsf{F}} \otimes T^{\mathsf{F}})_{(y_1, y_2), (x_1, x_2)} = T^{\mathsf{F}}_{y_1, x_1} T^{\mathsf{F}}_{y_2, x_2} = \delta_{y_1}(\mathsf{F}(x_1))\delta_{y_2}(\mathsf{F}(x_2)). \quad (5)$$

Definition 2 (Quasidifferential transition matrix [5]**).** *Let n and m be two positive integers and $\mathsf{F} : \mathbb{F}_2^n \to \mathbb{F}_2^m$ a function. The quasidifferential transition matrix D^{F} is defined as the matrix-representation of $T^{\mathsf{F}} \otimes T^{\mathsf{F}}$ with respect to the quasidifferential basis defined in Definition 1. That is, $D^{\mathsf{F}} = \mathscr{Q}_m (T^{\mathsf{F}} \otimes T^{\mathsf{F}}) \mathscr{Q}_n^{-1}$.*

As described in [5], the coordinates of D^{F} are pairs $(u, a) \in \mathbb{F}_2^n \times \mathbb{F}_2^n$ and $(v, b) \in \mathbb{F}_2^m \times \mathbb{F}_2^m$. By the orthogonality of the quasidifferential basis, it holds that $\mathscr{Q}_n^{-1} = \mathscr{Q}_n^{\mathsf{T}}/2^n$ and consequently

$$\begin{aligned} D^{\mathsf{F}}_{(v,b),(u,a)} &= \langle \delta_{(v,b)}, \mathscr{Q}_n(T^{\mathsf{F}} \otimes T^{\mathsf{F}})\mathscr{Q}_n^{\mathsf{T}}\delta_{(u,a)}\rangle/2^n = \langle \beta_{v,b}, (T^{\mathsf{F}} \otimes T^{\mathsf{F}})\beta_{u,a}\rangle/2^n \\ &= \frac{1}{2^n} \sum_{(x,y)\in\mathbb{F}_2^n\times\mathbb{F}_2^n} \chi_u(x)\chi_v(\mathsf{F}(x))\delta_a(x+y)\delta_b(\mathsf{F}(x)+\mathsf{F}(y)) \\ &= \frac{1}{2^n} \sum_{\substack{x\in\mathbb{F}_2^n \\ \mathsf{F}(x+a)=\mathsf{F}(x)+b}} (-1)^{u^{\mathsf{T}}x+v^{\mathsf{T}}\mathsf{F}(x)}. \end{aligned} \tag{6}$$

For $u = v = 0$, Eq. (6) reduces to the probability of the differential with input difference a and output difference b, that is, $D^{\mathsf{F}}_{(0,b),(0,a)} = 2^{-n}\mathsf{DDT}^{\mathsf{F}}_{(a,b)}$. For $a = b = 0$, the coordinates of the correlation matrix of F can be obtained. In particularly, $D^{\mathsf{F}}_{(v,0),(u,0)} = C^{\mathsf{F}}_{v,u}$. Overall, the coordinates of D^{F} express the correlations of probabilistic linear relations ("linear approximations") between the input and output values of the right pairs.

Motivated by the notion of *linear trails*, Beyne and Rijmen propose the definition of *quasidifferential trails* in Definition 3, and show that exact expression for the probabilities of differentials can be given in terms of the correlations of quasidifferential trails in Theorem 1. For key-alternating ciphers, the expressions are shown in Theorem 2.

Definition 3 ([5]). *A quasidifferential trail for a function* $\mathsf{F} = \mathsf{F}_r \circ \cdots \circ \mathsf{F}_1$ *is a sequence* $\omega_1, \ldots, \omega_{r+1}$ *of mask-difference pairs* $\omega_i = (u_i, a_i)$. *The correlation of this quasidifferential trail is defined as* $\prod_{i=1}^r D^{\mathsf{F}_i}_{\omega_{i+1},\omega_i}$.

Theorem 1 ([5]). *Let* $\mathsf{F} : \mathbb{F}_2^n \to \mathbb{F}_2^m$ *be a function such that* $\mathsf{F} = \mathsf{F}_r \circ \cdots \circ \mathsf{F}_1$. *The probability of a characteristic with differences* $a_1, \ldots, a_{r+1}$ *is equal to the sum of the correlations of all quasidifferential trails with the same intermediate differences:*

$$\Pr[\wedge_{i=1}^r \mathsf{F}_i(x_i + a_i) = \mathsf{F}_i(x_i) + a_{i+1}] = \sum_{u_2,\cdots,u_r} \prod_{i=1}^r D^{\mathsf{F}_i}_{(u_{i+1},a_{i+1}),(u_i,a_i)}, \tag{7}$$

with $u_1 = u_{r+1} = 0$, $x_i = \mathsf{F}_{i-1}(x_{i-1})$ *for* $i = 2, \ldots, r$ *and* x_1 *uniform random on* $\mathbb{F}_2^n$.

Theorem 2 ([5]). *Let* $\mathsf{F} = \mathsf{F}_r \circ \cdots \circ \mathsf{F}_1$ *with* $\mathsf{F}_i(x) = \mathsf{G}_i(x) + k_i$. *If* $\boldsymbol{k} = (\boldsymbol{k}_1, \ldots, \boldsymbol{k}_r)$ *is a uniform random variable on a set* $\mathcal{K}$, *then*

$$\Pr[\mathsf{F}(x+a) = \mathsf{F}(x) + b] = \sum_{\substack{u_2,\ldots,u_r \\ a_2,\ldots,a_r \\ (u_2,\ldots,u_r)\perp\mathcal{K}}} \prod_{i=1}^r D^{\mathsf{G}_i}_{(u_{i+1},a_{i+1}),(u_i,a_i)}, \tag{8}$$

where $u_1 = u_{r+1} = 0$ *and the probability is over a uniform random* x *and over the keys* $\boldsymbol{k}_1, \ldots, \boldsymbol{k}_r$. *In particular, for* $\mathcal{K} = \mathbb{F}_2^n$, *only quasidifferential trails with zero masks contribute to the key-averaged probability of the differential.*

2.2 Description of GIFT Family

GIFT. To describe the attacks on GIFT, notations in Table 2 are used. Proposed by Banik et al. at CHES 2017 [4], GIFT has two versions: GIFT-64 and GIFT-128. GIFT adopts an SPN structure, with a 64-bit input for GIFT-64 and a 128-bit input for GIFT-128, both using a 128-bit key. The round numbers for GIFT-64 and GIFT-128 are 28 and 40, respectively. The function for each round is the same for both versions, composed of three operations: SubCells, PermBits, and AddRoundKey.

Table 2. Notations used in describing the attacks on GIFT.

X_i	the input state of the round i
$X_i[j]$	the j-th bit of the state X_i, $j = 0, \ldots, 127$, $X_i[127]$ is the most significant bit of X_i
$X_i[j \cdots k]$	the j-th bit, ..., k-th bit of the state X_i
$X_i[j_{n-1} \sim j_0]$	consecutive n bits from j_{n-1}-th to j_0-th bit of the state X_i
X_i^S	the state after the operation SubCells of round i
X_i^P	the state after the operation PermBits of round i
X_{i+1}	the state after the operation AddRoundKeys of round i
ΔX	the difference in state X
RK_i	the round key of the round i
$RK_i[j]$	the j-th bit of the i-th round key RK_i
k_i	the 16-bit word of the master key, $i = 0, \ldots 7$
k_i^j	the j-th bit of a 16-bit word k_i of the master-key
$\ggg$	circular right shift
P	the plaintext
C	the ciphertext
T	the tag of the output of encryption for SUNDAE-GIFT
RK_i'	is equal to $\texttt{PermBits}^{-1}(RK_i)$
$X_i'^P$	is equal to X_{i+1}

SubCells. Both versions of GIFT use the same invertible 4-bit S-box GS. The S-box is applied to every nibble of the internal state and is given in Appendix A, Table 9 of the full paper.

PermBits. The bit permutation maps bits from bit position i of the internal state to bit position $P(i)$: $b_{P(i)} \leftarrow b_i, i \in \{0, 1, \ldots, 63\}$ for GIFT-64, and $i \in \{0, 1, \ldots, 127\}$ for GIFT-128. Two tables of bit permutation used in GIFT-64 and GIFT-128 are given in Appendix A, Table 10 and Table 11 of the full paper, respectively.

AddRoundKey. For GIFT-64, the 32-bit round key $RK = U||V = u_{15} \cdots u_0||v_{15} \cdots v_0$, and is XORed with the internal state in the following way:

$$b_{4i+1} \leftarrow b_{4i+1} \oplus u_i, \; b_{4i} \leftarrow b_{4i} \oplus v_i, \; i \in \{0, 1, \cdots, 15\}.$$

For GIFT-128, the 64-bit round key $RK = U||V = u_{31} \cdots u_0||v_{31} \cdots v_0$, and is XORed with the internal state in the following way:

$$b_{4i+2} \leftarrow b_{4i+2} \oplus u_i,\ b_{4i+1} \leftarrow b_{4i+1} \oplus v_i,\ i \in \{0, 1, \ldots, 31\}.$$

AddRoundConstants. The round constants are given in Appendix A, Table 12 of the full paper.

Key Schedule. The 128-bit master key is initialized as $k_7||k_6|| \cdots ||k_1||k_0$, where k_i is 16-bit. For GIFT-64, two 16-bit words of the key state are extracted as the round key $RK = U||V$. $U \leftarrow k_1$, $V \leftarrow k_0$. For GIFT-128, four 16-bit words of the key state are extracted as the round key $RK = U||V$. $U \leftarrow k_5||k_4$, $V \leftarrow k_1||k_0$.

The key state is then updated as follows:

$$k_7||k_6 \cdots ||k_1||k_0 \leftarrow (k_1 \ggg 2)||(k_0 \ggg 12)|| \cdots ||k_3||k_2.$$

SUNDAE-GIFT. SUNDAE-GIFT is based on the mode of operation SUNDAE [1] at ToSC 2019, and the underlying block cipher is GIFT-128. The encryption algorithm takes as input an encryption key $K \in \{0,1\}^{128}$, an associated data $A \in \{0,1\}^*$, and a message $M \in \{0,1\}^{128}$. A nonce N with fixed length for variants is prepended on and regarded as a part of the associated data A. The output of the encryption is a ciphertext $C \in \{0,1\}^{|M|}$ and a tag $T \in \{0,1\}^{128}$. The operation "$\times$" denotes the multiplication by 2 or 4 depending on the length of the last blocks of A and M.

3 Revisiting and Discussion on the Weak-Key Conditions with Quasidifferential Approach [5]

This section provides a brief description of how to use the quasidifferential to derive the weak-key conditions for a *key-alternating cipher*, as given in [5]. We also discuss the assumptions implicitly used in this approach.

In the normal differential cryptanalysis, an r-round differential characteristic of a function $\mathsf{F} = \mathsf{F}_r \circ \cdots \circ \mathsf{F}_1$ with $\mathsf{F}_i = \mathsf{G}_i + k_i$ is a sequence

$$\varepsilon = \{a_1, a_2, \ldots, a_{r+1}\},$$

where a_i is the input differences of the i-th round. In the quasidifferential cryptanalysis, according to Beyne and Rijmen [5], an r-round quasidifferential trail corresponding to the above characteristic ε is the following sequence,

$$t = \{(u_1, a_1), (u_2, a_2), \ldots, (u_{r+1}, a_{r+1})\},$$

where (u_i, a_i) is the input mask-difference pair of the i-th round.

The correlation of a quasidifferential trail can be calculated by the quasidifferential transition matrix D^{G_i} of G_i, which is

$$cor = \prod_{i=1}^{r} (-1)^{u_{i+1}^{\mathsf{T}} k_i} D^{\mathsf{G}_i}_{(u_{i+1}, a_{i+1}),(u_i, a_i)}$$

Let $c = \prod_{i=1}^{r} D^{\mathsf{G}_i}_{(u_{i+1},a_{i+1}),(u_i,a_i)}$, we have

$$cor = (-1)^{\mathcal{K}} \cdot c = (-1)^{\mathcal{K}} \cdot (-1)^{b} \cdot |c|, \tag{9}$$

where $\mathcal{K} = \sum_{i=1}^{r} u_{i+1}^{\mathsf{T}} k_i$, $|c|$ is the absolute value of c, and b represents the sign of c, i.e., when $b = 1$, $c < 0$, otherwise, $c > 0$.

It is easy to check, the correlation $cor > 0$ under a condition $\mathcal{K} = b$, and $cor < 0$ under a condition $\mathcal{K} = b + 1$. According to Theorem 1, given a differential characteristic ε with *key-averaged probability*, denoted by p_{avg}, the exact probability of ε, denoted by p, is equal to the sum of correlations of all its corresponding quasidifferential trails. By Eq. (9),

$$p = \sum_i cor_i = \sum_i (-1)^{\mathcal{K}_i} \cdot c_i = \sum_i (-1)^{\mathcal{K}_i} \cdot (-1)^{b_i} \cdot |c_i|. \tag{10}$$

Unfortunately, the number of quasidifferential trails is too enormous to exhaust, thus, we actually cannot collect all quasidifferential trails, so we can only approximate the exact p by considering a fraction of the trails. For example, in [5], Beyne and Rijmen consider the quasidifferential trails with $|c| = p_{avg}$ for the analysis of KNOT and RECTANGLE, and $|c| = 2^0 \cdot p_{avg}$ to $|c| = 2^{-4} \cdot p_{avg}$ for the analysis of SPECK-32.

This paper follows a similar strategy in that we only consider those trails that have a significant contribution to the exact p. Divide all quasidifferential trails corresponding to ε into two parts according to $|c| = p_{avg}$ and $|c| < p_{avg}$, we have

$$p = p_{|c|=p_{avg}} + p_{|c|<p_{avg}} = \sum_{i,|c_i|=p_{avg}} (-1)^{\mathcal{K}_i} \cdot (-1)^{b_i} \cdot |c_i| + \sum_{j,|c_j|<p_{avg}} (-1)^{\mathcal{K}_j} \cdot (-1)^{b_j} \cdot |c_j|. \tag{11}$$

Assumption 1. *The probability of a differential characteristic ε whose average probability is p_{avg} is dominated by those quasidifferential trails with $|c| = p_{avg}$.*

Based on the Assumption 1, we approximate that

$$p \approx p_{|c|=p_{avg}} = \sum_{i,|c_i|=p_{avg}} (-1)^{\mathcal{K}_i} \cdot (-1)^{b_i} \cdot |c_i|. \tag{12}$$

Remark. Assumption 1 is intuitive. However, it is similar to the cases in the traditional differential and linear cryptanalysis, where dominating trails are used to approximate the real probabilities or correlations. For our applications in this paper, we have done experiments to verify Assumption 1 on GIFT-64 and GIFT-128 in Sect. 4.4, the experimental results are exactly consistent with our assumption, showing that Assumption 1 works well.

4 Derive Weak-Key Distinguishers of GIFT

In this section, we introduce how to apply the quasidifferential cryptanalysis and derive weak-key distinguishers for GIFT. In Sect. 3, we have revisited the roles of the keys in the exact probability of a differential characteristic. In our analysis of GIFT, we tend to use the differential (multiple differential characteristics sharing the same input and output differences) to amplify the probability. Therefore, the method in Sect. 3 cannot be trivially used as needs to handle more quasidifferential trails simultaneously. In Sect. 4.1, we introduce a method how to obtain the weak-key conditions for a differential and choose a good weak-key space. In Sect. 4.2 and 4.3, we obtain the weak-key distinguishers on GIFT-64 and GIFT-128, respectively. Finally, we verify Assumption 1 experimentally on GIFT-64 and GIFT-128 in Sect. 4.4, respectively, the experimental results are consistent with our assumption.

4.1 Obtain a Good Weak-Key Space for a Differential

According to Sect. 3, if a characteristic with p_{avg} has m quasidifferential trails satisfying $|c| = p_{avg}$, then $p \leq m \cdot |c|$ (under Assumption 1). The "=" case holds only if we can add m conditions such that

$$\mathcal{K}_i = b_i, \quad i = 1, \ldots, m.$$

Each condition above corresponds to an equation of keys, thus the m conditions lead to a weak-key space. Furthermore, there might be redundancy among the m conditions, i.e., the rank of the m conditions might be smaller than m, which we denote by ℓ. Thus, the size of this weak-key space is of size $2^{n-\ell}$ (n is the length of the key). When a key falls into this weak-key space, $p = m \cdot p_{avg}$.

As mentioned, we want to use the differential to enhance our attack. If a differential contains d differential characteristics, denoted by $\varepsilon_1, \ldots, \varepsilon_d$, respectively. According to Theorem 2 and Eq. (12), the probability p of this differential can be expressed as

$$p = \sum_{i=1}^{d} p_{\varepsilon_i} = \sum_{i=1}^{d} \sum_{\substack{j \\ |c_j^i| = p_{avg}^i}} (-1)^{\mathcal{K}_j^i} \cdot (-1)^{b_j^i} \cdot |c_j^i|. \tag{13}$$

For each characteristic ε_i above, suppose its average probability is p_{avg}^i, $i = 1, \ldots, d$. By applying ℓ_i equations to the keys, we can make the probability of ε_i be maximum, i.e., $m_i \cdot p_{avg}^i$. The corresponding weak-key space is denoted by W_i.

Not all W_i are compatible. A good weak-key space should satisfy two points: (a) the number of key conditions should be as small as possible; (b) the probability of the differential in this weak-key space should be as large as possible. To choose a good weak-key space, we choose the W_i with the maximum $\log_2(p) - \ell_i$. The algorithm procedure pseudo-code is shown in Appendix B, Algorithm 1 of the full paper.

4.2 Weak-Key Distinguishers for GIFT-64

In this subsection, we automate the search for quasidifferential trails following [5], and obtain weak-key conditions for distinguishers of GIFT-64 according to the discussion in Sect. 4.1. The probability of the 13-round differential of GIFT-64 in [9], which is used to launch the known best published 21-round differential attack on GIFT-64, is improved from $2^{-62.06}$ to $2^{-57.82}$ with 4-bit conditions of master-key, and is close to zero in some fraction of master-key. The probability of a 13-round multiple differentials of GIFT-64, which has the same input difference patterns and same output difference, is improved from $2^{-58.96}$ to $2^{-55.67}$ with 4-bit conditions of master-key. The details of the analysis are as follows.

The 13-Round Differential of GIFT-64. For the dominant characteristic with average probability $p_{avg} = 2^{-64}$, denoted by ε_1, of the 13-round differential of GIFT-64 presented in [9], we search and find 64 quasidifferential trails with $|c| = p_{avg}$ corresponding to ε_1. Take one of 64 trails, denoted by t_1, corresponding to ε_1 as an example. The ε_1 and t_1 are both listed in Table 3. The function for each round is $\mathsf{F}_i = \mathsf{G}_i + rk_i$ for $i = 1, \ldots, r$, where G_i is the PermBits $\circ$ SubCells operation, and rk_i is the AddRoundKey operation. According to Eq. (9), we have the correlation for t_1 is that

$$cor_1 = (-1)^{\sum_{i=1}^{r} u_{i+1}^{\mathsf{T}} rk_i} \cdot (-1)^{\sum_{i=1}^{r} b_i} \cdot \prod_{i=1}^{r} |D^{\mathsf{G}_i}_{(u_{i+1},a_{i+1}),(u_i,a_i)}| = (-1)^{\mathcal{K}_1} \cdot (-1)^0 \cdot 2^{-64}, \tag{14}$$

where $\mathcal{K}_1 = rk_1^0 + rk_1^{16} + rk_3^2 + rk_3^{17} + rk_5^0 + rk_5^{16} + rk_7^2 + rk_7^{17} + rk_9^0 + rk_9^{16} + rk_{11}^2 + rk_{11}^{17}$. Thus, a weak-key condition $\mathcal{K}_1 = 0$ for t_1 is obtained to ensure that $cor_1 > 0$. After performing a similar analysis for the other 63 trails, a total of 64 conditions are obtained.

It is easy to convert the 64 conditions about round-key bits into conditions about master-key bits as the linear key-schedule of GIFT. We get 4-bit conditions of the master-key after the Gaussian elimination of the 64 conditions. Suppose that four rounds are added before the 13-round distinguisher to launch the key-recovery attack, we get a weak-key space with 4-bit conditions of master-key, denoted by W_1:

$$k_0^4 + k_0^{12} = 0, k_4^5 + k_4^{13} = 0, k_0^0 + k_0^8 = 0, k_4^1 + k_4^9 = 0. \tag{15}$$

The size of the weak-key space W_1 is $2^{128-4} = 2^{124}$. In the weak-key space W_1, the probability of characteristic ε_1 is increased from 2^{-64} to $2^6 \cdot 2^{-64} = 2^{-58}$, and the probability of the differential 0x0000000000000202 $\xrightarrow{13\text{-}r}$ 0x0000000500000005 is improved from $2^{-62.06}$ to $2^{-57.82}$ after applying Algorithm 1.

The 13-round Multiple Differentials of GIFT-64. According to the 13-round multiple differentials in [9], we search for all 13-round characteristics with $p_{avg} \geq 2^{-64}$ satisfying the output difference 0x0000000000001010, and find 196 characteristics with $p_{avg} = 2^{-64}$. Furthermore, we find 33 of the 196 characteristics having the same input difference patterns and the same weak-key space,

Table 3. A quasidifferential trail t_1 corresponding to a differential characteristic ε_1.

r	$a_r, \texttt{SubCell}(a_r)$ in ε_1, t_1	p^r_{avg}	$u_r, \texttt{SubCell}(u_r)$ in t_1	$c_r = D^{\mathsf{G}_r}_{(u_{r+1},a_{r+1}),(u_r,a_r)}$	$(-1)^{u^{\intercal}_{r+1} rk_r}$	b_r
1	0x0000000000000202	2^{-4}	0x0000000000000000	$D^{\mathsf{G}_1}_{(5,5),(0,2)} D^{\mathsf{G}_1}_{(5,5),(0,2)} = 2^{-4}$	$(-1)^{rk_1^0+rk_1^{16}}$	0
	0x0000000000000505		0x0000000000000505			
2	0x0000000500000005	2^{-6}	0x0000000500000005	$D^{\mathsf{G}_2}_{(0,2),(5,5)} D^{\mathsf{G}_2}_{(0,2),(5,5)} = 2^{-6}$		0
	0x0000000200000002		0x0000000000000000			
3	0x0000000002020000	2^{-4}	0x0000000000000000	$D^{\mathsf{G}_3}_{(5,5),(0,2)} D^{\mathsf{G}_3}_{(5,5),(0,2)} = 2^{-4}$	$(-1)^{rk_3^2+rk_3^{17}}$	0
	0x0000000005050000		0x0000000005050000			
4	0x0000005000000050	2^{-6}	0x0000005000000050	$D^{\mathsf{G}_4}_{(0,2),(5,5)} D^{\mathsf{G}_4}_{(0,2),(5,5)} = 2^{-6}$		0
	0x0000002000000020		0x0000000000000000			
5	0x0000000000000202	2^{-4}	0x0000000000000000	$D^{\mathsf{G}_5}_{(5,5),(0,2)} D^{5_1}_{(5,5),(0,2)} = 2^{-4}$	$(-1)^{rk_5^0+rk_5^{16}}$	0
	0x0000000000000505		0x0000000000000505			
6	0x0000000500000005	2^{-6}	0x0000000500000005	$D^{\mathsf{G}_6}_{(0,2),(5,5)} D^{\mathsf{G}_6}_{(0,2),(5,5)} = 2^{-6}$		0
	0x0000000200000002		0x0000000000000000			
7	0x0000000002020000	2^{-4}	0x0000000000000000	$D^{\mathsf{G}_7}_{(5,5),(0,2)} D^{\mathsf{G}_7}_{(5,5),(0,2)} = 2^{-4}$	$(-1)^{rk_7^2+rk_7^{17}}$	0
	0x0000000005050000		0x0000000005050000			
8	0x0000005000000050	2^{-6}	0x0000005000000050	$D^{\mathsf{G}_8}_{(0,2),(5,5)} D^{\mathsf{G}_8}_{(0,2),(5,5)} = 2^{-6}$		0
	0x0000002000000020		0x0000000000000000			
9	0x0000000000000202	2^{-4}	0x0000000000000000	$D^{\mathsf{G}_9}_{(5,5),(0,2)} D^{\mathsf{G}_9}_{(5,5),(0,2)} = 2^{-4}$	$(-1)^{rk_9^0+rk_9^{16}}$	0
	0x0000000000000505		0x0000000000000505			
10	0x0000000500000005	2^{-6}	0x0000000500000005	$D^{\mathsf{G}_{10}}_{(0,2),(5,5)} D^{\mathsf{G}_{10}}_{(0,2),(5,5)} = 2^{-6}$		0
	0x0000000200000002		0x0000000000000000			
11	0x0000000002020000	2^{-4}	0x0000000000000000	$D^{\mathsf{G}_{11}}_{(5,5),(0,2)} D^{\mathsf{G}_{11}}_{(5,5),(0,2)} = 2^{-4}$	$(-1)^{rk_{11}^2+rk_{11}^{17}}$	0
	0x0000000005050000		0x0000000005050000			
12	0x0000005000000050	2^{-6}	0x0000005000000050	$D^{\mathsf{G}_{12}}_{(0,2),(5,5)} D^{\mathsf{G}_{12}}_{(0,2),(5,5)} = 2^{-6}$		0
	0x0000002000000020		0x0000000000000000			
13	0x0000000000000202	2^{-4}	0x0000000000000000	$D^{\mathsf{G}_{13}}_{(0,5),(0,2)} D^{\mathsf{G}_{13}}_{(0,5),(0,2)} = 2^{-4}$		0
	0x0000000000000505		0x0000000000000000			

which are listed in Appendix C, Table 13 of the full paper. Suppose that three rounds are added before the 13-round multiple differential distinguisher to launch the key-recovery attack, we get a weak-key space with 4-bit conditions of master-key, denoted by W_2:

$$k_2^1 + k_2^9 = 0, k_2^5 + k_2^{13} = 0, k_6^0 + k_6^8 = 0, k_6^4 + k_6^{12} = 0. \tag{16}$$

The size of W_2 is 2^{124}. In W_2, the probability of the 13-round multiple differentials, which contains 33 characteristics, is improved from $2^{-58.96}$ to $2^{-55.67}$.

4.3 Weak-Key Distinguishers for GIFT-128

Similarly, we find that for GIFT-128, the probability of the 20-round differential (presented in [25]) is improved from $2^{-121.83}$ to $2^{-114.77}$ with 6-bit conditions of master-key, and the probability of a 21-round multiple differentials of GIFT-128 is improved from $2^{-128.38}$ to $2^{-122.77}$ with 4-bit conditions of master-key.

The 20-round Differentials of GIFT-128. For the 8 20-round differentials proposed in [25] (Table 7), which are used to launch the known best published 27-round differential attack on GIFT-128, a similar analysis is performed to obtain the weak-key spaces and probabilities. We find that the probability of differential 2 (0x000000000000000000000000000000a0 $\xrightarrow{20\text{-}r}$ 0x000000000000000000200000 0210000001), which contains 8 characteristics, is improved from $2^{-121.83}$ to $2^{-114.77}$ with 6-bit conditions of master-key. The size of the weak-key space is 2^{122}. The details are listed in Appendix D, Table 16 of the full paper. Suppose that four rounds are added before the 20-round distinguisher to launch the key-recovery attack, we get a weak-key space with 6-bit conditions of master-key, denoted by W_3:

$$k_0^9 + k_1^7 = 0, k_0^{11} + k_1^9 = 0, k_4^5 + k_5^1 = 0, k_6^9 + k_7^{11} = 0, k_6^{11} + k_7^{13} = 0, k_2^{15} = 1. \quad (17)$$

The 21-round Differentials of GIFT-128. We search for 21-round differentials that satisfy only one active S-box in the input difference, the output difference ΔOUT satisfies $\Delta OUT[127 \sim 64] = 0$ or $\Delta OUT[63 \sim 0] = 0$, and find 18 21-round differentials, which are listed in Appendix E, Table 19 of the full paper. Similarly, the quasidifferential trails for these differentials are searched, and the weak-key conditions for each differential are obtained. After that, we find 2 (differential 9 and 10 in Table 19 of the 18 differentials having the same input difference with the same 4-bit conditions of master-key. The details are listed in Appendix E, Table 20 of the full paper. Suppose that four rounds are added before the 21-round multiple differential distinguisher to launch the key-recovery attack, we get a weak-key space with 4-bit conditions of master-key, denoted by W_4:

$$k_4^4 + k_5^0 = 0, k_6^8 + k_7^{10} = 0, k_6^{10} + k_7^{12} = 0, k_2^1 = 1. \quad (18)$$

The size of W_4 is 2^{124}, and the probability of the 21-round multiple differentials, which contains 2 differentials, is improved from $2^{-128.38}$ to $2^{-122.77}$ in W_4.

4.4 Experiments

In Sect. 3 Assumption 1, we suppose that quasidifferential trails satisfying $|c| = p_{avg}$ are dominant for the probability of a characteristic. However, take the characteristic ε_1 in Table 3 as an example, when $\frac{|c|}{p_{avg}} \le 2^{-6}$, a large number of quasidifferential trails exist. The number of quasidifferential trails of ε_1 from $\frac{|c|}{p_{avg}} = 2^0$ to $\frac{|c|}{p_{avg}} = 2^{-9}$ are listed in Table 4. To verify the effect of quasidifferential trails with $|c| < p_{avg}$ on the probability of characteristic can be ignored, we have done experimental verification on GIFT-64 and GIFT-128, respectively.

Experiments on GIFT-64. The 13-round characteristic ε_1 (listed in Table 3) is divided into two consecutive 4-rounds and one consecutive 5-round to experiment with the probability in the weak-key space W_1.

Table 4. The numbers of trails (denoted by # t) from $\frac{|c|}{p_{avg}} = 2^0$ to $\frac{|c|}{p_{avg}} = 2^{-9}$.

$-\log_2 \frac{|c|}{p_{avg}}$	0	1	2	3	4	5	6	7	8	9
# t	64	0	0	0	0	0	1024	0	1536	$\geq$ 5856

For each consecutive round, we conduct experiments under three cases: (1) round-key bits of each round are randomly generated, corresponding to the *key-averaged probability* for *Markov ciphers*; (2) the 128-bit master-key used in the key-schedule is randomly generated, corresponding to the key space of size 2^{128}; (3) the 128-bit master-key used in the key-schedule satisfies 4-bit conditions of W_1 (Eq. (15)), corresponding to the weak-key space of size 2^{124}.

In each case, 100 times are performed. Each time, plaintext pairs satisfying the input difference are randomly generated, the number of corresponding consecutive rounds is encrypted, and the number of right pairs (satisfying all intermediate differences) is counted. The experimental results are listed in Table 5. $pairs_{exp}$ represents the number of randomly generated plaintext pairs in each time. $pairs_{right}$ represents the number of right pairs counted by 100 times, and $p_{exp} = \frac{pairs_{right}}{pairs_{exp}}$.

Table 5. Experimental results of GIFT-64.

round	p_{avg}	$pairs_{exp}$	Cases of key in the encryption					
			Random round-key		Random master-key		Fixed master-key	
			$pairs_{right}$	p_{exp}	$pairs_{right}$	p_{exp}	$pairs_{right}$	p_{exp}
1 to 4	2^{-20}	2^{25}	3325	$2^{-19.95}$	3385	$2^{-19.92}$	12786	$2^{-18.00}$
5 to 8	2^{-20}	2^{25}	3252	$2^{-19.98}$	3564	$2^{-19.84}$	12668	$2^{-18.01}$
9 to 13	2^{-24}	2^{29}	3204	$2^{-24.00}$	2842	$2^{-24.17}$	12805	$2^{-22.00}$

From the results in Table 5, the probabilities p_{exp} of case (3) in the weak-key space W_1 are much higher than case (2). The experimental probability of the characteristic ε_1 can be expressed as the product of two consecutive 4-rounds and one consecutive 5-round, i.e., $p \approx 2^{-58.01}$, which is close to 2^{-58} and exactly consistent with Assumption 1.

The numbers of right pairs of each experiment for three cases are shown in Fig. 1. In each subfigure, the lower triangles in yellow, the squares in blue, and the stars in red represent case (1), case (2), and case (3), respectively. It shows that the number of right pairs of case (2) is zero for some fraction of keys.

Experiments on ***GIFT-128***. We also perform the experiments for six consecutive 2-rounds for the two dominant 21-round characteristics, which are listed in Appendix E, Table 21 of the full paper, to verify that the probability in the weak-key space W_4. The results are listed in Table 6, showing that Assumption 1 is reasonable.

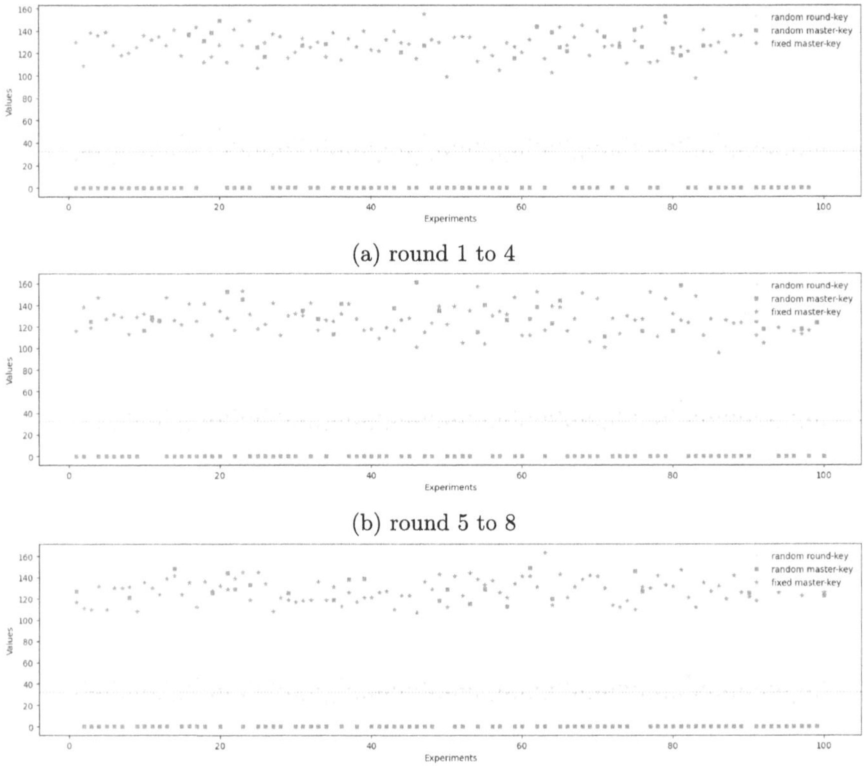

(a) round 1 to 4

(b) round 5 to 8

(c) round 9 to 13

Fig. 1. Numbers of right pairs of 100 times for three cases of the key of GIFT-64.

5 Improved Weak-Key Key-Recovery Attacks on GIFT

In this section, we mount and reevaluate the attacks on GIFT-64, and GIFT-128, by the differentials in the weak-key spaces proposed in Sect. 4, respectively.

5.1 Weak-Key Key-Recovery Attacks on GIFT-64

The 21-round Differential Attack on GIFT-64. By adding four rounds before and four rounds after the 13-round differential distinguisher, which is presented in Sect. 4.2 with probability $2^{-57.82}$ in the weak-key space W_1, we launch a 21-round weak-key key-recovery attack on GIFT-64. The key-recovery process is shown in Fig. 2.

To facilitate representation and simplify the process, we perform an equivalent substitution for the AddRoundkey operation in the bottom of the distinguisher, and move it before the PermBits operation. The RK' is equals to the inverse of PermBits of RK, i.e., $RK' = \texttt{PermBits}^{-1}(RK)$. Additionally, accord-

Table 6. Experimental results of GIFT-128.

round	p_{avg}	$pairs_{exp}$	Cases of key in the encryption					
			Random round-key		Random master-key		Fixed master-key	
			$pairs_{right}$	p_{exp}	$pairs_{right}$	p_{exp}	$pairs_{right}$	p_{exp}
5 to 6	2^{-19}	2^{25}	6468	$2^{-18.99}$	7238	$2^{-18.81}$	12690	$2^{-18.00}$
8 to 9	2^{-9}	2^{15}	12854	$2^{-8.00}$	12698	$2^{-8.00}$	12696	$2^{-8.00}$
10 to 11	2^{-21}	2^{25}	1525	$2^{-21.07}$	1098	$2^{-21.54}$	6394	$2^{-19.00}$
13 to 14	2^{-9}	2^{15}	12704	$2^{-8.00}$	12916	$2^{-7.98}$	12608	$2^{-8.00}$
16 to 17	2^{-20}	2^{25}	3233	$2^{-19.98}$	3432	$2^{-19.90}$	6340	$2^{-19.01}$
19 to 20	2^{-9}	2^{15}	9577	$2^{-8.42}$	9578	$2^{-8.42}$	9687	$2^{-8.40}$

ing to the key schedule of GIFT-64, the round key RK_i and RK_j involve the same 32-bit master key when $i \equiv j \ mod\ 4$.

Data Collection. GIFT's structure allows us to freely extend one round because there is no whitening key at the beginning. Specifically, the structure can be constructed at X_1^P, while the plaintext P can be obtained by applying the inverse operation of PermBits ($\texttt{PermBits}^{-1}$) and SubCell ($\texttt{SubCell}^{-1}$) to X_1^P. Then encrypt the plaintext and obtain the corresponding ciphertext. By iterating all 64-bit in X_1^P, i.e., 2^{64} plaintexts, we can generate about $\binom{2^{64}}{2} \approx 2^{127}$ plaintext pairs.

Key Recovery Phase. Suppose that after data collection, we have 2^n plaintext pairs and corresponding ciphertext pairs. The corresponding bits of the master-key that need to be guessed during the key-recovery phase are listed in Table 7. The time complexity of each step with initial 2^n pairs is listed in Table 8. The detailed analysis of guessing keys and filtering to get the right pairs is given below. ? represents one bit of undetermined difference.

1). Guess 32-bit of RK_1: Guess 2-bit value of $RK_1[1,0]$, make the SubCell operation on the first S-box, remain the pairs satisfying

$$\texttt{SubCell}(X_1^P[3 \sim 0] \oplus RK_1[1,0]) \oplus \texttt{SubCell}(X_1^P[3 \sim 0] \oplus RK_1[1,0]) = 00?0,$$

and about $2^n \times 2^{-3}$ pairs left. Similarly, for the other 30-bit value of RK_1, i.e., $RK_1[31 \sim 2]$, guess each 2-bit RK_1 and perform a 3-bit filtering, around the right candidate pairs remain. The similar procedures are performed 16 times in total. Step 1) guesses 32-bit RK_1 in total, and about 2^{n-48} pairs left.

2). Guess 8-bit of RK_2: Guess 2-bit value of $RK_2[9,8]$, make SubCell on the 5-th S-box, remain the pairs satisfying
small

$$\texttt{SubCell}(X_2^P[18 \sim 15] \oplus RK_2[9,8]) \oplus \texttt{SubCell}(X_2^P[18 \sim 15] \oplus RK_2[9,8]) = 010?,$$

and about $2^{n-48} \times 2^{-3}$ pairs left. Guess $RK_2[13,12]$, and perform a similar 3-bit filtering. Guess $RK_2[11,10]$, make `SubCell` on the 6-th S-box, and discard the pairs that do not satisfy $\Delta X_3^S[23 \sim 20]$ =?0?0. Then a 2-bit filtering is performed. Similarly, guess $RK_{15,14}$ and perform a 2-bit filtering. Step 2) guess 8-bit RK_2 in total, and about 2^{n-58} pairs left.

3). Guess 4-bit RK_3: For each of the 2 active S-boxes in ΔX_3^P, guess the corresponding 2-bit RK_3, make `SubCell`, and perform a 3-bit filtering. Step 3) guesses 4-bit RK_3 in total, and about 2^{n-64} pairs left.

4). Guess 32-bit RK'_{21}: Note that all 32-bit subkeys of RK'_{21} are already guessed in Step 1), thus, for each of the 16 active S-boxes in $\Delta X_{21}^{'P}$, make $\texttt{SubCell}^{-1}$ on the corresponding S-box. Step 4) does not perform the filtering, and about 2^{n-64} pairs left.

5). Guess 32-bit RK'_{20}: Guess 2-bit $RK'_{20}[1,0]$, make $\texttt{SubCell}^{-1}$, remain the pairs satisfying

$$\texttt{SubCell}^{-1}(X_{20}^{'P}[3 \sim 0] \oplus RK'_{20}[1,0]) \oplus \texttt{SubCell}^{-1}(X_{20}^{'P}[3 \sim 0] \oplus RK'_{20}[1,0]) = 0?0?,$$

and about $2^{n-64} \times 2^{-2}$ pairs left. For the other 15 active S-boxes in $\Delta X_{20}^{'P}$, 2-bit filtering is performed for each 2-bit RK'_{20} is guessed. The similar procedures are performed 16 times, and 32 bits RK'_{20} are guessed in Step 5) in total. After this step, there are about 2^{n-96} pairs left.

6). Guess 16-bit RK'_{19}: Similarly, for each one of 8 active S-boxes in $\Delta X_{19}^{'P}$, guess the corresponding 2-bit RK'_{19}, make $\texttt{SubCell}^{-1}$, and perform a 3-bit filtering. Step 6) guesses 16-bit RK'_{19}, and about 2^{n-120} pairs left.

7). Guess 4-bit RK'_{18}: Guess $RK'_{18}[1,0]$ and $RK'_{18}[17,16]$, make $\texttt{SubCell}^{-1}$, perform a 8-bit filtering in total. Step 7) guesses 4-bit RK'_{18}, and about 2^{n-128} pairs left.

Table 7. Involved keys in the 21-round differential attack on `GIFT`-64 of the 13-round differential. The keys in blue represent the bits that do not repeat the guess.

RK_1	$k_1^{15}k_0^{15}$	$k_1^{14}k_0^{14}$	$k_1^{13}k_0^{13}$	$k_1^{12}k_0^{12}$	$k_1^{11}k_0^{11}$	$k_1^{10}k_0^{10}$	$k_1^{9}k_0^{9}$	$k_1^{8}k_0^{8}$	$k_1^{7}k_0^{7}$	$k_1^{6}k_0^{6}$	$k_1^{5}k_0^{5}$	$k_1^{4}k_0^{4}$	$k_1^{3}k_0^{3}$	$k_1^{2}k_0^{2}$	$k_1^{1}k_0^{1}$	$k_1^{0}k_0^{0}$
RK_2									$k_3^{7}k_2^{7}$	$k_3^{6}k_2^{6}$	$k_3^{5}k_2^{5}$	$k_3^{4}k_2^{4}$				
RK_3							$k_5^{9}k_4^{9}$								$k_5^{1}k_4^{1}$	
RK_4																
RK'_{18}								$k_3^{14}k_2^{2}$								$k_3^{12}k_2^{0}$
RK'_{19}		$k_5^{7}k_4^{11}$		$k_5^{15}k_4^{3}$		$k_5^{6}k_4^{10}$		$k_5^{14}k_4^{2}$		$k_5^{5}k_4^{9}$		$k_5^{13}k_4^{1}$		$k_5^{4}k_4^{8}$		$k_5^{12}k_4^{0}$
RK'_{20}	$k_7^{3}k_6^{7}$	$k_7^{7}k_6^{11}$	$k_7^{11}k_6^{15}$	$k_7^{15}k_6^{3}$	$k_7^{2}k_6^{6}$	$k_7^{6}k_6^{10}$	$k_7^{10}k_6^{14}$	$k_7^{14}k_6^{2}$	$k_7^{1}k_6^{5}$	$k_7^{5}k_6^{9}$	$k_7^{39}k_6^{13}$	$k_7^{13}k_6^{1}$	$k_7^{0}k_6^{4}$	$k_7^{4}k_6^{8}$	$k_7^{8}k_6^{12}$	$k_7^{12}k_6^{0}$
RK'_{21}	$k_1^{5}k_0^{3}$	$k_1^{9}k_0^{7}$	$k_1^{13}k_0^{11}$	$k_1^{1}k_0^{15}$	$k_1^{4}k_0^{2}$	$k_1^{8}k_0^{6}$	$k_1^{12}k_0^{10}$	$k_1^{0}k_0^{14}$	$k_1^{3}k_0^{1}$	$k_1^{7}k_0^{5}$	$k_1^{11}k_0^{9}$	$k_1^{15}k_0^{13}$	$k_1^{2}k_0^{0}$	$k_1^{6}k_0^{4}$	$k_1^{10}k_0^{8}$	$k_1^{14}k_0^{12}$

Complexity and Success Probability. For the right key guesses, there are about $2^{n-64-57.82}$ pairs left, while for the wrong key guesses, about 2^{n-128} pairs left. We set $n = 121.82$ to ensure that at least one pair is remained for the right key guesses, while about $2^{-6.18}$ pairs are remained for the wrong key guesses. Therefore, the data complexity is about 2^{64} chosen-plaintexts, the time complexity is

Table 8. Time complexity of the 21-round differential attack on `GIFT-64` in each step.

Step	RK	# Key	Time(S-box operations)	Filtering probability	# Remaining pairs
1.	RK_1	2^{32}	$2 \times 2^n \times 2^3$	$2^{-3\times16}$	2^{n-48}
2.	RK_2	2^8	$2 \times 2^{32} \times 2^{n-48} \times 2^3$	$2^{-3\times2-2\times2}$	2^{n-58}
3.	RK_3	2^4	$2 \times 2^{40} \times 2^{n-58} \times 2^3$	$2^{-3\times2}$	2^{n-64}
4.	RK'_{21}	-	$2 \times 2^{44} \times 2^{n-64} \times 16$	-	2^{n-64}
5.	RK'_{20}	2^{32}	$2 \times 2^{44} \times 2^{n-64} \times 2^6$	$2^{-2\times16}$	2^{n-96}
6.	RK'_{19}	2^{16}	$2 \times 2^{76} \times 2^{n-96} \times 2^3$	$2^{-3\times8}$	2^{n-120}
7.	RK'_{18}	2^4	$2 \times 2^{92} \times 2^{n-120} \times 2^{2.32}$	$2^{-4\times2}$	2^{n-128}

dominated by Step 1), and about $2^{125.82} \cdot \frac{1}{16} \cdot \frac{1}{21} \approx 2^{117.42}$ 21-round operations, the memory complexity is about 2^{96}-bit. We use the formula presented by Selçuk in [17] to evaluate the success probability P_S:

$$P_S = \Phi\left(\frac{\sqrt{\mu S_N} - \Phi^{-1}(1 - 2^{-a})}{\sqrt{S_N + 1}}\right), \tag{19}$$

where p is the probability of the differential, N is the plaintext-ciphertext pairs, $\mu = pN$, S_N is the signal-to-noise, and a is an a-bit or higher advantage. We have $S_N = 2^{6.18}$. For $n = 121.82$, $\mu = 1$, $a = 5$, $P_S \approx 81.06\%$. For $n = 125$, $\mu = 2^{3.18}$, $a = 15$, $P_S \approx 99.41\%$, and time complexity is about $2^{120.6}$ 21-round operations.

Remark. The calculation of the time complexity of the 21-round differential attack proposed in [9], which is the combination of the 1-round attack and the 20-round, is not accurate, we reevaluate the time complexity utilizing their 13-round differential with average probability $2^{-62.06}$ based on the above analysis. Then $S_N = \frac{2^{n-64-62.06}}{2^{n-128}} = 2^{1.94}$. For $n = 126.06$ to ensure that at least one right pair left, $\mu = 1$, $P_S \approx 51.60\%$ for $a = 5$, and the time complexity is about $2^{121.66}$ 21-round operations. Our attack improves the success probability and complexity in the weak-key space W_1 compared to [9].

The 21-round Multiple Differential Attack on `GIFT-64`. Based on the 13-round multiple differentials proposed in Sect. 4.2 with probability $2^{-55.67}$ in the weak-key space W_2, we add three rounds before and five rounds after the distinguisher to mount the 21-round multiple differential attack on `GIFT-64` in Appendix C of the full paper. Thanks to increasing the probability of the 13-round multiple differential distinguisher in the weak-key space W_2, it allows us to boost the multiple differential attack on `GIFT-64` from 20 to 21 rounds.

Complexity and Success Probability. The data complexity is 2^{64} chosen-plaintexts, the time complexity is about $2^{123.27}$ 21-round operations, the memory complexity is about 2^{112}-bit, and the success probability is about 99.9%.

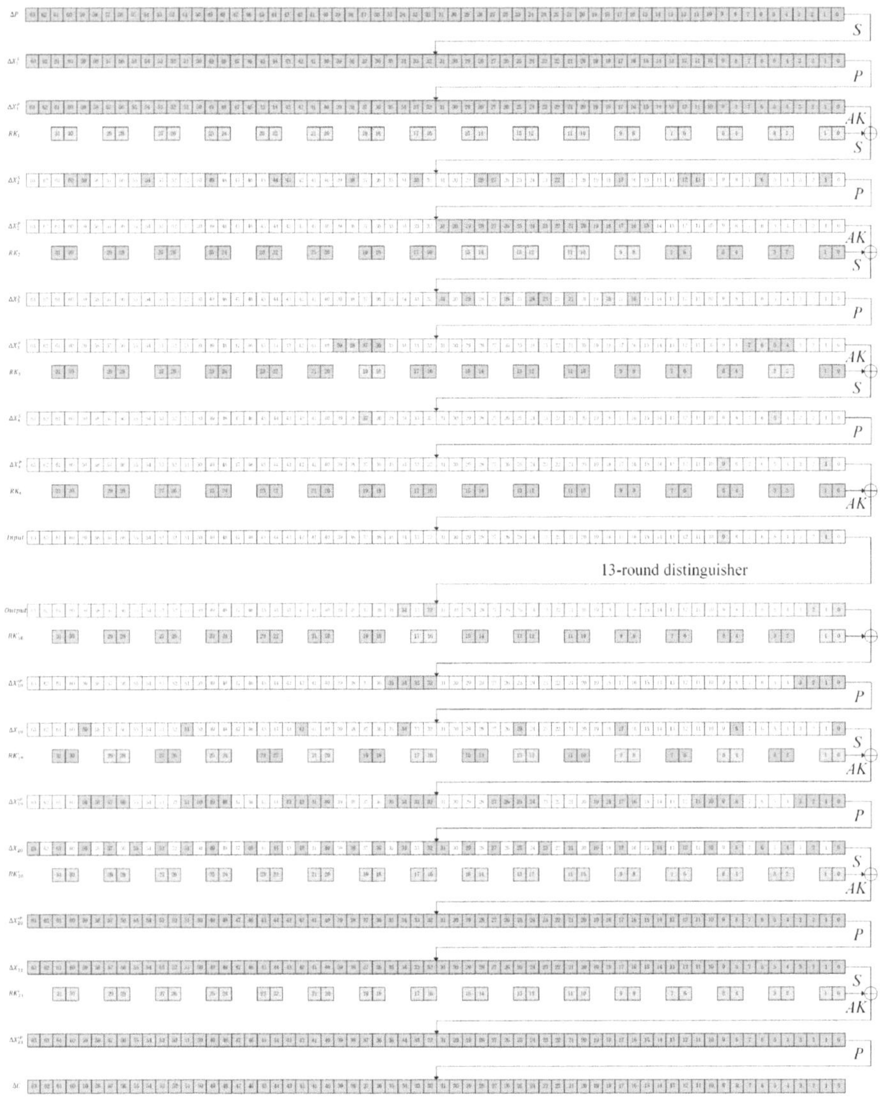

Fig. 2. 21-Round differential attack on GIFT-64. Each square represents one bit. The squares in white stand for the values of difference bits are '0'. The squares in green stand for the values of difference bits are '1'. The squares in grey stand for the values of difference bits that are indeterminate. The squares in orange stand for the bits of key are need to be guessed. The squares in blue stand for the bits of key that are omitted. (Color figure online)

5.2 Weak-Key Key Recovery Attacks on GIFT-128

The 27-round Differential Attack on GIFT-128. Using the 20-round differential with probability $2^{-114.77}$ in the weak-key space W_3, which is presented in

Sect. 4.3, we launch the differential attack on 27-round GIFT-128 by adding four rounds before and three rounds after the distinguisher in Appendix D of the full paper.

Complexity and Success Probability. The data complexity is about $2^{115.77}$ chosen-plaintexts, the time complexity is about $2^{110.85}$ 27-round operations, the memory complexity is about 2^{92}-bit, and the success probability is about 99.9%. Compared to the 27-round differential attack in [25], the complexity is reduced by about $2^{3.06}$ in a weak-key setting.

The 28-round Differential Attack on GIFT-128. Similarly, by adding four rounds before and three rounds after, the first 28-round multiple differential attack on GIFT-128 is launched based on the 21-round multiple differentials with probability $2^{-122.77}$ in the weak-key space W_4, which is proposed in Sect. 4.3. The details of the attack are presented in Appendix E of the full paper.

Complexity and Success Probability. The data complexity is about $2^{123.77}$ chosen-plaintexts, the time complexity is about $2^{123.77}$ 28-round operations, the memory complexity is about 2^{96}-bit, and the success probability is about 86.5%.

6 Distinguisher and Attack on SUNDAE-GIFT

We attack the initialization phase without plaintext data of version SUNDAE-GIFT-96 of SUNDAE-GIFT family with a 96-bit nonce, which is the primary member satisfying the requirements set by NIST. Our restriction for searching distinguishers is that the difference of the plaintext is only active in the high 96 bits by adding a certain number of rounds before the distinguisher. Then we find two 11-round differential characteristics, which are listed in Appendix F, Table 25 of the full paper with average probability 2^{-60}, that can be utilized to launch a 17-round differential attack by adding three rounds before and three rounds after the distinguisher. Similarly, we search for quasidifferential trails satisfying $|c| = p_{avg}$ and find only one quasidifferential trail with all-zero masks for each characteristic, thus, there are no weak-key conditions for these two characteristics.

The first 17-round differential attack on SUNDAE-GIFT utilizing the 11-round differential characteristic with probability 2^{-60} is proposed in Appendix F of the full paper.

Complexity and Success Probability : The data complexity is about $2^{62.5}$ chosen-plaintexts, the time complexity is about $2^{75.37}$ 17-round operations, the memory complexity is about 2^{66}-bit, and the success probability is about 99.9%.

7 Conclusion

In this paper, we continue the work on the quasidifferential transition matrix in differential cryptanalysis proposed by Beyne and Rijmen at CRYPTO 2022 and apply their approach to GIFT. By holding some conditions of master-key, the probabilities of some differential characteristics with small probabilities can be improved in a weak-key setting. Then the weak-key (multiple) differential key-recovery attacks on GIFT are obtained based on the weak-key distinguishers. For GIFT-64, the multiple differential attack can be boosted from 20 to 21 rounds, and the 21-round differential attack can be improved in terms of complexity. For GIFT-128, the complexity of the 27-round differential attack can be improved, and the first 28-round (multiple) differential attack is obtained. Finally, after checking the 11-round differential characteristic with quasidifferential trails, we mount the first differential attack on the 17-round SUNDAE-GIFT.

Acknowledgments. We sincerely thank the anonymous reviewers for providing valuable comments to help us improve the overall quality of the paper. This research is supported by the National Key R&D Program of China(Grant No. 2024YFA1013000, 2023YFA1009500), the National Natural Science Foundation of China (Grant No. 62032014, U2336207), Department of Science & Technology of Shandong Province(No.SYS202201), Quan Cheng Laboratory (Grant No. QCLZD202301, QCLZD202306). Kai Hu is supported by the National Natural Science Foundation of China (62402283), the Natural Science Foundation of Jiangsu Province (BK20240420), and Program of Qilu Young Scholars of Shandong University.

References

1. Banik, S., Bogdanov, A., Luykx, A., Tischhauser, E.: Sundae: small universal deterministic authenticated encryption for the internet of things. IACR Trans. Symmetric Cryptol. **2018**(3), 1–35 (2018). https://tosc.iacr.org/index.php/ToSC/article/view/7296
2. Banik, S., Bogdanov, A., Peyrin, T., Sasaki, Y., Tischhauser, S.M.E., Todo, Y.: Sundae-gift. Submission to Round, no. 1, 2019
3. Banik, S., et al.: Gift-cofb. Cryptology ePrint Archive, Paper 2020/738 (2020). https://eprint.iacr.org/2020/738
4. Banik, S., Pandey, S.K., Peyrin, T., Sasaki, Y., Sim, S.M., Todo, Y.: Gift: a small present. In: Fischer, W., Homma, N. (eds.) Cryptographic Hardware and Embedded Systems - CHES 2017, pp. 321–345. Springer International Publishing, Cham (2017)
5. Beyne, T., Rijmen, V.: Differential cryptanalysis in the fixed-key model. In: Dodis, Y., Shrimpton, T. (eds.) Advances in Cryptology - CRYPTO 2022 - 42nd Annual International Cryptology Conference, CRYPTO 2022, Santa Barbara, CA, USA, 15–18 August 2022, Proceedings, Part III. LNCS, vol. 13509, pp. 687–716. Springer, Cham (2022). https://doi.org/10.1007/978-3-031-15982-4_23
6. Biham, E., Shamir, A.: Differential cryptanalysis of des-like cryptosystems. In: Menezes, A.J., Vanstone, S.A. (eds.) Advances in Cryptology-CRYPTO' 90, pp. 2–21. Springer, Berlin, Heidelberg (1991)
7. Boura, C., David, N., Derbez, P., Boissier, R.H., Naya-Plasencia, M.: A generic algorithm for efficient key recovery in differential attacks - and its associated tool. In: Joye, M., Leander, G. (eds.) Advances in Cryptology - EUROCRYPT 2024 - 43rd Annual International Conference on the Theory and Applications of Cryptographic Techniques, Zurich, Switzerland, May 26-30, 2024, Proceedings, Part I.

LNCS, vol. 14651, pp. 217–248. Springer, Cham (2024). https://doi.org/10.1007/978-3-031-58716-0_8
8. Chakraborti, A., Datta, N., Jha, A., Nandi, M.: Hyena. Submission to the NIST Lightweight Cryptography project, 2019
9. Chen, H., Zong, R., Dong, X.: Improved differential attacks on GIFT-64. In: Zhou, J., Luo, X., Shen, Q., Xu, Z. (eds.) Information and Communications Security - 21st International Conference, ICICS 2019, Beijing, China, 15–17 December 2019, Revised Selected Papers. LNCS, vol. 11999, pp. 447–462. Springer, Cham (2019). https://doi.org/10.1007/978-3-030-41579-2_26
10. Daemen, J., Govaerts, R., Vandewalle, J.: Correlation matrices. In: Preneel, B. (ed.) Fast Software Encryption: Second International Workshop. Leuven, Belgium, 14–16 December 1994, Proceedings. LNCS, vol. 1008, pp. 275–285. Springer, Cham (1994). https://doi.org/10.1007/3-540-60590-8_21
11. Flórez-Gutiérrez, A., Todo, Y.: Improving linear key recovery attacks using walsh spectrum puncturing. In: Joye, M., Leander, G. (eds.) Advances in Cryptology - EUROCRYPT 2024 - 43rd Annual International Conference on the Theory and Applications of Cryptographic Techniques, Zurich, Switzerland, 26–30 May 2024, Proceedings, Part I. LNCS, vol. 14651, pp. 187–216. Springer, Cham (2024). https://doi.org/10.1007/978-3-031-58716-0_7
12. Ji, F., Zhang, W., Zhou, C., Ding, T.: Improved (related-key) differential cryptanalysis on gift. In: Dunkelman, O., Jacobson, M.J., Jr., O'Flynn, C. (eds.) Selected Areas in Cryptography, pp. 198–228. Springer International Publishing, Cham (2021)
13. Lai, X., Massey, J.L., Murphy, S.: Markov ciphers and differential cryptanalysis. In: Davies, D.W. (ed.) Advances in Cryptology - EUROCRYPT '91, Workshop on the Theory and Application of of Cryptographic Techniques, Brighton, UK, 8–11 April 1991, Proceedings. LNCS, vol. 547, pp. 17–38. Springer, Cham (1991). https://doi.org/10.1007/3-540-46416-6_2
14. Li, L., Wu, W., Zheng, Y., Zhang, L.: The relationship between the construction and solution of the milp models and applications. Cryptology ePrint Archive, Paper 2019/049 (2019). https://eprint.iacr.org/2019/049
15. Liu, Y., Sasaki, Y.: Related-key boomerang attacks on gift with automated trail search including bct effect. Cryptology ePrint Archive, Paper 2019/669 (2019). https://doi.org/10.1007/978-3-030-21548-4
16. Sasaki, Y.: Integer linear programming for three-subset meet-in-the-middle attacks: application to GIFT. In: Inomata, A., Yasuda, K. (eds.) Advances in Information and Computer Security - 13th International Workshop on Security, IWSEC 2018, Sendai, Japan, 3–5 September 2018, Proceedings. LNCS, vol. 11049, pp. 227–243. Springer, Cham (2018). https://doi.org/10.1007/978-3-319-97916-8_15
17. Selçuk, A.A.: On probability of success in linear and differential cryptanalysis. J. Cryptol. **21**, 131–147 (2008). **2008**, https://doi.org/10.1007/s00145-007-9013-7
18. Sun, L., Wang, W., Wang, M.: Accelerating the search of differential and linear characteristics with the SAT method. IACR Trans. Symmetric Cryptol. **2021**(1), 269–315 (2021). https://doi.org/10.46586/tosc.v2021.i1.269-315
19. Sun, L., Wang, W., Wang, M.: Improved attacks on GIFT-64. In: AlTawy, R., Hülsing, A. (eds.) Selected Areas in Cryptography - 28th International Conference, SAC 2021, Virtual Event, September 29–1 October 2021, Revised Selected Papers. LNCS, vol. 13203, pp. 246–265. Springer, Cham (2021). https://doi.org/10.1007/978-3-030-99277-4_12

20. Sun, L., Wang, W., Wang, M.: Linear cryptanalyses of three aeads with gift-128 as underlying primitives. IACR Trans. Symmetric Cryptol. **2021**(2), 199–221 (2021). https://tosc.iacr.org/index.php/ToSC/article/view/8909
21. Sun, L., Wang, W., Wang, M.: Addendum to linear cryptanalyses of three aeads with GIFT-128 as underlying primitives. IACR Trans. Symmetric Cryptol. **2022**(1), 212–219 (2022). https://doi.org/10.46586/tosc.v2022.i1.212-219
22. Wang, S., Liu, M., Hou, S., Lin, D.: Differential-linear cryptanalysis of GIFT family and gift-based ciphers. IACR Commun. Cryptol. **1**(1), 13 (2024). https://doi.org/10.62056/a6n5txol7
23. Zhu, B., Dong, X., Yu, H.: Milp-based differential attack on round-reduced GIFT. In: Matsui, M. (ed.) Topics in Cryptology - CT-RSA 2019 - The Cryptographers' Track at the RSA Conference 2019, San Francisco, CA, USA, 4–8 March 2019, Proceedings. LNCS, vol. 11405, pp. 372–390. Springer, Cham (2019). https://doi.org/10.1007/978-3-030-12612-4_19
24. Zhu, B., Dong, X., Yu, H.: Milp-based differential attack on round-reduced gift. In: Matsui, M. (ed.) Topics in Cryptology - CT-RSA 2019, pp. 372–390. Springer International Publishing, Cham (2019)
25. Zong, R., Dong, X., Chen, H., Luo, Y., Wang, S., Li, Z.: Towards key-recovery-attack friendly distinguishers: application to gift-128. IACR Trans. Symmetric Cryptol. **2021**(1), 156–184 (2021). https://tosc.iacr.org/index.php/ToSC/article/view/8836

Meet-in-the-Middle Attack on Primitives with Binary Matrix Linear Layer

Qingliang Hou[1], Kuntong Li[1], Guoyan Zhang[1,2(✉)], Yanzhao Shen[2], Qidi You[3,4], and Xiaoyang Dong[5]

[1] School of Cyber Science and Technology, Shandong University, Qingdao, China
{qinglianghou,likuntong}@mail.sdu.edu.cn, guoyanzhang@sdu.edu.cn
[2] Shandong Institute of Blockchain, Jinan, China
shenyanzhao@sdibc.cn
[3] State Key Laboratory of Space-Ground Integrated Information Technology, Beijing, China
youqd@spacestar.com.cn
[4] Space Star Technology Co., Ltd., Beijing, China
[5] Institute for Network Sciences and Cyberspace, BNRist, Tsinghua University, Beijing, China
xiaoyangdong@tsinghua.edu.cn

Abstract. Meet-in-the-middle (MitM) is a powerful approach for the cryptanalysis of symmetric primitives. In recent years, MitM has led to many improved records about key recovery, preimage and collision attacks with the help of automated tools. However, most of the previous work target AES-like hashing where the linear layer is an MDS matrix. And we observe that their automatic model for MDS matrix is not suitable for primitives using a binary matrix as their linear layer.

In this paper, we propose the n-XOR model to describe the XOR operation with an arbitrary number of inputs. And it can be applied to primitives with a binary matrix of arbitrary size. Then, we propose a check model to eliminate the possible inaccuracies caused by n-XOR. But the check model is limited by the input size (not greater than 4). Combined with the two new models, we find a MitM key recovery attack on 11-round Midori64. When the whitening keys are excluded, a MitM key recovery attack can be mounted on the 12-round Midori64. Compared with the previous best work, both of the above results have distinct advantages in terms of reducing memory and data complexity. At last, we apply the n-XOR model to the hashing modes of primitives with large size binary matrix. The preimage attack on weakened Camellia-MMO (without FL/FL^{-1} and whitening layers) and Aria-DM are both improved by 1 round.

Keywords: Meet-in-the-Middle · Binary Matrix · Key Recovery · Preimage · Midori64 · Camellia · Aria

First Author and Second Author contributed equally to this work.
The full version of this paper is available at https://eprint.iacr.org/2025/082.

A. Patra (Ed.): CT-RSA 2025, LNCS 15598, pp. 51–74, 2025.
https://doi.org/10.1007/978-3-031-88661-4_3

1 Introduction

The Meet-in-the-middle (MitM) is a powerful cryptanalysis strategy first proposed by Diffie and Hellman to attack Double DES [12]. The core idea is to identify two disjoint neutral sets of unknown values. Then, the whole computation path can be divided into two independent chunks, which are determined by two neutral sets and denoted by *forward chunk* and *backward chunk*, respectively. At last, the two chunks will meet at a common internal state where the consistency is checked to filter out candidate assignments of unknown values. From then on, MitM and its variants have been successfully applied to many block ciphers [9,19,30,33]. At SAC 2008, Aumasson *et al.* [3] first introduced the theory of MitM into preimage attacks on step-reduced MD5 and 3-pass HAVAL. Sequentially, many refined techniques were proposed to enhance the power of MitM, such as splice-and-cut [2], initial structure [31], bicliques [8], and so on. At FSE 2011, Sasaki [27] applied such MitM preimage attack to the PGV [26] hashing modes of AES and presented the first preimage attack on 7-round AES-MMO/MP/DM together with the partial indirect matching technique. Interestingly, these enhancements were finally found to be applicable in the key recovery attack on block ciphers. At ACISP 2011, Wei *et al.* [38] broke the full round KTANTAN using the splice-and-cut technique by connecting the plaintext and ciphertext with encryption or decryption oracles with only 4 chosen plaintexts.

Despite being clear that a MitM attack is entirely determined by its *characteristic*, i.e., the configuration for two chunks, it's still complicated and error-prone to explore the whole configuration space. Recently, automated tools were introduced to find the best characteristic by solving an optimization problem. At Eurocrypt 2021, Bao *et al.* [6] proposed an MILP-based MitM preimage attack on AES-like hash and Haraka v2. At CRYPTO 2021, Dong *et al.* [13] extended the automatic model into key-recovery and collision attacks and introduced a table-based method to solve the non-linear constraints imposed on neutral sets. At CRYPTO 2022, Bao *et al.* [7] considered the MitM attack in a view of superposition (SupP) states and bi-directional attribute propagation (BiDir) such that neutral sets are treated independently and can be imposed constraints in both computation paths. At Asiacrypt 2023, Hou *et al.* [17] introduced the SupP framework into Feistel-based hash functions. At Eurocrypt 2024, Chen *et al.* [10] considered the linearization of the S-Box in AES and allowed a linear combination of two neutral sets in the initial structure. Different from the above work, Schrottenloher and Stevens [34] studied a simple top-down modeling paradigm for both classical and quantum preimage attacks against permutations and was later extended to key recovery attack on block ciphers with simple key schedules [35]. The simplified attack excluded many details. In this paper, we adopt the bottom-up MitM framework in [7] and the table-based method in [13].

In the previous work, the targets are most built by a block cipher with an MDS matrix. Through the diffusion layer, each output cell is related to all the input cells. However, the primitives with binary matrix are rarely studied, where each output cell is represented as the XOR of partial input cells. In [13], Dong *et al.* introduced the 3-XOR model for SKINNY-n-$3n$. In their model, the number of input cells is fixed to be 4. All valid cases can be easily exhausted to form a system of inequalities using the convex hull method [37]. However, if more input cells are involved, the number of valid cases will increase extremely leading to larger size of system of inequalities, which can make model infeasible to compute. Hence, there is a gap to find an accurate and effective method to describe the MitM attribute propagation through a binary matrix of arbitrary size.

Our Contributions. In this paper, we propose a novel model called `n-XOR` under the encoding scheme in [7], to describe the propagation of MitM attributes through an `XOR` operation with an arbitrary number of input cells. And the number of inequalities formed by `n-XOR` is fixed, independent of the number of inputs. Hence, `n-XOR` can be applied to large binary matrices effectively. However, we also observe that only applying `n-XOR` will lead to subtle inaccuracies. An extremely explicit case is that the constraint on the same neutral bits may be double counted in two different `n-XOR` operations. Besides, there are more implicit cases depending on the specific linear layer. Hence, we propose an additional check model to eliminate these inaccuracies. But this model is limited by the input size n, that is, $n \leq 4$ in our paper.

As a low-energy lightweight cryptography, `Midori` [5] is well-suited for constrained environments, like the edge gateways and end devices in the blockchain on-chain and off-chain interactions. As a proof of work, we applied the two new models to `Midori64`, with 64-bit state and a 4×4 binary matrix as linear layer. Then, an 11-round key recovery attack is found with time complexity of 2^{124}. The data and memory complexity are 2^{36} and 2^{6}, respectively. When omitting the whitening layer, a 12-round MitM characteristic for weakened `Midori64` is found with time complexity of 2^{120}. The data and memory cost are 2^{48} and $2^{10.6}$, respectively. Besides, the data and memory complexity can be further reduced if the time complexity is relaxed to 2^{124}. Compared to the previous best records of `Midori64` [23,24,36], despite a little higher time complexity, our results have distinct advantages in reducing data and memory complexity.

It's a practical design strategy to build hash functions on widely used block cipher with a longstanding record of cryptanalysis. And `AES-MMO` was even internationally standardized by ISO [20]. Since `Camellia` [1] was also standardized by ISO [21] and `Aria` [22] was standardized by Korean Standard (KS X1213), the hashing modes of `Camellia` or `Aria` may be potential candidates used in practice. Indeed, their security have been evaluated in a series of works [4,16,28,32]. In this paper, we apply the `n-XOR` to describe the MitM attributes propagation through the large binary matrix of `Camellia` and `Aria`. Finally, we find a preimage attack on 14-round weakened `Camellia-MMO` (without FL/FL^{-1} and whitening layers) and a preimage attack on 6-round `Aria-DM`. Compared to the previous best records [16,29], the attack rounds are both improved by 1 round.

Our results are also summarized in Table 1 and Table 2. For the source code, please refer to https://github.com/wenny-kt/MITM-Binary-Matrix.

The rest of this paper is organized as follows. In Sect. 2, we give an overview of how the automated MitM attacks are deployed, along with some enhanced

Table 1. Single Key attacks on `Midori64`, where ID and $\mathcal{DS}$-MitM denote impossible differential and Demirci-Selçuk MitM attack, respectively.

Target	Rounds	Data	Memory(Bytes)	Time(Enc.)	Technique	Ref.
`Midori64`	11	2^{60}	$2^{95.8}$	$2^{116.6}$	ID	[24]
	11	2^{53}	$2^{92.2}$	2^{122}	$\mathcal{DS}$-MitM	[23]
	11	$\mathbf{2^{36}}$	$\mathbf{2^{6}}$	2^{124}	MitM	Sect. 4.1
	12	$2^{55.5}$	2^{109}	$2^{125.5}$	$\mathcal{DS}$-MitM	[23]
	$12^{\dagger}$	$2^{61.9}$	2^{44}	$2^{90.5}$	ID	[36]
	$12^{\dagger}$	$\mathbf{2^{48}}$	$\mathbf{2^{10.6}}$	2^{120}	MitM	Sect. 4.2
	$12^{\dagger}$	$\mathbf{2^{36}}$	$\mathbf{2^{5.6}}$	2^{124}	MitM	Sect. 4.2

† Weakened version without whitening layers.

Table 2. A Summary of the MitM Attacks on Hashing Modes.

Target	Attacks	Rounds	Time1	Time2	Memory	Technique	Ref.
`Camellia-MMO`	Preimage	$13^{\ddagger}$	2^{120}	2^{125}	2^{8}	MitM	[29]
		$14^{\ddagger}$	2^{120}	2^{125}	2^{8}	MitM	Sect. 5
`Aria-DM`	Preimage	5	2^{120}	2^{125}	2^{8}	MitM	[16]
		6	2^{120}	2^{125}	2^{112}	MitM	Sect. 6

- ‡ Weakened version without FL/FL^{-1} and whitening layers.
- Time1 represents the time complexity of pseudo-preimage. Time2 represents the time complexity of preimage attack converted from the pseudo-preimage attack according to [25, Fact9.99].

techniques. In Sect. 3, we introduce two new improved models embedded in the automated MitM framework, called `n-XOR` and check model. The applications to `Midori64`, `Camellia-MMO` and `Aria-DM` are presented in Sects. 4, 5 and 6, respectively. Finally, we conclude in Sect. 7.

2 Preliminaries: Automated Meet-in-the-Middle Attack

In this section, we provide an overview of how the MitM attack framework is constructed, and how it is encoded into the MILP language with specified configurations for the preimage and key recovery attack. Then, we recall two enhanced techniques to improve the power of MitM attack. The first one is the *table-based method* introduced in [13] to solving the non-linear constraints. Another one is the *Superposition (SupP) States and Bi-direction Attribute-Propagation (BiDir)* introduced in [7] to preserving more valid solutions.

2.1 Framework of the Meet-in-the-Middle Attack

The MitM attack framework is illustrated in Fig. 1. $\mathcal{S}^{\texttt{ENC}}$ and $\mathcal{S}^{\texttt{KEY}}$ are the starting states where there are $\lambda_{\mathcal{B}}^{\texttt{ENC}}$ and $\lambda_{\mathcal{B}}^{\texttt{KEY}}$ neutral bits for forward computation

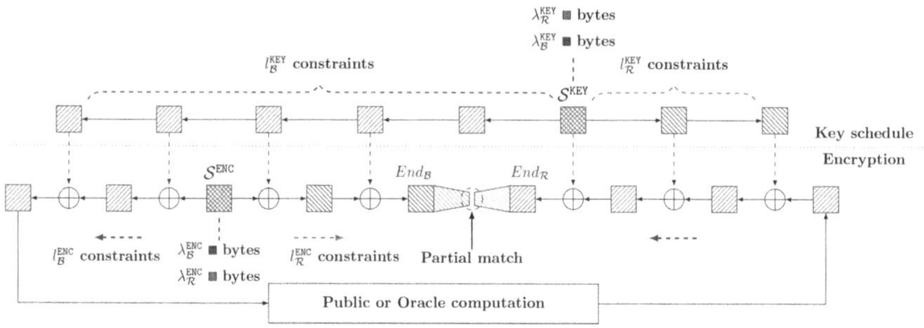

Fig. 1. A high-level overview of the MITM attacks [13]

denoted by ■, and there are $\lambda_{\mathcal{R}}^{\text{ENC}}$ and $\lambda_{\mathcal{R}}^{\text{KEY}}$ neutral bits for backward computation denoted by ■. After imposing $l_{\mathcal{R}}^{\text{ENC}}$ and $l_{\mathcal{R}}^{\text{KEY}}$ constraints on $\lambda_{\mathcal{R}}^{\text{ENC}}$ and $\lambda_{\mathcal{R}}^{\text{KEY}}$ backward neutral bits, respectively, ■ can be propagated to the matching points $End_{\mathcal{B}}$ independent of the ■ bits. The degree of freedom (DoF) for the ■ neutral space is computed by $d_{\mathcal{R}} = \lambda_{\mathcal{R}}^{\text{ENC}} + \lambda_{\mathcal{R}}^{\text{KEY}} - l_{\mathcal{R}}^{\text{ENC}} - l_{\mathcal{R}}^{\text{KEY}}$. Similarly, forward neutral bits are imposed on $l_{\mathcal{B}}^{\text{ENC}}$ and $l_{\mathcal{B}}^{\text{KEY}}$ constraints to cancel the effect of ■ in the backward computation. The DoF of the ■ neutral space can be computed by $d_{\mathcal{B}} = \lambda_{\mathcal{B}}^{\text{ENC}} + \lambda_{\mathcal{B}}^{\text{KEY}} - l_{\mathcal{B}}^{\text{ENC}} - l_{\mathcal{B}}^{\text{KEY}}$. Through a feed-forward mechanism or querying a public Encryption-Decryption oracle, $End_{\mathcal{R}}$ can be derived by ■. Instead of requiring the full states, the partial matching exploits the filtering ability derived by the deterministic relation "$End_{\mathcal{B}} = End_{\mathcal{R}}$" and denoted by d_m.

With the configurations of $(\lambda_{\mathcal{B}}^{\text{ENC}}, \lambda_{\mathcal{B}}^{\text{KEY}}, \lambda_{\mathcal{R}}^{\text{ENC}}, \lambda_{\mathcal{R}}^{\text{KEY}}, l_{\mathcal{B}}^{\text{ENC}}, l_{\mathcal{B}}^{\text{KEY}}, l_{\mathcal{R}}^{\text{ENC}}, l_{\mathcal{R}}^{\text{KEY}}, d_m)$, the basic attack procedure goes as follows:

1. Choose constants in $\mathcal{S}^{\text{ENC}}$ and $\mathcal{S}^{\text{KEY}}$ and $l_{\mathcal{B}}^{\text{ENC}} + l_{\mathcal{B}}^{\text{KEY}} + l_{\mathcal{R}}^{\text{ENC}} + l_{\mathcal{R}}^{\text{KEY}}$ constraints.
2. For $2^{d_{\mathcal{B}}}$ values of ■ neutral space, compute forward to $End_{\mathcal{B}}$ from the starting states, and store the values of ■ in table $L_{\mathcal{B}}[End_{\mathcal{B}}]$.
3. For $2^{d_{\mathcal{R}}}$ values of ■ neutral space, compute backward to $End_{\mathcal{R}}$ from the starting states, and store the values of ■ in table $L_{\mathcal{R}}[End_{\mathcal{R}}]$.
4. According to the indices, check the match between $L_{\mathcal{B}}$ and $L_{\mathcal{R}}$.
5. For the surviving pairs that pass the match, check for a full-state match.

Complexity Analysis. The above steps 2-5 form a MitM *episode*. To find an h-bit full match, $2^{h-(d_{\mathcal{B}}+d_{\mathcal{R}})}$ episodes are needed. Since each episode is performed with a time of $2^{\max\{d_{\mathcal{B}},d_{\mathcal{R}}\}} + 2^{d_{\mathcal{B}}+d_{\mathcal{R}}-d_m}$, the total time complexity is:

$$2^{h-(d_{\mathcal{B}}+d_{\mathcal{R}})} \cdot \left(2^{\max\{d_{\mathcal{B}},d_{\mathcal{R}}\}} + 2^{d_{\mathcal{B}}+d_{\mathcal{R}}-d_m}\right) \approx 2^{h-\min\{d_{\mathcal{B}},d_{\mathcal{R}},d_m\}} \tag{1}$$

Apparently, a MitM characteristic is valid, if and only if $\min\{d_{\mathcal{B}}, d_{\mathcal{R}}, d_m\} \geq 1$. For MitM key recovery attack, additional constraints must be fulfilled to ensure that the internal states in $\mathcal{S}^{\text{ENC}}$ can be totally determined by $\mathcal{S}^{\text{KEY}}$. This is equivalent to using up the DoFs of $\mathcal{S}^{\text{ENC}}$, i.e., $\lambda_{\mathcal{B}}^{\text{ENC}} - l_{\mathcal{B}}^{\text{ENC}} = 0$ and $\lambda_{\mathcal{R}}^{\text{ENC}} - l_{\mathcal{R}}^{\text{ENC}} = 0$. Besides, there should exists only one type of neutral bit in the plaintext or ciphertext, and at least 1-bit constant in the plaintext or ciphertext to avoid using up the full codebook. In [6], Bao *et al.* encoded the type of each byte in `AES` with a pair of boolean variables:

1. ■ $\mathcal{R}$, $(x, y) = (0, 1)$: Known byte only with backward computation.
2. ■ $\mathcal{B}$, $(x, y) = (1, 0)$: Known byte only with forward computation.
3. ■ $\mathcal{G}$, $(x, y) = (1, 1)$: Constant byte and known in both forward and backward computations.
4. □ $\mathcal{W}$, $(x, y) = (0, 0)$: Unknown byte in forward and backward computations.

Then, the propagation rules for `XOR` and `MixColumns` can be described as a system of inequalities based on the above definitions. A valid MitM characteristic is defined as a solution solved by the off-the-shelf MILP solvers, like Gurobi [15], with the objective function that maximizes the $\min\{d_{\mathcal{B}}, d_{\mathcal{R}}, d_m\}$. For the detailed MILP models of these propagation rules, please refer to [6] or [18, Appendix A].

2.2 Enhanced Techniques

Table-Based Method Solving Non-Linear Constraints. Note that Eq. (1) holds mostly when the constraints imposed on neutral bits can be solved in $O(1)$ time, such as linear equations. However, there are many practice MitM characteristics with non-linear constrained neutral bits, which can not be solved efficiently. In [13], Dong *et al.* proposed a precomputation method to compute the value of the constraints by enumerating the neutral bits. Specifically, after setting the value of constants in starting states, do as follows:

1. For $2^{\lambda_{\mathcal{B}}^{\texttt{ENC}}+\lambda_{\mathcal{B}}^{\texttt{KEY}}}$ ■ values, compute the values of $l_{\mathcal{B}}^{\texttt{ENC}} + l_{\mathcal{B}}^{\texttt{KEY}}$ constraints (denoted by $\mathfrak{c}_{\mathcal{B}} \in \mathbb{F}_2^{l_{\mathcal{B}}^{\texttt{ENC}}+l_{\mathcal{B}}^{\texttt{KEY}}}$) and store the $\lambda_{\mathcal{B}}^{\texttt{ENC}} + \lambda_{\mathcal{B}}^{\texttt{KEY}}$ ■ bits in $U[\mathfrak{c}_{\mathcal{B}}]$.
2. For $2^{\lambda_{\mathcal{R}}^{\texttt{ENC}}+\lambda_{\mathcal{R}}^{\texttt{KEY}}}$ ■ values, compute the values of $l_{\mathcal{R}}^{\texttt{ENC}} + l_{\mathcal{R}}^{\texttt{KEY}}$ constraints (denoted by $\mathfrak{c}_{\mathcal{R}} \in \mathbb{F}_2^{l_{\mathcal{R}}^{\texttt{ENC}}+l_{\mathcal{R}}^{\texttt{KEY}}}$) and store the $\lambda_{\mathcal{R}}^{\texttt{ENC}} + \lambda_{\mathcal{R}}^{\texttt{KEY}}$ ■ bits in $V[\mathfrak{c}_{\mathcal{R}}]$.

Then, in each MitM episode, for a given $\mathfrak{c}_{\mathcal{B}}$ and $\mathfrak{c}_{\mathcal{R}}$, the values in $U[\mathfrak{c}_{\mathcal{B}}]$ and $V[\mathfrak{c}_{\mathcal{R}}]$ can be searched in time $O(1)$. The time and memory cost for one precomputation phase are both $2^{\lambda_{\mathcal{B}}^{\texttt{ENC}}+\lambda_{\mathcal{B}}^{\texttt{KEY}}} + 2^{\lambda_{\mathcal{R}}^{\texttt{ENC}}+\lambda_{\mathcal{R}}^{\texttt{KEY}}}$.

SupP States and BiDir. In the SupP MitM framework of [7], neutral cells from both directions can be separated into two virtual states, called SupP states, to keep the linearity through linear operations. Then, ■ and ■ will be treated independently through linear operations, and the initial DoFs can be consumed in both directions. After a series of linear operations, two SupP states are finally combined before the next nonlinear operation. The color patterns and how the states are separated and combined are visualized in Fig. 2. BiDir allows neutral cells to be consumed in both two directions, but this may lead to dependency between one type of neutral cell with non-linear constraints imposed on another. In [11], Degré proposed a more generic table-based method to cancel this dependency. Combined with the SupP states and BiDir methods, the solution space is greatly enlarged, such that some attack configurations with lower time complexities may be found. In the rest of this paper, we simplify the representation of SupP states. The virtual states of pure ■/■/■/□ are omitted. And we denote the SupP states by the □ cell in which the blue cell and red cell occur simultaneously.

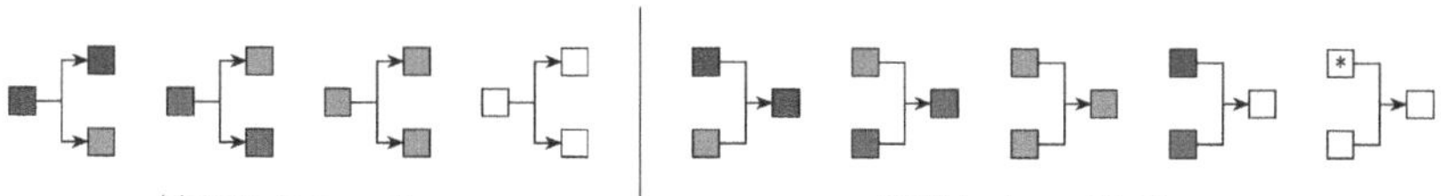

(a) Rules for separation (b) Rules for combination

Fig. 2. Rules for separation and combination, where "$*$" means any color

3 New Models for Linear Layer with Binary Matrix

In this section, we first propose an effective method to build an MILP model to describe the MitM attributes propagation through a `n-XOR` operation with SupP states. Interestingly, the number of input cells involved in the `XOR` operation can be arbitrary, but the size of MILP model will not increase. However, we also observer that this may lead to double counting of constraints on the same neutral cells. Then, we show that the inaccuracy can be easily eliminated by adding an additional check model.

3.1 N-XOR Model

To simulate the MitM attributes propagation through the linear layer, Bao *et al.* proposed the `MC-RULE` for the MDS matrix in `AES`-like hashing [6,7]. As shown in Fig. 3(a), each input cell has an effect on all output cells in MDS matrix. However, some primitives adopt a binary matrix in the diffusion layer where each output cell is computed by the `XOR` of partial input cells. As the `Midori64`'s binary matrix shown in Fig. 3(b), the first output cell is only related to the last three input cells. Apparently, this will lead to inaccurate propagation if we apply the `MC-RULE` for MDS matrix on binary matrix directly since one output cell is not related to all input cells.

(a) Coloring pattern of `MC-RULE` for MDS matrix (b) Coloring pattern for binary matrix

Fig. 3. A case of the difference of color pattern between MDS and binary matrix

In [13], Dong *et al.* proposed the `3-XOR-RULE` to model the key addition in `SKINNY`-n-$3n$. By enumerating four input cells, one output cell and one indicator variable for DoF cost, all valid color patterns can be restricted to a subset of $\mathbb{F}_2^{11}$, which can be described into a system of inequalities using the convex hull technique [37]. If we directly extend the strategy of `3-XOR-RULE` to the `XOR` operation with n input cells, then the enumeration scope will be restricted to a subset of $\mathbb{F}_2^{2n+3}$. When n is large, it's complicated and error-prone to enumerate all valid color patterns. And the size of the system of inequalities may be large, which renders the model infeasible to compute.

An alternative strategy is to apply the `XOR-RULE` in [6,7] for two-input `XOR` consecutively. This strategy is valid but may miss some valid patterns by introducing additional auxiliary variables. We take the attribute propagation through `Midori64`'s diffusion layer to state this fact as shown in Fig. 4. In the first step of Fig. 4(a), an auxiliary variable `auxi` is needed to carry on the output of $X[2] \oplus X[3]$. For the second step, $X[1]$ and $X[0]$ are `XOR`ed with `auxi` to compute $Y[0]$ and $Y[1]$, respectively. Then, one of the following cases will occur,

- If `auxi` is ■ by consuming one DoF, then $Y[0]$ will always be ■, and $Y[1]$ will always be ■.
- If `auxi` is ■, then $Y[1]$ will always be ■. $Y[0]$ can be either ■ or ■ by consuming one DoF.

However, with the `n-XOR` model in Fig. 4(b), step 1 and step 2 can be executed independently without correlated variables. Then, $Y[0]$ and $Y[1]$ can be ■ simultaneously by consuming 2 DoFs of ■, which can not be captured by the first strategy.

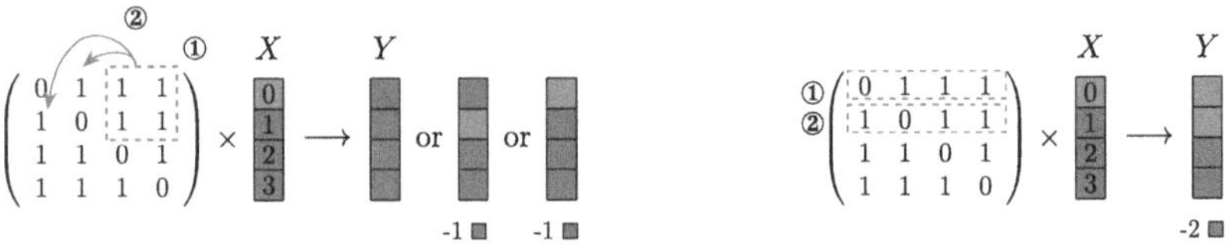

(a) Model of consecutive `XOR` (b) `n-XOR` Model

Fig. 4. The advantage of `n-XOR` model compared with consecutive `XOR`

In the following, we show how to convert the propagation of ■ cells through the `n-XOR` operation under SupP states into MILP language. All coloring patterns can be specified by the following set of rules denoted by `n-XOR-RULE`$^{-}$. The `n-XOR-RULE`$^{+}$ for ■ can be obtained in a similar way by exchanging ■ and ■ since they are dual.

- `n-XOR-RULE`$^{-}$-1. If there is at least one □ in input, then the output is □.
- `n-XOR-RULE`$^{-}$-2. If all cells of the input are ■, then the output must be ■.
- `n-XOR-RULE`$^{-}$-3. If there are ■ and ■ cells but no □ cell in the input, then one of the following situations will occur:
  - The output is ■ cell and no DoF is consumed.
  - The output is ■ by consuming one DoF of ■.

Let $(A[1], A[2], \cdots, A[n])$ be the input of `n-XOR` where $A[i] = (x_i^A, y_i^A)$. Let B be the output where $B = (x^B, y^B)$. Like [6], we introduce three boolean indicator variables μ, ν and η in the model. $\mu = 1$ if and only if there exists $i \in [1, 2, \cdots, n]$ such that $(x_i^A, y_i^A) = (0, 0)$. That is, n-XOR-RULE$^-$-1 is fulfilled. $\nu = 1$ if and only if $x_i^A = y_i^A = 1$ for all $1 \leq i \leq n$, which corresponds to n-XOR-RULE$^-$-2. When $\mu = \nu = 0$, n-XOR-RULE$^-$-3 is fulfilled. Besides, $\eta = 1$ when there exists one constraint imposed on input ■ cells. With the help of indicator variables, the n-XOR-RULE$^-$ can be converted into a system of inequalities shown in Eq. (2) and Eq. (3).

$$\begin{cases} \sum\limits_{i=0}^{n-1} y_i^A + \mu \leq n \\ \sum\limits_{i=0}^{n-1} y_i^A + n \cdot \mu \geq n \\ \sum\limits_{i=0}^{n-1} x_i^A - \nu \leq n - 1 \\ \sum\limits_{i=0}^{n-1} x_i^A - n \cdot \nu \geq 0 \end{cases} \quad (2) \qquad \begin{cases} y^B + \mu = 1 \\ x^B + \mu \leq 1 \\ \eta - x^B + \nu = 0 \\ \sum\limits_{i=0}^{n-1} x_i^A + x^B - 2 \cdot \nu \leq n - 1 \\ \sum\limits_{i=0}^{n-1} x_i^A + x^B - (n+1) \cdot \nu \geq 0 \end{cases} \quad (3)$$

At the end, we must emphasize that, in addition to preserving more valid coloring patterns, another advantage of n-XOR is that the size of model is fixed, independent of the number of input cells. And this makes it possible to describe the attributes propagation for primitives with large binary matrices, like Camellia and Aria.

3.2 Check Model: More Accurate Consumption of DoFs

We also observe that n-XOR model may lead to some subtle inaccuracies. We still take a possible propagation of Midori64's diffusion layer as an example to state this fact. A particularly explicit case is that the constraint on the same neutral cells may be double counted due to the independent computation of each output cell as shown in Fig. 5(a). Besides, there are some more implicit cases leading to inaccuracy as shown in Fig. 5(b).

Then, we introduce the check model to show how the inaccuracy can be eliminated, and describe it in the MILP language. We still state this by considering the ■ propagation through the n-XOR operation under SupP states. Let $A[j] = (x_j^A, y_j^A)$, for $1 \leq j \leq n$, be the input of the $n \times n$ binary matrix M. After the n-XOR Model, we can get $\boldsymbol{\eta} = (\eta_1, \cdots, \eta_n)$ denoted by the degree consumption vector where η_i is the indicator variable introduced in Eq. (3) and $\eta_i = 1$ means there exists one constraint imposed on the input ■ cells for the i-th row of M. Since only ■ cells are needed to be considered for DoF consumption, we introduce another $n \times n$ binary matrix M' to intuitively mark which ■ cells contribute to the DoF consumption. Then, M' is generated as follows:

- If $\eta_i = 1$ and $M_{i,j} = 1$ and $x_j^A = 0$, then $M'_{i,j} = 1$.
- If the first case is not satisfied, then $M'_{i,j} = 0$.

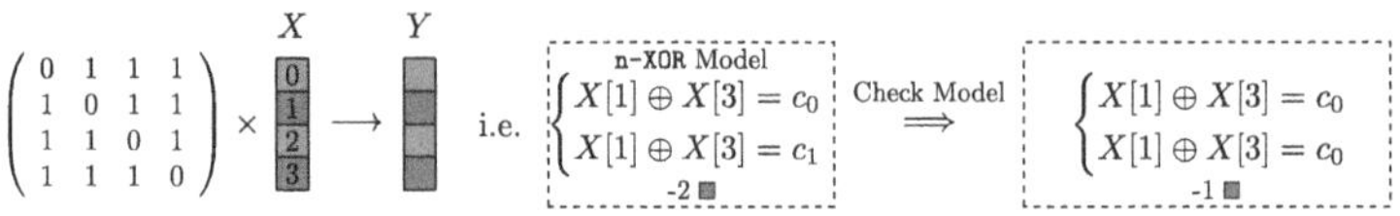

(a) Possible situation *I*

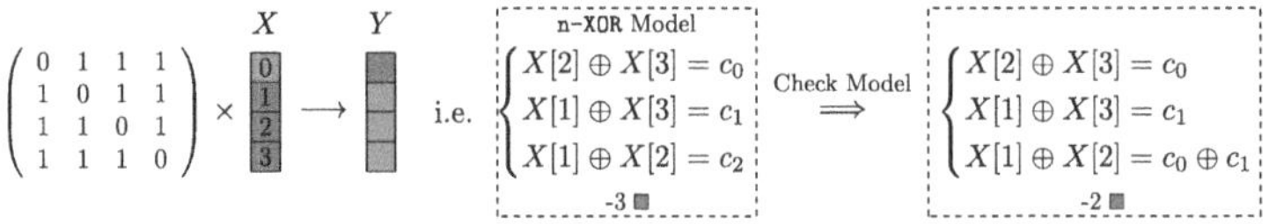

(b) Possible situation *II*

Fig. 5. Possible situations in our models.

For the first case, $\eta_i = 1$ means no □ in the involved input cells, and $M_{i,j} = 1$ and $x_j^A = 0$ means $A[j]$ is a ■ cell involved in the i-th XOR operation. We introduce a general variable η' to denote the rank of M', which equals to the accurate DoF consumption theoretically. Since M is a fixed matrix, we can conclude that the accurate DoF consumption can be determined by the other $2n$ variables $(x_1^A, \cdots, x_n^A, \eta_1, \cdots, \eta_n)$. Finally, the subset $(x_1^A, \cdots, x_n^A, \eta_1, \cdots, \eta_n, \eta')$ of $\mathbb{F}_2^{2n} \times \mathbb{F}_{n+1}$ can be restricted to a system of linear inequalities using the convex hull technique [37]. Different with the origin framework, the configuration $l_{\mathcal{R}}^{\text{ENC}} + l_{\mathcal{R}}^{\text{KEY}}$ should be calculated by accumulating the accurate DoF consumption determined by the n-XOR and check model, along with extra constraints imposed by other operations, such as KeyAddition. The configuration $l_{\mathcal{B}}^{\text{ENC}} + l_{\mathcal{B}}^{\text{KEY}}$ for degree consumption of ■ can also be gotten in the similar way due to the duality [7].

However, it should be noted that the cost of exhaustion to determine the accurate DoF consumption is still affected by the number of input cells. Hence, check model can not be applied to large binary matrix ($n > 4$ in this paper). Although it's trivial to compute the rank of a general matrix in $O(n^3)$, there is still no effective way to implement it in MILP model. Besides, in addition to finding out better modeling methods or more suitable optimizers, we can still combine theoretical models and manually checking to deal with large matrices, such as Sect. 5 and Sect. 6. In practice, by relaxing the constraint to $\min\{d_{\mathcal{B}}, d_{\mathcal{R}}, d_m\} \geq 1 - i$, where $i \geq 1$, we check the feasible solutions to find out valid characteristic. It also should be noted that the final results derived by the manually checking method may not be the optimal solution.

4 MitM Key Recovery Attack on Midori64

Midori64 is an SPN-based lightweight block cipher, consisting of 64-bit block and a 128-bit key. The state is seen as a 4×4 matrix of 4-bit cells, and its diffusion layer is 4×4 boolean matrix. The detailed specification is provided in [18, Appendix B.1].

In this section, we present an 11-round MitM key recovery attack on Midori64 with a time complexity of 2^{124}. For the weakened version of Midori64, without whitening key, a 12-round MitM characteristic is found with a time complexity of 2^{120}. Despite a little higher time complexity, the above two attacks can be applied with extremely low data and memory cost compared to the previous best work [24,36]. Besides, the data and memory of the attack on 12-round weakened `Midori64` can be further reduced if the time complexity is relaxed to 2^{124}.

4.1 MitM Key Recovery Attack on 11-Round Midori64

As shown in Fig. 6 and Fig. 7, an 11-round MitM key recovery attack is identified, where $|\mathcal{S}^{\texttt{ENC}}| = 16$ independent bytes in the encryption data path are set to be 0 as Line 1–2 in Algorithm 1, to ensure the values of all the other bytes are totally determined by the given key. And at least one 0 byte in the ciphertext C to avoid using the full codebook. The starting states are C and $(K^{(0)}, K^{(1)})$. The encryption data path provides $\lambda_{\mathcal{R}}^{\texttt{ENC}} = 9$ and $\lambda_{\mathcal{B}}^{\texttt{ENC}} = 0$ DoFs for ■ and ■, respectively. And the $\lambda_{\mathcal{R}}^{\texttt{ENC}} = 9$ ■ cells are used up when computing $A_{\texttt{ShC}}^{(9)}$ through an `MC` operation and $A_{\texttt{MC}}^{(8)}$ through an `XOR` operation in the backward computation path. For $(K^{(0)}, K^{(1)})$, the initial DoFs for ■ and ■ are $\lambda_{\mathcal{R}}^{\texttt{KEY}} = 3$ and $\lambda_{\mathcal{B}}^{\texttt{KEY}} = 2$, respectively. In the key schedule, $K^{(0)}[1] \oplus K^{(0)}[9]$ and $K^{(0)}[1] \oplus K^{(0)}[13]$ are restricted to constants, i.e., $l_{\mathcal{R}}^{\texttt{KEY}} = 2$. Hence, we get $\text{DoF}_{\mathcal{R}} = \lambda_{\mathcal{R}}^{\texttt{KEY}} - l_{\mathcal{R}}^{\texttt{KEY}} = 1$. Similarly, $K^{(0)}[5] \oplus K^{(1)}[5]$ is imposed on $l_{\mathcal{B}}^{\texttt{KEY}} = 1$ constraint, and then $\text{DoF}_{\mathcal{B}} = \lambda_{\mathcal{B}}^{\texttt{KEY}} - l_{\mathcal{B}}^{\texttt{KEY}} = 1$. The matching phase happens at the `MC` operation between $A_{\texttt{ShC}}^{(3)}$ and $A_{\texttt{MC}}^{(3)}$, providing $d_m = 1$ degree of matching by Eq. (4).

$$A_{\texttt{ShC}}^{(3)}[2] \oplus A_{\texttt{ShC}}^{(3)}[10] = A_{\texttt{MC}}^{(3)}[2] \oplus A_{\texttt{MC}}^{(3)}[10] \tag{4}$$

According to Eq. (1), the overall time complexity is $2^{4\times(32-\min\{1,1,1\})} \approx 2^{124}$. The data complexity is 2^{36} by traversing the $16 - 7 = 9$ non-constant cells in C. A detailed attack procedure is given in Algorithm 1. The memory cost is about 2^6 bytes to store $(\mathcal{S}_{\mathcal{R}}, \mathcal{S}_{\mathcal{B}}, L)$.

4.2 MitM Key Recovery Attack on 12-Round Weakened Midori64

In this section, we focus on the weakened version of `Midori64` omitting the whitening layers. And we found a MitM key recovery attack on the 12-round `Midori64` as shown in Fig. 8. As explained above, $|\mathcal{S}^{\texttt{ENC}}| = 16$ independent ■ bytes in the encryption data path are set as 0. The starting states are ciphertext C and two sub-key $(K^{(0)}, K^{(1)})$. In ciphertext, there are $\lambda_{\mathcal{R}}^{\texttt{ENC}} = 12$ and $\lambda_{\mathcal{B}}^{\texttt{ENC}} = 0$ initial DoFs for ■ and ■, respectively. And the DoFs of ■ are used up when computing $A_{\texttt{ShC}}^{(10)}$ through an `MC` operation and $A_{\texttt{MC}}^{(9)}$ through an `XOR` operation. The two sub-key $(K^{(0)}, K^{(1)})$ provide $\lambda_{\mathcal{R}}^{\texttt{KEY}} = 6$ and $\lambda_{\mathcal{B}}^{\texttt{KEY}} = 2$ initial DoFs for ■ and ■, respectively. For the key schedule, $K^{(0)}[0] \oplus K^{(0)}[4]$, $K^{(0)}[0] \oplus K^{(0)}[8]$, $K^{(0)}[1] \oplus K^{(0)}[5]$ and $K^{(0)}[1] \oplus K^{(0)}[13]$ are restricted to constants, i.e., $l_{\mathcal{R}}^{\texttt{KEY}} = 4$. Hence, we get $\text{DoF}_{\mathcal{R}} = \lambda_{\mathcal{R}}^{\texttt{KEY}} - l_{\mathcal{R}}^{\texttt{KEY}} = 2$ and $\text{DoF}_{\mathcal{B}} = \lambda_{\mathcal{B}}^{\texttt{KEY}} = 2$. The matching

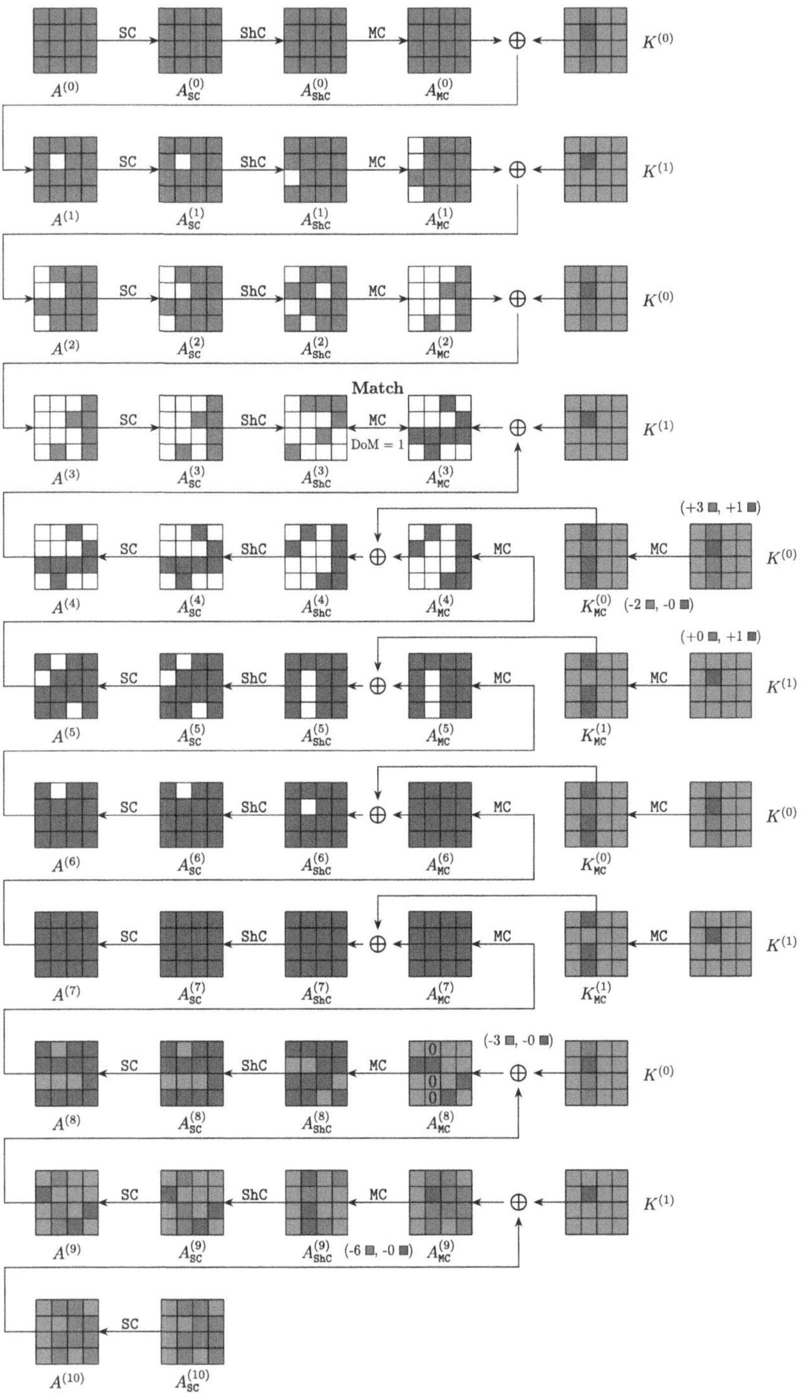

Fig. 6. Meet-in-the-Middle key recovery attack on 11-round Midori64

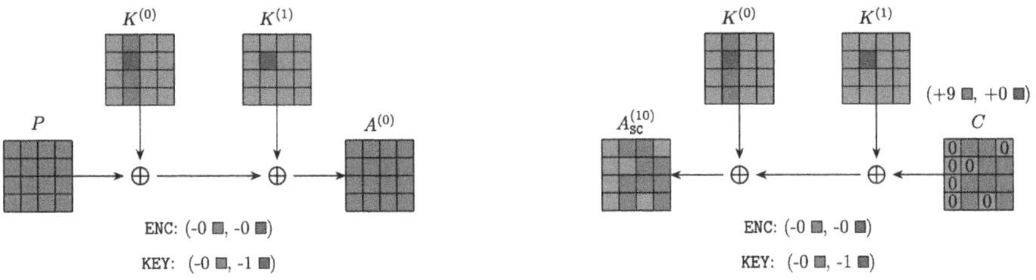

Fig. 7. The MitM characteristic through whitening layers of 11-round Midori64

Algorithm 1: MitM Key Recovery Attack on 11-round Midori64

Set the ■ bytes to be 0, i.e., $C[0,3,4,5,8,12,14] \leftarrow 0$, $A_{\mathtt{MC}}^{(8)}[1,9,13] \leftarrow 0$

$A_{\mathtt{MC}}^{(9)}[1] \oplus A_{\mathtt{MC}}^{(9)}[9] \leftarrow 0$, $A_{\mathtt{MC}}^{(9)}[1] \oplus A_{\mathtt{MC}}^{(9)}[13] \leftarrow 0$, $A_{\mathtt{MC}}^{(9)}[2] \oplus A_{\mathtt{MC}}^{(9)}[6] \leftarrow 0$, $A_{\mathtt{MC}}^{(9)}[2] \oplus A_{\mathtt{MC}}^{(9)}[10] \leftarrow 0$, $A_{\mathtt{MC}}^{(9)}[7] \oplus A_{\mathtt{MC}}^{(9)}[11] \leftarrow 0$, $A_{\mathtt{MC}}^{(9)}[7] \oplus A_{\mathtt{MC}}^{(9)}[15] \leftarrow 0$

Collecting plaintext-ciphertext pairs by traversing the non-constant $16 - 7 = 9$ cells in C, and storing them in table H

for *all possible values of the* ■ *cells in* $K^{(0)}$ *and* $K^{(1)}$ **do**

  $A_{\mathtt{SC}}^{(10)}[0,3,4,5,8,12,14] \leftarrow (K^{(0)} \oplus K^{(1)})[0,3,4,5,8,12,14]$

  for $(\mathfrak{c}_{\mathcal{R},1}, \mathfrak{c}_{\mathcal{R},2}, \mathfrak{c}_{\mathcal{B}}) \in \mathbb{F}_2^{3\times 4}$ **do**

    Derive the solution space $\mathcal{S}_{\mathcal{R}}$ of ■ cells by

$$\begin{cases} K^{(0)}[1] \oplus K^{(0)}[9] &= \mathfrak{c}_{\mathcal{R},1} \\ K^{(0)}[1] \oplus K^{(0)}[13] &= \mathfrak{c}_{\mathcal{R},2} \end{cases}$$

    Derive the solution space $\mathcal{S}_{\mathcal{B}}$ of ■ cells by $K^{(0)}[5] \oplus K^{(1)}[5] = \mathfrak{c}_{\mathcal{B}}$

    $L \leftarrow [\,]$

    for $v_{\mathcal{R}} \in \mathcal{S}_{\mathcal{R}}$ **do**

      Compute $A_{\mathtt{ShC}}^{(3)}[2,10]$ along the forward computation path:

      $A_{\mathtt{MC}}^{(8)} \to C \to Dec_K(C) \to A_{\mathtt{ShC}}^{(3)}$ by accessing H

      $L[A_{\mathtt{ShC}}^{(3)}[2] \oplus A_{\mathtt{ShC}}^{(3)}[10]] \leftarrow v_{\mathcal{R}}$

    end

    for $v_{\mathcal{B}} \in \mathcal{S}_{\mathcal{B}}$ **do**

      Compute $A_{\mathtt{MC}}^{(3)}[2,10]$ along the backward computation path: $C \to A_{\mathtt{MC}}^{(3)}$

      for *Candidate keys in* $L[A_{MC}^{(3)}[2] \oplus A_{MC}^{(3)}[10]]$ **do**

        Test the guessed key with several plaintext-ciphertext pairs

      end

    end

  end

end

---

phase happens at the MC operation between $A_{\mathtt{ShC}}^{(4)}$ and $A_{\mathtt{MC}}^{(4)}$, providing $d_m = 1$

degree of matching by Eq. (5).

$$A^{(4)}_{\mathtt{ShC}}[4] \oplus A^{(4)}_{\mathtt{ShC}}[12] = A^{(4)}_{\mathtt{MC}}[4] \oplus A^{(4)}_{\mathtt{MC}}[12] \tag{5}$$

In [14], Fuhr *et al.* proposed the *simultaneous matching* to decrease $2^{d_{\mathcal{B}}+d_{\mathcal{R}}-d_m}$ in Eq. (1) exponentially by testing the surviving keys with multiple plaintext-ciphertext pairs in parallel. Hence, the overall time is dominated by $2^{4\times(32-\min\{2,2\})} \approx 2^{120}$. The data complexity is 2^{48} by traversing the $16-4$ non-constant cells in C. A detailed attack procedure is given in Algorithm 2. The memory cost is $2^{10.6}$ bytes to store $(\mathcal{S}_{\mathcal{R}}, L)$.

When optimizing for data complexity, we found a MitM key recovery attack on 12-round `Midori64` with data complexity of 2^{36} by relaxing the time complexity to 2^{124}. The figure and algorithm are given in [18, Appendix C].

Algorithm 2: MitM Key Recovery Attack on 12-round weakened `Midori64`, optimized for time complexity

---

$C[2,6,10,14] \leftarrow 0$, $A^{(10)}_{\mathtt{ShC}}[1,4,7,9,12,15] \leftarrow 0$, $A^{(9)}_{\mathtt{MC}}[0,1,4,5,8,13] \leftarrow 0$

Collecting plaintext-ciphertext pairs by traversing the non-constant $16-4=12$ cells in C, and storing them in table H

for *all possible values of the* ■ *cells in* $K^{(0)}$ *and* $K^{(1)}$ **do**

  for $(\mathfrak{c}_{\mathcal{R},1}, \mathfrak{c}_{\mathcal{R},2}, \mathfrak{c}_{\mathcal{R},3}, \mathfrak{c}_{\mathcal{R},4}) \in \mathbb{F}_2^{4\times 4}$ **do**

    Derive the solution space $\mathcal{S}_{\mathcal{R}}$ of ■ cells by

$$\begin{cases} K^{(0)}[0] \oplus K^{(0)}[4] = \mathfrak{c}_{\mathcal{R},1} & K^{(0)}[0] \oplus K^{(0)}[8] = \mathfrak{c}_{\mathcal{R},2} \\ K^{(0)}[1] \oplus K^{(0)}[5] = \mathfrak{c}_{\mathcal{R},3} & K^{(0)}[1] \oplus K^{(0)}[13] = \mathfrak{c}_{\mathcal{R},4} \end{cases}$$

    $L \leftarrow [\,]$

    for $v_{\mathcal{R}} \in \mathcal{S}_{\mathcal{R}}$ **do**

      Compute $A^{(4)}_{\mathtt{ShC}}[4,12]$ along the forward computation path: $A^{(9)}_{\mathtt{MC}} \rightarrow C \rightarrow Dec_K(C) \rightarrow A^{(4)}_{\mathtt{ShC}}$ by accessing H

      $L[A^{(4)}_{\mathtt{ShC}}[4] \oplus A^{(4)}_{\mathtt{ShC}}[12]] \leftarrow v_{\mathcal{R}}$

    end

    for $2^{2\times 4}$ *possible values of* $K^{(1)}[7,12]$ **do**

      Compute $A^{(4)}_{\mathtt{MC}}[4,12]$ along the backward computation path: $C \rightarrow A^{(4)}_{\mathtt{MC}}$

      for *Candidate keys in* $L[A^{(4)}_{\mathtt{MC}}[4] \oplus A^{(4)}_{\mathtt{MC}}[12]]$ **do**

        Test the guessed key with several plaintext-ciphertext pairs

      end

    end

  end

end

---

5 MitM Preimage Attack on Weakened Camellia

`Camellia` is a Feistel-based block cipher with 128-bit block. The diffusion layer is a 8×8 boolean matrix. In this work, we only target on the version with a 128-bit key. The detailed specification is provided in [18, Appendix B.2].

5.1 The MitM Characteristic of 14-Round Weakened Camellia

We first applied the `n-XOR` model to describe the attributes propagation through the diffusion layer. However, the check model can not be deployed since the large size of the diffusion layer. We relaxed the constraint to $\min\{d_{\mathcal{B}}, d_{\mathcal{R}}, d_m\} \geq 1 - i$, where $i \geq 1$, as stated in Sect. 3.2, and manually checked the solution files to find out valid solutions (may not be optimal).

The final valid configuration of the pseudo-preimage MitM attack on 14-round weakened `Camellia-MMO` without FL/FL^{-1} and whitening layers is shown in Fig. 9. We deploy the `n-XOR` model by considering the `MixColumns` and `XOR` as a whole. The attack starts at $A^{(9)}$ and $B^{(9)}$ illustrated in Fig. 9(a), in which the initial DoFs for ■ and ■ are $\lambda_{\mathcal{B}} = \lambda_{\mathcal{R}} = 7$. In the forward computation path, in order to facilitate the propagation of ■ cells, there are $l_{\mathcal{R}} = 6$ linear constraints imposed on $A_{\texttt{SB}}^{(9)}[7] \oplus B^{(9)}[i]$, for $i \in \{0, 1, 2, 4, 5, 6\}$. Similarly, in the backward computation path, $l_{\mathcal{B}} = 6$ linear constraints are imposed on $A_{\texttt{SB}}^{(8)}[7] \oplus A^{(9)}[i]$, for $i \in \{0, 1, 2, 4, 5, 6\}$, to facilitate the propagation of ■ cells. Hence, we get $d_{\mathcal{B}} = \lambda_{\mathcal{B}} - l_{\mathcal{B}} = 1$ and $d_{\mathcal{R}} = \lambda_{\mathcal{R}} - l_{\mathcal{R}} = 1$.

Around the feed-forward mechanism of `MMO` mode, we set global constraints on round keys $(k_0, k_1, k_{12}, k_{13})$ to preserve some attributes like [29]. Specifically, for the given target $H_0 \| H_1$, $A_{\texttt{SB}}^{(0)}$ equals to $A_{\texttt{SB}}^{(13)}$ by setting $k_0 = k_{13} \oplus H_0$ globally. Since $B^{(0)} = \texttt{MC}(A_{\texttt{SB}}^{(13)}) \oplus A^{(12)} \oplus H_1$ and $A^{(1)} = B^{(0)} \oplus \texttt{MC}(A_{\texttt{SB}}^{(0)})$, then we can get $A^{(1)} = A^{(12)} \oplus H_1$. Similarly, $A^{(2)}$ equals to $B^{(12)} \oplus H_0$ by setting $k_1 = k_{12} \oplus H_1$. The cost to determine such proper subkeys is given in Sect. 5.2 and will not exceed the time complexity of main MitM procedure.

The matching points are $A^{(5)}$ and $B^{(5)}$ in Fig. 9(c). At first glance, there are no degree for the direct matching. However, after applying a linear transformation P^{-1} to $B^{(5)}$ as in Fig. 10, two-byte degree of match are derived. Since $d_{\mathcal{B}} = d_{\mathcal{R}} = 1$, we only use one-byte for match, i.e., $d_m = 1$. The specific matching equation is Eq. (6).

$$\bigoplus_{i \in [0,1,2,4,5,6]} B^{(3)}[i] \oplus A_{\texttt{SB}}^{(3)}[3] = \bigoplus_{i \in [0,1,2,4,5,6]} A^{(6)}[i] \oplus A_{\texttt{SB}}^{(5)}[3] \tag{6}$$

According to Eq. (1), the total time complexity is bounded by $2^{8 \times (16 - \min\{1,1,1\})} \approx 2^{120}$. A detailed attack procedure is given in Algorithm 3. The memory complexity of a hash table L is 2^8. And this attack can be converted to a second preimage attack with a time complexity of 2^{125} according to [25, Fact9.99].

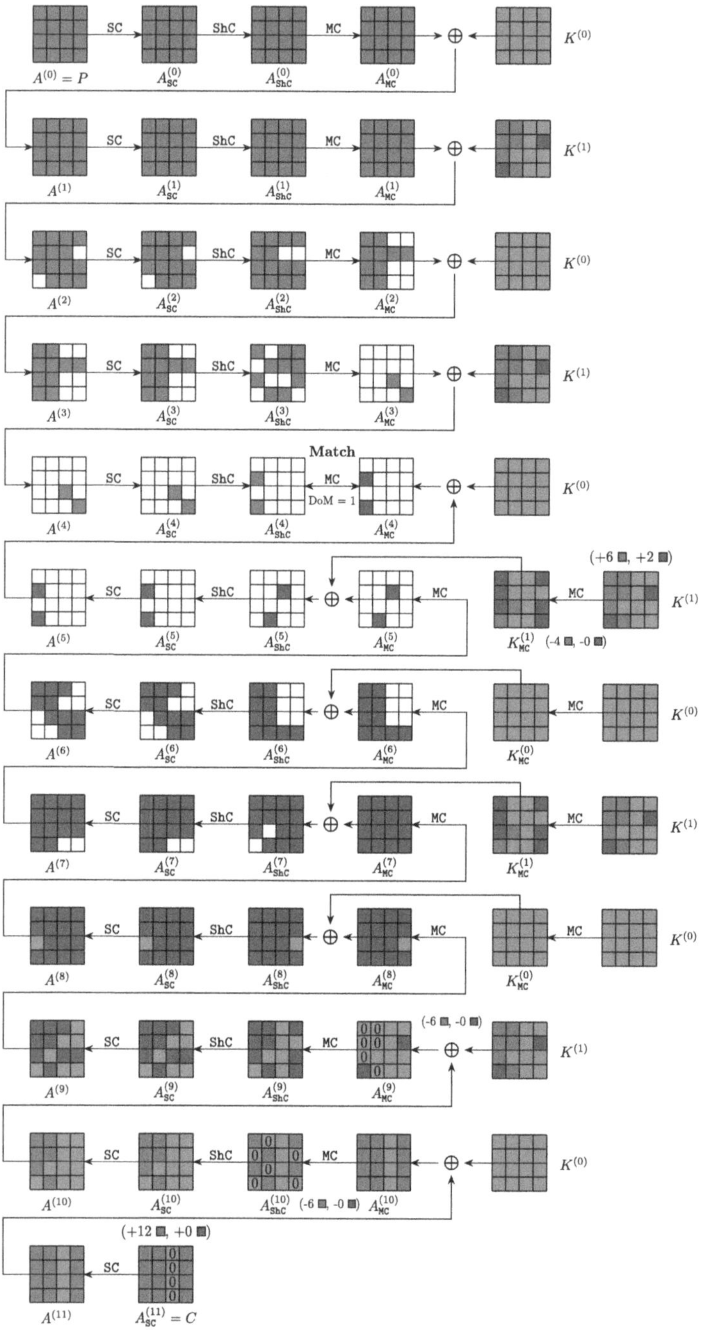

Fig. 8. Meet-in-the-Middle key recovery attack on 12-round weakened `Midori64`, optimized for time complexity

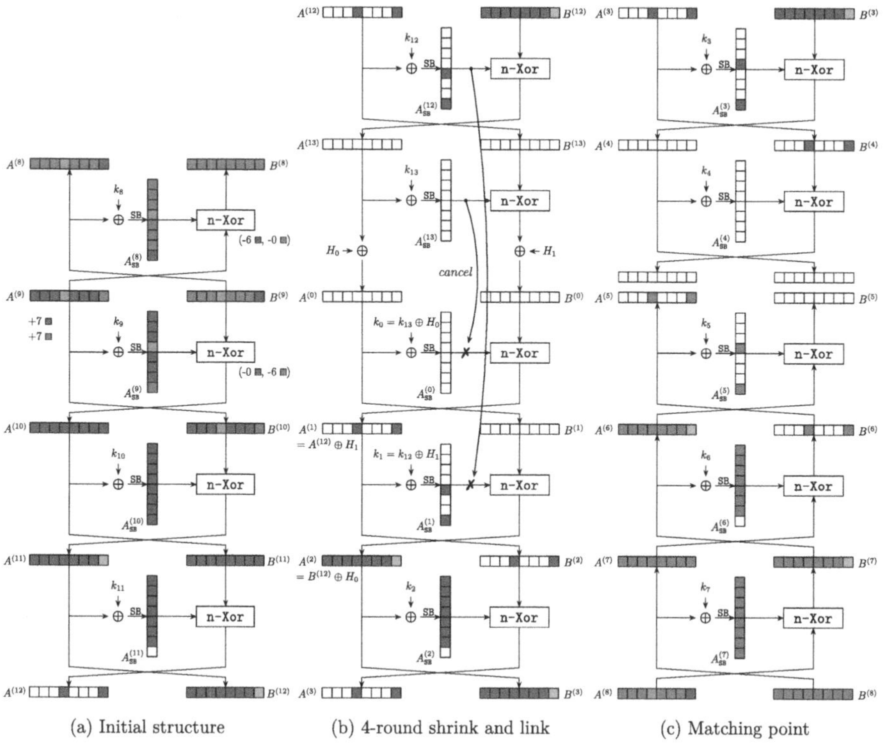

Fig. 9. Meet-in-the-Middle pseudo-preimage attack on 14-round weakened Camellia-MMO

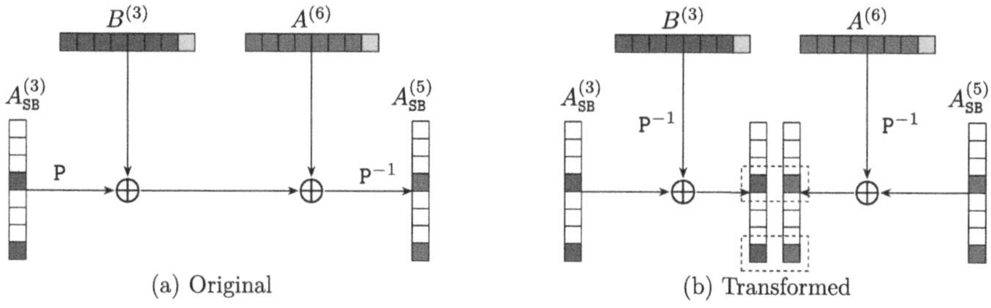

Fig. 10. The matching process of 14-round weakened Camellia-MMO

Algorithm 3: MitM Pseudo-Preimage Attack on 14-round weakened `Camellia-MMO`

Setting a global key satisfying $k_0 = k_{13} \oplus H_0$, $k_1 = k_{12} \oplus H_1$;
for 2^{16} *values of the* ■ *bytes in* $A^{(9)}[3] \| B^{(9)}[3]$ **do**
  for $\mathfrak{c}_{\mathcal{B}} \in \mathbb{F}_2^{8\times 6}$ **do**
    for $\mathfrak{c}_{\mathcal{R}} \in \mathbb{F}_2^{8\times 6}$ **do**
      $L \leftarrow [\,]$
      Solve the following system of equations to find the solution space $\mathcal{S}_{\mathcal{B}}$ of ■ in $A^{(9)}$ and $B^{(9)}$; /* $|\mathcal{S}_{\mathcal{B}}| = 2^{8\times(7-6)} = 2^8$ */

$$A^{(8)}_{\mathtt{SB}}[7] \oplus A^{(9)}[0] = \mathfrak{c}_{\mathcal{B}}[0],\ A^{(8)}_{\mathtt{SB}}[7] \oplus A^{(9)}[1] = \mathfrak{c}_{\mathcal{B}}[1],\ A^{(8)}_{\mathtt{SB}}[7] \oplus A^{(9)}[2] = \mathfrak{c}_{\mathcal{B}}[2],$$
$$A^{(8)}_{\mathtt{SB}}[7] \oplus A^{(9)}[4] = \mathfrak{c}_{\mathcal{B}}[3],\ A^{(8)}_{\mathtt{SB}}[7] \oplus A^{(9)}[5] = \mathfrak{c}_{\mathcal{B}}[4],\ A^{(8)}_{\mathtt{SB}}[7] \oplus A^{(9)}[6] = \mathfrak{c}_{\mathcal{B}}[5].$$

      Solve the following system of equations to find the solution space $\mathcal{S}_{\mathcal{R}}$ of ■ in $A^{(9)}$ and $B^{(9)}$; /* $|\mathcal{S}_{\mathcal{B}}| = 2^{8\times(7-6)} = 2^8$ */

$$A^{(9)}_{\mathtt{SB}}[7] \oplus B^{(9)}[0] = \mathfrak{c}_{\mathcal{R}}[0],\ B^{(9)}_{\mathtt{SB}}[7] \oplus A^{(9)}[1] = \mathfrak{c}_{\mathcal{R}}[1],\ A^{(9)}_{\mathtt{SB}}[7] \oplus B^{(9)}[2] = \mathfrak{c}_{\mathcal{R}}[2],$$
$$A^{(9)}_{\mathtt{SB}}[7] \oplus B^{(9)}[4] = \mathfrak{c}_{\mathcal{R}}[3],\ A^{(9)}_{\mathtt{SB}}[7] \oplus B^{(9)}[5] = \mathfrak{c}_{\mathcal{R}}[4],\ A^{(9)}_{\mathtt{SB}}[7] \oplus B^{(9)}[6] = \mathfrak{c}_{\mathcal{R}}[5].$$

      for $v_{\mathcal{B}} \in \mathcal{S}_{\mathcal{B}}$ **do**
        Compute forward to $A^{(3)}$ and $B^{(3)}$, derive 1-byte $End_{\mathcal{B}}$ by

$$End_{\mathcal{B}} \leftarrow P^{-1}\left(B^{(3)}\right)[3] \oplus A^{(3)}_{\mathtt{SB}}[3]$$

        $L[End_{\mathcal{B}}] \leftarrow v_{\mathcal{B}}$;
      end
      for $v_{\mathcal{R}} \in \mathcal{S}_{\mathcal{R}}$ **do**
        Compute backward to $A^{(6)}$ and $B^{(6)}$, derive 1-byte $End_{\mathcal{R}}$ by

$$End_{\mathcal{R}} \leftarrow P^{-1}\left(A^{(6)}\right)[3] \oplus A^{(5)}_{\mathtt{SB}}[3]$$

        for $v_{\mathcal{B}} \in L[End_{\mathcal{R}}]$ **do**
          Reconstruct the (candidate) message X; /* $2^{8\times(1+1-1)} = 2^8$ values passed the filter */
          if X *is a preimage* **then**
            Output X and stop;
          end
        end
      end
    end
  end
end

5.2 The Cost to Determine a Proper Key

The key schedule of `Camellia` with 128-bit key is shown in [18, Appendix B.2]. As explained above, we only need to focus on $(k_0, k_1, k_{12}, k_{13})$ [1],

$$k_0 \leftarrow K'_A,\ \ k_1 \leftarrow K''_A,\ \ k_{12} \leftarrow K''[30-63] \| K'[0-29],\ \ k_{13} \leftarrow K'[30-63] \| K''[0-29].$$

As shown in [18, Appendix B.2], every internal state can be derived for given K' and S_0. Hence, we get $K'' = F_0(K') \oplus S_0$ and $K''_A = F_2(F_1(S_0)) \oplus F_0(K')$.

According to the global constraints $k_0 = k_{13} \oplus H_0$ and $k_1 = k_{12} \oplus H_1$, the relation between K' and S_0 can be represented as Eq. (7).

$$F_2(F_1(S_0)) \oplus F_0(K') = \left(F_0(K') \oplus S_0\right)[30-63] \| K'[0-29] \oplus H_1 \quad (7)$$

Besides, we note that K' and S_0 can be placed at two sides of Eq. (8), respectively. The left-hand-side of Eq. (8) only contains variables in terms of K', while the right-hand-side of Eq. (8) depends on S_0.

$$F_0(K') \oplus F_0(K')[30-63] \| K'[0-29] \;=\; F_2(F_1(S_0)) \oplus S_0[30-63] \| \overbrace{0 \cdots 0}^{30} \oplus H_1 \quad (8)$$

Then, an algebraic meet-in-the-middle attack can be mounted by enumerating K' and S_0 independently to filter out valid pairs according to Eq. (8), i.e. $d_{\mathcal{B}} = d_{\mathcal{R}} = d_m = 64$. The time and memory complexity are both 2^{64}. Besides, the memory cost can be further reduced by extracting partial x bits of K' and S_0 as global variables. Then, the memory can be reduced by a fraction of 2^x, while the total time is bounded by 2^{64+x}. To avoid exceeding the time cost of main MitM procedure, $64 + x \leq 120$ should be fulfilled, i.e., x can take 56 at most. The corresponding memory cost is 2^8.

6 MitM Preimage Attack on 6-Round Aria

`Aria` is an SPN-based block cipher that supports a 128-bit block. In this work, we target on the version with a 128-bit key. The state is treated as a 4×4 matrix. And the diffusion layer is a 16×16 boolean matrix. The detailed specification of `Aria` is presented in [18, Appendix B.3].

Since the large size diffusion layer, only the `n-XOR` model can be applied to describe the MitM attribution propagation through the diffusion layer. By relaxing the constraint to $\min\{d_{\mathcal{B}}, d_{\mathcal{R}}, d_m\} \geq 1 - i$, where $i \geq 1$, as stated in Sect. 3.2, we finally found out a valid configuration of the pseudo-preimage MitM attack on 6-round `Aria-DM` as shown in Fig. 11 (may not be optimal). The attack starts at $A^{(1)}$ in which the initial DoFs for ■ and ■ are $\lambda_{\mathcal{B}} = 1, \lambda_{\mathcal{R}} = 14$, respectively. Since there are non-linear constraints on ■ cells to compute $A^{(2)}_{\mathtt{DL}}$ through the `DL` operation. We use the table-based method in [13] to solve such non-linear constraints.

Precomputation of Red Initial Values. By enumerating the ■ cells in $A^{(1)}$, in the backward computation path, two constraints imposed on ■ cells can be computed as follows:

$$\begin{cases} A^{(0)}_{\mathtt{DL}}[0] \oplus A^{(0)}_{\mathtt{DL}}[6] \oplus A^{(0)}_{\mathtt{DL}}[7] \oplus A^{(0)}_{\mathtt{DL}}[8] \oplus A^{(0)}_{\mathtt{DL}}[10] \oplus A^{(0)}_{\mathtt{DL}}[13] = \mathfrak{c}[0] \\ A^{(0)}_{\mathtt{DL}}[0] \oplus A^{(0)}_{\mathtt{DL}}[4] \oplus A^{(0)}_{\mathtt{DL}}[5] \oplus A^{(0)}_{\mathtt{DL}}[9] \oplus A^{(0)}_{\mathtt{DL}}[11] \oplus A^{(0)}_{\mathtt{DL}}[14] = \mathfrak{c}[1] \end{cases}$$

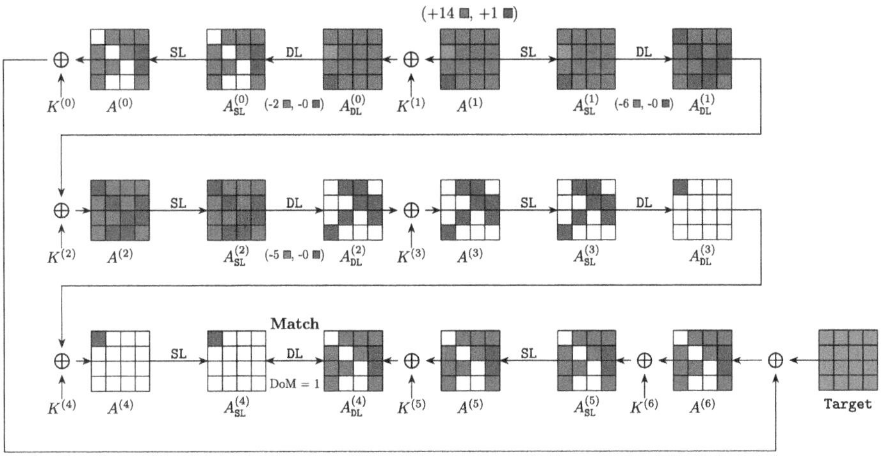

Fig. 11. Meet-in-the-Middle pseudo-preimage attack on 6-round Aria-DM

In the forward computation path, there are 11 constraints imposed on the ■ cells. During the DL operation in the 2nd round, 6 constraints are imposed on the ■ cells. The specific expression of the constraints is shown in as follows:

$$\begin{cases} A_{\mathrm{SL}}^{(1)}[4] \oplus A_{\mathrm{SL}}^{(1)}[6] \oplus A_{\mathrm{SL}}^{(1)}[8] \oplus A_{\mathrm{SL}}^{(1)}[9] \oplus A_{\mathrm{SL}}^{(1)}[13] \oplus A_{\mathrm{SL}}^{(1)}[14] = \mathfrak{c}[2] \\ A_{\mathrm{SL}}^{(1)}[4] \oplus A_{\mathrm{SL}}^{(1)}[9] \oplus A_{\mathrm{SL}}^{(1)}[10] \oplus A_{\mathrm{SL}}^{(1)}[14] \oplus A_{\mathrm{SL}}^{(1)}[15] = \mathfrak{c}[3] \\ A_{\mathrm{SL}}^{(1)}[2] \oplus A_{\mathrm{SL}}^{(1)}[5] \oplus A_{\mathrm{SL}}^{(1)}[6] \oplus A_{\mathrm{SL}}^{(1)}[8] \oplus A_{\mathrm{SL}}^{(1)}[13] \oplus A_{\mathrm{SL}}^{(1)}[15] = \mathfrak{c}[4] \\ A_{\mathrm{SL}}^{(1)}[0] \oplus A_{\mathrm{SL}}^{(1)}[6] \oplus A_{\mathrm{SL}}^{(1)}[7] \oplus A_{\mathrm{SL}}^{(1)}[8] \oplus A_{\mathrm{SL}}^{(1)}[10] \oplus A_{\mathrm{SL}}^{(1)}[13] = \mathfrak{c}[5] \\ A_{\mathrm{SL}}^{(1)}[5] \oplus A_{\mathrm{SL}}^{(1)}[7] \oplus A_{\mathrm{SL}}^{(1)}[10] \oplus A_{\mathrm{SL}}^{(1)}[11] = \mathfrak{c}[6] \\ A_{\mathrm{SL}}^{(1)}[10] \oplus A_{\mathrm{SL}}^{(1)}[11] \oplus A_{\mathrm{SL}}^{(1)}[12] \oplus A_{\mathrm{SL}}^{(1)}[15] = \mathfrak{c}[7] \end{cases}$$

Based on the above 6 constraints $(\mathfrak{c}[2], \mathfrak{c}[3], \mathfrak{c}[4], \mathfrak{c}[5], \mathfrak{c}[6], \mathfrak{c}[7])$, the effect of the ■ cells on the 7 cells $A_{\mathrm{DL}}^{(1)}[0, 5, 7, 10, 11, 13, 14]$ can be cancelled as follows:

$$\begin{cases} A_{\mathrm{SL}}^{(1)}[4] \oplus A_{\mathrm{SL}}^{(1)}[6] \oplus A_{\mathrm{SL}}^{(1)}[8] \oplus A_{\mathrm{SL}}^{(1)}[9] \oplus A_{\mathrm{SL}}^{(1)}[13] \oplus A_{\mathrm{SL}}^{(1)}[14] = \mathfrak{c}[2] \\ A_{\mathrm{SL}}^{(1)}[4] \oplus A_{\mathrm{SL}}^{(1)}[9] \oplus A_{\mathrm{SL}}^{(1)}[10] \oplus A_{\mathrm{SL}}^{(1)}[14] \oplus A_{\mathrm{SL}}^{(1)}[15] = \mathfrak{c}[3] \\ A_{\mathrm{SL}}^{(1)}[6] \oplus A_{\mathrm{SL}}^{(1)}[8] \oplus A_{\mathrm{SL}}^{(1)}[11] \oplus A_{\mathrm{SL}}^{(1)}[12] \oplus A_{\mathrm{SL}}^{(1)}[13] = \mathfrak{c}[2] \oplus \mathfrak{c}[3] \oplus \mathfrak{c}[7] \\ A_{\mathrm{SL}}^{(1)}[2] \oplus A_{\mathrm{SL}}^{(1)}[5] \oplus A_{\mathrm{SL}}^{(1)}[6] \oplus A_{\mathrm{SL}}^{(1)}[8] \oplus A_{\mathrm{SL}}^{(1)}[13] \oplus A_{\mathrm{SL}}^{(1)}[15] = \mathfrak{c}[4] \\ A_{\mathrm{SL}}^{(1)}[2] \oplus A_{\mathrm{SL}}^{(1)}[4] \oplus A_{\mathrm{SL}}^{(1)}[7] \oplus A_{\mathrm{SL}}^{(1)}[9] \oplus A_{\mathrm{SL}}^{(1)}[12] \oplus A_{\mathrm{SL}}^{(1)}[14] = \mathfrak{c}[2] \oplus \mathfrak{c}[4] \oplus \mathfrak{c}[6] \oplus \mathfrak{c}[7] \\ A_{\mathrm{SL}}^{(1)}[0] \oplus A_{\mathrm{SL}}^{(1)}[6] \oplus A_{\mathrm{SL}}^{(1)}[7] \oplus A_{\mathrm{SL}}^{(1)}[8] \oplus A_{\mathrm{SL}}^{(1)}[10] \oplus A_{\mathrm{SL}}^{(1)}[13] = \mathfrak{c}[5] \\ A_{\mathrm{SL}}^{(1)}[0] \oplus A_{\mathrm{SL}}^{(1)}[4] \oplus A_{\mathrm{SL}}^{(1)}[5] \oplus A_{\mathrm{SL}}^{(1)}[9] \oplus A_{\mathrm{SL}}^{(1)}[11] \oplus A_{\mathrm{SL}}^{(1)}[14] = \mathfrak{c}[2] \oplus \mathfrak{c}[5] \oplus \mathfrak{c}[6] \end{cases}$$

In a similar way, the 5 constraints $(\mathfrak{c}[8], \mathfrak{c}[9], \mathfrak{c}[10], \mathfrak{c}[11], \mathfrak{c}[12])$ imposed on the ■ cells through the DL in the 3rd round are enough to cancel the effect of the ■ cells on the 6 cells $A^{(2)}_{\mathtt{DL}}[4, 6, 8, 9, 13, 14]$. For the specific expression of the constraints, please refer to [18, Appendix C]. And the detailed DoFs consumption process is illustrated as follows:

$$\begin{cases} A^{(2)}_{\mathtt{SL}}[2] \oplus A^{(2)}_{\mathtt{SL}}[8] \oplus A^{(2)}_{\mathtt{SL}}[15] = \mathfrak{c}[8] \\ A^{(2)}_{\mathtt{SL}}[2] \oplus A^{(2)}_{\mathtt{SL}}[9] \oplus A^{(2)}_{\mathtt{SL}}[12] = \mathfrak{c}[8] \oplus \mathfrak{c}[12] \\ A^{(2)}_{\mathtt{SL}}[1] \oplus A^{(2)}_{\mathtt{SL}}[4] \oplus A^{(2)}_{\mathtt{SL}}[15] = \mathfrak{c}[9] \\ A^{(2)}_{\mathtt{SL}}[1] \oplus A^{(2)}_{\mathtt{SL}}[6] \oplus A^{(2)}_{\mathtt{SL}}[12] = \mathfrak{c}[9] \oplus \mathfrak{c}[11] \\ A^{(2)}_{\mathtt{SL}}[3] \oplus A^{(2)}_{\mathtt{SL}}[6] \oplus A^{(2)}_{\mathtt{SL}}[8] \ \ = \mathfrak{c}[10] \\ A^{(2)}_{\mathtt{SL}}[3] \oplus A^{(2)}_{\mathtt{SL}}[4] \oplus A^{(2)}_{\mathtt{SL}}[9] \ \ = \mathfrak{c}[10] \oplus \mathfrak{c}[11] \oplus \mathfrak{c}[12] \end{cases}$$

In summary, the values of $l_{\mathcal{R}} = 13$ constraints can be determined for given values of $\lambda_{\mathcal{R}} = 14$ ■ cells in $A^{(1)}$. Hence, we get $d_{\mathcal{B}} = 1$, $d_{\mathcal{R}} = \lambda_{\mathcal{R}} - l_{\mathcal{R}} = 1$.

Matching Process. The matching points are $A^{(4)}_{\mathtt{SL}}, A^{(4)}_{\mathtt{DL}}$, indirect matching through the DL provides one-byte match, i.e., DoM $= 1$. The specific matching process is Eq. (9).

$$A^{(4)}_{\mathtt{SL}}[0] \oplus A^{(4)}_{\mathtt{DL}}[13] \oplus A^{(4)}_{\mathtt{DL}}[14] = A^{(4)}_{\mathtt{DL}}[3] \oplus A^{(4)}_{\mathtt{DL}}[4] \oplus A^{(4)}_{\mathtt{DL}}[6] \oplus A^{(4)}_{\mathtt{DL}}[8] \oplus A^{(4)}_{\mathtt{DL}}[9] \tag{9}$$

Based on the above MitM framework, combined with the table-based technique for solving nonlinear constrained neutral words [13], the algorithm gives a detailed attack procedure and the complexity analysis described in [18, Appendix C].

Finally we get the total time complexity is 2^{120}, and the memory complexity is 2^{112}. This attack can be converted to a preimage attack with a time complexity of 2^{125} according to [25, Fact9.99].

7 Conclusion

In this paper, we propose the n-XOR model to simulate the XOR operation with an arbitrary number of input cells. Specifically, the size of n-XOR model is independent of the number of input cells, and thus it is well suitable for primitives with a binary matrix as the diffusion layer. To eliminate the subtle inaccuracies caused by n-XOR model, we introduce another check model to determine the exact DoFs consumption of MitM attributes propagation. However, the size of the check model is still limited by the number of input cells n and does not work well when $n > 4$ in this paper. We expect that there will be more elegant and efficient techniques to overcome this defect and we leave this as an open problem.

We apply the above two new models to a MitM key recovery attack on 11-round Midori64 with low data and memory. Besides, when omitting the whitening layers, two 12-round MitM characteristics for key recovery attack are found for optimizing time and data, respectively. For hash functions, we obtain improved preimage attack on 14-round weakened `Camellia-MMO` and 6-round `Aria-DM`. Both attacks are improved by 1 round compared to previous best records.

Acknowledgments. The authors would like to thank the reviewers for their valuable comments. This work is supported by the National Key R&D Program of China (2022YFB2702800), the Key R&D Program of Shandong Province, China (2024ZLGX05).

References

1. Aoki, K., et al.: *Camellia*: a 128-bit block cipher suitable for multiple platforms—design and analysis. In: Stinson, D.R., Tavares, S. (eds.) SAC 2000. LNCS, vol. 2012, pp. 39–56. Springer, Heidelberg (2001). https://doi.org/10.1007/3-540-44983-3_4
2. Aoki, K., Sasaki, Yu.: Preimage attacks on one-block MD4, 63-Step MD5 and more. In: Avanzi, R.M., Keliher, L., Sica, F. (eds.) SAC 2008. LNCS, vol. 5381, pp. 103–119. Springer, Heidelberg (2009). https://doi.org/10.1007/978-3-642-04159-4_7
3. Aumasson, J.-P., Meier, W., Mendel, F.: Preimage attacks on 3-pass HAVAL and step-reduced MD5. In: Avanzi, R.M., Keliher, L., Sica, F. (eds.) SAC 2008. LNCS, vol. 5381, pp. 120–135. Springer, Heidelberg (2009). https://doi.org/10.1007/978-3-642-04159-4_8
4. Baek, S., Kim, J.: Quantum rebound attacks on reduced-round ARIA-based hash functions. Cryptology ePrint Archive, Paper 2022/1604 (2022). https://eprint.iacr.org/2022/1604
5. Banik, S., et al.: Midori: a block cipher for low energy. In: Iwata, T., Cheon, J.H. (eds.) ASIACRYPT 2015. LNCS, vol. 9453, pp. 411–436. Springer, Heidelberg (2015). https://doi.org/10.1007/978-3-662-48800-3_17
6. Bao, Z., et al.: Automatic search of meet-in-the-middle preimage attacks on AES-like hashing. In: Canteaut, A., Standaert, F.-X. (eds.) EUROCRYPT 2021. LNCS, vol. 12696, pp. 771–804. Springer, Cham (2021). https://doi.org/10.1007/978-3-030-77870-5_27
7. Bao, Z., Guo, J., Shi, D., Tu, Y.: Superposition meet-in-the-middle attacks: updates on fundamental security of AES-like hashing. In: Dodis, Y., Shrimpton, T. (eds.) CRYPTO 2022. LNCS, vol. 13507, pp. 64–93. Springer, Cham (2022). https://doi.org/10.1007/978-3-031-15802-5_3
8. Bogdanov, A., Khovratovich, D., Rechberger, C.: Biclique cryptanalysis of the full AES. In: Lee, D.H., Wang, X. (eds.) ASIACRYPT 2011. LNCS, vol. 7073, pp. 344–371. Springer, Heidelberg (2011). https://doi.org/10.1007/978-3-642-25385-0_19
9. Bogdanov, A., Rechberger, C.: A 3-subset meet-in-the-middle attack: cryptanalysis of the lightweight block cipher KTANTAN. In: Biryukov, A., Gong, G., Stinson, D.R. (eds.) SAC 2010. LNCS, vol. 6544, pp. 229–240. Springer, Heidelberg (2011). https://doi.org/10.1007/978-3-642-19574-7_16
10. Chen, S., Guo, J., List, E., Shi, D., Zhang, T.: Diving deep into the preimage security of AES-like hashing. Cryptology ePrint Archive, Paper 2024/300 (2024). https://eprint.iacr.org/2024/300

11. Degré, M., Derbez, P., Lahaye, L., Schrottenloher, A.: New models for the cryptanalysis of ascon. Cryptology ePrint Archive, Paper 2024/298 (2024). https://eprint.iacr.org/2024/298
12. Diffie, W., Hellman, M.E.: Special feature exhaustive cryptanalysis of the NBS data encryption standard. Computer **10**(6), 74–84 (1977). https://doi.org/10.1109/C-M.1977.217750
13. Dong, X., Hua, J., Sun, S., Li, Z., Wang, X., Hu, L.: Meet-in-the-middle attacks revisited: key-recovery, collision, and preimage attacks. In: Malkin, T., Peikert, C. (eds.) CRYPTO 2021. LNCS, vol. 12827, pp. 278–308. Springer, Cham (2021). https://doi.org/10.1007/978-3-030-84252-9_10
14. Fuhr, T., Minaud, B.: Match box meet-in-the-middle attack against KATAN. In: Cid, C., Rechberger, C. (eds.) FSE 2014. LNCS, vol. 8540, pp. 61–81. Springer, Heidelberg (2015). https://doi.org/10.1007/978-3-662-46706-0_4
15. Gurobi Optimization, LLC.: Gurobi Optimizer Reference Manual (2023). https://www.gurobi.com
16. Hong, D., Koo, B., Kim, D.C.: Preimage and second-preimage attacks on PGV hashing modes of round-reduced aria, camellia, and serpent. IEICE T Fund Electr **95**(1), 372–380 (2012). https://api.semanticscholar.org/CorpusID:19830401
17. Hou, Q., Dong, X., Qin, L., Zhang, G., Wang, X.: Automated meet-in-the-middle attack goes to Feistel. In: Guo, J., Steinfeld, R. (eds.) ASIACRYPT 2023. LNCS, vol. 14440, pp. 370–404. Springer, Singapore (2023). https://doi.org/10.1007/978-981-99-8727-6_13
18. Hou, Q., Li, K., Zhang, G., Shen, Y., You, Q., Dong, X.: Meet-in-the-middle attack on primitives with binary matrix linear layer. Cryptology ePrint Archive, Paper 2025/082 (2025). https://eprint.iacr.org/2025/082
19. Isobe, T.: A single-key attack on the full GOST block cipher. J. Cryptol. **26**(1), 172–189 (2012). https://doi.org/10.1007/s00145-012-9118-5
20. ISO/IEC: 10118-2:2010 Information technology - Security techniques - Hash-functions - Part 2: Hash-functions using an n-bit block cipher, 3rd edn. (2010)
21. ISO/IEC 18033-3:2010 Information technology-Security techniques-Encryption Algorithms-Part 3: Block ciphers (2010)
22. Kwon, D., et al.: New block cipher: ARIA. In: Lim, J.-I., Lee, D.-H. (eds.) ICISC 2003. LNCS, vol. 2971, pp. 432–445. Springer, Heidelberg (2004). https://doi.org/10.1007/978-3-540-24691-6_32
23. Lin, L., Wu, W.: Meet-in-the-middle attacks on reduced-round midori64. IACR ToSC, pp. 215–239 (2017). https://doi.org/10.13154/tosc.v2017.i1.215-239
24. Liu, Y., Xiang, Z., Chen, S., Zhang, S., Zeng, X.: A novel automatic technique based on MILP to search for impossible differentials. In: Tibouchi, M., Wang, X. (eds.) ACNS 2023. LNCS, vol. 13905, pp. 119–148. Springer, Cham (2023). https://doi.org/10.1007/978-3-031-33488-7_5
25. Menezes, A.J., Vanstone, S.A., Oorschot, P.: Handbook of Applied Cryptography, 1st edn. CRC Press Inc., USA (1996)
26. Preneel, B., Govaerts, R., Vandewalle, J.: Hash functions based on block ciphers: a synthetic approach. In: Stinson, D.R. (ed.) CRYPTO 1993. LNCS, vol. 773, pp. 368–378. Springer, Heidelberg (1994). https://doi.org/10.1007/3-540-48329-2_31
27. Sasaki, Yu.: Meet-in-the-middle preimage attacks on AES hashing modes and an application to whirlpool. In: Joux, A. (ed.) FSE 2011. LNCS, vol. 6733, pp. 378–396. Springer, Heidelberg (2011). https://doi.org/10.1007/978-3-642-21702-9_22
28. Sasaki, Yu.: Preimage attacks on Feistel-SP functions: impact of omitting the last network twist. In: Jacobson, M., Locasto, M., Mohassel, P., Safavi-Naini, R. (eds.)

ACNS 2013. LNCS, vol. 7954, pp. 170–185. Springer, Heidelberg (2013). https://doi.org/10.1007/978-3-642-38980-1_11
29. Sasaki, Y.: Preimage attacks on Feistel-SP functions: impact of omitting the last network twist. IEICE Trans. Fund. Electr. **98**(1), 61–71 (2015). https://doi.org/10.1587/transfun.E98.A.61
30. Sasaki, Yu.: Integer linear programming for three-subset meet-in-the-middle attacks: application to GIFT. In: Inomata, A., Yasuda, K. (eds.) IWSEC 2018. LNCS, vol. 11049, pp. 227–243. Springer, Cham (2018). https://doi.org/10.1007/978-3-319-97916-8_15
31. Sasaki, Yu., Aoki, K.: Finding preimages in full MD5 faster than exhaustive search. In: Joux, A. (ed.) EUROCRYPT 2009. LNCS, vol. 5479, pp. 134–152. Springer, Heidelberg (2009). https://doi.org/10.1007/978-3-642-01001-9_8
32. Sasaki, Yu., Emami, S., Hong, D., Kumar, A.: Improved known-key distinguishers on Feistel-SP ciphers and application to camellia. In: Susilo, W., Mu, Y., Seberry, J. (eds.) ACISP 2012. LNCS, vol. 7372, pp. 87–100. Springer, Heidelberg (2012). https://doi.org/10.1007/978-3-642-31448-3_7
33. Sasaki, Yu., Wang, L., Sakai, Y., Sakiyama, K., Ohta, K.: Three-subset meet-in-the-middle attack on reduced XTEA. In: Mitrokotsa, A., Vaudenay, S. (eds.) AFRICACRYPT 2012. LNCS, vol. 7374, pp. 138–154. Springer, Heidelberg (2012). https://doi.org/10.1007/978-3-642-31410-0_9
34. Schrottenloher, A., Stevens, M.: Simplified MITM modeling for permutations: new (quantum) attacks. In: Dodis, Y., Shrimpton, T. (eds.) CRYPTO 2022. LNCS, vol. 13509, pp. 717–747. Springer, Cham (2022). https://doi.org/10.1007/978-3-031-15982-4_24
35. Schrottenloher, A., Stevens, M.: Simplified modeling of MITM attacks for block ciphers: new (quantum) attacks. IACR Trans. Symmetric Cryptol. **2023**, 146–183 (2023). https://doi.org/10.46586/tosc.v2023.i3.146-183
36. Shahmirzadi, A.R., Azimi, S.A., Salmasizadeh, M., Mohajeri, J., Aref, M.R.: Impossible differential cryptanalysis of reduced-round midori64 block cipher. In: ISCISC, pp. 99–104 (2017). https://doi.org/10.1109/ISCISC.2017.8488362
37. Sun, S., Hu, L., Wang, P., Qiao, K., Ma, X., Song, L.: Automatic security evaluation and (related-key) differential characteristic search: application to SIMON, PRESENT, LBlock, DES(L) and other bit-oriented block ciphers. In: Sarkar, P., Iwata, T. (eds.) ASIACRYPT 2014. LNCS, vol. 8873, pp. 158–178. Springer, Heidelberg (2014). https://doi.org/10.1007/978-3-662-45611-8_9
38. Wei, L., Rechberger, C., Guo, J., Wu, H., Wang, H., Ling, S.: Improved meet-in-the-middle cryptanalysis of KTANTAN (poster). In: Parampalli, U., Hawkes, P. (eds.) ACISP 2011. LNCS, vol. 6812, pp. 433–438. Springer, Heidelberg (2011). https://doi.org/10.1007/978-3-642-22497-3_31

Comprehensive Robustness Analysis of GCM, CCM, and OCB3

Akiko Inoue[1(✉)], Tetsu Iwata[2], and Kazuhiko Minematsu[1,3]

[1] NEC, Kawasaki, Japan
{a_inoue,k-minematsu}@nec.com
[2] Nagoya University, Nagoya, Japan
tetsu.iwata@nagoya-u.jp
[3] Yokohama National University, Yokohama, Japan

Abstract. Clarifying the robustness of authenticated encryption (AE) schemes, such as security under nonce misuse or Release of Unverified Plaintext (RUP), has significant importance due to the extensive use of AEs in real-world applications. We present a comprehensive analysis of the robustness of well-known standards, namely GCM, CCM, and OCB3. Despite many existing studies, we uncovered several robustness properties for them that were not known in the literature. In particular, we show that both GCM and CCM maintain authenticity under RUP. Moreover, CCM keeps this feature even if a nonce is misused. We show that this robust security is maintained if one block cipher call in CCM is omitted, resulting in an efficiency improvement of CCM since the proposal. Together with existing analysis, our work gives a complete picture of the robustness of these standards for the first time. Our results also imply several new robust AE schemes based on GCM and CCM.

Keywords: Authenticated Encryption · Robustness · GCM · CCM · OCB3

1 Introduction

Authenticated encryption (AE) [19,69][1] is a type of symmetric-key encryption that simultaneously ensures the confidentiality and authenticity of messages. AE is widely acknowledged as a fundamental tool in practical cryptography and is widely deployed in practice, such as TLS for the Internet and WPA for Wifi access. A wide class of AE is *nonce-based*; that is, it takes a nonce as input, a value that never repeats, in encryption. The most popular and widely accepted prerequisite for nonce-based AE is *nonce-respecting*; the assumption that a nonce is non-repeating is crucial as a repeat of the nonce implies an immediate break of IND-CPA, the standard cryptographic notion for privacy/confidentiality. Another common prerequisite for AE is that the decryption routine must return a single error message when verification fails so that any information on the "unverified plaintext" does not leak.

[1] AE with associated data (AEAD) is also a common name of our object of study.

A. Patra (Ed.): CT-RSA 2025, LNCS 15598, pp. 75–98, 2025.
https://doi.org/10.1007/978-3-031-88661-4_4

However, in practice, these two prerequisites are sometimes violated, *i.e.*, AE can be *misused*. Misuse can happen due to various reasons, say poor randomness for nonce generation, misconfiguration of protocol, or side-channel/fault attacks, and has a devastating impact on real-world applications, such as [26,66,76]. Studying the impact of violation of these prerequisites, *i.e.*, *robustness*, is thus quite essential and practically relevant. A well-known example is Joux's "forbidden" attacks against GCM [48], which shows that even a single nonce repeat allows a universal forgery attack. Padding oracle attack [77] is another famous example regarding the second prerequisite. After these examples, AE's robustness has been a central topic in the literature. Violation of the first prerequisite is called Nonce Misuse (NM), and that of the second is called Release of Unverified Plaintext (RUP) [14] (as a special case of [27]), and studying the robustness of a given scheme means studying security under NM or RUP or both. A number of formal security notions capturing robustness have been proposed and studied [14,16,74]. The robustness of GCM and other popular schemes is a frequent question raised by implementors/users [8–10] and received attention in IETF (see *e.g.*, Bozhko [28]). Robustness of modern AE schemes, such as the candidates to CAESAR competition [2] and NIST Lightweight Cryptography (LWC) [4], has been extensively studied [3,14,45,59,75,78]. In particular, NIST IR 8454 [3] mentioned that the robustness of the LWC finalists was considered for the final selection, together with a very detailed literature survey on the finalists, including their robustness analysis. The LWC winner Ascon also has received attention on its robustness [1,18,51].

Given this situation, it would be interesting to ask: do we fully understand the robustness of well-known standards, namely GCM [5], CCM [6], and OCB3 [50]? At first glance, it seems so since there are many existing studies (see Table 1 and Related Work), including the aforementioned forbidden attack by Joux. However, we reveal several robustness properties for them that are unknown (nor mentioned) in the literature. The purpose of this work is to report them in a comprehensive manner[2]. For the first time, we present the full picture of these standards' robustness together with existing analysis.

GCM and CCM are the two NIST AE standards (NIST SP800-38D [5] and SP800-38C [6]). They have been extensively used for TLS, IPSec, SSH, etc. CCM is the first specified AE mode for Wifi since WPA2 and is still mandated in the latest WPA3. It is also used for many resource-constrained networks, including LoRaWan, Bluetooth, and Zigbee, to name a few. See Rogaway's CRYPTREC report [72] for more information on their real-world applications. OCB3 is the third (and the final) version of the seminal OCB mode family and is an Internet standard (RFC 7253) [7].

For GCM, we show that it maintains authenticity even if it releases unverified plaintext, also known as INTegrity under RUP (INT-RUP) [14], irrespective of nonce length. Except for Ashur *et al.*'s result [16] (ADL17) on nonce misuse resilience privacy (see Table 1), GCM is considered to lack the robustness of any

[2] We do not consider leakage-resistance [22,23,64] as it requires additional security assumptions on side-channel attacks for implementations of (specific) components.

known kind. Our result shows that this is not the case, and hence, we think this is something unexpected.

For CCM, we show an even stronger result: it maintains INT-RUP even when nonce may repeat in encryption, which we refer to as Nonce-Misuse-Resistant (NMR) INT-RUP. This notion gives the strongest authenticity property that we consider in this paper. In addition, we show that CCM maintains privacy in the sense of Nonce Misuse resiLience (NML), a relaxed notion from nonce misuse resistance introduced by ADL17. These robustness properties are realized by CCM's prefix-free encoding applied to the internal CBC-MAC. The prefix-freeness was also the key of the existing nonce-respecting proofs [36,47,78], however, never used for proving robustness. These results indicate that CCM is much more robust than GCM (and OCB3, see Table 1). Despite its wide real-world adoption, CCM has received surprisingly less attention than GCM or OCB3 from a provable security perspective after Jonsson's initial proof [47]. Our results on CCM is connected to the existing results, say Petrank and Rackoff [65] for CBC-MAC taking prefix-free inputs. However, the structure of CCM is more involved which requires us to conduct careful dedicated analysis instead of a black-box use of existing results including Petrank and Rackoff. Our results could benefit protocols/applications adopting CCM to provide an in-depth defense.

For OCB3, the previous analysis covers most of the existing robustness notions. We present a study on nonce misuse resilience. Specifically, we show OCB3's privacy in the sense of nonce misuse resilience. Authenticity is broken in a general case, however, we point out that under a restriction on associated data, authenticity is also maintained. These results compensate for the original analysis of ADL17, which mainly focuses on the first version of OCB.

Table 1 shows the summary of our results together with existing results. For comparison, we also list the results for ChaCha20-Poly1305 [61], where all the robustness properties we consider are already known in the literature.

Benefits of Our Results. Our results have several implications on AE constructions. First, given that GCM and CCM are INT-RUP secure, we can convert them into a RUP-secure AE [14], a secure AE for both privacy and authenticity under RUP, in an efficient (near) black-box way, thanks to a method by Andreeva *et al.* [14]. An earlier RUP-secure AE based on GCM (GCM-RUP [16]) needs to modify the algorithm. No CCM-based scheme is known. RUP-secure AE is relevant as a countermeasure against real-world attacks such as Efail [66]. Second, our security proofs reveal that one block cipher call in CCM can be omitted, maintaining all the security properties, including those we prove in this paper. We call this optimized variant CCM2. Surprisingly, we found such an optimization after more than 15 years of being standardized by NIST. This improvement is particularly effective when messages are short [13]. Note that short inputs are common for wireless low-power communication protocols and even for Internet protocols, where CCM is often used.

Related Work. Provable security of GCM under the nonce-respecting scenario has been extensively studied [21,41,46,54,55,57,60,62]. Design issues such as

Table 1. Summary of results. GCM is NML-Priv secure only if nonce is 96 bits and broken otherwise. OCB3 is NML-Auth secure only if AD is fixed. CCM2 is our optimized version of CCM.

	RUP		NMR		NML		RUP+NMR
	Priv (PA1)	INT-RUP	Priv	Auth	Priv	Auth	Auth
GCM	✗ [14]	✓ Sect. 4	✗ [Classical]	✗ [48]	✓/ ✗ [16]	✗ [16]	✗ [48]
CCM/CCM2	✗ [14]	✓ Sect. 5	✗ [Classical]	✓ Sect. 5	✓ Sect. 6	✓ Sect. 5	✓ Sect. 5
OCB3	✗ [14]	✗ [14]	✗ [Classical]	✗ [78]	✓ Sect. 7	✓/ ✗ Sect. 7, [78]	✗ [78]
ChaChaPoly	✗ [14]	✓ [42,43]	✗ [Classical]	✗ [49]	✓ [16]	✓ [16]	✗ [49]

security degradation for short tag or weak keys have been discussed [11,34,38, 56,67]. Dodis *et al.* studied key committing security of GCM [32].

Provable security of CCM under the nonce-respecting scenario was proved by Jonsson [47]. Rogaway and Wagner [68] reviewed the design and pointed out several deficiencies. Fouque *et al.* [36] presented a security bound for a variant of CCM and forgery attacks on (a general form of) CCM based on nonce repeat. Their nonce-misuse forgery attack against the original CCM has birthday complexity and hence does not contradict our result. Gjiriti *et al.* [37] showed provable security of a variant of CCM with variable tag stretch. Menda *et al.* [58] showed key committing attack against CCM. Very recently, Zhang *et al.* [79] proved its multi-user security.

Provable security of OCB3 under the nonce-respecting scenario has been proved by Krovetz and Rogaway [50]. The bound was improved by Bhaumik and Nandi [25]. An authenticity attack under RUP was shown by [14]. Liénardy and Lafitte [52] pointed out an issue of the current specification on the valid nonce length.

Vaudenay and Vizár [78] showed a nonce-misuse analysis on CAESAR candidates and GCM, CCM and OCB3. Rogaway and Shrimpton [74] introduced the notion of nonce-misuse resistance and proposed SIV, an offline AE with nonce-misuse resistance. Robust AE (RAE) [39] is a class of (offline) AEs having full protection against nonce misuse and RUP. Online AE [35] is a class of nonce-based AE that has partial privacy protection against nonce misuse while online processing. Hoang *et al.* [40] discussed its practical relevance and limitation.

2 Preliminaries

2.1 Basic Notations

For non-negative integers i and j with $i < j$, let $[i..j] := \{i, i+1, i+2, \ldots, j\}$. For any list $X = (X[1], \ldots, X[x])$ and $i, j \in [1..x]$, $i < j$, we write $X[i..j]$ to mean $(X[i], \ldots, X[j])$. Let $\{0,1\}^*$ be the set of all bit strings, including the empty string ε, the single element in $\{0,1\}^0$. For $X \in \{0,1\}^*$, $|X|$ denotes its bit length and $|X|_n$ denotes $\lceil |X|/n \rceil$. We define the parsing of a string into n-bit blocks for a positive integer n by $(X[1], X[2], \ldots, X[m]) \xleftarrow{n} X$, where $X[1] \,\|\, X[2] \,\|\, \ldots \,\|\, X[m] = X$, $|X[i]| = n$ for $1 \leq i < m$ and $0 < |X[m]| \leq n$ when $|X| > 0$. When $|X| = 0$ (*i.e.*, $X = \varepsilon$), we let $X[1] \xleftarrow{n} X$ with $X[1] = \varepsilon$. A concatenation of bit strings X and Y is denoted as $X \,\|\, Y$, or XY, in case no confusion is possible. Let 0^i be the string of i zero bits. Hence, we write 10^i for $1 \,\|\, 0^i$. For $X \in \{0,1\}^*$ with $|X| \geq i$, $\mathtt{msb}_i(X)$ is the first (left) i bits of X, and $\mathtt{lsb}_i(X)$ is the last (right) i bits of X. Let $\langle X \rangle_c$ be the c-bit standard representation of $X \in [0..2^c - 1]$. If X is uniformly chosen from the set $\mathcal{X}$, we write $X \xleftarrow{\$} \mathcal{X}$. For any $X \in \{0,1\}^*$ and a positive integer n, let $\mathsf{pad}_n(X)$ be $X \,\|\, 00\ldots0$ so that $|\mathsf{pad}_n(X)|$ be the minimum number of multiple of n. If $|X|$ is a positive multiple of n, $\mathsf{pad}_n(X) = X$, and $\mathsf{pad}_n(\varepsilon) = \varepsilon$. Note that pad_n is not injective.

Oracles and Advantage. Suppose $\mathcal{A}$ is an adversary in a game. $\mathcal{A}$ can query to s oracles, $\mathcal{O}_1, \ldots, \mathcal{O}_s$, in any order. In the case of a distinguishing game, $\mathcal{A}$ outputs a bit after the queries, which is a random variable whose probability space is defined under $\mathcal{A}$ and $\{\mathcal{O}_i\}_{i \in [1..s]}$. Let $[\mathcal{A}^{\mathcal{O}_1, \ldots, \mathcal{O}_s} = 1]$ denote the event that this bit is 1. We call $\mathcal{O}_i$ the i-th oracle in the game. By writing $\mathbf{Adv}_{\Pi}^{\mathtt{xxx}}(\mathcal{A})$, we mean *advantage* of the adversary $\mathcal{A}$ in the game $\mathtt{xxx}$ involving Π. We say Π is $\mathtt{xxx}$-secure if the corresponding advantage is negligible for all computationally bounded adversaries.

(Tweakable) Block Cipher and Random Primitives. Any keyed function $F : \mathcal{K} \times \mathcal{X} \to \mathcal{Y}$ with key space $\mathcal{K}$, we may write $F_K(x)$ to denote $F(K, x)$. Unless otherwise specified, we assume $K \xleftarrow{\$} \mathcal{K}$ in evaluation of $F_K(x)$. A block cipher $E : \mathcal{K} \times \mathcal{M} \to \mathcal{M}$ is a keyed function such that for any $K \in \mathcal{K}$, $E(K, \cdot)$ is a permutation over the message space $\mathcal{M}$. We write $E_K^{-1}(\cdot)$ to denote the decryption function. A tweakable block cipher (TBC) [53] $\widetilde{E} : \mathcal{K} \times \mathcal{TW} \times \mathcal{M} \to \mathcal{M}$ is a keyed function such that for any $K \in \mathcal{K}$ and *tweak* $W \in \mathcal{TW}$, $\widetilde{E}(K, W, \cdot)$ is a permutation over $\mathcal{M}$. Tweak is typically used as a public/chosen value in contrast to the secret key. Let $\mathrm{Perm}(n)$ be the set of all permutations of n bits, and $\mathrm{Func}(n, m)$ be the set of all functions: $\{0,1\}^n \to \{0,1\}^m$. A uniform random permutation (URP) $\mathsf{P} : \{0,1\}^n \to \{0,1\}^n$ is a random permutation uniformly chosen over $\mathrm{Perm}(n)$. A uniform random function (URF) $\mathsf{R} : \{0,1\}^n \to \{0,1\}^m$ is a random function uniformly chosen over $\mathrm{Func}(n, m)$. A tweakable uniform random permutation (TURP) $\widetilde{\mathsf{P}} : \mathcal{TW} \times \mathcal{M} \to \mathcal{M}$ consists of $|\mathcal{TW}|$ independent instances of P over $\mathcal{M}$ and the first argument (tweak) specifies the URP used. The security of TBC $\widetilde{E}$ is defined as the following distinguishing probability.

$$\mathbf{Adv}_{\widetilde{E}}^{\mathtt{TPRP}}(\mathcal{A}) := |\Pr[\mathcal{A}^{\widetilde{E}_K} = 1] - \Pr[\mathcal{A}^{\widetilde{\mathsf{P}}} = 1]|, \tag{1}$$

where $\widetilde{\mathsf{P}}$ has the same domain and range as $\widetilde{E}_K$. When $\mathcal{TW}$ is a singleton, the security of block cipher E_K is obtained by the above security, denoted by $\mathbf{Adv}_{E}^{\mathtt{PRP}}(\mathcal{A})$.

H-Coefficient. All our proofs use the standard H-Coefficient technique [31,63]. See the full version for its basics.

2.2 Authenticated Encryption

A nonce-based AE scheme $\Pi = (\Pi.\mathcal{E}, \Pi.\mathcal{D})$ is defined over a key space $\mathcal{K}$, a nonce space $\mathcal{N}$, an associated data (AD) space $\mathcal{AD}$, a message space $\mathcal{M}$, and a tag space $\mathcal{T} = \{0,1\}^\tau$ for some fixed tag length τ. We use ν throughout the paper to denote the nonce length in bits, hence $\mathcal{N} = \{0,1\}^\nu$. An AD is information that is not to be kept confidential, but its integrity must be ensured. For example, network encryption will treat the protocol header as an AD. Formally, AE is a tuple of an encryption function $\Pi.\mathcal{E}\colon \mathcal{K} \times \mathcal{N} \times \mathcal{AD} \times \mathcal{M} \to \mathcal{M} \times \mathcal{T}$, and a decryption function $\Pi.\mathcal{D} : \mathcal{K} \times \mathcal{N} \times \mathcal{AD} \times \mathcal{M} \times \mathcal{T} \to \mathcal{M} \cup \{\bot\}$, where symbol $\bot$ indicates a verification failure. We require $\Pi.\mathcal{D}_K(N, A, C, T) = M$ if $\Pi.\mathcal{E}_K(N, A, M) = (C, T)$ for soundness. Moreover, we assume $|C| = |M|$; all our target schemes meet this condition. Basically, each nonce in encryption must be unique, which we call *nonce-respecting* (NR) model. Note that a nonce in decryption has no restrictions; it may repeat and it may collide with one used in encryption. A nonce-respecting adversary (NR adversary) may choose nonce arbitrarily in encryption, except that this condition must be respected [71]. Let $\Pi = (\Pi.\mathcal{E}, \Pi.\mathcal{D})$ be an AE scheme. Let \$ be the random-bit oracle that takes (N, A, M) and returns random $|M| + \tau$ bits. The standard security notions of Π against NR adversaries are Priv (confidentiality/privacy) and Auth (authenticity/integrity), defined below.

Definition 1 (Priv and Auth). *Let $\mathcal{A}$ be a* Priv *adversary against* Π *and let $\mathcal{B}$ be an* Auth *adversary against* Π.

$$\mathbf{Adv}_{\Pi}^{\mathsf{Priv}}(\mathcal{A}) := |\Pr[\mathcal{A}^{\Pi.\mathcal{E}_K} = 1] - \Pr[\mathcal{A}^{\$} = 1]|,$$
$$\mathbf{Adv}_{\Pi}^{\mathsf{Auth}}(\mathcal{B}) := \Pr[\mathcal{B}^{\Pi.\mathcal{E}_K, \Pi.\mathcal{D}_K} \text{ forges}],$$

where $\mathcal{A}$ and $\mathcal{B}$ are nonce-respecting. The event $[\mathcal{B}^{\Pi.\mathcal{E}_K, \Pi.\mathcal{D}_K}$ forges$]$ means that $\mathcal{B}$ receives some $M' \neq \bot$ from $\Pi.\mathcal{D}_K$. $\mathcal{B}$ does not forward queries from $\Pi.\mathcal{E}_K$ to $\Pi.\mathcal{D}_K$, namely, $\mathcal{B}$ does not query (N, A, C, T) to $\Pi.\mathcal{D}_K$ after obtaining (N, A, M, C, T) as a result of query-response to $\Pi.\mathcal{E}_K$.

It is also possible to consider a combined notion that captures Priv and Auth. While this is convenient, since our purpose is a fine-grained analysis, we always treat privacy and authenticity notions separately. This applies to the various robustness notions described in the next section.

3 Robustness Notions of Authenticated Encryption

3.1 Security Notions Under Nonce Misuse

Rogaway and Shrimpton [74] introduced the concept of *Nonce-Misuse Resistance* (NMR), best-possible security notions under possibly repeating nonces in encryptions. NMR security notions are as follows.

Definition 2 (NMR-Priv and NMR-Auth [74]**).** *Let $\mathcal{A}$ be an NMR-Priv adversary against Π and let $\mathcal{B}$ be an NMR-Auth adversary against Π.*

$$\boldsymbol{Adv}_{\Pi}^{\texttt{NMR-Priv}}(\mathcal{A}) := |\Pr[\mathcal{A}^{\Pi.\mathcal{E}_K} = 1] - \Pr[\mathcal{A}^{\$} = 1]|,$$
$$\boldsymbol{Adv}_{\Pi}^{\texttt{NMR-Auth}}(\mathcal{B}) := \Pr[\mathcal{B}^{\Pi.\mathcal{E}_K, \Pi.\mathcal{D}_K} \text{ forges}],$$

where $\mathcal{A}$ and $\mathcal{B}$ may query to the first oracle with repeating nonces, but does not query a repeated tuple of (N, A, M). $\mathcal{B}$ does not forward queries from the first oracle to the second oracle.

We remark that NMR-Priv requires $\Pi.\mathcal{E}$ to be offline, *i.e.*, any ciphertext bit must reflect the whole encryption input. This limits applicability in particular for long messages. GCM and OCB3 are online schemes; it is inherently impossible to meet this notion. CCM is not online, but the encryption part is nevertheless a counter mode and fails to meet NMR-Priv [78].

Nonce-Misuse Resilience. Ashur *et al.* [16] proposed the concept of *Nonce-Misuse resiLience* (NML), which is a relaxed form of NMR. Intuitively, NML security notions require that the attacker must win the game by making a query with a nonce that is not misused (repeated). Conversely, an AE scheme is NML-secure if a repeat of nonce N does not threaten the security of encryption/decryption with a different nonce from N. While weaker than NMR, NML notions can be fulfilled by online schemes. If nonce is determined by (*e.g.*) recipient ID or timestamp, NML is practically relevant.

Definition 3 (NML-Priv and NML-Auth [16]**).** *Let $\mathcal{A}$ be an NML-Priv adversary against Π and let $\mathcal{B}$ be an NML-Auth adversary against Π.*

$$\boldsymbol{Adv}_{\Pi}^{\texttt{NML-Priv}}(\mathcal{A}) := |\Pr[\mathcal{A}^{\Pi.\mathcal{E}_K, \Pi.\mathcal{E}_K} = 1] - \Pr[\mathcal{A}^{\$, \Pi.\mathcal{E}_K} = 1]|,$$
$$\boldsymbol{Adv}_{\Pi}^{\texttt{NML-Auth}}(\mathcal{B}) := \Pr[\mathcal{B}^{\Pi.\mathcal{E}_K, \Pi.\mathcal{D}_K} \text{ forges}],$$

where $\mathcal{A}$ is nonce-respecting with respect to the first oracle, i.e., let $\mathcal{N}_1$ and $\mathcal{N}_2$ be the multisets of nonces used by the queries to the first (nonce-respecting) and the second (nonce-misusing) oracles; $\mathcal{N}_1 \cap \mathcal{N}_2 = \emptyset$ and each $N \in \mathcal{N}_1$ has a multiplicity one. $\mathcal{N}_2$ may contain nonces with multiplicity ≥ 2. Similarly for $\mathcal{B}$, we define $\mathcal{N}_1$ and $\mathcal{N}_2$. Both may contain nonces with multiplicity ≥ 2. However, any $N \in \mathcal{N}_1 \cap \mathcal{N}_2$ must have multiplicity one in $\mathcal{N}_1$. In addition, as with the standard Auth *notion, a trivial forgery is prohibited.*

3.2 Security Notions Under Release of Unverified Plaintext

Release of Unverified Plaintext (RUP) was formalized by Andreeva *et al.* [14]. RUP is the game environment that leaks the unverified plaintext to the adversary at decryption independent of the verification result. To formalize RUP security games, we require that $\Pi.\mathcal{D}$ is decomposed into the unverified decryption function, $\Pi.u\mathcal{D} : \mathcal{K} \times \mathcal{N} \times \mathcal{AD} \times \mathcal{M} \times \mathcal{T} \to \mathcal{M}$ and the verification function, $\Pi.\mathcal{V} : \mathcal{K} \times \mathcal{N} \times \mathcal{AD} \times \mathcal{M} \times \mathcal{T} \to \{\top, \bot\}$. The normal decryption combines them as $\Pi.\mathcal{D}_K(N, A, C, T) = M$ if $\Pi.u\mathcal{D}_K(N, A, C, T) = M$ and $\Pi.\mathcal{V}_K(N, A, C, T) = \top$, and $\Pi.\mathcal{D}_K(N, A, C, T) = \bot$ if $\Pi.\mathcal{V}_K(N, A, C, T) = \bot$. That is, when $\Pi.u\mathcal{D}_K(N, A, C, T) = M$, M denotes the correct decrypted plaintext if the input tuple is authentic, and otherwise M is something that would be discarded by the decryption oracle in the classical authenticity notions. Most existing AE schemes, including our targets, fulfill the aforementioned assumption. We will write $\Pi = (\Pi.\mathcal{E}, \Pi.u\mathcal{D}, \Pi.\mathcal{V})$ when we discuss about RUP security of Π. As described, $\Pi.\mathcal{D}$ is uniquely determined from $\Pi.u\mathcal{D}$ and $\Pi.\mathcal{V}$.

Privacy notion under RUP is Plaintext Awareness (PA), and PA is classified into a basic notion (PA1) and a stronger notion (PA2). As they are irrelevant to our analysis, we omit the definitions here. The authenticity notion under RUP is called INT-RUP (for INTegrity under RUP) [14].

Definition 4 (INT-RUP). *Let $\mathcal{A}$ be the INT-RUP adversary against $\Pi = (\Pi.\mathcal{E}, \Pi.u\mathcal{D}, \Pi.\mathcal{V})$.*

$$\mathbf{Adv}_{\Pi}^{\text{INT-RUP}}(\mathcal{A}) := \Pr[\mathcal{A}^{\Pi.\mathcal{E}_K, \Pi.u\mathcal{D}_K, \Pi.\mathcal{V}_K} \text{ forges}],$$

where $\mathcal{A}$ is nonce-respecting, i.e., never repeats nonce in queries to $\Pi.\mathcal{E}$. Moreover, $\mathcal{A}$ does not forward queries from $\Pi.\mathcal{E}$ to $\Pi.\mathcal{V}$. Queries to $\Pi.u\mathcal{D}$ have no restrictions.

We can combine INT-RUP with the nonce-misuse scenario, yielding a more robust authenticity notion.

Definition 5 (NMR-INT-RUP). *The nonce-misuse resistance INT-RUP (NMR-INT-RUP) advantage, $\mathbf{Adv}_{\Pi}^{\text{NMR-INT-RUP}}(\mathcal{A})$, is defined in the same manner as INT-RUP, except that $\mathcal{A}$ is allowed to repeat nonces in queries to the first oracle.*

By definition, we have the following implications: (1) NMR-Priv $\rightarrow$ NML-Priv $\rightarrow$ Priv, and (2) NMR-Auth $\rightarrow$ NML-Auth $\rightarrow$ Auth, and (3) NMR-INT-RUP $\rightarrow$ INT-RUP, and (4) NMR-INT-RUP $\rightarrow$ NMR-Auth.

NMR-INT-RUP and related notions have been studied for on-line AE scheme [24], which is a class of AEs providing a relaxed NM security while enabling online processing [15]. We remark that none of our targets is an on-line AE.

4 Authenticity of GCM Under RUP

We show that GCM is INT-RUP secure. As described in the introduction, we think this result is kind of unexpected since GCM is considered to lack robustness other than NML-Priv with a restriction to 96-bit nonce [16].

4.1 Specification of GCM

We briefly present the specification of GCM. Let $n = 128$ and E be an n-bit block cipher. For $X \in \{0, 1\}^{\ell}$ such that $\langle X \rangle_{\ell} = x_{\ell-1} \cdots x_1 x_0$, let $\mathsf{int}(X)$ be an

Algorithm $\mathsf{GCM}.\mathcal{E}[E_K](N, A, M)$

1. $C \leftarrow \mathsf{GCTR}[E_K](N, C)$
2. $T \leftarrow \mathsf{GMAC}.\mathcal{T}[E_K](N, A, C)$
3. **return** (C, T)

Algorithm $\mathsf{GCM}.u\mathcal{D}[E_K](N, A, C, T)$

1. $M \leftarrow \mathsf{GCTR}[E_K](N, C)$
2. **return** M

Algorithm $\mathsf{GCM}.\mathcal{D}[E_K](N, A, C, T)$

1. $b = \mathsf{GCM}.\mathcal{V}[E_K](N, A, C, T)$
2. **if** $b = \bot$ **then return** $\bot$
3. **else** $M \leftarrow \mathsf{GCM}.u\mathcal{D}[E_K](N, A, C, T)$
4. **return** M

Algorithm $\mathsf{GCM}.\mathcal{V}[E_K](N, A, C, T)$

1. $\widehat{T} \leftarrow \mathsf{GMAC}.\mathcal{T}[E_K](N, A, C)$
2. **if** $T = \widehat{T}$ **then return** $\top$
3. **else return** $\bot$

Algorithm $\mathsf{GCTR}[E_K](N, M)$

1. $L \leftarrow E_K(0^n)$
2. **if** $\nu = 96$ **then** $\mathsf{Ctr0} \leftarrow N \,\|\, 0^{31}1$
3. **else then** $\mathsf{Ctr0} \leftarrow \mathsf{GHASH}_L(\varepsilon, N)$
4. $(M[1], \ldots, M[m]) \xleftarrow{n} M$
5. **for** $i = 1$ **to** m **do**
6. $\quad C[i] \leftarrow M[i] \oplus \mathtt{msb}_{|M[i]|}(E_K(\mathsf{inc}^i(\mathsf{Ctr0})))$
7. $C \leftarrow C[1] \,\|\, \cdots \,\|\, C[m-1] \,\|\, C[m]$
8. **return** C

Algorithm $\mathsf{GMAC}.\mathcal{T}[E_K](N, A, C)$

1. $L \leftarrow E_K(0^n)$
2. **if** $\nu = 96$ **then** $\mathsf{Ctr0} \leftarrow N \,\|\, 0^{31}1$
3. **else then** $\mathsf{Ctr0} \leftarrow \mathsf{GHASH}_L(\varepsilon, N)$
4. $\mathsf{Mask} \leftarrow \mathtt{msb}_\tau(E_K(\mathsf{Ctr0}))$
5. $T \leftarrow \mathsf{Mask} \oplus \mathtt{msb}_\tau(\mathsf{GHASH}_L(A, C))$
6. **return** T

Algorithm $\mathsf{GMAC}.\mathcal{V}[E_K](N, A, C, T)$

1. $\widehat{T} \leftarrow \mathsf{GMAC}.\mathcal{T}[E_K](N, A, C)$
2. **if** $T = \widehat{T}$ **return** $\top$
3. **else return** $\bot$

Algorithm $\mathsf{GHASH}_L(A, C)$

1. $X \leftarrow \mathsf{pad}_n(A) \,\|\, \mathsf{pad}_n(C) \,\|\, \langle |A| \rangle_{n/2} \,\|\, \langle |C| \rangle_{n/2}$
2. $(X[1], \ldots, X[x]) \xleftarrow{n} X$, $Y \leftarrow 0^n$.
3. **for** $i = 1$ **to** x **do** $Y \leftarrow L \cdot (Y \oplus X[i])$
4. **return** Y

Fig. 1. Algorithms of $\mathsf{GCM}[E_K]$. Note that $\nu := |N|$ and $\tau := |T|$ are fixed in advance. The operation "$\cdot$" in line 3 of GHASH denotes a multiplication over $\mathrm{GF}(2^n)$.

integer $\sum_{i=0}^{\ell-1} x_i 2^i$. Let $\mathsf{inc}(X) = \mathtt{msb}_{n-32}(X) \,\|\, \langle \mathsf{int}(\mathtt{lsb}_{32}(X)) + 1 \mod 2^{32} \rangle_{32}$. For $i \geq 0$, $\mathsf{inc}^i(X)$ means that applying inc on X for i times. When $i = 0$, $\mathsf{inc}^i(X) = X$.

GCM is basically a composition of counter mode and a nonce-based MAC using a polynomial hashing over $\mathrm{GF}(2^n)$. Figure 1 shows the algorithms of GCM using E_K, denoted as $\mathsf{GCM}[E_K]$. In addition to the normal decryption, Fig. 1 shows the unverified decryption and verification routines together with GMAC MAC function inside GCM. They will be needed for our analysis. Here, $N, A, C \in \{0,1\}^*$ and $\tau := |T| \in [1..n]$ (NIST recommends $\tau \geq 64$). We also require $\nu := |N| \in [1..2^{n/2} - 1]$, $|A| \in [0..2^{n/2} - 1]$, and $|M| \in [0..n(2^{32} - 2)]$. The parameters ν and τ must be fixed in advance. The derivation of the first counter block input depends on whether $\nu = 96$ or not. Note that $|C| = |M|$ holds. Figure 2 depicts the encryption.

4.2 INT-RUP Bounds of GCM

Let $\mathsf{GCM}[E] = (\mathsf{GCM}.\mathcal{E}[E], \mathsf{GCM}.u\mathcal{D}[E], \mathsf{GCM}.\mathcal{V}[E])$ employing a block cipher $E : \mathcal{K} \times \{0,1\}^n \to \{0,1\}^n$. Let $\mathcal{A}$ be an INT-RUP adversary who makes q_e queries to $\mathsf{GCM}.\mathcal{E}[E_K]$, q_d queries to $\mathsf{GCM}.u\mathcal{D}[E_K]$, and q_v queries to $\mathsf{GCM}.\mathcal{V}[E_K]$, with

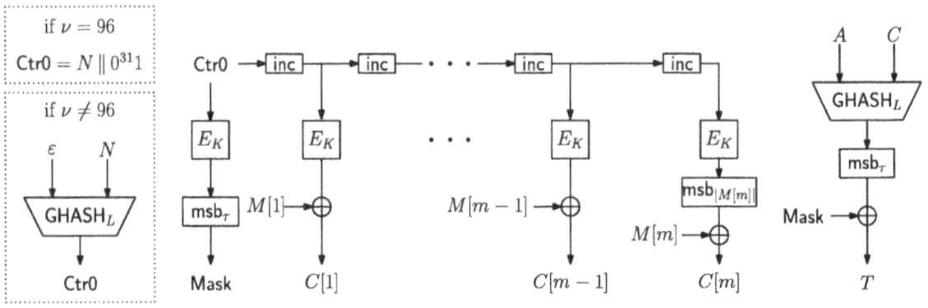

Fig. 2. Encryption of GCM.

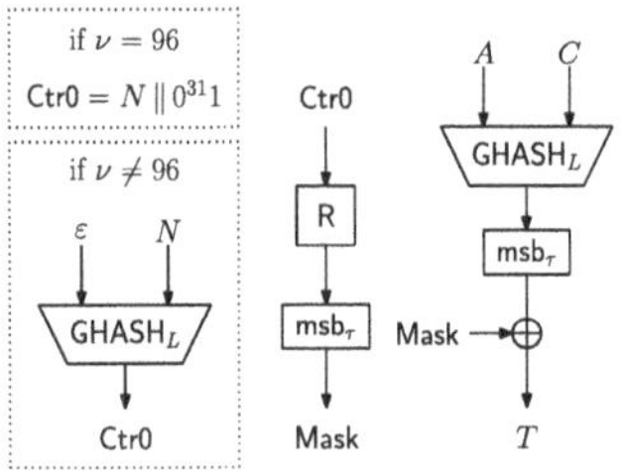

Fig. 3. $\mathsf{GMAC}.\mathcal{T}[\mathsf{R}]$.

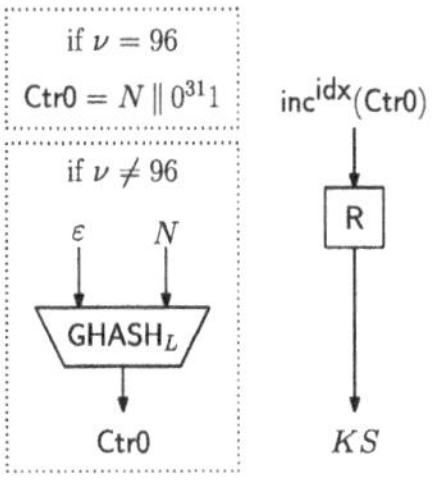

Fig. 4. $\mathcal{KS}_{\mathsf{G}}[\mathsf{R}]$, where $\mathsf{idx} \in [1..2^{32}-2]$.

time complexity t (where $K \xleftarrow{\$} \mathcal{K}$). After all the queries, $\mathcal{A}$ obtains a transcript written as

- $\{(N_i^e, A_i^e, M_i^e, C_i^e, T_i^e)\}_{i=1,\ldots,q_e}$ from $\mathsf{GCM}.\mathcal{E}[E_K]$,
- $\{(N_i^d, A_i^d, M_i^d, C_i^d, T_i^d)\}_{i=1,\ldots,q_d}$ from $\mathsf{GCM}.u\mathcal{D}[E_K]$,
- $\{(N_i^v, A_i^v, C_i^v, T_i^v, b_i)\}_{i=1,\ldots,q_v}$ from $\mathsf{GCM}.\mathcal{V}[E_K]$, where $b_i \in \{\top, \bot\}$.

Let σ_e, σ_d, and σ_v be the total number of plaintext/ciphertext blocks queried to $\mathsf{GCM}.\mathcal{E}[E]$, $\mathsf{GCM}.u\mathcal{D}[E]$, and $\mathsf{GCM}.\mathcal{V}[E]$ oracles, *i.e.*, $\sigma_e = \sum_{i=1}^{q_e} |M_i^e|_n$, $\sigma_d = \sum_{i=1}^{q_d} |C_i^d|_n$, and $\sigma_v = \sum_{i=1}^{q_v} |C_i^v|_n$. Let $\sigma_{\mathrm{all}} := \sigma_e + \sigma_d + \sigma_v + q_e + q_v + 1$ to denote the maximum of the total number of E calls in the game, which we call the effective total queried blocks. Let $\ell_N := \lceil \nu/n \rceil$ and ℓ_A be the maximum number of blocks of the input to GHASH in encryption and verification queries; thus, $|A_i^\#|_n + |C_i^\#|_n \leq \ell_A$ for $\# \in \{e, v\}$, $i \in [1..q_\#]$.

The following theorem shows that GCM is INT-RUP secure up to the birthday bound irrespective of nonce length.

Theorem 1. *For the adversary $\mathcal{A}$ defined as above with time complexity t,*

$$\begin{aligned}
\boldsymbol{Adv}_{\mathsf{GCM}[E]}^{\mathit{INT\text{-}RUP}}(\mathcal{A}) &\leq \boldsymbol{Adv}_E^{\mathit{PRP}}(\widehat{\mathcal{A}}) + \frac{\sigma_{all}^2}{2^{n+1}} \\
&+ \frac{(q_e^2 + 2q_e q_v + 2q_e + 2q_v + 2\sigma_e + 2\sigma_d)(\ell_N + 1)}{2^n} \\
&+ \frac{64(2q_e + q_d + q_v - 1)(\sigma_e + \sigma_d + q_e + q_d)(\ell_N + 1)}{2^n} + \frac{2q_v(\ell_A + 2)}{2^\tau}
\end{aligned}$$

holds for a PRP adversary $\widehat{\mathcal{A}}$ *with* σ_{all} *queries and time complexity* $t + O(\sigma_{all})$. *In particular, when* $\nu = 96$, *we have*

$$\mathbf{Adv}_{\mathsf{GCM}[E]}^{\mathit{INT\text{-}RUP}}(\mathcal{A}) \leq \mathbf{Adv}_{E}^{\mathit{PRP}}(\widehat{\mathcal{A}}) + \frac{\sigma_{all}^2}{2^{n+1}} + \frac{2q_v(\ell_A + 2)}{2^{\tau}}$$

for a PRP adversary $\widehat{\mathcal{A}}$ *with* σ_{all} *queries and time complexity* $t + O(\sigma_{all})$.

4.3 Proof Overview

We show an overview of the proof for Theorem 1. The complete one is shown in the full version. First, we focus on the idealized $\mathsf{GCM}[\mathsf{P}]$ obtained by replacing E with a uniform random permutation P. This introduces the gap $\mathbf{Adv}_E^{\mathsf{PRP}}(\widehat{\mathcal{A}})$ into the bound. We then apply the standard PRP/PRF switching lemma [20], thus, replacing all the invocations of P in the INT-RUP game of $\mathsf{GCM}[\mathsf{P}]$ with a uniform random function R, which leads to the term $\sigma_{\mathrm{all}}^2/2^{n+1}$.

Second, to analyze $\mathbf{Adv}_{\mathsf{GCM}[\mathsf{R}]}^{\mathtt{INT\text{-}RUP}}(\mathcal{A}')$, we reduce the INT-RUP game of $\mathsf{GCM}[\mathsf{R}]$ to *a variant* of UF-CMA (Unforgeability under Chosen Message Attack) game of $\mathsf{GMAC}[\mathsf{R}]$. For this reduction, we first define the tagging oracle $\mathsf{GMAC}.\mathcal{T}[\mathsf{R}]$ and the verification oracle $\mathsf{GMAC}.\mathcal{V}[\mathsf{R}]$ as shown in Figs. 1, 3. In the standard UF-CMA game, the advantage is defined as the probability that the adversary querying $\mathsf{GMAC}.\mathcal{T}$ and $\mathsf{GMAC}.\mathcal{V}$ successfully obtains $\top$ from $\mathsf{GMAC}.\mathcal{V}$. Note that we assume the adversary cannot repeat nonces in the queries to $\mathsf{GMAC}.\mathcal{T}$. We then easily see that $\mathsf{GMAC}.\mathcal{T}$ (resp. $\mathsf{GMAC}.\mathcal{V}$) in the UF-CMA can simulate the tag generation part (resp. tag verification part) of $\mathsf{GCM}.\mathcal{E}$ (resp. $\mathsf{GCM}.\mathcal{V}$) in the INT-RUP game. To simulate the other part/oracle in the INT-RUP game of GCM, we additionally define a function; let $\mathcal{KS}_{\mathsf{G}}[\mathsf{R}] : \{0,1\}^\nu \times [1..2^{32}-2] \rightarrow \{0,1\}^n$ be a function that outputs a block of keystream $KS \in \{0,1\}^n$ for the tuple of $N \in \{0,1\}^\nu$ and block index $\mathsf{idx} \in [1..2^{32}-2]$ using R. Concretely, we define $\mathcal{KS}_{\mathsf{G}}[\mathsf{R}](N, \mathsf{idx}) := \mathsf{R}(\mathsf{inc}^{\mathsf{idx}}(\mathsf{Ctr0}))$, where

$$\mathsf{Ctr0} := \begin{cases} N \,\|\, 0^{31}1 & \text{when } \nu = 96 \\ \mathsf{GHASH}_L(\varepsilon, N) & \text{when } \nu \neq 96, \end{cases} \tag{2}$$

and $L = \mathsf{R}(0^n)$. We also write it as $\mathcal{KS}_{\mathsf{G}}$. Figure 4 depicts $\mathcal{KS}_{\mathsf{G}}$. From the definition of $\mathcal{KS}_{\mathsf{G}}$, we see that $\mathcal{KS}_{\mathsf{G}}$ can simulate the keystream generation parts of $\mathsf{GCM}.\mathcal{E}/\mathsf{GCM}.\mathcal{V}$ and the whole of $\mathsf{GCM}.u\mathcal{D}$ in the INT-RUP. We then define a new UF-CMA-variant game, dubbed UF-CMA$^+$, involving $\mathsf{GMAC}.\mathcal{T}$, $\mathcal{KS}_{\mathsf{G}}$, and $\mathsf{GMAC}.\mathcal{V}$. Its definition is the UF-CMA game for $\mathsf{GMAC}[\mathsf{R}]$ with an additional oracle $\mathcal{KS}_{\mathsf{G}}$. For the detailed definition, see the full version. From the above discussion, we can prove that the INT-RUP game of GCM can be simulated by the UF-CMA$^+$ game of GMAC and we obtain $\mathbf{Adv}_{\mathsf{GCM}[\mathsf{R}]}^{\mathtt{INT\text{-}RUP}}(\mathcal{A}') \leq \mathbf{Adv}_{\mathsf{GMAC}[\mathsf{R}]}^{\mathtt{UF\text{-}CMA+}}(\mathcal{B})$. See the full version for the detailed proof.

Third, we analyze $\mathbf{Adv}_{\mathsf{GMAC}[\mathsf{R}]}^{\mathtt{UF\text{-}CMA+}}(\mathcal{B})$ using an H-coefficient technique. In this part, we mainly show that a non-trivial collision probability between any of the inputs of R is sufficiently low. For this evaluation, we can utilize the evaluation in [62], which shows the upper bound of the collision probability in the standard authentication proof of GCM. Whereas our proof technique and the one used in [62] are different, and we additionally allow the adversary to query $\mathcal{KS}_{\mathsf{G}}$, we can prove that a similar bound as in the normal Auth of GCM [62].

5 Authenticity of CCM Under RUP and Nonce Misuse, and Optimization of CCM

We show that CCM is NMR-INT-RUP secure. This also means CCM's INT-RUP and NMR-Auth security from the implications shown in Sect. 3. We also show that CCM maintains this robustness even if one omits a mask for the tag, which is derived by encrypting the nonce. We call this scheme CCM2.

5.1 Specifications of CCM and CCM2

We describe CCM, partially adopting the notations of Gjiriti *et al.* [37]. As in the case of GCM, we use $\nu := |N|$ and $\tau := |T|$ and assume they are fixed in advance. CCM fixes $n = 128$ and $\nu \in \{56, 64, 72, 80, 88, 96, 104\}$ and $\tau \in \{32, 48, 64, 80, 96, 112, 128\}$. All input and output variables of CCM are assumed to be byte strings. A valid AD A and a valid plaintext M must satisfy $0 \leq |A| < (2^{64}) \cdot 8$ and $0 \leq |M| < (2^{120-\nu}) \cdot 8$. CCM composes a counter mode (which we write as CCTR) and CBC-MAC in a way similar to MAC-then-Encryption, together with a certain input encoding applied to CBC-MAC.

Let $\mathsf{flags}(A)$ be a byte determined by AD A and ν and τ. As ν and τ are fixed, we do not write them as arguments. It is defined as $\mathsf{flags}(A) = (0 \,\|\, \mathsf{sign}(A = \varepsilon) \,\|\, \langle \tau/16 - 1 \rangle_3 \,\|\, \langle 14 - \nu/8 \rangle_3)$, where $\mathsf{sign}(\mathbf{S}) = 0$ if event $\mathbf{S}$ is true, $= 1$ otherwise. Let flags' be a byte $(0^5 \,\|\, \langle 14 - \nu/8 \rangle_3)$. Due to the range of τ, $\mathsf{flags}' \neq \mathsf{flags}(A)$ holds for any $A \in \{0,1\}^*$. Let $\mathsf{ecN}(N, i) = (\mathsf{flags}' \,\|\, N \,\|\, \langle i \rangle_{120-\nu})$ denote the i-th counter block. CBC-MAC takes an encoded sequence, $B = (B[0], B[1], \ldots, B[\ell])$, generated from (N, A, M). In particular, let $\mathsf{ecB}_0(N, A, M) := (\mathsf{flags}(A) \,\|\, N \,\|\, \langle |M|_8 \rangle_{120-\nu})$ which is used as $B[0]$. To determine the blocks after $B[0]$ in B, ecA encodes A as $\mathsf{ecA}(A) = \mathsf{pad}_n(\mathsf{lenA}(A) \,\|\, A)$. Here, $\mathsf{lenA}(A)$ denotes the length of A. Definitions of ecA and lenA are a bit complex and we omit the full details. See [33,68]. Our proof will only use the following facts: (1) $|\mathsf{ecA}(A)|$ is a multiple of n bits for any valid A, (2) $\mathsf{ecA}(A) \neq \mathsf{ecA}(A')$ for any valid and distinct A and A', and (3) $|\mathsf{ecA}(A)|_n \leq |A|_n + 1$ for any A. Finally, the rest of B blocks are determined by the message encoding function $\mathsf{ecM}(M) := \mathsf{pad}_n(M)$. CBC-MAC takes a full-block sequence of $\mathsf{ec}(N, A, M) := \mathsf{ecB}_0(N, A, M) \,\|\, \mathsf{ecA}(A) \,\|\, \mathsf{ecM}(M)$. The τ-bit output of CBC-MAC taking $\mathsf{ec}(N, A, M)$ is masked by the most significant τ-bit of the first CCTR output with a counter block $\mathsf{ecN}(N, 0)$, which becomes a tag. The plaintext M is encrypted by CCTR taking counter blocks $\mathsf{ecN}(N, i)$ for $i = 1, \ldots, |M|_n$. See Fig. 5 for the pseudocode and Fig. 6 for the illustration. As with Sect. 4, Fig. 5 contains the unverified and the verification routines for our analysis.

Algorithm $\mathsf{CCM}.\mathcal{E}[E_K](N, A, M)$

$V \leftarrow \mathsf{CBC\text{-}MAC}.\mathcal{T}[E_K](N, A, M)$
$C \leftarrow \mathsf{CCTR}[E_K](N, M)$
$U \leftarrow E_K(\mathsf{ecN}(N, 0))$
$T \leftarrow V \oplus \mathtt{msb}_\tau(U)$
return (C, T)

Algorithm $\mathsf{CCM}.u\mathcal{D}[E_K](N, A, C, T)$

$M \leftarrow \mathsf{CCTR}[E_K](N, C)$
return M

Algorithm $\mathsf{CCM}.\mathcal{D}[E_K](N, A, C, T)$

$b = \mathsf{CCM}.\mathcal{V}[E_K](N, A, C, T)$
if $b = \bot$ **then return** $\bot$
else $M \leftarrow \mathsf{CCM}.u\mathcal{D}[E_K](N, A, C, T)$
return M

Algorithm $\mathsf{CCM}.\mathcal{V}[E_K](N, A, C, T)$

$M \leftarrow \mathsf{CCM}.u\mathcal{D}[E_K](N, A, C, T)$
$V \leftarrow \mathsf{CBC\text{-}MAC}.\mathcal{T}[E_K](N, A, M)$
$U \leftarrow E_K(\mathsf{ecN}(N, 0))$
$\widehat{T} \leftarrow V \oplus \mathtt{msb}_\tau(U)$
if $T = \widehat{T}$ **then return** $\top$
else return $\bot$

Algorithm $\mathsf{CBC\text{-}MAC}.\mathcal{T}[E_K](N, A, M)$
(assumes N, A and M are of valid length)

$V \leftarrow 0^n$
$B[0] \leftarrow \mathsf{ecB}_0(N, A, M)$
$(B[1], \ldots, B[\ell]) \xleftarrow{n} \mathsf{ecA}(A) \,\|\, \mathsf{ecM}(M)$
for $i = 0$ **to** ℓ
  $V \leftarrow E_K(V \oplus B[i])$
$V \leftarrow \mathtt{msb}_\tau(V)$
return V

Algorithm $\mathsf{CBC\text{-}MAC}.\mathcal{V}[E_K](N, A, M, V)$
(assumes N, A and M are of valid length and $|V| = \tau$)

$\widehat{V} \leftarrow \mathsf{CBC\text{-}MAC}.\mathcal{T}[E_K](N, A, M)$
if $V = \widehat{V}$ **return** $\top$
else return $\bot$

Algorithm $\mathsf{CCTR}[E_K](N, M)$

$(M[1], \ldots, M[m]) \xleftarrow{n} M$
for $i = 1$ **to** $m - 1$
  $C[i] \leftarrow E_K(\mathsf{ecN}(N, i)) \oplus M[i]$
$C[m] \leftarrow \mathtt{msb}_{|M[m]|}(E_K(\mathsf{ecN}(N, m))) \oplus M[m]$
$C \leftarrow C[1] \,\|\, \ldots \,\|\, C[m]$
return C

Fig. 5. Algorithms of CCM. $\nu := |N|$ and $\tau := |T|$ are fixed parameters. Algorithms of our optimization CCM2 can be obtained by omitting gray boxes.

The specification of CCM2 is the same as that of CCM except that there is no mask for the tag. See Figs. 5, 6 for the definition.

Definition 6 (Prefix-free encoding). *The encoding function* $\mathsf{ec}(\cdot,\cdot,\cdot)$ *is said to be prefix-free if, for any input* (N, A, M)*, there is no input* (N', A', M') *s.t.* $(N', A', M') \neq (N, A, M)$ *and* $\mathsf{ec}(N', A', M') = \mathtt{msb}_j(\mathsf{ec}(N, A, M))$*, where* $j = |\mathsf{ec}(N', A', M')|$ *and* $j \leq |\mathsf{ec}(N, A, M)|$*. We also say* $\{B = \mathsf{ec}(N, A, M)\}$ *is prefix-free for any input* (N, A, M) *if* $\mathsf{ec}(\cdot,\cdot,\cdot)$ *is prefix-free.*

An important observation is that ec in CCM is indeed prefix-free [47]. This was used by several studies for both attack and proof sides [36,47]. It is known that CBC-MAC with a prefix-free input encoding realizes a PRF [65], however, CCTR and CBC-MAC in CCM share the key, and this shared-key structure does not allow to reuse this known result in a black-box way.

5.2 NMR-INT-RUP Bound of CCM and CCM2

We focus on CCM since the bound of CCM2 is almost the same as that of CCM. Let $\mathsf{CCM}[E_K] = (\mathsf{CCM}.\mathcal{E}[E_K], \mathsf{CCM}.u\mathcal{D}[E_K], \mathsf{CCM}.\mathcal{V}[E_K])$ for the underlying block cipher $E : \mathcal{K} \times \{0,1\}^n \rightarrow \{0,1\}^n$. We suppose the adversary $\mathcal{A}$ makes q_e queries to $\mathsf{CCM}.\mathcal{E}$, q_d queries to $\mathsf{CCM}.u\mathcal{D}$, and q_v queries to $\mathsf{CCM}.\mathcal{V}$. The adversary $\mathcal{A}$ obtains a transcript such that

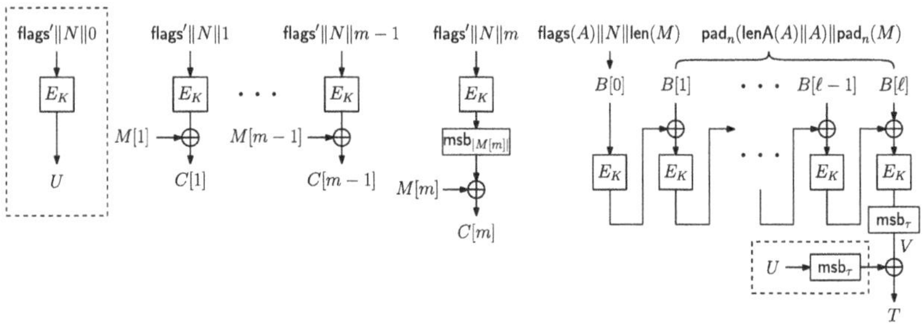

Fig. 6. $\mathsf{CCM}.\mathcal{E}[E_K]$. Our optimization (CCM2) omits the boxes with dashed lines.

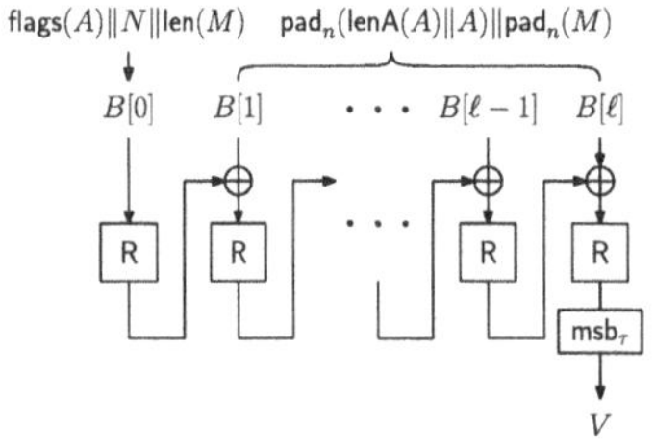

Fig. 7. $\mathsf{CBC\text{-}MAC}.\mathcal{T}[\mathsf{R}]$.

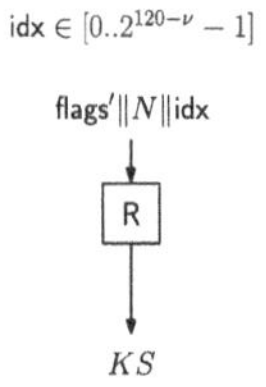

Fig. 8. $\mathcal{KS}_{\mathsf{C}}[\mathsf{R}]$.

- $\{(N_i^e, A_i^e, M_i^e, C_i^e, T_i^e)\}_{i=1,\ldots,q_e}$ from $\mathsf{CCM}.\mathcal{E}$,
- $\{(N_i^d, A_i^d, M_i^d, C_i^d, T_i^d)\}_{i=1,\ldots,q_d}$ from $\mathsf{CCM}.u\mathcal{D}$,
- $\{(N_i^v, A_i^v, C_i^v, T_i^v, b_i)\}_{i=1,\ldots,q_v}$ from $\mathsf{CCM}.\mathcal{V}$, where $b_i \in \{\top, \bot\}$.

Let σ_e, σ_d, and σ_v denote the total number of plaintext/ciphertext blocks queried in $\mathsf{CCM}.\mathcal{E}$, $\mathsf{CCM}u\mathcal{D}$, and $\mathsf{CCM}.\mathcal{V}$, respectively; thus, $\sigma_e = \sum_{i=1}^{q_e} |M_i^e|_n$, $\sigma_d = \sum_{i=1}^{q_d} |C_i^d|_n$, and $\sigma_v = \sum_{i=1}^{q_v} |C_i^v|_n$. Let σ'_e and σ'_v be the total number of input blocks to $\mathsf{CBC\text{-}MAC}.\mathcal{T}$ in $\mathsf{CCM}.\mathcal{E}$ and $\mathsf{CCM}.\mathcal{V}$, respectively; thus, $\sigma'_e = \sum_{i=1}^{q_e} |\mathsf{ec}(N_i^e, A_i^e, M_i^e)|_n$ and $\sigma'_v = \sum_{i=1}^{q_v} |\mathsf{ec}(N_i^v, A_i^v, M_i^v)|_n$, where $M_i^v = \mathsf{CCTR}(N_i^v, C_i^v)$. We define $\sigma_{\mathrm{all}} := \sigma_e + \sigma_d + \sigma_v + \sigma'_e + \sigma'_v + q_e + q_v$ to denote the total number of block cipher calls in the game.

We present an NMR-INT-RUP bound of CCM. The bound shows up-to-birthday-bound security, hence quantitatively equivalent to the normal Auth bound [47].

Theorem 2. *Let $\mathcal{A}$ be the NMR-INT-RUP adversary against $\mathsf{CCM}[E]$ defined as above with time complexity t. We have*

$$\boldsymbol{Adv}_{\mathsf{CCM}[E]}^{\mathit{NMR\text{-}INT\text{-}RUP}}(\mathcal{A}) \leq \boldsymbol{Adv}_E^{\mathit{PRP}}(\widehat{\mathcal{A}}) + \frac{\sigma_{all}^2}{2^{n+1}} + \frac{(\sigma'_e + \sigma'_v)(\sigma'_e + \sigma'_v + 2(q_e + q_v + \sigma_e + \sigma_d + \sigma_v))}{2^n} + \frac{4q_v}{2^\tau}$$

for a PRP adversary $\widehat{\mathcal{A}}$ with σ_{all} queries and time complexity $t + O(\sigma_{all})$.

For the bound of CCM2, the parameters can be determined in the same way as CCM, and we obtain the bound by replacing CCM and the third term of the bound in Theorem 2 with CCM2 and $(\sigma'_e + \sigma'_v)(\sigma'_e + \sigma'_v + 2(\sigma_e + \sigma_d + \sigma_v))/2^n$, respectively.

5.3 Proof Overview

We show an overview of the NMR-INT-RUP proofs for both CCM and CCM2. The complete ones are shown in the full version. As in the case of GCM, both proofs take two game hops: PRP/PRF switch and the security reduction to the UF-CMA$^+$ of the MAC part. By setting the MAC part as a pure CBC-MAC (not including the mask U), CCM and CCM2's NMR-INT-RUP bounds can be upper-bounded by the same UF-CMA$^+$ bound.

Let's consider $\mathbf{Adv}^{\texttt{NMR-INT-RUP}}_{\mathsf{CCM[R]}}(\mathcal{A}')$ and $\mathbf{Adv}^{\texttt{NMR-INT-RUP}}_{\mathsf{CCM2[R]}}(\mathcal{A}')$, that appear after replacing E in $\mathbf{Adv}^{\texttt{NMR-INT-RUP}}_{\mathsf{CCM}[E]}(\mathcal{A})$ and $\mathbf{Adv}^{\texttt{NMR-INT-RUP}}_{\mathsf{CCM2}[E]}(\mathcal{A})$ with P and then replace P with R. For the reduction to the UF-CMA$^+$ game, we define the tagging and the verification oracles of $\mathsf{CBC\text{-}MAC[R]}$, denoted by $\mathsf{CBC\text{-}MAC}.\mathcal{T}[\mathsf{R}]$ and $\mathsf{CBC\text{-}MAC}.\mathcal{V}[\mathsf{R}]$, as shown in Figs. 5, 7. Additionally, we define a keystream oracle similar to $\mathcal{KS}_\mathsf{G}$. Let $\mathcal{KS}_\mathsf{C}[\mathsf{R}]$ be a function invoking R which takes (an encoded form of) a nonce $N \in \{0,1\}^\nu$ and an index $\mathsf{idx} \in [0..2^{120-\nu} - 1]$ and outputs a block of keystream $KS \in \{0,1\}^n$. Specifically,

$$\mathcal{KS}_\mathsf{C}[\mathsf{R}](N, \mathsf{idx}) := \mathsf{R}(\mathsf{ecN}(N, \mathsf{idx})) = \mathsf{R}(\mathsf{flags}' \parallel N \parallel \langle \mathsf{idx} \rangle_{120-\nu}).$$

We also write it as $\mathcal{KS}_\mathsf{C}$. Figure 8 depicts $\mathcal{KS}_\mathsf{C}$. We then define the UF-CMA$^+$ game involving $\mathsf{CBC\text{-}MAC}.\mathcal{T}$, $\mathcal{KS}_\mathsf{C}$, and $\mathsf{CBC\text{-}MAC}.\mathcal{V}$ in the same manner as Sect. 4.3. Note that the adversary can repeat nonces in the queries to $\mathsf{CBC\text{-}MAC}.\mathcal{T}$. From the definition, we observe that $\mathsf{CBC\text{-}MAC}.\mathcal{T}$, $\mathcal{KS}_\mathsf{C}$, and $\mathsf{CBC\text{-}MAC}.\mathcal{V}$ in the UF-CMA$^+$ game can simulate $\mathsf{CCM}.\mathcal{E}$, $\mathsf{CCM}.u\mathcal{D}$, $\mathsf{CCM}.\mathcal{V}$ in the NMR-INT-RUP game, and the same holds for CCM2. Thus, we obtain $\mathbf{Adv}^{\texttt{NMR-INT-RUP}}_{\mathsf{CCM[R]}}(\mathcal{A}') \le \mathbf{Adv}^{\texttt{UF-CMA+}}_{\mathsf{CBC\text{-}MAC[R]}}(\mathcal{B})$ and $\mathbf{Adv}^{\texttt{NMR-INT-RUP}}_{\mathsf{CCM2[R]}}(\mathcal{A}') \le \mathbf{Adv}^{\texttt{UF-CMA+}}_{\mathsf{CBC\text{-}MAC[R]}}(\mathcal{B})$. See the full version for the detailed statement and the proof.

Finally, we evaluate $\mathbf{Adv}^{\texttt{UF-CMA+}}_{\mathsf{CBC\text{-}MAC[R]}}(\mathcal{B})$. Intuitively, CBC-MAC[R] should be secure because the standard CBC-MAC is secure when its input is prefix-free, and in this case, $\{B = \mathsf{ec}(N, A, M)\}$ is prefix-free even in the nonce-misuse setting. However, the adversary in the UF-CMA$^+$ game also has access to $\mathcal{KS}_\mathsf{C}$. Therefore, we need a careful discussion, and for that, we use an H-coefficient technique. In the proof, as in the case of GCM, we mainly show that a non-trivial collision probability between any of the inputs of R is sufficiently low. The tricky point is to count *non-trivial* collisions. Trivial collisions can be invoked easily since CBC-MAC with a nonce-misuse setting can have two queries sharing the prefix. Careful discussion and case analysis of queries enable us to count non-trivial collisions, and we obtain a birthday bound, which is quantitatively the same as the normal Auth of CCM [47].

6 Privacy of CCM and CCM2 Under Nonce Misuse

As Table 1 shows, CCM and CCM2 do not fulfill NMR-Priv. However, CCM and CCM2 still fulfill the weaker NML-Priv. The following theorem shows our bound.

Theorem 3. *Let q_r and q_m be the number of nonce-respecting and nonce-misusing queries of an adversary $\mathcal{A}$, and σ_{er} and σ_{em} be the total number of plaintext blocks queried to the nonce-respecting and nonce-misusing oracles. Let σ'_r and σ'_m be the total number of input blocks to underlying* CBC-MAC *in nonce-respecting and nonce-misusing queries. Let $\sigma_{all} := \sigma'_r + \sigma'_m + \sigma_{er} + \sigma_{em} + q_r + q_m$ and t be the time complexity of $\mathcal{A}$. We obtain*

$$\mathbf{Adv}^{\text{NML-Priv}}_{\mathsf{CCM}[E]}(\mathcal{A}) \le \mathbf{Adv}^{\text{PRP}}_{E}(\widehat{\mathcal{A}}) + \frac{\sigma_{all}^2}{2^{n+1}} + \frac{(\sigma'_r + \sigma'_m)(\sigma'_r + \sigma'_m + 2(\sigma_{er} + \sigma_{em} + q_r + q_m))}{2^n}$$

for a PRP adversary $\widehat{\mathcal{A}}$ with σ_{all} queries and time complexity $t + O(\sigma_{all})$. The bound of CCM2 is obtained by replacing CCM$[E]$ in the above equation with CCM2$[E]$ and changing σ_{all} to $\sigma_{all} := \sigma'_r + \sigma'_m + \sigma_{er} + \sigma_{em}$.

The proof is similar to the NMR-INT-RUP proof of CCM/CCM2 described in Sect. 5.3. Specifically, we define a new AE scheme, dubbed CCM+, that is the same as CCM, but CCM+.$\mathcal{E}$ outputs (C, U, V) instead of (C, T). The NML-Priv bounds of CCM and CCM2 can be upper-bounded by the NML-Priv bound of CCM+. We can evaluate $\mathbf{Adv}^{\texttt{NML-Priv}}_{\mathsf{CCM+}}(\mathcal{A})$ similarly to $\mathbf{Adv}^{\texttt{UF-CMA+}}_{\mathsf{CBC\text{-}MAC[R]}}(\mathcal{B})$, which is analyzed in the last step of the NMR-INT-RUP proof of CCM/CCM2. See the full version for the full proof.

7 Nonce Misuse Resilience of OCB3

As shown by Table 1, OCB3 has no security with respect to RUP and NMR for both privacy and authenticity. What about NML security? ADL17 provided NML security analysis of OCB. Concretely, they showed NML-Priv and NML-Auth attacks against *the first version of* OCB, also known as OCB1 [73]. These attacks exploit the incomplete domain separation of OCB1 between the encryption of plaintext blocks and the encryption of checksum and recover $E_K(0^n)$ via repeating nonces. ADL17 stated, "We focus on OCB version 1 [65], however, our results extend to all versions of OCB" [16, Appendix A.1]. While there is no concrete interpretation of this claim, we do show that OCB3 is *not* completely broken regarding NML security.

Theorem 4. *OCB3 has NML-Priv security.*

Theorem 5. *OCB3 does not have NML-Auth security, however, if AD is fixed to any value throughout the game, it maintains NML-Auth security.*

The proofs of Theorems 4 and 5 are straightforward. To prove NML-Priv, we observe that OCB3 can be interpreted as a mode of TBC built on a block cipher, called ΘCB3. It uses a TBC $\widetilde{E}$ based on XEX and XE modes by Rogaway [70] but with a more complex tweak space and mask derivation than the original (refer to [50] for the specification of $\widetilde{E}$). Thanks to the explicit domain separation via tweaks in ΘCB3, any output block in an encryption query with nonce N is of the form $\widetilde{E}_K^{(N,\mathtt{x})}(\alpha) \oplus \beta$ for some $\mathtt{x}$ (a tuple of size one or two) and some $\alpha, \beta \in \{0,1\}^n$ that do not involve computation of $\widetilde{E}_K^{(N,\mathtt{y})}$ for any possible $\mathtt{y}$. Suppose $\widetilde{E}_K$ is ideal (*i.e.*, a TURP $\widetilde{\mathsf{P}}$) and consider the real world in the NML-Priv game. The above observation implies that the responses from the first (nonce-respecting) oracle are completely random and independent of the responses from the second (nonce-misusing) oracles since the sets of used nonce values do not intersect. Therefore, ΘCB3 using $\widetilde{\mathsf{P}}$ is perfectly secure regarding NML-Priv. Thus, we obtain

$$\mathbf{Adv}^{\texttt{NML-Priv}}_{\mathsf{OCB3[P]}}(\mathcal{A}) = \mathbf{Adv}^{\texttt{NML-Priv}}_{\mathsf{\Theta CB3}[\widetilde{E}[\mathsf{P}]]}(\mathcal{A}) \leq \mathbf{Adv}^{\texttt{TPRP}}_{\widetilde{E}[\mathsf{P}]}(\widehat{\mathcal{A}}) + \mathbf{Adv}^{\texttt{NML-Priv}}_{\mathsf{\Theta CB3}[\widetilde{\mathsf{P}}]}(\mathcal{A}) \leq \frac{6\sigma^2}{2^n} \tag{3}$$

for any NML-Priv adversary $\mathcal{A}$ with σ total queried blocks, for a TPRP adversary $\widehat{\mathcal{A}}$ with σ queries. Here, $\widetilde{E}[\mathsf{P}]$ is a TBC built on n-bit URP P, and the last inequality follows from [50, Lemma 3][3].

For NML-Auth, if no restriction on AD is imposed, Vaudenay and Vizár [78] showed an attack, which exploits the fact that AD processing of ΘCB3/OCB3 does not involve nonce.

In contrast, the attack generally does not work if A is fixed to any value. In ΘCB3, AD processing function, Hash, uses distinct tweak values for the internal $\widetilde{\mathsf{P}}$ that are never used in the "core" encryption routine, G, because those used for Hash do not contain nonce while those for G always contain nonce. This fact implies that, if A is fixed to any value throughout the game, the encryption queries with repeating nonces do not contribute, hence can be ignored. Eventually, we can reuse the existing (nonce-respecting) Auth proof of ΘCB3 [50] including the bound. The final bound for OCB3 will be obtained by adding the TBC's security bound [50, Lemma 3]. A proof is straightforward and hence omitted.

Some ways to achieve NML-Auth security exist. A simple option is to change Hash of ΘCB3 so that it takes nonce as a part of the tweak for each AD block process. This also allows the reuse of existing Auth proof even if AD is not fixed, making the modified OCB3 NML secure for both privacy and authenticity. This comes at the cost of losing the property of efficient processing for static AD (*i.e.*, caching Hash(A)). Another option is to add Hash(A) to the checksum instead

[3] The TBC $\widetilde{E}$ reduces to (variants of) XEX and XE depending on the tweak used, and $\widetilde{E}$ is designed so that it is indistinguishable from TURP as long as the adversary performs CCA against XEX and performs only CPA against XE. This security property is needed for authenticity. We remark that OCB2 [70] used a similar, but wrong, combination, which leads to an attack [44]. However, the case of OCB3 is different and safe.

of the tag, *i.e.*, the tag is an encryption of the sum of checksum and Hash(A). This enables caching static AD, although the proof needs some revisions (future work).

8 Implications of Our Results

Proving robustness property is generally relevant as it gives defense in depth. Still, it is also natural to ask if there are real benefits. We show that this is indeed the case: our results enable 1) an efficient GCM-based RUP-secure AE and 2) an optimized version of CCM without losing security.

8.1 RUP-Secure AE

An AE scheme equipped with PA1/2 and INT-RUP security properties is often called *RUP-secure* AE. It has been studied extensively [12,14,16,30]. Andreeva *et al.* [14] (ABL+14) shows *nonce decoy*, a generic method to turn an AE scheme $\Pi = (\Pi.\mathcal{E}, \Pi.\mathcal{D})$ into a PA1-secure one if Π is PA1 secure under a random nonce setting. It takes an independently-keyed PRF, $G : \mathcal{K}' \times \{0,1\}^{\nu} \to \{0,1\}^{\nu}$, to encrypt the nonce N, and $G_{K'}(N)$ is given to $\Pi.\mathcal{E}$ as an input nonce. Nonce decoy preserves INT-RUP security of the baseline scheme if it has [14, Proposition 10]. ABL+14 also introduces another conversion scheme, called PRF-to-IV, from an AE scheme Π into a PA1 and INT-RUP secure one if Π is PA1 secure under a random nonce setting. While Π does not need to be INT-RUP secure, it also needs a variable-input-length PRF to take the whole input tuple of (N, A, M), imposing a significant computational overhead. ABL+14 shows that CTR is PA1 secure under a random nonce setting and that PA1 security of GCM and CCM can be reduced to that of CTR. Combining this result of ABL+14 and our INT-RUP results of GCM and CCM, nonce decoy with GCM or CCM implements RUP-secure AE *without modifying the algorithms of* GCM/CCM and *at a small computation overhead*. ADL17 introduces a RUP-secure variant of GCM, GCM-RUP, but this modifies the original algorithm, although the change is not extensive. Compared with GCM-RUP, nonce decoy works as a black-box conversion, enabling an easier adoption from the implementation point of view. Moreover, while the decryption of GCM-RUP cannot be online because of its MAC-then-Decrypt construction, the combination of nonce decoy and GCM preserves its online property. On the downside, as a nature of nonce decoy, the output must be expanded by ν bits from GCM. See the comparison in Table 2.

8.2 Optimizing CCM

CCM2 reduces the number of block cipher calls by one for any input. The gain may seem minor at first sight, however, we do not know any example among the popular standards that allow such optimization after their standardization. In addition, this optimization may be relevant in some applications. Adomnicăi *et al.* [13] showed that CCM needs at least four block cipher calls (overhead) for

Table 2. Comparison of RUP-secure AEs based on GCM. F and G are PRFs; $F : \mathcal{K}' \times \{0,1\}^* \rightarrow \{0,1\}^\nu$ and $G : \mathcal{K}' \times \{0,1\}^\nu \rightarrow \{0,1\}^\nu$ for some key space $\mathcal{K}'$.

Scheme	Black-box	Additional cost	Online (Dec)	Output expansion*
PRF-to-IV + GCM	✓	$F_K(N \parallel A \parallel M)$	✓	ν
GCM-RUP [16]	✗	$1\ E_K + 1\ \mathrm{GF}(2^n)$ Mul †	✗	$n - \nu$
Nonce decoy + GCM	✓	$G_K(N)$	✓	ν

* Additional output expansion in bits from the original GCM
† This can be none when the length of the last message block is in $[1..n - \tau]$.

Table 3. Number of block cipher calls for encryption of a 128-bit block of message without AD. $(2 + 1)$ means the first two calls are in parallel followed by one call.

Scheme	GCM	CCM	OCB3	COFB	CCM2
Calls	3* (3)	4 (2+2)	4 (2+2)	3 (1+1+1)	3 (2+1)

* GCM needs additional $\mathrm{GF}(2^{128})$ multiplications
(2 when $\nu = 96$ and 4 when $\nu \in [1..128] \setminus \{96\}$)

any non-empty message. As far as known in the literature, three is the minimum number of overhead achievable by a general-purpose (*i.e.*, taking variable-length inputs) AE mode, namely COFB [17,29]. See Table 3. Overhead is a critical measure to determine the performance for (very) short inputs. Consequently, CCM2 is yet another mode that achieves the minimum overhead of three calls, implying excellent performance for (very) short inputs, notably on microcontrollers [13].

9 Concluding Remarks

We have presented multiple new robustness properties for GCM, CCM, and OCB3. Our results provide a complete answer to the robustness of these standards and serve as a reference point for future research. Moreover, we showed that one block cipher call of CCM could be removed without harming robustness by presenting CCM2. Notably, CCM's strong robustness is somewhat surprising. This feature was probably not intended by the designers. We understand the design issues around CCM as pointed out by [68,72]. Still, our results will give some positive views on this classical mode.

Studying the tightness of our bounds would be an interesting future topic. Extending the targets to the modern schemes, including Sponge AE schemes, would also be interesting. Finally, designing a strongly robust AE mode with minimal overhead (an early attempt is CLOC [45]), not limited to be based on CCM, is also worth investigating.

References

1. Ascon. https://ascon.iaik.tugraz.at/publications.html
2. Competition for authenticated encryption: Security, applicability, and robustness. https://competitions.cr.yp.to/caesar.html
3. NIST internal report 8454: Status report on the final round of the NIST lightweight cryptography standardization process. https://nvlpubs.nist.gov/nistpubs/ir/2023/NIST.IR.8454.pdf
4. NIST lightweight cryptography. https://csrc.nist.gov/projects/lightweight-cryptography
5. Recommendation for Block Cipher Modes of Operation: Galois/Counter Mode (GCM) and GMAC. NIST Special Publication 800-38D (2007). National Institute of Standards and Technology
6. Recommendation for Block Cipher Modes of Operation: the CCM Mode for Authentication and Confidentiality. NIST Special Publication 800-38C (2007). National Institute of Standards and Technology
7. The OCB Authenticated-Encryption Algorithm. IRTF RFC 7253 (2014)
8. Why is release of unverified plaintext so Bad? StackExchange (2018). https://crypto.stackexchange.com/questions/59973/why-is-release-of-unverified-plaintext-so-bad
9. How bad it is using the same IV twice with AES/GCM? StackExchange (2019). https://crypto.stackexchange.com/questions/26790/how-bad-it-is-using-the-same-iv-twice-with-aes-gcm
10. AES GCM : is it acceptable to return the wrong plaintext if the tag is incorrect? StackExchange (2021). https://crypto.stackexchange.com/questions/89365/aes-gcm-is-it-acceptable-to-return-the-wrong-plaintext-if-the-tag-is-incorrect
11. Abdelraheem, M.A., Beelen, P., Bogdanov, A., Tischhauser, E.: Twisted polynomials and forgery attacks on GCM. In: Oswald, E., Fischlin, M. (eds.) EUROCRYPT 2015. LNCS, vol. 9056, pp. 762–786. Springer, Heidelberg (2015). https://doi.org/10.1007/978-3-662-46800-5_29
12. Abed, F., Forler, C., List, E., Lucks, S., Wenzel, J.: RIV for robust authenticated encryption. In: Peyrin, T. (ed.) FSE 2016. LNCS, vol. 9783, pp. 23–42. Springer, Heidelberg (2016). https://doi.org/10.1007/978-3-662-52993-5_2
13. Adomnicai, A., Minematsu, K., Shikata, J.: Authenticated encryption for very short inputs. In: Rosulek, M. (ed.) CT-RSA 2023. LNCS, pp. 553–572. Springer, Heidelberg (2023). https://doi.org/10.1007/978-3-031-30872-7_21
14. Andreeva, E., Bogdanov, A., Luykx, A., Mennink, B., Mouha, N., Yasuda, K.: How to securely release unverified plaintext in authenticated encryption. In: Sarkar, P., Iwata, T. (eds.) ASIACRYPT 2014. LNCS, vol. 8873, pp. 105–125. Springer, Heidelberg (2014). https://doi.org/10.1007/978-3-662-45611-8_6
15. Andreeva, E., Bogdanov, A., Luykx, A., Mennink, B., Tischhauser, E., Yasuda, K.: Parallelizable and authenticated online ciphers. In: Sako, K., Sarkar, P. (eds.) ASIACRYPT 2013. LNCS, vol. 8269, pp. 424–443. Springer, Heidelberg (2013). https://doi.org/10.1007/978-3-642-42033-7_22
16. Ashur, T., Dunkelman, O., Luykx, A.: Boosting authenticated encryption robustness with minimal modifications. In: Katz, J., Shacham, H. (eds.) CRYPTO 2017. LNCS, vol. 10403, pp. 3–33. Springer, Cham (2017). https://doi.org/10.1007/978-3-319-63697-9_1
17. Banik, S., et al.: GIFT-COFB. Submission to the NIST Lightweight Cryptography project (final round updates) (2022)

18. Baudrin, J., Canteaut, A., Perrin, L.: Practical cube attack against nonce-misused Ascon. IACR Trans. Symm. Cryptol. **2022**(4), 120–144 (2022). https://doi.org/10.46586/tosc.v2022.i4.120-144
19. Bellare, M., Namprempre, C.: Authenticated encryption: relations among notions and analysis of the generic composition paradigm. In: Okamoto, T. (ed.) ASIACRYPT 2000. LNCS, vol. 1976, pp. 531–545. Springer, Heidelberg (2000). https://doi.org/10.1007/3-540-44448-3_41
20. Bellare, M., Rogaway, P.: The security of triple encryption and a framework for code-based game-playing proofs. In: Vaudenay, S. (ed.) EUROCRYPT 2006. LNCS, vol. 4004, pp. 409–426. Springer, Heidelberg (2006). https://doi.org/10.1007/11761679_25
21. Bellare, M., Tackmann, B.: The multi-user security of authenticated encryption: AES-GCM in TLS 1.3. In: Robshaw, M., Katz, J. (eds.) CRYPTO 2016. LNCS, vol. 9814, pp. 247–276. Springer, Heidelberg (2016). https://doi.org/10.1007/978-3-662-53018-4_10
22. Bellizia, D., et al.: Mode-level vs. implementation-level physical security in symmetric cryptography. In: Micciancio, D., Ristenpart, T. (eds.) CRYPTO 2020. LNCS, vol. 12170, pp. 369–400. Springer, Cham (2020). https://doi.org/10.1007/978-3-030-56784-2_13
23. Berti, F., Guo, C., Pereira, O., Peters, T., Standaert, F.X.: TEDT: a leakage-resistant AEAD mode. IACR TCHES **2020**(1), 256–320 (2019). https://doi.org/10.13154/tches.v2020.i1.256-320. https://tches.iacr.org/index.php/TCHES/article/view/8400
24. Bhati, A.S., Andreeva, E., Vizár, D.: OAE-RUP: a strong online AEAD security notion and its application to SAEF. In: Galdi, C., Phan, D.H. (eds.) SCN 2024. LNCS, vol. 14974, pp. 117–139. Springer, Cham (2024)
25. Bhaumik, R., Nandi, M.: Improved security for OCB3. In: Takagi, T., Peyrin, T. (eds.) ASIACRYPT 2017. LNCS, vol. 10625, pp. 638–666. Springer, Cham (2017). https://doi.org/10.1007/978-3-319-70697-9_22
26. Böck, H., Zauner, A., Devlin, S., Somorovsky, J., Jovanovic, P.: Nonce-disrespecting adversaries: practical forgery attacks on GCM in TLS. In: WOOT. USENIX Association (2016)
27. Boldyreva, A., Degabriele, J.P., Paterson, K.G., Stam, M.: On symmetric encryption with distinguishable decryption failures. In: Moriai, S. (ed.) FSE 2013. LNCS, vol. 8424, pp. 367–390. Springer, Heidelberg (2014). https://doi.org/10.1007/978-3-662-43933-3_19
28. Bozhko, A.: Properties of AEAD Algorithms. Internet-Draft draft-irtf-cfrg-aead-properties-07, Internet Engineering Task Force (2024). https://datatracker.ietf.org/doc/draft-irtf-cfrg-aead-properties/07/, work in Progress
29. Chakraborti, A., Iwata, T., Minematsu, K., Nandi, M.: Blockcipher-based authenticated encryption: how small can we go? In: Fischer, W., Homma, N. (eds.) CHES 2017. LNCS, vol. 10529, pp. 277–298. Springer, Cham (2017). https://doi.org/10.1007/978-3-319-66787-4_14
30. Chang, D., et al.: Release of unverified plaintext: tight unified model and application to ANYDAE. IACR Trans. Symm. Cryptol. **2019**(4), 119–146 (2019). https://doi.org/10.13154/tosc.v2019.i4.119-146
31. Chen, S., Steinberger, J.: Tight security bounds for key-alternating ciphers. In: Nguyen, P.Q., Oswald, E. (eds.) EUROCRYPT 2014. LNCS, vol. 8441, pp. 327–350. Springer, Heidelberg (2014). https://doi.org/10.1007/978-3-642-55220-5_19

32. Dodis, Y., Grubbs, P., Ristenpart, T., Woodage, J.: Fast message franking: from invisible salamanders to encryptment. In: Shacham, H., Boldyreva, A. (eds.) CRYPTO 2018. LNCS, vol. 10991, pp. 155–186. Springer, Cham (2018). https://doi.org/10.1007/978-3-319-96884-1_6
33. Dworkin, M.: Recommendation for Block Cipher Modes of Operation: The CCM Mode for Authentication and Confidentiality. NIST-SP 800-38C (2007)
34. Ferguson, N.: Authentication Weaknesses in GCM. Public Comments to NIST (2005). http://csrc.nist.gov/groups/ST/toolkit/BCM/comments.html
35. Fleischmann, E., Forler, C., Lucks, S.: McOE: a family of almost foolproof on-line authenticated encryption schemes. In: Canteaut, A. (ed.) FSE 2012. LNCS, vol. 7549, pp. 196–215. Springer, Heidelberg (2012). https://doi.org/10.1007/978-3-642-34047-5_12
36. Fouque, P.-A., Martinet, G., Valette, F., Zimmer, S.: On the security of the CCM encryption mode and of a slight variant. In: Bellovin, S.M., Gennaro, R., Keromytis, A., Yung, M. (eds.) ACNS 2008. LNCS, vol. 5037, pp. 411–428. Springer, Heidelberg (2008). https://doi.org/10.1007/978-3-540-68914-0_25
37. Gjiriti, E., Reyhanitabar, R., Vizár, D.: Power yoga: variable-stretch security of CCM for energy-efficient lightweight IoT. IACR Trans. Symm. Cryptol. **2021**(2), 446–468 (2021). https://doi.org/10.46586/tosc.v2021.i2.446-468
38. Handschuh, H., Preneel, B.: Key-recovery attacks on universal hash function based MAC algorithms. In: Wagner, D. (ed.) CRYPTO 2008. LNCS, vol. 5157, pp. 144–161. Springer, Heidelberg (2008). https://doi.org/10.1007/978-3-540-85174-5_9
39. Hoang, V.T., Krovetz, T., Rogaway, P.: Robust authenticated-encryption AEZ and the problem that it solves. In: Oswald, E., Fischlin, M. (eds.) EUROCRYPT 2015. LNCS, vol. 9056, pp. 15–44. Springer, Heidelberg (2015). https://doi.org/10.1007/978-3-662-46800-5_2
40. Hoang, V.T., Reyhanitabar, R., Rogaway, P., Vizár, D.: Online authenticated-encryption and its nonce-reuse misuse-resistance. In: Gennaro, R., Robshaw, M. (eds.) CRYPTO 2015. LNCS, vol. 9215, pp. 493–517. Springer, Heidelberg (2015). https://doi.org/10.1007/978-3-662-47989-6_24
41. Hoang, V.T., Tessaro, S., Thiruvengadam, A.: The multi-user security of GCM, revisited: tight bounds for nonce randomization. In: Lie, D., Mannan, M., Backes, M., Wang, X. (eds.) ACM CCS 2018, pp. 1429–1440. ACM Press (2018). https://doi.org/10.1145/3243734.3243816
42. Imamura, K., Minematsu, K., Iwata, T.: Integrity analysis of authenticated encryption based on stream ciphers. In: Chen, L., Han, J. (eds.) ProvSec 2016. LNCS, vol. 10005, pp. 257–276. Springer, Cham (2016). https://doi.org/10.1007/978-3-319-47422-9_15
43. Imamura, K., Minematsu, K., Iwata, T.: Integrity analysis of authenticated encryption based on stream ciphers. Int. J. Inf. Sec. **17**(5), 493–511 (2018)
44. Inoue, A., Iwata, T., Minematsu, K., Poettering, B.: Cryptanalysis of OCB2: attacks on authenticity and confidentiality. In: Boldyreva, A., Micciancio, D. (eds.) CRYPTO 2019. LNCS, vol. 11692, pp. 3–31. Springer, Cham (2019). https://doi.org/10.1007/978-3-030-26948-7_1
45. Iwata, T., Minematsu, K., Guo, J., Morioka, S.: CLOC: authenticated encryption for short input. In: Cid, C., Rechberger, C. (eds.) FSE 2014. LNCS, vol. 8540, pp. 149–167. Springer, Heidelberg (2015). https://doi.org/10.1007/978-3-662-46706-0_8
46. Iwata, T., Ohashi, K., Minematsu, K.: Breaking and repairing GCM security proofs. In: Safavi-Naini, R., Canetti, R. (eds.) CRYPTO 2012. LNCS, vol. 7417,

pp. 31–49. Springer, Heidelberg (2012). https://doi.org/10.1007/978-3-642-32009-5_3
47. Jonsson, J.: On the security of CTR + CBC-MAC. In: Nyberg, K., Heys, H. (eds.) SAC 2002. LNCS, vol. 2595, pp. 76–93. Springer, Heidelberg (2003). https://doi.org/10.1007/3-540-36492-7_7
48. Joux, A.: Authentication Failures in NIST version of GCM. Public Comments to NIST (2006). http://csrc.nist.gov/groups/ST/toolkit/BCM/comments.html
49. KDDI Research, Inc.: Security Analysis of ChaCha20-Poly1305 AEAD. CRYPTREC-EX-2601-2016 (2017)
50. Krovetz, T., Rogaway, P.: The software performance of authenticated-encryption modes. In: Joux, A. (ed.) FSE 2011. LNCS, vol. 6733, pp. 306–327. Springer, Heidelberg (2011). https://doi.org/10.1007/978-3-642-21702-9_18
51. Lefevre, C., Mennink, B.: SoK: Security of the ascon modes. Cryptology ePrint Archive, Paper 2024/1969 (2024). https://eprint.iacr.org/2024/1969
52. Liénardy, J., Lafitte, F.: A weakness in OCB3 used with short nonces allowing for a break of authenticity and confidentiality. Inf. Process. Lett. **183**, 106404 (2024)
53. Liskov, M., Rivest, R.L., Wagner, D.: Tweakable block ciphers. In: Yung, M. (ed.) CRYPTO 2002. LNCS, vol. 2442, pp. 31–46. Springer, Heidelberg (2002). https://doi.org/10.1007/3-540-45708-9_3
54. Luykx, A., Mennink, B., Paterson, K.G.: Analyzing multi-key security degradation. In: Takagi, T., Peyrin, T. (eds.) ASIACRYPT 2017. LNCS, vol. 10625, pp. 575–605. Springer, Cham (2017). https://doi.org/10.1007/978-3-319-70697-9_20
55. Luykx, A., Preneel, B.: Optimal forgeries against polynomial-based MACs and GCM. In: Nielsen, J.B., Rijmen, V. (eds.) EUROCRYPT 2018. LNCS, vol. 10820, pp. 445–467. Springer, Cham (2018). https://doi.org/10.1007/978-3-319-78381-9_17
56. Mattsson, J., Westerlund, M.: Authentication key recovery on Galois/Counter Mode (GCM). In: Pointcheval, D., Nitaj, A., Rachidi, T. (eds.) AFRICACRYPT 2016. LNCS, vol. 9646, pp. 127–143. Springer, Cham (2016). https://doi.org/10.1007/978-3-319-31517-1_7
57. McGrew, D.A., Viega, J.: The security and performance of the Galois/Counter Mode (GCM) of operation. In: Canteaut, A., Viswanathan, K. (eds.) INDOCRYPT 2004. LNCS, vol. 3348, pp. 343–355. Springer, Heidelberg (2004). https://doi.org/10.1007/978-3-540-30556-9_27
58. Menda, S., Len, J., Grubbs, P., Ristenpart, T.: Context discovery and commitment attacks. In: Hazay, C., Stam, M. (eds.) EUROCRYPT 2023. LNCS, vol. 14007, pp. 379–407. Springer, Cham (2023). https://doi.org/10.1007/978-3-031-30634-1_13
59. Mileva, A., Dimitrova, V., Velichkov, V.: Analysis of the authenticated cipher MORUS (v1). In: Pasalic, E., Knudsen, L.R. (eds.) BalkanCryptSec 2015. LNCS, vol. 9540, pp. 45–59. Springer, Cham (2016). https://doi.org/10.1007/978-3-319-29172-7_4
60. Nandi, M.: Bernstein bound on WCS is tight. In: Shacham, H., Boldyreva, A. (eds.) CRYPTO 2018. LNCS, vol. 10992, pp. 213–238. Springer, Cham (2018). https://doi.org/10.1007/978-3-319-96881-0_8
61. Nir, Y., Langley, A.: ChaCha20 and Poly1305 for IETF protocols. IRTF RFC 7539 (2015). https://tools.ietf.org/html/rfc7539
62. Niwa, Y., Ohashi, K., Minematsu, K., Iwata, T.: GCM security bounds reconsidered. In: Leander, G. (ed.) FSE 2015. LNCS, vol. 9054, pp. 385–407. Springer, Heidelberg (2015). https://doi.org/10.1007/978-3-662-48116-5_19

63. Patarin, J.: The "coefficients H" technique. In: Avanzi, R.M., Keliher, L., Sica, F. (eds.) SAC 2008. LNCS, vol. 5381, pp. 328–345. Springer, Heidelberg (2009). https://doi.org/10.1007/978-3-642-04159-4_21
64. Pereira, O., Standaert, F.X., Vivek, S.: Leakage-resilient authentication and encryption from symmetric cryptographic primitives. In: Ray, I., Li, N., Kruegel, C. (eds.) ACM CCS 2015, pp. 96–108. ACM Press (2015). https://doi.org/10.1145/2810103.2813626
65. Petrank, E., Rackoff, C.: CBC MAC for real-time data sources. J. Cryptol. **13**(3), 315–338 (2000). https://doi.org/10.1007/s001450010009
66. Poddebniak, D., et al.: Efail: breaking S/MIME and OpenPGP email encryption using exfiltration channels. In: Enck, W., Felt, A.P. (eds.) USENIX Security 2018, pp. 549–566. USENIX Association (2018)
67. Procter, G., Cid, C.: On weak keys and forgery attacks against polynomial-based MAC schemes. In: Moriai, S. (ed.) FSE 2013. LNCS, vol. 8424, pp. 287–304. Springer, Heidelberg (2014). https://doi.org/10.1007/978-3-662-43933-3_15
68. Rogaway, P., Wagner, D.: A critique of CCM. Cryptology ePrint Archive, Report 2003/070 (2003). https://eprint.iacr.org/2003/070
69. Rogaway, P.: Authenticated-encryption with associated-data. In: Atluri, V. (ed.) ACM CCS 2002, pp. 98–107. ACM Press (2002). https://doi.org/10.1145/586110.586125
70. Rogaway, P.: Efficient instantiations of tweakable blockciphers and refinements to modes OCB and PMAC. In: Lee, P.J. (ed.) ASIACRYPT 2004. LNCS, vol. 3329, pp. 16–31. Springer, Heidelberg (2004). https://doi.org/10.1007/978-3-540-30539-2_2
71. Rogaway, P.: Nonce-based symmetric encryption. In: Roy, B., Meier, W. (eds.) FSE 2004. LNCS, vol. 3017, pp. 348–358. Springer, Heidelberg (2004). https://doi.org/10.1007/978-3-540-25937-4_22
72. Rogaway, P.: Evaluation of Some Blockcipher Modes of Operation. Investigation Reports on Cryptographic Techniques in FY 2010 (2011). http://www.cryptrec.go.jp/english/
73. Rogaway, P., Bellare, M., Black, J., Krovetz, T.: OCB: a block-cipher mode of operation for efficient authenticated encryption. In: Reiter, M.K., Samarati, P. (eds.) ACM CCS 2001, pp. 196–205. ACM Press (2001). https://doi.org/10.1145/501983.502011
74. Rogaway, P., Shrimpton, T.: A provable-security treatment of the key-wrap problem. In: Vaudenay, S. (ed.) EUROCRYPT 2006. LNCS, vol. 4004, pp. 373–390. Springer, Heidelberg (2006). https://doi.org/10.1007/11761679_23
75. Sasaki, Y., et al.: Minalpher v1.1. Submission to the CAESAR competition (2015)
76. Vanhoef, M., Piessens, F.: Release the kraken: new KRACKs in the 802.11 standard. In: Lie, D., Mannan, M., Backes, M., Wang, X. (eds.) ACM CCS 2018, pp. 299–314. ACM Press (2018). https://doi.org/10.1145/3243734.3243807
77. Vaudenay, S.: Security flaws induced by CBC padding—applications to SSL, IPSEC, WTLS... In: Knudsen, L.R. (ed.) EUROCRYPT 2002. LNCS, vol. 2332, pp. 534–545. Springer, Heidelberg (2002). https://doi.org/10.1007/3-540-46035-7_35
78. Vaudenay, S., Vizár, D.: Can Caesar beat Galois? In: Preneel, B., Vercauteren, F. (eds.) ACNS 2018. LNCS, vol. 10892, pp. 476–494. Springer, Cham (2018). https://doi.org/10.1007/978-3-319-93387-0_25
79. Zhang, X., Shen, Y., Wang, L.: Multi-user security of CCM authenticated encryption mode. In: CCS, pp. 4331–4345. ACM (2024)

Quantum Chosen-Ciphertext Attacks Based on Simon's Algorithm Against Unified Structures

Xiaoyu Wang[1], Zejun Xiang[2(✉)], Shasha Zhang[2], Siwei Chen[2], and Xiangyong Zeng[1]

[1] Faculty of Mathematics and Statistics, Hubei Key Laboratory of Applied Mathematics, Hubei University, Wuhan 430062, China
wangxiaoyu@stu.hubu.edu.cn, xiangyongzeng@aliyun.com

[2] School of Cyber Science and Technology, Hubei University, Wuhan 430062, China
xiangzejun@hubu.edu.cn

Abstract. Simon's algorithm, which constructs periodic functions from encryption and decryption oracles of a cipher, has shown great power in breaking symmetric ciphers. This paper studies the quantum chosen-ciphertext attacks (qCCA) distinguishers based on Simon's algorithm and the general technique to build such distinguishers. The qCCA distinguishers can be divided into distinguishers that use only the decryption oracle and those that use the encryption oracle. We refer to these two types of distinguishers as the qCCA^d distinguishers and the qCCA^e distinguishers, respectively. Firstly, we show the general methods of constructing qCCA^d distinguishers exploiting truncated differential, which can explain the previous work, that is, constructing Simon-based qCCA^d distinguishers of primitives case by case. Secondly, we explored the relations between periodic functions used by qCCA^e distinguishers and boomerang distinguishing attacks. Specifically, we deeply observed truncated boomerang attacks and introduced the definition of truncated boomerang differential to find the relations. The basic observation is that an improved truncated boomerang differential with probability 1 can be used to construct periodic functions, and two such constructions are presented. With these new construction techniques, we present new qCCA distinguishers of unified structures that unify the Feistel, Lai-Massey, MARS-like, and SM4-like structures. In particular, for the d-branch MARS-like and SM4-like structures, we prove the existence of $2d$-round qCCA distinguishers that are the best results so far as we know.

Keywords: Simon's Algorithm · Periodic Function · Quantum Chosen-ciphertext Attacks · Boomerang Attack · Cryptographic Structures

A. Patra (Ed.): CT-RSA 2025, LNCS 15598, pp. 99–122, 2025.
https://doi.org/10.1007/978-3-031-88661-4_5

1 Introduction

It is public knowledge that the development of quantum computing techniques has greatly influenced cryptography. The proposal of some quantum algorithms running on quantum computers with stronger computing power than classical computers has significantly affected the security of existing cryptographic schemes. The emergence of Shor's [25] algorithm can be said to open the prelude of quantum cryptanalysis. It can solve hard problems such as the factorization of large integers and the computation of discrete logarithms in polynomial time to break through public key cryptosystems. Shor's algorithm provides an exponential speed-up. Algorithmic speed-up using quantum computers can be applied to symmetric cryptosystems as well. For example, Grover's algorithm [9] achieves a quadratic acceleration for the exhaustive key search, halving the level of security for key-recovery provided by all block ciphers. Therefore, for such quantum attacks, the current consensus is that doubling the key length could restore an equivalent ideal security in the post-quantum world. In addition, some previous works demonstrate how to exploit Grover's algorithm and its generalization Quantum Amplitude Amplification (QAA) technique [26] to accelerate classical cryptanalysis techniques such as differential and linear attacks [16], Demirci and Selçuk meet-in-the-middle attacks [13], and integral attacks [3].

Research of quantum attacks on symmetric cryptosystems is not limited to the technique based on Grover's algorithm. The quantum Fourier transform is also a fundamental tool in quantum cryptanalysis. Lately, the quantum speed-up for multidimensional linear distinguishers [12] and quantum linear key-recovery attacks [24] are presented, with the quantum Fourier transform technique. Besides, Simon's algorithm [27] which relies on the quantum Fourier transform, has attracted much attention because it challenges the security of existing symmetric cryptographic schemes. In more detail, Simon's algorithm can be used to derive the period of periodic functions in polynomial time, by which the attacks on symmetric cryptographic structures can be conducted. The work of Kuwakado and Morii [17], proposing a quantum distinguishing attack for the 3-round Feistel structure, formally kicked off the quantum attacks based on Simon's algorithm. Later at CRYPTO 2016, Kaplan *et al.* [15] exploited Simon's algorithm to attack the most widely used authentication modes such as PMAC, GMAC, etc. Immediately afterwards, a quite different method which combines Grover's algorithm and Simon's algorithm was proposed by Leander *et al.* in [19] to attack the FX structure. The interest sparked by these important works resulted in the publication of attacks on many other constructions using Simon's algorithm [2,8,18], especially the distinguishing attacks [5–8,10,11,14,23,30]. It is not hard to notice that the core idea behind most of these attacks is to design periodic functions based on the target cryptographic scheme. So for the security analysis of the ability of cryptographic primitives to resist Simon's algorithm, it is feasible to consider how to construct periodic functions dependent on cryptographic primitives.

Recently, a general method of constructing periodic functions for block ciphers using truncated differentials is presented in [29]. Moreover, two types of periodic functions cover most quantum distinguishers based on Simon's algorithm. However, the application of this technique is restricted to the chosen-plaintext setting. In 2019, Ito *et al.* [14] constructed a 4-round distinguisher for the Feistel structure in the chosen-ciphertext setting instead of the chosen-plaintext setting. Naturally, the quantum distinguisher based on Simon's algorithm can be divided into two types: quantum chosen-plaintext distinguishers and quantum chosen-ciphertext distinguishers. In this paper, they are generally abbreviated as qCPA and qCCA distinguishers. According to the results of existing literature, the construction of the periodic function used by a qCPA distinguisher only uses the encryption oracle, while the construction of the periodic function used by a qCCA distinguisher must use the decryption oracle. The qCCA distinguisher can be divided into two types according to whether encryption oracle is used to construct corresponding periodic functions. To avoid ambiguity, we denote qCCA distinguishers using only the decryption oracle as qCCA^d distinguishers, and qCCA distinguishers using the encryption oracle as qCCA^e distinguishers. Given these, we show quantum distinguishers based on Simon's algorithm of several cryptographic structures in Table 1, where the details of non-linear components are not considered. From Table 1, it is easy to observe the lack of qCCA distinguishers, especially the qCCA^e distinguishers. On the one hand, inspired by the general approach of constructing qCPA distinguishers proposed in [29], we put forward some general techniques to build qCCA distinguishers. On the other hand, influenced by the work in [14,21], constructing a qCCA distinguisher longer than the qCPA distinguisher for some cryptographic structures is also worth further exploring.

Table 1. Quantum distinguishers of several cryptographic structures.

Structure	Setting					
	qCPA		qCCA			
			qCCA^d		qCCA^e	
	Round	Ref.	Round	Ref.	Round	Ref.
Feistel	3	[17]	–	–	4	[14]
Lai-Massey	3	[21]	–	–	4	[21]
d-Type-1 GFS	$3d-3$	[5,23]	d^2-d+1	[5,23]	–	–
$2d$-Type-2 GFS	$2d+1$	[5,7]	$2d+1$	[5]	–	–
d-Type-3 GFS	$d+1$	[11,30]	–	–	–	–
d-MARS	$2d-1$	[5]	$2d-1$	[5]	–	–
d-SM4	$2d-1$	[4,5,10]	$2d-1$	[5]	–	–
d-Skipjack-A	$3d-3$	[5]	d^2-d+1	[5]	-	-
d-Skipjack-B	d^2-d+1	[5]	$3d-3$	[5]	–	–

Contribution. To fill these gaps, we focus on the quantum chosen-ciphertext distinguishing attacks of symmetric primitives and investigate the construction of periodic functions exploited by qCCA distinguishers for round-reduced block ciphers in this paper. Our contributions are threefold.

- We reveal the links between boomerang attacks and the construction of qCCA^e distinguishers for the first time. We observe (truncated) boomerang attacks and introduce the definition of improved truncated boomerang differential of E. With the help of this concept, we present general approaches to constructing periodic functions using encryption and decryption oracles. Moreover, we present two types of periodic functions that cover existing qCCA^e distinguishers. This enables us to use classic differential cryptanalysis techniques to analyze the quantum security of cryptographic primitives.
- As an illustration, the new general techniques are applied to block cipher structures. It is proved that for a d-branch unified structure with a few restrictions, one can always construct a $2d$-round qCCA^e distinguisher. Specifically, this result applies to classical Feistel, Lai-Massey, MARS-like, and SM4-like structures. Therefore, for d-branch MARS-like and SM4-like structures, we find a $2d$-round qCCA distinguisher, one round longer than the previous best qCCA distinguisher.
- We indicate that the techniques proposed in [29] to construct qCPA distinguishers can also be used to construct qCCA^d distinguishers. Specifically, we use truncated differentials with probability 1 to build periodic functions, which cover qCCA^d distinguishers of structures in Table 1. The techniques avoid the tedious and complicated manual verification of the periodicity of the constructed function required in the previous work.

Organization. This paper is organized as follows. Section 2 introduces some notations and briefly revisits boomerang attacks. The approach to constructing periodic functions only using decryption oracles from truncated differentials is presented in Sect. 3. We introduce a new technique for constructing periodic functions used by qCCA^e distinguishers and extend such periodic functions in Sect. 4 and Sect. 5. Section 6 applies our technique to unified structures. Section 7 concludes the paper.

2 Preliminaries

2.1 Notation

This section introduces the notations that will be used throughout this paper. Let $\mathbb{F}_2$ denote the finite field with two elements, and $\mathbb{F}_2^n$ denote the n-dimensional vector space over $\mathbb{F}_2$. All vectors that appear in this paper are treated as column vectors. With a bit of abuse of notations, we let $a = (a_1, ..., a_n) \in \mathbb{F}_2^n$ denote a column vector, where we omit the transpose notation for clarity. 0^n represents an n-dimensional zero vector. In this paper, we consider an iterated design block cipher E, with a block size of n bits. We use E_r to denote a r-round reduced version of E, E^{-1} to denote the inverse of E, and E_r^{-1} to denote a r-round reduced version of E^{-1}. Denote the bit-wise XOR operations by $\oplus$. Let $b = (b_1, ..., b_n) \in \mathbb{F}_2^n$, $a \cdot b \triangleq a_1 b_1 \oplus \cdots \oplus a_n b_n$ denotes the inner product of a and b. Let V be a subset of $\mathbb{F}_2^n$, $V^\perp = \{x \in \mathbb{F}_2^n \mid x \cdot y = 0, \ \forall\ y \in V\}$ is the orthogonal complement of V. If V is a subspace, $V^\perp$ is the orthogonal complement subspace of V.

2.2 Simon's Algorithm

Our quantum attacks are based on Simon's algorithm, one of the most popular quantum algorithms. Next, we briefly introduce Simon's quantum algorithm [27]. This paper assumes that readers have basic knowledge about quantum computation. Simon's algorithm was originally proposed to solve the following Simon's problem.

Simon's Problem. Given a vectorial Boolean function $f : \mathbb{F}_2^n \rightarrow \mathbb{F}_2^m$ with the promise that there exists an $s \in \mathbb{F}_2^n \setminus \{0^n\}$, such that for any $x, y \in \mathbb{F}_2^n, f(x) = f(y) \Leftrightarrow x \oplus y \in \{0^n, s\}$, the goal is to find s.

According to the birthday bound, $O(2^{n/2})$ queries are needed to find s in the classical setting. However, Simon proposed a quantum algorithm that provides exponential speedup and requires only $O(n)$ quantum queries to find s. Concretely, assume that the attacker has access to a quantum oracle $U_f : |x\rangle|y\rangle \rightarrow |x\rangle|x \oplus f(y)\rangle$, Simon's algorithm whose circuit is shown in Fig. 1, returns a vector that is orthogonal to s by accessing the quantum oracle U_f. Repeat the circuit for a polynomial number of times to get $n-1$ linearly independent vectors, thus recovering s by solving the system of linear equations.

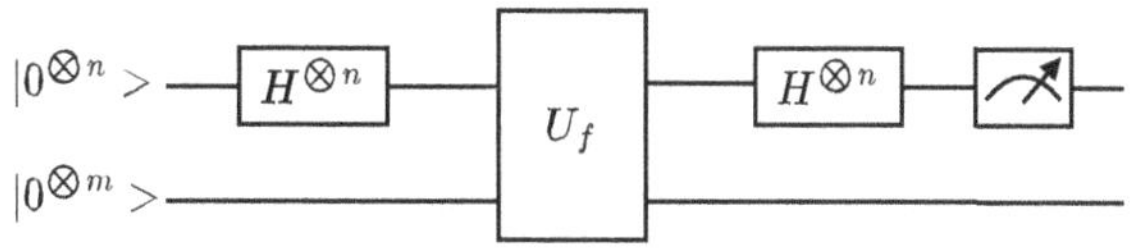

Fig. 1. The quantum circuit of Simon's algorithm.

The condition that $f(x) = f(y) \Leftrightarrow y = x \oplus s$ for any distinct x and y is called the *Simon's promise*. In practical settings, Simon's promise is not always completely satisfied. For example, f satisfies only the condition that $y = x \oplus s$ implies $f(x) = f(y)$ for any x. Further for this situation, we call such a function f a periodic function and s a period of f in the paper.

If f has other collisions besides s, then Simon's algorithm is not guaranteed to work. However, Kaplan *et al.* [15] considered the generalized versions of Simon's problem, indicating that Simon's algorithm still works for such f. Specifically, they introduced a parameter that quantifies how far the function is from satisfying Simon's promise and proved that Simon's algorithm can still be used to recover s with high probability, limiting the range of the parameter.

2.3 Quantum Distinguishers Based on Simon's Algorithm

Using Simon's algorithm, it is feasible to construct quantum distinguishers based on the recovery period. In more detail, suppose that we are given an oracle $\mathcal{O} : \mathbb{F}_2^n \rightarrow \mathbb{F}_2^n$ which is either a cryptographic primitive $E \in \text{Perm}(n)$ or a random permutation $\Pi \in \text{Perm}(n)$, where $\text{Perm}(n)$ denotes the set of all permutations over n-bit strings, the goal is to distinguish these two cases. Suppose that the quantum oracles $U_{\mathcal{O}}$ and $U_{\mathcal{O}^{-1}}$ can be queried. Let $f^{\mathcal{O}}$ be a vectorial Boolean function defined by accessing O, O^{-1}. Applying Simon's algorithm to $f^{\mathcal{O}}$, we can successfully recover its period only when $\mathcal{O} = E$. If we can construct such a function $f^{\mathcal{O}}$, then we can exploit Simon's algorithm to construct a distinguisher. But it is tricky for Kaplan *et al.*'s technique to evaluate an upper bound of the parameter. Subsequently, instead of using the period for the basis of the distinguisher, Ito *et al.* [14] further relaxed the condition to apply Simon's algorithm to build distinguishers. A distinguishing attack based on Simon's algorithm can be achieved as long as a periodic function is constructed, which is the theoretical support of this paper. Moreover, we consider distinguishing attacks where an adversary can query an oracle implementing a cryptographic primitive in a quantum superposition.

2.4 Boomerang Distinguishers

Boomerang attacks, introduced by Wagner in 1999 [28], is a differential attack that attempts to generate a quartet structure with specific differences at an intermediate state of the cipher. The attacker decomposes the cipher E into two subciphers E_0 and E_1, with $E = E_1 \circ E_0$, such that for E_0, E_1, there exist differential characteristics $\Delta \xrightarrow[E_0]{p} \Delta^*$, $\nabla \xrightarrow[E_1]{q} \nabla^*$ respectively, where $pq \gg 2^{-n/2}$. Then adversaries can distinguish E from a random permutation.

Further, it is proposed in [28] that the boomerang attacks can also be considered using truncated differentials instead of conventional differentials. Recently, Bariant *et al.* [1] have refined the work by proposing a generic framework to describe boomerang attacks based on truncated differentials.

The differential probability of a cipher and its inverse is the same. For truncated differentials, this fact in general is not correct. So unlike the standard boomerang attack described above, consider two truncated differentials $\mathcal{D}_{in}^0 \xrightarrow[E_0]{p} \mathcal{D}_{out}^0$, $\mathcal{D}_{out}^0 \xrightarrow[E_0^{-1}]{p'} \mathcal{D}_{in}^0$, $\mathcal{D}_{in}^1 \xrightarrow[E_1]{q} \mathcal{D}_{out}^1$, $\mathcal{D}_{out}^1 \xrightarrow[E_1^{-1}]{q'} \mathcal{D}_{in}^1$ with probabilities p, p' and q, q' on E_0 and E_1. The steps of boomerang attacks are the same as those for truncated boomerang attacks, which can be roughly referred to Fig. 2a. The truncated boomerang attacks proceed as follows:

1. Choose a random plaintext pair (P, P') with $P \oplus P' \in \mathcal{D}_{in}^0$, query the corresponding ciphertext pair (C, C').
2. Shift the ciphertext pair (C, C') into new pair $(\overline{C}, \overline{C'})$, such that $C \oplus \overline{C}, C' \oplus \overline{C'} \in \mathcal{D}_{out}^1$, and query the decryption of $(\overline{C}, \overline{C'})$ to $(\overline{P}, \overline{P'})$.

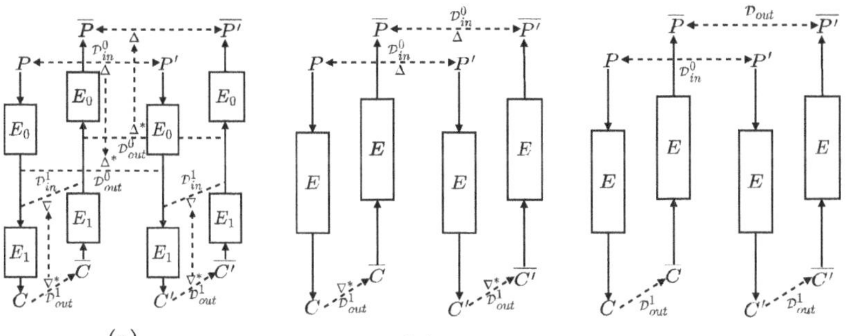

Fig. 2. The figure illustration of (truncated) boomerang differentials.

3. If $\overline{P} \oplus \overline{P'} \in \mathcal{D}_{in}^0$ holds, then $(P, P', \overline{P}, \overline{P'})$ is the truncated boomerang quartet. Then the attacker can use the difference in the probability that $(P, P', \overline{P}, \overline{P'})$ is a truncated boomerang quartet to accomplish the truncated boomerang distinguishing attack.

Next, we analyze the probability that $\overline{P} \oplus \overline{P'} \in \mathcal{D}_{in}^0$ holds. By the given truncated differential characteristics, we have $\Pr[E_0(P) \oplus E_0(P') \in \mathcal{D}_{out}^0] = p$, $\Pr[E_1^{-1}(C) \oplus E_1^{-1}(\overline{C}) \in \mathcal{D}_{in}^1] = q'$, $\Pr[E_1^{-1}(C') \oplus E_1^{-1}(\overline{C'}) \in \mathcal{D}_{in}^1] = q'$. Different from the standard boomerang attack, we cannot infer that the event $E_0(\overline{P}) \oplus E_0(\overline{P'}) \in \mathcal{D}_{out}^0$ must hold when the three events hold. We assume this conditional probability is r. And when $E_0(\overline{P}) \oplus E_0(\overline{P'}) \in \mathcal{D}_{out}^0$ is satisfied, we have $\overline{P} \oplus \overline{P'} \in \mathcal{D}_{in}^0$ with probability p'. Hence, assuming that all these events are independent, we can get

$$\Pr[\overline{P} \oplus \overline{P'} \in \mathcal{D}_{in}^0 \mid P \oplus P' \in \mathcal{D}_{in}^0, C \oplus \overline{C}, C' \oplus \overline{C'} \in \mathcal{D}_{out}^1] = p' \cdot p \cdot (q')^2 \cdot r.$$

However, for a random permutation, the probability is $|\mathcal{D}_{in}^0|/2^n$. Then adversaries can distinguish E from a random permutation.

3 Constructing the qCCA^d Distinguishers

In [29], Xiang *et al.* reveals the relations between periodic functions and truncated differentials. Concretely, it is proved that truncated differentials with probability 1 can be used to construct periodic functions. Subsequently, the general methods of constructing two types of periodic functions are presented using truncated differentials. Due to the space limitation, we choose the theory of constructing the Type-II periodic function in [29] as a representative to show here. We first introduce the definition of the *difference-annihilation matrix*, which is given in [29].

Definition 1 ([29]). *Let $\Delta_O \subset \mathbb{F}_2^n$ be a non-empty set of differences. Assume that there exists a non-zero matrix L and such that $Lx = \gamma$ for any $x \in \Delta_O$,* *where* $\gamma \in \mathbb{F}_2^n$ *is a fixed value. Then, we call* L *a difference-annihilation matrix of* Δ_O.

Definition 2 **([29]).** *Let* $E : \mathbb{F}_2^n \rightarrow \mathbb{F}_2^n$ *be a block cipher, which has an* r_2*-round truncated differential* $\Delta_I \rightarrow \Delta_O$ *of probability* 1*, and an* r_1*-round truncated differential* $\delta \rightarrow \Delta_I$ *of probability* 1 *with the restriction that one of the inputs belongs to an affine space* $w \oplus W$*. If there exists a difference-annihilation matrix* $M \in \mathbb{F}_2^{k\times n}$ *of* Δ_O *and the projection* $\delta^\perp$ *of* δ *on* $W^\perp$ *is known, then we can define a periodic function* $g : \mathbb{F}_2 \times \mathbb{F}_2^t \rightarrow \mathbb{F}_2^k, (b, x) \mapsto M \cdot E_{r_1+r_2}(w_b \oplus \varphi(x)) \oplus \gamma_b$*, where* $\varphi : \mathbb{F}_2^t \rightarrow W$ *is a bijective linear transformation,* $w_0 = w$*,* $w_1 = w \oplus \delta^\perp$*, and* γ_0, γ_1 *are two constants with* $\gamma = \gamma_0 \oplus \gamma_1$*. Moreover, we call such a periodic function a* ***Type-II periodic function*** *of* $E_{r_1+r_2}$*, where* $E_{r_1+r_2}$ *is the* $(r_1 + r_2)$*-round reduced version of* E.

The above definition provides a general approach to construct qCPA distinguishers for cryptographic primitives, and can also be used to explain many existing qCPA distinguishers based on Simon's algorithm. As mentioned earlier, the qCPA distinguisher only uses encryption oracle. Naturally, if we change the E in Definition 2 to E^{-1}, we can get a theory of constructing qCCA distinguisher using only the decryption oracle, i.e. qCCA^d distinguishers. As a result, we can easily translate the general techniques of constructing periodic functions by truncated differentials in [29] to constructing periodic functions underlying qCCA^d distinguishers. Furthermore, the technique can explain some existing qCCA^d distinguishers. The period functions used in qCCA^d distinguishers of Type-1 GFS [5,23], Type-2 GFS [5], SM4-like [5], MARS-like [5] and Skipjack-A/B [5] are also Type-II periodic functions.

4 Links Between qCCA^e Distinguishers and Boomerang Attacks

This section reveals the connection between boomerang attacks and qCCA^e distinguishers. In detail, we will present how to construct periodic functions from the boomerang distinguishers. Before formally introducing this, we need insight into the boomerang attacks.

4.1 Observations on Boomerang Attacks

The probability of getting boomerang quartets is directly determined by the chosen differential characteristics, as indicated by the above analysis. However, ignoring probability analysis, it is easy to observe that the internal differences Δ^* and ∇ are not used in boomerang distinguishing attacks, as shown in Fig. 2b. Boomerang quartets can also be detected with other internal differences. Motivated by this, we informally designate (Δ, ∇^*) as a boomerang differential of E to facilitate a more coherent narrative in the paper. The probability of the boomerang differential for E is defined by

$$\Pr[E^{-1}(E(P) \oplus \nabla^*) \oplus E^{-1}(E(P') \oplus \nabla^*) = \Delta \mid P \oplus P' = \Delta].$$

Throughout this paper, it will be assumed that $P, P', \overline{C}, \overline{C'}$ is uniformly distributed in $\mathbb{F}_2^n$, and the defined probability is taken over the distribution of $P, P', \overline{C}, \overline{C'}$. Likewise, we can also derive a similar definition for truncated boomerang distinguishing attacks.

Definition 3. *Let $E : \mathbb{F}_2^n \to \mathbb{F}_2^n$ be a block cipher, $\mathcal{D}_{in}^0$ and $\mathcal{D}_{out}^1$ be two subsets of $\mathbb{F}_2^n$. We define the probability of the truncated boomerang differential $(\mathcal{D}_{in}^0, \mathcal{D}_{out}^1)$ for E as* $\Pr[E^{-1}(\overline{C}) \oplus E^{-1}(\overline{C'}) \in \mathcal{D}_{in}^0 \mid P \oplus P' \in \mathcal{D}_{in}^0, E(P) \oplus \overline{C}, E(P') \oplus \overline{C'} \in \mathcal{D}_{out}^1]$.

4.2 Periodic Functions and Truncated Boomerang

In the above boomerang attack, for E_0 and E_1, if we can find suitable truncated differential characteristics such that $(P, P', \overline{P}, \overline{P'})$ must be a truncated boomerang quartet, we can construct periodic functions of E.

Theorem 1. *Let $E : \mathbb{F}_2^n \to \mathbb{F}_2^n$ be a block cipher, which has a truncated boomerang differential $(\mathcal{D}_{in}^0, \mathcal{D}_{out}^1)$ with probability 1. Assume that there exists a difference-annihilation matrix $M \in \mathbb{F}_2^{k\times n}$, such that $Mx = \gamma$ is a fixed constant for any $x \in \mathcal{D}_{in}^0$. Let γ_0 and γ_1 be two k-bit constants, such that $\gamma_0 \oplus \gamma_1 = \gamma$. Then, for any $\beta \in \mathcal{D}_{out}^1$ with $\beta \neq 0^n$, we can define a function g as*

$$\begin{aligned} g : \mathbb{F}_2 \times \mathbb{F}_2^n &\to \mathbb{F}_2^n \\ (b, x) &\mapsto M \cdot E^{-1}(E(x) \oplus \beta) \oplus \gamma_b. \end{aligned}$$

Then, g is a periodic function with $(1, s)$ being its period for any $s \in \mathcal{D}_{in}^0$.

Proof. $\forall\ \beta \in \mathcal{D}_{out}^1$, $s \in \mathcal{D}_{in}^0$, $x \in \mathbb{F}_2^n$, let $P = x, P' = x \oplus s, \overline{C} = E(P) \oplus \beta, \overline{C'} = E(P') \oplus \beta$. Since the probability of truncated boomerang differential $(\mathcal{D}_{in}^0, \mathcal{D}_{out}^1)$ is 1, we can get $E^{-1}(\overline{C}) \oplus E^{-1}(\overline{C'}) \in \mathcal{D}_{in}^0$ always holds by Definition 3. Thus we have

$$\begin{aligned} &g(0, x) \oplus g(1, x \oplus s) \\ =&M \cdot E^{-1}(E(x) \oplus \beta) \oplus \gamma_0 \oplus M \cdot E^{-1}(E(x \oplus s) \oplus \beta) \oplus \gamma_1 \\ =&M \cdot (E^{-1}(E(x) \oplus \beta) \oplus E^{-1}(E(x \oplus s) \oplus \beta)) \oplus \gamma \\ =&M \cdot (E^{-1}(\overline{C}) \oplus E^{-1}(\overline{C'})) \oplus \gamma = 0^k. \end{aligned}$$

This proves that g is a periodic function, and $(1, s)$ is a period of g for any $s \in \mathcal{D}_{in}^0$.

Corollary 1. *Let $E : \mathbb{F}_2^n \to \mathbb{F}_2^n$ be a block cipher, which has a boomerang differential (Δ, ∇^*) with probability 1. Let Δ_0 and Δ_1 be two n-bit constants, such that $\Delta_0 \oplus \Delta_1 = \Delta$. Define a function g as*

$$\begin{aligned} g : \mathbb{F}_2 \times \mathbb{F}_2^n &\to \mathbb{F}_2^n \\ (b, x) &\mapsto E^{-1}(E(x) \oplus \nabla^*) \oplus \Delta_b. \end{aligned}$$

Then, g is a periodic function with $(1, \Delta)$ being its period.

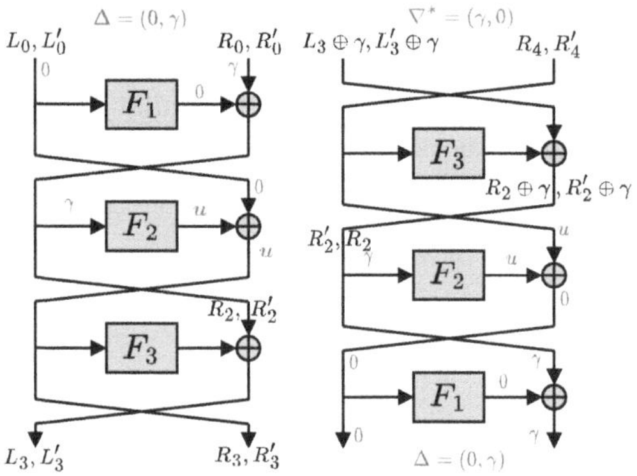

Fig. 3. The 3-round qCCA Distinguisher of the Feistel structure.

Example 1. For the 3-round Feistel structure $\mathcal{E}_3^{\texttt{Feistel}} : \mathbb{F}_2^n \times \mathbb{F}_2^n \to \mathbb{F}_2^n \times \mathbb{F}_2^n$, there exists $\Delta = (0^n, \gamma)$ and $\nabla^* = (\gamma, 0^n)$, $\gamma \neq 0^n$, such that the probability of boomerang differential (Δ, ∇^*) is 1, which can be obtained from Fig 3.

Let $\gamma_0, \gamma_1 \in \mathbb{F}_2^n$ be two arbitrarily chosen constants, such that $\gamma_0 \oplus \gamma_1 = \gamma$. According to Corollary 1, here it is easy to get the periodic function

$$g_1(b, y, z) = \mathcal{E}_3^{\texttt{Feistel},-1}[\mathcal{E}_3^{\texttt{Feistel}}(y, z) \oplus \nabla^*] \oplus (0^n, \gamma_b).$$

□

4.3 Periodic Functions and Improved Truncated Boomerang

The key to constructing a periodic function of E using Theorem 1 is to find a truncated boomerang differential with probability 1 for E. However, in general, this condition is more difficult to satisfy. Therefore, we propose that this condition can be relaxed appropriately to construct periodic functions.

In detail, supposing that the probability of the truncated boomerang differential $(\mathcal{D}_{in}^0, \mathcal{D}_{out}^1)$ of E is less than 1, it is possible to find $\mathcal{D}_{out}$ with $\mathcal{D}_{in}^0 \subsetneq \mathcal{D}_{out} \subsetneq \mathbb{F}_2^n$ to make $\Pr[E^{-1}(\overline{C}) \oplus E^{-1}(\overline{C'}) \in \mathcal{D}_{out} \mid P \oplus P' \in \mathcal{D}_{in}^0, E(P) \oplus \overline{C}, E(P') \oplus \overline{C'} \in \mathcal{D}_{out}^1] = 1$ hold. So in view of this case, we introduce Definition 4 referring to Fig. 2c. Furthermore, we can improve Theorem 1 to get Theorem 2.

Definition 4. *Let $E : \mathbb{F}_2^n \to \mathbb{F}_2^n$ be a block cipher, $\mathcal{D}_{in}^0$, $\mathcal{D}_{out}^1$ and $\mathcal{D}_{out}$ be three subsets of $\mathbb{F}_2^n$. We define the probability of the improved truncated boomerang differential $(\mathcal{D}_{in}^0, \mathcal{D}_{out}^1, \mathcal{D}_{out})$ of E as $\Pr[E^{-1}(\overline{C}) \oplus E^{-1}(\overline{C'}) \in \mathcal{D}_{out} \mid P \oplus P' \in \mathcal{D}_{in}^0, E(P) \oplus \overline{C}, E(P') \oplus \overline{C'} \in \mathcal{D}_{out}^1]$.*

Theorem 2. *Let $E : \mathbb{F}_2^n \to \mathbb{F}_2^n$ be a block cipher, which has an improved truncated boomerang differential $(\mathcal{D}_{in}^0, \mathcal{D}_{out}^1, \mathcal{D}_{out})$ with probability 1. Assume that there exists a difference-annihilation matrix $M \in \mathbb{F}_2^{k \times n}$, such that $Mx = \gamma$ is a* *fixed constant for any* $x \in \mathcal{D}_{out}$. *Let* γ_0 *and* γ_1 *be two k-bit constants, such that* $\gamma_0 \oplus \gamma_1 = \gamma$. *Then, for any* $\beta \in \mathcal{D}^1_{out}$ *with* $\beta \neq 0^n$, *let g be defined as*

$$\begin{aligned} g : \mathbb{F}_2 \times \mathbb{F}_2^n &\rightarrow \mathbb{F}_2^k \\ (b, x) &\mapsto M \cdot E^{-1}[E(x) \oplus \beta] \oplus \gamma_b. \end{aligned}$$

Then, g is a periodic function with $(1, s)$ *being its period for any* $s \in \mathcal{D}^0_{in}$.

Proof. $\forall\ \beta \in \mathcal{D}^1_{out}$, $s \in \mathcal{D}^0_{in}$, $x \in \mathbb{F}_2^n$, let $P = x, P' = x \oplus s, \overline{C} = E(P) \oplus \beta, \overline{C'} = E(P') \oplus \beta$. Since the probability of improved truncated boomerang differential $(\mathcal{D}^0_{in}, \mathcal{D}^1_{out}, \mathcal{D}_{out})$ is 1, we can get $E^{-1}(\overline{C}) \oplus E^{-1}(\overline{C'}) \in \mathcal{D}_{out}$ always holds by Definition 4. Thus,

$$\begin{aligned} &g(0, x) \oplus g(1, x \oplus s) \\ =&M \cdot E^{-1}[E(x) \oplus \beta] \oplus \gamma_0 \oplus M \cdot E^{-1}[E(x \oplus s) \oplus \beta] \oplus \gamma_1 \\ =&M \cdot [E^{-1}[E(x) \oplus \beta] \oplus E^{-1}[E(x \oplus s) \oplus \beta]] \oplus \gamma \\ =&M \cdot [E^{-1}(\overline{C}) \oplus E^{-1}(\overline{C'})] \oplus \gamma \\ =&\gamma \oplus \gamma = 0^k. \end{aligned}$$

This proves that g is a periodic function, and $(1, s)$ is a period of g for any $s \in \mathcal{D}^0_{in}$.

Definition 5. *Let* $E : \mathbb{F}_2^n \rightarrow \mathbb{F}_2^n$ *be a block cipher, which satisfies that* E_r *has an improved truncated boomerang differential* $(\mathcal{D}^0_{in}, \mathcal{D}^1_{out}, \mathcal{D}_{out})$ *with probability 1. If a difference-annihilation matrix of* $\mathcal{D}_{out}$ *exists, then we call the periodic function as constructed in Theorem 2 a* ***Type-III periodic function*** *of* E_r.

5 Extending the qCCA^e Distinguishers

5.1 The 4-Round qCCA^e Distinguisher of Feistel Structure

For the Feistel structure, if we try to use a Type-III periodic function to construct a distinguisher, we can only find a 3-round qCCA distinguisher as in Example 1. However, a qCCA distinguisher for the 4-round Feistel structure exists in [14]. The periodic function g_3' used by the distinguisher is defined as follows.

$$\begin{aligned} g_1' : \mathbb{F}_2 \times \mathbb{F}_2^n &\rightarrow \mathbb{F}_2^n \\ (b, x) &\mapsto L_0 \oplus \gamma_b, \end{aligned}$$

where $(L_0, R_0) = \mathcal{E}_4^{\mathtt{Feistel},-1}(L_4 \oplus \gamma, R_4), (L_4, R_4) = \mathcal{E}_4^{\mathtt{Feistel}}(\gamma_b, x)$, γ_0 and γ_1 are two different fixed constants with $\gamma_0 \oplus \gamma_1 = \gamma$. According to Fig. 4, to construct such a 4-round qCCA^e distinguisher, the input of left branch needs to be fixed to two distinct constants (γ_0 and γ_1) with a difference $\gamma = \gamma_0 \oplus \gamma_1$, such that the output difference of the first round function is a fixed unknown value $s = F_1(\gamma_0) \oplus F_1(\gamma_1)$, which is key-related. In this case, the output difference is $\Delta = (0^n, \gamma)$ after a round of encryption. Furthermore, there exists $\Delta = (0^n, \gamma)$ and $\nabla^* = (\gamma, 0^n)$, such that the corresponding boomerang probability is 1 for the

3-round Feistel structure. And $\mathcal{E}^{\mathtt{Feistel},-1}$ has a 1-round probability 1 truncated differential $\Delta = (0^n, \gamma) \to \{(\gamma, u) \mid u \in \mathbb{F}_2^n\}$. Thus, g_1' is a periodic function, and the 4-round qCCA^e distinguisher can be constructed.

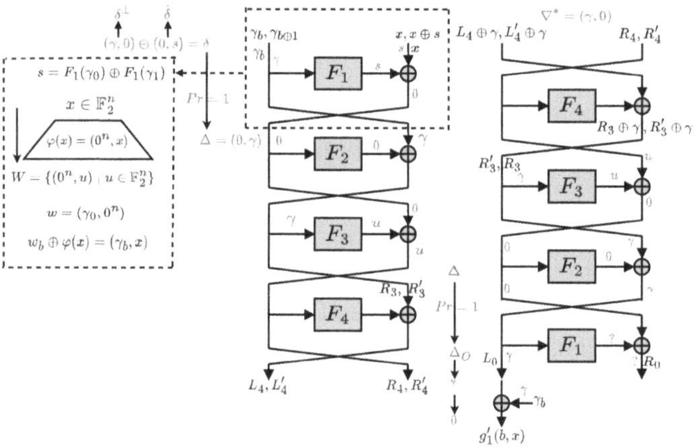

Fig. 4. The 4-round qCCA^e distinguisher of Feistel Structure.

5.2 Type-IV Periodic Functions

Inspired by the 4-round qCCA^e distinguisher of the Feistel structure, we further extend the Type-III periodic functions to construct new periodic functions.

Theorem 3. *Let $E : \mathbb{F}_2^n \to \mathbb{F}_2^n$ be a block cipher, which satisfies that E_{r_2} has an improved truncated boomerang differential $(\mathcal{D}_{in}^0, \mathcal{D}_{out}^1, \mathcal{D}_{out})$ with probability 1. Assume that there exists a probability* 1 *truncated differential $\mathcal{D}_{out} \to \Delta_O$ for $E_{r_1}^{-1}$, and a difference-annihilation matrix $M \in \mathbb{F}_2^{k \times n}$ with $Mx = \gamma$ for any $x \in \Delta_O$. Moreover, assume that E has a r_1-round difference transition $\delta \to \mathcal{D}_{in}^0$ with probability of 1 when one of the inputs belongs to a t-dimensional $(t < n)$ affine space $w \oplus W$, where $W = \mathrm{span}\{\zeta_1, \zeta_2, ..., \zeta_t\}$ (i.e., $\zeta_1, \zeta_2, ..., \zeta_t$ constitute a basis of W). Denote $\delta^{\perp}$ the projection of δ to $W^{\perp}$, and $\hat{\delta}$ the projection of δ to W. Let φ be a bijective linear transformation, and φ is defined as*

$$\varphi : \mathbb{F}_2^t \to W$$
$$(x_1, ..., x_t) \mapsto x_1\zeta_1 \oplus \cdots \oplus x_t\zeta_t.$$

Let $w_0 = w$, $w_1 = w \oplus \delta^{\perp}$, and γ_0, γ_1 be two constants such that $\gamma = \gamma_0 \oplus \gamma_1$. For any $\beta \in \mathcal{D}_{out}^1$ with $\beta \neq 0^n$, let g be defined as

$$g : \mathbb{F}_2 \times \mathbb{F}_2^t \to \mathbb{F}_2^k$$
$$(b, x) \mapsto M \cdot E_{r_1+r_2}^{-1}[E_{r_1+r_2}(w_b \oplus \varphi(x)) \oplus \beta] \oplus \gamma_b.$$

Then, g is a periodic function with a period $(1, s)$, where $s = \varphi^{-1}(\hat{\delta})$.

Proof. Since $\varphi(x) \in W$ for any $x \in \mathbb{F}_2^t$, $w_0 \oplus \varphi(x) = w \oplus \varphi(x) \in w \oplus W$. Thus, $w_0 \oplus \varphi(x)$, as one of the input to $E_{r_1+r_2}$, falls into $w \oplus W$. Moreover,

$$[w_0 \oplus \varphi(x)] \oplus [w_1 \oplus \varphi(x \oplus \varphi^{-1}(\hat{\delta}))] = w_0 \oplus w_1 \oplus \hat{\delta} = \delta^{\perp} \oplus \hat{\delta} = \delta.$$

According to the fact that the r_1-round difference transition $\delta \to \mathcal{D}_{in}^0$ for E has a probability of 1 when one of the inputs belongs to $w \oplus W$, it can deduced that

$$E_{r_1}(w_0 \oplus \varphi(x)) \oplus E_{r_1}(w_1 \oplus \varphi(x \oplus \varphi^{-1}(\hat{\delta}))) \in \mathcal{D}_{in}^0.$$

$\forall\, \beta \in \mathcal{D}_{out}^1$, $x \in \mathbb{F}_2^t$, let $P = E_{r_1}(w_0 \oplus \varphi(x)), P' = E_{r_1}(w_1 \oplus \varphi(x \oplus \varphi^{-1}(\hat{\delta})), \overline{C} = E_{r_2}(P) \oplus \beta, \overline{C'} = E_{r_2}(P') \oplus \beta, \overline{P} = E_{r_2}^{-1}(\overline{C}), \overline{P'} = E_{r_2}^{-1}(\overline{C'})$. Due to the probability of the improved truncated boomerang differential $(\mathcal{D}_{in}^0, \mathcal{D}_{out}^1, \mathcal{D}_{out})$ is 1, we can get $\overline{P} \oplus \overline{P'} \in \mathcal{D}_{out}$ always holds by Definition 4. And because E^{-1} has an r_1-round truncated differential $\mathcal{D}_{out} \to \Delta_O$ with probability 1, we can get $E_{r_1}^{-1}(\overline{P}) \oplus E_{r_1}^{-1}(\overline{P'}) \in \Delta_O$. Thus,

$$\begin{aligned}
&g(0,x) \oplus g(1, x \oplus s)\\
=&M \cdot E_{r_1+r_2}^{-1}[E_{r_1+r_2}(w_0 \oplus \varphi(x)) \oplus \beta] \oplus \gamma_0 \oplus M \cdot E_{r_1+r_2}^{-1}[E_{r_1+r_2}(w_1 \oplus \varphi(x \oplus s)) \oplus \beta] \oplus \gamma_1\\
=&M \cdot [E_{r_1+r_2}^{-1}[E_{r_2} \circ E_{r_1}(w_0 \oplus \varphi(x)) \oplus \beta] \oplus E_{r_1+r_2}^{-1}[E_{r_2} \circ E_{r_1}(w_1 \oplus \varphi(x \oplus s)) \oplus \beta]] \oplus \gamma\\
=&M \cdot [E_{r_1+r_2}^{-1}(E_{r_2}(P) \oplus \beta) \oplus E_{r_1+r_2}^{-1}(E_{r_2}(P') \oplus \beta)] \oplus \gamma\\
=&M \cdot [E_{r_1+r_2}^{-1}(\overline{C}) \oplus E_{r_1+r_2}^{-1}(\overline{C'})] \oplus \gamma\\
=&M \cdot [E_{r_1}^{-1} \circ E_{r_2}^{-1}(\overline{C}) \oplus E_{r_1}^{-1} \circ E_{r_2}^{-1}(\overline{C'})] \oplus \gamma\\
=&M \cdot [E_{r_1}^{-1}(\overline{P}) \oplus E_{r_1}^{-1}(\overline{P'})] \oplus \gamma = \gamma \oplus \gamma = 0^k.
\end{aligned}$$

This proves that g is a periodic function, and $(1, s)$ is a period, where $s = \varphi^{-1}(\hat{\delta})$.

Remark 1. It should be noted that only $\delta^{\perp}$ is used to construct the periodic function in Theorem 3. Thus, such δ is required to exist, and its projection to $W^{\perp}$ is known to the attacker.

Definition 6. *Let $E : \mathbb{F}_2^n \to \mathbb{F}_2^n$ be a block cipher, which satisfies that E_{r_2} has an improved truncated boomerang differential $(\mathcal{D}_{in}^0, \mathcal{D}_{out}^1, \mathcal{D}_{out})$ with probability 1. Moreover, E_{r_1} has a probability 1 truncated differential $\delta \to \mathcal{D}_{in}^0$ with the restriction that one of the inputs belongs to an affine space $w \oplus W$ and $E_{r_1}^{-1}$ has a probability 1 truncated differential $\mathcal{D}_{out} \to \Delta_O$. If a difference-annihilation matrix of Δ_O exists and the projection of δ to $W^{\perp}$ is known, then we call the periodic function as constructed in Theorem 3 a* ***Type-IV periodic function*** *of $E_{r_1+r_2}$.*

Remark 2. Fig. 5 briefly illustrates the construction of Type-IV periodic functions in Theorem 3 from a differential point of view. What is marked with red in the middle of Fig. 5 presents the intermediate differences during the encryption and decryption procedure.

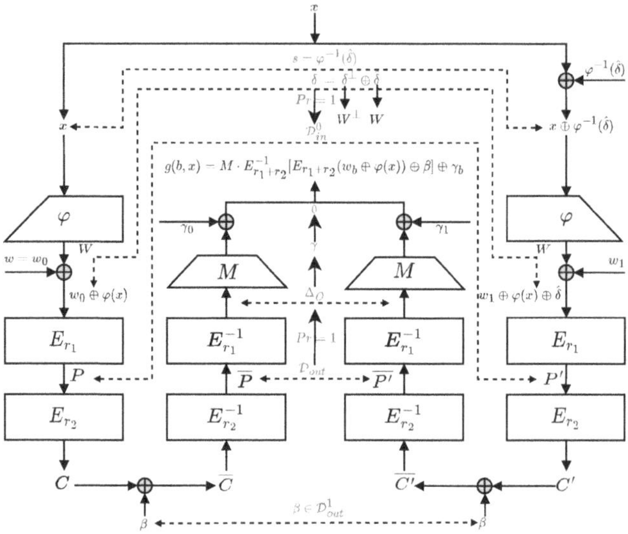

Fig. 5. An illustration of Type-IV periodic functions.

Remark 3. It is not difficult to notice that by interchanging E and E^{-1} in Theorem 2 (Theorem 3), the corresponding periodic functions still can be constructed. The method remains essentially unchanged, so the periodic function obtained by interchanging E and E^{-1} in Definition 5 (Definition 6) is also called a Type-III (Type-IV) periodic function.

Example 2. The periodic function used in the 4-round qCCA^e distinguisher of Feistel structure is a Type-IV periodic function as shown in Fig. 4. In this case, $r_2 = 3$, $r_1 = 1$, and the input affine space is $w \oplus W = (\gamma_0, 0^n) \oplus \{(0^n, u) \mid u \in \mathbb{F}_2^n\}$. Then the 1-round difference transition from $\delta^{\perp} \oplus \hat{\delta} = \delta = (\gamma, s) \rightarrow \Delta$ has a probability of 1 when the input belongs to $w \oplus W$. From Example 1, there exists the improved truncated boomerang differential $(\Delta, \nabla^*, \Delta)$ with probability 1 for $\mathcal{E}_3^{\texttt{Feistel}}$, where $\Delta = (0^n, \gamma)$ and $\nabla^* = (\gamma, 0^n)$, $\gamma \neq 0^n$. And $\mathcal{E}^{\texttt{Feistel},-1}$ has a 1-round truncated differential $\Delta = (0^n, \gamma) \rightarrow \Delta_O = \{(\gamma, u) \mid u \in \mathbb{F}_2^n\}$ with probability 1. And we know that the projection of δ to $W^{\perp}$ is $\delta^{\perp} = (\gamma, 0^n)$, define φ as $\varphi(x) = (0^n, x)$, where $x \in \mathbb{F}_2^n$. Let $w_0 = w = (\gamma_0, 0^n)$, $w_1 = w \oplus \delta^{\perp} = (\gamma_1, 0^n)$, $M_1 = (I\ O)$, where O and I denote the $n \times n$ zero and identity matrices over $\mathbb{F}_2$, respectively. Thus, according to Theorem 3, we can reconstruct the 4-round qCCA^e distinguisher as $g_1'(b, x) = L_0 \oplus \gamma_b = M_1 \cdot \mathcal{E}_4^{\texttt{Feistel},-1}[\mathcal{E}_4^{\texttt{Feistel}}(\gamma_b, x) \oplus \nabla^*] \oplus \gamma_b$. □

6 Applications to Unified Structures

Previous sections have presented definitions of two types of periodic functions, and give a method of finding such periodic functions. In the following, we apply our proposed new techniques to cryptographic structures ignoring the details of non-linear components to construct new qCCA distinguishers, that is, qCCA^e distinguishers, which is exactly what is lacking in existing research.

6.1 The Unified Structure

In [20], the authors presented a unified structure that covers the Feistel and Lai-Massey structures, as well as most generalized Feistel structures. The unified structure is illustrated in Fig. 6a, where A_i and B_i are the $m \times n$ and $n \times m$ matrices for $i = 1, 2, \ldots, d$; $f : \mathbb{F}_2^m \to \mathbb{F}_2^m$ is the round function; π is the branch permutation.

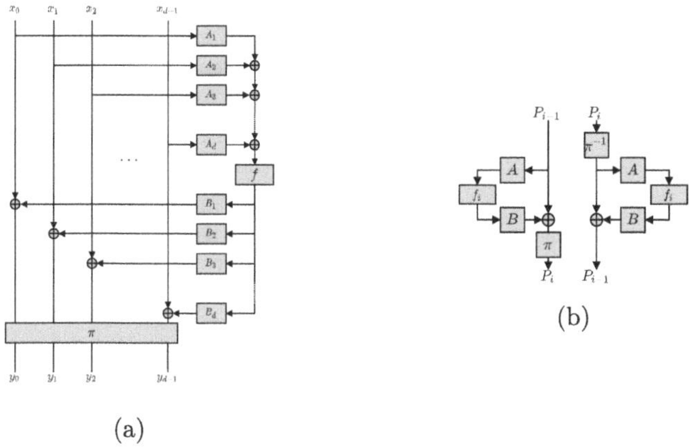

Fig. 6. The unified structure $f_{A,B,\pi}$ and its inverse $f^{-1}_{A,B,\pi}$.

In the following, we will denote an r-round unified structure by $\mathcal{F}_{A,B,\pi}$ $(f_1, ..., f_r)$, where f_i is the i-the round function, $A = (A_1 \ \cdots \ A_d)$, and $B = (B_1^{\mathrm{T}} \ \cdots \ B_d^{\mathrm{T}})^{\mathrm{T}}$. Further, if $AB = O$, then the unified structure $\mathcal{F}_{A,B,\pi}(f_1, ..., f_r)$ is invertible, denote the inverse structure as $\mathcal{F}^{-1}_{A,B,\pi}(f_1, ..., f_r)$. For simplicity, we use Fig. 6b to represent the unified structure and its inverse structure and denote

$$\mathcal{A}^r = \begin{pmatrix} A \\ A\pi \\ \vdots \\ A\pi^r \end{pmatrix}, \ \mathcal{B}^r = (B \ \pi B \ \cdots \ \pi^r B), \text{ which will be used in this paper.}$$

Proposition 1. *Let $\mathcal{F}_{A,B,\pi}(f_1, ..., f_{2d-1})$ be a unified structure with d branches and each of size n bits, where $A \in \mathbb{F}_2^{m \times nd}, B \in \mathbb{F}_2^{nd \times m}$. Moreover, $AB = O$, $\mathrm{rank}(\mathcal{A}^{d-2}) < nd$. Then, there always exists a boomerang differential (Δ, ∇^*) with probability 1 for $\mathcal{F}_{A,B,\pi}(f_1, ..., f_{2d-1})$.*

Proof. According to $\text{rank}(\mathcal{A}^{d-2}) < nd$, the matrix $\mathcal{A}^{d-2}$ is not of full column rank. So there exists a non-zero vector $\Delta_0 \in \mathbb{F}_2^{nd}$ such that $\mathcal{A}^{d-2}\Delta_0 = 0$. Let Δ_0 be the input difference to $\mathcal{F}_{A,B,\pi}(f_1, ..., f_{2d-1})$. Since $A\Delta_0 = A\pi\Delta_0 = \cdots = A\pi^{d-2}\Delta_0 = 0$, it can be deduced that the input difference to the first $(d-1)$ round functions are zero, and the output difference of the first $(d-1)$ rounds is $\pi^{d-1}\Delta_0$.

Let (P_0, P_0') be the plaintext pair input to $\mathcal{F}_{A,B,\pi}(f_1, ..., f_{2d-1})$ with $P_0 \oplus P_0' = \Delta_0$. Denote the output pair of the i-th round encryption by (P_i, P_i') for $i = 1, 2, \ldots, 2d-1$. Thus it is obtained that $P_{d-1} \oplus P_{d-1}' = \pi^{d-1}\Delta_0 = \pi^{-1}\Delta_0$ by the above differential analysis.

Let $(D_0, D_0') = (P_{2d-1} \oplus \pi^{d-1}\Delta_0, P_{2d-1}' \oplus \pi^{d-1}\Delta_0)$ be the new ciphertext pair input to $\mathcal{F}_{A,B,\pi}^{-1}(f_1, ..., f_{2d-1})$. Denote the output pair of the i-th round decryption by (D_i, D_i') for $i = 1, 2, \ldots, 2d-1$.

Next, we prove the fact that if $D_j = P_{2d-1-j} \oplus \pi^{d-1-j}\Delta_0$ holds, then we could deduce that $D_{j+1} = P_{2d-1-(j+1)} \oplus \pi^{d-1-(j+1)}\Delta_0$ for $j = 0, 1, \ldots, d-2$. From Fig. 6b, and $A\pi^{d-1-j-1}\Delta_0 = 0$, we have that

$$\begin{aligned} D_{j+1} =& \pi^{-1}D_j \oplus Bf_{2d-1-j}(A\pi^{-1}D_j) \\ =& \pi^{-1}(P_{2d-1-j} \oplus \pi^{d-1-j}\Delta_0) \oplus Bf_{2d-1-j}(A\pi^{-1}(P_{2d-1-j} \oplus \pi^{d-1-j}\Delta_0)) \\ =& \pi^{-1}P_{2d-1-j} \oplus \pi^{d-1-j-1}\Delta_0 \oplus Bf_{2d-1-j}(A\pi^{-1}P_{2d-1-j}) \\ =& P_{2d-1-j-1} \oplus \pi^{d-1-(j+1)}\Delta_0 \end{aligned}$$

And since $D_0 = P_{2d-1} \oplus \pi^{d-1}\Delta_0$, we can get $D_{d-1} = P_d \oplus \Delta_0$. Moreover, as $AB = O$, there is $AP_{d-1} = A[\pi^{-1}P_d \oplus Bf_d(A\pi^{-1}P_d)] = A\pi^{-1}P_d$. So

$$\begin{aligned} D_d &= \pi^{-1}D_{d-1} \oplus Bf_d(A\pi^{-1}D_{d-1}) \\ &= \pi^{-1}P_d \oplus \pi^{-1}\Delta_0 \oplus Bf_d(A\pi^{-1}P_d \oplus A\pi^{-1}\Delta_0) \\ &= \pi^{-1}P_d \oplus \pi^{-1}\Delta_0 \oplus Bf_d(A(P_{d-1} \oplus \pi^{-1}\Delta_0)) \\ &= \pi^{-1}P_d \oplus \pi^{-1}\Delta_0 \oplus Bf_d(AP_{d-1}') \end{aligned}$$

In the same way, it can be deduced that $D_d' = \pi^{-1}P_d' \oplus \pi^{-1}\Delta_0 \oplus Bf_d(AP_{d-1})$. As a result, $D_d \oplus D_d' = \pi^{-1}P_d \oplus Bf_d(AP_{d-1}) \oplus \pi^{-1}P_d' \oplus Bf_d(AP_{d-1}') = P_{d-1} \oplus P_{d-1}' = \pi^{-1}\Delta_0$. Thus, the output difference of the d-th round decryption is $\pi^{-1}\Delta_0$. And because $A\Delta_0 = A\pi\Delta_0 = \cdots = A\pi^{d-2}\Delta_0 = 0$, it can be deduced that the input difference to the last $(d-1)$ round functions is zero, and $D_{2d-1} \oplus D_{2d-1}' = \Delta_0$. In summary, there always exists $\Delta = \Delta_0$ and $\nabla^* = \pi^{-1}\Delta_0$ such that the probability of the boomerang differential (Δ, ∇^*) for $\mathcal{F}_{A,B,\pi}(f_1, ..., f_{2d-1})$ is 1.

The condition required in Proposition 1 holds for classical Feistel, Lai-Massey, SM4-like, MARS-like, Type-1 generalized Feistel structures. As a result, for SM4-like, MARS-like, and Type-1 generalized Feistel structures, we could design their Type-III periodic functions, which have not been mentioned in the existing research.

However, it is noted that from Proposition 1, we only know how to construct the Type-III periodic functions of some unified structures, and then get the corresponding qCCA^e distinguishers. In order to get longer qCCA^e distinguishers, we will consider how to design their Type-IV periodic functions to extend distinguishers.

Proposition 2. *Let $\mathcal{F}_{A,B,\pi}(f_1,...,f_{2d})$ be a unified structure with d branches and each of size n bits, where $A \in \mathbb{F}_2^{m\times nd}, B \in \mathbb{F}_2^{nd\times m}$. Moreover, $AB = O$, $\mathrm{rank}(\mathcal{A}^{d-2}) < nd$, and $\mathrm{rank}(B) < nd$. Then, there exists a Type-IV periodic function for $\mathcal{F}_{A,B,\pi}(f_1,...,f_{2d})$.*

Proof. According to the Proposition 1, there exists Δ_0 and $\pi^{-1}\Delta_0$ such that the boomerang probability of $\mathcal{F}_{A,B,\pi}(f_2,...,f_{2d})$ is 1, where $\Delta_0 \in \mathbb{F}_2^{nd}$ is a non-zero vector such that $\mathcal{A}^{d-2}\Delta_0 = 0$.

Obviously, $\mathcal{F}^{-1}_{A,B,\pi}(f_1,...,f_r)$ has a 1-round truncated differential $\Delta = \Delta_0 \to \Delta_O = \{\pi^{-1}\Delta_0 \oplus Bu \mid u \in \mathbb{F}_2^m\}$ with probability 1. And since $\mathrm{rank}(B) < nd$, then there exists a non-zero matrix M such that $MB = O$. Thus, $Mx = M(\pi^{-1}\Delta_0 \oplus Bu) = M\pi^{-1}\Delta_0 \oplus MBu = M\pi^{-1}\Delta_0$ is a fixed constant for any $x \in \Delta_O$.

Let $W = \{x \in \mathbb{F}_2^{nd} \mid Ax = 0\}$ and $w \in W^\perp$ be an arbitrarily chosen constant. Since A is known, W is also known. Consequently, we can define the corresponding bijective linear transformation φ. And the projection of $\pi^{-1}\Delta_0$ to $W^\perp$ is also known, denoted as $\delta^\perp$. For any $x \in W$, let $w \oplus x$, $w \oplus x \oplus \delta$ be two inputs of $\mathcal{F}_{A,B,\pi}(f_1,...,f_{2d})$, where $\delta = \pi^{-1}\Delta_0 \oplus B\beta_1$ and $\beta_1 = f_1(Aw) \oplus f_1(Aw \oplus A\delta^\perp)$. Since the output difference of the round function is $f_1(A(w \oplus x)) \oplus f_1(A(w \oplus x \oplus \delta)) = f_1(Aw) \oplus f_1(Aw \oplus A\delta^\perp) = \beta_1$, the output difference of the first round encryption is $\pi(\delta \oplus B\beta_1) = \Delta_0$. Thus the 1-round difference transition from $\delta = \pi^{-1}\Delta_0 \oplus B\beta_1 \to \Delta_0$ has a probability of 1 when the input belongs to $w \oplus W$. Since $AB\beta_1 = 0$, $B\beta_1 \in W$, the projection of δ to $W^\perp$ is the projection of $\pi^{-1}\Delta_0$ to $W^\perp$, which is known. In overview, from Definition 6, we can define a Type-IV periodic function for $\mathcal{F}_{A,B,\pi}(f_1,...,f_{2d})$.

It is not difficult to verify that structures such as classical Feistel, Lai-Massey, SM4-like, MARS-like, and Type-1 generalized Feistel all meet the condition of Proposition 2. Therefore, corresponding $2d$-round qCCA^e distinguishers can be constructed for these structures.

On the one hand, the results for classical Feistel and Lai-Massey structures are the same as the existing results; on the other hand, for SM4-like and MARS-like structures, the results are better than the existing results.

6.2 Distinguishers for SM4-Like Structures

Let $\mathcal{E}^{\mathtt{SM4}} : \mathbb{F}_2^{128} \to \mathbb{F}_2^{128}$ denote the unified structure derived from SM4, which means $\mathcal{E}^{\mathtt{SM4}}$ is a set of block ciphers identical to SM4 except the round functions. The corresponding parameters are as follows. $n = m = 32$, $d = 4$, $A_1 = B_2 = B_3 = B_4 = O$, $B_1 = A_2 = A_3 = A_4 = I$, where O and I denote the 32×32 zero and identity matrices over $\mathbb{F}_2$, respectively. Moreover, $A = (O\ I\ I\ I)$,

$B = (I\ O\ O\ O)^{\mathrm{T}}$, the branch permutation is

$$\pi = \begin{pmatrix} O & I & O & O \\ O & O & I & O \\ O & O & O & I \\ I & O & O & O \end{pmatrix}, \mathcal{A}^2 = \begin{pmatrix} O & I & I & I \\ I & O & I & I \\ I & I & O & I \end{pmatrix}.$$

Following the theory of matrix rank, we can get $\mathrm{rank}(\mathcal{A}^2) \leq 3n$. So $\mathcal{A}^2$ is not a full column rank matrix, i.e. $\mathrm{rank}(\mathcal{A}^{d-2}) < 4n = 128 = nd$.

Furthermore, there exists a non-zero vector $\Delta_0 = (\alpha, \alpha, \alpha, 0)$, such that $\mathcal{A}^2\Delta_0 = \mathcal{A}^2(\alpha, \alpha, \alpha, 0) = 0$, where $0 \neq \alpha \in \mathbb{F}_2^{32}$. According to the proof of Proposition 1, there exists $\Delta = \Delta_0 = (\alpha, \alpha, \alpha, 0)$ and $\nabla^* = \pi^{-1}\Delta_0 = \pi^3\Delta_0 = (0, \alpha, \alpha, \alpha)$, such that the probability of the boomerang differential (Δ, ∇^*) for $\mathcal{E}_7^{\mathsf{SM4}}$ is 1. Let α_0, α_1 be two 32-bit constants such that $\alpha_0 \oplus \alpha_1 = \alpha$. Therefore, we can design a Type-III periodic function $g_2(b, y)$ as

$$g_2 : \mathbb{F}_2 \times \mathbb{F}_2^{128} \to \mathbb{F}_2^{128}, (b, y) \mapsto \mathcal{E}_7^{\mathsf{SM4},-1}[\mathcal{E}_7^{\mathsf{SM4}}(y) \oplus (\alpha, \alpha, \alpha, 0)] \oplus (\alpha_b, \alpha_b, \alpha_b, 0)$$

for the 7-round SM4 structure $\mathcal{E}_7^{\mathsf{SM4}}$ by Corollary 1.

Moreover, since $B = (I\ O\ O\ O)^{\mathrm{T}}$, $\mathrm{rank}(B) < 128 = nd$. So, exploiting Proposition 2, we can further extend the 7-round qCCA^e distinguisher constructed from the Type-III periodic function $g_3(b, y)$. From the proof of Proposition 2, $\mathcal{E}^{\mathsf{SM4},-1}$ has a 1-round truncated differential

$$\Delta = \Delta_0 = (\alpha, \alpha, \alpha, 0) \to \Delta_O = \{\pi^{-1}\Delta_0 \oplus Bu \mid u \in \mathbb{F}_2^{32}\} = \{(u, \alpha, \alpha, \alpha) \mid u \in \mathbb{F}_2^{32}\}$$

with probability 1. Subsequently, a non-zero matrix $M_2 = (O\ I\ I\ I)$ exists such as $M_2 B = O$. Therefore, $M_2 y = M_2(\pi^{-1}\Delta_0 \oplus Bu) = \alpha$ for any $y \in \Delta_O$.

Slightly different from the construction demonstrated in the proof of Proposition 2, considering an arbitrary subspace of $\{x \in \mathbb{F}_2^{nd} \mid Ax = 0\}$ as W, the subsequent conclusions still hold. For the sake of simplicity, this extension requires $W = \{(x, 0, 0, 0) \mid x \in \mathbb{F}_2^{32}\} \subset \{x \in \mathbb{F}_2^{128} \mid Ax = 0\} = \{(x_1, x_2, x_3, x_4) \in (\mathbb{F}_2^{32})^4 \mid \bigoplus_{i=2}^4 x_i = 0\}$, $w = (0, \alpha_0, \alpha_0, \alpha_0) \in W^\perp$. The projection of $\pi^{-1}\Delta_0$ to $W^\perp$ is $\delta^\perp = (0, \alpha, \alpha, \alpha)$, and $\beta_1 = F_1(Aw) \oplus F_1(Aw \oplus A\delta^\perp) = F_1(\alpha_0) \oplus F_1(\alpha_1) = s$. Thus, the 1-round difference transition from $\delta = \pi^{-1}\Delta_0 \oplus B\beta_1 = (s, \alpha, \alpha, \alpha) \to \Delta_0$ has a probability of 1 when the input belongs to $w \oplus W$.

So we can construct a Type-IV periodic function $g_2'(b, x)$ as

$$g_2' : \mathbb{F}_2 \times \mathbb{F}_2^{32} \to \mathbb{F}_2^{32}, (b, x) \mapsto M_2 \cdot \mathcal{E}_8^{\mathsf{SM4},-1}[\mathcal{E}_8^{\mathsf{SM4}}(x, \alpha_b, \alpha_b, \alpha_b) \oplus (0, \alpha, \alpha, \alpha)] \oplus \alpha_b$$

for the 8-round SM4 structure $\mathcal{E}_8^{\mathsf{SM4}}$.

Therefore, we can build an 8-round distinguisher for the SM4 structure. To facilitate understanding, we provide Fig. 7, which intuitively illustrates the 8-round qCCA^e distinguisher of the SM4 structure, including the construction details of the boomerang differential and extension.

The same conclusion holds if the SM4 structure is generalized to the d-branch (d is even) SM4-like structure. The d-branch SM4-like structure $\mathcal{E}^{\mathsf{dSM4}} : \mathbb{F}_2^{nd} \to$

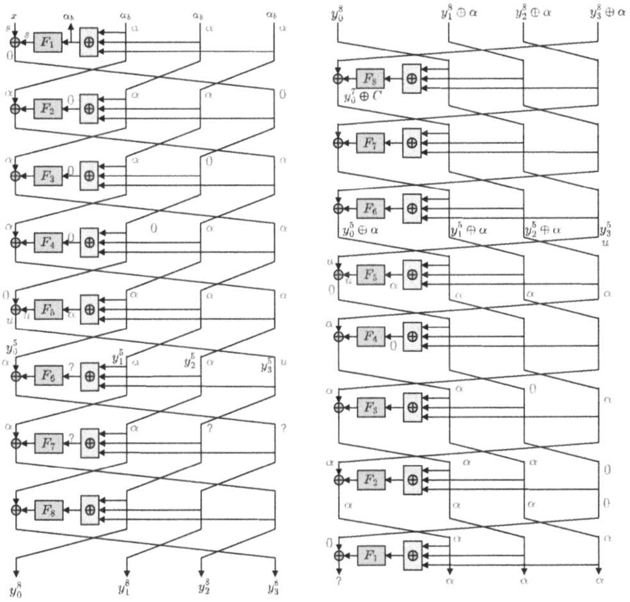

Fig. 7. A 8-round qCCA^e distinguisher of SM4 structures.

$\mathbb{F}_2^{nd}$ can also be regarded as a unified structure, whose corresponding parameters are as follows. $n = m, A_1 = B_2 = B_3 = \cdots = B_n = O, B_1 = A_2 = A_3 = \cdots = A_n = I$, where O and I denote the $n \times n$ zero and identity matrices over $\mathbb{F}_2$, respectively.

Therefore, we can build a $2d$-round distinguisher for the d-branch SM4-like structure. Nevertheless, for the d-branch SM4-like structure, the best result of quantum distinguishers based on Simon's algorithm given in [4,5,10] is $(2d-1)$-round. Namely, we can get a longer quantum distinguisher for the SM4-like structure with our new method.

6.3 Distinguishers for MARS-Like Structures

Let $\mathcal{E}^{\texttt{MARS}} : \mathbb{F}_2^{128} \to \mathbb{F}_2^{128}$ denote the unified structure derived from MARS, which means $\mathcal{E}^{\texttt{MARS}}$ is a set of block ciphers identical to MARS except the round functions. The corresponding parameters are as follows. $n = m = 32$, $d = 4$, $A_1 = B_2 = B_3 = B_4 = I$, $B_1 = A_2 = A_3 = A_4 = O$, where O and I denote the 32×32 zero and identity matrices over $\mathbb{F}_2$, respectively. Moreover, $A = (I\ O\ O\ O)$, $B = (O\ I\ I\ I)^{\mathrm{T}}$, the branch permutation is

$$\pi = \begin{pmatrix} O & I & O & O \\ O & O & I & O \\ O & O & O & I \\ I & O & O & O \end{pmatrix}, \mathcal{A}^2 = \begin{pmatrix} I & O & O & O \\ O & I & O & O \\ O & O & I & O \end{pmatrix}.$$

According to the theory of matrix rank, we can get $\mathrm{rank}(\mathcal{A}^2) \leq 3n$. So $\mathcal{A}^2$ is not a full column rank matrix, i.e. $\mathrm{rank}(\mathcal{A}^{d-2}) < 4n = 128 = nd$.

Furthermore, there exists a non-zero vector $\Delta_0 = (0,0,0,\alpha)$, such that $\mathcal{A}^2\Delta_0 = \mathcal{A}^2(0,0,0,\alpha) = 0$, where $0 \neq \alpha \in \mathbb{F}_2^{32}$. According to the proof of Proposition 1, there exists $\Delta = \Delta_0 = (0,0,0,\alpha)$ and $\nabla^* = \pi^{-1}\Delta_0 = \pi^3\Delta_0 = (\alpha,0,0,0)$, such that the probability of the boomerang differential (Δ, ∇^*) for $\mathcal{E}_7^{\mathtt{MARS}}$ is 1. Let α_0, α_1 be two 32-bit constants such that $\alpha_0 \oplus \alpha_1 = \alpha$. Then, we can build a Type-III periodic function $g_3(b,y)$ as

$$g_3 : \mathbb{F}_2 \times \mathbb{F}_2^{128} \to \mathbb{F}_2^{128}, (b,y) \mapsto \mathcal{E}_7^{\mathtt{MARS},-1}[\mathcal{E}_7^{\mathtt{MARS}}(y) \oplus (\alpha,0,0,0)] \oplus (0,0,0,\alpha_b)$$

for the 7-round MARS structure $\mathcal{E}_7^{\mathtt{MARS}}$ by Corollary 1.

Moreover, since $B = (O\ I\ I\ I)^{\mathrm{T}}$, $\mathrm{rank}(B) < 4n = 128 = nd$. So, according to Proposition 2, we can further extend the 7-round qCCA^e distinguisher constructed from the Type-III periodic function $g_3(b,y)$. From the proof of Proposition 2, $\mathcal{E}^{\mathtt{MARS},-1}$ has a 1-round truncated differential $\Delta = \Delta_0 = (0,0,0,\alpha) \to \Delta_O = \{\pi^{-1}\Delta_0 \oplus Bu \mid u \in \mathbb{F}_2^{32}\} = \{(u,\alpha,\alpha,\alpha) \mid u \in \mathbb{F}_2^{32}\}$ with probability 1. Subsequently, a non-zero matrix $M_3 = (I\ O\ O\ O)$ exists such as $M_3 B = O$. Therefore,

$$M_3 y = M_3(\pi^{-1}\Delta_0 \oplus Bu) = M_4\pi^{-1}\Delta_0 = \alpha$$

for any $y \in \Delta_O$. Similarly, we take the subspace $W = \{(0,x,x,x) \mid x \in \mathbb{F}_2^{32}\} \subset \{x \in \mathbb{F}_2^{128} \mid Ax = 0\} = \{(x_1,x_2,x_3,x_4) \in (\mathbb{F}_2^{32})^4 \mid x_1 = 0\}$, $w = (\alpha_0,0,0,0) \in W^{\perp}$. The projection of $\pi^{-1}\Delta_0$ to $W^{\perp}$ is $\delta^{\perp} = (\alpha,0,0,0)$, and $\beta_1 = F_1(Aw) \oplus F_1(Aw \oplus A\delta^{\perp}) = F_1(\alpha_0) \oplus F_1(\alpha_1) = s$. Thus, the 1-round difference transition from $\delta = \pi^{-1}\Delta_0 \oplus B\beta_1 = (\alpha,s,s,s) \to \Delta_0$ has a probability of 1 when the input belongs to $w \oplus W$.

Then, we can construct a Type-IV periodic function $g_3'(b,x)$ as

$$g_3' : \mathbb{F}_2 \times \mathbb{F}_2^{32} \to \mathbb{F}_2^{32}, (b,x) \mapsto M_3 \cdot \mathcal{E}_8^{\mathtt{MARS},-1}[\mathcal{E}_8^{\mathtt{MARS}}(\alpha_b,x,x,x) \oplus (\alpha,0,0,0)] \oplus \alpha_b$$

for the 8-round MARS structure $\mathcal{E}_8^{\mathtt{MARS}}$, which can be obtained directly from Fig. 8.

Hence, we can construct an 8-round qCCA^e distinguisher for the MARS structures, a polynomial-time quantum distinguisher. However, it has been proved that an r-round MARS structure becomes a classically secure strong pseudorandom permutation (SPRP) for $r \geq 8$ in [22], that is, it cannot be distinguished from a random permutation by polynomial-time chosen-ciphertext attacks when round functions are secure PRFs, round keys are chosen independently and uniformly at random.

But in this paper, we prove that when the adversary is allowed to make quantum superposition queries to keyed oracles, the 8-round MARS structure can be distinguished through polynomial-time chosen-ciphertext attacks. That is to say, the 8-round MARS structure is not a quantum pseudo-random permutation (qPRP). In other words, we have seen polynomial-time quantum distinguisher breaking the classical SPRP bound for the MARS structure.

The same conclusion holds if the MARS structure is generalized to the d-branch (d is even) MARS-like structure. The d-branch MARS-like structure

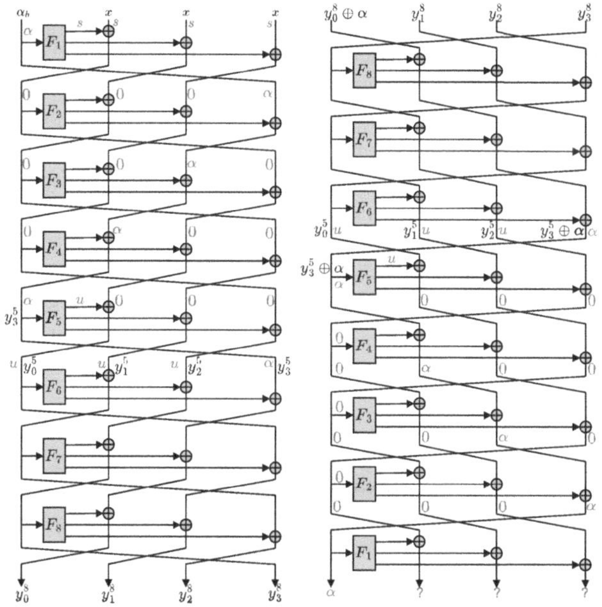

Fig. 8. A 8-round qCCA^e distinguisher of MARS structures.

$\mathcal{E}^{\mathtt{dMARS}} : \mathbb{F}_2^{nd} \rightarrow \mathbb{F}_2^{nd}$ can also be regarded as a unified structure, whose corresponding parameters are as follows. $n = m, A_1 = B_2 = B_3 = \cdots = B_n = I, B_1 = A_2 = A_3 = \cdots = A_n = O$, where O and I denote the $n \times n$ zero and identity matrices over $\mathbb{F}_2$, respectively. As a result, we can construct a Type-IV periodic function $g_3''(b, x)$ as

$$g_3'' : \mathbb{F}_2 \times \mathbb{F}_2^n \rightarrow \mathbb{F}_2^n, (b, x) \mapsto M_3' \cdot \mathcal{E}_{2d}^{\mathtt{dMARS},-1}[\mathcal{E}_{2d}^{\mathtt{dMARS}}(\alpha_b, x, x, \cdots, x) \oplus (\alpha, 0, 0, \cdots, 0)] \oplus \alpha_b$$

for the $2d$-round d-branch MARS-like structure $\mathcal{E}_{2d}^{\mathtt{dMARS}}$, where $M_3' = (O\ I\ I\ \cdots\ I)$.

Therefore, we can build a $2d$-round distinguisher for the d-branch MARS-like structure. However, for the d-branch MARS-like structure, the best result of quantum distinguishers based on Simon's algorithm given in [5] is $(2d-1)$-round. Consequently, we can improve such distinguishers for the MARS-like structure with our proposed method to construct a longer distinguisher.

7 Conclusion

In this paper, we study general techniques to construct quantum chosen-ciphertext attacks (qCCA) distinguishers based on Simon's algorithm. We further categorize the qCCA distinguishers into qCCA^d and qCCA^e distinguishers according to whether to access encryption oracles or not. Subsequently, we examine the general construction approaches of these two kinds of qCCA distinguishers respectively.

First, we find that extend the general construction technique of qCPA distinguishers to qCCA^e distinguishers. Then, we present how to build qCCA^d using truncated differentials with probability 1. Secondly, through observing the boomerang attack, we established the links between the periodic functions using encryption and decryption oracles and boomerang distinguishing attacks for the first time. Thereby a general approach to constructing qCCA^e distinguishers exploiting improved truncated boomerang differential with probability 1 is proposed in this paper, which can serve as a generic quantum cryptanalysis vector applicable to any block cipher. Furthermore, we apply our general techniques to unified structures, which cover Feistel, Lai-Massey, SM4-like, MARS-like structures, improving the Simon-based distinguisher of SM4-like and MARS-like structures.

Acknowledgments. We would like to thank all the anonymous reviewers for their valuable comments to improve the quality of this paper. This work was supported by the National Key R&D Program of China (No.2023YFA1011200), the National Natural Science Foundation of China (No.62272147, No.12401687), the Natural Science Foundation of Hubei Province of China (Grant No.2024AFB573), the innovation group project of the Natural Science Foundation of Hubei Province of China (No.2023AFA021).

References

1. Bariant, A., Leurent, G.: Truncated boomerang attacks and application to AES-based ciphers. In: Hazay, C., Stam, M. (eds.) Advances in Cryptology - EUROCRYPT 2023 - 42nd Annual International Conference on the Theory and Applications of Cryptographic Techniques, Lyon, France, 23–27 April 2023, Proceedings, Part IV. Lecture Notes in Computer Science, vol. 14007, pp. 3–35. Springer, Heidelberg (2023). https://doi.org/10.1007/978-3-031-30634-1_1
2. Bonnetain, X., Naya-Plasencia, M., Schrottenloher, A.: On quantum slide attacks. In: Paterson, K.G., Stebila, D. (eds.) SAC 2019. LNCS, vol. 11959, pp. 492–519. Springer, Cham (2020). https://doi.org/10.1007/978-3-030-38471-5_20
3. Bonnetain, X., Naya-Plasencia, M., Schrottenloher, A.: Quantum security analysis of AES. IACR Trans. Symmetric Cryptol. **2019**(2), 55–93 (2019). https://doi.org/10.13154/tosc.v2019.i2.55-93
4. Cid, C., Hosoyamada, A., Liu, Y., Sim, S.M.: Quantum cryptanalysis on contracting feistel structures and observation on related-key settings. In: Bhargavan, K., Oswald, E., Prabhakaran, M. (eds.) INDOCRYPT 2020. LNCS, vol. 12578, pp. 373–394. Springer, Cham (2020). https://doi.org/10.1007/978-3-030-65277-7_17
5. Cui, J., Guo, J., Ding, S.: Applications of Simon's algorithm in quantum attacks on Feistel variants. Quant. Inf. Process. **20**(3), 1–50 (2021). https://doi.org/10.1007/s11128-021-03027-x
6. Dong, X., Dong, B., Wang, X.: Quantum attacks on some feistel block ciphers. Des. Codes Crypt. **88**(6), 1179–1203 (2020). https://doi.org/10.1007/s10623-020-00741-y
7. Dong, X., Li, Z., Wang, X.: Quantum cryptanalysis on some generalized Feistel schemes. Sci. China Inf. Sci. **62**(2), 1–12 (2019). https://doi.org/10.1007/s11432-017-9436-7

8. Dong, X., Wang, X.: Quantum key-recovery attack on Feistel structures. Sci. China Inf. Sci. **61**(10), 1–7 (2018). https://doi.org/10.1007/s11432-017-9468-y
9. Grover, L.K.: A fast quantum mechanical algorithm for database search. In: Miller, G.L. (ed.) Proceedings of the Twenty-Eighth Annual ACM Symposium on the Theory of Computing, Philadelphia, Pennsylvania, USA, 22–24 May 1996, pp. 212–219. ACM (1996). https://doi.org/10.1145/237814.237866
10. Hodžić, S., Knudsen, L.R.: A quantum distinguisher for 7/8-round SMS4 block cipher. Quant. Inf. Process. **19**(11), 1–22 (2020). https://doi.org/10.1007/s11128-020-02929-6
11. Hodžić, S., Knudsen Ramkilde, L., Brasen Kidmose, A.: On quantum distinguishers for type-3 generalized feistel network based on separability. In: Ding, J., Tillich, J.-P. (eds.) PQCrypto 2020. LNCS, vol. 12100, pp. 461–480. Springer, Cham (2020). https://doi.org/10.1007/978-3-030-44223-1_25
12. Hosoyamada, A.: Quantum speed-up for multidimensional (zero correlation) linear distinguishers. In: Guo, J., Steinfeld, R. (eds.) Advances in Cryptology - ASIACRYPT 2023 - 29th International Conference on the Theory and Application of Cryptology and Information Security, Guangzhou, China, 4–8 December 2023, Proceedings, Part III. Lecture Notes in Computer Science, vol. 14440, pp. 311–345. Springer, Heidelberg (2023). https://doi.org/10.1007/978-981-99-8727-6_11
13. Hosoyamada, A., Sasaki, Yu.: Quantum Demiric-Selçuk meet-in-the-middle attacks: applications to 6-round generic feistel constructions. In: Catalano, D., De Prisco, R. (eds.) SCN 2018. LNCS, vol. 11035, pp. 386–403. Springer, Cham (2018). https://doi.org/10.1007/978-3-319-98113-0_21
14. Ito, G., Hosoyamada, A., Matsumoto, R., Sasaki, Yu., Iwata, T.: Quantum chosen-ciphertext attacks against feistel ciphers. In: Matsui, M. (ed.) CT-RSA 2019. LNCS, vol. 11405, pp. 391–411. Springer, Cham (2019). https://doi.org/10.1007/978-3-030-12612-4_20
15. Kaplan, M., Leurent, G., Leverrier, A., Naya-Plasencia, M.: Breaking symmetric cryptosystems using quantum period finding. In: Robshaw, M., Katz, J. (eds.) CRYPTO 2016. LNCS, vol. 9815, pp. 207–237. Springer, Heidelberg (2016). https://doi.org/10.1007/978-3-662-53008-5_8
16. Kaplan, M., Leurent, G., Leverrier, A., Naya-Plasencia, M.: Quantum differential and linear cryptanalysis. IACR Trans. Symmetric Cryptol. **2016**(1), 71–94 (2016). https://doi.org/10.13154/tosc.v2016.i1.71-94
17. Kuwakado, H., Morii, M.: Quantum distinguisher between the 3-round Feistel cipher and the random permutation. In: IEEE International Symposium on Information Theory, ISIT 2010, Austin, Texas, USA, 13–18 June 2010, Proceedings. pp. 2682–2685. IEEE (2010). https://doi.org/10.1109/ISIT.2010.5513654
18. Kuwakado, H., Morii, M.: Security on the quantum-type Even-Mansour cipher. In: Proceedings of the International Symposium on Information Theory and its Applications, ISITA 2012, Honolulu, HI, USA, 28–31 October 2012, pp. 312–316. IEEE (2012). https://ieeexplore.ieee.org/document/6400943/
19. Leander, G., May, A.: Grover meets simon – quantumly attacking the FX-construction. In: Takagi, T., Peyrin, T. (eds.) ASIACRYPT 2017. LNCS, vol. 10625, pp. 161–178. Springer, Cham (2017). https://doi.org/10.1007/978-3-319-70697-9_6
20. Liu, J., et al.: New wine old bottles: Feistel structure revised. IEEE Trans. Inf. Theory (2022)
21. Mao, S., Guo, T., Wang, P., Hu, L.: Quantum attacks on Lai-Massey structure. In: Cheon, J.H., Johansson, T. (eds.) Post-Quantum Cryptography - 13th Inter-

national Workshop, PQCrypto 2022, Virtual Event, 28–30 September 2022, Proceedings. Lecture Notes in Computer Science, vol. 13512, pp. 205–229. Springer, Heidelberg (2022). https://doi.org/10.1007/978-3-031-17234-2_11
22. Moriai, S., Vaudenay, S.: On the pseudorandomness of top-level schemes of block ciphers. In: Okamoto, T. (ed.) ASIACRYPT 2000. LNCS, vol. 1976, pp. 289–302. Springer, Heidelberg (2000). https://doi.org/10.1007/3-540-44448-3_22
23. Ni, B., Ito, G., Dong, X., Iwata, T.: Quantum attacks against type-1 generalized feistel ciphers and applications to CAST-256. In: Hao, F., Ruj, S., Sen Gupta, S. (eds.) INDOCRYPT 2019. LNCS, vol. 11898, pp. 433–455. Springer, Cham (2019). https://doi.org/10.1007/978-3-030-35423-7_22
24. Schrottenloher, A.: Quantum linear key-recovery attacks using the QFT. In: Handschuh, H., Lysyanskaya, A. (eds.) Advances in Cryptology - CRYPTO 2023 - 43rd Annual International Cryptology Conference, CRYPTO 2023, Santa Barbara, CA, USA, 20–24 August 2023, Proceedings, Part V. Lecture Notes in Computer Science, vol. 14085, pp. 258–291. Springer, Heidelberg (2023). https://doi.org/10.1007/978-3-031-38554-4_9
25. Shor, P.W.: Polynomial-time algorithms for prime factorization and discrete logarithms on a quantum computer. SIAM J. Comput. **26**(5), 1484–1509 (1997). https://doi.org/10.1137/S0097539795293172
26. Shyamsundar, P.: Non-boolean quantum amplitude amplification and quantum mean estimation. Quant. Inf. Process. **22**(12), 423 (2023). https://doi.org/10.1007/s11128-023-04146-3
27. Simon, D.R.: On the power of quantum computation. SIAM J. Comput. **26**(5), 1474–1483 (1997). https://doi.org/10.1137/S0097539796298637
28. Wagner, D.: The boomerang attack. In: Knudsen, L. (ed.) FSE 1999. LNCS, vol. 1636, pp. 156–170. Springer, Heidelberg (1999). https://doi.org/10.1007/3-540-48519-8_12
29. Xiang, Z., et al.: Links between quantum distinguishers based on simon's algorithm and truncated differentials. IACR Trans. Symmetric Cryptol. **2024**(2), 296–321 (2024). https://doi.org/10.46586/tosc.v2024.i2.296-321
30. Zhang, Z., Wu, W., Sui, H., Wang, B.: Quantum attacks on type-3 generalized Feistel scheme and unbalanced Feistel scheme with expanding functions. Chin. J. Electron. **32**(2), 209–216 (2023). https://doi.org/10.23919/cje.2021.00.294

Improved Key Recovery Attacks of Ascon

Shuo Peng[1,2,3], Kai Hu[1,2,3(✉)], Jiahui He[1,3], and Meiqin Wang[1,2,3]

[1] School of Cyber Science and Technology, Shandong University, Qingdao, Shandong, China
{pengshuo,hejiahui2020}@mail.sdu.edu.cn, {kai.hu,mqwang}@sdu.edu.cn
[2] Quan Cheng Shandong Laboratory, Jinan, China
[3] Key Laboratory of Cryptologic Technology and Information Security, Ministry of Education, Shandong University, Jinan, China

Abstract. Ascon, a family of algorithms that support hashing and Authenticated Encryption with Associated Data (AEAD), is the final winner of the NIST Lightweight Cryptography Project. As a research hotspot, Ascon has received substantial third-party security evaluation. Among all the results of Ascon-128 (the primary recommendation of AEAD), the key recovery attack can only be achieved by reducing the initialization phase to 7 rounds or fewer, regardless of whether it violates the security claims made by the designers (i.e., misuse of the nonce or exceeding data limits 2^{64}). In this paper, we, from two aspects (misuse-free setting and misused setting), improve the key recovery attack on Ascon-128 using the cube attack method. In one part, we present a faster method to recover the superpolies for a 64-dimensional cube in the output bits of the 7-round initialization, enabling us to recover the secret key with a time complexity of $2^{95.96}$ and a data complexity of 2^{64}. Our 7-round key recovery attack, based on the full key space, greatly improves the time complexity, making it the best result to date. Additionally, we utilize several techniques to extend state recovery to key recovery, answering the open problem of transitioning from full state recovery in the encryption phase to key recovery for Ascon-128 (ToSc Vol 4, 2022). By combining encryption phase state recovery with initialization phase key recovery, we can achieve 8-round and 9-round initialization phase key recovery in the nonce misuse scenario, with time complexities of 2^{101} and $2^{123.92}$, respectively. This represents an improvement of two rounds over previous results in the misused setting. Our first key recovery attack is also applicable to Ascon-128a, achieving the same result. In cases where the full state, prior to the encryption phase, can be recovered in other Ascon AEAD modes, our second key recovery attack will also be useful. It is worth noting that this work does not threaten the security of the full 12 rounds Ascon, but we expect that our results provide new insights into the security of Ascon.

Keywords: Ascon-128 · Cube attack · Superpoly recovery · Key recovery

A. Patra (Ed.): CT-RSA 2025, LNCS 15598, pp. 123–146, 2025.
https://doi.org/10.1007/978-3-031-88661-4_6

1 Introduction

Ascon [11], designed by Dobraunig, Eichlseder, Mendel, and Schläffer, is a family of lightweight Authenticated Encryptions with Associated Data (AEAD) and hash functions. As the winner of CAESAR competition, it is part of the final portfolio of the CAESAR competition in the "lightweight applications" category. Additionally, in February 2023, the NIST Lightweight Cryptography Team announced its decision to standardize the Ascon family for lightweight cryptographic applications, recognizing its suitability for a wide range of use cases where lightweight cryptography is essential. Consequently, assessing the security of Ascon is of critical importance.

The Ascon family supports authenticated ciphers Ascon-128, Ascon-128a, and Ascon-80pq, hash functions Ascon-Hash and Ascon-Hasha, and extendable output functions Ascon-XOF and Ascon-XOFa. In this paper, we focus on the AEAD modes, mainly Ascon-128, the primary recommendation of AEAD mode which aims to provide integrity, confidentiality, and authenticity. The designers of Ascon claim AEAD variants provide 128-bit security of privacy and authenticity when unique nonce values are used for the encryption under the same key. The maximum available plaintext and associated data blocks to the attacker are limited to 2^{64} per key.

Since being proposed, the security of the Ascon family has been widely analyzed. Cryptanalysis of Ascon in the AEAD context can be divided into different categories by whether the security claims are satisfied during the attack process. When the security claims are followed, many results cannot reach 7 rounds [10,16,19] and most 7-round key recovery attacks are based on the weak key condition [15,23]. The only known 7-round result based on the full key space is proposed by the authors in [22] with a time complexity of 2^{123}. In cases where the security claims are violated, some 7-round initialization key recovery attacks exceed the data limitations, although they remain within the nonce-respecting setting [15,19]. When it comes to that nonce is misused(nonce is reused under the same key), the state recovery during the encryption phase is typically the primary target of attacks, as seen in studies such as [3,7,19]. In [19], Li et al. provided key recovery attacks using a cube-like technique on a round-reduced version of Ascon with 7 rounds initialization in a nonce-misused setting. Another key recovery attack mentioned in [7] targeted the finalization phase of Ascon-128a and Ascon-80pq.

Although extensive analyses have been conducted on Ascon-128, none of the identified attacks pose a significant threat to the initialization phase of Ascon-128 for more than 7 rounds. Also, most 7-round initialization results either violate the security claims or are restricted to a weak key space. The only known 7-round key recovery attack, based on security claims, was proposed by the authors in [22] and exhibits a substantial time complexity of 2^{123}. Given the low degree of the round function in Ascon, algebraic attacks may prove more effective in the attack of Ascon. In this paper, we present some improved key recovery results for the initialization phase of Ascon-128 based on the cube attack, considering both misused and misuse-free settings.

Contributions. This paper focuses on key-recovery attacks against Ascon-128. We improve the key recovery attack from two aspects (misuse-free and misused settings) on Ascon-128. The details of our results are shown in Table 1.

Key Recovery in the Misuse-Free Setting. In the misuse-free setting, unique nonce values are used for encryption under the same key, with data complexity not exceeding 2^{64}. This limitation on data and the respective nonce prevent key recovery attack on Ascon-128. To adhere to the security claims of Ascon-128, we employ a cube attack methodology, specifically targeting the 7-round initialization phase of Ascon-128 while utilizing a 64-dimensional cube. We first present a faster method to efficiently recover the superpolies of the selected 64-dimensional cube in the output bits of the 7-round Ascon initialization. Based on the recovered superpolies, we can execute a key recovery attack. As a result, our attack can recover the secret key with a time complexity of $2^{95.96}$ and a data complexity of 2^{64}. Our key recovery attack operates over the full key space and significantly improves the time complexity compared to previous works.

Key Recovery in the Misused Setting. In [3], Baudrin et al. proposed a conditional cube attack capable of recovering the full state during the encryption phase of Ascon-128 within a practical time. However, extending this attack to achieve key recovery or forgery in Ascon-128 remains an open problem. To address this issue, we extend state recovery to key recovery by integrating state recovery during the encryption phase with key recovery during the initialization phase. Note a secret key is added to the state after the initialization phase, we exploit a cube distinguisher in the initialization phase. Then we traverse the key space to decrypt the recovered state until the end of the distinguisher. Since the correct key satisfies the conditions of the distinguisher, while the wrong key may not, the secret key space is reduced. To enhance the decryption process, we employ the partial sum technique, allowing us to append more rounds at the end of the distinguisher. For Ascon-128, we can recover the secret key with a complexity of 2^{101} for 8-round initialization and $2^{123.92}$ for 9-round initialization. Compared to the previous attack, which was limited to 7-round initialization, we have achieved an improvement of 2 rounds.

Outline. This paper is organized as follows: Sect. 2 presents some notations and definitions that will be used in this paper. The specification and some properties of Ascon are illustrated in Sect. 3. Section 4 introduces our key recovery in the misuse-free setting. The key recovery in the misused setting is shown in Sect. 5. Section 6 concludes the paper. The source codes and some results used in this paper are provided at https://github.com/keyrecoveryofascon/keyrecoveryofascon.

2 Preliminaries

Notations. Let $\mathbb{F}_2$ denote the finite field with two elements, while $\mathbb{F}_2^n$ denotes the vector space of dimension n over $\mathbb{F}_2$. We use bold italic lowercase letters to represent bit vectors. Given two vectors $\boldsymbol{u} = (u_0, u_1, \cdots, u_{n-1}), \boldsymbol{v} = (v_0, v_1, \cdots, v_{n-1}) \in \mathbb{F}_2^n$,

Table 1. Summary of key recovery attacks on Ascon AEAD. In the "Attack Type" column, "NR" denotes nonce-respecting attacks, while "NM" indicates nonce is misused. The "Var." column lists the Ascon variants, including Ascon-128, Ascon-128a, and Ascon-80pq. In the "Method" column, "Con." stands for conditional, "DL" refers to differential-linear, and "HDL" denotes higher-order differential-linear. The symbol † represents "weak-key space". "Valid.D" indicates whether the data complexity exceeds 2^{64}.

Attack Type	Phase	Var.	#R	Data/Time	Method	Valid.D	Source
NR key-recovery	Init.	all	4/12	$2^{18}/2^{18}$	DL	✓	[10]
		all	5/12	$2^{36}/2^{36}$	DL	✓	[10]
		all	5/12	$2^{35}/2^{35}$	Cube	✓	[10]
		all	5/12	$2^{26}/2^{26}$	Con.DL	✓	[21]
		all	5/12	$2^{24}/2^{36}$	Con.cube	✓	[20]
		all	5/12	$2^{22}/2^{32}$	Con.HDL	✓	[16]
		all	6/12	$2^{66}/2^{66}$	Cube	✗	[10]
		all	6/12	$2^{40}/2^{40}$	Con.cube	✓	[20]
		128(a)	7/12	$2^{77.2}/2^{77}$	Con.cube†	✗	[20]
		all	7/12	$2^{64}/2^{97}$	Cube†	✓	[23]
		all	7/12	$2^{63}/2^{115.2}$	Cube†	✓	[23]
		128(a)	7/12	$2^{72.1}/2^{72.1}$	Con.cube†	✗	[15]
		128(a)	7/12	$2^{63.32}/2^{115}$	Con.cube†	✓	[15]
		80pq	7/12	$2^{72.1}/2^{72.1}$	Con.cube†	✗	[15]
		128(a)	7/12	$2^{72.1}/2^{104.7}$	Con.cube	✗	[15]
		80pq	7/12	$2^{72.1}/2^{104.7}$	Con.cube	✗	[15]
		all	7/12	$2^{64}/2^{123}$	Cube	✓	[22]
		128(a)	7/12	$2^{64}/2^{95.96}$	Cube	✓	Section 4
NM key-recovery	Init.	all	7/12	$2^{97}/2^{97}$	Cube-like	✗	[19]
		128	8/12	$2^{101}/2^{101}$	Con.cube	✗	Section 5
		128	9/12	$2^{101}/2^{123.92}$	Con.cube	✗	Section 5

$\boldsymbol{u} \preccurlyeq \boldsymbol{v}$(resp. $\boldsymbol{u} \succcurlyeq \boldsymbol{v}$) stands for $u_i \leq v_i$ (resp. $u_i \geq v_i$), $\forall i \in \{0, \ldots, n-1\}$. The Hamming weight of vector $\boldsymbol{x} = (x_0, x_1, \cdots, x_{n-1})$, considered in $\mathbb{Z}$, is denoted as $wt(\boldsymbol{x})$, which is equal $\sum_{i=0}^{n-1} x_i$. We use "+" to denote all kinds of additions (of integers, field elements, Boolean functions, etc.). The actual meaning of a specific use instance should be clear from the context. Let I be a set, the complementary set of I is denoted $\bar{I}$. we use $|I|$ to represent the size of I. All elements in I but not in J are denoted by $I - J$. Given a set $I \subseteq \{0, \ldots, n-1\}$ of indexes, $\boldsymbol{x}[I]$ denotes the set of variables $\{x_i : i \in I\}$ and $\boldsymbol{x}^I$ denotes the monomial $\prod_{i \in I} x_i$. Let $f : \mathbb{F}_2^n \to \mathbb{F}_2$ with Algebraic Normal Form

$$f(\boldsymbol{x}) = \sum_{\boldsymbol{u} \in \mathbb{F}_2^n} \alpha_{\boldsymbol{u}} \boldsymbol{x}^{\boldsymbol{u}},$$

where $\boldsymbol{x} = (x_0, x_1, \ldots, x_{n-1})$, $\alpha_{\boldsymbol{u}} \in \mathbb{F}_2$ and $\boldsymbol{x}^{\boldsymbol{u}} = \prod_{i=0}^{n-1} x_i^{u_i}$, the coefficient of the monomial $\boldsymbol{x}^{\boldsymbol{u}}$ in f is denoted by $\alpha_{\boldsymbol{u}} = \mathrm{Coe}_f(\boldsymbol{x}^{\boldsymbol{u}})$.

Lemma 1 ([5,6]). *Given an oracle access to the Boolean function f, the coefficient of the monomial $\boldsymbol{x}^{\boldsymbol{u}}$ in f for a particular $\boldsymbol{u}$ can be computed as $Coe_f(\boldsymbol{x}^{\boldsymbol{u}}) = \sum_{\boldsymbol{x} \preccurlyeq \boldsymbol{u}} f(\boldsymbol{x})$ with $2^{wt(\boldsymbol{u})}$ evaluations of f.*

Lemma 2 ([5,6]). *The set of all coefficients $\{\alpha_{\boldsymbol{u}} = \sum_{\boldsymbol{x} \preccurlyeq \boldsymbol{u}} f(\boldsymbol{x}) : \boldsymbol{u} \in \mathbb{F}_2^n\}$ of the ANF can be obtained from the truth table of f with so-called fast Möbius transform with about $n2^n$ XOR operations.*

Keyed Boolean Functions. It is often necessary to distinguish controllable public variables from inaccessible secret variables. We denote public variables $\boldsymbol{x}$, and secret variables $\boldsymbol{k}$. With such a distinction, when a Boolean function depends on n public variables and m key variables, we look at it as

$$f(\boldsymbol{x}, \boldsymbol{k}) = \sum_{\boldsymbol{u} \in \mathbb{F}_2^n} \alpha_{\boldsymbol{u}}(\boldsymbol{k}) \boldsymbol{x}^{\boldsymbol{u}}, \tag{1}$$

where $\boldsymbol{x} \in \mathbb{F}_2^n$, $\boldsymbol{k} \in \mathbb{F}_2^m$. To distinguish from the Boolean function without secret variables, we also denote the keyed Boolean functions as $f_{\boldsymbol{k}}(\boldsymbol{x})$. When referring to the degree of a keyed Boolean function, we mean the degree in public variables: $\deg(f) := \max\{\mathbf{wt}(\boldsymbol{u}), \alpha_{\boldsymbol{u}} \neq 0\}$. In Eq. 1, the coefficient $\mathrm{Coe}_{f_k}(\boldsymbol{x}^{\boldsymbol{u}})$ actually is a Boolean function from $\mathbb{F}_2^m \to \mathbb{F}_2$ which maps $\boldsymbol{k}$ to $\alpha_{\boldsymbol{u}}(\boldsymbol{k})$.

Lemma 3 ([22]). *For the Boolean function shown in Eq. 1, it takes $2^{m+wt(\boldsymbol{u})}$ evaluations of f_k to recover $Coe_{f_k}(\boldsymbol{x}^{\boldsymbol{u}})$ for a certain u where $wt(\boldsymbol{u}) > log_2(m)$.*

Proof. According to Lemma 1, for any keyed Boolean function f_k and any given key, the value of $\mathrm{Coe}_f(\boldsymbol{x}^{\boldsymbol{u}})$ for all possible $\boldsymbol{k} \in \mathbb{F}_2^m$ can be obtained with $2^{m+wt(\boldsymbol{u})}$ evaluations of f. Then, applying Lemma 2, the ANF of the $\mathrm{Coe}_f(\boldsymbol{x}^{\boldsymbol{u}})$in $\boldsymbol{k}$ can be derived with about $m2^m = 2^{m+log_2(m)}$ XOR operations. If $wt(\boldsymbol{u}) > log_2(m)$, $2^{m+log_2(m)}$ XOR operations can be ignored.

Cube Attack. The cube attack was proposed at EUROCRYPT 2009 by Dinur and Shamir to analyze black-box tweakable polynomials [9]. For a set $I \subseteq \{0, \ldots, n-1\}$ with its complementary set $\bar{I} = \{0, \ldots, n-1\} - I$, the above keyed Boolean function can be represented as

$$f(\boldsymbol{x}, \boldsymbol{k}) = \boldsymbol{x}^I \cdot p_I(\boldsymbol{x}[\bar{I}], \boldsymbol{k}) + q(\boldsymbol{x}, \boldsymbol{k}),$$

where each term of $q(\boldsymbol{x}, \boldsymbol{k})$ misses some variables in $\boldsymbol{x}[I]$. We call $\boldsymbol{x}^I$ the cube term and $p_I(\boldsymbol{x}[\bar{I}], \boldsymbol{k})$ the superpoly of $\boldsymbol{x}^I$ in $f(\boldsymbol{x}, \boldsymbol{k})$. If we set the variables in $\boldsymbol{x}[\bar{I}]$ to some fixed constants, the superpoly $p_I(\boldsymbol{x}[\bar{I}], \boldsymbol{k})$ is a Boolean function of $\boldsymbol{k}$. Concerning the superpoly, we have the following lemma.

Lemma 4 ([9]). *For a set $I \subseteq \{0, \ldots, n-1\}$ and a keyed Boolean function*

$$f(\boldsymbol{x}, \boldsymbol{k}) = \sum_{\boldsymbol{u} \in \mathbb{F}_2^n} a_{\boldsymbol{u}}(\boldsymbol{k}) \boldsymbol{x}^{\boldsymbol{u}} = \boldsymbol{x}^I \cdot p_I(\boldsymbol{x}[\bar{I}], \boldsymbol{k}) + q(\boldsymbol{x}, \boldsymbol{k}),$$

we have $p_I(\boldsymbol{x}[\bar{I}], \boldsymbol{k}) = \sum_{\boldsymbol{x}[I] \in \mathbb{F}_2^{|I|}} f(\boldsymbol{x}, \boldsymbol{k})$.

In Lemma 4, if $I = \{0, 1, \cdots, n-1\}$, then the superpoly of $\boldsymbol{x}^I$ in $f(\boldsymbol{x}, \boldsymbol{k})$ equals to $\mathrm{Coe}_f(\boldsymbol{x}^I)$.

Division Property. Recovering the superpoly of $\boldsymbol{x}^I$ is challenging when the expressions of the $f_{\boldsymbol{k}}$ are complex and not readily available. Luckily, division properties proposed by Todo [24] have evolved into an effective and accurate method of probing the structure of Boolean functions. Its bit-based variants [26] together with their automatic search methods [29] have been found to have a great potential in accurately determining whether a monomial appears or disappears in an ANF that is not directly accessible [13,25,27,28]. In particular, bit-based division property can detect the presence or absence of a monomial in the target Boolean function, and therefore can be used to (partially) determine the algebraic structures of superpolies in cube attacks [13,14,17,25,27,28]. In fact, the division property has become a quite standard tool in assisting cube attacks. In this work, we adopt the Mixed Integer Linear Programming (MILP) approach to model the three-subset bit-based division property without unknown subset(3BDPwoU) [13], aiding in the recovery of the superpoly. A permutation can be decomposed into a sequence of basic operations, such as XOR, AND, and COPY. Therefore, it is sufficient to provide propagation rules of the 3BDPwoU for these basic operations. The concrete propagation rules and models of the 3BDPwoU are provided in Appendix A.

3 Ascon Specification and Useful Properties

At a high level, the Ascon AEAD algorithm takes as input a nonce N, a secret key K, an associated data A and a plaintext or message M, and produces a ciphertext C and a tag T. The authenticity of the associated data and message can be verified against the tag T. The Ascon AEAD adopts a MonkeyDuplex [4] mode with a stronger keyed initialization and keyed finalization phases as illustrated in Fig. 1. The Ascon AEAD family consists of three members, Ascon-128, Ascon-128a, and Ascon-80pq. All three variants have 128-bit nonce and Ascon-80pq takes half of the IV positions to allow 32 more key bits. The rates of the Ascon-128 and Ascon-80pq are 64 bits while 128 bits for Ascon-128a. The parameters are summarized in Table 2 and all three variants provide 128-bit security. The core components of all variants are the two 320-bit permutations p^a and p^b, with the permutation p of a and b rounds, respectively.

Table 2. Ascon-AEAD variants and their recommended parameters

Name	State size	Rate r	Size of			Rounds		IV
			Key	Nonce	Tag	p^a	p^b	
ASCON-128	320	64	128	128	128	12	6	80400c0600000000
AsCON-128a	320	128	128	128	128	12	8	80800c0800000000
ASCON-80pq	320	64	160	128	128	12	6	a0400c06

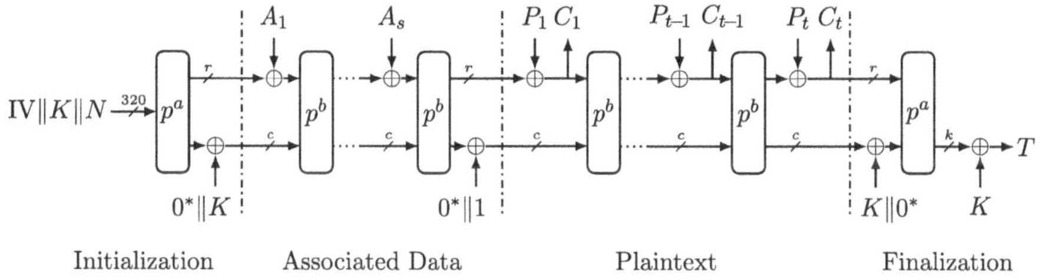

Fig. 1. Ascon AEAD encryption.

The permutation p is defined as the composition of a constant addition, a non-linear substitution layer, and a linear diffusion layer: $p = p_l \circ p_s \circ p_c$. The permutation operates on a 320-bit state, which is typically decomposed into five rows(Each row is a 64-bit word). The input state to the round function at r-th round is denoted by $X_0^r||X_1^r||X_2^r||X_3^r||X_4^r$ while the output state after p_s is given by $Y_0^r||Y_1^r||Y_2^r||Y_3^r||Y_4^r$. A bit of these words is denoted by $[\cdot]$ and X^r, Y^r refer to the full state. We denote $X_i^r[j]$ as the j-th (column) bit of the i-th (row) 64-bit word, where $0 \leq i \leq 4$ and $0 \leq j \leq 63$. Alternatively, $X_i^r[j]$ is also denoted as $X^r[64 * i + j]$. The state is constructed as a Substitution Permutation Network (SPN), as illustrated in Fig. 2. These operations in p are described as follows.

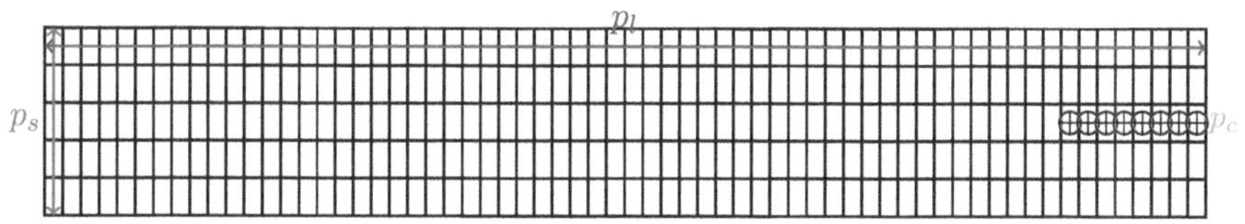

Fig. 2. The column-wise S-box layer, the row-wise linear layer and the constant addition.

Addition of Constants (p_c). The constant addition step consists in XORing an 8-bit constant to the positions $56, \cdots, 63$ of the 64-bit word X_2 at each round.

Substitution Layer (p_s). The substitution layer is made of 64 parallel calls to a single Substitution box (Sbox) on each state column. The Sbox used in Ascon is a quadratic 5-bit permutation. Equation 2 presents the ANFs of the Sbox in Ascon.

$$\begin{aligned}
Y_0[j] &= X_4[j]X_1[j] + X_3[j] + X_2[j]X_1[j] + X_2[j] + X_1[j]X_0[j] + X_1[j] + X_0[j]\\
Y_1[j] &= X_4[j] + X_3[j]X_2[j] + X_3[j]X_1[j] + X_3[j] + X_2[j]X_1[j] + X_2[j] + X_1[j] + X_0[j]\\
Y_2[j] &= X_4[j]X_3[j] + X_4[j] + X_2[j] + X_1[j] + 1\\
Y_3[j] &= X_4[j]X_0[j] + X_4[j] + X_3[j]X_0[j] + X_3[j] + X_2[j] + X_1[j] + X_0[j]\\
Y_4[j] &= X_4[j]X_1[j] + X_4[j] + X_3[j] + X_1[j]X_0[j] + X_1[j]
\end{aligned} \tag{2}$$

Linear Diffusion Layer(p_l). The linear diffusion layer is made of five calls to five different linear functions on each row of the state, as illustrated in Eq. 3.

$$
\begin{aligned}
X_0 &\leftarrow \sum_0(Y0) = Y_0 + (Y_0 >>> 19) + (Y_0 >>> 28) \\
X_1 &\leftarrow \sum_0(Y1) = Y_1 + (Y_1 >>> 61) + (Y_1 >>> 39) \\
X_2 &\leftarrow \sum_0(Y2) = Y_2 + (Y_2 >>> 1) + (Y_2 >>> 6) \\
X_3 &\leftarrow \sum_0(Y3) = Y_3 + (Y_3 >>> 10) + (Y_3 >>> 17) \\
X_4 &\leftarrow \sum_0(Y4) = Y_4 + (Y_4 >>> 7) + (Y_4 >>> 41)
\end{aligned}
\tag{3}
$$

This paper focuses on cube attack for Ascon-128. Based on the ANFs of the Ascon Sbox, several useful properties can be derived, which are commonly used in the cube attack of Ascon-128. In the following, we introduce some properties of Ascon-128 that will be used in our attack. Note that only the nonce X_3^0 and X_4^0 can be viewed as public variables in Ascon-128. We refer to the variables of X_3^0 and X_4^0 when discussing the degree.

Property 1. Among the 5 output bits of the Sbox, $X_4[j]$ never multiplies with $X_2[j]$.

Property 2. For $r \in \{0, \cdots, 7\}$, the degree of $X_i^r[j]$ is at most 2^r.

Property 3. If only one of the words X_3^0 and X_4^0 is treated as public variables, with the other set as constant, the degree of $X_i^r[j]$ is at most 2^{r-1}.

Property 1, 2 and 3 can be easily deduced from the quadratic Sbox in Ascon. To reduce the degree of $X_i^r[j]$, a condition can be imposed on the public variables, namely *Conditional Cube* [18]. In [22], the authors provided a condition that X_3^0 equals X_4^0 for Ascon-128. They then modelled the 3BDPwoU for the initialization phase of Ascon-128 using MILP to compute upper bounds on the degree of $X_i^r[j]$. We present their 7-round results in the following property.

Property 4 (Adapted form [22]). Under the condition that the public variables X_3^0 and X_4^0 are equal, the algebraic degrees of $X_0^7[j], X_1^7[j], \cdots, X_4^7[j]$ where $j \in \{0, \cdots, 63\}$ are 59, 59, 60, 60, and 58, respectively.

The concept *Borderline cube* whose superpoly depends only on a (relatively) small number of key bits is proposed in [8]. When the cube variables are not multiplied together in the first round, and the degree of $X_i^r[j]$ is 2^{r-1}, if a secret variable k_i is not multiplied with the cube variables in the first round, then the superpoly of a 2^{r-1} dimensional cube in $X_i^r[j]$ will be independent of k_i. According to the Property 1 and Property 3, a borderline cube can be constructed when only X_4^0 is regarded as cube variables, which was observed in [10]. We write their observations as the following Lemma.

Lemma 5 (Adapted from [10]). *If only X_4^0 can be regarded as public variables denoted $x_i (i \in 0, 1, \cdots, 63)$, for $1 \leq r \leq 7$ and $I = \{i_0, i_1, \ldots, i_{2^{r-1}-1}\} \subseteq \{0, 1, \ldots, 63\}$, the coefficient of the monomial $\boldsymbol{x}^I = \prod_{i \in I} x_i$ in $X_i^{(r)}[j]$ for $i \in \{0, \cdots, 4\}$ and $j \in \{0, \cdots, 63\}$ can be fully determined by the 2^{r-1} key bits in $\{k_{i_0}, \cdots, k_{i_{2^{r-1}-1}}\}$.*

4 Our Key Recovery Attack in the Misuse-Free Setting

In this section, we present our key recovery attack of 7-round initialization on Ascon-128 adhering to the security claims made by the designers(the nonce respective setting and the data complexity does not exceed 2^{64}). Our attack mode is illustrated in Fig. 3, employing a cube attack technique. The value in the first row of X_0^7 can be obtained by calculating $P_1 + C_1$. According to the inverse of the linear layer in Ascon, we can compute the value of Y_0^6 (the first row in the state after 7-round Sbox operation.) by X_0^7. Initially, we recover the superpolies of chosen cube in $Y_0^6[j]$, for $0 \leq j \leq 63$. The values of these superpolies can be evaluated through several calls to the 7-round initialization process. Subsequently, the recovered superpolies enable us to deduce crucial key information.

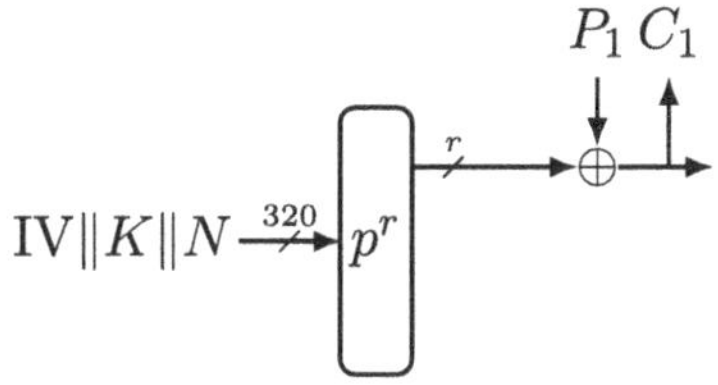

Fig. 3. Our attack mode.

4.1 Previous Work in [22]

In [22], the authors provided the first valid key recovery attack(which follows Ascon's security claims) on the 7-round initialization. In their work, they proposed a useful technique called *partial polynomial multiplication*, which enables the recovery of the superpoly of a given cube by multiplying the simplified versions of the involved Boolean functions.

More precisely, for a keyed Boolean function $f(\boldsymbol{x}, \boldsymbol{k}) = \sum_{u \in \mathbb{F}_2^n} \alpha_u(\boldsymbol{k}) \boldsymbol{x}^u$ where $\boldsymbol{x} \in \mathbb{F}_2^n$ and $\boldsymbol{k} \in \mathbb{F}_2^m$, if it can be expressed in the following form

$$f(\boldsymbol{x}, \boldsymbol{k}) = \varepsilon(\boldsymbol{x}, \boldsymbol{k}) + \sum_{t=0}^{l-1} p^{(t)}(\boldsymbol{x}, \boldsymbol{k}) q^{(t)}(\boldsymbol{x}, \boldsymbol{k})$$

such that $\deg(p^{(t)}) \leq n/2$, $\deg(q^{(t)}) \leq n/2$ and $\deg(\varepsilon) < n$ (here, We emphasize that $\deg(f)$ refers to the algebraic degree in $\boldsymbol{x}$) where n is even, then for $I = \{0, \cdots, n-1\}$

$$Coe_f(\boldsymbol{x}^I) = Coe_{\sum_{t=0}^{l-1} p^{(t)}q^{(t)}}(\boldsymbol{x}^I) = \sum_{t=0}^{l-1} Coe_{p^{(t)}q^{(t)}}(\boldsymbol{x}^I)$$

.

Since the degrees of $p^{(t)}$ and $q^{(t)}$ are no greater than $n/2$, only the degree-$n/2$ monomials in $p^{(t)}$ multiplying with the degree-$n/2$ monomials in $q^{(t)}$ might contribute to the coefficient of the monomial $\boldsymbol{x}^I$. Therefore, We only need to care the coefficients of degree-$n/2$ monomials in both $p^{(t)}$ and $q^{(t)}$ when computing the coefficient of $\boldsymbol{x}^I$, as shown in the following,

$$Coe_{p^{(t)}q^{(t)}}(\boldsymbol{x}^I) = \sum_{J \subsetneq I, |J|=n/2} Coe_{p(t)}(\boldsymbol{x}^J) Coe_{q(t)}(\boldsymbol{x}^{I-J})$$

The authors in [22] applied this technique to the key recovery of 7-round Ascon initialization, successfully recovering the superpoly of a 64-dimensional cube by multiplying the coefficients of degree-32 monomials in the bits of 6-th round state($X_i^r[j]$). With an overall time complexity of approximately 2^{123} calls for 7-round Ascon permutations, they successfully recovered the superpoly. In their work, the process of computing the ANFs of $X_i^6[j]$ dominates the overall time complexity of superpoly recovery, which requires approximately 2^{123} calls of 7-round Ascon permutation.

In this paper, we extend the *partial polynomial multiplication* technique proposed in [22] to a more general case and apply it to the superpoly recovery of the 7-round Ascon-128 initialization. Specifically, to recover the superpoly of a 64-dimensional cube, we compute it by multiplying the coefficients of monomials of an earlier round state (in our case, the 5-th round state, rather than the 6-th round state). Compared to the computation of the ANFs of $X_i^6[j]$, evaluating the ANFs of $X_i^5[j]$ is significantly faster. Another challenge addressed in this work is the increased frequency of multiplying the coefficients of two monomials. To mitigate this, instead of expanding the product into a polynomial in terms of $\boldsymbol{k}$, we exploit its product form, which reduces the overall computational time.

4.2 Our Superpoly Recovery (Offline Phase)

In the above, we briefly describe the *partial polynomial multiplication* proposed in [22]. Actually, the partial polynomial multiplication can be extended to a more general case. For a keyed Boolean function $f(\boldsymbol{x}, \boldsymbol{k}) = \sum_{\boldsymbol{u} \in \mathbb{F}_2^n} \alpha_{\boldsymbol{u}}(\boldsymbol{k}) \boldsymbol{x}^{\boldsymbol{u}}$ where $\boldsymbol{x} \in \mathbb{F}_2^n$ and $\boldsymbol{k} \in \mathbb{F}_2^m$, if it can be represented as the following form

$$f(\boldsymbol{x}, \boldsymbol{k}) = \varepsilon(\boldsymbol{x}, \boldsymbol{k}) + \sum_{t=0}^{l-1} (\prod_{s=0}^{i-1} p_{(s)}^{(t)}(\boldsymbol{x}, \boldsymbol{k})) \quad (4)$$

such that $\deg(p_{(s)}^{(t)}) \leq n/i$, and $\deg(\varepsilon) < n$ where n is divisible by i. This representation of $f(\boldsymbol{x}, \boldsymbol{k})$ contains l monomials of $p(\boldsymbol{x}, \boldsymbol{k})$, i.e., the product of i polynomials $p(\boldsymbol{x}, \boldsymbol{k})$. Then for $I = \{0, \cdots, n-1\}$

$$Coe_f(\boldsymbol{x}^I) = Coe_{\sum_{t=0}^{l-1}(\prod_{s=0}^{i-1} p_{(s)}^{(t)})}(\boldsymbol{x}^I) = \sum_{t=0}^{l-1} Coe_{\prod_{s=0}^{i-1} p_{(s)}^{(t)}}(\boldsymbol{x}^I) \quad (5)$$

Similarly, in $p(\boldsymbol{x},\boldsymbol{k})$, only the coefficient of degree-(n/i) monomial can contribute to $\mathrm{Coe}_f(\boldsymbol{x}^I)$. Thus, we can only focus on the coefficient of degree-(n/i) monomials in each $p(\boldsymbol{x},\boldsymbol{k})$.

An R-round Ascon $f(\boldsymbol{x},\boldsymbol{k})$ can be further decomposed into a composition of simple vectorial Boolean functions as follows,

$$f(\boldsymbol{x},\boldsymbol{k}) = f^{(R-1)} \circ f^{(R-2)} \circ \cdots f^{(0)}(\boldsymbol{x},\boldsymbol{k}),$$

where quadratic round function $f^{(r)} : \mathbb{F}_2^n \to \mathbb{F}_2^n$ $(0 \le r \le R-1)$. In the condition of $R \le 7$, if we choose a proper number r_0, where $r_0 \in \{0,\cdots,R-1\}$, $f(\boldsymbol{x},\boldsymbol{k})$ can be represented the sum of monomials of X^{r_0}, which is the form as Eq. 4, where now $p(\boldsymbol{x},\boldsymbol{k})$ is a bit of X^{r_0} and $i = 2^{R-r_0}$. Thus, the coefficient of $\boldsymbol{x}^I$ in $f(\boldsymbol{x},\boldsymbol{k})$ can be computed by Eq. 5.

In our superpoly recovery process for Ascon-128, we set $r_0 = 5$ and i will be 4. Consequently, the state Y_0^6 can be expressed as a polynomial composed of monomials of X^5. Known the representation of $f(\boldsymbol{x},\boldsymbol{k})$ as Eq. 4, the superpoly recovery process can be divided into two parts: (1) compute the ANFs of all bits in X^5 with respect to variables $\boldsymbol{x}$ and $\boldsymbol{k}$, and (2) compute the superpoly according Eq. 5.

The superpoly recovery process is performed entirely offline and needs to be done only once for all (secret key). For sake of clarity, we take the first bit of Y_0^6 as an example to demonstrate how we recover the superpoly of $\boldsymbol{x}^I$ in $Y_0^6[0]$.

Choose Cube. According to Lemma 5, when all bits of X_3^0 are set to 0 and all bits of X_4^0 are treated as cube variables, the superpoly corresponding to this cube in 7the -th round depends solely on the 64 bits secret key, namely X_1^0. In this configuration, the word X_4^0 is viewed as cube variables denoted as $x_0, x_1, \cdots, x_{63}$, while X_1^0 and X_2^0 represent secret variables, denoted as $k_0, k_1, \cdots, k_{127}$ (with only $k_0, k_1, \cdots, k_{63}$ are involved in the superpoly). We specifically chose this 64-dimensional borderline cube for the superpoly recovery because a smaller number of variables simplifies both the superpoly and key recovery processes. Consequently, in our superpoly recovery, the cube set $\boldsymbol{x}[I]$ we choose is $\{x_0, x_1, \cdots, x_{63}\}$.

Compute all Monomials of $X_i^5[j]$ Containing $\boldsymbol{x}^I$ in $Y_0^6[0]$. $Y_0^6[0]$ can be expressed as a polynomial composed of monomials of X^5. According to property 3, the degree of $X_i^5[j]$ is 16 and the degree of $Y_0^6[0]$ is 64. Therefore, only the monomial of X^5 with four factors may contain $\boldsymbol{x}^I$, which will contribute to $\mathrm{Coe}_{Y_0^6[0]}(\boldsymbol{x}^I)$. Without loss of generality, we denoted the monomial of X^5 containing $\boldsymbol{x}^I$ as the following form,

$$X^5[p]X^5[q]X^5[s]X^5[t]$$

where p, q, s and t are different values in $\{0,1,\cdots,319\}$. While there are too many monomials of X^5 in the representations of $Y_0^6[0]$, we use the MILP tool and the three-subset bit-based division property without unknown subset(3BDPwoU) [13] to help us finding all monomials containing $\boldsymbol{x}^I$. The details of the MILP model rule for 3BDPwoU are shown in the Appendix A.

We first compute all monomials with four factors($X_i^5[j]$) using Gurobi [1], by solving a MILP model for the 6-th round and 7-th round (exclude the linear layer). Subsequently, for each obtained monomial, we test whether it can contain $\boldsymbol{x}^I$ by solving a MILP model for the first five rounds of Ascon.

In total, we identify 121 monomials that contribute to $\mathrm{Coe}_{Y_0^6[0]}(\boldsymbol{x}^I)$. The corresponding source code and results are available in the github repository at https://github.com/keyrecoveryofascon/keyrecoveryofascon/tree/main/forward_extension.

Step1: Compute the Coefficients of Degree-16 monomials in $X_i^5[j]$. According to Lemma 5, for a given $J = \{i_0, \cdots, i_{15}\} \subseteq I = \{0, \cdots, 63\}$, the coefficient of $\boldsymbol{x}^J$ in $X_i^5[j]$ is a Boolean function in variables $\{k_{i_0}, \cdots, k_{i_{15}}\}$, involving 15 secret key variables. The truth table for this Boolean function can be obtained after $2^{16} \times 2^{16} = 2^{32}$ evaluations of the 5-round Ascon permutation, where for each possible value of $(k_{i_0}, \cdots, k_{i_{15}}) \in \mathbb{F}_2^{16}$, we evaluate the coefficient value of $\boldsymbol{x}^J$ based on Lemma 1. Since one evaluation of the 5-round Ascon permutation gives the coefficient value of $\boldsymbol{x}^J$ in the full state $X_i^5[j]$, after $2^{16} \times 2^{16} = 2^{32}$ evaluations of the 5-round Ascon permutation, we obtain the 320 truth tables for the coefficients of $\boldsymbol{x}^J$ in $X_i^5[j]$.

By applying the fast Möbius transform to the 320 truth tables, we obtain the ANFs of $Coe_{X_i^5[j]}(\boldsymbol{x}^J)$ for $i \in \{0, \cdots 4\}$ and $j \in \{0, \cdots, 63\}$, with about $320 \times 16 \times 2^{16}$ XOR operations. In summary, the time complexity of recovering the ANF of $Coe_{X_i^5[j]}(\boldsymbol{x}^J)$ for $i \in \{0, \cdots 4\}$ and $j \in \{0, \cdots, 63\}$ is dominated by 2^{32} evaluations of the 5-round Ascon permutation. Since there are totally $\binom{64}{16} \approx 2^{48.8}$ different sets $J \subseteq I$ with $|J|=16$, it takes $2^{48.8+32} \approx 2^{80.8}$ calls to the 5-round Ascon permutation to obtain the ANFs of $Coe_{X_i^5[j]}(\boldsymbol{x}^J)$ ($i \in \{0, \cdots, 4\}$ and $j \in \{0, \cdots, 63\}$) for all possible $J \subseteq I$ with $|J| = 16$. Then we store each $Coe_{X_i^5[j]}(\boldsymbol{x}^J)$ as a 2^{16}–bit string into a hash table $\mathbb{T}_i[j]$ at address $addr(\boldsymbol{x}^J) \in \mathbb{F}_2^{64}$. Finally, we obtain 320 tables $\mathbb{T}_i[j]$ ($i \in \{0, \cdots, 4\}$ and $j \in \{0, \cdots, 63\}$), which requires about $320 \times \binom{64}{16} \times 2^{16} \approx 2^{73.12}$ bits of memory.

Step2: Compute $\mathrm{Coe}_{Y_0^6[0]}(\boldsymbol{x}^I)$. In the above, we identify 121 monomials that contribute to $\mathrm{Coe}_{Y_0^6[0]}(\boldsymbol{x}^I)$. To compute the coefficient of $\boldsymbol{x}^I$ in $Y_0^6[0]$, we need to calculate the contribution of each monomial and then sum them. Next, we outline the process for calculating the contribution of a single monomial, using $X^5[p]X^5[q]X^5[s]X^5[t]$ as an illustrative example.

1. Firstly, we compute the coefficients of all degree-32 monomials in $X^5[p]X^5[q]$ and $X^5[s]X^5[t]$. Here, we use x^L where $L \subseteq I$ and $|L| = 32$ to denote a degree-32 monomial. For $X^5[p]X^5[q]$ and $X^5[s]X^5[t]$, we use the hash tables $\mathbb{L}_{p,q}$ and $\mathbb{L}_{s,t}$ to store the coefficients of the degree-32 monomials. The coefficient of $\boldsymbol{x}^L$ in $X^5[p]X^5[q]$ (resp. $X^5[s]X^5[t]$) is stored at address $addr(x^L) \in \mathbb{F}_2^{64}$ of the hash table $\mathbb{L}_{p,q}$ (resp. $\mathbb{L}_{s,t}$).
   For clarity, we take $X^5[p]X^5[q]$ as an example to show how we compute the coefficients of all degree-32 monomials in them and $X^5[s]X^5[t]$ is similar. For a degree-16 monomial $\boldsymbol{x}^{J_1}$ in $X^5[p]$ and a degree-16 monomial $\boldsymbol{x}^{J_2}$ in $X^5[q]$, they will produce a degree-32 monomial if $|J_1 \cup J_2| = 32$. We then store the

coefficient of $\boldsymbol{x}^{J_1}$ and $\boldsymbol{x}^{J_2}$ at the address $addr(\boldsymbol{x}^{J_1 \cup J_2}) \in \mathbb{F}_2^{64}$ of the hash table $\mathbb{L}_{p,q}$. It is worth noting that instead of storing it as a polynomial in terms of $\boldsymbol{k}$, we just store the address of the coefficient of $\boldsymbol{x}^{J_1}$ and $\boldsymbol{x}^{J_2}$.
There are $\binom{64}{16}$ degree-16 monomials in $X^5[p]$. For each degree-16 monomial in $X^5[p]$, there are $\binom{48}{16}$ degree-16 monomials in $X^5[q]$ that will be multiplied with it to produce a degree-32 monomial. Thus, the time complexity is $\binom{64}{16} \times \binom{48}{16} \approx 2^{48.80+41.04} = 2^{89.84}$ memory accesses of hash table $\mathbb{L}_{p,q}$. For a degree-32 monomial, there will be $\binom{32}{16}$ terms in its coefficient. The memory complexity is $\binom{64}{32} \times \binom{32}{16} \times (64+64) \approx 2^{60.67+29.16+7} = 2^{96.83}$. Considering $X^5[s]X^5[t]$ and there are 121 monomials to be handled, the time complexity is $2^{97.76}$ and the memory complexity is $2^{104.85}$. Note that there are many duplicate items of $X^5[p]X^5[q]$ and $X^5[s]X^5[t]$ in the 121 monomials. The complexity can be reduced further, but here we omit it.

2. Then, we compute the coefficient of $\boldsymbol{x}^I$ in $X^5[i]X^5[j]X^5[s]X^5[t]$. For a degree-32 monomial in $X^5[i]X^5[j]$, only one degree-32 monomials in $X^5[s]$ $X^5[t]$ can multiply with it to produce a degree-64 monomial, namely $\boldsymbol{x}^I$. Let $\boldsymbol{x}^{L_1}$ be a degree-32 monomial in $X^5[i]X^5[j]$ and $\boldsymbol{x}^{L_2}$ be a degree-32 monomial in $X^5[s]X^5[t]$, where $|L_1 \cup L_2| = 64$. We can obtain the coefficient of x^I provided by multiplying the coefficient of $\boldsymbol{x}^{L_1}$ with the coefficient of $\boldsymbol{x}^{L_2}$. Also, we use the product form rather than expand it into a polynomial. It will cost $2 + 2\binom{32}{16}$ memory accesses (one memory access of $\mathbb{L}_{p,q}$ and $\mathbb{L}_{s,t}$, $2\binom{32}{16}$ memory accesses of $\mathbb{T}_i[j]$). There are $\binom{64}{32}$ degree-32 monomials in $X^5[i]X^5[j]$. The time complexity in this procedure is $\binom{64}{32} \times 2 \times \binom{32}{16} \approx 2^{60.67+29.16+1} = 2^{90.84}$ memory access (one memory access of $\mathbb{L}_{p,q}$ and $\mathbb{L}_{s,t}$ can be ignored). Considering 121 monomials, the time complexity is $2^{97.76}$.

If all coefficients of $\boldsymbol{x}^I$ in the 121 monomials of X^5 are computed, $\mathrm{Coe}_{Y_0^6[0]}(\boldsymbol{x}^I)$ equals the sum of them. In total, in this step, the time complexity is $2^{98.76}(2^{97.76} + 2^{97.76})$ memory accesses and the memory complexity is $2^{104.85}$ bits.

Generate the Comparison Tables for Key Candidates. With the 64 recovered superpolies $\mathrm{Coe}_{Y_0^6[0]}(\boldsymbol{x}^I), \mathrm{Coe}_{Y_0^6[1]}(\boldsymbol{x}^I), \ldots, \mathrm{Coe}_{Y_0^6[63]}(\boldsymbol{x}^I)$, we can define a vectorial Boolean function $F : \mathbb{F}_2^{64} \rightarrow \mathbb{F}_2^{64}$ mapping $(k_0, k_1, \ldots, k_{63})$ to $\left(\mathrm{Coe}_{Y_0^6[0]}(\boldsymbol{x}^I), \ldots, \mathrm{Coe}_{Y_0^6[63]}(\boldsymbol{x}^I)\right)$. Then, we store each $(k_0, k_1, \ldots, k_{63}) \in \mathbb{F}_2^{64}$ into a hash table $\mathbb{H}$ at address $F(k_0, k_1, \ldots, k_{63})$, which requires about $2^{64} \times 64 = 2^{70}$ bits of memory.

Experiment. Since the superpoly of a 64-dimensional cube in an output bit of the 7-round initialization is too large to be practically recovered, we conduct an experiment to recover the superpoly of a 32-dimensional cube in an output bit of the 6-round initialization. In our experiment, we impose the following condition on the public variable:

$$X_3^0[j] = \begin{cases} X_4^0[j] + 1 & \text{if } j = 0 \text{ or } j = 1, \\ X_4^0[j] & \text{if } j \in \{2, 3, \ldots, 63\}. \end{cases}$$

The degree of X_0^6 is 30 when $X_3^0[j] = X_4^0[j]$ for $j \in \{0, 1, \ldots, 63\}$. However, when the first two bits of $X_3^0[j]$ and $X_4^0[j]$ are not equal, the degree of X_0^6 becomes 32. It appears that the appearance of degree-32 monomials is mainly due to the first two bits of $X_3^0[j]$ and $X_4^0[j]$ are not equal. The main reason for this condition is that the superpoly of a 32-dimension cube may be sparse. The cube set we have chosen is $\{x_0, x_1, x_2, x_3, x_{36}, x_{37}, \cdots, x_{63}\}$ and the superpoly involves 64 bits secret key. While the superpoly can be recovered at a time complexity of 2^{96} evaluations according to Lemma 1, we are able to recover it within 36 h using our superpoly recovery method. The experiment was conducted on a server equipped with 36 Intel(R) Xeon(R) Gold 6240 CPU @ 2.60 GHz and 534 GB of memory. Some of the programs were run in parallel, as long as the memory is enough. The corresponding source code and the recovered superpoly are available in the GitHub repository at https://github.com/keyrecoveryofascon/keyrecoveryofascon.

4.3 Key Recovery (Online Phase)

Considering the cube set $\boldsymbol{x}[I] = (x_0, x_1, \ldots, x_{63}) \in \mathbb{F}_2^{64}$ that we have chosen, we begin by selecting a random 64-bit plaintext P and encrypt it using Ascon, obtaining the ciphertext C. The first 64-bit output after 7 rounds Ascon, namely X_0^7 is computed as $P + C$. According to the inverse of the linear layer in Ascon, Y_0^6 can be obtained from X_0^7. By summing all Y_0^6 over all $\boldsymbol{x} \in \mathbb{F}_2^{64}$, we obtain the 64-bit cube sum, denoted as $(z_0, z_1, \ldots, z_{63})$. Then the key candidates are obtained from $\mathbb{H}[(z_0, z_1, ..., z_{63})]$. Based on the assumption that the superpoly for 7-round Ascon is (almost) balanced Boolean functions, on average, only one key candidate is suggested. Such an assumption is common and also used in the previous works [20,22]. The complexity of this step is 2^{64} queries to Ascon. The remaining 64-bit key can be obtained by an exhaustive search, which requires another 2^{64} queries. The total complexity in the online phase is then 2^{65} queries for 7-round Ascon permutations.

4.4 Complexity Evaluation

Time Complexity. In our attack, the process of superpoly recovery(offline phase) dominates the main complexity. In Step 1, the time complexity is $2^{80.8}$ calls to the 5-round permutation, which can regarded as $5/7 \times 2^{80.8} = 2^{80.38}$ calls to 7-round permutation. In Step 2, the time complexity is $2^{98.76}$ memory accesses. In a conventional method, one memory access can be regarded as one Sbox operation. In this paper, we regard one memory access to a big table as one single round of Ascon permutation, considering the worst case. But our results are still a significant improvement over previous work. Thus, the time complexity of our attack $2^{98.76}/7 \approx 2^{95.96}$ calls of 7-round permutation. Following computing 64 superpolies in a parallel fashion used in [22], the total time complexity is $2^{95.96}$ calls for 7-round Ascon permutation.

Memory Complexity. In our attack, the memory complexity is dominated by the process of the superpoly recovery in Subsect. 4.2. In the superpoly recovery process, step 1 requires $2^{73.12}$ bits memory while step 2 requires a memory of $2^{104.85}$ bits. When generating the comparison tables for key candidates, the memory complexity is 2^{70} bits of memory. Therefore, the total memory complexity in our attack is around $2^{104.85}$.

Data Complexity. Since our attack utilizes only a 64-dimensional cube, it requires 2^{64} data to compute the cube sum. Consequently, the data complexity is 2^{64}, which satisfies the security claim of Ascon.

5 Our Key Recovery in the Misused Setting

In [3], Baudrin et al. proposed a conditional cube attack on Ascon-128 that is capable of recovering the full state prior to the encryption phase within a practical time. However, the extension of this attack to achieve key recovery or forgery in Ascon-128 remains an unresolved open problem. In this paper, we provide an answer of the problem by executing a key recovery attack on Ascon-128 under the condition of the full state prior to the encryption phase being recovered. Our attack is in the misused setting, specifically, the nonce will be reused, and the data exceeds 2^{64}. We first present our key recovery attack on the 8-round initialization of Ascon-128 in Subsect. 5.1. Then, in Subsect. 5.2, we introduce our key recovery attack when the initialization phase is reduced to 9 rounds.

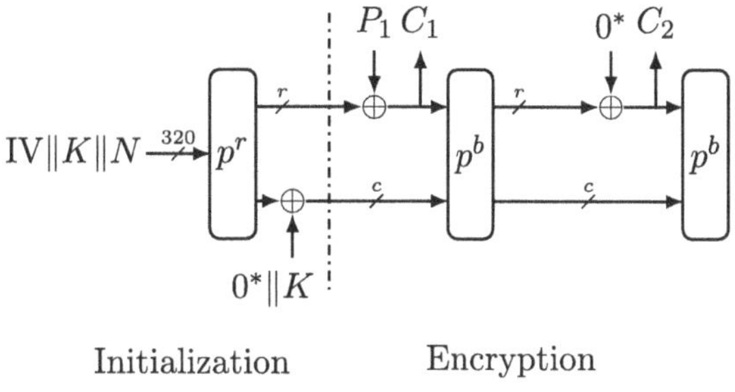

Fig. 4. Our attack mode.

5.1 Key Recovery on the 8-Round Initialization

In our attack process, we focus on both the initialization phase and the encryption phase, as illustrated in Fig. 4. We omit the associated data phase since the associated data is public and will never affect our attack results. For convenience, the state prior to the encryption phase is denoted as E. Accordingly, the bit in

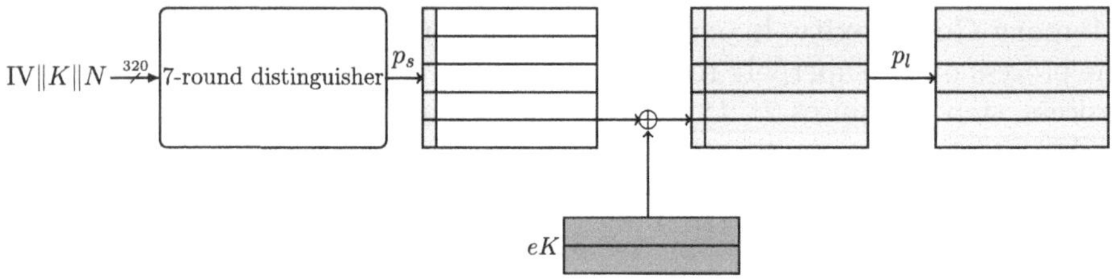

Fig. 5. Key recovery of 8-round initialization of Ascon-128.

i-th row and j-th column is $E_i[j]$. The details of our attack process on 8-round initialization are as follows.

Choose a Distinguisher for the Initialization Phase. In [22], Rohit et al., detected the degree upper bound of Ascon in the condition of $X_3^0 = X_4^0$. The 7-round results are shown in Property 4. When a cube size $|I|$ is larger than the degree upper bound ($|I| > deg(f)$) in $X_i^7[j]$, the superpoly of the monomial $\boldsymbol{x}^I$ in $X_i^7[j]$, namely $\text{Coe}_{X_i^7[j]}(\boldsymbol{x}^I)$, must be 0, which distinguishes the 7-round Ascon permutation from random. According to Property 4, we choose a 61 dimension cube in the condition of $X_3^0 = X_4^0$. Then, the value of all superpolies of the 61 dimension cube in all bits of $X_i^7[j]$ is 0. Namely, $\text{Coe}_{X_i^7[j]}(\boldsymbol{x}^I) = \sum_{\boldsymbol{x}[I]\in\mathbb{F}_2^{|I|}} f(\boldsymbol{x},\boldsymbol{k}) = 0$. This gives us a distinguisher for 7-round initialization. In this distinguisher, the number of nonces we used is 2^{61} to compute the cube sums.

Recover the State Prior to the Encryption Phase. For the 2^{61} nonces, we will recover all states prior to the encryption phase, which is denoted as E. The authors in [3] proposed a method to recover the value of E for Ascon-128 with a time complexity less than 2^{40}. To obtain the values of E for 2^{61} different nonces, we employ the method introduced in [3]. In total, we can recover all E at a time complexity less than 2^{101} calls to an 8-round permutation in the initialization phase and a 6-round permutation in the encryption phase.

Recover the Secret Key. Since the secret key is added to the 4-th and 5-th words after the initialization phase, we can guess the secret key and decrypt E to the end of the chosen distinguisher. The correctness of the guess is determined by whether the guessed key satisfies the end condition of the distinguisher.

As shown in Fig. 5, we append one additional round at the end of the distinguisher, targeting the 8-round initialization. The constant operation p_c is simple and does not affect our attack, so we omit it. Furthermore, since both the linear layer p_l and key addition are linear, we swap the order of these two operations in the final round and introduce the equivalent keys eK.

By recovering all information of eK, we can deduce the original secret key using the linear layer of the Ascon permutation. The substitution layer of the Ascon permutation consists of 64 parallel Sbox calls on each state column, allowing the equivalent key bits to be guessed separately. For example, we first guess

2 equivalent key bits in the first column to determine the input to the first Sbox in the 8-th round, i.e., $X_i^7[0]$ for $i \in \{0, \ldots, 4\}$.

For 2^{61} states E, the time complexity is 2^{63} Sbox operations. If the guessed bits are correct, the sum of 2^{61} values of $X_i^7[0]$ should be zero for $i \in \{0, \ldots, 4\}$, forming a 5-bit filtering condition. As a result, only one candidate remains for the guessed equivalent key bits. For the 64 Sboxes, this procedure requires 2^{69} Sbox operations.

Complexity. In the attack process, the state recovery dominates the complexity. Thus, the data complexity and time complexity are around 2^{101}. The memory complexity is $2^{61+8.32} = 2^{69.32}$ bits.

5.2 Key Recovery on 9-Round Initialization

In the above, we introduce our key recovery target the 8-round initialization by appending one round at the end of a 7-round distinguisher of the initialization. Actually, we can recover the secret key for the 9-round initialization at a complexity less than an exhaustive search by appending two rounds after the 7-round distinguisher. There is a challenge in that the diffusion of the inverse of p_s and p_l in Ascon is relatively fast. Equation 6 presents the ANFs of the inverse of the Sbox which can be easily obtained by SageMath [2].

$$
\begin{aligned}
X_0[j] =& Y_4[j]Y_3[j]Y_2[j] + Y_4[j]Y_3[j]Y_1[j] + Y_4[j]Y_3[j]Y_0[j] + Y_3[j]Y_2[j]Y_0[j] \\
&+ Y_3[j]Y_2[j] + Y_3[j] + Y_2[j] + Y_1[j]Y_0[j] + Y_1[j] + 1, \\
X_1[j] =& Y_4[j]Y_2[j]Y_0[j] + Y_4[j] + Y_3[j]Y_2[j] + Y_2[j]Y_0[j] + Y_1[j] + Y_0[j], \\
X_2[j] =& Y_4[j]Y_3[j]Y_1[j] + Y_4[j]Y_3[j] + Y_4[j]Y_2[j]Y_1[j] + Y_4[j]Y_2[j] \\
&+ Y_3[j]Y_1[j]Y_0[j] + Y_3[j]Y_1[j] + Y_2[j]Y_1[j]Y_0[j] + Y_2[j]Y_1[j] \\
&+ Y_2[j] + 1 + a_1, \\
X_3[j] =& Y_4[j]Y_2[j]Y_1[j] + Y_4[j]Y_2[j]Y_0[j] + Y_4[j]Y_2[j] + Y_4[j]Y_1[j] + Y_4[j] \\
&+ Y_3[j] + Y_2[j]Y_1[j] + Y_2[j]Y_0[j] + Y_1[j], \\
X_4[j] =& Y_4[j]Y_3[j]Y_2[j] + Y_4[j]Y_2[j]Y_1[j] + Y_4[j]Y_2[j]Y_0[j] + Y_4[j]Y_2[j] \\
&+ Y_3[j]Y_2[j]Y_0[j] + Y_3[j]Y_2[j] + Y_3[j] + Y_2[j]Y_1[j] + Y_2[j]Y_0[j] \\
&+ Y_1[j]Y_0[j].
\end{aligned} \tag{6}
$$

For the inverse of the linear layer, the state Y_i^{r-1}(state before the linear layer) can be regarded as $M_i \times X_i^r$, where i refers to the i-th row, $i \in \{0, 1, \cdots, 4\}$. The binary matrices M_i used in the inverse of the linear layer are 64×64 circulant matrices, which are shown in Appendix B.

Similarly to the key recovery of the 8-round case, we change the order of the last linear layer in 9-th round and the addition key operation by introducing eK. Thus, the last linear layer can be ignored, and the state before the last linear layer, denoted C, can be calculated by the linear layer of Ascon.

Firstly, we try to write out explicitly the mapping f from $C_i[j]$ to any one bit of $X^{(7)}$. Without loss of generality, here we take the bit in the first row and first column $X_0^7[0]$ as an example. Since the Boolean function of the mapping f

is too complicated, we split it into three steps, clearly indicating how each step maps to the next.

Step 1: Express $X_0^7[0]$ by Y^7. We first express $X_0^7[0]$ in a polynomial of Y^7, according to the ANF of the inverse of the Sbox.

$$\begin{aligned} X_0^7[0] = \; & Y_4^7[0]Y_3^7[0]Y_2^7[0] + Y_4^7[0]Y_3^7[0]Y_1^7[0] + Y_4^7[0]Y_3^7[0]Y_0^7[0] \\ & + Y_3^7[0]Y_2^7[0]Y_0^7[0] + Y_3^7[0]Y_2^7[0] + Y_3^7[0] \\ & + Y_2^7[0] + Y_1^7[0]Y_0^7[0] + Y_1^7[0] + 1 \end{aligned}$$

There are five bits involved in the ANF of $X_0^7[0]$. If we have known the $Y_i^7[0]$ for $0 \le i \le 4$, we can compute the value of $X_0^7[0]$.

Step 2: Express $Y_i^7[0]$ for $0 \le i \le 4$ by X^8.

$$Y_i^7[0] = M_i[0] \cdot (X_i^8[0], X_i^8[1], \ldots, X_i^8[63])^T = \textstyle\sum_{j \in I_i} X_i^8[j],$$

where I_i is a set of indices corresponding to the coefficient of $M_i[0](M_i[j]$ is the j-th row of $M_i)$. According to M_i, $Y_i^7[0]$ can be computed by the sum of 31, 33, 33, 33 and 35 bits of $X_i^8[0]$ respectively, where $i \in \{0, 1, \cdots, 4\}$.

Step 3: Express $X_i^8[j]$ for $0 \le i \le 4$ by Y^8.

According to the ANF of the inverse of Sbox, each bit of $X_i^8[j]$ can be represented by $Y^{(8)}$ easily. Here we only take $X_0^8[j]$ as an example and others are similar.

$$\begin{aligned} X_0^8[j] = \; & Y_4^8[j]Y_3^8[j]Y_2^8[j] + Y_4^8[j]Y_3^8[j]Y_1^8[j] + Y_4^8[j]Y_3^8[0]Y_0^8[j] \\ & + Y_3^8[j]Y_2^8[j]Y_0^8[j] + Y_3^8[j]Y_2^8[j] + Y_3^8[j] \\ & + Y_2^8[j] + Y_1^8[j]Y_0^8[j] + Y_1^8[j] + 1, \end{aligned}$$

In the end, an equivalent key eK is added to Y^8 at the position of 3-th and 4-th rows. Thus, we can build a relation between the Y^8 and C. Towards the first three rows of Y^8, we can directly obtain $Y_i^8[j] = C_i[j]$ where $i \in \{0, 1, 2\}$ and $j \in \{0, \cdots, 63\}$. For the 4-th row of Y^8, we can represent them by $Y_3^8[j] = C_3[j] + eK_0[j]$, where $j \in \{0, \cdots, 63\}$. For the 5-th row of Y^8, we can represent them by $Y_4^8[j] = C_4[j] + eK_1[j]$, where $j \in \{0, \cdots, 63\}$.

As a result, we can further represent $Y_i^7[0]$ for $0 \le i \le 4$ by C and eK. Here, we only take $Y_i^7[0]$ as an example and others are similar.

$$\begin{aligned}
Y_0^7[0] &= \sum_{j\in I_0} X_0^8[j] \\
&= \sum_{j\in I_0} Y_4^8[j]Y_3^8[j]Y_2^8[j] + \sum_{j\in I_0} Y_4^8[j]Y_3^8[j]Y_1^8[j] + \sum_{j\in I_0} Y_4^8[j]Y_3^8[j]Y_0^8[j] \\
&+ \sum_{j\in I_0} Y_3^8[j]Y_2^8[j]Y_0^8[j] + \sum_{j\in I_0} Y_3^8[j]Y_2^8[j] + \sum_{j\in I_0} Y_3^8[j] \\
&+ \sum_{j\in I_0} Y_2^8[j] + \sum_{j\in I_0} Y_1^8[j]Y_0^8[j] + \sum_{j\in I_0} Y_1^8[j] + 1, \qquad (7) \\
&= \sum_{j\in I_0} (C_4[j] + ek_1[j])(C_3[j] + ek_0[j])(C_2[j] + C_1[j] + C_0[j]) \\
&+ \sum_{j\in I_0} (C_3[j] + ek_1[j])C_2[j]C_0[j] + \sum_{j\in I_0} (C_3[j] + ek_1[j])C_2[j] \\
&+ \sum_{j\in I_0} (C_3[j] + ek_1[j]) + \sum_{j\in I_0} C_2[j] + \sum_{j\in I_0} C_1[j]C_0[j] + \sum_{j\in I_0} C_1[j] + 1
\end{aligned}$$

According to Eq. 7, $Y_0^7[0]$ involves $2\times|I_0|=62$ bits of eK. It is similar for $Y_i^7[0]$ where $i \in \{1,2,3,4\}$, the involved eK is 33, 33, 33 and 35 bits respectively, which are shown in Fig. 6. If we decrypt C to $X_i^7[j]$ directly, many key bits are involved which will cause the complexity increasing quickly. Fortunately, the technique, *partial sum*, can be used to reduce the complexity.

The partial-sum technique was initially introduced by Ferguson et al. in [12] to reduce the time complexity of integral attacks. In Ascon, the small Sboxes are applied separately and the output of $M_i \times X_i^r$ is a linear combination of $X_i^r[j]$. Then, the secret key bits are divided into relatively independent parts and can be guessed one after another, which will reduce the complexity. When a part of the secret key is guessed, the corresponding value obtained by decrypting C, can be compressed with the information and stored for further calculation.

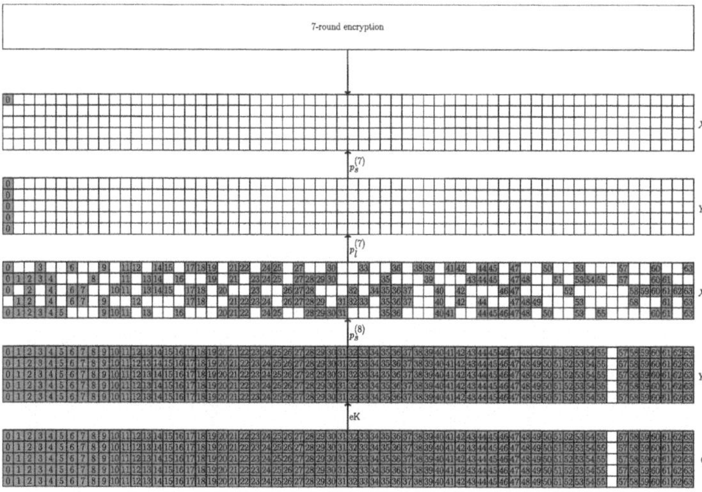

Fig. 6. Key recovery of 9-round initialization.

Guess Strategy. According to Fig. 6, we can identify only 63 columns are involved to calculate the sum of $X_0^7[0]$, which can be guessed separately. Firstly, for each 2-bit guess, decrypt through $p_s^{(8)}$ and $p_l^{(7)}$ and calculate the contribution to $Y_i^7[0]$ for $0 \leq i \leq 4$. We treat the cost of the operation at once as 2 times 5-bit Sbox computations. Since there are 2^{61} C distributed over 315 bits, the average amount of data reduced each time a 2-bit key is guessed is $2^{0.97}$. The maximum complexity of the step to guess the key of the last column is $2^{127.97}$ 5-bit Sbox computations. We then decrypt $Y_i^7[0]$ to $X_i^{(7)}[0]$ for $0 \leq i \leq 4$. Due to there are 2^{126} bit guessed equivalent key, the time complexity is $2^{(126+5)} \times 2$ 5-bit sbox computation.

The key space by a factor of 2^{-1} for the 126-bit guess. Actually, the superpolies of the 61 dimension cube in $X_i^7[0]$ for $0 \leq i \leq 4$ are all 0. The key space can be reduced by 2^{-5}. For the remaining key space, we just exhaustive search all possibilities.

Complexity. In the state recovery phase, we need recover the 2^{61} states of E, with a time complexity of less than $2^{61} \times 2^{40} = 2^{101}$, which can be omitted. In the guessing equivalent key phase, the complexity is dominated by decrypting $Y_i^7[0]$ to $X_i^{(7)}[0]$ for $0 \leq i \leq 4$, which involves around 2^{132} 5-bit Sbox computations. There are 64 5-bit Sbox computations in p_s of Ascon and we only regard a p_s operation as equivalent to one round permutation. The corresponding complexity represented by 9-round initialization is $2^{132}/(64 \times 9) \approx 2^{122.83}$. Since there are 2^{123} possibilities in the remaining key space, 2^{123} exhaustive search are needed. The total time complexity is $2^{122.83} + 2^{123} \approx 2^{123.92}$ calls for 9-rounds permutation of Ascon.

Since there are 2^{61} states to be recovered, the data complexity is 2^{101} and the memory complexity is $2^{61+8.32} = 2^{69.32}$ bits.

6 Conclusion

In this paper, we improve the key recovery attack on Ascon-128 both in misuse-free and misused settings. In a misuse-free setting, we present a faster method to recover the superpolies for a 64-dimension cube in the output bits of 7-round initialization, by which we can recover the full key with a time complexity of $2^{98.76}$ and a data complexity of 2^{64}. Additionally, we employ several techniques to extend state recovery to key recovery, answering the open question of how to transition from full state recovery in the encryption phase to key recovery for Ascon-128 (ToSc Vol 4, 2022). We achieve a 8-round and 9-round key recovery in the nonce misuse scenario, with complexities of 2^{101} and $2^{123.92}$ for Ascon-128, respectively. This represents an improvement of two rounds over previous results. We believe our attacks will be helpful in understanding the security of Ascon.

Acknowledgment. We sincerely thank the anonymous reviewers for providing valuable comments to help us improve the overall quality of the paper. This research is supported by the National Key R&D Program of China (Grant No. 2024YFA1013000), the National Natural Science Foundation of China (Grant No. 62032014, U2336207), Department of Science & Technology of Shandong Province (No. SYS202201), Quan Cheng Laboratory (Grant No. QCLZD202301, QCLZD202306). Kai Hu is also supported by the National Natural Science Foundation of China (62402283), Natural Science Foundation of Jiangsu Province (BK20240420), and Program of Qilu Young Scholars of Shandong University.

Appendix

A MILP Model for the Three-Subset Bit-Based Division Property [13]

In the following, we will give the model method of 3BDPwoU trail propagation for some basic operations.

COPY Operation. For the COPY operation, 3BDPwoU MILP model $u \to (v_1, v_2)$ can use the following constraints

$$\begin{cases} u, v_1, v_2 \text{ are binary variables} \\ u = v_1 \vee v_2 \end{cases}$$

XOR Operation. For the XOR operation, 3BDPwoU MILP model $(u_1, u_2) \to v$ can use the following constraints

$$\begin{cases} u_1, u_2, v \text{ are binary variables} \\ v = u_1 + u_2 \end{cases}$$

AND Operation. For the AND operation, 3BDPwoU MILP model $(u_1, u_2) \to v$ can use the following constraints

$$\begin{cases} u_1, u_2, v \text{ are binary variables} \\ u_1 = v, u_2 = v \end{cases}$$

For the nonlinear layer Sbox, we can model the exact vectorial Boolean functions of Sbox in each round.

B The Binary Matrices M_i

The binary matrices M_i used in the inverse of the linear layer are 64×64 circulant matrices, as follows.

$$\begin{aligned}
M_0 = \mathrm{cir}([&1,0,0,1,0,0,1,0,0,1,0,1,1,0,1,1,0,1,1,1,0,1,1,0,1,1,0,1,0,0,1,0,\\
&0,1,0,0,1,0,1,1,0,1,1,0,1,1,0,1,0,0,1,0,0,1,0,0,0,1,0,0,1,0,0,1]),\\
M_1 = \mathrm{cir}([&1,1,1,1,1,0,0,0,1,0,0,1,0,1,1,0,1,0,0,1,0,1,0,1,1,1,0,1,1,1,1,0,\\
&0,0,0,1,0,0,0,1,0,0,0,1,1,1,0,1,1,0,0,1,0,1,1,1,0,1,0,0,1,1,0,0]),\\
M_2 = \mathrm{cir}([&1,0,1,0,1,0,1,1,0,0,1,1,0,1,1,1,0,1,1,0,1,0,0,1,0,0,1,1,1,0,0,0,\\
&1,0,1,1,1,1,0,0,1,0,1,0,0,0,1,1,0,0,0,0,1,0,0,0,0,0,1,1,1,1,1,1]),\\
M_3 = \mathrm{cir}([&0,1,1,0,1,0,1,1,0,1,0,0,1,0,0,0,0,1,1,0,0,1,1,1,1,0,1,1,1,1,0,1,\\
&1,1,0,1,1,1,0,0,1,0,1,0,1,0,0,1,1,1,0,0,0,1,0,0,0,0,1,0,0,1,0,1]),\\
M_4 = \mathrm{cir}([&1,1,1,1,1,1,0,0,0,1,1,1,0,1,0,0,1,0,0,0,1,1,1,0,1,1,0,0,1,1,1,1,\\
&0,0,0,1,1,0,0,0,1,1,0,0,1,1,1,1,1,0,1,0,0,1,0,1,0,0,0,0,1,1,0,1]).
\end{aligned}$$

References

1. Gurobi optimization. https://www.gurobi.com
2. Sagemath. https://www.sagemath.org/
3. Baudrin, J., Canteaut, A., Perrin, L.: Practical cube attack against nonce-misused ascon. IACR Trans. Symmetric Cryptol. 2022(4), 120–144 (2022). https://doi.org/10.46586/TOSC.V2022.I4.120-144
4. Bertoni, G., Daemen, J., Peeters, M., Van Assche, G.: Permutation-based encryption, authentication and authenticated encryption. In: Directions in Authenticated Ciphers, pp. 159–170 (2012)
5. Canteaut, A.: Lecture notes on cryptographic boolean functions. Inria, Paris, France **3** (2016)
6. Carlet, C., Crama, Y., Hammer, P.L.: Boolean functions for cryptography and error-correcting codes (2010)
7. Chang, D., Hong, D., Kang, J., Turan, M.S.: Resistance of ascon family against conditional cube attacks in nonce-misuse setting. IEEE Access **11**, 4501–4516 (2023). https://doi.org/10.1109/ACCESS.2022.3223991
8. Dinur, I., Morawiecki, P., Pieprzyk, J., Srebrny, M., Straus, M.: Cube attacks and cube-attack-like cryptanalysis on the round-reduced Keccak sponge function. In: Oswald, E., Fischlin, M. (eds.) EUROCRYPT 2015. LNCS, vol. 9056, pp. 733–761. Springer, Heidelberg (2015). https://doi.org/10.1007/978-3-662-46800-5_28
9. Dinur, I., Shamir, A.: Cube attacks on tweakable black box polynomials. In: Joux, A. (ed.) EUROCRYPT 2009. LNCS, vol. 5479, pp. 278–299. Springer, Heidelberg (2009). https://doi.org/10.1007/978-3-642-01001-9_16
10. Dobraunig, C., Eichlseder, M., Mendel, F., Schläffer, M.: Cryptanalysis of Ascon. In: Nyberg, K. (ed.) CT-RSA 2015. LNCS, vol. 9048, pp. 371–387. Springer, Cham (2015). https://doi.org/10.1007/978-3-319-16715-2_20
11. Dobraunig, C., Eichlseder, M., Mendel, F., Schläffer, M.: Ascon v1.2: lightweight authenticated encryption and hashing. J. Cryptol. **34**(3), 33 (2021). https://doi.org/10.1007/S00145-021-09398-9
12. Ferguson, N., et al.: Improved cryptanalysis of Rijndael. In: Goos, G., Hartmanis, J., van Leeuwen, J., Schneier, B. (eds.) FSE 2000. LNCS, vol. 1978, pp. 213–230. Springer, Heidelberg (2001). https://doi.org/10.1007/3-540-44706-7_15

13. Hao, Y., Leander, G., Meier, W., Todo, Y., Wang, Q.: Modeling for three-subset division property without unknown subset. In: Canteaut, A., Ishai, Y. (eds.) EUROCRYPT 2020. LNCS, vol. 12105, pp. 466–495. Springer, Cham (2020). https://doi.org/10.1007/978-3-030-45721-1_17
14. Hebborn, P., Lambin, B., Leander, G., Todo, Y.: Lower bounds on the degree of block ciphers. In: Moriai, S., Wang, H. (eds.) ASIACRYPT 2020, Part I. LNCS, vol. 12491, pp. 537–566. Springer, Cham (2020). https://doi.org/10.1007/978-3-030-64837-4_18
15. Hu, K.: Improved conditional cube attacks on ascon AEADs in nonce-respecting settings - with a break-fix strategy. IACR Cryptol. ePrint Arch. 743 (2024). https://eprint.iacr.org/2024/743
16. Hu, K., Peyrin, T., Tan, Q.Q., Yap, T.: Revisiting higher-order differential-linear attacks from an algebraic perspective. In: Guo, J., Steinfeld, R. (eds.) ASIACRYPT 2023, Part III. LNCS, vol. 14440, pp. 405–435. Springer, Cham (2023). https://doi.org/10.1007/978-981-99-8727-6_14
17. Hu, K., Sun, S., Wang, M., Wang, Q.: An algebraic formulation of the division property: revisiting degree evaluations, cube attacks, and key-independent sums. In: Moriai, S., Wang, H. (eds.) ASIACRYPT 2020. LNCS, vol. 12491, pp. 446–476. Springer, Cham (2020). https://doi.org/10.1007/978-3-030-64837-4_15
18. Huang, S., Wang, X., Xu, G., Wang, M., Zhao, J.: Conditional cube attack on reduced-round Keccak sponge function. In: Coron, J.-S., Nielsen, J.B. (eds.) EUROCRYPT 2017. LNCS, vol. 10211, pp. 259–288. Springer, Cham (2017). https://doi.org/10.1007/978-3-319-56614-6_9
19. Li, Y., Zhang, G., Wang, W., Wang, M.: Cryptanalysis of round-reduced ASCON. Sci. China Inf. Sci. **60**(3), 38102 (2017). https://doi.org/10.1007/S11432-016-0283-3
20. Li, Z., Dong, X., Wang, X.: Conditional cube attack on round-reduced ASCON. IACR Trans. Symmetric Cryptol. **2017**(1), 175–202 (2017). https://doi.org/10.13154/TOSC.V2017.I1.175-202
21. Liu, M., Lu, X., Lin, D.: Differential-linear cryptanalysis from an algebraic perspective. In: Malkin, T., Peikert, C. (eds.) CRYPTO 2021. LNCS, vol. 12827, pp. 247–277. Springer, Cham (2021). https://doi.org/10.1007/978-3-030-84252-9_9
22. Rohit, R., Hu, K., Sarkar, S., Sun, S.: Misuse-free key-recovery and distinguishing attacks on 7-round ascon. IACR Trans. Symmetric Cryptol. **2021**(1), 130–155 (2021). https://doi.org/10.46586/TOSC.V2021.I1.130-155
23. Rohit, R., Sarkar, S.: Diving deep into the weak keys of round reduced ascon. IACR Trans. Symmetric Cryptol. **2021**(4), 74–99 (2021). https://doi.org/10.46586/TOSC.V2021.I4.74-99
24. Todo, Y.: Structural evaluation by generalized integral property. In: Oswald, E., Fischlin, M. (eds.) EUROCRYPT 2015. LNCS, vol. 9056, pp. 287–314. Springer, Heidelberg (2015). https://doi.org/10.1007/978-3-662-46800-5_12
25. Todo, Y., Isobe, T., Hao, Y., Meier, W.: Cube attacks on non-blackbox polynomials based on division property. In: Katz, J., Shacham, H. (eds.) CRYPTO 2017, Part III. LNCS, vol. 10403, pp. 250–279. Springer, Cham (2017). https://doi.org/10.1007/978-3-319-63697-9_9
26. Todo, Y., Morii, M.: Bit-based division property and application to SIMON family. In: Peyrin, T. (ed.) FSE 2016. LNCS, vol. 9783, pp. 357–377. Springer, Heidelberg (2016). https://doi.org/10.1007/978-3-662-52993-5_18
27. Wang, Q., Hao, Y., Todo, Y., Li, C., Isobe, T., Meier, W.: Improved division property based cube attacks exploiting algebraic properties of superpoly. In: Shacham,

H., Boldyreva, A. (eds.) CRYPTO 2018, Part I. LNCS, vol. 10991, pp. 275–305. Springer, Cham (2018). https://doi.org/10.1007/978-3-319-96884-1_10
28. Wang, S., Hu, B., Guan, J., Zhang, K., Shi, T.: MILP-aided method of searching division property using three subsets and applications. In: Galbraith, S.D., Moriai, S. (eds.) ASIACRYPT 2019, Part III. LNCS, vol. 11923, pp. 398–427. Springer, Cham (2019). https://doi.org/10.1007/978-3-030-34618-8_14
29. Xiang, Z., Zhang, W., Bao, Z., Lin, D.: Applying MILP method to searching integral distinguishers based on division property for 6 lightweight block ciphers. In: Cheon, J.H., Takagi, T. (eds.) ASIACRYPT 2016, Part I. LNCS, vol. 10031, pp. 648–678. Springer, Heidelberg (2016). https://doi.org/10.1007/978-3-662-53887-6_24
30. Yan, H., Lai, X., Wang, L., Yu, Y., Xing, Y.: New zero-sum distinguishers on full 24-round Keccak-F using the division property. IET Inf. Secur. **13**(5), 469–478 (2019). https://doi.org/10.1049/IET-IFS.2018.5263

Public-Key Cryptography

DSKE: Digital Signatures with Key Extraction

Zhipeng Wang[1(✉)], Orestis Alpos[2], Alireza Kavousi[3], Harry W. H. Wong[4], Sze Yiu Chau[4], Duc V. Le[5], and Christian Cachin[2]

[1] Imperial College London, London, UK
zhipeng.wang20@imperial.ac.uk
[2] University of Bern, Bern, Switzerland
christian.cachin@unibe.ch
[3] University College London, London, UK
a.kavousi@cs.ucl.ac.uk
[4] The Chinese University of Hong Kong, Hong Kong, China
{whwong,sychau}@ie.cuhk.edu.hk
[5] Visa Research, Foster City, CA, USA

Abstract. This work introduces DSKE, digital signatures with key extraction. In a DSKE scheme, the private key can be extracted if more than a threshold number of signatures on different messages are ever created while, within the threshold, each signature continues to authenticate the signed message. We propose a formal definition of DSKE, as well as two provably secure constructions, one from hash-based digital signatures and one from polynomial commitments. We demonstrate that DSKE is useful for various applications, such as cryptographic deniability and spam prevention. First, we introduce the GroupForge signature scheme, leveraging DSKE to achieve deniability in digital communication. GroupForge integrates DSKE with a Merkle tree and timestamps to produce a forward-forgeable signature equipped with extractable sets, ensuring deniability under a fixed public key. We illustrate that GroupForge can serve as a viable alternative to Keyforge in the non-attributable email protocol of Specter, Park, and Green (USENIX Sec '21), thereby eliminating the need for continuous disclosure of outdated private keys. GroupForge can also operate as a short-lived signature, providing deniability non-interactively and agnostic to time. Second, we leverage the inherent extraction property of DSKE to develop a Rate-Limiting Nullifier (RLN) scheme. RLN efficiently identifies and expels spammers once they exceed a predetermined action threshold, thereby jeopardizing their private keys.

Moreover, we implement both variants of the DSKE to demonstrate their performance and show they are comparable to existing signature schemes. We also implement GroupForge from the polynomial commitment-based DSKE and illustrate the practicality of our proposed scheme.

A. Patra (Ed.): CT-RSA 2025, LNCS 15598, pp. 149–173, 2025.
https://doi.org/10.1007/978-3-031-88661-4_7

1 Introduction

Digital signature schemes [21] play an important role in protecting the integrity of data transmitted over the Internet. In some jurisdictions [12,25,31], a digital signature applied to data can serve as evidence of the sender's authorship of the data. Moreover, the signature of a message remains valid until either the underlying signature scheme is broken or the private key is compromised. However, as pointed out by Borisov, Goldberg, and Brewer in their work on off-the-record (OTR) communication [16], this "long-lived" property is unsuitable for certain types of messages [6]. For instance, if Alice wishes to communicate privately with Bob, she can encrypt her messages using Bob's public key (i.e., for confidentiality) and sign them with her private key (i.e., for authenticity). However, if Eve compromises Bob's computer at some point in the future, Eve will be able to read all of Bob's previous messages from Alice, and use the signatures to prove to Judy that the messages indeed originated from Alice.

To address this problem, OTR messaging requires an interactive key agreement protocol between the sender and the recipient to agree on session keys before exchanging messages. Hence, participants can achieve plausible deniability by revealing the message authentication code (MAC) key at the end of the conversation; thus, no one can prove that any person is the author of the messages. However, this pair-wise key agreement required in OTR is not scalable for applications such as email protocols, in which there is often no prior end-to-end interaction among the participating parties.

Another way to achieve deniability is to simply require the sender to periodically rotate keys and publish their old private keys [22]. This method enables anyone to forge signatures using the published private keys and thus offers deniability to old transcripts. In fact, this method is being suggested to offer deniability in domain keys identified mail (DKIM) [2], where SMTP servers sign outgoing emails on behalf of the whole domain using a single key, as a way to safeguard against email spoofing. A server sending an email cryptographically signs it so that the recipient can verify that it has originated from the reported server. A side effect of this action is *email attributability* which stems from the fact that the digital signature remains valid for a long time, potentially forever [22]. As a result, a malicious actor, who at any time gains access to these emails, can provably link them to their sender, which in turn incentivizes extortion and retaliation, among others.

Problem Statement. In this paper, we focus on answering the following question that arises naturally from the limitations of existing attempts [3,16,22]:

Is it possible to design a signature scheme that allows the recipients to verify the validity of the signature, while enabling the sender to gain plausible deniability, without requiring the constant release of old key materials or relying on any additional components?

It is worth noting that the question itself is seemingly a contradiction due to the non-repudiation property of the digital signature. In this work, we propose digital signatures with key extraction (DSKE) scheme to answer the aforementioned question affirmatively. We first propose a general framework, showing that any one-time hash-based signature scheme, such as Lamport [28] and Winternitz OTS [17,32], can be turned into a DSKE scheme, and present two concrete constructions. We then propose another DSKE construction based on polynomial commitments [26]. This type of signature scheme comes with an *extractable set*, a set of signatures from which the private key can be extracted *asynchronously*.

Independently, the key extraction property of DKSE is particularly useful when there is a need to disincentivize or penalize the creation of more than a certain number of signatures. As concrete examples, one may consider the issue of double-spending [40] or double-signing on executable code [19]. Both could be mitigated by putting the user under the threat of key leakage.[1]

Contributions. Our contributions can be summarized as follows:

- We formally define the notion of DSKE. It comes with an *extractable set*, a set of signatures that can be used to extract the private key.
- We introduce a framework to make one-time hash-based DSKE, and present two constructions for $\mathsf{DSKE}_{\mathsf{hash}}$. One is based on Lamport [28] and the other is based on Winternitz signatures [17,32]. We demonstrate that generating multiple signatures while reusing a private key in one-time hash-based signatures results in an extractable set with an overwhelming probability.
- We propose a polynomial commitment-based DSKE, and present a concrete construction $\mathsf{DSKE}_{\mathsf{poly}}$ based on the KZG commitment scheme [26]. In comparison to hash-based DSKE, $\mathsf{DSKE}_{\mathsf{poly}}$ offers shorter signature size and more flexibility to the signer in customizing the size of the extractable set.
- We use $\mathsf{DSKE}_{\mathsf{poly}}$ to present two concrete applications. First, we introduce GroupForge, a forward-forgeable signature with extractable set for deniability under a fixed public key. This makes GroupForge a potential replacement for Keyforge (USENIX Sec '21) [41] with additional benefit like eliminating the reliance on a trusted party and the need for continual disclosure of outdated private keys. We show how GroupForge can also serve as a *short-lived signature* [3] without using expensive timed cryptography. Second, we harness the inherent extraction property of DSKE to build a Rate-Limiting Nullifier (RLN) protocol, which can identify and expel spammers once they exceed a certain threshold in some action.
- We implement and evaluate both DSKE and GroupForge constructions to highlight their practicality.

[1] We remark that DSKE in this sense resembles an existing primitive in the literature, named double-authentication-preventing signatures (DAPS). However, there are crucial differences between the two primitives, as we elaborate in Sect. 9.

2 Preliminaries

Notation. We denote by 1^λ the security parameter and by $\mathsf{negl}(\lambda)$ a negligible function of λ. We express by (pk, sk) a pair of public and private keys. We let $[n]$ denote the set $\{1, \ldots, n\}$. Moreover, we require that pk can always be efficiently derived from sk, and we denote $\mathsf{extractPK}(sk) = pk$ to be the deterministic function for doing so. For a field $\mathbb{F}$, we denote $\mathbb{F}^{\leq d}(X)$ the set of polynomials in $\mathbb{F}[X]$ with degree at most d. We denote by $\mathcal{M}$ the message space and $\mathcal{S}$ the signature space. For a non-negative integer j, we let $f^{(j)}$ be the j-th iterate of the function f, i.e., $f^{(j)}(x) = f(f(\cdots f(x)\cdots))$ where f is repetitively calculated j times. We use the notation $p(x) \leftarrow \mathsf{Interpolate}(\{x_i, y_i\}_{i \in [d+1]})$ to denote using Lagrange interpolation to obtain a degree-d polynomial given $d+1$ evaluation points and their corresponding evaluations.

Hash Functions. Our constructions employ the following standard properties of cryptographic hash functions. We use $H : \mathcal{K} \times \mathcal{M} \rightarrow \{0,1\}^\lambda$ to denote a family of hash functions that is parameterized by a key $k \in \mathcal{K}$ and message $m \in \mathcal{M}$ and outputs a binary string of length λ. For this work, we consider cryptographic hash functions [39], satisfying preimage resistance and collision resistance properties. In practice, the key for standard hash functions is public; therefore, from this point, we refer to the cryptographic hash function h sampled from a family of hash functions as a fixed function $H : \mathcal{M} \rightarrow \{0,1\}^\lambda$.

Polynomial Commitment Schemes. A polynomial commitment scheme (PCS) allows a prover to commit to a polynomial $f(X) \in \mathbb{F}^{\leq d}(X)$ and later open $f(X)$ at arbitrary points x, revealing only the value $f(x)$.

Definition 1 (Polynomial Commitment). *A PCS consists of the following algorithms.*

- $(ck, vk) \leftarrow \mathsf{Setup}(1^\lambda, d)$: *The setup algorithm takes as input a security parameter* λ, *a maximum degree* $d \in \mathbb{N}$, *and outputs the public commitment key* ck, *which allows committing to polynomials in* $\mathbb{F}^{\leq d}(X)$, *and the public verification key* vk.
- $C_f \leftarrow \mathsf{Com}(ck, f(X))$: *The commitment algorithm takes as input the commitment key* ck, *a polynomial* $f(X) \in \mathbb{F}^{\leq d}(X)$, *and outputs a commitment* $C_f \in G$ *to the polynomial* $f(X)$.
- $(\pi, y) \leftarrow \mathsf{Open}(ck, C_f, x, f(X))$: *The algorithm takes as input a commitment key* ck, *a commitment* C_f, *an evaluation point* x, *the polynomial* $f(X)$, *and outputs* $y = f(x) \in \mathbb{F}$ *and a proof* $\pi \in G$.
- $0/1 \leftarrow \mathsf{Check}(vk, C_f, x, y, \pi)$: *The algorithm takes as input the verification key* vk, *the commitment* C_f, *a point* x, *the claimed evaluation* y, *the opening proof* π, *and outputs* 1 *iff* $y = f(x)$.

A PSC is secure if it can guarantee *correctness*, *computational hiding*, *evaluation binding*, *polynomial binding*, and *interpolation binding* properties from the polynomial commitment scheme.

Definition 2 (Correctness [26]**).** *Let* $(ck, vk) \leftarrow \mathsf{Setup}(1^\lambda, d)$, $f(X) \in \mathbb{F}^{\leq d}(X)$, *and* $C_f \leftarrow \mathsf{Com}(ck, f(X))$. *Then for any* (π, y) *output by* $\mathsf{Open}(ck, C_f, x, f(X))$, *we have* $\mathsf{Check}(vk, C_f, x, y, \pi) = 1$.

Definition 3 (Computational Hiding [26]**).** *Given* $(ck, vk) \leftarrow \mathsf{Setup}(1^\lambda, d)$, *the commitment* $C_f = \mathsf{Com}(ck, f(X))$, *and* $\hat{d}$ *valid openings* (y_i, π_i) *for points* x_i, *where* $i \in \{1, \ldots, \hat{d}\}$, $\hat{d}$ *is the degree of* $f(X)$, *and* $\hat{d} \leq d$, *no PPT adversary can determine the value* $f(x')$, *for* $x' \notin \{x_1, \ldots, x_{\hat{d}}\}$, *except with a negligible probability.*

Definition 4 (Evaluation Binding [26]**).** *Given* $(ck, vk) \leftarrow \mathsf{Setup}(1^\lambda, d)$, *no PPT adversary can compute commitment* C_f, *point* x, *and two openings* (π_1, y_1), (π_2, y_2) *for* x, *such that* $\mathsf{Check}(vk, C_f, x, y_1, \pi_1) = 1$, $\mathsf{Check}(vk, C_f, x, y_2, \pi_2) = 1$, *and* $y_1 \neq y_2$.

Definition 5 (Polynomial Binding [26]**).** *Given* $(ck, vk) \leftarrow \mathsf{Setup}(1^\lambda, d)$, *no PPT adversary can compute polynomials* $f(X)$ *and* $f'(X)$, *such that* $f(X) \neq f'(X)$ *and* $\mathsf{Com}(ck, f(X)) = \mathsf{Com}(ck, f'(X))$.

Abraham *et al.* [1] recently introduced a new property termed *interpolation binding* for polynomial commitment schemes. This property implies that if a sufficient number of valid evaluations of the committed polynomial are provided, the polynomial interpolated from these points must be identical to the originally committed polynomial.

Definition 6 (Interpolation Binding [1]**).** *Given* $(ck, vk) \leftarrow \mathsf{Setup}(1^\lambda, d)$, *no PPT adversary can output* $(C_f, \{x_i, y_i, \pi_i\}_{i\in[d+1]})$ *such that* $x_j \neq x_k$ *for all* $j \neq k$, $\mathsf{Check}(vk, C_f, x_i, y_i, \pi_i) = 1$ *for all* $i \in [d+1]$, *and* $C_f \neq \mathsf{Com}(ck, f'(X))$ *where* $f'(X) = \mathsf{Interpolate}(\{x_i, y_i\}_{i\in[d+1]})$.

3 Digital Signatures with Key Extraction (DSKE)

In this section, we formally define the notion of digital signatures with key extraction (DSKE). We adopt the standard digital signature definition and introduce a new algorithm to capture the capability of extracting the private key from a set of signatures.

Definition 7 ((k, δ)-Digital Signature with Key Extraction). *A signature scheme* Σ, *with key extraction consists of five algorithms:*

- $par \leftarrow \mathsf{Setup}(1^\lambda)$: *The setup algorithm takes a security parameter* 1^λ *and outputs a set of public parameters par. This algorithm runs once, and the public parameters are implicitly input to all subsequent algorithms.*
- $(pk, sk) \leftarrow \mathsf{KeyGen}(par)$: *The key generation is a* probabilistic *algorithm that outputs a pair of public and private keys* (pk, sk).
- $\sigma \leftarrow \mathsf{Sign}(sk, m)$: *The signing algorithm is a* probabilistic *algorithm that takes a private key sk and a message* $m \in \mathcal{M}$ *as input, and outputs a signature* σ *in the signature space* $\mathcal{S}$.

- $b \leftarrow \mathsf{Verify}(pk, m, \sigma)$: *The verification algorithm is a* deterministic *algorithm that takes a public key pk, a message m, a signature σ as input, and outputs the validity of the signature,* $b \in \{0, 1\}$.
- $sk \leftarrow \mathsf{Extract}(\{(m_i, \sigma_i)\}_{i\in[k]}, pk)$: *The extraction algorithm is a* deterministic *algorithm that takes as input a set of distinct message-signature pairs* $(m_i, \sigma_i)_{i\in[k]}$ *and the public key pk such that* $\mathsf{Verify}(pk, m_i, \sigma_i) = 1$, *and outputs the underlying private key sk with probability δ and ⊥ with probability* $1 - \delta$.

Besides the straightforward correctness definition, we consider other properties of DSKE: existential unforgeability (Definition 8), the extractability with trusted generation (Definition 9) and untrusted generation (Definition 10).

To define existential unforgeability, we consider the following experiment.
d-times signature experiment $\mathsf{SignExp}^d_{\mathcal{A},\Sigma}(\lambda)$**.**

1. $\mathsf{Setup}(1^\lambda)$ and $\mathsf{KeyGen}(par)$ are run to obtain keys (pk, sk).
2. $\mathcal{A}$ is given pk and can ask up to d queries to the signing oracle $\mathsf{Sign}(sk, \cdot)$. Let $Q_{\mathcal{A}}^{\mathsf{Sign}(sk,\cdot)} = \{m_i\}_{i\in[d]}$ be the set of all messages for which $\mathcal{A}$ queries $\mathsf{Sign}(sk, \cdot)$, where the ith query is a message $m_i \in \mathcal{M}$. Eventually, $\mathcal{A}$ outputs a pair $(m^*, \sigma^*) \in \mathcal{M} \times \mathcal{S}$.
3. The output of the experiment is defined to be 1 if and only if $m^* \notin Q_{\mathcal{A}}^{\mathsf{Sign}(sk,\cdot)}$ and $\mathsf{Verify}(pk, m^*, \sigma^*) = 1$.

Definition 8 (Existential Unforgeability). *A digital signature scheme Σ is* existentially unforgeable under a d-times adaptive chosen-message attack, *or* d-times-secure, *if for all PPT adversaries $\mathcal{A}$ the success probability in the d-times signature experiment is negligible:* $\Pr[\mathsf{SignExp}^d_{\mathcal{A},\Sigma}(\lambda) = 1] \le \mathsf{negl}(\lambda)$.

We proceed to define the extractability with trusted generation, in which the private key becomes extractable upon accumulating an adequate quantity of signatures generated by an honest signer. This property can be useful for applications where the signer wants to achieve deniability.

Definition 9 (Extractability with Trusted Generation). *A digital signature scheme has a (k, δ)-extractable set when the algorithm* $\mathsf{Extract}(\cdot)$ *on input k distinct message-signature pairs* $\{(m_i, \sigma_i)\}_{i\in[k]}$ *and the public key pk, such that each σ_i is a valid signature on m_i under pk, outputs the private key sk with probability δ. That is:*

$$\Pr\left[\begin{array}{l} par \leftarrow \mathsf{Setup}(1^\lambda), (pk, sk) \leftarrow \mathsf{KeyGen}(par), \\ m_i \leftarrow \mathcal{M},\ s.t.\ m_i \neq m_j,\ for\ i, j \in [k], i \neq j, \\ \sigma_i \leftarrow \mathsf{Sign}(sk, m_i), \\ sk' \leftarrow \mathsf{Extract}\left(\{(m_i, \sigma_i)\}_{i\in[k]}, pk\right) \end{array} : pk = \mathsf{extractPK}(sk')\right] = \delta$$

We further define the extractability with untrusted generation, in which the signatures are generated by an adversary. Such property can be used to construct spam prevention by revealing the secret key. Intuitively, this property prevents an adversary from creating more message-signature pairs than the pre-defined threshold.

Definition 10 (Extractability with Untrusted Generation). *A digital signature scheme has a (k, δ)-extractable set when the algorithm* Extract$(\cdot)$ *on input k distinct message-signature pairs $\{(m_i, \sigma_i)\}_{i\in[k]}$ and the public key pk generated by an adversary $\mathcal{A}$, outputs the private key sk with probability δ:*

$$\Pr\left[\begin{array}{l} par \leftarrow \mathsf{Setup}(1^\lambda), (pk, \{(m_i, \sigma_i)\}_{i\in[k]}) \leftarrow \mathcal{A}(1^\lambda, par), \\ s.t.\ \mathsf{Verify}(pk, m_i, \sigma_i) = 1, \\ m_i \neq m_j,\ for\ i, j \in [k], i \neq j, \\ sk' \leftarrow \mathsf{Extract}\left(\{(m_i, \sigma_i)\}_{i\in[k]}, pk\right) \end{array} : pk = \mathsf{extractPK}(sk')\right] = \delta$$

4 DSKE from Hash-Based Signature Schemes

Hash-based signature schemes (such as Lamport [28] and Winternitz OTS [17]) leverage the security of one-way functions to construct digital signatures.

In hash-based signature schemes, the private key is often a list that is derived from a succinct seed, and based on the message, the signature reveals "partial" information about the private key. In essence, having a *sufficiently* large number of signatures allows us to obtain enough information for the reconstruction of the private key.

In this section, we provide DSKE constructions based on the hash-based signature schemes, denoted as $\mathsf{DSKE_{hash}}$. We also assume that $\mathsf{DSKE_{hash}}$ follows the hash-then-sign paradigm, where a message is first hashed (converted into a fixed-length string) using a cryptographic hash function $H(\cdot)$. We first give a generic definition to capture the private key leakage of hash-based signature schemes and then provide two DSKE constructions that are based on the Lamport signature scheme and Winternitz OTS (see the full version of this paper [42]).

Definition 11 (Leakage of Hash-based Signature). *A hash-based signature, Σ_{hash}, consists of the four algorithms* Setup, KeyGen, Sign, *and* Verify *as defined in Definition 7, as well as a leakage algorithm defined as follows:*

- $S/\bot \leftarrow \mathsf{Leak}((m, \sigma), pk)$: *This leakage algorithm is a* deterministic *algorithm that takes as input a message-signature pairs, (m, σ) and a public key pk. If* $\mathsf{Verify}(pk, m, \sigma) = 1$, *it outputs a list S, containing a fraction of the private key; Otherwise, it outputs $\bot$.*

We can then propose a hash signature-based DSKE:

Definition 12 (Hash-based DSKE). *A hash-based DSKE scheme, $\mathsf{DSKE_{hash}}$, consists of the four algorithms,* Setup, KeyGen, Sign, *and* Verify *which are same as a hash-based signature, as well as an* Extract *algorithm defined as follows:*

- $sk/\bot \leftarrow \mathsf{Extract}(\{(m_i, \sigma_i)\}_{i\in[k]}, pk)$: *The extraction algorithm is a deterministic algorithm that receives a set of distinct message-signature pairs* $\{m_i, \sigma_i\}_{i\in[k]}$, *and the public key* pk *as inputs. For each* (m_i, σ_i), *this algorithm runs* $S_i \leftarrow \mathsf{Leak}((m_i, \sigma_i), pk)$, *and computes* $sk' = \bigcup_{i=1}^{k}(S_i)$. *The algorithm outputs the private key* sk' *if* $pk = \mathsf{extractPK}(sk')$; *otherwise, it outputs* $\bot$.

We subsequently introduce a definition aimed at quantifying the probability that an element of the private key is not revealed even after receiving k hash-based signatures. This definition serves as a tool to compute the probability of a successful output of the private key by running the Extract() function.

Definition 13. *Consider* k *distinct messages* $\{m_i\}_{i\in[k]}$ *which are sampled from* $\mathcal{M}$, *a key pair* (pk, sk) *generated by* KeyGen() *where* $sk = (sk_j)_{[\lambda]}$, k *signatures* $\{\sigma_i\}_{i\in[k]}$ *such that each* σ_i *is a valid signature on* m_i *under* pk, *an element* sk_j *which is a part of the secret key* sk. *We assume that a hash function* $H(\cdot)$ *is used for hash-then-sign in the signature scheme and* $H(\cdot)$ *is modeled as a random oracle. We define* p_k^{leak} *as the probability that* sk_j *is not leaked after running* Leak() *on all message-signature pairs* $\{(m_i, \sigma_i)\}_{i\in[k]}$.

$$\mathsf{p}_k^{leak} = \Pr\left[\begin{array}{l} par \leftarrow \mathsf{Setup}(1^\lambda), (pk, sk) \leftarrow \mathsf{KeyGen}(par) \\ m_i \leftarrow \mathcal{M},\ s.t.\ m_i \neq m_j,\ for\ i, j \in [k], i \neq j, \\ \sigma_i \leftarrow \mathsf{Sign}(sk, m_i), S_i \leftarrow \mathsf{Leak}((m_i, \sigma_i), pk) \\ sk_j \in sk \end{array} : sk_j \notin \bigcup_{i=1}^{k} S_i\right]$$

The following theorem shows that the lower bound of δ in any hash-based DSKE scheme can be determined by p_k^{leak}.

Theorem 1 (Extractability with Trusted Generation). *Given a hash-based DSKE scheme with a private key of size* λ, *if all underlying hash functions are modeled as a random oracle, then* $\mathit{DSKE}_{\mathsf{hash}}$ *has a* (k, δ)*-extractable set, where:* $\delta \geq 1 - \lambda \cdot \mathsf{p}_k^{leak} - \mathsf{negl}(\lambda)$.

In this paper, we provide two DSKE constructions based on the Lamport signature scheme and Winternitz OTS, respectively. We will show that, for a Lamport signature scheme, p_k^{leak} is determined by the number of given signatures (i.e., k), $\mathsf{p}_k^{leak} = \frac{1}{2^{k-1}}$ (see Sect. 4.1); and for a Winternitz OTS, $\mathsf{p}_k^{leak} = \frac{w^k}{(w+1)^k}$, where w are a parameter for the Winternitz OTS (see the full version of our paper [42]).

4.1 Lamport Signature-Based Construction

The Lamport signature scheme is parameterized by a preimage-resistant hash function F and a collision-resistant hash function H. The private key SK contains 2λ binary strings uniformly sampled from $\{0,1\}^\lambda$, where λ is the security parameter. The public key PK consists of 2λ binary strings that are evaluations of F on each element in the private key. To form a signature σ on a message m, the signer reveals components of the private key SK, according to the binary representation of $H(m)$ as the signature. To verify the signature, the verifier uses the binary representation of the digest, $H(m)$, to validate if each element contained in the signature is the actual preimage of the public key elements.

Extracting Private Key from Message-Signature Pairs. As shown in Fig. 1, the intuition behind the extracting function is that each signature σ_i is a subset of the private key SK. To extract the complete private key, one needs to compute the union of k different signatures $\{\sigma_i\}_{i\in[k]}$. Since the underlying hash function is unpredictable, the probability of successfully extracting the private key depends on the number of distinct message-signature pairs (i.e., k). Based on the above intuition, we propose a hash-based construction, $\mathsf{DSKE}_{\mathsf{lamp}}$, as follows.

Leakage Function for Lamport Signatures. As illustrated in Fig. 1, within a Lamport signature scheme, each signature encapsulates half of the information about the privacy key SK. The leakage function is employed to extract the divulged information of the privacy key from the signature.

- $\mathsf{Leak}((m,\sigma),PK)$: Check if $\mathsf{Verify}(PK,m,\sigma) = 1$; otherwise, output $\perp$. Compute $d = H(m) = (d_i)_{i\in[\lambda]}$, and parse $\sigma = (\sigma_i)_{i\in[\lambda]}$. For each $i \in [\lambda], b \in \{0,1\}$, if $d_i = b$, then let $S_i[b] = \sigma_i$ and $S_i[1-b] = \perp$. Output $S = (S_i[b])_{i\in[\lambda],b\in\{0,1\}}$.

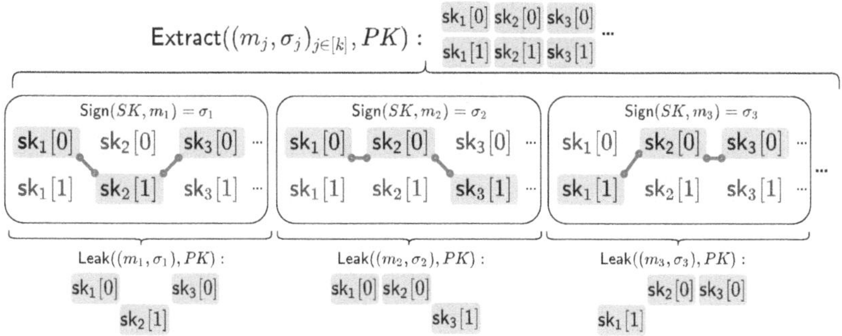

Fig. 1. Example of the algorithm $\mathsf{Extract}$ for $\mathsf{DSKE}_{\mathsf{lamp}}$. The elements of a signature σ are linked via red lines. In this example, the original private key can be collectively reconstructed from $\{(m_i,\sigma_i)\}_{i\in[3]}$. (Color figure online)

We the proceed to define the Lamport-Based DSKE.

Lamport-Based DSKE. A Lamport-based DSKE scheme, $\mathsf{DSKE}_{\mathsf{lamp}}$, includes:

- $\mathsf{Setup}(1^\lambda)$: On input the security parameter λ, the algorithm outputs a parameter, par, containing a hash function, $F : \{0,1\}^\lambda \to \{0,1\}^\lambda$, chosen from a family of preimage-resistant hash functions, and a hash function, $H : \mathcal{M} \to \{0,1\}^\lambda$, chosen from a family of collision-resistant hash function. The public parameters are implicitly input to all subsequent algorithms.
- $\mathsf{KeyGen}(par)$: For each $i \in [\lambda]$, $b \in \{0,1\}$, sample $sk_i[b] \xleftarrow{\$} \{0,1\}^\lambda$; output the private key, $SK = (sk_i[b])_{i\in[\lambda],b\in\{0,1\}}$, and the public key, $PK = (pk_i[b])_{i\in[\lambda],b\in\{0,1\}}$, where $pk_i[b] = F(sk_i[b])$.
- $\mathsf{Sign}(SK, m)$: Parse $SK = (sk_i[b])_{i\in[\lambda],b\in\{0,1\}}$, compute $d = H(m) = (d_i)_{i\in[\lambda]}$, and output $\sigma = (sk_i[d_i])_{i\in[\lambda]}$.
- $\mathsf{Verify}(PK, m, \sigma)$: Parse PK, σ, and compute $d = H(m) = (d_i)_{i\in[\lambda]}$. For all $i \in [\lambda]$, if $F(\sigma_i) \neq pk_i[d_i]$, return 0. Otherwise, return 1.
- $\mathsf{Extract}(\{m_j, \sigma_j\}_{j\in[k]}, PK)$: For each message-signature pair (m_j, σ_j), compute $d_j = H(m_j) = (d_{ji})_{i\in[\lambda]}$, and parse $\sigma_j = (\sigma_{ji})_{i\in[\lambda]}$. For each $j \in [k], i \in [\lambda], b \in \{0,1\}$, if $\exists d_{ji} = b$, then let $sk_i[b] = \sigma_{ji}$. Set $SK = (sk_i[b])_{i\in[\lambda],b\in\{0,1\}}$ and parse $PK = (pk_i[b])_{i\in[\lambda],b\in\{0,1\}}$. If $\forall i \in [\lambda]$ and $b \in \{0,1\}$, $pk_i[b] = pk_i[d_i] = F(\sigma_i) = F(sk_i[b])$, then output SK. Otherwise, the algorithm outputs $\perp$.

$\mathsf{DSKE}_{\mathsf{lamp}}$ satisfies unforgeability and extractability with trusted generation depending on the number of distinct message-signature pairs. We refer readers to our detailed proofs in the full version of this paper [42].

Theorem 2 (Existential Unforgeability). *$\mathsf{DSKE}_{\mathsf{lamp}}$ is existentially unforgeable under a 1-time adaptive chosen-message attack, that is,*

$$\Pr[\mathsf{SignExp}^1_{\mathcal{A},\mathsf{DSKE}_{\mathsf{lamp}}}(\lambda) = 1] \leq \mathsf{negl}(\lambda)$$

Lemma 1. *In a Lamport-based DSKE scheme, if $H(\cdot)$ is modeled as a random oracle, the probability that an element of the private key will not be leaked after receiving k distinct signatures is $\mathsf{p}_k^{leak} = \frac{1}{2^{k-1}}$.*

Proof. We define $d_i = H(m_i)$. All d_i for $i \in \{1,\ldots,k\}$ form a $k \times \lambda$ matrix:

$$\begin{pmatrix} H(m_1) \\ \vdots \\ H(m_k) \end{pmatrix} = \begin{pmatrix} d_1 \\ \vdots \\ d_k \end{pmatrix} = \begin{pmatrix} d_{1,1} & \ldots & d_{1,\lambda} \\ \vdots & \ddots & \vdots \\ d_{k,1} & \ldots & d_{k,\lambda} \end{pmatrix}$$

where $d_{i,j} \in \{0,1\}$.

For $j \in [\lambda], b \in \{0,1\}$, to extract the value of $sk_j[b]$, there should be at least one d_{ij} that satisfies $d_{ij} = b$, i.e., for $j \in [\lambda]$, d_{ij} should not all be $1 - b$. Therefore, to be able to extract an element sk_j, we do not want any columns in the matrix that contain all 0s or all 1s.

Since $H(\cdot)$ is modeled as a random oracle, p_k^{leak} is the probability that one single column consists of all 0s or all 1s:

$$\mathsf{p}_k^{leak} = \Pr\left[x \xleftarrow{\$} \{0,1\}^k : x = 0^k \vee x = 1^k\right] = \frac{1}{2^{k-1}}$$

By combining Theorem 1 and Lemma 1, we can deduce Theorem 3.

Theorem 3 ($\mathsf{DSKE}_{\mathsf{lamp}}$ Extractability with Trusted Generation). *If $H(\cdot)$ is modeled as a random oracle, then $\mathsf{DSKE}_{\mathsf{lamp}}$ has a (k, δ)-extractable set, where:* $\delta \geq 1 - \dfrac{\lambda}{2^{k-1}} - \mathsf{negl}(\lambda)$.

Limitations of $\mathsf{DSKE}_{\mathsf{hash}}$. Although the scheme $\mathsf{DSKE}_{\mathsf{hash}}$ satisfies our definition of a signature scheme with key extraction, it has several inherent weaknesses: (1) The key and signature sizes are linear with the security parameter λ, making it inefficient in practice; (2) $\mathsf{Extract}$ may not always output the secret key and depends on the size of the extractable set k^2; (3) $\mathsf{DSKE}_{\mathsf{hash}}$ does not satisfy the extractability with an untrusted generation, as a (malicious) signer can manipulate the hash results of messages. For instance, within $\mathsf{DSKE}_{\mathsf{lamp}}$, a signer may selectively choose messages to manipulate the hash results: the first bit of the hash results $(H(m_1), H(m_2), \dots)$ consistently remains 0, thus ensuring that the private key will never get extracted.

5 DSKE from Polynomial Commitment Schemes

In this section, we construct a DSKE scheme $\mathsf{DSKE}_{\mathsf{poly}}$ from a polynomial commitment scheme Π without the drawbacks of $\mathsf{DSKE}_{\mathsf{hash}}$. The idea is to use the polynomial $f(X)$ of degree d as the private key with the corresponding public key being the polynomial commitment. Then, the signature on a message m is the evaluation of $f(X)$ at point $x = H(m)$, where H is a collision-resistant hash function. For key extraction, we employ polynomial interpolation: any set of $d + 1$ valid message-signature pairs (m_i, σ_i) can reconstruct $f(X)$.

Definition 14 (Polynomial Commitment-based DSKE). *A polynomial commitment-based DSKE scheme, $\mathsf{DSKE}_{\mathsf{poly}}$, consists of:*

- $\mathsf{Setup}(1^\lambda, d)$: *On input the security parameter λ and degree $d \in \mathbb{N}$, it runs $\Pi.\mathsf{Setup}(1^\lambda, d)$ to obtain (ck, vk), which allows a signer to commit to polynomials in $\mathbb{F}^{\leq d}(X)$. It samples a collision-resistant hash function $H : \mathcal{M} \rightarrow \mathbb{F}$. The public parameters, par, contain ck, vk, d, and the specification of H.*
- $\mathsf{KeyGen}(par)$: *It samples $f(X) \xleftarrow{\$} \mathbb{F}^{\leq d}(X)$ as a d-degree polynomial and computes $\Pi.\mathsf{Com}(ck, f(X)) \rightarrow C_f$. Let $sk = f(X)$, $pk = C_f$*[3]*.*
- $\mathsf{Sign}(sk, m)$: *It parses $sk = f(X)$, computes $x = H(m)$, and runs $\Pi.\mathsf{Open}(ck, C_f, x, f(X)) \rightarrow (\pi, y)$. It outputs the signature $\sigma = (\pi, y)$.*

[2] This drawback can be circumvented by requiring signers to add an extra nonce to k different messages so that the set of these signatures guarantees the existence of the extractable set.

[3] For applications that require deniability, the signer can flexibly choose to commit to any polynomial of degree $\ell \in [1, d]$ and has no incentive to commit to a polynomial of degree larger than ℓ, since that would cost them the deniability property, as we discuss in the following sections.

- $\mathsf{Verify}(pk, m, \sigma)$: *It parses* $pk = C_f$ *and* $\sigma = (\pi, y)$, *computes* $x = H(m)$, *and outputs* $\Pi.\mathsf{Check}(vk, C_f, x, y, \pi) \in \{0, 1\}$.
- $\mathsf{Extract}(\{(m_i, \sigma_i)\}_{i\in[k]}, pk)$: *If the number of distinct* m_i *is less than* d, *or* $\mathsf{Verify}(pk, m_i, \sigma_i) = 0$ *for some* $i \in [k]$, *then return* $\perp$. *Otherwise, it computes* $x_i = H(m_i)$ *and parses* $\sigma_i = (\pi_i, y_i)$, *for* $i \in [k]$, *and outputs* $f'(X) \leftarrow \mathsf{Interpolate}(\{x_i, y_i\}_{i\in[d+1]})$

In the following, we show that $\mathsf{DSKE_{poly}}$ can achieve existential unforgeability, extractability with both trusted and untrust generation. Moreover, in this construction, $\mathsf{extractPK}(\cdot) = \Pi.\mathsf{Com}(\cdot)$.

Theorem 4 (Existential Unforgeability). *Assuming the security of underlying polynomial commitment scheme* Π, *and that* H *is a hash function modeled as random oracle, the DSKE scheme* $\mathit{DSKE}_{\mathsf{poly}}$ *is* existentially unforgeable *under* d*-times adaptive chosen-message attack. That is,* $\Pr[\mathsf{SignExp}^d_{\mathcal{A},\mathit{DSKE}_{\mathsf{poly}}}(\lambda) = 1] \leq \mathsf{negl}(\lambda)$.

We refer readers to our detailed proofs of Theorem 4 in the full version of this paper [42].

Theorem 5 (Extractability with Trusted Generation). *Assuming the security of underlying polynomial commitment scheme* Π, *the DSKE scheme* $\mathit{DSKE}_{\mathsf{poly}}$ *has a* $(k, 1 - \mathsf{negl}(\lambda))$*-extractable set with trusted generation for any* $k \geq d + 1$. *That is,*

$$\Pr\left[\begin{array}{l} par \leftarrow \mathsf{Setup}(1^\lambda), (pk, sk) \leftarrow \mathsf{KeyGen}(par) \\ m_i \leftarrow \mathcal{M}, s.t.\ m_i \neq m_j,\ for\ i, j \in [k], i \neq j \\ \sigma_i \leftarrow \mathsf{Sign}(sk, m_i),\ for\ i \in [k] \\ sk' \leftarrow \mathsf{Extract}\left(\{(m_i, \sigma_i)\}_{i\in[k]}, pk\right) \end{array} : pk = \mathsf{extractPK}(sk')\right] = 1 - \mathsf{negl}(\lambda)$$

Proof. The proof follows from two facts. First, since the key generation is trusted, the degree of the polynomial must be less than d and the signer does not commit to polynomials of degree bigger than d. Second, from the *evaluation binding property* and since the points (x_i, y_i) correspond to valid signatures, we know that $y_i = f(x_i)$, for some polynomial $f(X) \in \mathbb{F}^{\leq d}(X)$ and for all $i \in [k]$, except with negligible probability. Due to the uniqueness of polynomial interpolation, we know that any $d+1$ distinct points (x_i, y_i) define a unique polynomial $\phi(X)$ of degree at most d, hence $\phi(X)$ must be the same as $f(X)$, hence $sk = sk'$ with probability $1 - \mathsf{negl}(\lambda)$.

Theorem 6 (Extractability with Untrusted Generation). *Assuming the security of underlying polynomial commitment scheme* Π, *the DSKE scheme* $\mathit{DSKE}_{\mathsf{poly}}$ *has a* $(k, 1 - \mathsf{negl}(\lambda))$*-extractable set with untrusted generation for any* $k \geq d + 1$. *That is,*

$$\Pr\left[\begin{array}{l} par \leftarrow \mathsf{Setup}(1^\lambda), (pk, \{(m_i, \sigma_i)\}_{i\in[k]}) \leftarrow \mathcal{A}(1^\lambda, par), \\ s.t.\ \mathsf{Verify}(pk, m_i, \sigma_i) = 1, \\ m_i \neq m_j,\ for\ i \neq j, \\ sk' \leftarrow \mathsf{Extract}\left(\{(m_i, \sigma_i)\}_{i\in[k]}, pk\right) \end{array} : pk = \mathsf{extractPK}(sk')\right] = 1 - \mathsf{negl}(\lambda)$$

Proof. Consider an adversary $\mathcal{A}$ capable of submitting a public key pk and k signatures $\sigma_1, \ldots, \sigma_k$ on distinct messages $m_1, \ldots, m_k$ such that $\mathsf{Verify}(pk, m_i, \sigma_i) = 1$ for $i \in [1, k]$ and $k \geq d + 1$. If the private key $f(X)$ cannot be extracted from their corresponding signatures, we encounter two possible scenarios:

1. The k messages $m_1, \ldots, m_k$ generate fewer than $d + 1$ inputs for $f(X)$, implying the existence of some m_i and m_j ($i \neq j$, $i, j \in [k]$) for which $H(m_i) = H(m_j)$, which breaks the collision-resistance property of H.
2. $\mathcal{A}$ directly breaks the interpolation binding property of PCS: Parse $\sigma_i = (\pi_i, y_i)$ and set $x_i = H(m_i)$ for $i \in [1, d + 1]$, we can submit $(pk, \{x_i, y_i, \pi_i\}_{i \in [1,d+1]})$ which immediately breaks interpolation binding of the polynomial commitment scheme Π.

Both scenarios occur with negligible probability, leading to $\delta = 1 - \mathsf{negl}(\lambda)$.

5.1 DSKE from KZG Polynomial Commitment

KZG Polynomial Commitment Scheme. We now revisit the KZG scheme [26] as a concrete polynomial commitment construction. It works over a bilinear pairing group $\mathbb{G} = \langle e, G, G_t \rangle$, where G is a group of prime order p, e is a symmetric pairing $e : G \times G \to G_t$, and g and $\hat{h}$ are generators of G.

- $(\mathbb{G}, \mathsf{ck}, \mathsf{vk}) \leftarrow \mathsf{Setup}(1^\lambda, d)$: The algorithm outputs a representation of the bilinear group $\mathbb{G}$, commitment key $ck = \{g, g^\alpha, \ldots, g^{\alpha^d}\}$, and verification key $vk = \hat{h}^\alpha$, for an $\alpha \in \mathbb{Z}_p$.
- $C_f \leftarrow \mathsf{Com}(ck, f(X))$: The algorithm computes $C_f = g^{f(\alpha)}$ using ck and outputs C_f.
- $(\pi, y) \leftarrow \mathsf{Open}(ck, C_f, x, f(X))$: The algorithm computes $y = f(x)$ and the quotient polynomial $q(X) = \frac{f(X)-y}{X-x}$, and outputs y and $\pi = C_q = \mathsf{Com}(ck, q(X))$.
- $0/1 \leftarrow \mathsf{Check}(vk, C_f, x, y, \pi)$: The algorithm outputs 1 if $e(C_f \cdot g^{-y}, \hat{h}) = e(C_q, \hat{h}^\alpha \cdot \hat{h}^{-x})$, and 0 otherwise.

Kate *et al.* [26] proved that KZG scheme satisfies *correctness*, *computational hiding*, *evaluation binding*, *polynomial binding* properties, provided the DL and d-SDH assumptions hold in $\mathbb{G}$ [26]. Recently, Abraham *et al.* [1] proved that KZG PCS satisfies *interpolation binding* property assuming the hardness of the Strong Diffie-Hellman problem in the Algebraic Group Model.

KZG-Based DKSE Scheme. We now show $\mathsf{DSKE}_{\mathsf{poly}}$, a concrete construction of $\mathsf{DSKE}_{\mathsf{poly}}$ from the Π_{kzg} polynomial commitment scheme [26].

- $\mathsf{Setup}(1^\lambda, d)$: Run $\Pi_{\mathsf{kzg}}.\mathsf{Setup}(1^\lambda, d)$ to obtain the commitment key, $ck = \{g, g^\alpha, \ldots, g^{\alpha^d}\}$, and the verification key, $vk = \hat{h}^\alpha \in G$. It samples a collision-resistant hash function $H : \mathcal{M} \to \mathbb{Z}_p$ The algorithm returns the public parameters, par, containing ck, vk, d, and the specification of H.

- $\mathsf{KeyGen}(1^\lambda)$: Sample $f(X) \xleftarrow{\$} \mathbb{F}^d(X)$. The algorithm returns the public key, $pk = C_f = \Pi_{\mathsf{kzg}}.\mathsf{Com}(ck, f(X)) = g^{f(\alpha)} \in G$ and the secret key, $sk = f(X)$.
- $\mathsf{Sign}(sk, m)$: Parse $sk = f(X)$, compute $x = H(m)$, and output the signature $\sigma = (\pi, y) = \Pi_{\mathsf{kzg}}.\mathsf{Open}(ck, C_f, x, f(X)) \in G \times \mathbb{Z}_p$.
- $\mathsf{Verify}(pk, m, \sigma)$: Parse $pk = C_f$ and $\sigma = (\pi, y)$, compute $x = H(m)$, and output $\Pi_{\mathsf{kzg}}.\mathsf{Check}(vk, C_f, x, y, \pi) \in \{0, 1\}$.
- $\mathsf{Extract}(\{(m_i, \sigma_i)\}_{i\in[k]}, pk)$: As in the general construction, check the validity of σ_i, for $i \in [k]$, interpolate $\phi(X)$ from points (x_i, y_i) output $sk' = \phi(X) \in \mathbb{F}^d(X)$.

$\mathtt{DSKE}_{\mathsf{kzg}}$ can satisfy existential unforgeability (see Theorem 4), and the extractability with trusted generation (see Theorem 5) as well as untrusted generation (see Theorem 6).

6 Applications

In this section, we present two concrete applications of DSKE.

6.1 Non-attributable Email

Non-attributable Email. The notion of non-attributable emails [41] addresses the inherent drawbacks of DKIM by deploying a forward-forgeable signature (FFS) scheme. An FFS scheme consists of the standard $\mathsf{KeyGen}(1^\lambda)$, $\mathsf{Sign}(sk, m)$, and $\mathsf{Verify}(pk, m, \sigma)$ algorithms, and additionally an $\mathsf{Expire}(sk, \mathcal{T})$ algorithm, that generates expiry information η for a private key sk, possibly using additional information $\mathcal{T}$, and a $\mathsf{Forge}(\eta, m)$ algorithm, that, given the expiry information of a key, outputs a signature on a message m. The scheme satisfies the standard *correctness* and *unforgeability* properties, and the *forgeability on expiry* property.

Definition 15 (Forgeability on Expiry [41]). *A digital signature scheme satisfies the* forgeability on expiry *property if no PPT adversary can distinguish a signature created with private key sk from a signature created with the expiry information η of sk. Formally, for any $m \in \mathcal{M}$ and any PPT distinguisher $\mathcal{D}$, there is a negligible function* $\mathsf{negl}(\cdot)$, *such that for all* λ,

$$\Pr\left[\begin{array}{l} (pk, sk) \leftarrow \mathsf{KeyGen}(1^\lambda), \sigma_0 \leftarrow \mathsf{Sign}(sk, m) \\ \eta \leftarrow \mathsf{Expire}(sk, \mathcal{T}), \sigma_1 \leftarrow \mathsf{Forge}(\eta, m) \\ b \xleftarrow{\$} \{0,1\}, b' \leftarrow \mathcal{D}(\sigma_b, \eta, m, pk) \end{array} : b = b' \right] \leq \frac{1}{2} + \mathsf{negl}(\lambda)$$

The authors in [41] provide two constructions, KeyForge and Timeforge. Both satisfy the FFS properties by requiring signers either to publish old private keys or to issue signed updates to a publicly verifiable timekeeping service, respectively. KeyForge is an FFS scheme where signatures expire after a predefined delay Δ. The expiry information is the private key itself, which has to be published by the server every Δ time. KeyForge uses a hierarchical tree structure with four levels to manage private keys, where each level corresponds to distinct timespans, namely, years, months, days, and minutes. Each leaf represents a private key of a unique 15-minute time chunk. This structure is realized by a hierarchical identity-based signature scheme (HIBS), which allows any node to derive the private keys of its children. The underlying HIBS enables email servers to keep the expiration information succinct. Instead of storing all private keys for a day as the expiration information, it is enough to store the private key that corresponds to the node that encodes that day on the third level.

GroupForge from DSKE. In the following, we show how a DSKE scheme, such as $\mathsf{DSKE}_{\mathsf{poly}}$, can be used in a non-attributable email protocol [41]. DSKE removes the requirement for email servers to periodically publish expiration information. Looking ahead, we introduce GroupForge, an FFS scheme that builds on top of a DSKE and achieves the same properties as KeyForge, while it does not require the email servers to publish *any* expiry information, i.e., algorithm Expire() requires only information already published by the servers.

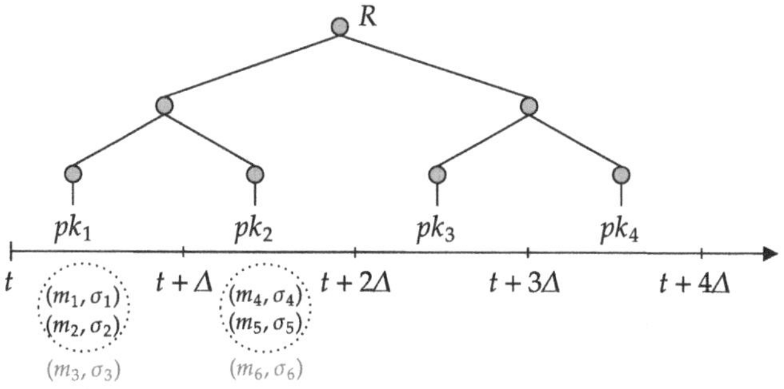

Fig. 2. An example of GroupForge for $h_T = 2$ and between the interval $[t, t + 2^{h_T} \cdot \Delta]$. In this example, $\{(m_i, \sigma_i)\}_{i\in[2]}$ can potentially act as the deniable group (see Sect. 8 for detailed discussions) for the message-signature pair (m_3, σ_3), and $\{(m_i, \sigma_i)\}_{i\in\{4,5\}}$ can act as the deniable group for the message-signature pair (m_6, σ_6).

GroupForge uses a DSKE scheme Σ_{DSKE} with extractable sets of size k, a collision-resistant hash function $H()$, and a clock $\mathsf{Time}(\cdot)$ that returns the current time. GroupForge works as follows.

- $\mathsf{KeyGen}(1^\lambda, \Delta, h_T, t)$: On input the security parameter λ, the length Δ, the height of the Merkle tree $h_T \in \mathbb{N}$, and the starting time t, it invokes $\Sigma_{\mathsf{DSKE}}.\mathsf{Setup}(1^\lambda)$, and generates 2^{h_T} key pairs $\{(pk_i, sk_i)\}_{i\in[2^{h_T}]}$ using the algorithm $\Sigma_{\mathsf{DSKE}}.\mathsf{KeyGen}(par)$. The algorithm then uses the hash function $H()$ to construct a Merkle tree from $\{pk_i\}_{i\in[2^{h_T}]}$. Let R be the root of this Merkle tree. Then it sets $PK = (R, \Delta, h_T, t)$ and $SK = (R, \Delta, h_T, t, \{sk_i\}_{i\in[2^{h_T}]})$, and outputs (SK, PK).

- $\mathsf{Sign}(SK, m)$: On input the key, $SK = (R, \Delta, h_T, t, \{sk_i\}_{i\in[2^{h_T}]})$, it obtains the current time $t' \leftarrow \mathsf{Time}()$, and computes $i = \lfloor (t'-t)/\Delta \rfloor$ (the current time chunk $\lfloor (t'-t)/\Delta \rfloor$). It invokes $s = \Sigma_{\mathsf{DSKE}}.\mathsf{Sign}(sk_i, m)$, the authenticity proof proof_i for the path from leaf_i to the root R, and outputs the signature $\sigma = (s, pk_i, \mathsf{leaf}_i, \mathsf{proof}_i)$.
- $\mathsf{Verify}(PK, m, \sigma)$: On input the public key PK, the message m, and the signature σ, it parses $PK = (R, \Delta, h_T, t)$, and $\sigma = (s, pk_i, \mathsf{leaf}_i, \mathsf{proof}_i)$, obtains the current time $t' \leftarrow \mathsf{Time}()$, and computes $i' = \lfloor (t'-t)/\Delta \rfloor$. If $i \neq i'$ (i.e., messages arrived late), then returns 0. It validates proof_i starting from leaf_i; if invalid, it returns 0. Otherwise, returns $\Sigma_{\mathsf{DSKE}}.\mathsf{Verify}(pk_i, m, s)$.
- $\mathsf{Expire}(PK, \{(m_j, \sigma_j)\}_{j\in[k]})$: On input the public key PK and k message-signature pairs $\{(m_j, \sigma_j)\}_{j\in[k]}$, the algorithm checks that the messages are pairwise different, i.e., for all $j_1, j_2 \in [k]$, $m_{j_1} \neq m_{j_2}$, that all signatures are valid, i.e., for all $j \in [k]$, $\mathsf{Verify}(PK, m_j, \sigma_j) = 1$, and that all signatures are created in the same time chunk, i.e., there exists $i \in [2^{h_T}]$ such that for all $j \in [k]$, $\sigma_j = (s_j, pk_i, \mathsf{leaf}_i, \mathsf{proof}_i)$. If the conditions do not hold, it returns $\perp$. Otherwise, it calls $\Sigma_{\mathsf{DSKE}}.\mathsf{Extract}(\{(m_j, \sigma_j)\}_{j\in[k]}, pk_i)$. If this call returns $\perp$, then $\mathsf{Expire}()$ also returns $\perp$. If it returns an extracted key sk_i, then $\mathsf{Expire}()$ returns the expiry information $\mathsf{info} = (\mathsf{leaf}_i, \mathsf{proof}_i, sk_i)$.
- $\mathsf{Forge}(PK, m, \mathsf{info})$: On input the public key PK, a message m, and the expiry information $\mathsf{info} = (\mathsf{leaf}_i, \mathsf{proof}_i, sk_i)$, for some $i \in [2^{h_T}]$, the algorithm computes $s = \Sigma_{\mathsf{DSKE}}.\mathsf{Sign}(sk_i, m)$ and returns the signature $\sigma = (s, pk_i, \mathsf{leaf}_i, \mathsf{proof}_i)$, where $pk_i = \mathsf{extractPK}(sk_i)$ is the public key of leaf_i.

Figure 2 provides a pictorial example of how GroupForge works. GroupForge satisfies the *correctness*, *unforgeability*, and *forgeability on expiry* properties of an FFS scheme (see the detailed proof in [42]).

Remark 1. A close notion to FSS is the concept of short-lived signatures [3], where the signature becomes non-attributable after some time without requiring further actions from the signer like releasing expiry information. We later in Sect. 8 discuss that GroupForge can also work as a short-lived signature.

6.2 Rate-Limiting Nullifier

Rate Limiting Nullifier. A Rate-Limiting Nullifier (RLN) [36] is a scheme aimed at restricting the number of user actions, thereby facilitating a robust mechanism for spam prevention. This approach has been extensively discussed in a range of real-world applications [10,11]. Generally, RLN achieves spam deterrence by either increasing the difficulty of duplicating identities or disclosing of a user's private key once a certain number of actions are exceeded. In the following, we propose a RLN construction that is directly derived from our $\mathtt{DSKE}_{\mathsf{poly}}$ scheme. The formal study and construction of secure RLN schemes has, to the best of our knowledge, not appeared in academic literature before.

RLN from $\mathtt{DSKE}_{\mathsf{poly}}$. A RLN scheme typically consists of four parts, *setup*, *registration*, *interaction*, and *slashing*, run between two types of participants, a *user* $\mathcal{U}$ and a *server* $\mathcal{T}$. Our $\mathtt{DSKE}_{\mathsf{poly}}$-based RLN works as follows:

- $\mathsf{Setup}(1^\lambda, d, \mathcal{U}, \mathcal{T})$: On input the security parameter λ and degree $d \in \mathbb{N}$, it runs $\mathsf{DSKE_{poly}.Setup}(1^\lambda, d)$ to obtain (ck, vk), which allows a signer to commit to polynomials in $\mathbb{F}^{\leq d}(X)$. It samples a collision-resistant hash function $h : \mathcal{M} \rightarrow \mathbb{F}$. The public parameters par contain ck, vk, d, and h. The parameters are publicly known for the user $\mathcal{U}$ and the server $\mathcal{T}$.
- $\mathsf{Registration}(1^\lambda, \mathcal{U}, \mathcal{T})$: The user $\mathcal{U}$ runs $\mathsf{DSKE_{poly}.KeyGen}(1^\lambda, d)$ to obtain the private key $sk_{\mathcal{U}} = f(X)$ and the public key $pk_{\mathcal{U}} = C_f$. The public key $pk_{\mathcal{U}}$ is registered and stored on the server $\mathcal{T}$. $\mathcal{T}$ initializes a counter $\mathsf{MsgNum}_{\mathcal{U}} = 0$ to record the number of messages signed by $\mathcal{U}$.
- $\mathsf{Interaction}(m, \mathcal{U}, \mathcal{T})$: The interaction algorithm is run between $\mathcal{U}$ and $\mathcal{T}$ in order to sign and verify a message m. User $\mathcal{U}$ parses $sk = f(X)$, computes $x = h(m)$ and the signature $\sigma = \mathsf{DSKE_{poly}.Open}(ck, C_f, x, f(X)) = (\pi, y)$, and sends σ to the server $\mathcal{T}$. Upon receiving σ, server $\mathcal{T}$ parses the user's $pk_{\mathcal{U}} = C_f$ and $\sigma = (\pi, y)$, computes $x = h(m)$, and outputs $\mathsf{DSKE_{poly}.Check}(vk, C_f, x, y, \pi) \in \{0, 1\}$. If $\mathsf{DSKE_{poly}.Check}(vk, C_f, x, y, \pi) = 1$, then $\mathcal{T}$ increases the counter $\mathsf{MsgNum}_{\mathcal{U}}$ and stores the message-signature pair (m, σ).
- $\mathsf{Slashing}(\{(m_i, \sigma_i)\}_{i \in [\mathsf{MsgNum}]}, pk_{\mathcal{U}}, \mathcal{T})$: If server $\mathcal{T}$ has received more than d message-signature pairs from the user $\mathcal{U}$, i.e., $\mathsf{MsgNum} > d$, then $\mathcal{T}$ runs the algorithm $\mathsf{Extract}(\{(m_i, \sigma_i)\}_{i \in [\mathsf{MsgNum}]}, pk_{\mathcal{U}})$ of $\mathsf{DSKE_{kzg}}$ to extract $sk_{\mathcal{U}}$. Subsequently, $\mathcal{T}$ publishes $sk_{\mathcal{U}}$ and removes $\mathcal{U}$ from the system.

Spam Prevention in $\mathsf{DSKE_{poly}}$-based RLN. The key extraction property of a $\mathsf{DSKE_{ploy}}$ (see Theorem 5) empowers the server to extract the private key of a user who issues more than d messages with their signatures. Here, d serves as a predefined parameter, influencing the polynomial's degree that the user can select. Consequently, in a $\mathsf{DSKE_{poly}}$-based RLN, a user is prevented from generating excessive spam (exceeding d messages) because their private key would be publicly disclosed, leading to their expulsion from the system.

Table 1. Performance of $\mathsf{DSKE_{lamp}}$ and $\mathsf{DSKE_{kzg}}$. Note that the probability of extracting the key in $\mathsf{DSKE_{lamp}}$ is overwhelming in k, so the actual size of the extractable group can be smaller than $k = 64$.

Scheme	Group Size	Key Generation	Signing	Verification	Extraction
$\mathsf{DSKE_{lamp}}$(SHA256)	$k = 64$	451.583 μs	17.625 μs	160.458 μs	45.083 μs
$\mathsf{DSKE_{kzg}}$(BLS12-377)	$k = 16$	2.795 ms	2.425 ms	4.949 ms	1.785 ms
	$k = 32$	2.825 ms	2.523 ms	6.123 ms	7.813 ms
	$k = 64$	2.852 ms	2.756 ms	7.202 ms	35.341 ms
	$k = 128$	3.624 ms	3.404 ms	8.045 ms	166.433 ms

Table 2. Performance of GroupForge Constructions with $\Delta = 0.5$ hour.

Scheme	Parameters: Tree height (Duration)	Key Generation	Signing	Verification
$\text{GroupForge}_{\mathsf{hash}}$ (SHA256)	$h_T = 14$ (0.93 years)	7.407 s	21.791 μs	176.541 μs
	$h_T = 15$ (1.87 years)	14.815 s	34.708 μs	177.416 μs
	$h_T = 16$ (3.74 years)	29.631 s	41.291 μs	178.083 μs
	$h_T = 17$ (7.48 years)	59.262 s	45.916 μs	179.374 μs
$\text{GroupForge}_{\mathsf{kzg}}$ (SHA256, BLS12-377, $k = 32$)	$h_T = 14$ (0.93 years)	46.294 s	1.554ms	6.139ms
	$h_T = 15$ (1.87 years)	92.588 s	1.591 ms	6.140 ms
	$h_T = 16$ (3.74 years)	185.175 s	1.611 ms	6.141 ms
	$h_T = 17$ (7.48 years)	370.350 s	1.722 ms	6.143 ms

Using RLN in Anonymous Setting. As discussed in existing works [9–11,37], we can utilize non-interactive zero-knowledge proofs to hide the public key $pk_{\mathcal{U}}$ of a user $\mathcal{U}$, thereby achieving anonymity for an RLN scheme. Nevertheless, a significant challenge persists in obtaining the extractable set, which consists of signatures from the same user. The full anonymity provided by zero-knowledge proofs leaks nothing about the signer, preventing anyone to obtain this set. A feasible approach might be to weaken the full anonymity to the linkable anonymity by including a linkable tag into the signed message. It allows the server to link the signatures and track the number of messages originating from the same user (without revealing the public key). Incorporating these techniques for privacy protection (e.g., blockchain privacy solutions [44]) into our $\mathsf{DSKE_{poly}}$-enhanced RLN represents a promising direction for future work.

7 Evaluation

In this section, we evaluate the performance of hash-based and polynomial commitment-based DSKE, as well as the performance of GroupForge.

Testbed. We evaluate our schemes on a macOS Monterey machine with an Apple M1 chip (8-core, 3.2 GHz), 8 GB of RAM.

DSKE Constructions. We have implemented prototypes of our proposed constructions of $\mathsf{DSKE_{lamp}}$ and $\mathsf{DSKE_{poly}}$ in Rust. For our $\mathsf{DSKE_{lamp}}$, we use the SHA-256 implementation. For $\mathsf{DSKE_{poly}}$, we used the KZG polynomial commitment implementation using the curve BLS12-377 from `arkworks` library[4].

Table 1 provides a comprehensive overview of the performance metrics for both $\mathsf{DSKE_{lamp}}$ and $\mathsf{DSKE_{poly}}$. Remarkably, the execution time of functions within $\mathsf{DSKE_{lamp}}$ consistently remains below $1ms$, indicating efficient processing across various $\mathsf{DSKE_{lamp}}$ functions. The extraction time of $\mathsf{DSKE_{poly}}$ appears as approximately a quadratic function of the group size k. This is because the complexity of $\phi(X)$ in $\mathsf{DSKE_{poly}}$ increases quadratically as k grows.

[4] https://github.com/arkworks-rs/poly-commit.

GroupForge Constructions. We also implement two GroupForge constructions based on $\mathsf{DSKE}_{\mathsf{lamp}}$ and $\mathsf{DSKE}_{\mathsf{poly}}$ respectively. We leverage the Merkle tree library using SHA-256 from **arkworks**[5] to construct our GroupForge. We implement GroupForge$_{\mathsf{hash}}$ with $\mathsf{DSKE}_{\mathsf{lamp}}$, and GroupForge$_{\mathsf{poly}}$ with $\mathsf{DSKE}_{\mathsf{poly}}$ using BLS12-377 curve and the group size $k = 32$. Table 2 summarizes the performance of GroupForge constructions. We evaluate our constructions with Merkle tree heights of 14, 15, 16, and 17, which correspond to a duration of 0.93, 1.87, 3.74 and 7.48 years respectively (given a time chunk of $\Delta = 0.5$ hour). For both GroupForge$_{\mathsf{hash}}$ and GroupForge$_{\mathsf{poly}}$, the most expensive computation is the key generation. This is because we need to generate 2^{h_T} key pairs, where h_T is the Merkle tree height.

8 Discussion

In this part, we discuss relevant properties and examine potential future directions and improvements for our constructions.

GroupForge with Forward-secure Signature Schemes. Forward-secure signature schemes (FSS)[6] [7] allow signers to derive future keys from past keys while preventing users from deriving past keys from future keys. This property of FSS can be combined with GroupForge to demonstrate that if there is a deniable group at some point, the same group can be used as a deniable proof for all message-signature pairs before that point. In particular, to achieve this property, the signer can produce several FSS key pairs from a master private key, and use them in reverse order in the leaves of the Merkle hash tree. For instance, a private key sk_i used in the interval $[t_i, t_i + \Delta]$ can produce all previous private keys sk_j used before t_i. Hence, it is not difficult to see that, if a deniable group exists at some time t', the same group can derive all private keys before t'.

Figure 3 gives a high-level example of how FSS can help improve GroupForge.

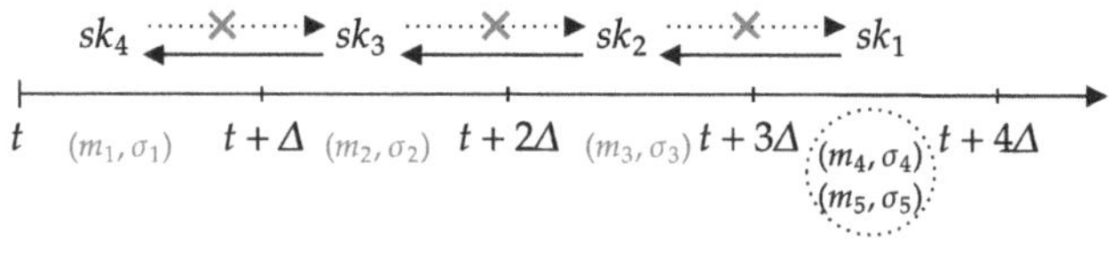

Fig. 3. An example of GroupForge using FSS. The group $\{(m_i, \sigma_i)\}_{i \in \{4,5\}}$ can act as a deniable group that can reconstruct the private key to deny all message-signature pairs in the past, $\{(m_i, \sigma_i)\}_{i \in [3]}$.

[5] https://github.com/arkworks-rs/crypto-primitives.
[6] FSS is not to be confused with forward-forgeable signatures.

GroupForge as a Short-lived Signature. There is a subtle difference between forward-forgeable signature scheme and a short-lived signature scheme. While FFS provides non-attributability by selective release of some *expiry* information, short-lived signatures *automatically* become non-attributable after some time without further action. GroupForge, proposed in Sect. 6.1, can essentially offer both types of functionality. In other words, as the deniability property of GroupForge relies on the *number* of generated signatures, it essentially can be considered a short-lived signature in scenarios where the signer is supposed to generate a *certain* number of signatures, achieving deniability for free without requiring any trusted service or computing costly Verifiable Delay Functions (VDFs) [3]. As mentioned, GroupForge can also be modeled as a forward-forgeable signature, achieving forgeability without constantly publishing key materials that are problematic in practice due to unreliable distribution [41].

Trusted Setup. The KZG scheme used in $\mathsf{DSKE_{poly}}$ requires a trusted setup to generate the public parameters. Although the scheme can leverage a trusted third party to run the setup, such a reliance on a trusted party is typically not welcome in various settings. To remove this trusted assumption, practitioners and the academic community have developed practical solutions to securely generate these parameters, knows as ceremony [33]. Also, one may deploy polynomial commitment schemes that do not require a trusted setup, such as the one constructed from Bulletproofs [18].

Time-Agnostic Forgeability. Although not explicitly mentioned, making a synchronous assumption on the communication is required to ensure parties (i.e., group of size k) receive their signatures in the respective time chuck. Moreover, the proper operation of the system relies on parties having access to a local clock that advances at the same pace. The original work of [41] requires the stronger assumption of a shared global clock. However, we observe that the forgeability aspect of the DSKE is generally independent of the notion of time as it comes from the availability of a sufficient number of signatures for key extraction. This essentially opens up the door to use DSKE for adding forgeability property in settings where reliance on time is not desirable.

Compacting the Keys and Signatures. We can also consider extending $\mathsf{DSKE_{poly}}$ to *multi-signature schemes*, where a group of individuals, each holding their own key pairs, collectively sign a message and the resulting signature is verifiable under the respective set of public keys. In recent years, there has been a surge of interest in multi-signature schemes that support an aggregation property for the public key and the signature, aiming to reduce the size of blockchains, especially in the consensus layer [4,14]. Leveraging the homomorphic property of the underlying KZG polynomial commitment scheme, these key and signature aggregation techniques are also applicable to $\mathsf{DSKE_{kzg}}$, offering a high level of space efficiency.

Table 3. Comparison of signature schemes with deniability.

Scheme	Without Requiring Future Actions (e.g., Publishing Keys)	Without Requiring External Services (e.g., Random Beacon)	Without Requiring VDF
KeyForge [41]	✗	✓	✓
TimeForge [41]	✓	✗	✓
Short-lived signature [3]	✓	✗	✗
GroupForge$_{\mathsf{hash}}$ (based on $\mathsf{DSKE_{hash}}$)	✓	✓	✓
GroupForge$_{\mathsf{poly}}$ (based on $\mathsf{DSKE_{poly}}$)	✓	✓	✓

Reduce the Size of the Private Key. The private key in $\mathsf{DSKE_{poly}}$, i.e., the polynomial $f(X)$, contains d elements of $\mathbb{F}$, i.e., the coefficients $f_0, \dots, f_{d-1}$. A possible optimization is to employ a pseudorandom function (PRF) $F : \{0,1\}^\lambda \times \mathbb{Z} \rightarrow \mathbb{F}$ and pick a $k \in \{0,1\}^\lambda$ as the private key. The coefficients are derived as $f_i = F(k, i)$, for $i \in 0, \dots, d-1$. In the security proof the challenger now chooses k uniformly at random and uses the PRF to derive $f(X)$. From the security definition of PRF, $f(X)$ still looks random to the simulator $\mathcal{B}$. Observe, however, that $\mathsf{Extract}()$ would still return all d coefficients. Similarly, the KeyGen algorithm in GroupForge generates 2^h private keys for the underlying Σ_{DSKE} scheme, i.e., $\{sk_i\}_{i\in[2^h]}$, which are then stored in the private key SK. Using again a PRF $F' : \{0,1\}^\lambda \times \mathbb{Z} \rightarrow \mathbb{Z}$ and a private key $k' \in \{0,1\}^\lambda$ we can generate them as $sk_i = F'(k', i)$, for $i \in 1, \dots, 2^h$, and store only k' in SK. As long as 2^h is polynomial in λ the outputs of F' are pseudorandom and security holds. We leave the formalization of these optimizations as future work.

Further Applications. DSKE can facilitate more applications where the need for authenticity is momentary and signers desire long-term deniability. Such examples are electronic voting and monetary donations. It has been argued that, even if future adversaries cannot go back to change the integrity or the result of a finished election, the privacy requirements of voters in the face of retaliation are everlasting [20]. Similarly, leaked donation records have reportedly caused individuals to be targeted and threatened [34], and transaction deniability might be desirable in such scenarios as well.

9 Related Work

DAPS. Designing digital signature scheme with a key-extraction property has already been explored in the context of double authentication preventing signatures (DAPS). DAPS are genuinely designed with the purpose of double or multiple authentication prevention [8,19,35,40], and they particularly aim at messages of special form, namely $m = (a, p)$, where a is an address and p is a payload. In case a signer signs two (or more) messages with the same address but different payloads, its private key is leaked. However, DSKE essentially provides key extractability as an inherent feature without making assumptions about the type of message, increasing its applicability. In particular, the key extraction in our polynomial commitment-based DSKE (i.e., $\mathsf{DSKE}_{\mathsf{poly}}$) directly comes from the polynomial interpolation theorem. Note that one major downside of many DAPS schemes is their limited address space, i.e., exponentially large address space is not supported. Moreover, a notable difference between DSKE and DAPS is that the former has a sole design similar to the typical signature scheme in the literature like BLS [15], while the latter has a hybrid design, containing different components. For instance, DAPS of [8] builds on trapdoor identification schemes and that of [19] involves encryption scheme and secret sharing. This, in turn, results in DAPS having considerably larger key pairs and also signature sizes compared to the normal signatures [19].

Forward-forgeable and Short-lived Signatures. Specter, Park, and Green formally defined the notion of FFS [41] and showed how FFS can be used to achieve deniability in the email protocol. The main idea of their scheme is to make the signatures become forgeable after a fixed delay. They present two concrete constructions: KeyForge and TimeForge. In the KeyForge construction, the email server needs to periodically publish expired keys to claim deniability over sent emails, and in the TimeForge construction, the signers need to rely on a trusted publicly verifiable time-keeping (PVTK) service to provide them with a verifiable clock time proof. The forgeability comes from the possibility of obtaining a valid proof by querying the PVTK service after a fixed delay.

Arun, Bonneau, and Clark proposed a similar notion to FFS called short-lived signatures [3]. The main idea of their work is to leverage a disjunctive statement to achieve deniability, building up on the previous efforts in the literature, e.g., designated verifier proofs [24], proofs-of-work-or-knowledge (PoWorKs) [5], ring signatures [38], and one-out-of-many proofs [23]. In particular, the construction in Arun *et al.*'s work [3] deploys verifiable delay functions [13,43] as its main building block together with a (trusted) randomness beacon. They use a statement of the form: *I know the witness, x (e.g., private key), or someone solved a VDF on a beacon value derived from the trusted beacon before a time, t.* Hence, their construction offers deniability to the prover because anyone can produce a valid proof by evaluating the VDF through sequential computation. Moreover, a recent analysis report [29] of the VDF implementation shows that VDFs in practice, such as Minroot [27], the VDF for the Ethereum blockchain, might be prone to various potential attacks, which have yet not been explored thoroughly. This work offers a simpler approach without requiring costly VDF evaluations and a trusted random beacon. We provide a comparison of our work and state-of-the-art signature schemes with deniability in Table 3.

Rate-Limiting Nullifier. A Rate-Limiting Nullifier (RLN) [36] is a mechanism designed to restrict users in the number of actions within a system, thereby facilitating an effective spam prevention mechanism. RLN can be used in anonymous voting schemes [10], privacy-preserving P2P networks [37], and decentralized blockchain applications [9]. RLN has been extensively discussed by the blockchain community and implemented in practice [30]. However, to our knowledge, no academic initiative has been undertaken to formally propose and establish secure RLN constructions as we do in this work with DSKE. In addition, it is feasible to extend DSKE-based RLN to an anonymous setting by employing non-interactive zero-knowledge proofs.

10 Conclusion

This paper introduces DSKE, a novel signature scheme featuring key extraction capabilities. We present concrete DSKE constructions based on the hash-based signature schemes and polynomial commitment schemes. We provide formal proof of security for our constructions, demonstrating that signers can consistently achieve deniability by presenting a set of signatures utilized to regenerate (old) private keys. Furthermore, we illustrate how DSKE can serve as the foundation for constructing both GroupForge signatures and RLN schemes. We posit that DSKE holds promise to be applicable in settings that require short-term authenticity.

References

1. Abraham, I., Jovanovic, P., Maller, M., Meiklejohn, S., Stern, G.: Bingo: adaptivity and asynchrony in verifiable secret sharing and distributed key generation. In: Advances in Cryptology - CRYPTO. Springer, Heidelberg (2023). https://doi.org/10.1007/978-3-031-38557-5_2
2. Allman, E., Callas, J., Delany, M., Libbey, M., Fenton, J., Thomas, M.: Domainkeys identified mail (dkim) signatures. Technical report, RFC 4871 (2007)
3. Arun, A., Bonneau, J., Clark, J.: Short-lived zero-knowledge proofs and signatures. In: ASIACRYPT 2022. Springer, Heidelberg (2022). https://doi.org/10.1007/978-3-031-22969-5_17
4. Azouvi, S., Cachin, C., Le, D.V., Vukolic, M., Zanolini, L.: Modeling resources in permissionless longest-chain total-order broadcast. In: 26th International Conference on Principles of Distributed Systems, OPODIS 2022, Brussels, Belgium, 13–15 December 2022, vol. 253 of LIPIcs, pp. 19:1–19:23. Schloss Dagstuhl - Leibniz-Zentrum für Informatik (2022)
5. Baldimtsi, F., Kiayias, A., Zacharias, T., Zhang, B.: Indistinguishable proofs of work or knowledge. In: Cheon, J.H., Takagi, T. (eds.) ASIACRYPT 2016. LNCS, vol. 10032, pp. 902–933. Springer, Heidelberg (2016). https://doi.org/10.1007/978-3-662-53890-6_30
6. Beck, G., Choudhuri, A.R., Green, M., Jain, A., Tiwari, P.R.: Time-deniable signatures. In: Proceedings on Privacy Enhancing Technologies (2023)
7. Bellare, M., Miner, S.K.: A forward-secure digital signature scheme. In: Wiener, M. (ed.) CRYPTO 1999. LNCS, vol. 1666, pp. 431–448. Springer, Heidelberg (1999). https://doi.org/10.1007/3-540-48405-1_28

8. Bellare, M., Poettering, B., Stebila, D.: Deterring certificate subversion: efficient double-authentication-preventing signatures. In: Fehr, S. (ed.) PKC 2017. LNCS, vol. 10175, pp. 121–151. Springer, Heidelberg (2017). https://doi.org/10.1007/978-3-662-54388-7_5
9. Blagoj. Private message sharing for eth2 validators (2021). https://ethresear.ch/t/private-message-sharing-for-eth2-validators/10664
10. Blagoj. Rate limiting nullifier: A spam-protection mechanism for anonymous environments (2021). https://medium.com/privacy-scaling-explorations/rate-limiting-nullifier-a-spam-protection-mechanism-for-anonymous-environments-bbe4006a57d
11. Blagoj and WhiteHat Barry. Decentralised cloudflare - using rln and rich user identities (2021). https://ethresear.ch/t/decentralised-cloudflare-using-rln-and-rich-user-identities/10774
12. Blythe, S.E.: Digital signature law of the United Nations, European Union, United Kingdom and United States: promotion of growth in e-commerce with enhanced security. Richmond J. Law Technol. **11**(2), 6 (2005)
13. Boneh, D., Bonneau, J., Bünz, B., Fisch, B.: Verifiable delay functions. In: Shacham, H., Boldyreva, A. (eds.) CRYPTO 2018. LNCS, vol. 10991, pp. 757–788. Springer, Cham (2018). https://doi.org/10.1007/978-3-319-96884-1_25
14. Boneh, D., Drijvers, M., Neven, G.: Compact multi-signatures for smaller blockchains. In: Peyrin, T., Galbraith, S. (eds.) ASIACRYPT 2018. LNCS, vol. 11273, pp. 435–464. Springer, Cham (2018). https://doi.org/10.1007/978-3-030-03329-3_15
15. Boneh, D., Lynn, B., Shacham, H.: Short signatures from the weil pairing. In: Boyd, C. (ed.) ASIACRYPT 2001. LNCS, vol. 2248, pp. 514–532. Springer, Heidelberg (2001). https://doi.org/10.1007/3-540-45682-1_30
16. Borisov, N., Goldberg, I., Brewer, E.: Off-the-record communication, or, why not to use pgp. In: Proceedings of the 2004 ACM Workshop on Privacy in the Electronic Society, pp. 77–84 (2004)
17. Buchmann, J., Dahmen, E., Ereth, S., Hülsing, A., Rückert, M.: On the security of the winternitz one-time signature scheme. In: Nitaj, A., Pointcheval, D. (eds.) AFRICACRYPT 2011. LNCS, vol. 6737, pp. 363–378. Springer, Heidelberg (2011). https://doi.org/10.1007/978-3-642-21969-6_23
18. Bünz, B., Bootle, J., Boneh, D., Poelstra, A., Wuille, P., Maxwell, G.: Bulletproofs: short proofs for confidential transactions and more. In: IEEE Symposium on Security and Privacy (SP), pp. 315–334. IEEE (2018)
19. Derler, D., Ramacher, S., Slamanig, D.: Short double-and n-times-authentication-preventing signatures from ecdsa and more. In: IEEE European Symposium on Security and Privacy (EuroS&P), pp. 273–287. IEEE (2018)
20. Ge, H., et al.: Koinonia: verifiable e-voting with long-term privacy. In: Proceedings of the 35th Annual Computer Security Applications Conference, pp. 270–285 (2019)
21. Goldwasser, S., Micali, S., Rivest, R.L.: A digital signature scheme secure against adaptive chosen-message attacks. SIAM J. Comput. **17**(2), 281–308 (1988)
22. Green, M.: Ok Google: please publish your DKIM secret keys (2020). https://blog.cryptographyengineering.com/2020/11/16/ok-google-please-publish-your-dkim-secret-keys/
23. Groth, J., Kohlweiss, M.: One-out-of-many proofs: or how to leak a secret and spend a coin. In: Oswald, E., Fischlin, M. (eds.) EUROCRYPT 2015. LNCS, vol. 9057, pp. 253–280. Springer, Heidelberg (2015). https://doi.org/10.1007/978-3-662-46803-6_9

24. Jakobsson, M., Sako, K., Impagliazzo, R.: Designated verifier proofs and their applications. In: Maurer, U. (ed.) EUROCRYPT 1996. LNCS, vol. 1070, pp. 143–154. Springer, Heidelberg (1996). https://doi.org/10.1007/3-540-68339-9_13
25. Karanikolas, N.: Digital signature legality in different jurisdictions: Legally binding issues (2019)
26. Kate, A., Zaverucha, G.M., Goldberg, I.: Constant-size commitments to polynomials and their applications. In: Abe, M. (ed.) ASIACRYPT 2010. LNCS, vol. 6477, pp. 177–194. Springer, Heidelberg (2010). https://doi.org/10.1007/978-3-642-17373-8_11
27. Khovratovich, D., Maller, M., Tiwari, P.R.: Minroot: Candidate sequential function for ethereum vdf. Cryptology ePrint Archive (2022)
28. Lamport, L.: Constructing digital signatures from a one way function (1979)
29. Leurent, G., Mennink, B., Pietrzak, K., Rijmen, V.: Analysis of minroot: Public report (2023). https://crypto.ethereum.org/events/minrootanalysis2023.pdf
30. Lim, W.: Rln on kzg polynomial commitment scheme (2023). https://zkresear.ch/t/rln-on-kzg-polynomial-commitment-scheme-cross-posted/114
31. Mason, S.: Electronic signatures in law. University of London Press (2016)
32. Merkle, R.C.: A certified digital signature. In: Brassard, G. (ed.) CRYPTO 1989. LNCS, vol. 435, pp. 218–238. Springer, New York (1990). https://doi.org/10.1007/0-387-34805-0_21
33. Nikolaenko, V., Ragsdale, S., Bonneau, J., Boneh, D.: Powers-of-tau to the people: Decentralizing setup ceremonies. Cryptology ePrint Archive (2022)
34. Ottawa Citizen. Threats close stella luna gelato café after owner's name appears in givesendgo data leak (2022). https://ottawacitizen.com/news/local-news/threats-close-stella-luna-gelato-cafe-after-owners-name-appears-in-givesendgo-data-leak
35. Poettering, B., Stebila, D.: Double-authentication-preventing signatures. In: Kutyłowski, M., Vaidya, J. (eds.) ESORICS 2014. LNCS, vol. 8712, pp. 436–453. Springer, Cham (2014). https://doi.org/10.1007/978-3-319-11203-9_25
36. Privacy and Scaling Explorations team, Ethereum Foundation. Rate-limiting nullifier (2024). https://rate-limiting-nullifier.github.io/rln-docs/rln.html
37. Vac Research. Privacy-preserving p2p economic spam protection in waku v2 (2021). https://vac.dev/rlog/rln-relay/
38. Rivest, R.L., Shamir, A., Tauman, Y.: How to leak a secret. In: Boyd, C. (ed.) ASIACRYPT 2001. LNCS, vol. 2248, pp. 552–565. Springer, Heidelberg (2001). https://doi.org/10.1007/3-540-45682-1_32
39. Rogaway, P., Shrimpton, T.: Cryptographic hash-function basics: definitions, implications, and separations for preimage resistance, second-preimage resistance, and collision resistance. In: Roy, B., Meier, W. (eds.) FSE 2004. LNCS, vol. 3017, pp. 371–388. Springer, Heidelberg (2004). https://doi.org/10.1007/978-3-540-25937-4_24
40. Ruffing, T., Kate, A., Schröder, D.: Liar, liar, coins on fire! penalizing equivocation by loss of bitcoins. In: CCS 2015 (2015)
41. Specter, M.A., Park, S., Green, M.: KeyForge:non-attributable email from Forward-Forgeable Signatures. In: 30th USENIX Security Symposium (USENIX Security 21), pp. 1755–1773 (2021)
42. Wang, Z., et al.: DSKE: digital signatures with key extraction. Cryptology ePrint Archive, Paper 2022/1753 (2022). https://eprint.iacr.org/2022/1753
43. Wesolowski, B.: Efficient verifiable delay functions. In: Annual International Conference on the Theory and Applications of Cryptographic Techniques (2019)
44. Wicht, F.-X., Wang, Z., Le, D.V., Cachin, C.: A transaction-level model for blockchain privacy. Cryptology ePrint Archive (2023)

Simplified Adaptively Secure Threshold BLS Signatures

Benoît Libert(✉)

Zama, Paris, France
benoit.libert@zama.ai

Abstract. Recently (Crypto'24), Das and Ren proposed an adaptively secure variant of threshold BLS signatures. Unlike the initial threshold BLS signature described by Boldyreva (PKC'03), their variant can be proven secure in the adaptive corruption setting while preserving the useful features of the scheme (i.e., non-interactivity, uniqueness of signatures, and optimal signature size). In this work, we present a simplification of their scheme where the sizes of partial signatures and secret key shares are decreased by $\approx 20\%$ and 33%, respectively. In addition, we reduce the communication cost of the distributed key generation phase by a factor 2. We can still prove the security of our simplified variant under adaptive corruptions in the random oracle model and under the same assumptions (namely, the co-CDH assumption and the DDH assumption in the first source group of the pairing) as Das and Ren.

Keywords: Non-interactive threshold signatures · adaptive corruptions · BLS signatures

1 Introduction

Threshold cryptography [15,24,27,28] involves primitives where secret keys are split into $n > 1$ shares, held by distinct parties, with the motivation of increasing the system's resilience to failures and its security. In (t, n)-threshold signatures, signature generation requires the cooperation of at least $t + 1$ out of n servers. In terms of security, an adversary that corrupts up to t servers remains unable to forge signatures. Threshold signatures thus enhance the security of highly sensitive private keys, like those of certification authorities, since the adversary is forced to break into multiple locations to compromise the security of the system. The recent years, they received a revived interest from the research community as they have proven to be useful tools in blockchain applications.

Thresholdizing existing digital signatures (including Schnorr [56] or ECDSA signatures [3]) often requires several rounds of interaction among shareholders. In contrast, non-interactive threshold signatures require no communication between shareholders who can even generate their partial signature without being aware of one another.

A. Patra (Ed.): CT-RSA 2025, LNCS 15598, pp. 174–197, 2025.
https://doi.org/10.1007/978-3-031-88661-4_8

In [11], Boldyreva proposed a practical non-interactive threshold variant of Boneh-Lynn-Shacham (BLS) signatures [13]. Besides its appealing non-interactive signing procedure, Boldyreva's scheme retains the advantages of centralized BLS signatures, including their optimal signature length (with signatures comprised of only one element of a pairing-friendly group) and their unique signatures. In particular, the latter property makes the scheme suitable to the construction of distributed verifiable random functions [52], distributed coin flipping protocols [16] and randomness beacons in blockchain applications.

On the downside, Boldyreva's threshold signature [11] was only proven secure under static corruptions, meaning that the adversary has to declare the set of corrupted parties at the very beginning of the attack game, before the generation of the public key. In an adaptive corruption model, adversaries are allowed to choose whom to corrupt at any time, based on the previously collected information. In particular, they can interleave signing queries and corruption queries in arbitrary order.

Das and Ren [23] proposed an adaptively secure threshold BLS signature which retains the main advantages of Boldyreva's construction, including its optimal signature length as well as its uniqueness and the fact that signatures can be verified exactly in the same way as in the centralized scheme [13]. Their construction, however, increases the length of secret key shares by a factor 3. In addition, it involves partial signatures that come along with longer proofs of correctness showing the validity of partial signatures.

A natural question to ask is then whether we can reduce the overhead incurred by security proofs under adaptive corruptions (without introducing further idealizations such as the algebraic group model [32]) compared to their analogue [11] that is only proven secure under static corruptions.

1.1 Our Contribution

We present a simplified version of the adaptively secure threshold BLS signature recently proposed by Das and Ren [23]. Like [23], we prove security under adaptive corruptions in the random oracle model under the co-CDH assumption and assuming the hardness of DDH in $\mathbb{G}$, which allows instantiating the scheme in Type-2 and Type-3 pairings.

We improve upon [23] in several aspects: (i) We have shorter secret-key shares consisting of only two field elements instead of three; (ii) Each proof that a partial signature was correctly generated is shorter and faster to compute/verify than in [23]; (iii) Verification keys $(\mathsf{vk}_1, \ldots, \mathsf{vk}_n) \in \mathbb{G}^n$ are also shorter as they live in the same source group $\mathbb{G}$ as the signature whereas [23] requires verification keys in $\hat{\mathbb{G}}^n$ if signatures live in $\mathbb{G}$; (iii) The distributed key generation protocol has a smaller communication cost as each player only broadcasts one element of $\hat{\mathbb{G}}$ and $t+1$ elements of $\mathbb{G}$ (instead of $t+1$ elements of $\hat{\mathbb{G}}$ in [23]).

Concretely, we shorten the size of secret key shares by 33% and the size (as well as the generation cost) of partial signature evaluation proofs by 25%. Each secret key share is only twice (instead of three times in [23]) as large as the secret key of the centralized scheme [13]. We note that, in Boldyreva's construction [11], secret key shares are as short as secret keys in centralized BLS signatures, which means that we obtain adaptive security by only doubling the share size.

If the scheme is instantiated with BLS12-381 curves [8], each element of $\hat{\mathbb{G}}$ is as long as two elements of $\mathbb{G}$. We then decrease the size of verification keys and the communication cost of the distributed key generation protocol by a factor 2. With other pairing-friendly curves, this factor only becomes larger: for example, in KSS16 curves [41], elements of $\hat{\mathbb{G}}$ are three times as long as those of $\mathbb{G}$.

1.2 Technical Overview

In asymmetric pairings $e : \mathbb{G} \times \hat{\mathbb{G}} \to \mathbb{G}_T$ of prime order p, BLS signatures [13] are of the form $\sigma = H_0(M)^s$, where $s \in \mathbb{Z}_p$ is the secret key and $H_0 : \{0,1\}^* \to \mathbb{G}$ is a hash function modeled as a random oracle. Using the public key $\hat{g}^s$, signatures can be verified by testing if $e(\sigma, \hat{g}) = e(H_0(M), \hat{g}^s)$. Due to its linearly homomorphic property over the key space, the scheme is well-suited to non-interactive threshold signing protocols. If each secret key share $\mathsf{sk}_i = s(i)$ consists of a Shamir secret sharing [58] of $s = s(0)$ for some degree-t polynomial $s[X]$, then partial signature can be generated $\sigma_i = H_0(m)^{s(i)}$. A combiner can then reconstruct $\sigma = H_0(M)^s$ via a simple Lagrange interpolation in the exponent.

When it comes to proving security under adaptive corruptions, the difficulty is that partial signatures $\sigma_i = H_0(M)^{s(i)}$ information-theoretically commit to the underlying secret key share $\mathsf{sk}_i = s(i)$, so that $t+1$ partial signatures commit to the entire secret key. In the adaptive corruption setting, it prevents a reduction from the security of the centralized scheme. Indeed, without knowing the shared secret key s, the reduction is only be able to consistently simulate the internal state of at most t servers. So, at the first (signing or corruption) query involving the i-th server, the reduction has to decide if it will "know" sk_i or not. Clearly, the reduction can only succeed if it guesses in advance the set of corrupted players (which causes a super-polynomial security loss if the number of n servers is super-logarithmic) since an adaptive adversary can obtain n partial signatures before making a first corruption query.

In order to prove adaptive security, the construction of [23] uses modified partial signatures of the form $\sigma_i = H_0(M)^{s(i)} H_1(M)^{r(i)}$, where $H_1\{0,1\}^* :\to \mathbb{G}$ is another random oracle and $\{r(i)\}_{i=1}^n$ is a Shamir secret sharing of 0 (for a random polynomial $r[X]$ such that $r(0) = 0$). This modification still allows reconstructing $\sigma = H_0(M)^s$ by Lagrange interpolation in the exponent. In addition, it allows making partial signatures "non-committing" in a sequence of games that steps through an intermediate game where random oracle outputs $(H_0(M), H_1(M))$ are correlated. Specifically, the scheme involves verification keys $\{\mathsf{vk}_i\}_{i=1}^n$ where each $\mathsf{vk}_i \in \hat{\mathbb{G}}$ is a commitment to $(s(i), r(i))$, which helps prove the correctness of partial signatures. In order to minimize the information that an unbounded adversary learns about $(s(i), r(i))$ for uncorrupted users i, the security proof considers a hybrid game where, for all messages M that differ from the forgery message $M^\star$, $(H_0(M), H_1(M))$ lives in the one-dimensional subspace spanned by a public vector $(g, h) \in \mathbb{G}^2$ (this technique was previously used in [46]). Under the DDH assumption in $\mathbb{G}$, the modified distribution of $\{(H_0(M), H_1(M))\}_{M \neq M^\star}$

will not affect the adversary's behavior. After this change, the proof of [23] replaces the real $r[X]$ by a polynomial $r[X]$ such that $r(0) = 1$ without the adversary noticing (as long as it corrupts at most t players). The latter polynomial switching has the effect of deviating the public key towards a "rigged" public key $\hat{g}^s = \hat{g}^{s(0)} \cdot h^{r(0)} = \hat{g}^{s(0)} \cdot h$, where g, h are part of a co-Diffie-Hellman instance. At this point, if the reduction programs $H_0(M^\star)$ in a suitable way, it can use the forgery $\sigma^\star = H_0(M^\star)^{s(0)+\log_g(h)}$ to solve its co-Diffie-Hellman instance.

To apply the above approach, one issue arises from verification keys $\{\mathsf{vk}_i\}_{i=1}^n$ that contain commitments to $\{(s(i), r(i))\}_{i=1}^n$ and help prove the validity of partial signatures. In order to hide the replacement of $r(0) = 0$ by $r(0) = 1$ to any adversary corrupting at most t players, each vk_i should statistically hide the underlying $(s(i), r(i))$ (recall that this is possible after the transition ensuring that $\{(H_0(M), H_1(M))\}_{M \neq M^\star}$ all live in the subspace spanned by (g, h)). Since the public key and $\{\mathsf{vk}_i\}_{i=1}^n$ are generated in a distributed key generation (DKG) protocol where players send verifiable secret sharings to one another, Das and Ren [23] use verification keys of the form $\mathsf{vk}_i = \hat{g}^{s(i)} \cdot \hat{h}^{r(i)} \cdot \hat{v}^{r(i)}$, where $\hat{h}, \hat{v} \in \hat{\mathbb{G}}$ are public generators and $u[x]$ is an additional degree-t polynomial such that $u(0) = 0$. This modification has the consequence of increasing the size of secret key shares (which now consist of 3 scalars $\mathsf{sk}_i = (s(i), r(i), u(i))$) and the length of evaluation proofs showing that each σ_i is consistent with vk_i.

We adopt a different solution to the above problem and use verification keys $\mathsf{vk}_i = g^{s(i)} h^{r(i)}$ in the first source group $\mathbb{G}$ of the pairing, which allows secret key share $\mathsf{sk}_i = (s(i), r(i))$ made of two scalars. Note that we cannot simply set $\mathsf{vk}_i = \hat{g}^{s(i)} \hat{h}^{r(i)} \in \hat{\mathbb{G}}$ in the second source group as this would require $\log_{\hat{g}}(\hat{h}) = \log_g(h)$ in order to preserve the entropy of $(s(i), r(i))$ (recall that partial signatures reveal $g^{s(i)} h^{r(i)}$). The problem is that publicizing such an $\hat{h}$ would not be compatible with a reduction from the DDH assumption in a game transition leading to vectors $\{(H_0(M), H_1(M))\}_{M \neq M^\star}$ in the subspace $\langle (g, h) \rangle$. Fortunately, we do not have this issue with verification keys $\mathsf{vk}_i = g^{s(i)} h^{r(i)} \in \mathbb{G}$. Without using an additional polynomial $u[X]$ as a source of entropy, we can still prove (in Lemma 3) that an unbounded adversary that corrupts at most t parties is unable to distinguish between games where $r(0) = 0$ and $r(1)$.

When the public key is generated using a distributed key generation protocol (which is realized using a one-round Pedersen-like protocol [55] as in [23, 46]), one additional difficulty is that $s[X]$ is obtained by summing polynomials $\{s_j[X]\}_{j \in \mathcal{Q}}$ chosen by non-disqualified players in a set $\mathcal{Q}$. So, each verification key $\mathsf{vk}_i = g^{s(i)} h^{r(i)}$ is obtained by homomorphically combining Pedersen commitments to polynomial evaluations $\{(s_j(i), r_j(i))\}_{j \in \mathcal{Q}}$. The issue is that verification keys vk_i live in $\mathbb{G}$ while the key generation protocol has to produce a public key $\hat{g}^{s(0)}$ in $\hat{\mathbb{G}}$. If we directly adapt the DKG protocol of [23] by reversing the roles of $\mathbb{G}$ and $\hat{\mathbb{G}}$, each party $j \in \mathcal{Q}$ only sends a commitment $C_{j0} = g^{s_j(0)} h^{r_j(0)} = g^{s_j(0)}$ and simply multiplying these commitments leads to a public key $\prod_{j \in \mathcal{Q}} C_{j0} = g^{s(0)}$ in $\mathbb{G}$ instead of $\hat{\mathbb{G}}$. Hence, we require each player j to also send $\hat{C}_{j0} = \hat{g}^{s_j(0)} \hat{h}^{r_j(0)} = \hat{g}^{s_j(0)}$ in the DKG protocol (which does not require $\hat{h}$ since $r_j(0) = 0$) and have all parties check that $e(g, \hat{C}_{j0}) = e(C_{j0}, \hat{g})$. This public key can then be obtained as $\hat{g}^{s(0)} = \prod_{j \in \mathcal{Q}} \hat{C}_{j0}$. The use of verification keys in $\mathbb{G}$ has the benefit of decreasing the communication cost of the DKG phase by a factor 2 since each player only has to broadcast one element of $\hat{\mathbb{G}}$ and about t elements of $\mathbb{G}$ instead of $\approx t$ elements of $\hat{\mathbb{G}}$ in [23]. Another difference with the DKG protocol of [23] is that each player P_i no longer has to prove knowledge of $\log_g(C_{i0})$ via a Σ-protocol since the equality $e(g, \hat{C}_{i0}) = e(C_{i0}, \hat{g})$ already serves as an argument that $r_i(0) = 0$.

1.3 Related Work

Threshold signatures were suggested by Desmedt [27]. Since then, a large body of work was devoted to threshold extensions of existing standard signature schemes (see [9–12,17,19,25,34–37,39,43,44,48,59,60,62,64] and references therein). Most of these works only considered static corruptions due to the difficulty of consistently explaining the internal state of adaptively corrupted players. Also, very few schemes are non-interactive. One reason is that distributing the signing process of digital signatures [10,20,22,36,61] derived from the Fiat-Shamir paradigm [29] inherently requires more than one round as (unless they involve a message-independent pre-processing round [44,45]) the parties usually need at least one round of interaction to jointly generate a secret randomness. The same holds for threshold (EC)DSA signatures [17,19,34,49].

Non-interactive statically secure schemes. Shoup described [60] efficient non-interactive RSA-based threshold signatures. Boldyreva's scheme [11] can be seen as a pairing-based analogue of [60]. Katz and Yung [43] proposed factoring-based threshold signatures. Wee [64] put forth an abstract framework for the realization of threshold signatures which implies a variant of [43].

Boneh *et al.* introduced universal thresholdizers [12] as a compiler allowing to turn any signature scheme into a non-interactive threshold signature. While generic, their approach incurs a significant overhead as it requires to homomorphically evaluate the circuit of the signing algorithm in a (threshold) fully homomorphic encryption scheme.

Adaptive corruptions. Canetti *et al.* [18] and Frankel *et al.* [30,31] independently proposed interactive adaptively secure threshold signatures by introducing a technique called “single inconsistent player” (SIP). The idea is that, at any step of the security proof, there is only one player whose internal state cannot be consistently simulated by the reduction. Since this inconsistent player is initially chosen at random by the reduction, it only gets corrupted with probability $\leq 1/2$ as long as there is a majority of uncorrupted players (i.e., $n > 2t$). The SIP technique initially assumed reliable erasures in order to properly stimulate corrupted players. It was subsequently combined with other tools [1,40,50] to achieve adaptive security avoid relying on erasures. It was also used to build adaptively secure threshold RSA [2] and Waters [63] signatures. These constructions require interaction among shareholders at each signature generation.

Non-interactive threshold signature with adaptive security were proposed in [47] assuming reliable erasures. In [46], Libert, Joye and Yung came up with a non-interactive realization without relying on erasures. While their scheme has a BLS-like structure, it departs from [11] and from standard BLS signatures in its verification algorithm. In particular, it loses the signature uniqueness property[1] and the optimal signature length by requiring two group elements per signature. Bacho and Loss [4] showed that Boldyreva's original scheme [11] can be proven adaptively secure in the combined algebraic group [32] and random oracle model under an interactive one-more discrete logarithm assumption. They further proved that the one-more assumption cannot be avoided in any proof of adaptive security with or without the algebraic group model.

The recent work of Das and Ren [23] bypassed the impossibility result of [4] by modifying Boldyreva's scheme [11] and the shape of secret key shares and partial signatures (while preserving the shape of BLS signatures after its reconstruction from partial signatures).

Several recent works [5–7,22,42] re-investigated the adaptive security of pairing-free threshold signatures. These schemes, however, require interaction during the signing process and sometimes rely on interactive one-more assumptions [22]. Similarly to [23], we focus on non-interactive schemes based on standard assumptions in this work.

2 Background

NOTATIONS. For integers $a, b \in \mathbb{N}$, we denote by $[a]$ and $[a, b]$ the sets $\{1, 2, \ldots, a\}$ and $\{a, a+1, \ldots, b\}$, respectively.

2.1 Definitions for Threshold Signatures

A non-interactive (t, n)-threshold signature scheme is a tuple $\Sigma = (\mathsf{DKG}, \mathsf{Share\text{-}Sign}, \mathsf{Share\text{-}Verify}, \mathsf{Verify}, \mathsf{Combine})$ of efficient algorithms or protocols such that:

DKG$(\mathsf{params}, \lambda, t, n)$**:** is an interactive protocol involving n players $P_1, \ldots, P_n$, which all take as input common public parameters params, a security parameter $\lambda \in \mathbb{N}$ as well as a pair of integers $t, n \in \mathsf{poly}(\lambda)$ such that $1 \leq t \leq n$. The outcome of the protocol is the generation of a public key pk, a vector of private key shares $\mathbf{sk} = (\mathsf{sk}_1, \ldots, \mathsf{sk}_n)$ where P_i only obtains sk_i for each $i \in [n]$, and a public vector of verification keys $\mathbf{vk} = (\mathsf{vk}_1, \ldots, \mathsf{vk}_n)$. At the end of this protocol, some players may be disqualified, in which case their shares are replaced by zeroes. We call $\mathcal{Q}$ the set of non-disqualified players.

Share-Sign(sk_i, M)**:** is a possibly randomized algorithm that takes in a message M and a private key share sk_i. It outputs a signature share σ_i and (optionally) a proof π_{σ_i} that σ_i was correctly generated.

[1] While their signing algorithm is deterministic, signatures are not unique.

Share-Verify$(\mathsf{pk}, \mathbf{vk}, M, (i, \sigma_i, \pi_{\sigma,i}))$**:** is a deterministic algorithm that takes as input a message M, the public key pk, the verification key $\mathbf{vk}$ and a triple $(i, \sigma_i, \pi_{\sigma,i})$ consisting of an index $i \in [n]$ and signature share σ_i and a proof $\pi_{\sigma,i}$. It outputs 1 if $(\sigma_i, \pi_{\sigma,i})$ is deemed valid and 0 otherwise.

Combine$(\mathsf{pk}, \mathbf{vk}, M, \{(i, \sigma_i, \pi_{\sigma,i})\}_{i \in S})$**:** takes as input a public key pk, a message M and a subset $S \subset [n]$ of size $|S| = t + 1$ with triples $\{(i, \sigma_i, \pi_{\sigma,i})\}_{i \in S}$ such that $i \in [n]$ and σ_i is a signature share and $\pi_{\sigma,i}$ a proof of validity for σ_i. This algorithm outputs either a full signature σ or $\perp$ if $\{(i, \sigma_i, \pi_{\sigma,i})\}_{i \in S}$ is found to contain invalid partial signatures.

Verify(pk, M, σ)**:** is a deterministic algorithm that takes as input a message M, the public key pk and a signature σ. It outputs 1 or 0 depending on whether σ is deemed valid or not.

We use the same communication model as in, e.g., [35–37], which is partially synchronous. Namely, communications proceed in synchronized rounds and sent messages are always received within some time bound in the same round. All players have access to a public broadcast channel, which the adversary can use as a sender and a receiver. However, the adversary cannot modify messages sent over this channel, nor prevent their delivery. In addition, we assume private and authenticated channels between all pairs of players.

In the adaptive corruption setting, the security of non-interactive threshold signatures is captured by Definition 1, where we assume a majority of honest parties (i.e., $n \geq 2t + 1$).

Definition 1. *A non-interactive (t, n)-threshold signature scheme Σ is* **adaptively secure** *against* **chosen-message attacks** *if no PPT adversary $\mathcal{A}$ has non-negligible advantage in the game hereunder. At any time, we denote by $\mathcal{C} \subset \{1, \ldots, n\}$ and $\mathcal{G} := \{1, \ldots, n\} \backslash \mathcal{C}$ the dynamically evolving subsets of corrupted and honest players, respectively. Initially, we set $\mathcal{C} = \emptyset$.*

1. *The game begins with an execution of* $\mathsf{DKG}(\mathsf{params}, \lambda, t, n)$ *where the challenger plays the role of honest players P_i and $\mathcal{A}$ can corrupt players at any time. When $\mathcal{A}$ chooses to corrupt a player P_i, the challenger sets $\mathcal{G} = \mathcal{G} \backslash \{i\}$, $\mathcal{C} = \mathcal{C} \cup \{i\}$ and returns the internal state of P_i. Moreover, $\mathcal{A}$ is allowed to act on behalf of P_i from this point forward. The protocol ends with the generation of a public key* pk*, a vector of private key shares* $\mathbf{sk} = (\mathsf{sk}_1, \ldots, \mathsf{sk}_n)$ *and the corresponding verification keys* $\mathbf{vk} = (\mathsf{vk}_1, \ldots, \mathsf{vk}_n)$*. At the end of this phase, the public key* pk *and* $\{\mathsf{sk}_i\}_{i \in \mathcal{C}}$ *are available to $\mathcal{A}$.*
2. *On polynomially many occasions, $\mathcal{A}$ adaptively interleaves two kinds of queries.*
   - *Corruption query: At any time, $\mathcal{A}$ can choose to corrupt a server. To this end, $\mathcal{A}$ chooses $i \in \{1, \ldots, n\}$ and the challenger returns* sk_i *before setting $\mathcal{G} = \mathcal{G} \backslash \{i\}$ and $\mathcal{C} = \mathcal{C} \cup \{i\}$.*
   - *Signing query: For any $i \in \mathcal{G}$, $\mathcal{A}$ can also submit a pair (i, M) and ask for a signature share on a message M on behalf of player P_i. The challenger responds by computing* $\sigma_i \leftarrow \mathsf{Share\text{-}Sign}(\mathsf{sk}_i, M)$ *and returning σ to $\mathcal{A}$.*

3. *$\mathcal{A}$ outputs a message $M^\star$ and a signature $\sigma^\star$. We define $\mathcal{V} = \mathcal{C} \cup \mathcal{S}[M^\star]$, where $\mathcal{S}[M^\star] \subset \{1, \ldots, n\}$ is the subset of players for which $\mathcal{A}$ made a signing query of the form $(i, M^\star)$. The experiment returns 1 (meaning that $\mathcal{A}$ wins) if the following conditions hold: (i) $|\mathcal{V}| < t+1$; (ii) $\mathsf{Verify}(\mathsf{pk}, M^\star, \sigma^\star) = 1$. Otherwise, the experiment returns 0.*

The adversary's advantage is defined as the probability that the experiment return 1, taken over all random choices.

Since we focus on non-interactive schemes, Definition 1 allows the adversary to individually query each partial signing oracle whereas usual definitions only provide the adversary with an oracle that runs the distributed signing protocol on behalf of all honest players. We also remark that Definition 1 allows the adversary to obtain some partial signatures on the forgery message $M^\star$ as long as its output remains a non-trivial forgery.

The following two definitions are adapted from [14, Chapter 22] with slight changes to capture adaptive adversaries.

Definition 2. *A non-interactive threshold signature scheme Σ provides* **correctness** *if, for all security parameters λ, any public parameters* params*, any integers $t < n \in \mathsf{poly}(\lambda)$, any adversary $\mathcal{A}$, any possible output*

$$(\mathsf{pk}, \mathbf{sk} = (\mathsf{sk}_1, \ldots, \mathsf{sk}_n), \mathbf{vk} = (\mathsf{vk}_1, \ldots, \mathsf{vk}_n))$$

of $\mathsf{DKG}(\mathsf{params}, \lambda, t, n)$, and any message M, we have

$$\forall i \in [n] : \Pr[\ \mathsf{Share\text{-}Verify}\big(\mathsf{pk}, \mathbf{vk}, M, (i, (\sigma_i, \pi_{\sigma,i}))\big) = 1 \mid (\sigma_i, \pi_{\sigma,i}) \leftarrow \mathsf{Share\text{-}Sign}(i, \mathsf{sk}_i, M)\ ] = 1.$$

Definition 3. *A non-interactive threshold signature scheme Σ provides* **consistency** *if no PPT adversary $\mathcal{A}$ has non-negligible advantage in the game below.*

1. *The challenger executes $\mathsf{DKG}(\mathsf{params}, \lambda, t, n)$ in interaction with the adversary $\mathcal{A}$. It plays the role of honest players P_i and $\mathcal{A}$ can corrupt players at any time. This protocol ends with the generation of a public key pk, a vector of secret key shares $\mathbf{sk} = (\mathsf{sk}_1, \ldots, \mathsf{sk}_n)$ and the corresponding verification keys $\mathbf{vk} = (\mathsf{vk}_1, \ldots, \mathsf{vk}_n)$. At the end of this phase, pk and $\{\mathsf{sk}_i\}_{i \in \mathcal{C}_0}$ are available to $\mathcal{A}$, where $\mathcal{C}_0$ denotes the set of corrupted players. Let $\mathcal{Q} \subseteq [n]$ the set of non-disqualified players at the end of DKG.*
2. *$\mathcal{A}$ is given the secret key shares $\{\mathsf{sk}_i\}_{i \in [n] \setminus \mathcal{C}_0}$ of all honest players and their entire view of the DKG protocol at step 1.*
3. *$\mathcal{A}$ outputs a message M, a set $S \subseteq \mathcal{Q}$ of size $t+1$ with partial signatures $\{\sigma_i\}_{i \in S}$ and proofs $\{\pi_{\sigma,i}\}_{i \in S}$ of validity. The experiment returns 1 if the following conditions hold and 0 otherwise:*
   (i) $\mathsf{Share\text{-}Verify}\big(\mathsf{pk}, \mathbf{vk}, M, (i, (\sigma_i, \pi_{\sigma,i}))\big) = 1$ for each $i \in S$;
   (ii) $\mathsf{Verify}(\mathsf{pk}, M, \sigma^\star) = 0$, where $\sigma^\star \leftarrow \mathsf{Combine}(\mathsf{pk}, \mathbf{vk}, M, \{(i, \sigma_i, \pi_{\sigma,i})\}_{i \in S})$.

The adversary's advantage is defined as the probability that the experiment return 1, taken over all random choices.

Similarly to [14, Chapter 22], a non-interactive threshold signature provides **robustness** if it provides both correctness and consistency.

2.2 Hardness Assumptions

We first recall the definition of the Decision Diffie-Hellman problem.

Definition 4. *In a cyclic group* $\mathbb{G}$ *of prime order* p*, the* **Decision Diffie-Hellman Problem** *(DDH) in* $\mathbb{G}$*, is to distinguish the distributions* (g, g^a, g^b, g^{ab}) *and* (g, g^a, g^b, g^c)*, with* $a, b, c \stackrel{R}{\leftarrow} \mathbb{Z}_p$*. The Decision Diffie-Hellman assumption is the intractability of DDH for any PPT distinguisher.*

We use bilinear maps $e : \mathbb{G} \times \hat{\mathbb{G}} \to \mathbb{G}_T$ over groups of prime order p. We will work in asymmetric pairings, where we have $\mathbb{G} \neq \hat{\mathbb{G}}$ so as to allow the DDH assumption to hold in $\mathbb{G}$ (see, e.g., [57]). In certain asymmetric pairing configurations (i.e. Type-3 pairings), DDH is even believed to hold in both $\mathbb{G}$ and $\hat{\mathbb{G}}$. However, we only need it to hold in $\mathbb{G}$, so that we can use either Type-2 or Type-3 pairings in the terminology of [33].

Definition 5. *In pairing-friendly groups* $(\mathbb{G}, \hat{\mathbb{G}}, \mathbb{G}_T)$ *of prime order* p*, the* **co-CDH Problem** *(co-CDH), is to compute* g^{ab} *given* $(g, \hat{g}, g^a, g^b, \hat{g}^a)$ *for random* $a, b \stackrel{R}{\leftarrow} \mathbb{Z}_p$*. The co-CDH assumption is the PPT intractability of co-CDH.*

3 A Simplification of the Das-Ren Non-interactive Threshold BLS Signature

As in [23,46], the key generation phase uses the one-round DKG protocol of Pedersen [55], which is known [35] to *not* guarantee a uniform distribution for the resulting public key (indeed, a rushing adversary can always bias the public key distribution [35,37]). As shown in [36], it nevertheless remains possible to use this protocol if we prove the security of the global scheme in a non-modular way, without a reduction from the security of the centralized scheme.

3.1 Description

We assume that all players agree on public parameters params consisting of asymmetric bilinear groups $(\mathbb{G}, \hat{\mathbb{G}}, \mathbb{G}_T)$ of prime order $p > 2^{2\lambda}$ with random generators $\hat{g} \in_R \hat{\mathbb{G}}$, $g, h \in_R \mathbb{G}$, a hash function $H : \{0,1\}^* \to \mathbb{G}^2$ that ranges over $\mathbb{G} \times \mathbb{G}$ and an additional hash functions $H_{\mathsf{FS}} : \{0,1\}^* \to \mathbb{Z}_p$ that will be used to generate Fiat-Shamir-based non-interactive Schnorr-like proofs [56]. These hash functions are modeled as a random oracle in the security analysis.

Importantly, no party should know $\log_g(h)$. However, this does not require a trusted setup since h is just a random group element.

$\mathsf{DKG}(\mathsf{params}, \lambda, t, n)$: Given $\mathsf{params} = \{(\mathbb{G}, \hat{\mathbb{G}}, \mathbb{G}_T), g, h, \hat{g}, H, H_{\mathsf{FS}}\}$, a security parameter λ and integers $t, n \in \mathbb{N}$ such that $n \geq 2t + 1$, each player P_i conducts the following steps.

1. Each player P_i shares a pair $(s_{i0}, 0)$ for a random $s_{i0} \in \mathbb{Z}_p$. To this end, P_i does the following:

a. Choose random polynomials

$$s_i[X] = s_{i0} + s_{i1}X + \cdots + s_{it}X^t, \qquad r_i[X] = r_{i1}X + \cdots + r_{it}X^t$$

of degree t such that $r_i(0) = 0$. Commit to the coefficients by computing $\mathsf{Com}_i = \big(\hat{C}_{i0}, (C_{i\ell})_{\ell\in[0,t]}\big)$, where

$$\begin{aligned}\hat{C}_{i0} &= \hat{g}^{s_{i0}} \\ C_{i0} &= g^{s_{i0}} \\ C_{i\ell} &= g^{s_{i\ell}} \cdot h^{r_{i\ell}} \qquad\qquad \forall \ell \in [1,t]\end{aligned}$$

Then, P_i broadcasts

$$\big(\mathsf{Com}_i = \big(\hat{C}_{i0}, (C_{i\ell})_{\ell\in[0,t]}\big)\big).$$

b. For $j = 1$ to n, privately send $(s_i(j), r_i(j))$ to P_j.

2. For each $(s_j(i), r_j(i))$ received from another player P_j, P_i checks that

$$g^{s_j(i)} \cdot h^{r_j(i)} = \prod_{\ell=0}^{t} C_{j\ell}^{i^\ell}. \tag{1}$$

P_i also verifies that $e(C_{j0}, \hat{g}) = e(g, \hat{C}_{j0})$. If these conditions do not both hold, P_i broadcasts a complaint against the faulty sender P_j.
3. Any player receiving strictly more than t complaints is disqualified. Each player P_i that received a complaint from another player P_j responds by returning the correct shares $(s_i(j), r_i(j))$ and a valid proof $\pi_{i,0}$. If any of these new shares/proof does not satisfy (1) or if $e(C_{i0}, \hat{g}) \neq e(g, \hat{C}_{i0})$, P_i is disqualified. Let $\mathcal{Q} \subset \{1, \ldots, n\}$ be the set of non-disqualified players at the end of step 3.
4. The public key $\mathsf{pk} = \hat{g}^s$ is obtained as $\mathsf{pk} = \prod_{i\in\mathcal{Q}} \hat{C}_{i0} = \hat{g}^{\sum_{i\in\mathcal{Q}} s_{i0}}$. Each P_i locally defines its private key share

$$\mathsf{sk}_i = (s(i), r(i)) = \Big(\sum_{j\in\mathcal{Q}} s_j(i), \sum_{j\in\mathcal{Q}} r_j(i)\Big)$$

and anyone can publicly compute his verification key as

$$\mathsf{vk}_i = g^{s(i)} \cdot h^{r(i)} = \prod_{j\in\mathcal{Q}} \prod_{\ell=0}^{t} C_{j\ell}^{i^\ell}$$

By convention, for any disqualified player $i \in \{1, \ldots, n\}\backslash\mathcal{Q}$, the i-th private key share is set as $\mathsf{sk}_i = (0,0)$ and the corresponding verification key is $\mathsf{vk}_i = 1_{\mathbb{G}}$.

This completes the generation of the private key shares $\mathbf{sk} = (\mathsf{sk}_1, \ldots, \mathsf{sk}_n)$, the verification keys $\mathbf{vk} = (\mathsf{vk}_1, \ldots, \mathsf{vk}_n)$ and the public key, which is

$$\mathsf{pk} = \Big(\mathsf{params},\ \hat{g}^s\Big).$$

When DKG ends, the private key shares $s(i)$ and $r(i)$ lie on t-degree polynomials $s[X] = \sum_{j\in\mathcal{Q}} s_j[X]$ and $r[X] = \sum_{j\in\mathcal{Q}} r_j[X]$ such that $r(0) = 0$.

Share-Sign(i, sk_i, M)**:** To generate a partial signature on a message $M \in \{0,1\}^*$ using his private key share $\mathsf{sk}_i = (s(i), r(i))$, P_i first computes the hash value $(H_0(M), H_1(M)) = H(M) \in \mathbb{G}^2$ and generates the partial signature as

$$\sigma_i = H_0(M)^{s(i)} \cdot H_1(M)^{r(i)} \in \mathbb{G}$$

In addition, P_i proves that σ_i is consistent with vk_i by generating a NIZK proof of knowledge of $(s(i), r(i))$ such that

$$\mathsf{vk}_i = g^{s(i)} \cdot h^{r(i)}, \qquad \sigma_i = H_0(M)^{s(i)} \cdot H_1(M)^{r(i)} \tag{2}$$

This proof is $\pi_{\sigma,i} \triangleq (c_i, z_{s,i}, z_{r,i}) \in \mathbb{Z}_p^3$, where

$$c_i = H_{\mathsf{FS}}(\mathsf{vk}_i, \sigma_i, M, g^{u_i} h^{v_i}, H_0(M)^{u_i} H_1(M)^{v_i})$$

and

$$(z_{s,i}, z_{r,i}) = (u_i + c_i \cdot s(i), v_i + c_i \cdot r(i)) \in \mathbb{Z}_p^2,$$

for random $u_i, v_i \xleftarrow{R} \mathbb{Z}_p$, and P_i returns $(\sigma_i, \pi_{\sigma,i})$

Share-Verify$(\mathsf{pk}, \mathbf{vk}, M, (i, (\sigma_i, \pi_{\sigma,i})))$**:** Given the partial signature $\sigma_i \in \mathbb{G}$ and the verification key $\mathsf{vk}_i \in \mathbb{G}$, compute $(H_0(M), H_1(M)) = H(M) \in \mathbb{G}^2$. Parse $\pi_{\sigma,i} = (c_i, z_{s,i}, z_{r,i}) \in \mathbb{Z}_p^3$ and return 1 if

$$c_i = H_{\mathsf{FS}}\big(\mathsf{vk}_i, \sigma_i, M, g^{z_{s,i}} h^{z_{r,i}} \mathsf{vk}_i^{-c_i}, H_0(M)^{z_{s,i}} H_1(M)^{z_{r,i}} \sigma_i^{-c_i}\big).$$

Otherwise, return 0.

Combine$(\mathsf{pk}, \mathbf{vk}, M, \{(i, \sigma_i, \pi_{\sigma,i})\}_{i\in S})$**:** Given a set of $(t+1)$-set with valid partial signatures $\{(i, \sigma_i)\}_{i\in S}$ for which the proof $\pi_{\sigma,i}$ verifies, compute and return

$$\sigma = \prod_{i\in S} \sigma_i^{\Delta_{i,S}(0)},$$

where $\Delta_{i,S}(0)$ denotes the i-th Lagrange coefficient.

Verify(pk, M, σ)**:** Given a candidate signature $\sigma \in \mathbb{G}$ and a public key pk containing $\hat{g}^s$, compute $(H_0(M), H_1(M)) = H(M) \in \mathbb{G}^2$. Return 1 if the following equality holds and 0 otherwise:

$$e(\sigma, \hat{g}) = e(H_0(M), \hat{g}^s)$$

3.2 Efficiency

The total size $|\sigma_i| + |\pi_{\sigma,i}|$ of partial signatures and their proofs of correctness amounts to 144 bytes on a BLS12-381 curve. In [23], it amounts to 176 bytes on the same curves.[2] We estimate that the computation of $(\sigma_i, \pi_{\sigma,i})$ is faster than in [23] by more than 25%. The reason is that, on BLS12-381 curves, exponentiations in $\hat{\mathbb{G}}$ are about twice as expensive as in $\mathbb{G}$ and we replace a triple exponentiation of the form $\hat{g}^{\alpha_i}\hat{h}^{\beta_i}\hat{v}^{\gamma_i}$ in $\hat{\mathbb{G}}$ by a double exponentiation of the form $g^{u_i}h^{v_i}$ in $\mathbb{G}$.

In the Share-Verify algorithm, we similarly replace a multi-exponentiation $\hat{g}^{\alpha_i}\hat{h}^{\beta_i}\hat{u}^{\delta_i}\hat{\mathsf{vk}}_i^{-c_i}$ in $\hat{\mathbb{G}}$ by a multi-exponentiation $g^{z_{s,i}}h^{z_{r,i}}\mathsf{vk}_i^{-c_i}$ in $\mathbb{G}$. This speeds up the verification of partial signatures $\pi_{\sigma,i}$ by more than 33% if we count an exponentiation in $\hat{\mathbb{G}}$ as having the same cost as two exponentiations in $\mathbb{G}$.

The distributed key generation protocol differs from the one of [23] in that each P_i only sends one commitment $\hat{C}_{i0}$ in $\hat{\mathbb{G}}$ and $t+1$ commitments $\{C_{i\ell}\}_{\ell\in[0,t]}$ in $\mathbb{G}$ (instead of $O(t)$ commitments in $\hat{\mathbb{G}}$) and no proof of knowledge of $\log_g(C_{i0})$ is required to guarantee that $r_i(0) = 0$ (otherwise, $\hat{C}_{i0}$ would not be computable without $\hat{g}^{\log_g(h)}$). This reduces the communication cost of DKG by a factor 2 because each element of $\hat{\mathbb{G}}$ is as long as two elements of $\mathbb{G}$ on BLS12 curves.

We note that, unlike [23], our DKG protocol requires each player P_i to compute pairings in order to check that $\log_{\hat{g}}(\hat{C}_{j0}) = \log_g(C_{j0})$ for each $j \neq i$ at step 2. However, instead of naively computing $2n$ pairings, P_i can choose random a random $\omega \xleftarrow{R} \mathbb{Z}_p$ and test the equality

$$e\Big(\prod_{j=1,j\neq i}^{n} C_{j0}^{\omega^{j-1}}, \hat{g}\Big) = e\Big(g, \prod_{j=1,j\neq i}^{n} \hat{C}_{j0}^{\omega^{j-1}}\Big), \tag{3}$$

which only requires two pairings when all $\{P_j\}_{j\neq i}$ follow the specification. By the Schwartz-Zippel lemma, the latter equality can only hold with negligible probability n/p if there exists $j \in [n]\backslash\{i\}$ such that $e(C_{j0}, \hat{g}) \neq e(g, \hat{C}_{j0})$. If the batch verification test fails (3), then P_i can proceed with $2n$ pairing evaluations to sieve out inconsistent pairs $(C_{j0}, \hat{C}_{j0})$.

4 Security

We now prove security in the programmable random oracle model. In the proof of unforgeability, we also assume an honest majority.

4.1 Unforgeability Under Adaptive Corruptions

Theorem 1. *The scheme provides adaptive security under the DDH assumption in $\mathbb{G}$ and the co-CDH assumption in the random oracle model. Namely, for any*

[2] [23, Section 9.2] reports a 224-byte size when signatures live in $\hat{\mathbb{G}}$. We believe that their scheme allows signatures to live in $\mathbb{G}$, in which case the size of verifiable partial signatures is 176 bytes.

PPT adversary $\mathcal{A}$, there exist either DDH distinguishers $\mathcal{B}_0$ and $\mathcal{B}_1$ in $\mathbb{G}$ or a co-CDH solver $\mathcal{B}_2$ in $(\mathbb{G}, \hat{\mathbb{G}})$ such that the adversary's advantage is at most

$$\mathbf{Adv}_{\mathcal{A}}(\lambda) \leq \mathbf{Adv}_{\mathcal{B}_0}^{\mathrm{DDH}_1}(\lambda) + \tfrac{1}{p} + 2 \cdot \Big(\exp(1) \cdot (Q_s + 1)\Big) \cdot \Big(\mathbf{Adv}_{\mathcal{B}_1}^{\mathrm{DDH}_1}(\lambda) + \mathbf{Adv}_{\mathcal{B}_2}^{\text{co-CDH}}(\lambda) + \tfrac{1}{p}\Big),$$

where Q_s denotes the number of signing queries.

Proof. The proof uses a sequence of games that begins with Game_0, which is the real game, and ends with Game_6, where we show that a successful adversary implies a PPT algorithm that breaks the co-CDH assumption. For each $j \in [0, 6]$, we call W_j the event that the experiment of Definition 1 returns 1 in Game_j.

We assume w.l.o.g. that the adversary $\mathcal{A}$ always queries the random oracle H before any signing query for the same message M. The challenger can always enforce this by making random oracle queries for itself. We also assume that random oracle queries are distinct.

Game_0: This is the real game. The challenger runs the DKG protocol on behalf of all uncorrupted players. Whenever $\mathcal{A}$ decides to corrupt a player P_i, the challenger sets $\mathcal{C} = \mathcal{C} \cup \{i\}$, $\mathcal{G} = \mathcal{G} \backslash \{i\}$ and faithfully reveals the internal state of P_i, which includes P_i's private key share $\mathsf{sk}_i = (s(i), r(i))$ and its polynomials $(s_i[X], r_i[X])$ if the corruption query occurs after step 1.a of DKG. Whenever a player P_i is corrupted, $\mathcal{A}$ obtains full control over P_i, which can then arbitrarily deviate from the protocol. Queries to the random oracle H are answered by returning uniformly random group elements in $\mathbb{G}^2$. Signing queries (i, M) are answered by returning the partial signatures $\sigma_i = H_0(M)^{r(i)} H_1(M)^{s(i)}$ together with a faithfully generated proof $\pi_{\sigma,i} = (c_i, z_{s,i}, z_{r,i})$. At the end of the game, $\mathcal{A}$ outputs a message-signature pair $(M^\star, \sigma^\star)$. We assume that the adversary queries $H(M^\star)$ before producing its forgery. We denote by W_0 the event that $\mathcal{A}$ satisfies all its winning conditions in the experiment of Definition 1.

We define $s[X] = \sum_{i \in \mathcal{Q}} s_i[X]$ and $r[X] = \sum_{i \in \mathcal{Q}} r_i[X]$ as well as their degree-0 coefficients $(s_0, r_0) = (\sum_{i \in \mathcal{Q}} s_{i0}, \sum_{i \in \mathcal{Q}} r_{i0})$. We observe that, at the end of the DKG protocol, the challenger knows the polynomials $s_j[X], r_j[X]$ and the additive shares (s_{j0}, r_{j0}) of all non-disqualified players $j \in \mathcal{Q}$. Indeed, for each $j \in \mathcal{Q} \cap \mathcal{C}$ such that P_j was corrupted before step 1.a of the distributed key generation phase, it obtained at least $t+1$ shares $(s_j(i), r_j(i))$, which is sufficient for reconstructing $(s_j[X], r_j[X])$. For any other player P_j such that $j \in \mathcal{Q}$, the challenger honestly chose their sharing polynomials at step 1.a of DKG.

Game_1: This game is the same as Game_0 with the difference that the challenger replaces the output of the experiment by 0 in the event bad_1 that, at the end of the DKG protocol, there is an index $j \in \mathcal{Q} \cap \mathcal{C}$ such that $r_j(0) \neq 0$. Clearly, $|\Pr[W_1] - \Pr[W_0]| \leq \Pr[\mathsf{bad}_1]$. Lemma 1 shows that $\Pr[\mathsf{bad}_1]$ is negligible under the DDH assumption in $\mathbb{G}$. Concretely, it builds a DDH distinguisher $\mathcal{B}_0$ such that $\Pr[\mathsf{bad}_1] \leq \mathbf{Adv}_{\mathcal{B}_0}^{\mathrm{DDH}}(\lambda) + 1/p$.

Game$_2$: This game is identical to Game$_1$ with the following difference. For each random oracle query $H(M)$, the challenger flips a biased coin $\vartheta_M \in \{0,1\}$ that takes the value 1 with probability $1/(Q_s+1)$ and the value 0 with probability $Q_s/(Q_s+1)$. When the game ends, $\mathcal{B}$ considers the event bad_2 that either of the following conditions holds:

- For the message $M^\star$, the coin $\vartheta_{M^\star} \in \{0,1\}$ flipped for the hash query $H(M^\star)$ was $\vartheta_{M^\star} = 0$.
- There exists signing query (i, M) with $M \neq M^\star$ for which $\vartheta_M = 1$.

If bad_2 occurs (which $\mathcal{B}$ can detect at the end of the game), $\mathcal{B}$ replaces the output of the experiment by 0. The same analysis as [21] shows that

$$\Pr[\neg\mathsf{bad}_2] = \frac{1}{Q_s+1} \cdot \left(1 - \frac{1}{Q_s+1}\right)^{Q_s} \geq \frac{1}{\exp(1)\cdot(Q_s+1)}.$$

The transition from Game 0 to Game 1 is thus a transition based on a failure event of large probability [26] and we thus have

$$\Pr[W_2] = \Pr[W_1]\cdot\Pr[\neg\mathsf{bad}_2] = \Pr[W_1]\cdot\frac{1}{Q_s+1}\cdot\left(1-\frac{1}{Q_s+1}\right)^{Q_s}$$

Game$_3$: This game is like Game$_2$ except that the challenger initially picks a random index $i^\diamond \stackrel{R}{\leftarrow} [n]$. At the end of the game, the challenger outputs 0 if the adversary decided to corrupt player $P_{i^\diamond}$. We call bad_3 the latter event. We have $W_3 = W_2 \wedge \neg\mathsf{bad}_3$ by definition. Moreover, since $i^\diamond$ is chosen uniformly and independently of $\mathcal{A}$'s view, we have $\Pr[W_3] = \Pr[W_2]\cdot\Pr[\neg\mathsf{bad}_3]$, where $\Pr[\neg\mathsf{bad}_3] = \binom{n-1}{t}/\binom{n}{t}$. This yields

$$\Pr[W_3] = \frac{\binom{n-1}{t}}{\binom{n}{t}}\cdot\Pr[W_2] = \frac{n-t}{n}\cdot\Pr[W_2] \geq \frac{1+1/n}{2}\cdot\Pr[W_2] > \frac{1}{2}\cdot\Pr[W_2]$$

since $n \geq 2t+1$.

Game$_4$: This game is like Game$_3$ with the difference that the experiment immediately halts and outputs 0 in the following events: (i) $\mathcal{A}$ chooses to corrupt $P_{i^\diamond}$; (ii) The coin $\vartheta_M \in \{0,1\}$ takes the value 1 for more than one message involved in signing queries. This modification does not change the output distribution of the experiment because the only difference is that the challenger halts and outputs 0 as soon as it realizes that its output will be 0 at the end of the game. We then have $\Pr[W_4] = \Pr[W_3]$.

Game$_5$: We replace the random oracle $H : \{0,1\}^* \to \mathbb{G}^2$ by a pseudorandom oracle under the DDH assumption in $\mathbb{G}$. The simulation of each random oracle query $H(M)$ depends on the random coin $\vartheta_M \in \{0,1\}$.

- If $\vartheta_M = 0$, the challenger $\mathcal{B}$ chooses a random $\alpha_M \stackrel{R}{\leftarrow} \mathbb{Z}_p$, and programs the random oracle so as to have $H(M) = (g^{\alpha_M}, h^{\alpha_M})$. Note that the resulting $(H_0(M), H_1(M)) \in \mathbb{G}^2$ is no longer uniform in $\mathbb{G}^2$ but lives in the one-dimensional subspace spanned by $(g,h) \in \mathbb{G}^2$.

- If $\vartheta_M = 1$, $\mathcal{B}$ chooses a truly random pair $(g_M, h_M) \stackrel{R}{\leftarrow} \mathbb{G}^2$ and outputs
$$H(M) = (H_0(M), H_1(M)) = (g_M, h_M).$$

Lemma 2 shows that $|\Pr[W_5] - \Pr[W_4]| \leq \mathbf{Adv}_{\mathcal{B}_1}^{\mathrm{DDH}_1}(\lambda)$, so that Game_5 and Game_4 are indistinguishable if the DDH assumption holds in $\mathbb{G}$.

Game_6: We modify the simulation of $P_{i^\diamond}$ at step 1.a of DKG. Instead of choosing a polynomial $r_{i^\diamond}[X]$ such that $r_{i^\diamond}(0) = 0$, the challenger chooses a random "fake" polynomial $r_{i^\diamond}[X] = 1 + \sum_{\ell=1}^{t} r_{i^\diamond \ell} \cdot X^\ell$ such that $r_{i^\diamond 0}(0) = 1$. In details, when the challenger generates public parameters containing $g, h \in \mathbb{G}$, and $\hat{g} \in \hat{\mathbb{G}}$, it also chooses $\hat{h} \in \hat{\mathbb{G}}$ such that $\log_{\hat{g}}(\hat{h}) = \log_g(h)$, which is used to compute $\mathsf{Com}_{i^\diamond} = \big(\hat{C}_{i^\diamond 0}, (C_{i^\diamond \ell})_{\ell \in [0,t]}\big)$ as

$$\begin{aligned} \hat{C}_{i^\diamond 0} &= \hat{g}^{s_{i^\diamond 0}} \cdot \hat{h} \\ C_{i^\diamond 0} &= g^{s_{i^\diamond 0}} \cdot h \\ C_{i^\diamond \ell} &= g^{s_{i^\diamond \ell}} \cdot h^{r_{i^\diamond \ell}} \qquad \forall \ell \in [1,t] \end{aligned} \tag{4}$$

for random $s_{i^\diamond \ell} \stackrel{R}{\leftarrow} \mathbb{Z}_p$ for each $\ell \in [0,t]$ and $r_{i^\diamond \ell}$ for $\ell \in [1,t]$. Lemma 3 shows that $\mathcal{A}$'s view remains the same as in Game_5, so that $\Pr[W_6] = \Pr[W_5]$.

In Game_6, Lemma 4 shows that $\Pr[W_6] \leq \mathbf{Adv}_{\mathcal{B}_2}^{\text{co-CDH}}(\lambda) + 1/p$ as the adversary implies an algorithm $\mathcal{B}_2$ solving the co-CDH problem.

By tracing through the sequence of games, we obtain the stated upper bound on the adversary's advantage $\mathbf{Adv}_{\mathcal{A}}(\lambda) = \Pr[W_0]$. □

Lemma 1. Game_1 *is indistinguishable from* Game_0 *under the DDH assumption in* $\mathbb{G}$. *There is a PPT algorithm* $\mathcal{B}_0$ *such that* $\Pr[\mathsf{bad}_1] \leq \mathbf{Adv}_{\mathcal{B}_0}^{\mathrm{DDH}_1}(\lambda) + 1/p$.

Proof. Let us assume that event bad_1 happens with non-negligible probability $\varepsilon = \Pr[\mathsf{bad}_1]$. We describe an algorithm $\mathcal{B}_0$ that uses $\mathcal{A}$ to decide if $T = g^{ab}$ given (g, g^a, g^b, T) with non-negligible advantage $\varepsilon - 1/p$.

Algorithm $\mathcal{B}_0$ sets $h = g^a$ and runs $\mathcal{A}$ until the end of the distributed key generation protocol where it faithfully simulates all honest players. Let $j \in \mathcal{Q} \cap \mathcal{C}$ such that $r_j(0) \neq 0$ at the end of DKG. Since $j \in \mathcal{Q}$, the challenger obtained at least $t+1$ correct shares $(s_j(i), r_j(i))$ satisfying (1). Let $S \subset [n]$ an arbitrary subset of $t+1$ correct shares. We then have

$$g^{s_j(0)} \cdot h^{r_j(0)} = \prod_{i \in S} \Big(\prod_{\ell=0}^{t} C_{j\ell}^{i^\ell} \Big)^{\Delta_{i,S}(0)} = C_{j0}$$

with $r_j(0) \neq 0$. However, at step 1.a of DKG, $\mathcal{A}$ must have supplied a proof $\hat{C}_{j0}$ such that $e(g, \hat{C}_{j0}) = e(C_{j0}, \hat{g})$, which implies that $\log_{\hat{g}}(\hat{C}_{j0}) = \log_g(C_{j0})$ and thus $\hat{C}_{j,0} = \hat{g}^{s_j(0)} \cdot (\hat{g}^a)^{r_j(0)}$. Then, $\mathcal{B}_0$ can compute $\hat{\eta} = \hat{g}^a = (\hat{C}_{j,0} \cdot \hat{g}^{-s_j(0)})^{1/r_j(0)}$.

Using $\hat{\eta} = \hat{g}^a$, it can then check if its DDH candidate satisfies the equality $e(g^b, \hat{g}^a) = e(T, \hat{g})$. If so, $\mathcal{B}_0$ outputs 1. Otherwise, it outputs 0. The claim of the lemma follows since, if $T = g^{ab}$, $\mathcal{B}_0$ outputs 1 with probability ε. If $T \in_R \mathbb{G}$, then $\mathcal{B}_0$ only outputs 1 with probability $1/p$. □

Lemma 2. *Under the DDH assumption in* $\mathbb{G}$, Game_5 *is computationally indistinguishable from* Game_4.

Proof. The proof is identical to the one of [46, Lemma 1]. The reduction $\mathcal{B}$ is given a DDH instance (g, g^a, g^b, T) and has to decide if $T = g^{ab}$ or $T \in_R \mathbb{G}$. To do so, $\mathcal{B}$ defines $h = g^a$. It runs the DKG protocol in the same way as in the real scheme. During the game, $\mathcal{B}$ always faithfully answers signing queries and corruption queries. As in Game_4, it halts and outputs a random bit if one of the events bad_1, bad_2 or bad_3 occurs.

As in Game_4, the simulation of random oracle queries depends on the random variable $\vartheta_M \in \{0,1\}$. When $\vartheta_M = 0$, $\mathcal{B}$ exploits the random self-reducibility of DDH and constructs many DDH instances out of one.

- If $\vartheta_M = 0$, $\mathcal{B}$ chooses $\alpha_M, \beta_M \stackrel{R}{\leftarrow} \mathbb{Z}_p$, computes
$$(g_M, h_M) = ((g^b)^{\alpha_M} \cdot g^{\beta_M}, T^{\alpha_M} \cdot (g^a)^{\beta_M})$$
and programs $H(M) = (H_0, H_1) = (g_M, h_M)$. We note that, if $T = g^{ab}$, then $(H_0, H_1) = (g_M, h_M)$ has the same distribution as in Game_4 as it can be written $(H_0, H_1) = (g^{z_M}, h^{z_M})$ with $z_M = b \cdot \alpha_M + \beta_M$. If $T \in_R \mathbb{G}$, then we can write $T = g^{ab+z}$ for a random $z \in_R \mathbb{Z}_p$. In this case, we have $(H_0, H_1) = (g_M, g_M^a \cdot g^{z \cdot \alpha_M})$, so that $(H_0, H_1) \in_R \mathbb{G}^2$.
- If $\vartheta_M = 1$, $\mathcal{B}$ chooses $g_M, h_M \stackrel{R}{\leftarrow} \mathbb{G}^2$ and defines $H(M) = (g_M, h_M)$.

When $\mathcal{A}$ halts, the distinguisher $\mathcal{B}$ outputs 1 if $\mathcal{A}$ succeeds and 0 otherwise.

Clearly, if $T = g^{ab}$, $\mathcal{A}$'s view is exactly as in Game_5. If T is uniform in $\mathbb{G}$, then $\mathcal{A}$'s view is identical to that of Game_4. $\square$

Lemma 3. Game_6 *is perfectly indistinguishable from* Game_5 *in* $\mathcal{A}$*'s view.*

Proof. In Game_6, we observe that $P_{i^\diamond}$'s commitments to the polynomial coefficients (4) can be written

$$\hat{C}_{i^\diamond 0} = \hat{g}^{\bar{s}_{i^\diamond 0}}$$
$$C_{i^\diamond 0} = g^{\bar{s}_{i^\diamond 0}}$$
$$C_{i^\diamond \ell} = g^{s_{i^\diamond \ell}} \cdot h^{r_{i^\diamond \ell}} \qquad \forall \ell \in [1, t]$$

with $\bar{s}_{i^\diamond 0} = s_{i^\diamond 0} + a$, where $a = \log_g(h)$. We claim that $\mathcal{A}$'s view of Game_6 is the same as if $P_{i^\diamond}$'s polynomials were defined as

$$\bar{s}_{i^\diamond}[X] = \bar{s}_{i^\diamond 0} + \bar{s}_{i^\diamond 1} X + \ldots + \bar{s}_{i^\diamond t} X^t \qquad (5)$$
$$\bar{r}_{i^\diamond}[X] = 0 + \bar{r}_{i^\diamond 1} X + \ldots + \bar{r}_{i^\diamond t} X^t.$$

for coefficients $\{(\bar{s}_{i^\diamond \ell}, \bar{r}_{i^\diamond \ell})\}_{\ell=1}^t$ such that

$$\bar{s}_{i^\diamond}[X] + a \cdot \bar{r}_{i^\diamond}[X] = s_{i^\diamond}[X] + a \cdot r_{i^\diamond}[X] \qquad (6)$$

and

$$(\bar{s}_{i^\diamond}(i), \bar{r}_{i^\diamond}(i)) = (s_{i^\diamond}(i), r_{i^\diamond}(i)) \qquad \forall i \in \mathcal{V} = \mathcal{C} \cup \mathcal{S}[M^\star] \tag{7}$$

with the notations of Definition 1. For given degree-t $(s_{i^\diamond}[X], r_{i^\diamond}[X])$, there always exist degree-t polynomials $(\bar{s}_{i^\diamond}[X], \bar{r}_{i^\diamond}[X])$ satisfying $\bar{r}_{i^\diamond}(0) = 0$ and conditions (6)–(7) since $|\mathcal{V}| \leq t$. We now argue that the simulated polynomials (5) and the fake polynomials $(s_{i^\diamond}[X], r_{i^\diamond}[X])$ are equally compatible with $\mathcal{A}$'s view.

Indeed, we first note that, due to (6), the simulated polynomials (5) satisfy

$$g^{\bar{s}_{i^\diamond}(i)} \cdot h^{\bar{r}_{i^\diamond}(i)} = g^{s_{i^\diamond}(i)} \cdot h^{r_{i^\diamond}(i)} = \prod_{\ell=0}^{t} C_{i^\diamond \ell}^{\,i^\ell} \qquad \forall i \in [n] \tag{8}$$

so that $\{(\bar{s}_{i^\diamond}(i), \bar{r}_{i^\diamond}(i))\}_{i\in[n]}$ pass the test (1) at step 2 of DKG. So, at the end of DKG, the information that $\mathcal{A}$ learned about the fake polynomials $s_{i^\diamond}[X]$ and $r_{i^\diamond}[X]$ consists of $s_{i^\diamond}(i) + a \cdot r_{i^\diamond}(i)$ (which is revealed by (8)) and the evaluations $\{(s_{i^\diamond}(i), r_{i^\diamond}(i))\}_{i\in\mathcal{C}_0} = \{(\bar{s}_{i^\diamond}(i), \bar{r}_{i^\diamond}(i))\}_{i\in\mathcal{C}_0}$, where $\mathcal{C}_0$ is the set of corrupted players after the distributed key generation phase.

Next, at step 2 of the unforgeability experiment, we only need to consider the information that $\mathcal{A}$ obtains about $r_{i^\diamond}[X]$ and $\bar{r}_{i^\diamond}[X]$ since they uniquely determine $s_{i^\diamond}[X]$ and $\bar{s}_{i^\diamond}[X]$ from (8). Adaptive corruption queries reveal $\{r_{i^\diamond}(i)\}_{i\in\mathcal{C}}$ since we do not rely on erasures. At each signing query (i, M), $\mathcal{A}$ also obtains

$$\begin{aligned} \sigma_i = H_0(M)^{s(i)} \cdot H_1(M)^{r(i)} &= \prod_{j\in\mathcal{Q}} \left(H_0(M)^{s_j(i)} \cdot H_1(M)^{r_j(i)}\right) \qquad (9)\\ &= H_0(M)^{s_{i^\diamond}(i)} \cdot H_1(M)^{r_{i^\diamond}(i)} \cdot \prod_{j\in\mathcal{Q}\setminus\{i^\diamond\}} \left(H_0(M)^{s_j(i)} \cdot H_1(M)^{r_j(i)}\right) \end{aligned}$$

For signing queries on $M \neq M^\star$, we have $(H_0(M), H_1(M)) = (g^{\alpha_M}, h^{\alpha_M})$ due to the change introduced in Game_5. Therefore

$$H_0(M)^{s_{i^\diamond}(i)} \cdot H_1(M)^{r_{i^\diamond}(i)} = \left(g^{s_{i^\diamond}(i)} \cdot h^{r_{i^\diamond}(i)}\right)^{\alpha_M},$$

is completely determined by $g^{s_{i^\diamond}(i)} \cdot h^{r_{i^\diamond}(i)}$ and α_M in the right-hand-side member of (9) and we have $H_0(M)^{s_{i^\diamond}(i)} \cdot H_1(M)^{r_{i^\diamond}(i)} = H_0(M)^{\bar{s}_{i^\diamond}(i)} \cdot H_1(M)^{\bar{r}_{i^\diamond}(i)}$. Moreover, when $M \neq M^\star$, the two pairs of polynomials $(\bar{s}_{i^\diamond}[X], \bar{r}_{i^\diamond}[X])$ and $(s_{i^\diamond}[X], r_{i^\diamond}[X])$ lead to the same distribution of proofs $\pi_{\sigma,i} \triangleq (c_i, z_{s,i}, z_{r,i}) \in \mathbb{Z}_p^3$ for all $i \in [n]$. To see this, we define

$$\bar{s}[X] = \bar{s}_{i^\diamond}[X] + \sum_{j\in\mathcal{Q}\setminus\{i^\diamond\}} s_j[X], \qquad \bar{r}[X] = \bar{r}_{i^\diamond}[X] + \sum_{j\in\mathcal{Q}\setminus\{i^\diamond\}} r_j[X], \tag{10}$$

and observe that (8) implies

$$\begin{aligned}\mathsf{vk}_i = g^{s(i)} \cdot h^{r(i)} &= g^{s_{i^\diamond}(i)} \cdot h^{r_{i^\diamond}(i)} \cdot \prod_{j \in \mathcal{Q} \setminus \{i^\diamond\}} \left(g^{s_j(i)} \cdot h^{r_j(i)}\right) \\ &= g^{\bar{s}_{i^\diamond}(i)} \cdot h^{\bar{r}_{i^\diamond}(i)} \cdot \prod_{j \in \mathcal{Q} \setminus \{i^\diamond\}} \left(g^{s_j(i)} \cdot h^{r_j(i)}\right) = g^{\bar{s}(i)} \cdot h^{\bar{r}(i)} \qquad \forall i \in [n]\end{aligned}$$

and $\sigma_i = H_0(M)^{s(i)} \cdot H_1(M)^{r(i)} = H_0(M)^{\bar{s}(i)} \cdot H_1(M)^{\bar{r}(i)} = \mathsf{vk}_i^{\alpha_M}$. Hence, each evaluation proof $\pi_{\sigma,i} = (c_i, z_{s,i}, z_{r,i}) \in \mathbb{Z}_p^3$ for $M \neq M^\star$ is a perfectly witness indistinguishable (see, e.g., [54]) proof of knowledge of an opening of a Pedersen commitment vk_i, meaning that two distinct representations $(s(i), r(i)), (\bar{s}(i), \bar{r}(i))$ of $\mathsf{vk}_i = g^{s(i)} \cdot h^{r(i)} = g^{\bar{s}(i)} \cdot h^{\bar{r}(i)}$ lead to the same distribution of $\pi_{\sigma,i}$.

If we now consider signing queries $(i, M^\star)$ on the forgery message $M^\star$, we have

$$\begin{aligned}\sigma_i &= H_0(M^\star)^{s(i)} \cdot H_1(M^\star)^{r(i)} \\ &= H_0(M^\star)^{s_{i^\diamond}(i)} \cdot H_1(M^\star)^{r_{i^\diamond}(i)} \cdot \prod_{j \in \mathcal{Q} \setminus \{i^\diamond\}} \left(H_0(M^\star)^{s_j(i)} \cdot H_1(M^\star)^{r_j(i)}\right) \\ &= g_{M^\star}^{s_{i^\diamond}(i)} \cdot h_{M^\star}^{r_{i^\diamond}(i)} \cdot \prod_{j \in \mathcal{Q} \setminus \{i^\diamond\}} \left(H_0(M^\star)^{s_j(i)} \cdot H_1(M^\star)^{r_j(i)}\right)\end{aligned}$$

where $(g_{M^\star}, h_{M^\star})$ is linearly independent of (g, h). We thus consider that these queries reveal $(s(i), r(i))$ for $i \in \mathcal{S}[M^\star]$ in the information-theoretic sense. However, by (7), we have $(s_{i^\diamond}(i), r_{i^\diamond}(i)) = (\bar{s}_{i^\diamond}(i), \bar{r}_{i^\diamond}(i))$ for all $i \in \mathcal{V}$, so that the polynomials $(\bar{s}[X], \bar{r}[X])$ of (10) satisfy $(\bar{s}(i), \bar{r}(i)) = (s(i), r(i))$ for all $i \in \mathcal{V}$.

We have shown that there exist simulated polynomials $(\bar{s}_{i^\diamond}[X], \bar{r}_{i^\diamond}[X])$ satisfying (5)–(7) and explaining $\mathcal{A}$'s view. We now show that, conditionally on $\mathcal{A}$'s view, these simulated polynomials have the same distribution as $(s_{i^\diamond}[X], r_{i^\diamond}[X])$ in Game_5. Indeed, we have $|\mathcal{V}| = |\mathcal{C} \cup \mathcal{S}[M^\star]| \leq t$ at the end of the experiment of Definition 1. If we parse $\mathcal{V}$ as $\mathcal{V} = \{i_1, \ldots, i_t\}$, the coefficients $(\bar{r}_{i^\diamond 1}, \ldots, \bar{r}_{i^\diamond t})$ of $\bar{r}_{i^\diamond}[X]$ are the unique solution of the linear system

$$\begin{bmatrix} i_1 & i_1^2 & \ldots & i_1^t \\ i_2 & i_2^2 & \ldots & i_2^t \\ \vdots & & & \vdots \\ i_t & i_t^2 & \ldots & i_t^t \end{bmatrix} \cdot \begin{bmatrix} \bar{r}_{i^\diamond 1} \\ \bar{r}_{i^\diamond 2} \\ \vdots \\ \bar{r}_{i^\diamond t} \end{bmatrix} = \begin{bmatrix} r_{i^\diamond}(i_1) \\ r_{i^\diamond}(i_2) \\ \vdots \\ r_{i^\diamond}(i_t) \end{bmatrix}$$

of which the right-hand-side member is uniformly distributed in $\mathbb{Z}_p^t$ since the polynomial $r_{i^\diamond}[X] = 1 + \sum_{\ell=1}^{t} r_{i^\diamond \ell} \cdot X^\ell$ acts as a t-wise independent function on non-zero inputs.

This concludes the proof that Game_6 is identical to Game_5 in the view of any adversary $\mathcal{A}$ that complies with the rules of Definition 1. □

Lemma 4. *In* Game_6 *, the adversary* $\mathcal{A}$ *implies a PPT algorithm* $\mathcal{B}_2$ *for which we have* $\Pr[W_6] \leq \mathbf{Adv}_{\mathcal{B}_2}^{\text{co-CDH}}(\lambda) + 1/p$.

Proof. In Game_6, the polynomials $(s[X], r[X]) = (\sum_{i \in \mathcal{Q}} s_i[X], \sum_{i \in \mathcal{Q}} r_i[X])$ are such that $r(0) = \sum_{i \in \mathcal{Q}} r_{i0} = 1$ since $r_{i^\diamond 0} = 1$ is the only non-zero summand due to the changes introduced in Game_1 and Game_6.

Then, if the adversary $\mathcal{A}$ is a successful forger, its output $\sigma^\star$ must satisfy the BLS verification Eq.

$$e(\sigma^\star, \hat{g}) = e(H_0(M^\star), \hat{g}^{s(0)+\log_g(h)}) \tag{11}$$

for a "rigged" public key $\hat{g}^s = \hat{g}^{s(0)+\log_g(h) \cdot r(0)} = \hat{g}^{s(0)+\log_g(h)}$.

Our co-CDH solver $\mathcal{B}_2$ takes as input a co-CDH instance $(g, \hat{g}, g^a, g^b, \hat{g}^a)$ and extracts g^{ab} from its interaction with $\mathcal{A}$ in Game_8 . To this end, it defines $h = g^a$, $\hat{h} = \hat{g}^a$ and feeds $\mathcal{A}$ with public parameters params containing $(g, h = g^a, \hat{g})$. Then, it draws a random index $i^\diamond \xleftarrow{R} [n]$ for the single inconsistent player and interacts with $\mathcal{A}$ in the following way.

It runs DKG on behalf of all uncorrupted players $\mathcal{G} = [n] \backslash \mathcal{C}$. For each player P_i with $i \in \mathcal{G} \backslash \{i^\diamond\}$, it follows the specification of DKG. For the single inconsistent player $P_{i^\diamond}$, it proceeds as in Game_7. Namely, it chooses random polynomials $s_{i^\diamond}[X] = \sum_{\ell=0}^{t} s_{i^\diamond \ell} \cdot X^\ell$ and $r_{i^\diamond}[X] = 1 + \sum_{\ell=1}^{t} r_{i^\diamond \ell} \cdot X^\ell$. Then, it computes $\mathsf{Com}_{i^\diamond} = \big(\hat{C}_{i^\diamond 0}, (C_{i^\diamond \ell})_{\ell \in [0,t]}\big)$ as

$$\begin{aligned} \hat{C}_{i^\diamond 0} &= \hat{g}^{s_{i^\diamond 0}} \cdot \hat{h} \\ C_{i^\diamond 0} &= g^{s_{i^\diamond 0}} \cdot h \\ C_{i^\diamond \ell} &= g^{s_{i^\diamond \ell}} \cdot h^{r_{i^\diamond \ell}} \qquad \forall \ell \in [1, t] \end{aligned} \tag{12}$$

The simulation of random oracles proceeds as in Game_6. When $\mathcal{A}$ queries $H(M)$, $\mathcal{B}_2$ flips a coin $\vartheta_M \in \{0, 1\}$ that takes the value 1 with probability $1/(Q_s + 1)$.

- If $\vartheta_M = 0$, $\mathcal{B}_2$ chooses a random $\alpha_M \xleftarrow{R} \mathbb{Z}_p$, and returns

$$H(M) = (H_0(M), H_1(M)) = (g^{\alpha_M}, h^{\alpha_M}).$$

- If $\vartheta_M = 1$, $\mathcal{B}$ chooses $\theta_M \xleftarrow{R} \mathbb{Z}_p$, $h_M \xleftarrow{R} \mathbb{G}$ and returns

$$H(M) = (H_0(M), H_1(M)) = \big((g^b)^{\theta_M}, h_M\big).$$

If $\mathcal{A}$ chooses to corrupt $P_{i^\diamond}$ at any time during the game, $\mathcal{B}_2$ aborts and reports failure since it cannot provide a consistent state for $P_{i^\diamond}$. For any other player P_i with $i \in \mathcal{G} \backslash \{i\}$, $\mathcal{B}_2$ can faithfully return the secret key shares $\mathsf{sk}_i = (s(i), r_(i))$ and whatever P_i has seen so far (including the polynomial evaluations $(s_j(i), r_j(i))$ that P_i obtained in the key generation phase for $j \neq i$).

For all players $i \in \mathcal{G}$ (including the inconsistent player $P_{i^\diamond}$), signing queries (i, M) are always answered by computing $\sigma_i = H_0(M)^{s(i)} \cdot H_1(M)^{r(i)}$ and generating a real proof π_{σ_i}. As in Game_6, $\mathcal{B}_2$ aborts and fails if $\mathcal{A}$ makes signing queries (i, M) for more than one message such that $\vartheta_M = 1$.

When $\mathcal{A}$ halts, it outputs a pair $(M^\star, \sigma^\star)$ and $\mathcal{B}_2$ fails if $\vartheta_{M^\star} = 1$. Otherwise, $\mathcal{B}_2$ retrieves the value $\theta_{M^\star} \in \mathbb{Z}_p$ that was chosen when it programmed $H(M^\star) = (H_0(M^\star), H_1(M^\star)) = \big((g^b)^{\theta_{M^\star}}, h_M\big)$. Since $\sigma^\star$ must satisfy the verification equation (11) for the rigged public key

$$\hat{g}^{s(0)+\log_g(h)} = \hat{g}^{s(0)} \cdot (\hat{g}^a),$$

we must have $e(\sigma^\star, \hat{g}) = e\big((g^b)^{\theta_{M^\star}}, \hat{g}^{s(0)+a}\big)$ or, equivalently,

$$e\big(\sigma^\star \cdot (g^b)^{-\theta_{M^\star} \cdot s(0)}, \hat{g}\big) = e(g^b, \hat{g}^a)^{\theta_{M^\star}}.$$

This implies that $g^{ab} = \big(\sigma^\star \cdot (g^b)^{-\theta_{M^\star} \cdot s(0)}\big)^{1/\theta_{M^\star}}$ is computable by $\mathcal{B}_2$ unless $\theta_{M^\star} = 0$, which only happens with negligible probability $1/p$. □

Remark. As mentioned in the introduction, a difference between the above scheme and the one of Das and Ren [23] is that the latter has verification keys $\{\mathsf{vk}_i\}_{i \in [n]}$ that live in the second source group $\hat{\mathbb{G}}$ (instead of $\mathbb{G}$). This prevents from simply defining them as $\mathsf{vk}_i = \hat{g}^{s(i)} \cdot \hat{h}^{r(i)}$ because it would require to include $\hat{h}$ in the public parameters. However, it would be necessary to maintain the equality $\log_{\hat{g}}(\hat{h}) = \log_g(h)$ in order to make sure that vk_i and σ_i leak redundant information about $(s(i), r(i))$. This would not be compatible with a reduction from DDH in the proof of Lemma 2 since revealing $\hat{h} = \hat{g}^a$ would clearly invalidate the assumption. Such a reduction would actually be impossible because, in Game_5, partial signatures $\sigma_i = H_0(M)^{s(i)} H_1(M)^{r(i)}$ would satisfy $e(\sigma_i, \hat{g}) = e(H_0(M) \cdot H_1(M), \mathsf{vk}_i)$ and not in Game_4, thus yielding an immediate distinguisher between Game_4 and Game_5.

To address this problem, the scheme of [23] uses verification keys of the form $\mathsf{vk}_i = \hat{g}^{s(i)} \cdot \hat{h}^{r(i)} \cdot \hat{v}^{u(i)}$, where $\hat{v} \in \hat{\mathbb{G}}$ is an additional public generator and $u[X]$ as another polynomial such that $u(0) = 0$. By doing so, they can prevent the aforementioned distinguishing attack (since introducing $u(i)$ makes the condition $\log_{\hat{g}}(\hat{h}) = \log_g(h)$ unnecessary) at the expense of longer secret key share $\mathsf{sk}_i = (s(i), r(i), u(i))$. This approach also increases the length of evaluation proofs $\pi_{\sigma,i} = (c_i, z_{s,i}, z_{r,i}, z_{u,i}) \in \mathbb{Z}_p^4$, which involve 3 witnesses $(s(i), r(i), u(i))$ in order to prove that $\sigma_i = H_0(M)^{s(i)} H_1(M)^{r(i)}$ is consistent with vk_i.

In our variant of the scheme, we can use verification keys $\mathsf{vk}_i = g^{s(i)} \cdot h^{r(i)}$ in the first source group $\mathbb{G}$. This allows a reduction from DDH in the transition from Game_4 to Game_5 since we do not need to publicize $\hat{h} = \hat{g}^a$. We note that, in Game_6, the challenger needs $\hat{h} = \hat{g}^a$ to simulate $\hat{C}_{i \diamond 0}$. Fortunately, $\hat{h}$ does not have to appear in public parameters. It is only internally used by the security proof in a game where we are done with the DDH assumption.

4.2 Robustness

The correctness of the scheme follows immediately from the perfect completeness of the Σ-protocol allowing to prove the validity of partial signatures. We thus focus on the consistency property.

Theorem 2. *In the ROM, no PPT adversary $\mathcal{A}$ has non-negligible advantage in the game of Definition 3 under the DDH assumption in $\mathbb{G}$.*

Proof. Assuming that an adversary $\mathcal{A}$ has non-negligible advantage ε in the game Definition 3, we build a DDH distinguisher with almost the same advantage.

To do this, we call Game_0 the game of Definition 3 and define W_0 to be the event that the adversary $\mathcal{A}$ wins in this game. By definition, $\varepsilon = \Pr[W_0]$. We consider a modified game Game_1 where the random oracle $H : \{0,1\}^* \to \mathbb{G}^2$ is replaced by a pseudorandom oracle that always outputs vectors $(H_0(M), H_1(M))$ in the subspace spanned by (g, h). Namely, at each query $H(M)$, the oracle returns $(H_0(M), H_1(M)) = (g^{\alpha_M}, h^{\alpha_M})$ for a random $\alpha_M \stackrel{R}{\leftarrow} \mathbb{Z}_p$. By the same proof as in Lemma 2, we can show that $\mathcal{A}$'s probability of success remains about the same as in Game_0 if the DDH assumption holds. If we call W_1 the event that $\mathcal{A}$ succeeds in Game_1, we have $|\Pr[W_0] - \Pr[W_1]| \leq \mathbf{Adv}_{\mathcal{B}}^{\mathrm{DDH}}(\lambda)$.

We now prove that, in Game_1, the probability $\Pr[W_1]$ is negligible. As part of its output in Game_1, $\mathcal{A}$ produces partial signatures $\{\sigma_i\}_{i \in S}$ and evaluation proofs $\{\pi_{\sigma,i}\}_{i \in S}$. Unless $\mathcal{A}$ managed to break the soundness of one of the evaluation proofs, for each $i \in S$, there exists $(s_i, r_i) \in \mathbb{Z}_p^2$ such that $\sigma_i = H_0(M)^{s_i} \cdot H_1(M)^{r_i}$ and $\mathsf{vk}_i = g^{s_i} \cdot h^{r_i}$ and thus $\sigma_i = \mathsf{vk}_i^{\alpha_M}$, where $H_0(M) = g^{\alpha_M}$ and $H_1(M) = h^{\alpha_M}$. If we denote by $\phi : \mathbb{G} \to \hat{\mathbb{G}}$ the isomorphism such that $\hat{g} = \phi(g)$ (which is assumed to be not efficiently computable), we note that the public key $\mathsf{pk} = \hat{g}^s$ satisfies $\mathsf{pk} = \prod_{i \in S} \phi(\mathsf{vk}_i)^{\Delta_{i,S}(0)}$ due to the way it is generated at step 4 of DKG. Since the final signature is obtained as $\sigma = \prod_{i \in S} \sigma_i^{\Delta_{i,S}(0)}$, we have

$$
\begin{aligned}
e(\sigma, \hat{g}) &= e\Big(\prod_{i \in S} \sigma_i^{\Delta_{i,S}(0)}, \hat{g}\Big) = e\Big(\prod_{i \in S} (\mathsf{vk}_i^{\alpha_M})^{\Delta_{i,S}(0)}, \hat{g}\Big) \\
&= e\Big(\prod_{i \in S} \mathsf{vk}_i^{\Delta_{i,S}(0)}, \hat{g}^{\alpha_M}\Big) = e\Big(g^{\alpha_M}, \prod_{i \in S} \phi(\mathsf{vk}_i)^{\Delta_{i,S}(0)}\Big) = e(H_0(M), \mathsf{pk}),
\end{aligned}
$$

which means that $\mathsf{Combine}$ successfully obtains the valid signature for M. Hence, the only way for $\mathcal{A}$ to succeed in Game_1 is to fake an evaluation proof $\pi_{\sigma,i}$ for an incorrect partial signature $\sigma_i \neq \mathsf{vk}_i^{\alpha_M}$. Since H_{FS} is a random oracle and by the special-soundness of the Σ-protocol used in $\pi_{\sigma,i}$, this implies $\Pr[W_1] \leq Q_{H,\mathsf{FS}}/p$ if where $Q_{H,\mathsf{FS}}$ is the number of queries made by $\mathcal{A}$ to H_{FS}. □

5 Extensions

5.1 Adaptively Secure Distributed PRFs

The construction can be modified to provide a simple adaptively secure distributed PRF. The idea is to remove the Verify algorithm and instantiate the construction in a DDH-hard group *without* a bilinear map. To do this, we can apply the DKG protocol as it is and set $\mathbb{G} = \hat{\mathbb{G}}$. The pairing is no longer necessary at step 2 of DKG since $C_{j0} = \hat{C}_{j0}$. The rest of the scheme is unchanged.

With these changes, we obtain a simple adaptively secure variant of the Naor-Pinkas-Reingold DPRF [53], whose pseudorandomness relies on the DDH assumption in the random oracle model.

5.2 Adaptively Secure Distributed VRFs

A useful feature of BLS signatures is that their signatures are unique. They thus provide an efficient verifiable random function (VRF) [52] in the random oracle model, which can be used as a randomness beacon in blockchain applications.

It is known [52] that unique signatures (a.k.a. verifiable unpredictable functions) can be generically turned into verifiable random functions by means of Goldreich-Levin predicates [38]. However, BLS signatures enable a direct, much more efficient construction that bypasses the use of Goldreich-Levin predicates.

The verification key is the public key $\mathsf{pk} = \hat{g}^s$ of the signature scheme and contains an additional group element $\hat{g}^t$. The VRF evaluation on an input x consists of $y = e(H_0(x)^s, \hat{g}^t) \in \mathbb{G}_T$, which is pseudorandom under the Decision Bilinear Diffie-Hellman assumption. To prove the correctness of the evaluation y, the owner of the secret key $\mathsf{sk} = s$ can reveal the BLS signature $\pi = H_0(x)^s$, which convinces the verifier if $e(\pi, \hat{g}) = e(H_0(x), \hat{g}^s)$ and $y = e(\pi, \hat{g}^t)$.

Our threshold BLS signatures extends into an adaptively secure distributed VRF since partial VRF evaluations can be obtained as the image of partial signatures via the mapping that sends σ_i to $e(\sigma_i, \hat{g}^t)$ (see, e.g., [51, Section 4.4]). This makes them straightforward to simulate in the security proof.

In addition, the resulting threshold VRF inherits the useful key-homomorphic and aggregation properties [51] of the BLS-based verifiable random function.

References

1. Abe, M., Fehr, S.: Adaptively secure Feldman VSS and applications to universally-composable threshold cryptography. In: Crypto (2004)
2. Almansa, I., Damgård, I., Nielsen, J.-B.: Simplified threshold RSA with adaptive and proactive security. In: Eurocrypt (2006)
3. ANSI X9.62-1998. Public Key Cryptography For The Financial Services Industry: The Elliptic Curve Digital Signature Algorithm (ECDSA). Working Draft - Version 2.0 (1998)
4. Bacho, R., Loss, J.: On the adaptive security of the threshold BLS signature scheme. In: ACM-CCS (2022)
5. Bacho, R., Loss, J., Stern, G., Wagner, B.: HARTS: high-threshold, adaptively secure, and robust threshold Schnorr signatures. In: Asiacrypt (2024)
6. Bacho, R., Loss, J., Tessaro, S., Wagner, B., Zhu, C.: Twinkle: threshold signatures from DDH with full adaptive security. In: Eurocrypt (2024)
7. Bacho, R., Wagner, B.: Tightly secure threshold signatures over pairing-free group. Cryptology ePrint Archive Report 2024/1557
8. Barreto, P., Lynn, B., Scott, M.: Constructing elliptic curves with prescribed embedding degrees. In: SCN (2002)
9. Bellare, M., Crites, E., Komlo, C., Maller, M., Tessaro, S., Zhu, C.: Better than advertised security for non-interactive threshold signatures. In: Crypto (2022)
10. Benhamouda, F., Halevi, S., Krawczyk, H., Ma, Y., Rabin, T.: SPRINT: high-throughput robust distributed Schnorr signatures. In: Eurocrypt (2024)
11. Boldyreva, A.: Efficient threshold signature, multisignature and blind signature schemes based on the Gap-Diffie-Hellman-group signature scheme. In: PKC (2003)

12. Boneh, D., et al.: Threshold cryptosystems from threshold fully homomorphic encryption. In: Crypto (2018)
13. Boneh, D., Lynn, B., Shacham, H.: Short signatures from the Weil pairing. In: Asiacrypt (2001)
14. Boneh, D., Shoup, V.: A graduate course in applied cryptography Version 0.6 (2023). https://toc.cryptobook.us/
15. Boyd, C.: Digital multisignatures. In: Cryptography and Coding (1989)
16. Cachin, C., Kursawe, K., Shoup, V.: Random oracles in constantinople: practical asynchronous byzantine agreement using cryptography. In: PODC (2000)
17. Canetti, R., Gennaro, R., Goldfeder, S., Makriyannis, N., Peled, U.: UC non-interactive, proactive, threshold ECDSA with identifiable aborts. In: ACM-CCS (2020)
18. Canetti, R., Gennaro, R., Jarecki, S., Krawczyk, H., Rabin, T.: Adaptive security for threshold cryptosystems. In: Crypto (1999)
19. Canetti, R., Makriyannis, N., Peled, U.: UC non-interactive, proactive, threshold ECDSA. Cryptology ePrint Archive Report 2020/492 (2020)
20. Chu, H., Gerhart, P., Ruffing, T., Schröder, D.: Practical Schnorr threshold signatures without the algebraic group model. In: Crypto (2023)
21. Coron, J.-S.: On the exact security of Full Domain Hash. In: Crypto (2000)
22. Crites, E., Komlo, C., Maller, M.: Fully adaptive Schnorr threshold signatures. In: Crypto (2023)
23. Das, S., Ren, L.: Adaptively secure BLS threshold signatures from DDH and co-CDH. In: Crypto (2024)
24. De Santis, A., Desmedt, Y., Frankel, Y., Yung, M.: How to share a function securely. In: STOC (1994)
25. del Pino, R., Katsumata, S., Maller, M., Mouhartem, F., Prest, T., Saarinen, M.-J.: Threshold raccoon: practical threshold signatures from standard lattice assumptions. In: Eurocrypt (2024)
26. Dent, A.: A note on game hopping proofs. Cryptology ePrint Archive Report 2006/260
27. Desmedt, Y.: Society and group oriented cryptography: a new concept. In: Crypto (1987)
28. Desmedt, Y., Frankel, Y.: Threshold cryptosystems. In: Crypto (1989)
29. Fiat, A., Shamir, A.: How to prove yourself: practical solutions to identification and signature problems. In: Crypto (1986)
30. Frankel, Y., Gemmell, P., MacKenzie, P., Yung, M.: Optimal-resilience proactive public-key cryptosystems. In: FOCS (1997)
31. Frankel, Y., MacKenzie, P., Yung, M.: Adaptively-secure distributed public-key systems. In: ESA (1999)
32. Fuchsbauer, G., Kiltz, E., Loss, J.: The algebraic group model and its applications. In: Crypto (2018)
33. Galbraith, S., Paterson, K., Smart, N.: Pairings for cryptographers. Discrete Appl. Math. **156**(16) (2008)
34. Gennaro, R., Jarecki, S., Krawczyk, H., Rabin, T.: Robust threshold DSS signatures. In: Eurocrypt (1996)
35. Gennaro, R., Jarecki, S., Krawczyk, H., Rabin, T.: Secure distributed key generation for discrete-log based cryptosystems. In: Eurocrypt (1999)
36. Gennaro, R., Jarecki, S., Krawczyk, H., Rabin, T.: Secure applications of pedersen's distributed key generation protocol. In: CT-RSA (2003)
37. Gennaro, R., Jarecki, S., Krawczyk, H., Rabin, T.: Secure distributed key generation for discrete-log based cryptosystems. J. Cryptol. **20**(1) (2007)

38. Goldreich, O., Levin, L.: A hard-core predicate for all one-way functions. In: STOC (1989)
39. Haitner, I., Lindell, Y., Nof, A., Ranellucci, S.: Fast secure multiparty ECDSA with practical distributed key generation and applications to cryptocurrency custody. In: ACM-CCS (2018)
40. Jarecki, S., Lysyanskaya, A.: Adaptively secure threshold cryptography: Introducing concurrency, removing erasures. In: Eurocrypt (2000)
41. Kachisa, E., Schaefer, E., Scott, M.: Constructing Brezing-Weng pairing-friendly elliptic curves using elements in the cyclotomic field. In: Pairing (2008)
42. Katsumata, S., Reichle, M., Takemure, K.: Adaptively secure 5 round threshold signatures from MLWE/MSIS and DL with rewinding. In: Crypto (2024)
43. Katz, J., Yung, M.: Threshold cryptosystems based on factoring. In: Asiacrypt (2002)
44. Komlo, C., Goldberg, I.: FROST: flexible round-optimized Schnorr threshold signatures. In: SAC (2020)
45. Komlo, C., Goldberg, I.: Arctic: lightweight and stateless threshold Schnorr signatures. Cryptology ePrint Archive Report 2024/466 (2024)
46. Libert, B., Joye, M., Yung, M.: Born and raised distributively: fully distributed non-interactive adaptively-secure threshold signatures with short shares. In: PODC (2014)
47. Libert, B., Yung, M.: Adaptively secure non-interactive threshold cryptosystems. In: ICALP (2011)
48. Lindell, Y.: Simple three-round multiparty Schnorr signing with full simulatability. Cryptology ePrint Archive Report 2022/374
49. Lindell, Y.: Fast secure two-party ECDSA signing. In: Crypto (2017)
50. Lysyanskaya, A., Peikert, C.: Adaptive security in the threshold setting: from cryptosystems to signature schemes. In: Asiacrypt (2001)
51. Malavolta, G.: Key-homomorphic and aggregate verifiable random functions. In: TCC (2024)
52. Micali, S., Rabin, M., Vadhan, S.: Verifiable random functions. In: FOCS (1999)
53. Naor, M., Pinkas, B., Reingold, O.: Distributed pseudo-random functions and KDCs. In: Eurocrypt (1999)
54. Okamoto, T.: Provably secure and practical identification schemes and corresponding signature schemes. In: Crypto (1992)
55. Pedersen, T.: Non-interactive and information-theoretic secure veriable secret sharing. In: Crypto (1991)
56. Schnorr, C.-P.: Efficient identification and signatures for smart cards. In: Crypto (1989)
57. Scott, M.: Authenticated id-based key exchange and remote log-in with simple token and pin number. Cryptology ePrint Archive: Report 2002/164 (2002)
58. Shamir, A.: How to share a secret. Commun. ACM (1979)
59. Shoup, V.: The many faces of Schnorr. Cryptology ePrint Archive Report 2023/1019
60. Shoup, V.: Practical threshold signatures. In: Eurocrypt (2000)
61. Stinson, D., Strobl, R.: Provably secure distributed Schnorr signatures and a (t, n) threshold scheme for implicit certificates. In: ACISP (2001)
62. Tessaro, S., Zhu, C.: Threshold and multi-signature schemes from linear hash functions. In: Eurocrypt (2023)
63. Wang, Z., Qian, H., Li, Z.: Adaptively secure threshold signature scheme in the standard model. Informatica **20**(4) (2009)
64. Wee, H.: Threshold and revocation cryptosystems via extractable hash proofs. In: Eurocrypt (2011)

Non-interactive Threshold BBS+ from Pseudorandom Correlations

Sebastian Faust[1], Carmit Hazay[2], David Kretzler[1], Leandro Rometsch[3], and Benjamin Schlosser[1](✉)

[1] Technical University of Darmstadt, Darmstadt, Germany
{sebastian.faust,david.kretzler,benjamin.schlosser}@tu-darmstadt.de
[2] Bar-Ilan University, Ramat Gan, Israel
carmit.hazay@biu.ac.il
[3] Hamburg University of Technology, Hamburg, Germany
leandro.rometsch@tuhh.de

Abstract. The BBS+ signature scheme is one of the most prominent solutions for realizing anonymous credentials. Its prominence is due to properties like selective disclosure and efficient protocols for creating and showing possession of credentials. Traditionally, a single credential issuer produces BBS+ signatures, which poses significant risks due to a single point of failure.

In this work, we address this threat via a novel t-out-of-n threshold BBS+ protocol. Our protocol supports an arbitrary security threshold $t \leq n$ and works in the so-called preprocessing setting. In this setting, we achieve non-interactive signing in the online phase and sublinear communication complexity in the number of signatures in the offline phase, which, as we show in this work, are important features from a practical point of view. As it stands today, none of the widely studied signature schemes, such as threshold ECDSA and threshold Schnorr, achieve both properties simultaneously. In this work, we make the observation that presignatures can be directly computed from pseudorandom correlations which allows servers to create signatures shares without additional cross-server communication. Both our offline and online protocols are actively secure in the Universal Composability model. Finally, we evaluate the concrete efficiency of our protocol, including an implementation of the online phase and the expansion algorithm of the pseudorandom correlation generator (PCG) used during the offline phase. The online protocol without network latency takes less than 14 ms for $t \leq 30$ and credentials sizes up to 10. Further, our results indicate that the influence of t on the online signing is insignificant, $\leq 6\%$ for $t \leq 30$, and the overhead of the thresholdization occurs almost exclusively in the offline phase. Our implementation of the PCG expansion shows that even for a committee size of 10 servers, each server can expand a correlation of up to 2^{17} presignatures in less than 100 ms per presignature.

Keywords: Threshold Signature · BBS+ · Pseudorandom Correlation Functions · Pseudorandom Correlation Generators

A. Patra (Ed.): CT-RSA 2025, LNCS 15598, pp. 198–222, 2025.
https://doi.org/10.1007/978-3-031-88661-4_9

1 Introduction

Anonymous credentials schemes, as introduced by Chaum in 1985 [25] and subsequently refined by a line of work [9,19–21,39,54], allow an issuing party to create credentials for users, which then can prove individual attributes about themselves without revealing their identities. The essential properties these schemes satisfy are *unlinkability*, ensuring that verifiers cannot link two disclosures of credentials of the same identity, and *selective disclosure*, allowing parties to decide which individual attributes of their credentials to disclose. The former makes anonymous credentials a useful privacy tool on the web, allowing clients to authenticate themselves for access to web-based services while preventing service providers from gathering information about the client's usage patterns. The latter makes anonymous credentials an essential building block for self-sovereign identity frameworks, as it enables clients to not only take responsibility for storing their credentials but also to filter the disclosure of their credentials.

The BBS+ signature scheme [4,18,49] named after the group signature scheme of Boneh, Boyen, and Shacham [10] is one of the most prominent solutions for realizing anonymous credential schemes. Abstractly speaking, a BBS+ signature over a set of attributes constitutes credentials, and the holder of such credentials can prove possession of individual attributes using efficient zero-knowledge protocols. The importance of BBS+ is illustrated by the renewed attention in the research community [30,49], several industrial implementations [1,40,41], ongoing standardization efforts by the W3C Verifiable Credentials Group and IETF [8,38], and adaption in further applications [4,17,18].

In traditional credential systems, the credential issuer who is in possession of the signing key constitutes a single point of failure. A powerful and widely adapted tool mitigating such a single point of failure is to distribute the cryptographic task (e.g., [2,23,24,26,33,47] and many more) via so-called *threshold cryptography*. Here, the cryptographic key is shared among a set of servers such that any subset of t servers can produce a signature, while the underlying signature scheme remains secure even if up to $t-1$ servers are corrupted. The thresholdization of digital signature schemes comes with significant overhead in computation, communication, and round complexity. This is particularly the case for randomized signature schemes, where a random secret nonce has to be generated and used in combination with the shared secret key by the set of servers. In the signing protocol, this nonce is then used together with the shared key to produce the signature. Concretely, for BBS+ signing, we require a distributed protocol to compute the exponentiation of the inverse of the secret key added to the random nonce securely.

A straightforward approach to compute the inverse is based on the inversion protocol by Bar-Ilan and Beaver [6] and requires server interaction. In order to strengthen the protection against failure and corruption, we assess it as likely for servers to be located in different jurisdictional and geographic regions. In such a setting, any additional communication round involves a significant performance overhead. Therefore, a threshold BBS+ scheme is desired to have a non-interactive signing phase that enables servers to respond to signature requests without any cross-server interaction.

A popular approach in secure distributed computation to cope with the high complexities of protocols is to split the computation into an input-independent offline and input-dependent online phase [28,42,50,51]. The offline phase provides precomputation material, which in the context of a digital signature scheme is called presignatures [31]. These presignatures are produced during idle times of the system and facilitate an efficient online phase. In recent years, Boyle et al. [12,14,15] put forth a novel concept to generate precomputation material. The main advantage of this concept is the generation of precomputation material with sublinear communication complexity in the amount of precomputation material generated. Recently, this technique also attracted interest for use in threshold signature protocols [2,36]. The technique allows parties to precompute values via a pseudorandom correlation generator (PCG) or a pseudorandom correlation function (PCF). These primitives include an interactive setup phase where short keys are generated and distributed. Then, in the evaluation phase, every party locally evaluates on its key and a common input. The outputs look pseudorandom but still satisfy some correlation, e.g., vector oblivious linear evaluation (VOLE), oblivious transfer (OT), or multiplication triples.

1.1 Contribution

We propose a novel t-out-of-n threshold BBS+ signature scheme in the offline-online model with an arbitrary security threshold $t \leq n$. The centerpiece of our protocol is the design of specifically tailored presignatures that can be directly instantiated from PCG or PCF evaluations and can be used by servers to create signature shares without any additional cross-server communication. This way, our scheme simultaneously provides a non-interactive online signing phase and an offline phase with sublinear communication complexity in the number of signatures. Even for the widely studied signature schemes ECDSA and Schnorr, no threshold protocol exists that achieves both features simultaneously. Moreover, we are the first to present a PCG/PCF-based protocol that supports t-out-of-n threshold, while previous protocols support only n-out-of-n. We formally analyze the active security of all our protocols in the Universal Composability framework under static corruption.

We present two instantiations of the offline phase, one based on PCGs and one based on PCFs. Conceptually, PCFs are better suited than PCGs for preprocessing signatures as PCFs allow servers to compute presignatures only when needed. In contrast, PCGs require the generation of a large batch of presignatures at once that need to be stored on the server side. Nevertheless, existing PCG constructions provide better efficiency than PCF constructions. Therefore, we present protocols for both primitives. For the sake of presentation, we focus on PCGs in the main body and present the a new definition of PCFs and the PCF-based offline phase in the full version of this paper [32].

Unlike prior work using silent preprocessing in the context of threshold signatures [2], we use the PCG and PCF primitive in a black-box way, allowing for a modular treatment. In this process, we identify several issues in using the primitives in a black-box way, extend the definitional frameworks accordingly, and prove the security of existing constructions under the adapted properties.

On a practical level, we provide an extensive evaluation of our protocol, including an implementation and experimental evaluation of the online phase and the seed expansion of the PCG-based offline phase. Since state-of-the-art PCF constructions lack concrete efficiency, we focus our evaluation on the PCG-based preprocessing. Given preprocessed presignatures, the total runtime of the online signing protocol is below 13.486 ms plus one round trip time of the slowest client-server connection for $t \leq 30$ signers and message arrays of size $k \leq 10$. Our benchmarks show that the influence of the number of signers on the runtime of the online protocol is minimal; increasing the number of signers from 2 to 30 increases the runtime by just 1.13%–6.02% (for message array sizes between 2 and 50). Further, our results show that the cost of thresholdization occurs almost exclusively in the offline phase; a threshold signature on a single message array takes 7.286 ms in our protocol, while a non-threshold signature, including verification of the received signature, takes 6.971 ms; ignoring network delays which are the same in both settings. Our implementation of the PCG seed expansion shows that batches of up to 2^{17} presignatures can be expanded with less than 100 ms per presignature for $n \leq 10$.

1.2 Technical Overview

BBS+ Signatures. The BBS+ signature scheme was first described by Au et al. [4] as a modification of the Boneh, Boyen, and Shacham group signature scheme [10]. Recently, Tessaro and Zhu [49] showed how to reduce the size of BBS+ signatures by one group element. In this paper, we follow the improved scheme by Tessaro and Zhu [49] and discuss how to adapt our protocol to the legacy scheme of Au et al. [4] in the full version of this paper [32].

Let $\mathbb{G}_1, \mathbb{G}_2$, and $\mathbb{G}_T$ be groups of prime order p with generators $g_1 \in \mathbb{G}_1$ and $g_2 \in \mathbb{G}_2$ and let map $\mathsf{e} : \mathbb{G}_1 \times \mathbb{G}_2 \to \mathbb{G}_T$ be a bilinear pairing. A BBS+ signature on a message array $\{m_\ell\}_{\ell \in [k]}$ is a tuple (A, e) with $A = (g_1 \cdot \prod_{\ell \in [k]} h_\ell^{m_\ell})^{\frac{1}{x+e}}$ for a random nonce $e \in_R \mathbb{Z}_p$, secret key $x \in \mathbb{Z}_p$ and a set of random elements $\{h_\ell\}_{\ell \in [k]}$ in $\mathbb{G}_1$. To verify under public key g_2^x, check if $\mathsf{e}(A, g_2^x \cdot g_2^e) = \mathsf{e}(g_1 \cdot \prod_{\ell \in [k]} h_\ell^{m_\ell}, g_2)$ (see the full version of this paper [32] for a more formal description).

Distributed Inverse Calculation. The main difficulty in thresholdizing the BBS+ signature algorithm comes from the signing operation requiring the computation of the inverse of $x + e$ without leaking x. This non-linear operation is expensive to be computed in a distributed way. Similar challenges are known from other signature schemes relying on exponentiation (or a scalar multiplication in additive notion) of the inverse of secret values, e.g., ECDSA [2,5,23]. The typical approach (cf. [6]) to compute $M^{\frac{1}{y}}$ for a group element M and a secret shared y is to separately open $B = M^a$ and $\delta = a \cdot y$ for a freshly shared random a. The desired result can be reconstructed by computing $M^{\frac{1}{y}} = B^{\frac{1}{\delta}}$.

Since δ is the product of two secret shared values, it still is a non-linear operation requiring interaction between the parties. Nevertheless, as δ is independent of the actual message, several such values can be precomputed in an *offline* phase. As explained next, a similar, yet more involved, approach can be applied to the BBS+ protocol, allowing an efficient, non-interactive online signing based on correlated precomputation material.

The Threshold BBS+ Online Protocol. We describe a simplified, n-out-of-n version of our threshold BBS+ protocol. Assume a BBS+ secret key x, elements $\{h_\ell\}_{\ell\in[k]}$ in $\mathbb{G}_1$, a random blinding factor $a \in \mathbb{Z}_p$ and n servers, each having access to a preprocessed pair $(a_i, \beta_i) \in \mathbb{Z}_p^2$, in the following called *presignatures*, such that $\sum_{\ell\in[n]} \beta_\ell = a \cdot x$ for $a = \sum_{\ell\in[n]} a_\ell$.

To sign a message array $\mathbf{m} = \{m_\ell\}_{\ell\in[k]}$, each server first obtains the random nonce e via a call to a random oracle H, i.e., $e = \mathsf{H}(\mathsf{sid}||\mathsf{ssid}||\mathbf{m}||[n])$, where sid and ssid are identifiers for the signing session such that the nonce is fresh for each signing request. Then, each server computes $A_i := (g_1 \cdot \prod_{\ell\in[k]} h_\ell^{m_\ell})^{a_i}$ and $\delta_i = \beta_i + a_i \cdot e$ and outputs a partial signature $\sigma_i := (A_i, \delta_i)$. This allows the receiver of the partial signatures to reconstruct δ and compute

$$A = (\prod_{i\in[n]} A_i)^{\frac{1}{\delta}} = ((g_1 \cdot \prod_{\ell\in[k]} h_\ell^{m_\ell})^a)^{\frac{1}{a(x+e)}}$$

such that the tuple (A, e) constitutes a valid BBS+ signature [49]. Each signature requires a new preprocessed pair to prevent straightforward forgeries.

The specialized layout of our presignatures allows us to realize a non-interactive signing procedure. In contrast, using plain multiplication triples, as often done in multiparty computation protocols [7,28], would require one additional round of communication. Further, our online protocol provides active security at a low cost. This is achieved by verifying the received signatures and works since the presignatures are created securely.

The Preprocessing Protocol. The presignatures required by our online phase consist of two values. Each party P_i obtains a share a_i of a random value a and a share β_i of the product $\beta = a \cdot x$. Since a and x are both secret shared values, we can write $\beta = (a_1 + \ldots + a_n) \cdot (x_1 + \ldots + x_n) = a_1x_1 + \ldots + a_1x_n + \ldots + a_nx_1 + \ldots + a_nx_n$, i.e. β is the sum of all cross products. While each party P_i can compute the cross product a_ix_i on its own, party P_i must communicate with P_j to compute the cross products a_ix_j and a_jx_i. Importantly, while the share a_i must be a fresh random value for each presignature, the secret key share x_i is fixed for all presignatures. This fact allows us to obtain additive shares of the cross products via *vector oblivious linear evaluation* (VOLE) correlations. A VOLE correlation is a two-party correlation, in which party P_1 gets a tuple of two random values (a, u) and party P_2 gets a tuple (s, v), where s is fixed for all correlation tuples and v is random. Moreover, the tuples satisfy the correlation $a \cdot s = u + v$. Using VOLE correlations, where the fixed s is set to be the secret key share x_i, parties P_i and P_j obtain additive shares $u_{j,i}, v_{j,i}$ of the cross product a_jx_i. The same applies for the cross product a_ix_j. After obtaining additive shares of all cross products, every party P_i calculates β_i by summing up the additive shares and the cross product $a_i x_i$.

An appealing choice for instantiating the preprocessing protocol is to use pseudorandom correlation generators (PCG) or functions (PCF), as they enable the efficient generation of correlated random tuples. More precisely, PCGs and PCFs allow two parties to expand short seeds to fresh correlated random tuples locally. While the distributed generation of the seeds requires more involved protocols and typically relies on general-purpose multiparty computation, the seed size and the communication complexity of the generating protocols are sublinear in the size of the expanded correlated tuples [12,14]. Using PCG or PCF constructions, we can efficiently compute VOLE correlations [12,15,16,27,43]. Note that the a_i value must be the same for all cross terms, so we require the VOLE PCG/PCF to provide the reusability feature. This allows party P_i to use the same input value a_i in all VOLE correlations for the cross terms $a_i x_j$ with $j \neq i$.

Using PCGs/PCFs in a Black-Box Way. Pseudorandom correlation generators (PCGs) and pseudorandom correlation functions (PCFs) are introduced in [12] and [15]. Concrete constructions of both primitives for simple correlations, such as VOLE, are presented in a line of work including [12,15,16,27,43]. In our work, we aim to deal with PCGs/PCFs in a black-box way such that we can instantiate our protocols with arbitrary constructions as long as they fulfill our requirements. These requirements include supporting VOLE correlations, supporting the active security setting, and providing the opportunity to reuse inputs, as emphasized above. A first step towards black-box usage of PCGs was taken by [14]. This work defines an ideal functionality for correlated randomness, which they show can be instantiated by PCGs. However, the definition does not support reusing inputs to PCGs.

[14] and [15] lay the foundation of the reusability property for PCGs and PCFs. However, their definitions consider passive security only and are unsuitable for black-box usage. Therefore, we introduce new notions called *reusable PCG* and *reusable PCF*, which capture the active security setting, support reusability, and permit black-box use.

Identical to prior definitions of PCGs and PCFs, our primitives consist of a key generation Gen and an expansion algorithm Expand or evaluation algorithm Eval. The reusability feature allows both parties to specify an input to the key generation, which is used to derive the correlation tuples. Additionally, our reusable primitives must satisfy four properties. Three of these properties are stated by [14] and [15], two of which we slightly modified. Our new insight is the requirement of the *key indistinguishability* property, which we specifically introduce to cover malicious parties. The key indistinguishability property states that the adversary cannot learn information about the honest party's input to the key generation, even if the corrupted party chooses its input arbitrarily. This property makes our notion suitable for the active security setting. We state and prove that existing PCG and PCF constructions fulfill our new definition.

The t-out-of-n Setting. So far, we discussed a setting where n-out-of-n servers must contribute to the signature creation. However, in many use cases, we need to support the more flexible t-out-of-n setting with $t \leq n$. In this setting, the secret key material is distributed to n servers, but only t must contribute to the signing protocol. A threshold $t \leq n$ improves the flexibility and robustness of the signing process, as not all servers must be online.

The typical approach in the t-out-of-n setting is to share the secret key material using Shamir's secret sharing [46] instead of an additive sharing as done above. While additive shares are reconstructed by summation, Shamir-style shares must be aggregated using Lagrange interpolation, either on the client or server side. In this work, we reconstruct on the server side due to technical details of our precomputation protocols. Note that prior threshold signature schemes leveraging PCF/PCGs (e.g., [2,36]) only support an n-out-of-n setting.

On a technical level, the challenge for client-side reconstruction is due to VOLE correlations providing us with two-party additive sharings of multiplications, e.g., $u_{i,j} + v_{i,j} = a_i x_j$. The additive shares $u_{i,j}$ and $v_{i,j}$ are sufficient for the n-out-of-n setting (see above). However, it is unclear how VOLE outputs can be transformed into Shamir sharings of $a \cdot x$ so that a client can reconstruct in a t-out-of-n setting.

We, therefore, incorporate a share conversion mechanism from Shamir-style shared key material into additively shared presignatures on the server side. Our mechanism consists of the servers applying the corresponding Lagrange interpolation directly to the outputs of the VOLE correlation. More precisely, as described above, each party P_i gets additive shares of the cross terms $a_i x_j$ and $a_j x_i$ for every other party P_j, where x_ℓ denotes the Shamir-style key share of P_ℓ. Let $u_{i,j}$ be the additive share of $a_i x_j$, then party P_i multiplies the required Lagrange coefficient $L_{j,\mathcal{T}}$ to this share and $L_{i,\mathcal{T}}$ to $v_{j,i}$, where $\mathcal{T}$ is the set of t signers. The client provides the set of servers as part of the signing request to enable the servers to compute the interpolation. While the secret key is shared using Shamir's secret sharing, we can define the random blinding factor a as the additive sharing of all t involved signers, i.e., $a = \sum_{\ell \in \mathcal{T}} a_\ell$. Since there is at least one honest signer in $\mathcal{T}$, a is still random and unknown to the adversary.

1.3 Related Work

Most related to our work are the works by Gennaro et al. [34] and Doerner et al. [30], proposing threshold protocols for the BBS+ signing algorithm. While [34] focuses on a group signature scheme with threshold issuance based on the BBS signatures, their techniques can be directly applied to BBS+. [30] presents a threshold anonymous credential scheme based on BBS+. Both schemes compute the inverse using classical techniques of Bar-Ilan and Beaver [6]. Moreover, they realize the multiplication of two secret shared values by multiplying each pair of shares. While [34] uses a two-round multiplication protocol based on an additively homomorphic encryption scheme, [30] integrates a two-round OT-based multiplier. Although the OT-based multiplier requires a one-time setup, both schemes do not use precomputed values per signing request. This is in contrast to our scheme but at the cost of requiring several rounds of communication during the signing. Parts of their protocols are independent of the message that will be signed; thus, in principle, these steps can be moved to a presigning phase. In this case, the signing phase is non-interactive, but on the downside, the communication complexity of the presigning phase has linear complexity. In contrast, our protocol achieves both a non-interactive online phase and an offline phase with sublinear complexity. In addition, both works [30,34] consider a security model tailored to the BBS+ signature scheme while we show security with respect to a more generic threshold signature ideal functionality.

Wong et al. [53] presented another threshold BBS+ signature scheme. However, their work focuses on providing strong robustness using a linearly homomorphic encryption scheme with threshold decryption. The cost of achieving this property is a four-round protocol.

Another anonymous credential scheme with threshold issuance, called Coconut, is proposed by Sonnino et al. [48] and analyzed and improved by Rial and Piotrowska [45]. Their scheme is based on the Pointcheval-Sanders (PS) signature scheme, which allows them to have a non-interactive issuance phase without coordination or precomputation. We emphasize that the PS signature scheme is less popular than BBS+ and not subject to standardization efforts. The security of PS and Coconut is based on a modified variant of the LRSW assumption introduced in [44]. This assumption is interactive in contrast to the q-Strong Diffie-Hellman assumption on which the security of BBS+ is based. While PS and Coconut also support multi-attribute credentials, the secret and public key size increases linearly in the number of attributes. In BBS+, the key size is constant. Further, PS and, therefore, the Coconut scheme relies on Type-3 pairings, while our scheme can be instantiated with any pairing type. The security of Coconut was not shown under concurrent composition while our scheme is analyzed in the Universal Composability framework.

Like our work, [2] and [36] leverage pseudorandom correlations for threshold signatures. [2] presents an ECDSA scheme, while [36] focuses on Schnorr signatures. [2] constructs a tailored PCG generating ECDSA- presignatures while our scheme uses existing VOLE PCGs/PCFs in a black-box way. Further, in contrast to our work, [2] presents an n-out-of-n protocol without a flexible threshold. [36] introduces the new notion of a discrete log PCF and constructs a two-party protocol based on this primitive. In contrast to our work, [36] captures only the 2-out-of-2 setting. Both schemes [2,36] require additional per-presignature communication. Depending on the phase this communication is assigned to, the schemes either have linear communication in the offline phase or require two rounds of communication in the online phase.

2 Preliminaries

Throughout this work, we denote the security parameter by $\lambda \in \mathbb{N}$, the set $\{1, \ldots, k\}$ as $[k]$, the set $\{0, 1, \ldots, k\}$ as $[0..k]$, the number of parties by n and a specific party by P_i. The set of indices of corrupted parties is denoted by $\mathcal{C} \subsetneq [n]$

and honest parties are denoted by $\mathcal{H} = [n]\backslash\mathcal{C}$. We denote vectors of elements via bold letters, e.g., $\mathbf{a}$, and the i-th element of a vector $\mathbf{a}$ by $\mathbf{a}[i]$.

We model our protocol in the Universal Composability (UC) framework by Canetti [22]. In our constructions, we denote by $\mathcal{Z}$ the UC environment and use sid and ssid to denote session and subsession identifier. We consider a malicious adversary statically corrupting up to $t-1$ parties and the synchronous communication model.

We make use of a bilinear mapping following the definition of [10,11]. A bilinear mapping is described by three cyclic groups $(\mathbb{G}_1, \mathbb{G}_2, \mathbb{G}_T)$ of prime order p, generators $g_1 \in \mathbb{G}_1, g_2 \in \mathbb{G}_2$, and a pairing $\mathsf{e} : \mathbb{G}_1 \times \mathbb{G} \rightarrow \mathbb{G}_T$. We call e a bilinear map iff it can be computed efficiently, $\mathsf{e}(u^a, v^b) = \mathsf{e}(u, v)^{ab}$ for all $(u, v, a, b) \in \mathbb{G}_1 \times \mathbb{G}_2 \times \mathbb{Z}_p \times \mathbb{Z}_p$, and $\mathsf{e}(g_1, g_2) \neq 1$ for all generators g_1 and g_2. We refer to [11] for a more formal specification.

3 Reusable Pseudorandom Correlation Generators

In this section we introduce our definition of reusable PCGs, extending the definition of programmable PCGs from [14] and [16].

In a nutshell, pseudorandom correlation generators allow two parties to generate a large amount of correlated randomness from short seeds. They are useful in many two- and multiparty protocols in the offline-online-model [28,42,50,51]. Examples for frequently used correlations are vector oblivious linear evaluations, oblivious transfer and multiplication triples.

Our modifications and extensions of the definitions of [13] and [16] reflect the challenges we faced when using PCGs as black-box primitives in our threshold BBS+ protocol. We present our definition and highlight these challenges and changes in the following. We note that Boyle et al. [14] presents an ideal functionality for corruptible, correlated randomness which can be instantiated by PCGs. While this notion allows to abstract from concrete PCG constructions, their ideal functionality does not cover the reusability feature required in our setting. Therefore, we present a suitable definition extending the game-based definitions of [13] and [16].

3.1 Definition

As mentioned above, a PCF/PCG realizes a target correlation $\mathcal{Y}$. For some correlations, like VOLE, parts of the correlation outputs are fixed over all outputs. In the example of VOLE, where the correlation is $v = as + u$ over some ring R, the s value is fixed for all tuples.

Additionally, in a multiparty setting, we like PCG/PCF constructions that allow parties to obtain the same values for parts of the correlation output in multiple instances. Concretely, assume party P_i evaluates one VOLE PCG/PCF instance with party P_j and one with party P_k. P_i evaluates the PCG/PCF to $(a_{i,j}, u_{i,j})$ for the first instance and $(a_{i,k}, u_{i,k})$ for the second instance. Here, we want to give party P_i the opportunity to get $a_{i,j} = a_{i,k}$ when applied on the same input. This property is necessary to construct multiparty correlations from two-party PCG/PCF instances.

To formally model the abovementioned properties, we define a *target correlation* as a tuple of probabilistic algorithms $(\mathsf{Setup}, \mathcal{Y})$, where Setup takes two inputs and creates a master key mk. These inputs enable fixing parts of the correlation, e.g., the fixed value s in VOLE correlations, and obtaining the same values over multiple instances, e.g., by reusing the values s in multiple VOLE correlations. Algorithm $\mathcal{Y}$ uses the master key to sample correlation outputs.

Finally, we follow [13,16] and require a target correlation to be reverse-sampleable to facilitate a suitable definition of PCGs. In contrast to [14,16], our definition of a target correlation explicitly considers the reusability of values over multiple invocations.

Definition 1 (Reverse-sampleable target correlation with setup). *Let* $\ell_0(\lambda), \ell_1(\lambda) \leq \mathsf{poly}(\lambda)$ *be output length functions. Let* $(\mathsf{Setup}, \mathcal{Y})$ *be a tuple of probabilistic algorithms, such that* Setup *on input* 1^λ *and two parameters* ρ_0, ρ_1 *returns a master key* mk*; algorithm* $\mathcal{Y}$ *on input* 1^λ *and* mk *returns a pair of outputs* $(y_0^{(i)}, y_1^{(i)}) \in \{0,1\}^{\ell_0(\lambda)} \times \{0,1\}^{\ell_1(\lambda)}$.

We say that the tuple $(\mathsf{Setup}, \mathcal{Y})$ *defines a* reverse-sampleable target correlation with setup *if there exists a probabilistic polynomial time algorithm* RSample *that takes as input* $1^\lambda, \mathsf{mk}, \sigma \in \{0,1\}, y_\sigma^{(i)} \in \{0,1\}^{\ell_\sigma(\lambda)}$ *and outputs* $y_{1-\sigma}^{(i)} \in \{0,1\}^{\ell_{1-\sigma}(\lambda)}$*, such that for all* $\sigma \in \{0,1\}$*, for all* $\mathsf{mk}, \mathsf{mk}'$ *in the range of* Setup *for arbitrary but fixed input* ρ_σ *the following distributions are statistically close:*

$$\{(y_0, y_1) | (y_0, y_1) \xleftarrow{\$} \mathcal{Y}(1^\lambda, \mathsf{mk})\}$$
$$\{(y_0, y_1) | (y_0', y_1') \xleftarrow{\$} \mathcal{Y}(1^\lambda, \mathsf{mk}'),$$
$$y_\sigma \leftarrow y_\sigma', y_{1-\sigma} \leftarrow \mathsf{RSample}(1^\lambda, \mathsf{mk}, \sigma, y_\sigma)\}.$$

Given the definition of a reverse-sampleable correlation with setup, we define our primitive called *reusable PCG (rPCG)*.

The security properties in the original notion of programmable PCGs assumes randomly selected seeds that are inserted into the key generation. This reflects a passive or semi-honest setting in which the adversary cannot deviate from the protocol description such that the seeds are indeed random. We are interested in the active security setting, where an adversary can insert arbitrary seeds into the key generation. Therefore, we adapted the pseudorandom $\mathcal{Y}$-correlated outputs and the security property. Additionally, we introduced a key indistinguishability property. This property is helpful in security proofs of protocols where we want to use PCGs in a black-box way. In particular, it allows us to switch from fake to real PCG seeds/keys and show indistinguishability between two hybrids via a reduction to the property. Next, we formally propose the notion of *rPCG*.

Definition 2 (Reusable pseudorandom correlation generator (rPCG)). *Let* $(\mathsf{Setup}, \mathcal{Y})$ *be a reverse-sampleable correlation with setup which has output* *length functions* $\ell_0(\lambda), \ell_1(\lambda)$*, let* $\lambda \leq \eta(\lambda) \leq \mathsf{poly}(\lambda)$ *be the sample size function. Let* $(\mathsf{PCG.Gen_p}, \mathsf{PCG.Expand})$ *be a pair of algorithms with the following syntax:*

- $\mathsf{PCG.Gen_p}(1^\lambda, \rho_0, \rho_1)$ *is a probabilistic polynomial-time algorithm that on input the security parameter* 1^λ *and reusable inputs* ρ_0, ρ_1 *outputs a pair of keys* $(\mathsf{k}_0, \mathsf{k}_1)$.
- $\mathsf{PCG.Expand}(\sigma, \mathsf{k}_\sigma)$ *is a deterministic polynomial-time algorithm that on input* $\sigma \in \{0, 1\}$ *and key* k_σ *outputs* $\mathbf{y}_\sigma \in \{0,1\}^{\ell_\sigma(\lambda) \times \eta(\lambda)}$*, i.e. an array of size* $\eta(\lambda)$ *with elements being bit-strings of length* $\ell_\sigma(\lambda)$.

We say $(\mathsf{PCG.Gen_p}, \mathsf{PCG.Expand})$ *is a* reusable pseudorandom correlation generator (rPCG) *for* $(\mathsf{Setup}, \mathcal{Y})$*, if the following conditions hold:*

- ***Programmability.*** *There exist public efficiently computable functions* ϕ_0, ϕ_1*, such that for all* $\rho_0, \rho_1 \in \{0,1\}^*$

$$\Pr\left[\begin{array}{l}(\mathsf{k}_0, \mathsf{k}_1) \xleftarrow{\$} \mathsf{PCG.Gen_p}(1^\lambda, \rho_0, \rho_1) \\ (\mathbf{x}_0, \mathbf{z}_0) \leftarrow \mathsf{PCG.Expand}(0, \mathsf{k}_0), \\ (\mathbf{x}_1, \mathbf{z}_1) \leftarrow \mathsf{PCG.Expand}(1, \mathsf{k}_1)\end{array} : \begin{array}{l}\mathbf{x}_0 = \phi_0(\rho_0) \\ \mathbf{x}_1 = \phi_1(\rho_1)\end{array}\right] \geq 1 - \mathsf{negl}(\lambda).$$

- ***Pseudorandom*** $\mathcal{Y}$***-correlated outputs.*** *For every non-uniform adversary* $\mathcal{A}$ *of size* $\mathsf{poly}(\lambda)$ *it holds that*

$$\left|\Pr[\mathsf{Exp}^{\mathsf{pr\text{-}g}}_{\mathcal{A}}(\lambda) = 1] - \frac{1}{2}\right| \leq \mathsf{negl}(\lambda)$$

for all sufficiently large λ*, where* $\mathsf{Exp}^{\mathsf{pr\text{-}g}}_{\mathcal{A}}(\lambda)$ *is as defined in Fig. 1.*
- ***Security.*** *For each* $\sigma \in \{0,1\}$ *and non-uniform adversary* $\mathcal{A}$ *of size* $\mathsf{poly}(\lambda)$*, it holds that*

$$\left|\Pr[\mathsf{Exp}^{\mathsf{sec\text{-}g}}_{\mathcal{A},\sigma}(\lambda) = 1] - \frac{1}{2}\right| \leq \mathsf{negl}(\lambda)$$

for all sufficiently large λ*, where* $\mathsf{Exp}^{\mathsf{sec\text{-}g}}_{\mathcal{A},\sigma}(\lambda)$ *is as defined in Fig. 1.*
- ***Key indistinguishability.*** *For any* $\sigma \in \{0,1\}$ *and non-uniform adversary* $\mathcal{A} = (\mathcal{A}_0, \mathcal{A}_1)$*, it holds*

$$\Pr[\mathsf{Exp}^{\mathsf{key\text{-}ind\text{-}g}}_{\mathcal{A},\sigma}(\lambda) = 1] \leq \frac{1}{2} + \mathsf{negl}(\lambda)$$

for all sufficiently large λ*, where* $\mathsf{Exp}^{\mathsf{key\text{-}ind\text{-}g}}_{\mathcal{A},\sigma}$ *is as defined in Fig. 1.*

3.2 Correlations

Our VOLE correlation of size N over a finite field $\mathbb{F}$ is given by $\mathbf{z}_1 = \mathbf{x}_0 \cdot x_1 + \mathbf{z}_0$, where $\mathbf{z}_1, \mathbf{x}_0, \mathbf{z}_0 \in \mathbf{F}_p^N$ and x_1 is a fixed scalar in $\mathbf{F}_p$. Moreover, we require $\mathbf{x}_0$ being computed by a pseudorandom generator (PRG). We formally define the

$\mathsf{Exp}^{\mathsf{pr\text{-}g}}_{\mathcal{A}}(\lambda)$:
$b \xleftarrow{\$} \{0,1\}, N \leftarrow \eta(\lambda), (\rho_0, \rho_1) \leftarrow \mathcal{A}_0(1^\lambda)$
$\mathsf{mk} \xleftarrow{\$} \mathsf{Setup}(1^\lambda, \rho_0, \rho_1)$
$(\mathsf{k}_0, \mathsf{k}_1) \xleftarrow{\$} \mathsf{PCG.Gen_p}(1^\lambda, \rho_0, \rho_1)$
if $b = 0$ **then** $(\mathbf{y}_0, \mathbf{y}_1) \xleftarrow{\$} \mathcal{Y}(1^\lambda, \mathsf{mk})$
else $\mathbf{y}_\sigma \leftarrow \mathsf{PCG.Expand}(\sigma, k_\sigma)$ for $\sigma \in \{0,1\}$
$b' \leftarrow \mathcal{A}_1(1^\lambda, \mathbf{y}_0, \mathbf{y}_1)$, **return** $b' = b$

$\mathsf{Exp}^{\mathsf{key\text{-}ind\text{-}g}}_{\mathcal{A},\sigma}(\lambda)$:
$b \xleftarrow{\$} \{0,1\}, \rho_\sigma \leftarrow \mathcal{A}_0(1^\lambda)$
$\rho^{(0)}_{1-\sigma}, \rho^{(1)}_{1-\sigma} \xleftarrow{\$} \{0,1\}^*, \rho_{1-\sigma} \leftarrow \rho^{(b)}_{1-\sigma}$
$(\mathsf{k}_0, \mathsf{k}_1) \leftarrow \mathsf{PCG.Gen_p}(1^\lambda, \rho_0, \rho_1)$
$b' \leftarrow \mathcal{A}_1(1^\lambda, \mathsf{k}_\sigma, \rho^{(0)}_{1-\sigma})$ **return** $b' = b$

$\mathsf{Exp}^{\mathsf{sec\text{-}g}}_{\mathcal{A},\sigma}(\lambda)$:
$b \xleftarrow{\$} \{0,1\}, N \leftarrow \eta(\lambda), (\rho_0, \rho_1) \leftarrow \mathcal{A}_0(1^\lambda)$
$\mathsf{mk} \xleftarrow{\$} \mathsf{Setup}(1^\lambda, \rho_0, \rho_1), (\mathsf{k}_0, \mathsf{k}_1) \xleftarrow{\$} \mathsf{PCG.Gen_p}(1^\lambda, \rho_0, \rho_1)$
$\mathbf{y}_\sigma \xleftarrow{\$} \mathsf{PCG.Expand}(\sigma, k_\sigma)$
if $b = 0$ **then** $(\mathbf{y}_{1-\sigma}) \leftarrow \mathsf{PCG.Expand}(1-\sigma, k_{1-\sigma})$
else $\mathbf{y}_{1-\sigma} \leftarrow \mathsf{RSample}(1^\lambda, \mathsf{mk}, \sigma, \mathbf{y}_\sigma)$
$b' \leftarrow \mathcal{A}_1(1^\lambda, \mathbf{y}_0, \mathbf{y}_1)$, **return** $b' = b$

Fig. 1. Security games for reusable PCGs.

reverse-sampleable target correlation with setup $(\mathsf{Setup}_{\mathsf{VOLE}}, \mathcal{Y}_{\mathsf{VOLE}})$ of size N over field $\mathbb{F}_p$ as

$$\mathsf{mk} = (\rho, x_1) \leftarrow \mathsf{Setup}_{\mathsf{VOLE}}(1^\lambda, \rho, x_1),$$
$$((F(\rho), \mathbf{z}_0), (x_1, \mathbf{z}_1)) \leftarrow \mathcal{Y}_{\mathsf{VOLE}}(1^\lambda, \mathsf{mk}) \quad \text{such that}$$
$$\mathbf{z}_0 \xleftarrow{\$} \mathbb{F}_p^N \text{ and } \mathbf{z}_1 = F_0(\rho_0) \cdot x_1 + \mathbf{z}_0,$$

where F being a PRG. The reverse-sampling algorithm is defined such that $(x_1, F(\rho) \cdot \mathbf{x}_1 + \mathbf{z}_0) \leftarrow \mathsf{RSample}_{\mathsf{VOLE}}(1^\lambda, \mathsf{mk}, 0, (F(\rho), \mathbf{z}_0))$ and $(F(\rho), \mathbf{z}_1 - F(\rho) \cdot x_1) \leftarrow \mathsf{RSample}_{\mathsf{VOLE}}(1^\lambda, \mathsf{mk}, 1, (x_1, \mathbf{z}_1))$.

We state a PCG construction realizing this definition of a VOLE correlation in the full version of this paper [32].

4 Threshold Online Protocol

In this section, we present our threshold BBS+ protocol. This protocol yields a signing phase without interaction between the signers and a flexible threshold parameter t.

We show the security of our protocol against a malicious adversary statically corrupting up to $t-1$ parties in the UC framework. We show that our scheme implements a modification of the generic ideal functionality for threshold signature schemes introduced by Canetti et al. [23]. We deliberately chose the generic threshold signature functionality by Canetti et al. [23] over a specific BBS+ functionality such as the one used in [30]. Proving security under a generic threshold functionality enables our threshold BBS+ protocol to be used whenever a threshold signature scheme is required (e.g., for the construction of a more complex protocol such as an anonymous credential system). We present the ideal functionality and discuss the changes with respect to the original version in the full version of this paper [32].

Our protocol uses precomputation to accelerate online signing and requires a random oracle. An intuitive description of the random oracle usage and the precomputation used is given in Sect. 1.2. We formally model the random oracle and the precomputation by describing our protocol in a hybrid model where parties can access a global random oracle functionality H and a hybrid preprocessing functionality $\mathcal{F}_{\mathsf{Prep}}$. Using a hybrid model allows us to abstract from the concrete instantiation of the preprocessing functionality. We present concrete instantiations of $\mathcal{F}_{\mathsf{Prep}}$ in Sect. 5 and in the full version of this paper [32].

4.1 Global Random Oracle Functionality

We follow the formalism of Canetti et al. [23] to model a global random oracle in the UC framework. This model constitutes an abstraction of a hash function that is used within and outside of the analyzed system. We refer the reader to [23] and references within for further discussions.

<u>Functionality H</u>

Parameter: Output domain $\mathbb{Z}_p$.
Upon receiving ($\texttt{query}, x$) from party P, do:
- If a tuple (x, a) is stored, then output ($\texttt{answer}, a$) to P.
- Else, sample $a \leftarrow \mathbb{Z}_p$ and store (x, a).
  Output ($\texttt{answer}, a$) to P.

4.2 Ideal Preprocessing Functionality

The preprocessing functionality consists of two phases. First, the *Initialization* phase samples a private/public key pair. Second, the *Tuple* phase provides correlated tuples upon request. In the second phase, the output values of the honest parties are reverse sampled, given the corrupted parties' outputs. To explicitly model the Tuple phase as non-interactive, we require the simulator to specify a function Tuple during the Initialization. This function defines the corrupted parties' output values in the Tuple phase and is computed first to reverse sample the honest parties' outputs.

Functionality $\mathcal{F}_{\mathsf{Prep}}$

The functionality $\mathcal{F}_{\mathsf{Prep}}$ interacts with parties $P_1, \ldots, P_n$ and ideal-world adversary $\mathcal{S}$. The functionality is parameterized by a threshold parameter t. During the initialization, $\mathcal{S}$ provides a tuple function $\mathsf{Tuple}(\cdot,\cdot,\cdot) \to \mathbb{Z}_p^2$.
Initialization. Upon receiving $(\texttt{init}, \mathsf{sid})$ from all parties,

1. Sample the secret key $\mathsf{sk} \xleftarrow{\$} \mathbb{Z}_p$.
2. Send $\mathsf{pk} = (g_2^{\mathsf{sk}})$ to $\mathcal{S}$. Upon receiving $(\mathsf{ok}, \mathsf{Tuple}(\cdot,\cdot,\cdot))$ from $\mathcal{S}$, send pk to every honest party.

Tuple. On input $(\texttt{tuple}, \mathsf{sid}, \mathsf{ssid}, \mathcal{T})$ from party P_i where $i \in \mathcal{T}$, $\mathcal{T} \subseteq [n]$ of size t do:

- If $(\mathsf{ssid}, \mathcal{T}, \{(a_\ell, \beta_\ell)\}_{\ell \in \mathcal{T}})$ is stored, send (a_i, β_i) to P_i.
  Else, compute $(a_j, \beta_j) \leftarrow \mathsf{Tuple}(\mathsf{ssid}, \mathcal{T}, j)$ for every corrupted party P_j where $j \in \mathcal{C} \cap \mathcal{T}$. Next, sample $a \xleftarrow{\$} \mathbb{Z}_p$ and tuples (a_j, β_j) over $\mathbb{Z}_p$ for $j \in \mathcal{H} \cap \mathcal{T}$ such that

$$\sum_{\ell \in \mathcal{T}} a_\ell = a \qquad \sum_{\ell \in \mathcal{T}} \beta_\ell = a \cdot \mathsf{sk} \tag{1}$$

  Store $(\mathsf{sid}, \mathsf{ssid}, \mathcal{T}, \{(a_\ell, \beta_\ell)\}_{\ell \in \mathcal{T}})$ and send $(\mathsf{sid}, \mathsf{ssid}, a_i, \beta_i)$ to honest P_i.

Abort. On input $(\texttt{abort}, \mathsf{sid})$ from $\mathcal{S}$, send $\texttt{abort}$ to all honest parties and halt.

4.3 Online Signing Protocol

Next, we formally state our threshold BBS+ protocol. We refer the reader to the technical overview in Sect. 1.2 for a high-level description of our protocol. Further, we discuss extensions for anonymous credentials systems and blind signing in the full version of this paper [32].

Construction 1: $\pi_{\mathsf{TBBS+}}$

We describe the protocol from the perspective of an honest party P_i.
Public Parameters. Number of parties n, maximal number of signatures N, size of message arrays k, security threshold t, a bilinear mapping tuple $(\mathbb{G}_1, \mathbb{G}_2, \mathbb{G}_T, p, g_1, g_2, \mathsf{e})$ and randomly sampled $\mathbb{G}_1$ elements $\{h_\ell\}_{\ell \in [k]}$. Let $\mathsf{Verify}_{\mathsf{pk}}(\cdot,\cdot)$ be the BBS+ verification algorithm.
KeyGen.

- Upon receiving $(\texttt{keygen}, \mathsf{sid})$ from $\mathcal{Z}$, send $(\texttt{init}, \mathsf{sid})$ to $\mathcal{F}_{\mathsf{Prep}}$ and receive pk in return.
- Upon receiving $(\texttt{pubkey}, \mathsf{sid})$ from $\mathcal{Z}$ output $(\texttt{pubkey}, \mathsf{sid}, \mathsf{Verify}_{\mathsf{pk}}(\cdot,\cdot))$.

Sign. Upon receiving $(\texttt{sign}, \mathsf{sid}, \mathsf{ssid} \in [N], \mathcal{T}, \mathbf{m} = \{m_\ell\}_{\ell\in[k]})$ from $\mathcal{Z}$ with $P_i \in \mathcal{T}$ and no tuple $(\mathsf{sid}, \mathsf{ssid}, \cdot)$ is stored, perform the following steps:

1. Send $(\texttt{tuple}, \mathsf{sid}, \mathsf{ssid}, \mathcal{T})$ to $\mathcal{F}_{\mathsf{Prep}}$ and receive tuple $(\mathsf{sid}, \mathsf{ssid}, a_i, \beta_i)$.
2. Store $(\mathsf{sid}, \mathsf{ssid}, \mathbf{m})$, send $(\texttt{query}, \mathsf{sid}||\mathsf{ssid}||\mathbf{m}||\mathcal{T})$ to H and receive $(\texttt{answer}, e)$. Then, send $(\mathsf{sid}, \mathsf{ssid}, \mathcal{T}, A_i := (g_1 \cdot \prod_{\ell\in[k]} h_\ell^{m_\ell})^{a_i}, \delta_i := \beta_i + a_i \cdot e)$ to each party $P_j \in \mathcal{T}$.
3. Once $(\mathsf{sid}, \mathsf{ssid}, \mathcal{T}, A_j, \delta_j)$ is received from every party $P_j \in \mathcal{T}\backslash\{P_i\}$,
   a) Send $(\texttt{query}, \mathsf{sid}||\mathsf{ssid}||\mathbf{m}||\mathcal{T})$ to H and receive $(\texttt{answer}, e)$. Next, compute $\epsilon = \left(\sum_{\ell\in\mathcal{T}} \delta_\ell\right)^{-1}$ and $A = (\Pi_{\ell\in\mathcal{T}} A_\ell)^\epsilon$.
   b) If $\mathsf{Verify}_{\mathsf{pk}}(\mathbf{m}, (A, e)) = 1$, set $\mathsf{out} = \sigma = (A, e)$. Otherwise, set $\mathsf{out} = \texttt{abort}$. Then, output $(\texttt{sig}, \mathsf{sid}, \mathsf{ssid}, \mathcal{T}, \mathbf{m}, \mathsf{out})$.

Verify. Upon receiving $(\texttt{verify}, \mathsf{sid}, \mathbf{m} = \{m_\ell\}_{\ell\in[k]}, \sigma, \mathsf{Verify}_{\mathsf{pk}'}(\cdot,\cdot))$ from $\mathcal{Z}$ output $(\texttt{verified}, \mathsf{sid}, \mathbf{m}, \sigma, \mathsf{Verify}_{\mathsf{pk}'}(\mathbf{m}, \sigma))$.

Remark. While we simplified our UC model to capture the scenario where every signer obtains the final signature, we expect real-world scenarios to have a dedicated client which is the only party to obtain the signature. In the latter case, the signers send the partial signature in Step 2 only to the client and Steps 3a and 3b are performed by the client. We stress that in both cases the communication follows a request-response pattern which is the minimum for MPC protocols. Moreover, note that the $(\texttt{tuple}, \cdot, \cdot, \cdot)$-call to $\mathcal{F}_{\mathsf{Prep}}$ does not involve additional communication when being instantiated based on PCGs or PCFs as done in this work. Using such an instantiation, the $(\texttt{tuple}, \cdot, \cdot, \cdot)$-call is realized by local evaluation of the PCF or local expansion of the PCG so that no interaction between the parties is needed.

Theorem 1. *Assuming the strong unforgeability of BBS+, protocol $\pi_{\mathsf{TBBS+}}$ UC-realizes $\mathcal{F}_{\mathsf{tsig}}$ in the $(\mathcal{F}_{\mathsf{Prep}}, \mathsf{H})$-hybrid model in the presence of malicious adversaries controlling up to $t-1$ parties.*

The proof is given in the full version of this paper [32].

5 PCG-Based Threshold Preprocessing Protocol

We state our threshold BBS+ signing protocol in Sect. 4 in a $\mathcal{F}_{\mathsf{Prep}}$-hybrid model. Now, we present an instantiation of the $\mathcal{F}_{\mathsf{Prep}}$ functionality using pseudorandom correlation generators (PCGs). Our $\pi_{\mathsf{Prep}}^{\mathsf{PCG}}$ protocol builds solely on PCGs for VOLE correlations. The resulting protocol consists of an interactive *Initialization* and a non-interactive *Tuple* phase, consisting only of the retrieval of stored PCG tuples and additional local computation.

Our preprocessing protocol consists of four steps: the first three are part of the Initialization phase, and the fourth one builds the Tuple phase. First, the parties set up a secret and corresponding public key. For the BBS+ signature scheme, the public key is $\mathsf{pk} = g_2^x$, while the secret key is $\mathsf{sk} = x$, which is secret-shared using Shamir's secret sharing. This procedure constitutes a standard distributed key generation protocol for a DLOG-based cryptosystem. Therefore, we abstract from the concrete instantiation of this protocol and model the key generation as a hybrid functionality $\mathcal{F}_{\mathsf{KG}}$. Second, the parties set up the keys for the PCG instances. The protocol uses two-party PCGs, meaning each pair of parties sets up required instances. We model the PCG key generation as a hybrid functionality $\mathcal{F}_{\mathsf{Setup}}^{\mathsf{PCG}}$. Third, every party expands the local seeds to the required VOLE correlations and store them in their storage. The fourth step constitutes the Tuple phase and is executed by every party in the signer set $\mathcal{T}$ of a signing request. In this phase party P_i generates (a_i, β_i), where the values fulfill correlation (1). For a signing request with ssid, P_i uses the ssid-th component of the previously expanded correlation vector $\mathbf{a}$ as a_i. Note that the a_i values constitute an additive secret sharing of a value a (cf. (1)). Then, $\sum_{\ell \in \mathcal{T}} \beta_\ell = a \cdot \mathsf{sk}$ can be rewritten as $a \cdot \mathsf{sk} = \sum_{\ell \in \mathcal{T}} a_\ell \cdot \sum_{j \in \mathcal{T}} L_{j,\mathcal{T}} \cdot \mathsf{sk}_j = \sum_{\ell \in \mathcal{T}} \sum_{j \in \mathcal{T}} a_\ell \cdot \mathsf{sk}_j \cdot L_{j,\mathcal{T}}$. Recall that the sk_j values constitute a Shamir sharing of sk so that we need to integrate LaGrange coefficients for interpolation. The multiplication $a_\ell \mathsf{sk}_j$ is equal to the additive shares of a VOLE correlation, i.e., $c_1 - c_0 = a_\ell \mathsf{sk}_j$. For $\ell \neq j$, the parties obtain these additive shares via the stored VOLE correlations that were expanded in the third step. Note that the parties use again the ssid-th component of the vectors to get consistent values. Finally, party P_i applies the appropriate LaGrange coefficients to the output of its PCG expansion and adds $a_i \cdot \mathsf{sk}_i \cdot L_{i,\mathcal{T}}$ to get an additive sharing of $a \cdot \mathsf{sk}$. Note that while the value a is a fresh random values for each signing request, sk is fixed. Therefore, the parties can use VOLE correlations to compute $a\mathsf{sk}$.

Note that party P_i uses PCG instances for computing additive shares of $a_i \mathsf{sk}_j$ and $a_i \mathsf{sk}_\ell$ for two different parties P_j and P_ℓ. Since a_i must be the same for both products, we use reusable PCGs so parties can fix a_i over multiple PCG instances. Based on these two requirements, our protocol relies on reusable PCGs defined in Sect. 3.

Key Generation Functionality. We abstract from the concrete instantiation of the key generation. Therefore, we state a very simple key generation functionality for discrete logarithm-based cryptosystems similar to the functionality of [52]. The functionality describes a standard distributed key generation for discrete logarithm-based cryptosystems and can be realized by [35, 52] or the key generation phase of [23] or [30].

Functionality $\mathcal{F}_{\mathsf{KG}}$

The functionality is parameterized by the order of the group from which the secret key is sampled p, a generator for the group of the public key g_2, and a threshold parameter t. The key generation functionality interacts with parties $P_1, \ldots, P_n$ and ideal-world adversary $\mathcal{S}$.

Key Generation. Upon receiving $(\texttt{keygen}, \mathsf{sid})$ from every party P_i and $(\texttt{corruptedShares}, \mathsf{sid}, \{\mathsf{sk}_j\}_{j \in \mathcal{C}})$ from $\mathcal{S}$:

1. Sample random polynomial $F \in \mathbb{Z}_p[X]$ of degree $t-1$ such that $F(j) = \mathsf{sk}_j$ for every $j \in \mathcal{C}$.
2. Set $\mathsf{sk} = F(0)$, $\mathsf{pk} = g_2^{\mathsf{sk}}$, $\mathsf{sk}_\ell = F(\ell)$ and $\mathsf{pk}_\ell = g_2^{\mathsf{sk}_\ell}$ for $\ell \in [n]$.
3. Send $(\mathsf{sid}, \mathsf{sk}_i, \mathsf{pk}, \{\mathsf{pk}_\ell\}_{\ell \in [n]})$ to every party P_i.

Setup Functionality. The setup functionality gets random values, secret key shares, and partial public keys as input from every party. Then, it first checks if the secret key shares and the partial public keys match and next generates the PCG keys using the random values. Finally, it returns the generated PCG keys to the parties.

In order to provide modularity, we abstract from concrete instantiation by specifying this functionality. Nevertheless, $\mathcal{F}_{\mathsf{Setup}}$ can be instantiated using general-purpose MPC or tailored protocols similar to distributed seed generation protocols from prior work [2,16]. We leave a formal specification of a tailored protocol as future work.

Functionality $\mathcal{F}_{\mathsf{Setup}}^{\mathsf{PCG}}$

Let $\mathsf{PCG}_{\mathsf{VOLE}}.\mathsf{Gen}_{\mathsf{p}}$ be an rPCG for VOLE correlations. The setup functionality interacts with parties $P_1, \ldots, P_n$.

Setup. Upon receiving $(\texttt{setup}, \mathsf{sid}, \rho_a^{(i)}, \mathsf{sk}_i, \{\mathsf{pk}_\ell^{(i)}\}_{\ell \in [n]})$ from every party P_i:

1. Check if $g_2^{\mathsf{sk}_\ell} = \mathsf{pk}_\ell^{(i)}$ for every $\ell, i \in [n]$. If the check fails, send $\texttt{abort}$ to all parties.
   Else, compute $(\mathsf{k}_{i,j,0}^{\mathsf{VOLE}}, \mathsf{k}_{i,j,1}^{\mathsf{VOLE}}) \leftarrow \mathsf{PCG}_{\mathsf{VOLE}}.\mathsf{Gen}_{\mathsf{p}}(1^\lambda, \rho_a^{(i)}, \mathsf{sk}_j)$ for each tuple (P_k, P_j) with $k, j \in [n], k \neq j$.
2. Send keys $(\mathsf{sid}, \{\mathsf{k}_{i,j,0}^{\mathsf{VOLE}}, \mathsf{k}_{j,i,1}^{\mathsf{VOLE}}\}_{j \in [n] \setminus i})$ to party P_i for $i \in [n]$.

PCG-Based Preprocessing Protocol. In this section, we formally present our PCG-based preprocessing protocol in the $(\mathcal{F}_{\mathsf{KG}}, \mathcal{F}_{\mathsf{Setup}}^{\mathsf{PCG}})$-hybrid model.

Construction 2: $\pi^{\mathsf{PCG}}_{\mathsf{Prep}}$

Let $(\mathsf{PCG}_{\mathsf{VOLE}}.\mathsf{Gen}_{\mathsf{p}}, \mathsf{PCG}_{\mathsf{VOLE}}.\mathsf{Expand})$ be an rPCG for VOLE correlations.
We describe the protocol from the perspective of P_i.
Initialization. Upon receiving input $(\mathtt{init}, \mathsf{sid})$, do:

1. Send $(\mathtt{keygen}, \mathsf{sid})$ to $\mathcal{F}_{\mathsf{KG}}$.
2. Upon receiving $(\mathsf{sid}, \mathsf{sk}_i, \mathsf{pk}, \{\mathsf{pk}_\ell^{(i)}\}_{\ell\in[n]})$ from $\mathcal{F}_{\mathsf{KG}}$, sample $\rho_a^{(i)} \in \{0,1\}^\lambda$ and send $(\mathtt{setup}, \mathsf{sid}, \rho_a^{(i)}, \mathsf{sk}_i, \{\mathsf{pk}_\ell^{(i)}\}_{\ell\in[n]})$ to $\mathcal{F}^{\mathsf{PCG}}_{\mathsf{Setup}}$.
3. Upon receiving $(\mathsf{sid}, \{\mathsf{k}^{\mathsf{VOLE}}_{i,j,0}, \mathsf{k}^{\mathsf{VOLE}}_{j,i,1}\}_{j\neq i})$ from $\mathcal{F}^{\mathsf{PCG}}_{\mathsf{Setup}}$, compute and store for every $j \in [N]\backslash\{i\}$:
   a) $(\mathbf{a}_i, \mathbf{c}^{\mathsf{VOLE}}_{i,j,0}) = \mathsf{PCG}_{\mathsf{VOLE}}.\mathsf{Expand}(0, \mathsf{k}^{\mathsf{VOLE}}_{i,j,0})$,
   b) $(\mathsf{sk}_i, \mathbf{c}^{\mathsf{VOLE}}_{j,i,1}) = \mathsf{PCG}_{\mathsf{VOLE}}.\mathsf{Expand}(1, \mathsf{k}^{\mathsf{VOLE}}_{j,i,0})$,
4. Output pk.

Tuple: Upon receiving input $(\mathtt{tuple}, \mathsf{sid}, \mathsf{ssid}, \mathcal{T})$, compute:

5. Let $a_i = \mathbf{a}_i[\mathsf{ssid}]$, $c^{\mathsf{VOLE}}_{(i,j,0)} = \mathbf{c}^{\mathsf{VOLE}}_{(i,j,0)}[\mathsf{ssid}]$, $c^{\mathsf{VOLE}}_{(j,i,1)} = \mathbf{c}^{\mathsf{VOLE}}_{(j,i,1)}[\mathsf{ssid}]$ for $j \in \mathcal{T}\backslash\{i\}$.
6. Compute $\beta_i = a_i \cdot L_{i,\mathcal{T}} \cdot \mathsf{sk}_i + \sum_{j\in\mathcal{T}\backslash\{i\}} \left(L_{i,\mathcal{T}} \cdot c^{\mathsf{VOLE}}_{j,i,1} - L_{j,\mathcal{T}} \cdot c^{\mathsf{VOLE}}_{i,j,0}\right)$
7. Output $(\mathsf{sid}, \mathsf{ssid}, a_i, \beta_i)$.

Theorem 2. *Let* $\mathsf{PCG}_{\mathsf{VOLE}}$ *be an rPCG for VOLE correlations. Then, protocol* $\pi^{\mathsf{PCG}}_{\mathsf{Prep}}$ *UC-realizes* $\mathcal{F}_{\mathsf{Prep}}$ *in the* $(\mathcal{F}_{\mathsf{KG}}, \mathcal{F}^{\mathsf{PCG}}_{\mathsf{Setup}})$*-hybrid model in the presence of malicious adversaries controlling up to* $t-1$ *parties.*

We state our simulator, a proof sketch and the full indistinguishability proof in the full version of this paper [32].

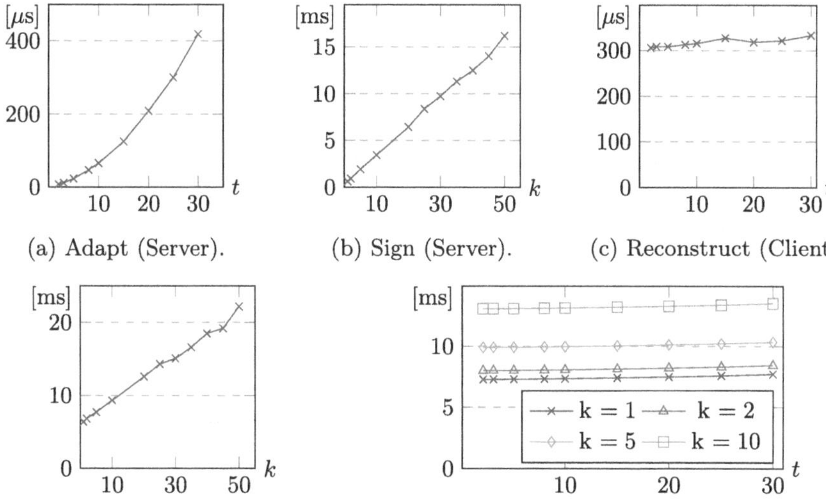

(a) Adapt (Server). (b) Sign (Server). (c) Reconstruct (Client).
(d) Verify (Client). (e) Total.

Fig. 2. The runtime of individual protocol phases (a)-(d) and the total online protocol (e). The *Adapt* phase, describing Steps 6 of protocol $\pi^{\mathsf{PCG}}_{\mathsf{Prep}}$, and the *Reconstruct* phase, describing Step 3a of $\pi_{\mathsf{TBBS+}}$, depend on security threshold t. The *Sign* phase, describing Step 2 of $\pi_{\mathsf{TBBS+}}$, and the signature verification, describing Step 3b of $\pi_{\mathsf{TBBS+}}$, depend on the message array size k.

6 Evaluation

This section presents the evaluation of the online phase of our protocol and compares it to related work. We refer the reader to the full version of this paper [32] for an evaluation of the offline phase and an evaluation of our threshold protocol based on the legacy BBS+ scheme by Au et al. [4].

6.1 Online, Signing Request-Dependent Phase

We evaluate the online, signing request-dependent phase by implementing the protocol, running benchmarks, and reporting the runtime and the communication complexity. For comparison, we also implement and benchmark the non-threshold BBS+ signing algorithm. We open-source our prototype implementation to foster future research in this area.[1]

Implementation and Experimental Setup. Our implementation and benchmarks of the online phase are written in Rust (compiled using rustc 1.68.2 (9eb3afe9e)) and based on the BLS12_381 curve.[2] Note, since the BLS12_381 curve defines an elliptic curve, we use the additive group notation in the following. This differs from the multiplicative group notation used in the protocol description. Our code, including the benchmarks and rudimentary tests, comprises 1,400 lines.

For our benchmarks, we split the protocol into four phases: *Adapt* (Steps 6 of protocol $\pi_{\mathsf{Prep}}^{\mathsf{PCG}}$), *Sign* (Step 2 of $\pi_{\mathsf{TBBS+}}$), *Reconstruct* (Step 3a of $\pi_{\mathsf{TBBS+}}$) and *Verify* (Step 3b of $\pi_{\mathsf{TBBS+}}$). Adapt and Sign are executed by the servers. Reconstruct and Verify are executed by the client. Together, these phases cover the whole online signing protocol. The runtime of our protocol is influenced by the security threshold t and the message array size k. We perform benchmarks for $2 \leq t \leq 30$ and $1 \leq k \leq 50$. The range for parameter t is chosen to provide comparability with [30] and we deem $k \leq 50$ a realistic setting for the use-cases of credential certificates. Moreover, both ranges illustrate the trend for increasing parameters. The influence of the total number of servers n is insignificant to non-existent. Our benchmarks do not account for network latency, which heavily depends on the location of clients and servers. Network latency, in our protocol, incurs the same overhead as in the non-threshold setting. It can be incorporated by adding the round-trip time of messages up to 2KB over the client's (slowest) server connection to the total runtime. As the online phase of our protocol is non-interactive, we benchmark servers and clients individually. We execute all benchmarks on a single machine with a 14-core Intel Xeon Gold 5120 CPU @ 2.20GHz processor and 64GB of RAM. We repeat each benchmark 100 times to account for statistical deviations and report the average. For comparability, we report the runtime of basic arithmetic operations in the full version [32].

[1] https://github.com/AppliedCryptoGroup/NI-Threshold-BBS-Plus-Code.

[2] We have used [3] for all curve operations.

Experimental Results. We report the results of our benchmarks in Fig. 2. These results reflect our expectations as outlined in the following. The *Adapt* phase transforming PCF/PCG outputs to signing request-dependent presignatures involves only field operations and is much faster than the other phases for small t. The runtime increases for larger t due to the computation of LaGrange coefficient which scales quadratically with the number of signers. The *Sign* phase requires the servers to compute $k+1$ scalar multiplications in $\mathbb{G}_1$, each taking 100 times more time than the slowest field operation (cf. benchmarks in the full version). The *Reconstruct* phase involves a single $\mathbb{G}_1$ scalar multiplication and less expensive hashing and field operations. The *Verify* phase requires the client to compute two pairing operations, a single scalar multiplication in $\mathbb{G}_2$, k scalar multiplications $\mathbb{G}_1$, and multiple additions in $\mathbb{G}_1$ and $\mathbb{G}_2$. The pairing operations and the scalar multiplication in $\mathbb{G}_2$ are responsible for the constant costs visible in the graph. The scalar multiplications in $\mathbb{G}_1$ cause the linear increase. The influence of $\mathbb{G}_1$ and $\mathbb{G}_2$ additions is insignificant because they take at most 1.4% of scalar multiplication in $\mathbb{G}_1$. The *Total* runtime mainly depends on the size of the signed message array, k, due to the scalar multiplications in the signing and verification step. The number of signers, t, has only a minor influence on the online runtime; increasing the number of signers from 2 to 30 increases the runtime by 1.13% – 6.02%. Consequently, the online protocol can essentially support any number of servers as long as the preprocessing, which is expected to scale worse, can be instantiated efficiently for the number of servers and the storage complexity of the generated preprocessing material does not exceed the servers' capacities (cf. the offline evaluation in the full version of this paper [32]).

To measure the *overhead of thresholdization*, we compare the runtime of our online protocol to the runtime of signature creation in the non-threshold setting in Fig. 3. The overhead of our online protocol mainly consists of a single scalar multiplication in $\mathbb{G}_1$, assuming that clients also verify received signatures in the non-threshold setting. This observation reflects our protocol pushing all the overhead of the distributed signing to the offline phase.

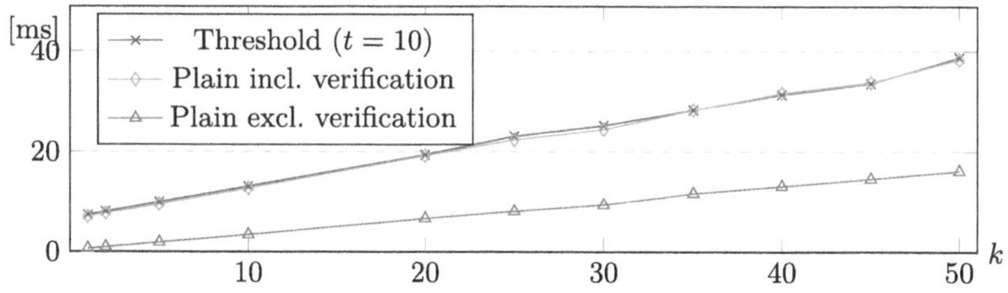

Fig. 3. The total runtime of our online protocol compared to plain, non-threshold signing with and without signature verification in dependence of k. The number of signers t is insignificant (cf. Fig. 2e).

Communication Complexity. The client has to send one signing request of size $(k \cdot \lceil \log p \rceil) + (t \cdot \lceil \log n \rceil)$ bits to each of the t selected servers. By deriving the signer set via a random oracle, we can reduce the size of the request to $(k \cdot \lceil \log p \rceil)$. Each selected server has to send a partial signature of size $(\lceil \log p \rceil + |\mathbb{G}_1|)$. In case of the BLS12_381 curve, $\lceil \log p \rceil$ equals 381 bits whereas $|\mathbb{G}_1|$ equals 762 bits. Parties can also encode $\mathbb{G}_1$ elements with 381 bits by only sending the x-coordinate of the curve point and requiring the sender to compute the y-coordinate itself.

Note that our UC functionality models a scenario where every signer obtains the final signature. Therefore, the partial signatures are sent to all other signers. However, by incorporating a dedicated client into the model, the signers can send the partial signatures only to the client. While we expect this to be sufficient for real-life settings, it makes the model messier. We emphasize that this request-response behavior is the minimum interaction for distributed protocols. As there is no interaction between the servers, this setting is referred to as non-interactive in the literature [2,23].

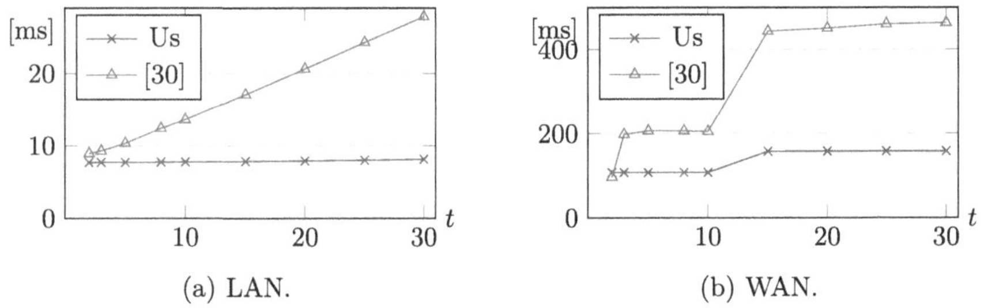

Fig. 4. Runtime of the signing protocol of [30] compared to the network adjusted runtime of our signing protocol in the LAN and WAN setting.

6.2 Comparison to [30]

Independently of our work, [30] presented the first t-out-of-n threshold protocol for the legacy BBS+ scheme. This protocol incorporates a lightweight setup independent of the number of generated signatures but requires an interactive signing protocol. In contrast, our scheme offers a trade-off that provides an efficient, non-interactive online phase at the cost of a more complex offline phase. This trade-off aims to minimize the time it takes to answer a signing request. To show that our online phase's efficiency indeed benefits from the costly preprocessing, we compare our online signing phase to their interactive signing protocol.[3] We stress that the advantage of our online phase comes at the cost of a significantly more complex offline phase. However, our online phase is independent of the concrete instantiation of the offline phase. In particular, less memory-consuming but more communication-intensive instantiations, e.g., based on oblivious transfer or somewhat homomorphic encryption, are also possible.

[3] We thank the authors of [30] for sharing concrete numbers of their evaluation.

As our implementation, their implementation is in Rust and based on the BLS12_381 curve. When comparing the benchmarking machines, $\mathbb{G}_1$ and $\mathbb{G}_2$ scalar multiplications are 15–25% faster on our machine, while signature verifications are 20% faster on their machine. Although not explicitly stated, the numbers strongly indicate the choice $k = 1$ in [30]; the reported runtime of non-threshold BBS+ signing is slightly larger than three $\mathbb{G}_1$ scalar multiplications. Due to the interactivity of their protocol, their benchmarks incorporate network delays for different settings (LAN, WAN). We add network delays to our results to compare our benchmarks to theirs. All machines used in their evaluation are *Google Cloud c2d-standard-4* instances. In the LAN setting, all instances are located at the us-east1-c zone. [29] reports a LAN latency of 0.146 ms for this zone. We add a delay of 0.3 ms to our results. In the WAN setting, the first 12 instances in their benchmarks are located in the US, while other machines are in Europe or the US. According to [37], we add 100 ms to our results for $t < 13$ and 150 ms for $t \geq 13$.

In Fig. 4, we compare the runtime, including latency, of our online signing protocol to the runtimes reported in [30] for the LAN and the WAN setting. The graphs show that our protocol outperforms the one of [30] in both settings for every number of servers. The only exception is the runtime for $t = 2$ in the WAN setting. This exception seems caused by an unusually low connection latency between the first two servers and the client in [30]. The overhead of [30] is mainly caused by the two additional rounds of cross-server interaction. This overhead rises with the number of servers as each server has to communicate with each other servers and is especially severe in the WAN setting.

Due to the high efficiency and non-interactivity of our online phase, our protocol is more suited for settings where servers have a sufficiently long setup interval and storage capacities to deal with the complexity of the preprocessing phase. On the other hand, the protocol of [30] is more suited for use cases with more lightweight servers, especially in a LAN environment where the network delay of the additional communication is less significant.

Acknowledgments. The first, third, and fifth authors were supported by the German Research Foundation (DFG) CRC 1119 CROSSING (project S7), by the German Federal Ministry of Education and Research and the Hessen State Ministry for Higher Education, Research and the Arts within their joint support of the National Research Center for Applied Cybersecurity ATHENE, by the European Research Council (ERC) under the European Union's Horizon 2020 and Horizon Europe research and innovation programs (grant CRYPTOLAYER-101044770), and by the Hessen Agentur, LOEWE-Förderrichtlinie 3, 1376/22-81. The second author was partially supported by the Algorand Centres of Excellence programme managed by Algorand Foundation. Any opinions, findings, and conclusions or recommendations expressed in this material are those of the author(s) and do not necessarily reflect the views of the Algorand Foundation and the United States-Israel Binational Science Foundation (BSF) through Grant No. 2020277.

Disclosure of Interests. The authors have no competing interests to declare that are relevant to the content of this article.

References

1. Github - trinsic-id/bbs. https://github.com/trinsic-id/bbs. Accessed 14 Oct 2024
2. Abram, D., Nof, A., Orlandi, C., Scholl, P., Shlomovits, O.: Low-bandwidth threshold ECDSA via pseudorandom correlation generators. In: IEEE SP (2022)
3. Algorand. BLS12-381 Rust crate. https://github.com/algorand/pairing-plus. Accessed 14 Oct 2024
4. Au, M.H., Susilo, W., Mu, Y., Chow, S.S.M.: Constant-size dynamic k -times anonymous authentication. IEEE Syst. J. (2013)
5. Aumasson, J-P., Hamelink, A., Shlomovits, O.: A survey of ECDSA threshold signing. IACR Cryptol. ePrint Arch. (2020)
6. Bar-Ilan, J., Beaver, D.: Non-cryptographic fault-tolerant computing in constant number of rounds of interaction. In: PODC (1989)
7. Beaver, D.: Efficient multiparty protocols using circuit randomization. In: CRYPTO (1991)
8. Bernstein, G., Sporny, M.: Data integrity bbs cryptosuites v1.0 (2024). https://w3c.github.io/vc-di-bbs/. Accessed 14 Oct 2024
9. Blömer, J., Bobolz, J., Diemert, D., Eidens, F.: Updatable anonymous credentials and applications to incentive systems. In: CCS (2019)
10. Boneh, D., Boyen, X., Shacham, H.: Short group signatures. In: CRYPTO (2004)
11. Boneh, D., Franklin, M.K.: Identity-based encryption from the weil pairing. In: CRYPTO (2001)
12. Boyle, E., Couteau, G., Gilboa, N., Ishai, Y.: Compressing vector OLE. In: CCS (2018)
13. Boyle, E., ET AL.: Efficient two-round OT extension and silent non-interactive secure computation. In: CCS (2019)
14. Boyle, E., Couteau, G., Gilboa, N., Ishai, Y., Kohl, L., Scholl, P.: Efficient pseudorandom correlation generators: silent OT extension and more. In: CRYPTO (2019)
15. Boyle, E., Couteau, G., Gilboa, N., Ishai, Y., Kohl, L., Scholl, P.: Correlated pseudorandom functions from variable-density LPN. In: FOCS (2020)
16. Boyle, E., Couteau, G., Gilboa, N., Ishai, Y., Kohl, L., Scholl, P.: Efficient pseudorandom correlation generators from ring-LPN. In: CRYPTO (2020)
17. Brickell, E., Li, J.: Enhanced privacy ID from bilinear pairing for hardware authentication and attestation. Int. J. Inf. Priv. Secur. Integr. (2011)
18. Camenisch, J., Drijvers, M., Lehmann, A.: Anonymous attestation using the strong Diffie Hellman assumption revisited. In: TRUST (2016)
19. Camenisch, J., Dubovitskaya, M., Haralambiev, K., Kohlweiss, M.: Composable and modular anonymous credentials: definitions and practical constructions. In: ASIACRYPT (2015)
20. Camenisch, J., Lysyanskaya, A.: An efficient system for non-transferable anonymous credentials with optional anonymity revocation. In: EUROCRYPT (2001)
21. Camenisch, J., Lysyanskaya, A.: Signature schemes and anonymous credentials from bilinear maps. In: CRYPTO (2004)
22. Canetti, R.: Universally composable security: a new paradigm for cryptographic protocols. In: FOCS (2001)
23. Canetti, R., Gennaro, R., Goldfeder, S., Makriyannis, N., Peled, U.: UC non-interactive, proactive, threshold ECDSA with identifiable aborts. In: CCS (2020)
24. Castagnos, G., Laguillaumie, F., Tucker, I.: Threshold linearly homomorphic encryption on $\mathbf{Z}/2^k\mathbf{Z}$. In: ASIACRYPT (2022)

25. Chaum, D.: Security without identification: transaction systems to make big brother obsolete. ACM Commun. (1985)
26. Chu, H., Gerhart, P., Ruffing, T., Schröder, D.: Practical schnorr threshold signatures without the algebraic group model. In: CRYPTO (2023)
27. Couteau, G., Rindal, P., Raghuraman, S.: Silver: silent VOLE and oblivious transfer from hardness of decoding structured LDPC codes. In: CRYPTO (2021)
28. Damgård, I., Pastro, V., Smart, N.P., Zakarias, S.: Multiparty computation from somewhat homomorphic encryption. In: CRYPTO (2012)
29. Phanekham, R.J.D.: How much is google cloud latency (GCP) between regions? (2020). https://cloud.google.com/blog/products/networking/using-netperf-and-ping-to-measure-network-latency. Accessed 14 Oct 2024
30. Doerner, J., Kondi, Y., Lee, E., Shelat, A., Tyner, L.: Threshold BBS+ signatures for distributed anonymous credential issuance. In: IEEE SP (2023)
31. Even, S., Goldreich, O., Micali, S.: On-line/off-line digital signatures. J. Cryptol. **9**(1), 35–67 (1996). https://doi.org/10.1007/BF02254791
32. Faust, S., Hazay, C., Kretzler, D., Rometsch, L., Schlosser, B.: Non-interactive threshold BBS+ from pseudorandom correlations. Cryptology ePrint Archive, Paper 2023/1076 (2023). https://eprint.iacr.org/2023/1076
33. Gennaro, R., Goldfeder, S.: Fast multiparty threshold ECDSA with fast trustless setup. In: CCS (2018)
34. Gennaro, R., Goldfeder, S., Ithurburn, B.: Fully distributed group signatures (2019)
35. Gennaro, R., Jarecki, S., Krawczyk, H., Rabin, T.: Secure distributed key generation for discrete-log based cryptosystems. In: EUROCRYPT (1999)
36. Kondi, Y., Orlandi, C., Roy, L.: Two-round stateless deterministic two-party schnorr signatures from pseudorandom correlation functions. In: CRYPTO (2023)
37. Kumar, C.: How much is google cloud latency (GCP) between regions? (2022). https://geekflare.com/google-cloud-latency/. Accessed 14 Oct 2024
38. Looker, T., Kalos, V., Whitehead, A., Lodder, M.: The BBS Signature Scheme. Internet-Draft draft-irtf-cfrg-bbs-signatures-02, Internet Engineering Task Force (2023). (Work in Progress)
39. Lysyanskaya, A., Rivest, R.L., Sahai, A., Wolf, S.: Pseudonym systems. In: SAC (1999)
40. MATTR. mattrglobal/bbs-signatures: an implementation of bbs+ signatures for node and browser environments. https://github.com/mattrglobal/bbs-signatures. Accessed 14 Oct 2024
41. Microsoft. microsoft/bbs-node-reference: Typescript/node reference implementation of bbs signature. https://github.com/microsoft/bbs-node-reference. Accessed 14 Oct 2024
42. Nielsen, J.B., Nordholt, P.S., Orlandi, C., Burra, S.S.: A new approach to practical active-secure two-party computation. In: CRYPTO (2012)
43. Orlandi, C., Scholl, P., Yakoubov, S.: The rise of paillier homomorphic secret sharing and public-key silent OT. In: EUROCRYPT (2021)
44. Pointcheval, D., Sanders, O.: Short randomizable signatures. In: CT-RSA (2016)
45. Rial, A., Piotrowska, A.M.: Security analysis of coconut, an attribute-based credential scheme with threshold issuance. *IACR Cryptol. ePrint Arch* (2022)
46. Shamir, A.: How to share a secret. Commun. ACM (1979)
47. Smart, N.P., Talibi Alaoui, Y.: Distributing any elliptic curve based protocol. In: IMA (2019)
48. Sonnino, A., Al-Bassam, M., Bano, S., Meiklejohn, S., Danezis, G.: Coconut: threshold issuance selective disclosure credentials with applications to distributed ledgers. In: NDSS (2019)

49. Tessaro, S., Zhu, C.: Revisiting BBS signatures. In: EUROCRYPT (2023)
50. Wang, X., Ranellucci, S., Katz, J.: Authenticated garbling and efficient maliciously secure two-party computation. In: CCS (2017)
51. Wang, X., Ranellucci, S., Katz, J.: Global-scale secure multiparty computation. In: CCS (2017)
52. Wikström, D.: Universally composable DKG with linear number of exponentiations. In: SCN (2004)
53. Wong, H.W.H., Ma, J.P.K., Chow, S.S.M.: Secure multiparty computation of threshold signatures made more efficient. In: NDSS (2024)
54. Yu, Z., Au, M.H., Yang, R.: Accountable anonymous credentials. In: Advances in Cyber Security: Principles, Techniques, and Applications (2019)

Updatable Public Key Encryption with Strong CCA Security: Security Analysis and Efficient Generic Construction

Kyoichi Asano[1(✉)] and Yohei Watanabe[1,2]

[1] The University of Electro-Communications, 1–5–1 Chofugaoka, Chofu, Tokyo 182–8585, Japan
{k.asano,watanabe}@uec.ac.jp
[2] National Institute of Advanced Industrial Science and Technology, 2–3–26 Aomi, Koto-ku, Tokyo 135–0064, Japan

Abstract. With applications in secure messaging, Updatable Public Key Encryption (UPKE) was proposed by Jost et al. (EUROCRYPT '19) and Alwen et al. (CRYPTO '20). It is a natural relaxation of forward-secure public-key encryption. In UPKE, we can update secret keys by using update ciphertexts which any sender can generate. The UPKE schemes proposed so far that satisfy the strong CCA security are Haidar et al.'s concrete construction (CCS '22) and Dodis et al.'s generic construction that use Non-Interactive Zero-Knowledge (NIZK) arguments. Yet, even despite the aid of random oracles, their concrete efficiency, except for the recent independent work (EUROCRYPT '24), is quite far from the most efficient CPA-secure scheme. In this paper, we first demonstrate a simple and efficient attack against Dodis et al.'s strongly CCA-secure scheme, and show how to fix it. Then, based on the observation from the attack and fix, we propose a new strongly CCA-secure generic construction for a UPKE scheme with random oracles and show that its instantiation is almost as concretely efficient as the most efficient CPA-secure one. Our construction does not rely on either NIZKs, the AGM, or GGM.

1 Introduction

Forward security (or *forward secrecy*), which is practically crucial for secure communication protocols such as Transport Layer Security (TLS) and secure-messaging protocols such as Signal, guarantees that even if users' secret keys are compromised, messages previously exchanged before the compromise remain secure. In the symmetric-key setting, forward security can be easily achieved with Pseudo-Random Generator (PRG) [4]; one has an initial seed s_0 and iteratively runs $\mathsf{PRG} : \{0,1\}^\lambda \to \{0,1\}^{2\lambda}$ to generate (k_i, s_i) from s_{i-1}, where k_i is a one-time key and s_i is a seed for the next update. However, the symmetric-key approach does not scale since it is hard to efficiently and dynamically add or

A. Patra (Ed.): CT-RSA 2025, LNCS 15598, pp. 223–246, 2025.
https://doi.org/10.1007/978-3-031-88661-4_10

remove users to or from a group. Although an interactive group key-agreement protocol (e.g., [26]) allows users to join and leave the group dynamically, it could take longer to run, especially when some users are offline.[1] The requirement that all users are always active and behave faithfully is unrealistic, particularly in the context of secure messaging.

Forward-Secure Public-Key Encryption (FS-PKE) [7] provides efficient key-evolving functionality in the public-key setting; any sender can update a public key "$\cdots \rightarrow \mathsf{pk}_i \rightarrow \mathsf{pk}_{i+1} \rightarrow \cdots$" consistently with the corresponding secret key "$\cdots \rightarrow \mathsf{sk}_i \rightarrow \mathsf{sk}_{i+1} \rightarrow \cdots$", which is only updated by a receiver.[2] Any ciphertexts encrypted under pk_i can be decrypted with sk_i, and the key chain guarantees the one-wayness of secret keys, i.e., forward security; even if sk_i is exposed, no ciphertexts encrypted under pk_j for any $j < i$ are compromised. However, a major drawback of FS-PKE is efficiency. Canetti et al. [7] showed that Hierarchical Identity-Based Encryption (HIBE) [20,24] implies an asymptotically efficient FS-PKE scheme. Although HIBE can be instantiated from various assumptions over bilinear groups [5,6], lattices [8], and even pairing-free groups [14], these concrete HIBE schemes (and, therefore, the resulting FS-PKE schemes) either require relatively expensive techniques such as pairings or are considerably less efficient than many simple PKE schemes.

Another important security requirement for modern secure messaging protocols is *backward security* (or *post-compromise security*), which guarantees that once the exposure of secret keys ends, security can be restored by updating secret keys. Unfortunately, FS-PKE never supports backward security since the public-key update procedure is deterministic; the adversary who has an exposed secret key sk_i can obtain a sequence of the future secret keys $\mathsf{sk}_{i+1}, \mathsf{sk}_{i+2}, \ldots$. Although several key-evolving PKE schemes support backward security [9,10,13], they seem to essentially require computational costs at least as expensive as HIBE, as in FS-PKE.

Updatable Public-Key Encryption. Motivated by practically efficient forward and backward security in secure messaging protocols, Jost et al. [25] and Alwen et al. [1] recently put forward a notion of Updatable Public-Key Encryption (UPKE), a mild variant of the above key-evolving PKE schemes.[3] UPKE allows any sender to initiate key updates, whereas senders are forced to synchronize key-update intervals with the receiver, who has a secret key in FS-PKE. Specifically, any sender can update pk_i to pk_{i+1} and generate (encrypted) update information up_{i+1}, called an *update ciphertext*. The receiver updates sk_i to sk_{i+1} with up_{i+1} so as to be consistent with pk_{i+1}. Indeed, UPKE meets

[1] A trivial solution in the public-key setting, i.e., refresh all users' pairs of public and secret keys, has the same problem and requires all users to be online for each update.

[2] In the seminal work [7], FS-PKE allows receivers to update their secret keys sk_i without updating the corresponding public keys pk. Nevertheless, FS-PKE can be viewed as a key-evolving PKE by setting $\mathsf{pk}_i = (\mathsf{pk}, i)$.

[3] To be precise, UPKE does not always support backward security, though it meets forward security in any case. Nevertheless, UPKE clearly differs in the *possibility* of backward security from FS-PKE (see [25, Sec. 4] for the detailed discussion).

both forward and backward security (in the above sense) and can close the gap in the efficiency between the existing key-evolving PKE and standard PKE schemes; Jost et al. [25] and Alwen et al. [1] showed a UPKE scheme based on the hashed ElGamal PKE scheme, i.e., from the computational Diffie–Hellman (CDH) assumption in the Random Oracle Model (ROM). Following these seminal works, various UPKE schemes have been proposed. Eaton et al. [16] proposed the first post-quantum secure UPKE schemes from isogenies. Dodis et al. [11] got rid of the random oracles and proposed two concrete UPKE schemes from Decisional Diffie–Hellman (DDH) and the Learning with Errors (LWE) assumptions in the standard model, respectively. Haidar et al. [22] showed a UPKE scheme from the Decisional Composite Residuosity (DCR) assumption without random oracles, and Haidar et al. [23] proposed a new UPKE scheme from the LWE assumption in the standard model, which is more efficient than Dodis et al.'s scheme. Duparc et al. [15] showed the first isogeny-based UPKE scheme which is not based on isogeny group actions, called SILBE. Very recently (and independently of our work), Alwen et al. [2] proposed an efficient UPKE scheme with advanced security notions over bilinear groups in the ROM and algebraic group model (AGM).

Chosen-Randomness Security vs. Chosen-Update Security. In addition to standard security notions against Chosen-Plaintext Attacks (CPA) and Chosen-Ciphertext Attacks (CCA), there are two kinds of security notions for update operations in UPKE: *Chosen-Randomness* (CR) and *Chosen-Update* (CU) security. The seminal works [1,25] originally considered the former in the context of secure messaging protocols; it captures the exposure of intermediate values of computations (including the randomness r' used for key updates) during sessions, and therefore an adversary can obtain vulnerable secret keys sk'_i updated by the exposed randomness r'. For that matter, the adversary is even allowed to arbitrarily choose "bad" randomness to have the target receiver update secret keys with it. The UPKE constructions listed in the last paragraph all satisfy CR-CPA security.

Dodis et al. [11] introduced CU security; it allows the adversary to provide a (maliciously-generated) public key pk'_i and update ciphertext up'_i to the target receiver, instead of the exposed randomness r'. It is clear that CU security is stronger than CR since the CU adversary does not necessarily follow the update procedure and choice of randomness. Taking into account the presence of such malicious senders who attempt to impersonate honest ones, CU security is much closer to reality. Thus, we mainly focus on CU security in this paper. To date, there are only two approaches to achieving CU security. The first is generic transformations in the standard model, as proposed by Dodis et al. [11]. Specifically, they showed two generic transformations that lift CPA to CCA security and CR to CU security, respectively. Hence, any CR-CPA-secure UPKE scheme can be transformed into a CU-CCA-secure one. Both transformations employ one-time, strong, true-simulation f-extractable Non-Interactive Zero-Knowledge (NIZK) arguments. Although the NIZK arguments with those properties can be instantiated by, e.g., Groth–Sahai proof [21], its practically efficient instantiation is unclear. The second one is concrete constructions with efficient NIZK arguments for specific languages in the ROM [2,22,23]. Haidar et al. [22] constructed CR-CPA-secure schemes and then lifted to CU-CCA-secure ones without using an inefficient NIZK argument; instead, they built a Σ-protocol for a specific Schnorr-like language and applied the Fiat-Shamir transformation to construct an efficient NIZK argument. Although Haidar et al. [23] gave a CU-CCA secure generic construction from any CR-CPA secure UPKE scheme and computationally sound NIZK argument, one should clarify the corresponding language and NIZK construction to instantiate the UPKE scheme so that the NIZK argument works well with the underlying CR-CPA scheme. They indeed showed a concrete language, and the corresponding NIZK argument can be obtained by applying the existing work [27]. The independent work by Alwen et al. [2] provides a very efficient UPKE scheme, which requires simulation-extractable zero-knowledge proofs for a specific language, called the "Proof of Logarithm" system. Therefore, though the above schemes require random oracles to lift CR to CU security, the constructions are more practical than Dodis et al.'s transformation. Yet, despite the aid of random oracles, the concrete efficiency of the CU-CCA-secure schemes (with the exception of the independent work [2]; which we discuss later in this section) remains significantly below that of Jost et al.'s CR-CPA-secure UPKE scheme (see Table 1).

Going back to the original motivation of UPKE [1,25], it was introduced and investigated in the hope of being used for secure messaging protocols. Therefore, in that sense, the concrete rather than asymptotic efficiency of UPKE is a crucial issue; to be put to practical use, i.e., used as a critical primitive in secure messaging protocols, UPKE has to be comparable to the existing primitives, such as the X3DH protocol [28] and the double ratchet protocol [30] in the Singal [32]. Thus, the question we ask in this paper is:

How efficiently can we make a CU-CCA-secure UPKE scheme? In particular, is it possible to realize a CU-CCA-secure UPKE scheme almost as concretely efficient as Jost et al.'s scheme?

Independent Work. We must also mention the recent independent work by Alwen et al. [2]. Their CU-CCA-secure UPKE scheme achieves concrete efficiency comparable to that of Jost et al.'s scheme [25]. However, the security of their scheme relies on the AGM. The AGM is an appealing and powerful cryptographic model since it seems weaker than the generic group model (GGM). However, Zhang et al. [33] recently demonstrated that hardness in the AGM may not necessarily imply hardness in the GGM. In this regard, it would be preferable to achieve a concretely efficient CU-CCA-secure UPKE scheme without relying on the AGM or GGM. Notably, our construction does not require either the AGM or GGM.

1.1 Our Contributions

In this paper, we give an affirmative answer to the above question; we show a CU-CCA-secure UPKE scheme almost as concretely efficient as the most-efficient-ever UPKE scheme, i.e., Jost et al.'s scheme. Our construction requires random oracles but does not rely on either NIZKs, AGM, or GGM. Jost et al.'s UPKE scheme is just a variant of hashed ElGamal PKE, and therefore, our results show that UPKE could reach the same efficiency level as standard PKE. Specifically, our contributions are two-fold.

First, along the way to our main result above, we show a practical attack breaking CR/CU-CCA-security of Dodis et al.'s CPA-to-CCA transformation [11] and how to modify it. Specifically, we formalize a special property of UPKE, called *non-influential randomness*, and show that it contradicts CCA security but *not* CPA. Indeed, all the existing CR-CPA-secure UPKE schemes [1,11,22,25] satisfy this property. We then show that our attack is effective and efficient against CCA-secure UPKE schemes obtained via Dodis et al.'s CPA-to-CCA transformation (even in a CR setting) if the underlying CPA-secure UPKE scheme meets the non-influential randomness. To put it differently, the property is carried over to the resulting CCA-secure scheme. We also show how to modify their transformation, namely, how not to take over the special property in the transformation.

Second, as our main result, we propose a new generic transformation from CR-CPA to CU-CCA security in the ROM. Unlike the existing transformation, our generic construction no longer requires NIZK arguments and is almost as concretely efficient as the underlying CR-CPA-secure UPKE scheme (see Table 1). Namely, as in the seminal works [1,25], we use random oracles to circumvent a circular-security issue and make the resulting scheme efficient, and we differently employ random oracles for the lifting of CR to CU security; we apply the *double Fujisaki-Okamoto (FO) transformation* for that aim, whereas the Haidar's CU-CCA-secure schemes [22,23] employ the specific NIZK arguments in the ROM. In that sense, we only require the *one-wayness* of CR-CPA security, i.e., OW-CR-CPA security, not indistinguishability (IND-CR-CPA security).

Efficiency Comparison. Table 1 compares the efficiency of the CR/CU-CCA-secure UPKE schemes among existing schemes and our schemes instantiated with Jost et al.'s CR-CPA-secure scheme [25]. We here omit lattice-based schemes [11,23] since it is hard to estimate concrete parameters, and they obviously require larger parameters than Jost et al.'s scheme. For example, the CR-CCA-secure scheme [23] requires 24,000 bits for ciphertexts and 96,000 bits for update ciphertexts (see [23] for the detailed estimation). As a reference, we also show a comparison between Jost et al.'s CR-CPA-secure scheme in the ROM and Haidar et al.'s CR-CPA secure scheme in the standard model. Specifically, we compare the sizes of secret keys, public keys, ciphertexts, and update ciphertexts when satisfying 128-bit security. Based on this comparison, we can say that our CR/CU-CCA-secure UPKE schemes are more efficient than Haidar et al.'s CR/CU-CCA-secure UPKE schemes. Specifically, it can be seen that our schemes are efficient by an order of magnitude (2 to 100 times) for each parameter size. Alwen et al.'s CU-CCA-secure scheme achieves comparable parameter sizes to ours; the main difference between our scheme and Alwen et al.'s scheme is that our construction requires only random oracles. We note that the compar-

Table 1. Comparison for existing UPKE schemes with 128-bit security. The asterisk (*) means no public verifiablity.

Scheme	Secret key	Public key	Ciphertext	Update ciphertext	Security	ROM	NIZK	AGM
Jost et al. [25]	256 b	512 b	512 b	512 b	CR-CPA	✓	–	–
Dodis et al. [11]	1.3 kb	328 kb	328 kb	419 Mb	CR-CPA	–	–	–
Haidar et al. [22]	4.6 kb	6.1 kb	12 kb	12 kb	CR-CPA	–	–	–
Ours (with [25])	256 b	512 b	512 b	1 kb	CU-CPA*	✓	–	–
Haidar et al. [22]	4.6 kb	6.1 kb	66 kb	12 kb	CR-CCA	✓	✓	–
Ours (with [25])	256 b	640 b	768 b	512 b	CR-CCA	✓	–	–
Ours (with [22])	4.6 kb	6.1 kb	15 kb	12 kb	CR-CCA	✓	–	–
Haidar et al. [22]	4.6 kb	9.2 kb	91 kb	105 kb	CU-CCA	✓	✓	–
Alwen et al. [2]	384 b	384 b	768 b	768 b	CU-CCA	✓	✓	✓
Ours (with [22])	4.6 kb	9.2 kb	24 kb	105 kb	CU-CCA*	✓	–	–
Ours (with [25])	256 b	640 b	768 b	1 kb	CU-CCA*	✓	–	–

ison in Table 1 does not take into account the security loss caused by security proofs, so it is necessary to consider the effect of the security loss when conducting a rigorous parameter evaluation. Although, as can be seen above, our transformation is quite efficient, the resulting CU-CPA/CCA secure scheme does not achieve public verifiability, which is an important property for CU security; we leave it as an open problem.

1.2 Technical Overview

In this section, we give an overview of our results.

Updatable Public-Key Encryption. We start describing the syntax of UPKE: it consists of standard PKE algorithms $(\mathsf{Gen}, \mathsf{Enc}, \mathsf{Dec})$ and the following update algorithms $(\mathsf{UpdPk}, \mathsf{UpdSk})$ for public and secret keys:

$$(\mathsf{pk}_i, \mathsf{up}_i) \leftarrow \mathsf{UpdPk}(\mathsf{pk}_{i-1}; r_i), \quad \mathsf{sk}_i \leftarrow \mathsf{UpdSk}(\mathsf{pk}_{i-1}, \mathsf{sk}_{i-1}, (\mathsf{pk}_i, \mathsf{up}_i)),$$

where r_i is update randomness used in UpdPk, up_i is an update ciphertext, and it holds $\mathsf{Dec}(\mathsf{pk}_i, \mathsf{sk}_i, \mathsf{Enc}(\mathsf{pk}_i, \mathsf{M})) = \mathsf{M}$ for any epoch i. Any sender can initiate the update procedure and execute UpdPk to update pk_{i-1} to pk_i and generate an update ciphertext up_i. Receiving $(\mathsf{pk}_i, \mathsf{up}_i)$, a receiver updates the corresponding secret key sk_{i-1} to sk_i.

As described earlier, there are two kinds of security notions related to the update procedures of UPKE: CR and CU security. Loosely speaking, CR security captures "leakage and malicious modifications to update randomness," whereas CU security captures "leakage and malicious modifications to whole update information (including update randomness)".

- *CR Security*: A CR adversary is allowed to arbitrarily choose update randomness r_i^* and force the target receiver to run the UpdPk algorithm with r_i^*. It is worth noting that the CR adversary may choose the update randomness over arbitrary probability distribution. If chosen uniformly at random, it captures that the CR adversary observes the leakage of update randomness.
- *CU Security*: A CU adversary can create maliciously-generated public keys pk_i^* and update ciphertexts up_i^* and force the target receiver to use them for the UpdSk algorithms. Note that the CU adversary may not follow the protocol, whereas pk_i^* and up_i^* are honestly generated except for the choice of the update randomness in CR security. Hence, CU security is a stronger security notion than CR.

Combined with CPA and CCA security, there are four security notions for UPKE, CR-CPA, CU-CPA, CR-CCA, and CU-CCA, where the first is the weakest, and the last is the strongest.

Existing Construction Approaches for CU-CCA-Secure UPKE. All related works [1,11,22,23,25] have begun working on constructing CR-CPA-secure schemes directly, and then some of the works extended them to strongly secure ones, e.g., CU-CCA-secure schemes. In particular, only two existing ways to enhance CR-CPA security to CU-CCA.

- *CU-CCA Security in the ROM* [22,23]: Haidar et al. [22] and Haidar et al. [23] extended their CR-CPA-secure UPKE constructions from the DCR and LWE assumptions, respectively, to CU-CCA-secure schemes in the ROM by using specific and efficient NIZK arguments that support limited languages (but compatible with their CR-CPA-secure schemes). In particular, in the DCR-based construction [22], they employed the variant of Naor–Yung transformation [29] with the Fiat–Shamir heuristic [17] to construct such an efficient NIZK argument. The downside of this approach is that this specific NIZK argument cannot be applied to other CR-CPA-secure UPKE schemes.
- *CU-CCA Security in the Standard Model* [11]: Dodis et al. proposed two transformations for UPKE: the one lifts CPA security to CCA, and the other lifts CR security to CU, which we call the *CPA-to-CCA* and *CR-to-CU* transformations. These transformations also employ NIZK arguments. In particular, since Dodis et al. viewed (CR-CPA-secure) UPKE schemes as a kind of PKE schemes with circular security and leakage resilience, they required strong properties of NIZK arguments to lift CPA security to CCA *even in the leakage-resilient setting.* It is worth noting that the two transformations do not require random oracles, though it is unclear how to efficiently instantiate such a strong NIZK argument.

As seen above, both approaches are based on NIZK arguments, which seem to be an efficiency bottleneck: if one wants to realize CU-CCA-secure schemes without random oracles, inefficient NIZK arguments seem necessary; even with random oracles, one has to narrow down the language the NIZK supports to keep efficiency. Although Haidar et al.'s CU-CCA-secure scheme requires random oracles, their CR-CPA-secure UPKE scheme does not require any random oracles, so its parameter sizes are relatively large.

A Simple Attack against Dodis et al.'s CPA-to-CCA Transformation. Along the way to pursuing efficient CU-CCA-secure UPKE schemes, we find a simple and efficient attack against Dodis et al.'s CPA-to-CCA transformation. To be precise, this attack works if the underlying CPA-secure UPKE scheme satisfies a certain property, however, all the existing CPA-secure UPKE schemes [1,11, 22,23,25] indeed meet it.

Let us briefly explain here with an instantiation of the CPA-to-CCA transformation from Jost et al.'s scheme [25]. A public and secret keys are given by:

$$\mathsf{pk}_i := (g, h := g^x, \mathsf{CRS}) \text{ and } \mathsf{sk}_i := x,$$

where g is a generator of a cyclic group $\mathbb{G}$ of order q, $x \in \mathbb{Z}_q$, and CRS is a common reference string of the underlying NIZK argument. The UpdPk and UpdSk algorithms are defined as follows.

- $\mathsf{UpdPk}(\mathsf{pk}_i)$: Choose update randomness $r \leftarrow_{\$} \mathbb{Z}_q$ and output $\mathsf{pk}_{i+1} := (g, h \cdot g^r, \mathsf{CRS})$ and $\mathsf{up}_{i+1} \leftarrow \mathsf{Enc}(\mathsf{pk}_i, r)$.
- $\mathsf{UpdSk}(\mathsf{pk}_i, \mathsf{sk}_i, (\mathsf{pk}_{i+1}, \mathsf{up}_{i+1}))$: Run $r \leftarrow \mathsf{Dec}(\mathsf{pk}_i, \mathsf{sk}_i, \mathsf{up}_{i+1})$ and output $\mathsf{sk}_{i+1} := x + r \bmod q$.

Here, let us briefly explain the CU-CCA-security game between an adversary $\mathcal{A}$ and a challenger $\mathcal{C}$. The adversary $\mathcal{A}$ can make either update or challenge queries: upon an update query on the update randomness r_i, where i denotes the current epoch, the challenger $\mathcal{C}$ generates updated public and secret keys such that $\mathsf{pk}_{i+1} := (g, h \cdot g^{r_i}, \mathsf{CRS})$ and $\mathsf{sk}_{i+1} := x + r_i \bmod q$; upon the challenge query $(\mathsf{M}_0^*, \mathsf{M}_1^*)$, $\mathcal{A}$ receives the challenge ciphertext ct^*, which is encrypted by pk_{i^*}, where i^* is the challenge epoch. Although $\mathcal{A}$ is not allowed to make a decryption query on ct^* at the challenge epoch i^* to prevent a trivial attack, $\mathcal{A}$ can make a decryption query on ct^* once the public and secret keys are updated, i.e., the epoch goes by.

Now, $\mathcal{A}$ tries to break the CU-CCA security as follows. At the challenge epoch i^*, $\mathcal{A}$ sets update randomness $r_{i^*} := 0$ and makes an updated query on r_{i^*}. Then, $\mathcal{A}$ forces $\mathcal{C}$ to compute $(\mathsf{pk}_{i^*+1}, \mathsf{sk}_{i^*+1})$ such that $(\mathsf{pk}_{i^*+1}, \mathsf{sk}_{i^*+1}) = (\mathsf{pk}_{i^*}, \mathsf{sk}_{i^*})$, since $\mathsf{pk}_{i^*+1} := (g, h \cdot g^0, \mathsf{CRS})$ and $\mathsf{sk}_{i^*+1} := \mathsf{sk}_{i^*} + 0 \bmod q$. As described above, $\mathcal{A}$ can now make a decryption query on the challenge ciphertext. Since $(\mathsf{pk}_{i^*+1}, \mathsf{sk}_{i^*+1}) = (\mathsf{pk}_{i^*}, \mathsf{sk}_{i^*})$, $\mathcal{A}$ obtains the decryption result of the challenge ciphertext and breaks the CU-CCA security.

Why Does the Attack Succeed? The attack succeeds since if the underlying CPA-secure UPKE scheme meets the property that there exists update randomness r^* such that $(\mathsf{pk}_{i^*+1}, \mathsf{sk}_{i^*+1}) = (\mathsf{pk}_{i^*}, \mathsf{sk}_{i^*})$, the CPA-to-CCA transformation inherits it. In the main part, we formally reveal and define the property as *non-influential randomness*, and demonstrate a generalized version of the above attack. We want to emphasize that the property of non-influential randomness contradicts CCA security but does not contradict CPA, and all the existing CPA-secure schemes meet it.

How to Fix the Flaw. The above attack enables the adversary to get the decryption result of the challenge ciphertext since the adversary can create a situation for generating the same public and secret keys as those at the challenge epoch. To prevent this attack, they must have essentially different key pairs of public and secret keys in different epochs. We give an overview of our modification of Dodis et al.'s CPA-to-CCA transformation below.

1. Change the public key $\mathsf{pk}_i = (g, h, \mathsf{CRS})$ (and the corresponding relation) to $(g, h, \boxed{i}, \mathsf{CRS})$ to make it explicit that the public key has an epoch.
2. Change the Enc and Dec algorithms so that an epoch is embedded into a ciphertext $\mathsf{ct} \leftarrow \mathsf{Enc}(\mathsf{pk}_i, \boxed{[i \| \mathsf{M}]})$, instead of $\mathsf{Enc}(\mathsf{pk}_i, \mathsf{M})$.

Our Efficient Generic Construction. Going back to our main goal: *to construct an efficient CU-CCA-secure UPKE scheme.* As mentioned earlier, towards our goal, it is preferable to avoid using NIZK arguments to achieve CU-CCA security. Therefore, we employ the Fujisaki-Okamoto (FO) transformation [18,19] *twice* to lift both CPA and CR security to CCA and CU, respectively.

First, let us see the encryption procedure of the original FO transformation below.

$$\mathsf{ct} := (\mathsf{Enc}(\mathsf{pk}, \sigma; \mathsf{H}(\sigma, \mathsf{SKE.Enc}(\mathsf{G}(\sigma), \mathsf{M})),\ \mathsf{SKE.Enc}(\mathsf{G}(\sigma), \mathsf{M}))\,,$$

where

- $\mathsf{SKE.Enc}$ is an encryption algorithm of symmetric-key encryption that takes as input a common secret key and a plaintext M.
- σ is a random value chosen from the plaintext space of PKE,
- G and H are random oracles.

The above encryption procedure is sufficient to achieve CCA security of traditional (i.e., non-updatable) PKE, but it is actually *insufficient* for the CCA security of UPKE. As discussed in the last paragraph, we need to embed the epochs into the public keys and ciphertexts not to have the property of non-influential randomness. We fix the above for UPKE by embedding the epoch i into H as follows.

$$\mathsf{ct} := (\mathsf{Enc}(\mathsf{pk}_i, \sigma; \mathsf{H}(i, \sigma, \mathsf{SKE.Enc}(\mathsf{G}(\sigma), \mathsf{M}))),\ \mathsf{SKE.Enc}(\mathsf{G}(\sigma), \mathsf{M})).$$

Thanks to the above modification, the challenger in the CCA security game can easily reject the ciphertexts which generated at the different epoch j. Indeed, our attack described earlier no longer works. This is our CPA-to-CCA transformation without NIZK arguments; it yields better efficiency than the existing ones and is applicable to all the existing CPA-secure UPKE schemes.

Although our CR-to-CU transformation can be realized similarly to the above, we can fine-tune our variant of the FO transformation since, roughly speaking, there is no challenge query in the sense of update queries. Specifically, we do not need to embed an epoch into update ciphertexts since the challenger does not return the update information to the adversary, unlike the challenge query.

2 Preliminaries

Notation. Throughout the paper, λ denotes a security parameter. For an i-bit binary string $\mathsf{s}_1 \in \{0,1\}^i$ and a j-bit binary string $\mathsf{s}_2 \in \{0,1\}^j$, let $[\mathsf{s}_1 \| \mathsf{s}_2] \in \{0,1\}^{i+j}$ denote an $(i+j)$-bit concatenation of s_1 and s_2. For a finite set S, $s \leftarrow_\$ S$ denotes a sampling of an element of s from S uniformly at random and let$|S|$ denotes a cardinality of S. Probabilistic polynomial time is abbreviated as PPT.

Lemma 1 (Difference Lemma [31]). *Let A, B, and F be events defined in some probability distribution, and suppose that $A \wedge B \Leftrightarrow B \wedge \neg F$. Then, $|\Pr[A] - \Pr[B]| \leq \Pr[F]$ holds.*

2.1 Updatable Public Key Encryption

Syntax. Let $\mathcal{M}$ and $\mathcal{R}$ be the message and the randomness spaces determined only by the security parameter, respectively. A UPKE scheme Π consists of the five algorithms $(\mathsf{Gen}, \mathsf{Enc}, \mathsf{Dec}, \mathsf{UpdPk}, \mathsf{UpdSk})$ as follows:

$\mathsf{Gen}(1^\lambda) \rightarrow (\mathsf{pk}_0, \mathsf{sk}_0)$: On input the security parameter λ, it outputs an initial public key pk_0 and an initial secret key sk_0.

$\mathsf{Enc}(\mathsf{pk}_i, \mathsf{M}) \rightarrow \mathsf{ct}$: On input a public key pk_i for epoch i and a plaintext M, it outputs a ciphertext ct.

$\mathsf{Dec}(\mathsf{pk}_i, \mathsf{sk}_i, \mathsf{ct}) \rightarrow \mathsf{M}$ or $\perp$: On input a public key pk_i, a secret key for epoch i, and a ciphertext ct, it outputs the plaintext M or $\perp$, which indicates the failure of decryption.

$\mathsf{UpdPk}(\mathsf{pk}_i) \rightarrow (\mathsf{pk}_{i+1}, \mathsf{up}_{i+1})$: On input a public key pk_i for epoch i, it outputs a new public key pk_{i+1} and an update ciphertext up_{i+1} for next epoch $i+1$.

$\mathsf{UpdSk}(\mathsf{pk}_i, \mathsf{sk}_i, (\mathsf{pk}_{i+1}, \mathsf{up}_{i+1})) \rightarrow \mathsf{sk}_{i+1}$ or $\perp$: On input a pubic key pk_i, a secret key sk_i for epoch i, and an update ciphertext up_{i+1}, it outputs a new secret key sk_{i+1} for next epoch $i+1$.

Correctness. For all $\lambda \in \mathbb{N}$, all $\ell \in \mathbb{N}$, all $(\mathsf{pk}_0, \mathsf{sk}_0) \leftarrow \mathsf{Gen}(1^\lambda)$, all $\mathsf{M} \in \mathcal{M}$, all $i \in \{0, \ldots, \ell\}$, it is required that $\mathsf{Dec}(\mathsf{pk}_i, \mathsf{sk}_i, \mathsf{Enc}(\mathsf{pk}_i, \mathsf{M})) = \mathsf{M}$ holds with overwhelming probability, where $(\mathsf{pk}_j, \mathsf{up}_j) \leftarrow \mathsf{UpdPk}(\mathsf{pk}_{j-1})$, $\mathsf{sk}_j \leftarrow \mathsf{UpdSk}(\mathsf{pk}_{j-1}, \mathsf{sk}_{j-1}, (\mathsf{pk}_j, \mathsf{up}_j))$ for $j = 1, \ldots, \ell$.

Security. In this paper, we almost follow the security notions defined by Dodis et al. [11].

Definition 1 (IND-CR-CPA Security [11]). *The IND-CR-CPA security of a UPKE scheme Π is defined by a game between an adversary $\mathcal{A}$ and a challenger $\mathcal{C}$ as follows:*

Init: *$\mathcal{C}$ runs $(\mathsf{pk}_0, \mathsf{sk}_0) \leftarrow \mathsf{Gen}(1^\lambda)$ and gives pk_0 to $\mathcal{A}$.*
Phase 1: *$\mathcal{A}$ is allowed to make the following update queries to $\mathcal{C}$.*
Update query: *$\mathcal{A}$ is allowed to make the query on $r_i \in \mathcal{R}$ where i is the current epoch. Upon the query, $\mathcal{C}$ runs $(\mathsf{pk}_{i+1}, \mathsf{up}_{i+1}) \leftarrow \mathsf{UpdPk}(\mathsf{pk}_i; r_i)$ and $\mathsf{sk}_{i+1} \leftarrow \mathsf{UpdSk}(\mathsf{pk}_i, \mathsf{sk}_i, (\mathsf{pk}_{i+1}, \mathsf{up}_{i+1}))$.*
Challenge query: *$\mathcal{A}$ is allowed to make the query only once. Upon $\mathcal{A}$'s query on $(\mathsf{M}_0^*, \mathsf{M}_1^*) \in \mathcal{M}^2$, where M_0^* and M_1^* have the same length. Then $\mathcal{C}$ flips a coin $\mathsf{coin}^* \leftarrow_\$ \{0,1\}$ and runs $\mathsf{ct}^* \leftarrow \mathsf{Enc}(\mathsf{pk}_{t_c}, \mathsf{M}^*_{\mathsf{coin}^*})$ where t_c is the current epoch. Finally, $\mathcal{C}$ returns ct^* to $\mathcal{A}$.*
Phase 2: *$\mathcal{A}$ is allowed to make update queries as in Phase 1.*
Reveal query: *For the query $\perp$ from $\mathcal{A}$, $\mathcal{C}$ chooses a randomness $r^* \leftarrow_\$ \mathcal{R}$, and runs $(\mathsf{pk}^*_{t_r}, \mathsf{up}^*) \leftarrow \mathsf{UpdPk}(\mathsf{pk}_{t_r-1}; r^*)$ and $\mathsf{sk}^*_{t_r} \leftarrow \mathsf{UpdSk}(\mathsf{pk}_{t_r-1}, \mathsf{sk}_{t_r-1}, (\mathsf{pk}^*_{t_r}, \mathsf{up}^*_{t_r}))$ where t_r is the current epoch. Then, $\mathcal{C}$ returns $(\mathsf{pk}^*_{t_r}, \mathsf{up}^*_{t_r}, \mathsf{sk}^*_{t_r})$ to $\mathcal{A}$.*
Guess: *At the end of the game, $\mathcal{A}$ returns $\widehat{\mathsf{coin}} \in \{0,1\}$ as a guess of coin.*

The adversary $\mathcal{A}$ wins in the above game if $\widehat{\mathsf{coin}} = \mathsf{coin}^*$ and the advantage is defined to

$$\mathsf{Adv}^{\textit{IND-CR-CPA}}_{\Pi,\mathcal{A}}(\lambda) := |\Pr\left[\widehat{\mathsf{coin}} = \mathsf{coin}^*\right] - \frac{1}{2}|.$$

If $\mathsf{Adv}^{\textit{IND-CR-CPA}}_{\Pi,\mathcal{A}}(\lambda)$ is negligible in the security parameter λ for all PPT adversaries $\mathcal{A}$, a UPKE scheme Π is said to satisfy IND-CR-CPA security.

Next, we define IND-CU-CCA security, the strongest security notion in UPKE, based on Dodis et al.'s one [11,12]. We suppose UpdSk also performs the consistency check in our definition, whereas Dodis et al. separately defined UpdSk and $\mathsf{VerifyUpd}$ algorithms.[4]

Definition 2 (IND-CU-CCA Security). *The IND-CU-CCA security of a UPKE scheme Π is defined by a game between an adversary $\mathcal{A}$ and a challenger $\mathcal{C}$ as follows:*

Init: *$\mathcal{C}$ runs $(\mathsf{pk}_0, \mathsf{sk}_0) \leftarrow \mathsf{Gen}(1^\lambda)$ and gives pk_0 to $\mathcal{A}$.*
Phase 1: *$\mathcal{A}$ is allowed to make the following two types of queries to $\mathcal{C}$.*
Update query: *$\mathcal{A}$ is allowed to make the query on $(\mathsf{pk}_{i+1}, \mathsf{up}_{i+1})$ where i is the current epoch. Upon the query, $\mathcal{C}$ runs $\mathsf{UpdSk}(\mathsf{pk}_i, \mathsf{sk}_i, (\mathsf{pk}_{i+1}, \mathsf{up}_{i+1}))$ and rejects update if it outputs $\perp$.*
Decryption query: *$\mathcal{A}$ is allowed to make the query on ct. Upon the query, $\mathcal{C}$ runs $\mathsf{Dec}(\mathsf{pk}_i, \mathsf{sk}_i, \mathsf{ct})$ and returns the result, where i is the current epoch.*

[4] This implies that our syntax does not support public verifiablity, and hence, fully offline updates in the CU setting. We leave it as an open problem to how we realize an efficient CR-to-CU transformation in the publicly verifiable setting.

Challenge query: *$\mathcal{A}$ is allowed to make the query only once. Upon $\mathcal{A}$'s query on* $(\mathsf{M}_0^*, \mathsf{M}_1^*) \in \mathcal{M}^2$, *where* M_0^* *and* M_1^* *have the same length. Then* $\mathcal{C}$ *flips a coin* $\mathsf{coin}^* \leftarrow_\$ \{0,1\}$ *and runs* $\mathsf{ct}^* \leftarrow \mathsf{Enc}(\mathsf{pk}_{t_c}, \mathsf{M}^*_{\mathsf{coin}^*})$ *where* t_c *is the current epoch. Finally,* $\mathcal{C}$ *returns* ct^* *to* $\mathcal{A}$.

Phase 2: *$\mathcal{A}$ is allowed to make the queries as in Phase 1 with the following exceptions:*

Decryption query: *$\mathcal{A}$ is not allowed to make the query on* ct^* *without making an update query. In other words, $\mathcal{A}$'s query* ct *on a epoch i satisfies* $(i, \mathsf{ct}) \neq (t_c, \mathsf{ct}^*)$.

Reveal query: *For the query $\perp$ from $\mathcal{A}$, $\mathcal{C}$ chooses a randomness* $r^* \leftarrow_\$ \mathcal{R}$, *and runs* $(\mathsf{pk}^*_{t_r}, \mathsf{up}^*_{t_r}) \leftarrow \mathsf{UpdPk}(\mathsf{pk}_{t_r}; r^*)$ *and* $\mathsf{sk}^*_{t_r} \leftarrow \mathsf{UpdSk}(\mathsf{pk}_{t_r-1}, \mathsf{sk}_{t_r-1}, (\mathsf{pk}^*_{t_r}, \mathsf{up}^*_{t_r}))$ *where* t_r *is the current epoch. Then,* $\mathcal{C}$ *returns* $(\mathsf{pk}^*_{t_r}, \mathsf{up}^*_{t_r}, \mathsf{sk}^*_{t_r})$ *to* $\mathcal{A}$.

Guess: *At the end of the game,* $\mathcal{A}$ *returns* $\widehat{\mathsf{coin}} \in \{0,1\}$ *as a guess of* coin.

The adversary $\mathcal{A}$ wins in the above game if $\widehat{\mathsf{coin}} \in \{0,1\}$ *as a guess of* coin.

$$\mathsf{Adv}^{\mathit{IND\text{-}CU\text{-}CCA}}_{\Pi,\mathcal{A}}(\lambda) := |\Pr\left[\widehat{\mathsf{coin}} = \mathsf{coin}^*\right] - \frac{1}{2}|.$$

If $\mathsf{Adv}^{\mathit{IND\text{-}CU\text{-}CCA}}_{\Pi,\mathcal{A}}(\lambda)$ *is negligible in the security parameter λ for all PPT adversaries $\mathcal{A}$, a UPKE scheme Π is said to satisfy IND-CU-CCA security.*

2.2 Symmetric Key Encryption

Syntax. Let $\mathcal{M}$ and $\mathcal{SK}$ be the message and the secret key spaces determined only by the security parameter, respectively. An SKE scheme Γ consists of the two algorithms $(\mathsf{SKE.Enc}, \mathsf{SKE.Dec})$ as follows:

$\mathsf{SKE.Enc}(k, \mathsf{M}) \rightarrow \mathsf{ct}$: On input a secret key k and a plaintext M, it outputs a ciphertext.

$\mathsf{SKE.Dec}(k, \mathsf{ct}) \rightarrow \mathsf{M}$ or $\perp$: On input a secret key and a ciphertext ct, it outputs the plaintext M.

Correctness. For all $\lambda \in \mathbb{N}$, all $k \in \mathcal{SK}$, all $\mathsf{M} \in \mathcal{M}$, it is required that $\mathsf{Dec}(k, \mathsf{Enc}(k, \mathsf{M})) = \mathsf{M}$ holds.

Definition 3 (OT-CPA security). *The OT-CPA security of an SKE scheme Γ is defined by a game between an adversary $\mathcal{A}$ and a challenger $\mathcal{C}$. The game is parameterized by the security parameter λ. The game proceeds as follows: $\mathcal{A}$ sends* $(\mathsf{M}_0^*, \mathsf{M}_1^*) \in \mathcal{M}^2$ *to $\mathcal{C}$. $\mathcal{C}$ chooses* $\mathsf{coin}^* \leftarrow_\$ \{0,1\}$, $k \leftarrow_\$ \mathcal{SK}$, *runs* $\mathsf{ct}^* \leftarrow \mathsf{SKE.Enc}(k, \mathsf{M}^*_{\mathsf{coin}^*})$, *and sends* ct^* *to $\mathcal{A}$. Finally, $\mathcal{A}$ outputs* $\widehat{\mathsf{coin}}$ *as a guess of* coin^* *and terminates the game. In this game, $\mathcal{A}$'s advantage is defined by*

$$\mathsf{Adv}^{\mathit{OT\text{-}CPA}}_{\Gamma,\mathcal{A}}(\lambda) := |\Pr\left[\widehat{\mathsf{coin}} = \mathsf{coin}^*\right]|.$$

If $\mathsf{Adv}^{\mathit{OT\text{-}CPA}}_{\Gamma,\mathcal{A}}(\lambda)$ *is negligible in the security parameter λ for all PPT adversaries $\mathcal{A}$, an SKE scheme Γ is said to satisfy OT-CPA security.*

2.3 Non-interactive Zero-Knowledge

Syntax. A NIZK argument for a polynomial relation R consists of the three algorithms as follows:

$\mathsf{Setup}(1^\lambda) \to (\mathsf{CRS}, \mathsf{tk}, \mathsf{ek})$: On input the security parameter λ, it outputs a common reference string (CRS), a trapdoor key tk, and an extraction key ek. [5]

$\mathsf{Prove}(\mathsf{CRS}, x, w) \to \pi$: On input a CRS, a statement x, and a witness w with $R(x, w) = 1$, it outputs a proof π.

$\mathsf{Vrfy}(\mathsf{CRS}, x, \pi) \to 1$ or 0: On input a CRS, a statement x, and a proof π, it outputs 1 or 0.

In the generic constructions by Dodis et al. [11,12], a NIZK is used that satisfies completeness, soundness, zero knowledge, and strong extractability. In this paper, we only introduce the definition of completeness because we only use completeness for the attack.

Definition 4 (Completeness). *For all* $\lambda \in \mathbb{N}$, *all* $(x, w) \in R$, *and all* $(\mathsf{CRS}, \mathsf{tk}, \mathsf{ek}) \leftarrow \mathsf{Setup}(1^\lambda)$, *it is required that* $\mathsf{Vrfy}(\mathsf{CRS}, x, \mathsf{Prove}(\mathsf{CRS}, x, w)) = 1$ *holds.*

3 Security Analysis of Dodis et al.'s UPKE Scheme

There are only two existing ways to achieve CU-CCA-secure UPKE schemes.

- Haidar et al. [22] and Haidar et al. [23] provided direct CR-CPA-secure UPKE constructions from the DCR and LWE assumptions, respectively, and extended them to CU-CCA-secure schemes with the aid of random oracles and efficient NIZK arguments for specific language. Alwen et al. [2] also took a similar approach, though they directly constructed a CU-CCA-secure scheme from a Proof-of-Logarithm (PoL) system and co-DL assumption in the ROM and AGM.
- Dodis et al. [11] proposed two transformations for UPKE: the one converts CR/CU-CPA security into CR/CU-CCA, called the *CPA-to-CCA transformation*, and the other converts CR-CPA/CCA security into CU-CPA/CCA, called the *CR-to-CU transformation.* Since CR-CPA-secure UPKE schemes from the DDH and LWE assumptions, respectively, in the standard model, one obtains CU-CCA-secure UPKE schemes from those assumptions. It is worth noting that the two transformations do not require random oracles, though they employ NIZK arguments with strong properties instead.

In this section, we point out that Dodis et al.'s CPA-to-CCA transformation has a fatal flaw when the underlying CPA-secure UPKE scheme satisfies the property of *non-influential randomness*, which is introduced in Sect. 3.1. We can break the CCA security of the CPA-to-CCA transformation with our

[5] tk and ek are used to define security notions such as zero knowledge and strong extractability, although we omit their definitions.

simple and efficient attack demonstrated in Sect. 3.2. Indeed, all existing CR-CPA-secure schemes [1,11,22,23,25] satisfy the particular property; therefore, *our security analysis shows that the CPA-to-CCA transformation does not work with any existing CPA-secure UPKE scheme.* Nevertheless, we also show that the transformation can be fixed with a slight modification in Sect. 3.3.

3.1 UPKE with Non-Influential Randomness

We reveal and formalize the property that all the existing CPA-secure UPKE schemes have, called *non-influential randomness.* Roughly speaking, we say a UPKE scheme has non-influential randomness if there exists efficiently computable randomness r^* such that it holds $(\mathsf{pk}_{i+1}, \mathsf{sk}_{i+1}) = (\mathsf{pk}_i, \mathsf{sk}_i)$ for some epoch i, where $(\mathsf{pk}_{i+1}, \mathsf{up}_{i+1}) \leftarrow \mathsf{UpdPk}(\mathsf{pk}_i; r^*)$, $\mathsf{sk}_{i+1} \leftarrow \mathsf{UpdSk}(\mathsf{pk}_i, \mathsf{sk}_i, (\mathsf{pk}_{i+1}, \mathsf{up}_{i+1}))$. Namely, the randomness r^* has no influence on key updates. Note that such non-influential randomness can be a sequence; namely, if there exists a sequence of randomness $(r_i^*, r_{i+1}^*, \ldots, r_{i+\ell}^*)$ such that it holds $(\mathsf{pk}_{i+\ell}, \mathsf{sk}_{i+\ell}) = (\mathsf{pk}_i, \mathsf{sk}_i)$ for some epoch i, where $(\mathsf{pk}_{i+j}, \mathsf{up}_{i+j}) \leftarrow \mathsf{UpdPk}(\mathsf{pk}_{i+j-1}; r^*)$, $\mathsf{sk}_{i+j} \leftarrow \mathsf{UpdSk}(\mathsf{pk}_{i+j-1}, \mathsf{sk}_{i+j-1}, (\mathsf{pk}_{i+j}, \mathsf{up}_{i+j}))$ for every $j = 1, \ldots, \ell$.

Definition 5 (UPKE with Non-Influential Randomness). *Let* $\Pi = (\mathsf{Gen}, \mathsf{Enc}, \mathsf{Dec}, \mathsf{UpdPk}, \mathsf{UpdSk})$ *be a UPKE scheme. Consider a game between a PPT adversary* $\mathcal{A}^*$ *and a challenger* $\mathcal{C}$ *as follows:*

Init: $\mathcal{C}$ *sets a counter* $\mathsf{ctr} = 0$ *and runs* $(\mathsf{pk}_0, \mathsf{sk}_0) \leftarrow \mathsf{Gen}(1^\lambda)$ *and gives* pk_0 *to* $\mathcal{A}^*$.

Update query: $\mathcal{A}^*$ *is allowed to iteratively make the update query. Upon the query,* $\mathcal{C}$ *sets* $\mathsf{ctr} = \mathsf{ctr} + 1$, *and runs* $(\mathsf{pk}_{\mathsf{ctr}}, \mathsf{up}_{\mathsf{ctr}}) \leftarrow \mathsf{UpdPk}(\mathsf{pk}_{\mathsf{ctr}-1})$ *and* $\mathsf{sk}_{\mathsf{ctr}} \leftarrow \mathsf{UpdSk}(\mathsf{pk}_{\mathsf{ctr}-1}, \mathsf{sk}_{\mathsf{ctr}-1}, (\mathsf{pk}_{\mathsf{ctr}}, \mathsf{sk}_{\mathsf{ctr}}))$. $\mathcal{C}$ *returns* $(\mathsf{pk}_{\mathsf{ctr}}, \mathsf{up}_{\mathsf{ctr}}, \mathsf{sk}_{\mathsf{ctr}})$.

Challenge query: *Upon* $\mathcal{A}^*$*'s query on* $(r_1^*, r_2^*, \ldots, r_\ell^*)$, *which is issued only once, where* ℓ *is polynomial in* λ. *For every* $j = 1, 2, \ldots, \ell$, $\mathcal{C}$ *runs* $(\mathsf{pk}_{\mathsf{ctr}+j}, \mathsf{up}_{\mathsf{ctr}+j}) \leftarrow \mathsf{UpdPk}(\mathsf{pk}_{\mathsf{ctr}+j-1}; r_j^*)$ *and* $\mathsf{sk}_{\mathsf{ctr}+j} \leftarrow \mathsf{UpdSk}(\mathsf{pk}_{\mathsf{ctr}+j-1}, \mathsf{sk}_{\mathsf{ctr}+j-1}, (\mathsf{pk}_{\mathsf{ctr}+j}, \mathsf{sk}_{\mathsf{ctr}+j}))$. $\mathcal{C}$ *returns* $(\mathsf{pk}_{\mathsf{ctr}+\ell}, \mathsf{sk}_{\mathsf{ctr}+\ell})$ *and* $(\mathsf{pk}_{\mathsf{ctr}}, \mathsf{sk}_{\mathsf{ctr}})$ *as the output of the game and halts the game.*

We say that the UPKE scheme has non-influential randomness if for all PPT adversaries $\mathcal{A}^*$, *it holds*

$$(\mathsf{pk}_{\mathsf{ctr}+\ell}, \mathsf{sk}_{\mathsf{ctr}+\ell}) = (\mathsf{pk}_{\mathsf{ctr}}, \mathsf{sk}_{\mathsf{ctr}}),$$

with overwhelming probability in λ.

It is worth noting that the above property does not contradict CR/CU-CPA security since the property brings the CPA adversary no benefit; even if the CPA adversary has the challenger produce $(\mathsf{pk}_{t_c+\ell}, \mathsf{sk}_{t_c+\ell})$ such that $(\mathsf{pk}_{t_c+\ell}, \mathsf{sk}_{t_c+\ell}) = (\mathsf{pk}_{t_c}, \mathsf{sk}_{t_c})$ for some $\ell \in \mathbb{N}$ and t_c is the challenge epoch, all information the CPA adversary can obtain after the challenge query is the response to the reveal query $(\mathsf{pk}_{t_r}^*, \mathsf{up}_{t_r}^*, \mathsf{sk}_{t_r}^*)$, which is randomized with fresh randomness chosen by the challenger.

Indeed, all the existing CR-CPA secure UPKE schemes [1,11,22,23,25] satisfy the property of non-influential randomness. For simplicity, we give a concrete example of non-influential randomness with a *variant* of Jost et al.'s CR-CPA secure scheme, which is the simplest UPKE scheme.[6] Let $\mathcal{M}$ and $\mathsf{H} : \{0,1\}^* \to \mathcal{M}$ denote a plaintext space and random oracle, respectively.

$\mathsf{Gen}(1^\lambda) \to (\mathsf{pk}_0, \mathsf{sk}_0)$: Choose a cyclic group $\mathbb{G}$ of order q with a generator g, which is determined by the security parameter λ, and choose $x \leftarrow_\$ \mathbb{Z}_q$. Output $\mathsf{pk}_0 := (g, g^x)$ and $\mathsf{sk}_0 := x$.
$\mathsf{Enc}(\mathsf{pk}_i, \mathsf{M}) \to \mathsf{ct}$: Parse $\mathsf{pk}_i = (g, h)$ and output $\mathsf{ct} = (g^s, h^s \cdot \mathsf{M})$, where $s \leftarrow_\$ \mathbb{Z}_q$.
$\mathsf{Dec}(\mathsf{pk}_i, \mathsf{sk}_i, \mathsf{ct}) \to \mathsf{M}$: Parse $\mathsf{sk}_i = x$ and $\mathsf{ct} = (a, b)$, and output b/a^x.
$\mathsf{UpdPk}(\mathsf{pk}_i) \to (\mathsf{pk}_{i+1}, \mathsf{up}_{i+1})$: Parse $\mathsf{pk}_i = (g, h)$, choose $r \leftarrow_\$ \mathbb{Z}_q$, and output $\mathsf{pk}_{i+1} := (g, h \cdot g^r)$ and $\mathsf{up}_{i+1} := (g^s, \mathsf{H}(h^s) \oplus r)$, where $s \leftarrow_\$ \mathbb{Z}_q$.
$\mathsf{UpdSk}(\mathsf{pk}_i, \mathsf{sk}_i, (\mathsf{pk}_{i+1}, \mathsf{up}_{i+1})) \to \mathsf{sk}_{i+1}$: Parse $\mathsf{sk}_i = x$ and $\mathsf{up}_{i+1} = (a, b)$, calculate $r := \mathsf{H}(a^x) \oplus b$, and output $\mathsf{sk}_{i+1} := x + r \bmod q$.

We can construct the adversary $\mathcal{A}^*$ against the game in Def. 5 of the above scheme as follows: the challenger $\mathcal{C}$ generates $(\mathsf{pk}_0, \mathsf{sk}_0) = ((g, g^x), x)$ and gives pk_0 to $\mathcal{A}^*$. $\mathcal{A}^*$ makes a challenge query $r^* := 0$ and the challenger runs the UpdPk and the UpdSk algorithms. Then, the public and secret keys at the epoch 1 is $(\mathsf{pk}_1, \mathsf{sk}_1) = ((g, g^x \cdot g^0), x + 0) = ((g, g^x), x)$, which is the same as $(\mathsf{pk}_0, \mathsf{sk}_0)$. Therefore, Jost et al.'s UPKE scheme indeed has non-influential randomness.

Remark 1. In the above attack against the variant of Jost et al.'s scheme, we demonstrated the simplest case; we use the fact that 0 is the identity element of the secret key space $\mathbb{Z}_q$ and $g^0 = 1$ is also the identity element of the public key space $\mathbb{G}$. A naive countermeasure is to modify UpdPk and UpdSk so that they halt if the randomness r is the identity element. However, as stated in Definition 5, the adversary is allowed to make multiple update queries, and we can improve the above attack to circumvent the countermeasure: Suppose the adversary randomly chooses $r_1, r_2, \ldots, r_i \in \mathbb{Z}_q$ and use them as i update queries. Now the challenger has a correctly generated key-pair $(\mathsf{pk}_i, \mathsf{sk}_i)$. the adversary arbitrarily chooses i and ℓ, and randomly chooses $r'_1, r'_2, \ldots, r'_\ell \in \mathbb{Z}_q$ such that $\sum_{j=1}^{\ell} r'_j = 0 \bmod q$. After the challenge query on $(r'_1, r'_2, \ldots, r'_\ell)$, it obviously holds $(\mathsf{pk}_{i+\ell}, \mathsf{sk}_{i+\ell}) = (\mathsf{pk}_i, \mathsf{sk}_i)$. Although one can check all the previous keys to detect the above attack, it seems unrealistic and inefficient.

Although the property of non-influential randomness may coexist with CPA security by definition, in contrast, it hinders CCA security due to decryption queries. Specifically, the CCA adversary is allowed to make decryption queries on even the challenge ciphertext after the epoch when the challenge query is made.

[6] Since Dodis et al.'s CPA-to-CCA transformation requires a NIZK for a relation $R = \{((\mathsf{pk}_i, \mathsf{ct}), (\mathsf{M}, r)) \mid \mathsf{ct} = \mathsf{Enc}(\mathsf{pk}_i, \mathsf{M}; r)\}$, we need to get rid of a RO from the Enc algorithm of Jost et al.'s scheme to apply the transformation. Therefore, we here show the variant of Jost et al.'s CR-CPA-secure scheme, which is secure under the DDH assumption in the ROM; the Enc algorithm, which is the same as that of the hashed ElGamal PKE, is replaced with the standard ElGamal PKE's one.

Therefore, the adversary easily breaks CCA security by issuing a decryption query on the challenge ciphertext at the epoch ℓ such that $(\mathsf{pk}_{t_c+\ell}, \mathsf{sk}_{t_c+\ell}) = (\mathsf{pk}_{t_c}, \mathsf{sk}_{t_c})$, where t_c is the epoch when the adversary makes the challenge query.

3.2 Security Analysis of Dodis et al's CPA-to-CCA Transformation

We show a simple and efficient attack against the CPA-to-CCA transformation proposed by Dodis et al. [11]. It clearly stems from the non-influential randomness property of the CCA-secure UPKE scheme obtained by the transformation. Put differently, if the underlying CPA-secure scheme has non-influential randomness, the CPA-to-CCA transformation takes over the property. In that sense, our attack does not work if the underlying CPA-secure UPKE scheme does not meet the property; however, as mentioned above, all the known CPA-secure schemes do.

We describe the CPA-to-CCA transformation from any CR/CU-CPA-secure UPKE scheme $\Pi = (\mathsf{Gen}, \mathsf{Enc}, \mathsf{Dec}, \mathsf{UpdPk}, \mathsf{UpdSk})$ and any NIZK argument $\Omega = (\mathsf{Setup}, \mathsf{Prove}, \mathsf{Vrfy})$ for the relation $R = \left\{((\mathsf{pk}_i, \mathsf{ct}), (\mathsf{M}, r)) \mid \mathsf{ct} = \mathsf{Enc}(\mathsf{pk}_i, \mathsf{M}; r)\right\}$ to a CR/CU-CCA-secure UPKE scheme $\Sigma = (\mathsf{Gen}', \mathsf{Enc}', \mathsf{Dec}', \mathsf{UpdPk}', \mathsf{UpdSk}')$ as follows.

$\mathsf{Gen}'(1^\lambda) \to (\mathsf{pk}_0', \mathsf{sk}_0')$**:** Generate an initial key pair as follows.
- $(\mathsf{pk}_0, \mathsf{sk}_0) \leftarrow \mathsf{Gen}(1^\lambda)$,
- $(\mathsf{CRS}, \mathsf{tk}, \mathsf{ek}) \leftarrow \mathsf{Setup}(1^\lambda)$.

Output $\mathsf{pk}_0' := (\mathsf{pk}_0, \mathsf{CRS})$ and $\mathsf{sk}_0' := \mathsf{sk}_0$.

$\mathsf{Enc}'(\mathsf{pk}_i', \mathsf{M}) \to \mathsf{ct}'$**:** Parse $\mathsf{pk}_i' = (\mathsf{pk}_i, \mathsf{CRS})$ and run
- $r \leftarrow_\$ \mathcal{R}$,
- $\mathsf{ct} \leftarrow \mathsf{Enc}(\mathsf{pk}_i, \mathsf{M}; r)$,
- $\pi \leftarrow \mathsf{Prove}(\mathsf{CRS}, (\mathsf{pk}_i, \mathsf{ct}), (\mathsf{M}, r))$.

Output $\mathsf{ct}' = (\mathsf{ct}, \pi)$.

$\mathsf{Dec}'(\mathsf{pk}_i', \mathsf{sk}_i', \mathsf{ct}') \to \mathsf{M}$ or $\perp$**:** Parse $\mathsf{pk}_i' = (\mathsf{pk}_i, \mathsf{CRS})$, $\mathsf{sk}_i' = \mathsf{sk}_i$, and $\mathsf{ct}' = (\mathsf{ct}, \pi)$. If $1 \leftarrow \mathsf{Vrfy}(\mathsf{CRS}, (\mathsf{pk}_i, \mathsf{ct}), \pi)$ holds, then run and output $\mathsf{Dec}(\mathsf{pk}_i, \mathsf{sk}_i, \mathsf{ct})$. Otherwise, output $\perp$.

$\mathsf{UpdPk}'(\mathsf{pk}_i') \to (\mathsf{pk}_{i+1}', \mathsf{up}_{i+1}')$**:** Parse $\mathsf{pk}_i' = (\mathsf{pk}_i, \mathsf{CRS})$ and run $(\mathsf{pk}_{i+1}, \mathsf{up}_{i+1}) \leftarrow \mathsf{UpdPk}(\mathsf{pk}_i)$. Then, output $\mathsf{pk}_{i+1}' = (\mathsf{pk}_{i+1}, \mathsf{CRS})$ and $\mathsf{up}_{i+1}' = \mathsf{up}_{i+1}$.

$\mathsf{UpdSk}'(\mathsf{pk}_i', \mathsf{sk}_i', (\mathsf{pk}_{i+1}', \mathsf{up}_{i+1}')) \to \mathsf{sk}_{i+1}'$**:** Parse $\mathsf{pk}_i' = (\mathsf{pk}_i, \mathsf{CRS})$, $\mathsf{sk}_i' = \mathsf{sk}_i$, $\mathsf{pk}_{i+1}' = (\mathsf{pk}_{i+1}, \mathsf{CRS})$, and $\mathsf{up}_{i+1}' = \mathsf{up}_{i+1}$. Run $\mathsf{sk}_{i+1} \leftarrow \mathsf{UpdSk}(\mathsf{pk}_i, \mathsf{sk}_i, (\mathsf{pk}_{i+1}, \mathsf{up}_{i+1}))$ and output $\mathsf{sk}_{i+1}' := \mathsf{sk}_{i+1}$.

Theorem 1. *Let* $\Sigma = (\mathsf{Gen}', \mathsf{Enc}', \mathsf{Dec}', \mathsf{UpdPk}', \mathsf{UpdSk}')$ *be the UPKE scheme constructed above. Then, if the underlying IND-CU-CPA-secure (resp., IND-CR-CPA-secure) UPKE scheme has non-influential randomness, there exists a PPT algorithm* $\mathcal{A}$ *that breaks IND-CU-CCA security (resp., IND-CR-CCA security).*

Proof. It is sufficient to show how to break the IND-CU-CCA security of the above UPKE scheme if the underlying UPKE scheme has non-influential randomness, so we omit the case of IND-CR-CCA security. For this purpose, we use a PPT adversary $\mathcal{A}^*$, which can efficiently find non-influential randomness via the game in Definition 5, to construct a PPT adversary $\mathcal{A}$ that breaks IND-CU-CR-CCA security as follows. The challenger $\mathcal{C}$ begins the IND-CU-CCA security game, runs $(\mathsf{pk}'_0 = (\mathsf{pk}_0, \mathsf{CRS}), \mathsf{sk}'_0 = \mathsf{sk}_0) \leftarrow \mathsf{Gen}'(1^\lambda)$, and gives pk'_0 to $\mathcal{A}$. $\mathcal{A}$ then gives pk_0 to $\mathcal{A}^*$. $\mathcal{A}^*$ iteratively makes update queries to $\mathcal{A}$; for an i-th update query from $\mathcal{A}^*$, $\mathcal{A}$ runs $\mathsf{UpdPk}(\mathsf{pk}_{i-1})$ to get $(\mathsf{pk}_i, \mathsf{up}_i)$, and gives $(\mathsf{pk}'_i, \mathsf{up}'_i) := ((\mathsf{pk}_i, \mathsf{CRS}), \mathsf{up}_i)$ to $\mathcal{C}$. At some point (suppose that the current epoch is i^*), $\mathcal{A}$ receives a challenge query $(r_1^*, r_2^*, \ldots, r_\ell^*)$ for some $\ell \in \mathbb{N}$ from $\mathcal{A}^*$. Then, $\mathcal{A}$ chooses $\mathsf{M}_0^*, \mathsf{M}_1^* \leftarrow_\$ \mathcal{M}$ such that $|\mathsf{M}_0^*| = |\mathsf{M}_1^*| \wedge \mathsf{M}_0^* \neq \mathsf{M}_1^*$ and makes the challenge query on $(\mathsf{M}_0^*, \mathsf{M}_1^*)$. Upon $\mathcal{A}$'s challenge query, $\mathcal{C}$ chooses $\mathsf{coin}^* \leftarrow \{0,1\}$, runs $\mathsf{ct}^* = (\mathsf{ct}, \pi) \leftarrow \mathsf{Enc}'(\mathsf{pk}'_{i^*}, \mathsf{M}^*_{\mathsf{coin}^*})$, and returns ct^* to $\mathcal{A}$. $\mathcal{A}$ then makes an update query on $(\mathsf{pk}'_{i^*+j}, \mathsf{up}'_{i^*+j})$ for $j = 1, 2, \ldots, \ell$ by executing $\mathsf{UpdPk}(\mathsf{pk}_{i^*+j-1}; r_j) \rightarrow (\mathsf{pk}_{i^*+j}, \mathsf{up}_{i^*+j})$ and setting $(\mathsf{pk}'_{i^*+j}, \mathsf{up}'_{i^*+j}) := ((\mathsf{pk}_{i^*+j}, \mathsf{CRS}), \mathsf{up}_{i^*+j})$. Upon the update query, $\mathcal{C}$ runs $\mathsf{UpdSk}(\mathsf{pk}_{i^*+j-1}, \mathsf{up}_{i^*+j-1}, (\mathsf{pk}_{i^*+j}, \mathsf{up}_{i^*+j}))$ and gets sk'_{i^*+j}. Then, due to the non-influential randomness property, it holds that $(\mathsf{pk}_{i^*+\ell}, \mathsf{sk}_{i^*+\ell}) = (\mathsf{pk}_{i^*}, \mathsf{sk}_{i^*})$ with overwhelming probability. Finally, $\mathcal{A}$ makes a decryption query on the challenge ciphertext $\mathsf{ct}^* = (\mathsf{ct}, \pi)$. Since the current secret key $\mathsf{sk}_{i^*+\ell}$ is the same as the secret key sk_{i^*} at the challenge epoch, $\mathcal{A}$ obtains the decryption result of the challenge ciphertext, which clearly breaks the IND-CU-CCA security.

Note that, in the above attack, we only use the non-influential randomness and correctness properties of the CR/CU-CPA-secure UPKE scheme Π, and the completeness of the NIZK argument Ω.

3.3 Fixing the Transformation

The reason why the attack in the previous section succeeds is that the transformation inherits the property of non-influential randomness that the underlying CPA secure UPKE scheme has. The non-influential randomness allows the adversary to get the decryption result of the challenge ciphertext since the adversary can have the challenger generate the same public and secret keys as those at the challenge epoch. To prevent this attack, they must have essentially different key pairs of public and secret keys in different epochs.

One may come up with the following naive approach: just appending epoch information to public and secret keys, i.e., $(\mathsf{pk}'_i, \mathsf{sk}'_i) := ((\mathsf{pk}_i, i, \mathsf{CRS}), (\mathsf{sk}_i, i))$, instead of $(\mathsf{pk}'_i, \mathsf{sk}'_i) := ((\mathsf{pk}_i, \mathsf{CRS}), \mathsf{sk}_i)$. Unfortunately, this approach does not work since the key pairs are not *essentially* different; although it holds $(\mathsf{pk}'_i, \mathsf{sk}'_i) \neq (\mathsf{pk}'_{i+\ell}, \mathsf{sk}'_{i+\ell})$ for any i, ℓ, the parts of the secret keys sk_i and $\mathsf{sk}_{i+\ell}$ could still be equivalent due to the non-influential randomness property, and therefore $\mathsf{sk}_{i+\ell}$ might be able to decrypt the challenge ciphertext encrypted at the epoch i.

Based on the above observation, we show two simple modifications of Dodis et al.'s CPA-to-CCA transformation not to inherit the property by embedding epochs in not only public keys but also ciphertexts. One is changing the relation from $R = \{((\mathsf{pk}_i, \mathsf{ct}), (\mathsf{M}, r)) \mid \mathsf{ct} = \mathsf{Enc}(\mathsf{pk}_i, \mathsf{M}; r)\}$ to $R' =$

$\{((\mathsf{pk}_i, i, \mathsf{ct}, j), (\mathsf{M}, r)) \mid \mathsf{ct} = \mathsf{Enc}(\mathsf{pk}_i, \mathsf{M}; r) \wedge i = j\}$, where j is an epoch ct was made. The other is also changing the relation but only changing a witness, not a statement. To this end, we make two minor changes as follows. First, we change the public key $\mathsf{pk}'_i = (\mathsf{pk}_i, \mathsf{CRS})$ to $(\mathsf{pk}_i, i, \mathsf{CRS})$ to make it explicit that the public key has an epoch, and the corresponding relation to $R' = \{((\mathsf{pk}_i, i, \mathsf{ct}), (\mathsf{M}, r)) \mid \mathsf{ct} = \mathsf{Enc}(\mathsf{pk}_i, [i\|\mathsf{M}]\,; r)\}$. Second, accordingly, we also change the Enc' and Dec' algorithms as follows:

$\mathsf{Enc}'(\mathsf{pk}'_i, \mathsf{M}) \to \mathsf{ct}'$: Parse $\mathsf{pk}'_i = (\mathsf{pk}_i, i, \mathsf{CRS})$ and run
- $r \leftarrow_\$ \mathcal{R}$,
- $\mathsf{ct} \leftarrow \mathsf{Enc}(\mathsf{pk}_i, [i\|\mathsf{M}]\,; r)$,
- $\pi \leftarrow \mathsf{Prove}(\mathsf{CRS}, (\mathsf{pk}_i, i, \mathsf{ct}), (\mathsf{M}, r))$.

Output $\mathsf{ct}' = (\mathsf{ct}, \pi)$.

$\mathsf{Dec}'(\mathsf{pk}'_i, \mathsf{sk}'_i, \mathsf{ct}') \to \mathsf{M}$ or $\perp$: Parse $\mathsf{pk}'_i = (\mathsf{pk}_i, i, \mathsf{CRS})$, $\mathsf{sk}'_i = \mathsf{sk}_i$, and $\mathsf{ct}' = (\mathsf{ct}, \pi)$. If $1 \leftarrow \mathsf{Vrfy}(\mathsf{CRS}, (\mathsf{pk}_i, i, \mathsf{ct}), \pi)$, then run $[i\|\mathsf{M}] \leftarrow \mathsf{Dec}(\mathsf{pk}_i, \mathsf{sk}_i, \mathsf{ct})$ and output M. Ohterwise, output $\perp$.

By making the above change, even if the adversary makes a decryption query on a challenge ciphertext ct^* after the update queries, the challenger can return $\perp$ thanks to the Vrfy algorithm.

Theorem 2. *If Π is an IND-CU-CPA-secure (resp., IND-CR-CPA-secure) UPKE scheme and Ω is a strong one-time true-simulation f-extractable NIZK argument,* [7] *the UPKE scheme $\Sigma = (\mathsf{Gen}', \mathsf{Enc}', \mathsf{Dec}', \mathsf{UpdPk}', \mathsf{UpdSk}')$ constructed above meets IND-CU-CCA security (resp., IND-CR-CCA security).*

We omit the proof since it is almost the same as in the original transformation [11].

4 Efficient Generic Construction of CU-CCA-Secure UPKE

As seen above, fortunately, although Dodis et al.'s CPA-to-CCA transformation is fixable, it still employs NIZK arguments with strong requirements. Their original motivation to use such a strong NIZK argument is to lift CPA security to CCA in the context of UPKE, which is regarded as PKE with circular security and leakage resilience by Dodis et al. Their technique can rule out random oracles; however, it is unclear how the strong NIZK arguments can be efficiently instantiated.

Haidar et al. [22] showed another method to achieving CCA security of UPKE is to apply a specific variant of the Naor–Yung transformation [29] to their CPA-secure UPKE scheme from the DCR assumption. They proposed a concrete Σ-protocol to prove plaintext equality so that it is compatible to their specific CPA-secure UPKE scheme, and applied the Fiat–Shamir heuristic [17] to make the Σ-protocol non-interactive in the ROM. Although this approach preserves

[7] See the original paper [11] for the detailed definition of such a NIZK argument.

the efficiency of the underlying CPA-secure scheme, there are two issues with applicability and concrete efficiency: first, the Σ-protocol (and the NIZK via the Naor–Yung transformation) supports a specific language, and therefore it cannot be combined with other CPA-secure schemes; second, though the variant of the Naor–Yung transformation does not lose the efficiency of the underlying UPKE scheme that much, the CPA security of the underlying UPKE scheme was proved without random oracles, and hence it (and the resulting CCA-secure scheme) requires relatively larger concrete parameters compared to Jost et al.'s scheme [25]. Haidar et al. [23] also took a similar approach and proposed a CCA-secure UPKE scheme from the LWE assumption with an efficient NIZK argument for a specific language. The above NIZK issues seem to be an unavoidable dilemma; even with random oracles, one has to narrow down the language the NIZK supports to keep efficiency.

Towards concretely efficient CCA-secure UPKE schemes, we take an alternative approach: applying random oracles to convert *any* CPA-secure UPKE scheme to a CCA-secure scheme without using NIZK. To this end, we employ the FO transformation [18,19] *twice* to lift both CPA and CR to CCA and CU, respectively. Therefore, the one-wayness of CR-CPA security suffices to build our construction, which will be introduced in Sect. 4.1.

4.1 Definitions for UPKE

We define the security notion considering one-wayness called the OW-CR-CPA security, as in OW-CPA security in PKE.

Definition 6 (OW-CR-CPA Security). *The OW-CR-CPA security of a UPKE scheme Π is defined by a game between an adversary $\mathcal{A}$ and a challenger $\mathcal{C}$, which is the same as the IND-CR-CPA security game defined in Definition 1 except for the following change:*

Challenge query: *$\mathcal{A}$ is allowed to make the query only once. Upon $\mathcal{A}$'s query on $\perp$, $\mathcal{C}$ chooses $\mathsf{M}^* \leftarrow \mathcal{M}$ and runs $\mathsf{ct}^* \leftarrow \mathsf{Enc}(\mathsf{pk}_{t_c}, \mathsf{M}^*)$ where t_c is the current epoch. Finally, $\mathcal{C}$ returns ct^* to $\mathcal{A}$.*

Guess: *At the end of the game, $\mathcal{A}$ returns $\widehat{\mathsf{M}}$ as a guess of M^*.*

The relationship between OW-CR-CPA and IND-CR-CPA security can be easily derived below. We omit the proofs, which can be proved similarly to traditional PKE.

Proposition 1. *If a UPKE scheme Π satisfies IND-CR-CPA security, it also satisfies OW-CR-CPA security.*

Proposition 2. *There exists a UPKE scheme Π that satisfies OW-CR-CPA security but does not meet IND-CR-CPA security.*

We next define γ-spread for UPKE based on the same property of PKE [18, 19].

Definition 7 (γ-spread). *A UPKE scheme* $\Pi = (\mathsf{Gen}, \mathsf{Enc}, \mathsf{Dec}, \mathsf{UpdPk}, \mathsf{UpdSk})$ *is* γ*-spread if for all* $\lambda, \ell \in \mathbb{N}$ *all* $(\mathsf{pk}_0, \mathsf{sk}_0) \leftarrow \mathsf{Gen}(1^\lambda)$*, all* $\mathsf{M} \in \mathcal{M}$*, all* $i \in \{0, \ldots, \ell\}$*, we have*

$$-\log \left(\max_{\mathsf{ct} \in \{0,1\}^*} \Pr\left[h \leftarrow_\$ \mathcal{R} : \mathsf{ct} = \mathsf{Enc}((\mathsf{pk}_i, \mathsf{M}; h)\right] \right) \geq \gamma,$$

where $(\mathsf{pk}_j, \mathsf{up}_j) \leftarrow \mathsf{UpdPk}(\mathsf{pk}_{j-1})$*,* $\mathsf{sk}_j \leftarrow \mathsf{UpdSk}(\mathsf{pk}_{j-1}, sk_{j-1}, (\mathsf{pk}_j, \mathsf{up}_j))$ *for* $j = 1, \ldots, \ell$*.*

Our construction requires UPKE schemes to meet γ-spread, where γ is at least $O(\lambda)$. Indeed, all the existing CR-CPA-secure UPKE schemes satisfy this requirement and can be used to instantiate our construction. Even if CR-CPA-secure UPKE schemes with insufficient γ-spread are proposed in the near future, as in [18,19], one can strengthen the γ-spread to the $(\gamma + \gamma')$-spread by appending a random value $r \leftarrow_\$ \{0,1\}^{\gamma'}$ to the end of ciphertexts.

4.2 Our Construction

We combine the two FO transformations and fine-tune them to achieve an efficient CU-CCA-secure UPKE scheme. Specifically, the second FO transformation could be a weaker form since CU security requires the consistency check but no (kind of) challenge queries.

Formally, we construct an IND-CU-CCA-secure UPKE scheme $\Sigma = (\mathsf{Gen}', \mathsf{Enc}', \mathsf{Dec}', \mathsf{UpdPk}', \mathsf{UpdSk}')$ from an OW-CR-CPA-secure UPKE scheme $\Pi = (\mathsf{Gen}, \mathsf{Enc}, \mathsf{Dec}, \mathsf{UpdPk}, \mathsf{UpdSk})$, an OT-CPA-secure SKE scheme $\Gamma = (\mathsf{SKE.Enc}, \mathsf{SKE.Dec})$, and four random oracles $\mathsf{G} : \{0,1\}^* \to \mathcal{SK}_{\mathsf{sym}}$, $\mathsf{H} : \{0,1\}^* \times \{0,1\}^* \times \{0,1\}^* \to \mathcal{R}_{\mathsf{asy}}$, $\widehat{\mathsf{G}} : \{0,1\}^* \to \mathcal{SK}_{\mathsf{sym}}$, and $\widehat{\mathsf{H}} : \{0,1\}^* \times \{0,1\}^* \to \mathcal{R}_{\mathsf{asy}}$,[8] where $\mathcal{M}_{\mathsf{asy}}$, $\mathcal{R}_{\mathsf{asy}}$, and $\mathcal{SK}_{\mathsf{sym}}$ are the spaces of plaintexts of Π, randomness of Π, and secret keys of Γ, respectively.

$\mathsf{Gen}'(1^\lambda) \to (\mathsf{pk}'_0, \mathsf{sk}'_0)$: Run $(\mathsf{pk}_0, \mathsf{sk}_0) \leftarrow \mathsf{Gen}(1^\lambda)$ and output $\mathsf{pk}'_0 := (\mathsf{pk}_0, 0)$ and $\mathsf{sk}'_0 := \mathsf{sk}_0$.

$\mathsf{Enc}'(\mathsf{pk}'_i, \mathsf{M}) \to \mathsf{ct}$: Parse $\mathsf{pk}'_i = (\mathsf{pk}_i, i)$. Run
- $\sigma \leftarrow_\$ \mathcal{M}_{\mathsf{asy}}$,
- $k := \mathsf{G}(\sigma)$,
- $\mathsf{ct}_{\mathsf{sym}} \leftarrow \mathsf{SKE.Enc}(k, \mathsf{M})$,
- $h := \mathsf{H}(i, \sigma, \mathsf{ct}_{\mathsf{sym}})$,
- $\mathsf{ct}_{\mathsf{asy}} \leftarrow \mathsf{Enc}(\mathsf{pk}_i, \sigma; h)$.

Output $\mathsf{ct} := (\mathsf{ct}_{\mathsf{asy}}, \mathsf{ct}_{\mathsf{sym}})$.

$\mathsf{Dec}'(\mathsf{pk}'_i, \mathsf{sk}'_i, \mathsf{ct}) \to \mathsf{M}$ or $\perp$: Parse $\mathsf{pk}'_i = (\mathsf{pk}_i, i)$, $\mathsf{sk}'_i = \mathsf{sk}_i$, and $\mathsf{ct} = (\mathsf{ct}_{\mathsf{asy}}, \mathsf{ct}_{\mathsf{sym}})$. Run
- $\sigma \leftarrow \mathsf{Dec}(\mathsf{pk}_i, \mathsf{sk}_i, \mathsf{ct}_{\mathsf{asy}})$.

[8] One may merge G and $\widehat{\mathsf{G}}$ (and also H and $\widehat{\mathsf{H}}$) into one by using a bit flag, though we use the random oracles separately to make the security proof simple. For instance, one may set $\mathsf{G}(0\|\cdot)$ and $\mathsf{G}(1\|\cdot)$ instead of $\mathsf{G}(\cdot)$ and $\widehat{\mathsf{G}}(\cdot)$, where '$\|$' denotes concatenation.

Output $\perp$ if $\sigma \notin \mathcal{M}_{\mathsf{asy}}$. Otherwise, run
- $h := \mathsf{H}(i, \sigma, \mathsf{ct}_{\mathsf{sym}})$.

Output $\perp$ if $\mathsf{ct}_{\mathsf{asy}} \neq \mathsf{Enc}(\mathsf{pk}_i, \sigma; h)$. Otherwise, run
- $k := \mathsf{G}(\sigma)$.

Finally, run and output $\mathsf{SKE.Dec}(k, \mathsf{ct}_{\mathsf{sym}})$.

$\mathsf{UpdPk}'(\mathsf{pk}'_i) \rightarrow (\mathsf{pk}'_{i+1}, \mathsf{up}'_{i+1})$: Parse $\mathsf{pk}'_i = (\mathsf{pk}_i, i)$. Run
- $r \leftarrow_{\$} \mathcal{M}_{\mathsf{asy}}$,
- $s := \widehat{\mathsf{G}}(r)$
- $(\mathsf{pk}_{i+1}, \mathsf{up}_{i+1}) \leftarrow \mathsf{UpdPk}(\mathsf{pk}_i; s)$,
- $h := \widehat{\mathsf{H}}(r, \mathsf{pk}_{i+1}, \mathsf{up}_{i+1})$,
- $\mathsf{ct}_{\mathsf{aux}} \leftarrow \mathsf{Enc}(\mathsf{pk}_i, r; h)$.

Output $\mathsf{pk}'_{i+1} := (\mathsf{pk}_{i+1}, i+1)$ and $\mathsf{up}'_{i+1} := (\mathsf{up}_{i+1}, \mathsf{ct}_{\mathsf{aux}})$.

$\mathsf{UpdSk}'(\mathsf{pk}'_i, \mathsf{sk}'_i, (\mathsf{pk}'_{i+1}, \mathsf{up}'_{i+1})) \rightarrow \mathsf{sk}'_{i+1}$ or $\perp$: Parse $\mathsf{pk}'_i = (\mathsf{pk}_i, i)$, $\mathsf{sk}'_i = \mathsf{sk}_i$, $\mathsf{pk}'_{i+1} = (\mathsf{pk}_{i+1}, i+1)$, and $\mathsf{up}'_{i+1} = (\mathsf{up}_{i+1}, \mathsf{ct}_{\mathsf{aux}})$.[9] Run
- $r \leftarrow \mathsf{Dec}(\mathsf{pk}_i, \mathsf{sk}_i, \mathsf{ct}_{\mathsf{aux}})$.

Output $\perp$ if $r \notin \mathcal{M}_{\mathsf{asy}}$ holds. Otherwise, run
- $h := \widehat{\mathsf{H}}(r, \mathsf{pk}_{i+1}, \mathsf{up}_{i+1})$,
- $s := \widehat{\mathsf{G}}(r)$.

Output $\perp$ if at least one of the following holds:
- $\mathsf{ct}_{\mathsf{aux}} \neq \mathsf{Enc}(\mathsf{pk}_i, r; h)$,
- $(\mathsf{pk}_{i+1}, \mathsf{up}_{i+1}) \neq \mathsf{UpdPk}(\mathsf{pk}_i; s)$.

Otherwise, run $\mathsf{sk}_{i+1} \leftarrow \mathsf{UpdSk}(\mathsf{pk}_i, \mathsf{sk}_i, (\mathsf{pk}_{i+1}, \mathsf{sk}_{i+1}))$ and output $\mathsf{sk}'_{i+1} := \mathsf{sk}_{i+1}$.

4.3 Correctness

We prove the correctness of our UPKE construction as follows.

Theorem 3. *Our UPKE scheme Σ satisfies correctness if the underlying UPKE scheme Π and SKE scheme Γ satisfy correctness.*

Due to the page limitation, we defer the proof of Theorem 3 to the full version of this paper [3].

4.4 Security

Theorem 4. *If the underlying UPKE scheme Π is γ-spread and satisfies OW-CR-CPA security, SKE scheme Γ satisfies OT-CPA security, and* G, H, $\widehat{\mathsf{G}}$, *and* $\widehat{\mathsf{H}}$ *are random oracles, then our proposed UPKE scheme Σ satisfies IND-CU-CCA security.*

[9] To be precise, one has to confirm whether the second element of $\mathsf{pk}'_{i+1} = (\mathsf{pk}_{i+1}, j)$ denotes the next epoch of i, i.e., $j = i+1$; we omit the procedure since one can easily check it by just incrementing the second element of $\mathsf{pk}'_i = (\mathsf{pk}_i, i)$ and comparing it with j.

Due to the page limitation, we defer the formal proof to the full version of this paper [3] and provide the proof sketch below.

Proof (Sketch). As we described earlier, our construction employs the FO transformation for each of the ciphertexts and the update ciphertexts. Although we can prove the theorem in a manner similar to the original FO transformation, we must address several minor modifications as follows. (1) we require that the hash functions H and $\widehat{\mathsf{H}}$ additionally take epochs and updated public keys as input, respectively; and (2) we apply the FO transformation twice for CCA and CU security.

The overview of the proof is as follows. First, we show how to simulate the decryption and update queries without the secret keys by simulating H and $\widehat{\mathsf{H}}$. To do so, we define *valid* (update) ciphertexts; we say that a ciphertext (resp., an update ciphertext) is valid if it satisfies the validity check in the Dec' algorithm (resp., UpdSk' algorithm). Now consider the case in which the queries cannot be simulated. In this case, the adversary generates *valid* ciphertexts or *valid* update ciphertexts without using H and $\widehat{\mathsf{H}}$. This case occurs with a negligible probability thanks to the γ-spread property of Π. Next, we show how to change the ways to generate the challenge ciphertext and the update ciphertext at the reveal query; namely, sample the randomness uniformly at random, instead of using the random oracles. The above change is indistinguishable from the adversary's point of view thanks to OW-CR-CPA security of Π. Finally, from OT-CPA security of Γ, the adversary cannot distinguish the challenge ciphertext is an encryption of M_0^* or M_1^*. Thus, we complete the proof of Theorem 4. □

5 Conclusion

In this paper, we demonstrated that Dodis et al.'s CPA-to-CCA transformation [11] does not satisfy CCA security if the underlying UPKE schemes have non-influential randomness, a special property of UPKE that we introduced in this paper. The property enables the adversary to have the challenger generate the same public and secret keys as those at the challenge epoch. Then, the adversary can get the decryption result of the challenge ciphertext by making the decryption query. To prevent the above attack, we modified their CPA-to-CCA transformation by embedding epochs in public keys and cipheretexts.

We also proposed a new generic construction of the IND-CU-CCA secure UPKE scheme from any OW-CR-CPA-secure UPKE scheme in the ROM. By employing the FO transformation [18,19] twice instead of using inefficient NIZK arguments, we can obtain the most efficient IND-CR-CCA/IND-CU-CCA secure UPKE schemes from the most efficient IND-CR-CPA-secure UPKE scheme by Jost et al. [25].

Although our CU-CCA-secure scheme is quite efficient, it does not support public verifiability. It would be interesting to realize a transformation that supports public verifiability with almost the same efficiency as ours since it is an important property in the CU setting.

Acknowledgments. The authors would like to thank Shuichi Katsumata, Keita Xagawa, Calvin Abou Haidar, Yevgeniy Dodis, and Harish Karthikeyan for their valuable comments. The authors also thank Paul Rösler for spotting typos in the UPKE security definitions. This work was supported by JSPS KAKENHI Grant Numbers JP23H00479, JP23KJ0968, JP23K21668, JP21H03341, JP21H03395, JP18H05289, JST CREST JPMJCR23M2, and MEXT Leading Initiative for Excellent Young Researchers.

References

1. Alwen, J., Coretti, S., Dodis, Y., Tselekounis, Y.: Security analysis and improvements for the IETF MLS standard for group messaging. In: CRYPTO, pp. 248–277 (2020)
2. Alwen, J., Fuchsbauer, G., Mularczyk, M.: Updatable public-key encryption, revisited. In: EUROCRYPT, pp. 346–376 (2024)
3. Asano, K., Watanabe, Y.: Updatable public key encryption with strong CCA security: security analysis and efficient generic construction. IACR Cryptol. ePrint Arch. 976 (2023). https://eprint.iacr.org/2023/976
4. Bellare, M., Yee, B.S.: Forward-security in private-key cryptography. In: CT-RSA, pp. 1–18 (2003)
5. Boneh, D., Boyen, X.: Efficient selective-ID secure identity-based encryption without random oracles. In: EUROCRYPT, pp. 223–238 (2004)
6. Boneh, D., Boyen, X., Goh, E.: Hierarchical identity based encryption with constant size ciphertext. In: EUROCRYPT, pp. 440–456 (2005)
7. Canetti, R., Halevi, S., Katz, J.: A forward-secure public-key encryption scheme. In: EUROCRYPT, pp. 255–271 (2003)
8. Cash, D., Hofheinz, D., Kiltz, E., Peikert, C.: Bonsai trees, or how to delegate a lattice basis. J. Cryptol. 601–639 (2012)
9. Dodis, Y., Franklin, M.K., Katz, J., Miyaji, A., Yung, M.: Intrusion-resilient public-key encryption. In: CT-RSA, pp. 19–32 (2003)
10. Dodis, Y., Franklin, M.K., Katz, J., Miyaji, A., Yung, M.: A generic construction for intrusion-resilient public-key encryption. In: CT-RSA, pp. 81–98 (2004)
11. Dodis, Y., Karthikeyan, H., Wichs, D.: Updatable public key encryption in the standard model. In: TCC, pp. 254–285 (2021)
12. Dodis, Y., Karthikeyan, H., Wichs, D.: Updatable public key encryption in the standard model. IACR Cryptol. ePrint Arch. 68 (2022). https://eprint.iacr.org/2022/068
13. Dodis, Y., Katz, J., Xu, S., Yung, M.: Key-insulated public key cryptosystems. In: EUROCRYPT, pp. 65–82 (2002)
14. Döttling, N., Garg, S.: Identity-based encryption from the Diffie-Hellman assumption. In: CRYPTO, pp. 537–569 (2017)
15. Duparc, M., Fouotsa, T.B., Vaudenay, S.: SILBE: an updatable public key encryption scheme from lollipop attacks. In: SAC (2024, to appear)
16. Eaton, E., Jao, D., Komlo, C., Mokrani, Y.: Towards post-quantum key-updatable public-key encryption via supersingular isogenies. In: SAC, pp. 461–482 (2021)
17. Fiat, A., Shamir, A.: How to prove yourself: practical solutions to identification and signature problems. In: CRYPTO, pp. 186–194 (1986)
18. Fujisaki, E., Okamoto, T.: Secure integration of asymmetric and symmetric encryption schemes. In: CRYPTO, pp. 537–554 (1999)

19. Fujisaki, E., Okamoto, T.: Secure integration of asymmetric and symmetric encryption schemes. J. Cryptol. 80–101 (2013)
20. Gentry, C., Silverberg, A.: Hierarchical id-based cryptography. In: ASIACRYPT, pp. 548–566 (2002)
21. Groth, J., Sahai, A.: Efficient non-interactive proof systems for bilinear groups. In: EUROCRYPT, pp. 415–432 (2008)
22. Haidar, C.A., Libert, B., Passelègue, A.: Updatable public key encryption from DCR: efficient constructions with stronger security. In: CCS 2022, pp. 11–22 (2022)
23. Haidar, C.A., Passelègue, A., Stehlé, D.: Efficient updatable public-key encryption from lattices. In: ASIACRYPT, pp. 342–373 (2023)
24. Horwitz, J., Lynn, B.: Toward hierarchical identity-based encryption. In: EUROCRYPT, pp. 466–481 (2002)
25. Jost, D., Maurer, U., Mularczyk, M.: Efficient ratcheting: almost-optimal guarantees for secure messaging. In: EUROCRYPT, pp. 159–188 (2019)
26. Kim, H., Lee, S., Lee, D.H.: Constant-round authenticated group key exchange for dynamic groups. In: ASIACRYPT, pp. 245–259 (2004)
27. Lyubashevsky, V., Nguyen, N.K., Plançon, M.: Lattice-based zero-knowledge proofs and applications: shorter, simpler, and more general. In: CRYPTO, pp. 71–101 (2022)
28. Marlinspike, M., Perrin, T.: The X3DH key agreement protocol. https://signal.org/docs/specifications/x3dh/
29. Naor, M., Yung, M.: Public-key cryptosystems provably secure against chosen ciphertext attacks. In: STOC, pp. 427–437 (1990)
30. Perrin, T., Marlinspike, M.: The double ratchet algorithm. https://signal.org/docs/specifications/doubleratchet/
31. Shoup, V.: Sequences of games: a tool for taming complexity in security proofs. IACR Cryptol. ePrint Arch. 332 (2004). http://eprint.iacr.org/2004/332
32. Signal protocol: Signal protocol: Technical documentation. https://signal.org/doc
33. Zhang, C., Zhou, H.S., Katz, J.: An analysis of the algebraic group model. In: ASIACRYPT, pp. 310–322 (2022)

Hardware and Software Implementations

Masking Gaussian Elimination at Arbitrary Order with Application to Multivariate-and Code-Based PQC

Quinten Norga[1(✉)], Suparna Kundu[1], Uttam Kumar Ojha[2], Anindya Ganguly[3], Angshuman Karmakar[3], and Ingrid Verbauwhede[1]

[1] COSIC, KU Leuven, Leuven, Belgium
{quinten.norga,suparna.kundu,ingrid.verbauwhede}@esat.kuleuven.be
[2] Indian Statistical Institute Kolkata, Kolkata, India
uttamkumarojha1729@gmail.com
[3] Indian Institute of Technology Kanpur, Kanpur, India
{anindyag,angshuman}@cse.iitk.ac.in

Abstract. Gaussian Elimination (GE) is a critical operation in the signing procedure of multivariate- and code-based schemes. In this paper, we provide a masking scheme for GE with back substitution to defend against arbitrary-order attacks. We propose a masked algorithm for transforming a system of linear equations into row-echelon form. This is realized by introducing techniques for efficiently making leading (pivot) elements one while avoiding costly conversions between Boolean and multiplicative masking at all orders. We also propose a technique for efficient masked back substitution, which eventually enables a secure unmasking of the output. All novel gadgets are proven secure in the t-probing model. Additionally, we evaluate the overhead of our countermeasure for several post-quantum candidates and their different security levels at first-, second-, and third-order, including UOV, MAYO, SNOVA, QR-UOV, and MQ-Sign. Notably, the operational cost of first-, second-, and third-order masked GE is 2.3× higher, and the randomness cost is 1.2× higher in MAYO compared to UOV for security levels III and V. In contrast, these costs are similar in UOV and MAYO for one version of level I. We also show detailed performance results for first-, second- and third-order masked GE implementations on the Arm Cortex-M4 and compare them with unmasked cycle counts. Our first-order masked implementation has an overhead of factor 15.1×, 15.2×, and 15.4× compared to the unprotected implementation of UOV-I, UOV-III and UOV-V.

Keywords: PQC · Masking · Gaussian Elimination · Digital Signatures · UOV

1 Introduction

NIST announced a standardization process [28] for additional post-quantum Digital Signature (DS) schemes. Gaussian Elimination (GE) is a key compo-

Extended version: https://eprint.iacr.org/2024/1777.

A. Patra (Ed.): CT-RSA 2025, LNCS 15598, pp. 249–272, 2025.
https://doi.org/10.1007/978-3-031-88661-4_11

nent of the signing procedure in many of the schemes selected for the second round of NIST PQC DS on-ramp [29], used for finding the unique solution of a system of linear equations. All MQ-based signature schemes, such as (i) UOV [7], (ii) MAYO [6], (iii) SNOVA [35], (iv) QR-UOV [19], (v) MQ-Sign [33], (vi) PROV [22], (vii) VOX [12], (viii) TUOV [18], (ix) VDOO [20], and (x) IPRainbow [8] rely on GE during signing. Recently it has also been used in some code-based (CB) signature schemes such as Wave [2]. As the secret key is used during the signing and the GE procedure, it is a potential target for Side-Channel Analysis (SCA).

SCA can have severe impacts on cryptographic implementations, and post-quantum schemes are equally vulnerable [23,25,34]. SCA attacks extract secret data of the mathematically secure cryptographic algorithm from the cryptographic device by observing the computation and its physical behavior. Such attacks can be prevented by ensuring that any computation in the cryptographic algorithm is independent of any secret variables.

Masking [9] is a provably secure widely used countermeasure of such attacks [17,26,32]. Various SCAs have been demonstrated on the UOV-based signature schemes in the literature [1,30,36]. However, there is almost no research on countermeasures for MQ and CB digital signature schemes, including UOV, to prevent potential SCAs. Even more so, no specialized gadgets for the GE operation, a critical and costly component during signing, have been proposed.

Contributions. We propose *first- and higher-order* masked algorithms for solving a system of linear equations using (masked) Gaussian elimination with back substitution (`SecRowEch` & `SecBackSub`), a critical component in MQ and CB signature schemes. We propose masked gadgets for the following sub-operations in Sect. 3:

- For efficiently solving the linear system, it needs to be in *row-echelon form.* We propose the *conditional addition* gadget for making the pivot element non-zero, by securely adding different rows to the pivot-row if it is zero.
- Subsequently, the pivot coefficient needs to be reduced to value one. As directly computing its inverse would require unmasking the pivot element, our approach is based on switching *masking representations* for computing its multiplicative inverse and using share-wise multiplication.
- Finally, we devise an efficient masked gadget for back substituting the linear equations. We propose unmasking the final output *early* and *partitioned* to minimize the amount of masked operations.

We formally prove the t-order security of all proposed (sub-)gadgets in the t-probing model. We apply our techniques on several promising, UOV-based DS schemes (UOV, MAYO, SNOVA, QR-UOV & MQ-Sign) and compare their operation and randomness cost for masking the GE with back substitution, at first-, second-, and third-order (see Sect. 4). We provide an arbitrary-order masked implementation (Arm M4 C code[1]) of our masked GE and evaluate the performance of our methods for UOV parameters on an Arm Cortex-M4 processor (see

[1] https://github.com/KULeuven-COSIC/Masking-Gaussian-Elimination.

Sect. 5). Our masked implementation targeting UOV parameters has an overhead of factor 15.1×, 15.2×, and 15.4× compared to the unprotected implementation for NIST security level I, III, and V.

2 Preliminaries

We denote a finite field with q elements by $\mathbb{F}_q$, with q always a positive integer. $\mathbb{F}_q^*$ is used to present $\mathbb{F}_q \setminus \{0\}$. All the polynomials, vectors, and matrices are defined over $\mathbb{F}_q$ (or $\mathbb{F}_q^*$). We used lower-case letters to denote field elements/coefficients (e.g., x), bold lower-case letters to denote vectors (e.g., $\mathbf{b}$), and bold upper-case letters to denote matrices (e.g., $\mathbf{P}$). Please note that all the vectors are in column form and $\mathbf{P}^T$ represents the transposition of a matrix $\mathbf{P}$. The assignment of a variable is written as $:=$ and $x \leftarrow A$ denotes sampling an element uniformly random from set A and assignment to variable x. All logarithms are in base 2. We denote the selection of coordinates in a vector and matrix as $\mathbf{b}_{[j]}$ and $\mathbf{P}_{[j,k]}$. The selection of a specific bit of a field element x is denoted by $x^{[i]}$. A sequence of n variables $(x_1, \cdots, x_n)$ (e.g., shares of variable x) is represented as $(x_i)_{1 \leq i \leq n}$ or in short as (x_i) if the sequence length is obvious from context.

2.1 Gaussian Elimination

Gaussian elimination, $\boldsymbol{x} \leftarrow \texttt{Gaussian Elimination}(\mathbf{A}, \mathbf{b})$, is an old technique to solve a linear system of the form $\mathbf{Ax} = \mathbf{b}$, where $\mathbf{A} \in \mathbb{F}_q^{m \times m}$ and vector $\mathbf{b} \in \mathbb{F}_q^m$ are given. Let us assume that $\mathbf{T} = [\mathbf{A} \mid \mathbf{b}]$. In Line 4 of Algorithm 1, it is attempted to make the pivot element $\mathbf{T}_{[j,j]}$ non-zero by adding the following rows if it is zero. In Line 8, it is checked if the pivot is still a non-zero pivot, and else the computation is aborted as the matrix $\mathbf{A}$ is not invertible in this case (Line 16). Subsequently, in Line 11, each current row element is multiplied with the inverse of the pivot element, making the pivot $\mathbf{T}_{[j,j]} = 1$. The loop in Line 13–14 subtracts a scalar multiple of row j from all rows below the current pivot row, making the elements below the pivot zero. Finally, to find $\mathbf{x}$, Line 18 back-substitutes the variables into the system of equations.

2.2 Masking to Thwart SCA Attacks

Masking [9] is a well-known countermeasure against side-channel attacks. Here the sensitive variables x are split into multiple, randomized shares $(x_1, \ldots, x_n)$. As a result, an attacker who does not have access to all shares (x_i) does not learn anything about the secret variable x. The relation between x and its shares $(x_1, \ldots, x_n)$ is some group operation that changes depending on the masking methods. The most utilized masking method in the literature is Boolean masking, where $x = x_1 + \cdots + x_n$ and the addition is a simple XOR ($\oplus$). In this work, we also use multiplicative masking, where $x = x_1 \otimes x_2 \cdots \otimes x_n$ and $\otimes$ denotes a multiplication between two elements of $\mathbb{F}_q$.

Algorithm 1: `Gaussian Elimination` [7,11]

Data: Linear equation $\mathbf{Ax} = \mathbf{b}$, where matrix $\mathbf{A} \in \mathbb{F}_q^{m \times m}$ and vector $\mathbf{b} \in \mathbb{F}_q^m$
Result: Unique $\mathbf{x} \in \mathbb{F}_q^m$ such that $\mathbf{Ax} = \mathbf{b}$

$\mathbf{T} := [\mathbf{A} \mid \mathbf{b}]$ /* $\mathbf{T} \in \mathbb{F}_q^{m \times (m+1)}$ */
for $j = 1$ *upto* m **do**
  `## Try to make pivot` $\mathbf{T}_{[j,j]}$ `non-zero`
  for $k = j + 1$ *upto* m **do**
    if $T_{[j,j]} == 0$ **then**
      $\mathbf{T}_{[j,j:m+1]} = \mathbf{T}_{[j,j:m+1]} + \mathbf{T}_{[k,j:m+1]}$
  `## Check if pivot is non-zero`
  if $T_{[j,j]} \neq 0$ **then**
    `## Multiply row` j `with the inverse of its pivot`
    $p := \mathbf{T}_{[j,j]}{}^{-1}$
    $\mathbf{T}_{[j,j:m+1]} = p \cdot \mathbf{T}_{[j,j:m+1]}$
    `## Subtract scalar multiple of row` j `from the rows below`
    for $k = j + 1$ *upto* m **do**
      $\mathbf{T}_{[k,j:m+1]} = \mathbf{T}_{[k,j:m+1]} - \mathbf{T}_{[k,j]} \cdot \mathbf{T}_{[j,j:m+1]}$
  else return $\perp$
for $j = m$ *downto* 2 **do**
  for $k = 1$ *upto* j **do**
    $\mathbf{T}_{[k,m+1]} = \mathbf{T}_{[k,m+1]} + \mathbf{T}_{[j,k]} \cdot \mathbf{T}_{[j,m+1]}$
return $\boldsymbol{x} := \boldsymbol{T}_{[:,m+1]}$

To argue about the security level of a masked implementation and its attackers, Ishai et al. [24] introduced the t-probing model. It assumes an adversary can probe up to t variables during a cryptographic computation. An implementation is t-probing secure if any t intermediate values leak no information about the unshared secret and thus can be simulated without the knowledge of this secret. Below, we recall several security notions which are used throughout this work.

Definition 1 (t-(Strong-)Non-Interference (t-(S)NI) security [3]). *A gadget with one output sharing and m_i input shares is t-Non-Interference (t-NI) (resp. t-Strong Non-Interference (t-SNI)) secure if any set of at most t_1 probes on its internal wires and t_2 probes on wires from its output sharings such that $t_1 + t_2 \leq t$ can be simulated with $t_1 + t_2$ (resp. t_1) shares of each of its m_i input sharings.*

Definition 2 (free-t-Strong-Non-Interference (free-t-SNI) security [15]). *A gadget with output sharing (b_i) and n input shares (m_i) is free-t-SNI secure if for any set of at most t_1 probes on its internal wires such that $t_1 \leq t$, there exists a subset I of input indices with $|I| \leq t_1$, such that the t_1 intermediate variables and the output shares $b_{|I}$ can be perfectly simulated from $m_{|I}$, while for any $O \subsetneq [1, n] \setminus I$ the output variables in $b_{|O}$ are uniformly and independently distributed, conditioned on the probed variables and $c_{|I}$.*

Definition 3 (t-Non-Interference with public outputs (t-NIo) security [4]). *A gadget with public output b and m_i input sharings is t-Non-Interference with public outputs (t-NIo) secure if any set of at most t_1 probes on its internal wires such that $t_1 \leq t$ can be simulated with t_1 shares of each of its m_i input sharings and b.*

3 Masked Gaussian Elimination with Back Substitution

We now describe a method for solving a system of linear equations using GE and back substitution in a masked manner. Our approach is generic and can be applied at first- and higher-order. The main algorithms are the conversion of a matrix to its row-echelon form (`SecRowEch`, Algorithm 6) and the back substitution (`SecBackSub`, Algorithm 7).

First, in Sects. 3.1–3.5, we introduce several novel masked gadgets that are used as subroutines in the main algorithms, including:

- `SecCondAdd`: conditional addition of two Boolean shared vectors (rows). This allows us to securely add two rows together, only if the pivot element of the first row is zero, without directly revealing any information about the pivot.
- `SecScalarMult`: multiplication of a (Boolean) shared vector with a multiplicative shared scalar. This allows us to multiply a row with the masked pivot of a different row, without unmasking and revealing the scalar value.
- `B2Minv`: Boolean to multiplicative inverse mask conversion, which allows us to make a pivot element one by multiplying the row with its inverse, so efficient back substitution can subsequently be performed.

All components are put together to achieve fully masked GE with back substitution in Sects. 3.6–3.7. Table 1 gives an overview of all the used gadgets in this work, including gadgets from previous works. We also include a short description of the computed functionality and the assumed security properties.

Methodology. All novel gadgets are described by a t-order algorithm ($n = t + 1$ shares) and accompanied with a detailed description. We also prove the t-(S)NI security in the probing model of all algorithms/gadgets. The proofs are simulation-based: we show how probes on intermediate and output variables in the algorithms can be perfectly simulated with only a limited number of input shares. For algorithms that are composed of smaller gadgets, we rely on the t-(S)NI properties of the sub-gadgets. By iterating over all possible intermediate (and output) variables of each sub-gadget, starting at the output and moving to the input of the algorithm, all required probes for simulation are summed. Crucially, the set of probes required from the input shares of a t-SNI gadget is independent from the amount of probes on its output shares.

Table 1. Overview of used gadgets in this work, with $n = t + 1$ shares.

Algorithm	Description	Security	Reference
`Refresh`	Refresh of Boolean masking	t-NI	[3,5]
`StrongRefresh`	Strong refresh of Boolean masking	t-SNI	[3]
`FullAdd`	Refresh and combine Boolean shares	t-NI	[4,14]
`B2M`	Boolean to multiplicative mask conversion	t-SNI	[21,27]
`B2Minv`	Boolean to multiplicative inverse conversion	t-SNI	Algorithm 5
`SecMult`	Multiplication of Boolean shares	t-SNI	[3,24]
`SecNonzero`	Nonzero check of Boolean shares	t-SNI	[10]
`SecCondAdd`	Secure conditional addition	t-SNI	Algorithm 2
`SecScalarMult`	Masked scalar multiplication	t-SNI	Algorithm 3
`SecMultSub`	Masked multiplication and subtraction	t-NI	Algorithm 4
`SecRowEch`	Matrix conversion to row echelon form	t-NIo	Algorithm 6
`SecBackSub`	Masked back substitution with public output	t-NIo	Algorithm 7

3.1 Masked Conditional Addition

The conditional addition of two Boolean shared row vectors $(\mathbf{x}_i)$ and $(\mathbf{y}_i)$ is described in Algorithm 2. Depending on the condition, represented by a Boolean shared bit (b_i), the result $\mathbf{s} = \mathbf{x} + \mathbf{y}$ or $\mathbf{s} = \mathbf{x}$ is computed (Line 3) and returned. For each coefficient in the vector, the shared term that is added to $(\mathbf{x}[j]_i)$ is computed using the `SecAND` gadget (Line 2). This gadget can be seen as a specific invocation of the `SecMult` gadget for GF(2) (bit-wise logical AND).

Algorithm 2: `SecCondAdd`

Data: 1. A Boolean sharing $(\mathbf{x}_i)$ of a (row) vector $\mathbf{x} \in \mathbb{F}_q^l$.
2. A Boolean sharing $(\mathbf{y}_i)$ of a (row) vector $\mathbf{y} \in \mathbb{F}_q^l$.
3. A Boolean sharing (b_i) of a coefficient (bit) b.

Result: A Boolean sharing $(\mathbf{s}_i)$ of the vector $\mathbf{s} = \mathbf{x} + b \cdot \mathbf{y} \in \mathbb{F}_q^l$

1 **for** $j = 1$ *upto* l **do**
2 $\quad(\mathbf{a}[j]_i) :=$ `SecAND`$((\mathbf{y}[j]_i), (b_i^{[w:1]}))$ /* extend b to $w = \lceil \log(q) \rceil$ bits */
3 $\quad(\mathbf{s}[j]_i) := (\mathbf{x}[j]_i + \mathbf{a}[j]_i)$
4 $\quad(\mathbf{s}[j]_i) =$ `StrongRefresh`$((\mathbf{s}[j]_i))$
5 **return** $(\mathbf{s}_i)$

3.1.1 Complexity

Here, we discuss the run-time complexity (number of operations) and randomness complexity of the `SecCondAdd` operation. We follow the approach proposed in [13,32]. We denote the run-time and randomness complexity of an operation `Operation` by $T_{\texttt{Operation}}$ and $R_{\texttt{Operation}}$, respectively. We also assume that the run-time cost of random number generation is unit time and operands are $w = \lceil \log(q) \rceil$ bits wide.

$$T_{\texttt{SecCondAdd}}(n, l) = (5n^2 - 3n)l, \quad R_{\texttt{SecCondAdd}}(n, l, w) = (n^2 - n)lw.$$

3.1.2 Security We now show Algorithm 2 to be t-SNI secure with $n = t + 1$ shares. This means it provides resistance against an adversary with t probes and allows the algorithm to be used in larger compositions.

Lemma 1. *The gadget* `SecCondAdd` *(Algorithm 2) is t-SNI secure.*

Proof. We first show that a single iteration j is t-SNI secure, which is shown in an abstract diagram in Fig. 1. Apart from the gadgets listed in Table 1, we model the share-wise addition on Line 3 as t-NI (G_2). An adversary can probe each gadget (G_i) internally or at its output. The number of internal and output probes for each gadget is denoted as t_{G_i} and o_{G_i}, respectively. We show that any set of t probes can be perfectly simulated with $\leq t_{A_2} = \sum_{i=1}^{3} t_{G_i} + \sum_{i=1}^{2} o_{G_i}$ input shares. Firstly, to simulate the internal and output probes on gadget G_3, only t_{G_3} shares of the output of G_2 are required. This is a direct result of the t-SNI property of G_3. Secondly, the simulation of the probes on gadgets G_1-G_2 requires $t_{G_1} + t_{G_2} + o_{G_2}$ shares of inputs $(\mathbf{x}_i)$, $(\mathbf{y}_i)$ and (b_i), as G_2 is t-NI secure. Due to the t-SNI property of gadget G_1, t_{G_1} input shares are required to simulate t_{G_1} intermediate probes and o_{G_1} output shares. Finally, we sum up the required shares of the inputs for the simulation of all gadgets $|I|$. As $|I| = t_{G_1} + t_{G_2} + o_{G_2} + t_{G_3} \leq t_{A_2}$ and independent from its output shares$|O| = o_{G_3}$, iteration j of Algorithm 2 is t-SNI.

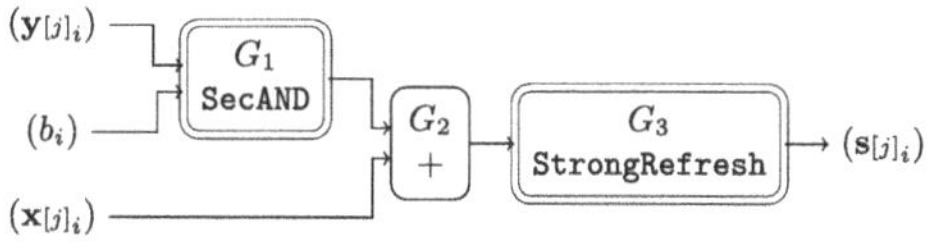

Fig. 1. An abstract diagram of an iteration j in `SecCondAdd` (Algorithm 2). t-NI gadgets are depicted with a single border, t-SNI gadgets with a double border. These notations are used in all the figures.

Now we remark that each iteration j is independent and can be executed in parallel, meaning that an adversary who places t probes across all iterations can simulate them with no more number of input shares. All gadgets can thus be summarized into a single gadget (across iterations), meaning the entire loop is t-SNI. □

3.2 Masked Scalar Multiplication

The `SecScalarMult` gadget is described in Algorithm 3. The operation is used to multiply one row-vector ($\mathbf{x}$) of a matrix with a non-zero scalar value (p), its pivot-element. It computes the multiplication $y = p \cdot x$, with one Boolean shared operand $(\mathbf{x}_i)$ and a multiplicative shared operand (p_i). The end-result is also Boolean shared, as is preferred for succeeding operations.

Our approach does not rely on first converting both operands to the same sharing type. The conversion of $(\mathbf{x}_i)$ to the multiplicative domain (`B2M`) would allow for simple share-wise computation of the multiplication, but would require another conversion back (`M2B`). The conversion of p_i to the Boolean domain (`M2B`) would result in the requirement for `SecMult` for the multiplication, which has a higher cost than `SecScalarMult`.

Algorithm 3: `SecScalarMult`

Data: 1. A Boolean sharing $(\mathbf{x}_i)$ of vector $x \in \mathbb{F}_q^l$.
2. A multiplicative sharing (p_i) of a coefficient $p \in \mathbb{F}_q$.
Result: A Boolean sharing $(\mathbf{y}_i)$ of the vector $y = p \cdot x \in \mathbb{F}_q^l$

1 $(\mathbf{y}_i) := (\mathbf{x}_i)$
2 **for** $j = 1$ *upto* n **do**
3   **for** $k = 1$ *upto* l **do**
4         $(\mathbf{y}[k]_i) = (p_j \cdot \mathbf{y}[k]_i)$
5         $(\mathbf{y}[k]_i) =$ `Refresh`$((\mathbf{y}[k]_i))$
6 **return** $(\mathbf{y}_i)$

We propose to perform the multiplication on a Boolean and multiplicative shared operand. The multiplicative shares are multiplied with all shares of the first operand, one share at a time (Line 2–5). To ensure no shares of (p_i) are re-combined during the operation, the intermediate results are refreshed (Line 5).

3.2.1 Complexity

The run-time and randomness complexity of `SecScalarMult` are:

$$T_{\texttt{SecScalarMult}}(n, l) = (5n^2 - 3n)l, \quad R_{\texttt{SecScalarMult}}(n, l, w) = (n^2 - n)lw.$$

3.2.2 Security

We now show that `SecScalarMult` is t-SNI secure with $n = t+1$ shares. This means it provides resistance against an adversary with t probes and allows the algorithm to be used in larger compositions.

Lemma 2. *The gadget* `SecScalarMult` *(Algorithm 3) is t-SNI secure.*

Proof. Before proving that the entire (outer) loop is t-SNI secure (Line 2–5), we show that the inner loop (Line 3–5) is t-NI secure, and its operations can be modeled as single t-NI gadgets. This follows directly from each iteration being independent and assumed to be executed in parallel (on individual coefficients). As a result, we can summarize the operations in the inner loop into single t-NI gadgets G_1 (share-wise multiplication) and G_2 (`Refresh`), which operate on the entire vector.

Figure 2 depicts an abstract diagram of a single iteration j in Algorithm 3. Since there are n iterations, an adversary cannot place probes in at least one iteration, which we refer to as j^*. We first consider the case where an adversary places all probes after or at the output of iteration $j = j^*$. As shown in [5], any set of output shares of `Refresh` with size $\leq n-1$ is uniformly distributed (Lemma 1). Thus, all probes can be perfectly simulated with fresh randomness, including the outputs of the entire gadget.

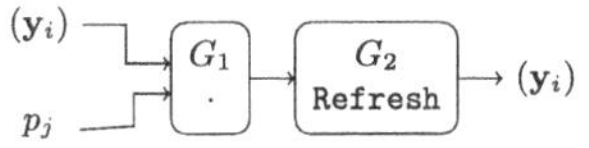

Fig. 2. An abstract diagram of an iteration j in `SecScalarMult` (Algorithm 3).

We now show that when an adversary places t probes before j^*, these can be simulated with no more number of shares of input $(\mathbf{x}_i)$ and (p_i). If the share-wise multiplication (G_1) and/or refresh (G_2) is probed, all probes (across iterations) can be simulated with the same (or fewer) number of input shares of $(\mathbf{x}_i)$. Now we determine the amount of shares of (p_i) required to simulate all possible probes. If all t probes are placed in a single iteration $j = j^{'}$, only $p_{j^{'}}$ is required for successful simulation. If G_2 (`Refresh`) in successive iterations $j = j^{'} - 1$ and $j = j^{'}$ are probed, only $p_{j^{'}}$ is required for simulation. And finally, if probes are placed in non-consecutive iterations of G_2, no shares of (p_i) are required. The simulation is sound as the outputs of the `Refresh` gadget are uniformly random, and any such combination of probes can be perfectly simulated with fresh randomness. We now remark that the size of the required set of shares of (p_i) never exceeds the number of placed probes. In conclusion, as the output of the entire loop can be perfectly simulated without any input shares and the required set of input shares of all intermediate probes is less or equal to the amount of placed probes, the entire algorithm is t-SNI. □

3.3 Masked Multiplication and Subtraction

The `SecMultSub` gadget (Algorithm 4) is used to first multiply a Boolean shared (row-)vectors $(\mathbf{x}_i)$ with a Boolean shared coefficient (c_i). For this, we rely on the `SecMult` gadget (Line 2). We do not convert to the multiplicative domain, as the coefficients can be zero and thus would require handling the zero-problem as discussed in [21,27]. The result of the multiplication is subsequently subtracted from a second Boolean shared vector $(\mathbf{y}_i)$ in Line 3.

3.3.1 Complexity The run-time and randomness complexity of `SecMultAdd` are:

$$T_{\texttt{SecMultAdd}}(n, l) = \frac{7n^2 - 3n}{2} \cdot l, \quad R_{\texttt{SecMultAdd}}(n, l, w) = \frac{n^2 - n}{2} \cdot lw.$$

Algorithm 4: `SecMultSub`

Data: 1. Two Boolean sharings $(\mathbf{x}_i), (\mathbf{y}_i)$ of vector $x, y \in \mathbb{F}_q^l$.
2. A Boolean sharing (c_i) of a coefficient $c \in \mathbb{F}_q$.
Result: A Boolean sharing $(\mathbf{z}_i)$ of the vector $z = x * c + y \in \mathbb{F}_q^l$

for $j = 1$ *upto* l **do**
  $(\mathbf{t}[j]_i) :=$ `SecMult`$((\mathbf{x}[j]_i), (c_i))$ /* $\mathbf{t}_i \in \mathbb{F}_q^l$ */
  $(\mathbf{z}[j]_i) := (\mathbf{y}[j]_i - \mathbf{t}[j]_i)$
return $(\mathbf{z}_i)$

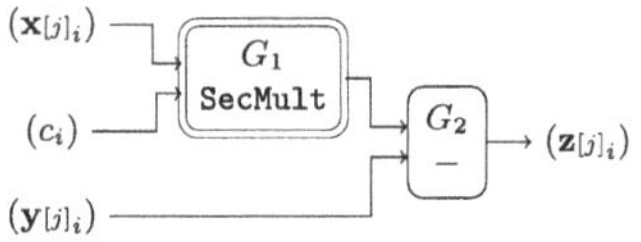

Fig. 3. An abstract diagram of an iteration j in `SecMultSub` (Algorithm 4).

3.3.2 Security

We now show that Algorithm 4 is t-NI secure with $n = t + 1$ shares. This means it provides resistance against an adversary with t probes and allows the algorithm to be used in larger compositions.

Lemma 3. *The gadget* `SecMultSub` *(Algorithm 4) is t-NI secure.*

Proof. Figure 3 depicts a single iteration j in `SecMultSub`. We model the `SecMult` gadget as G_1 and the share-wise subtraction as t-NI gadget G_2. An adversary can probe intermediate values of both gadgets t_{G_i} and the ouput of G_1 (o_{G_1}). We now show that all probes in iteration j can be simulated with no more number of shares of the inputs $(|I|)$ of the iteration: $|I| \leq t_{A_4} = \sum_{i=1}^{2} t_{G_i} + o_{G_1}$. If that is the case, and an adversary can place t probes across different (independent) iterations, those can still be simulated with no more number of input shares. Due to the t-NI property of G_2 and t-SNI security of G_1, it follows directly that $|I| = t_{G_1} + t_{G_2}$, and Lemma 4 is proven. As t-SNI security allows to simulate the intermediate and output probes of a gadget with a number of input shares, independent from the amount of probed output shares. Finally, as each iteration j is independent and can be executed in parallel, we can summarize the gadgets in each iteration as a single gadget across all iterations. As a result, the entire loop is t-NI. □

3.4 Boolean to Multiplicative Inverse Conversion

We now introduce a method for converting from a Boolean to a multiplicative inverse masked representation (Algorithm 5). In order to make a pivot element in a matrix one, as required for it to be in the row-echelon form, we multiply it with its inverse. As the computation of an inverse prefers multiplicative masking, the Boolean shared input (x_i) is first converted to a multiplicative sharing (m_i) (Line

1). We rely on the Boolean to multiplicative conversion proposed in [21], which is recalled in Sect. 3.5. Finally, in Line 2, a share-wise inversion is performed.

Algorithm 5: `B2Minv`

Data: A Boolean sharing (x_i) of a coefficient $x \in \mathbb{F}_q^*$

Result: A multiplicative inverse sharing (p_i) such that $x^{-1} = \prod_{i=1}^{n} p_i$

1 $(m_i) :=$ `B2M`$((x_i))$
2 $(p_i) := (m_i^{-1})$ `/* multiplicative inverse */`
3 **return** (p_i)

3.4.1 Complexity

The run-time and randomness complexity of `B2Minv` are:

$$T_{\mathtt{B2Minv}}(n) = \frac{5n^2 - 5n + 4}{2}, \quad R_{\mathtt{B2Minv}}(n, w) = \frac{n^2 - n}{2} \cdot w.$$

3.4.2 Security

We now show that Algorithm 5 is t-SNI secure with $n = t + 1$ shares. As a result, it provides resistance against an adversary with t probes and allows the algorithm to be used in larger compositions.

Lemma 4. *The gadget* `B2Minv` *(Algorithm 5) is t-SNI secure.*

Proof. `B2M` is a t-SNI Boolean to multiplicative conversion, as shown in [27]. The multiplicative inversion on Line 2 can be modeled as a t-NI gadget, as it is performed share-wise. Logically, it follows that Algorithm 5 is t-SNI secure. □

3.5 Auxiliary Gadgets

Before discussing our approach to masking the Gaussian elimination and back substitution, we first recall (the functionality of) several auxiliary gadgets. We refer to their original work for their full algorithm, security proof and details on complexity, unless specified.

`Refresh & StrongRefresh` [3, Alg. 4a & 4b]. Both types of mask refresh gadgets are used throughout this work, being proven t-NI and t-SNI in [5] and [3], respectively.

`FullAdd` [4,14]. We use this gadget for secure share recombination. It consists of two steps: the *strong* mask refreshing and the share combination (unmasking). In the context of secure unmasking, a strong refresh refers to a free-t-SNI mask refreshing. It is shown in [16] that the `StrongRefresh` gadget satisfies the free-t-SNI notion. Thanks to the free-SNI notion, all outputs (y_i) are simulatable if the simulator is given the unmasked value y. As a result, we can recombine the output shares of the gadget while ensuring all intermediate variables can be perfectly simulated.

As shown in [16,17], the FullAdd gadget satisfies the t-NIo definition when the output y is made public. Or, to prove the probing security of a composed circuit, the full gadget can be modeled as t-NI if the simulator has knowledge of the encoded output y.

SecNonzero [10]. The algorithm is t-SNI and checks if a Boolean shared operand (x_i) is non-zero, if unmasked, and returns the result as a single Boolean shared bit (b_i). The run-time and randomness complexity of SecNonzero are:

$$T_{\texttt{SecNonzero}}(n) = (5n^2 + 2n - 1) + \lceil \log(w+1) \rceil \cdot (5n^2 - n + 2),$$
$$R_{\texttt{SecNonzero}}(n, w) = \frac{\lceil \log(w+1) \rceil^2 - \lceil \log(w+1) \rceil}{2} \cdot (n^2 - n).$$

B2M [21, AMtoMM]. The t-SNI security of the B2M conversion is proven in [27, A.2]. Intuitively, the algorithm sequentially replaces each Boolean share x_i by a multiplicative one (z_i).

3.6 Masked Row Echelon Conversion

A critical step in multivariate-based post-quantum signature schemes, including UOV, is solving a system of linear equations. In this (and the next) section, we propose a method for solving a Boolean shared set of linear equations $((\mathbf{T}_i) = [\mathbf{A}_i \mid \mathbf{b}_i])$ using masked Gaussian elimination. Our strategy consists of reducing a shared matrix, containing the set of equations, to its (masked) row echelon form using (SecRowEch). Subsequently, solving the system the system requires performing masked back substitution (SecBackSub).

An important step in the computation is the (repeated) checking if the matrix $\mathbf{T}$ is invertible, as this leads to a unique solution. We propose an efficient approach, which relies on verifying if pivot elements are (non-)zero in a masked manner. Note that we do not leak (unmask) the pivot element itself, but securely compute and reveal if it is zero (or not). Leaking that the matrix is not invertible is not an issue for security, as the matrix is discarded and the algorithm is re-started in this case. We now discuss the four steps of gadget SecRowEch in detail.

Step 1: try to make pivot $\mathbf{T}_{[j,j]}$ non-zero. As each pivot element (and the rest of the row) is multiplied with its inverse, in order to make it one (row echelon form), it needs to be non-zero. If the selected pivot element is zero (SecNonzero & SecNOT[2]), one of r rows below is added to the 'pivot-row' j using SecCondAdd to make it non-zero, all in the masked domain (Line 7). One needs to iterate over all rows to ensure there are no timing side-channel leakages.

Step 2: check if pivot $\mathbf{T}_{[j,j]}$ is non-zero. A masked non-zero check is performed on the pivot element (Line 9), resulting in a Boolean masked bit (t_i).

[2] $(y_i) = \texttt{SecNOT}((x_i)) = \neg x_1 + \cdots + x_n$.

Algorithm 6: `SecRowEch`

Data: 1. A Boolean sharing $(\mathbf{A}_i)$ of matrix $\mathbf{A} \in \mathbb{F}_q^{m \times m}$
2. A Boolean sharing $(\mathbf{b}_i)$ of the vector $\mathbf{b} \in \mathbb{F}_q^m$

Result: Masked conversion to row echelon form or $\perp$

1 $(\mathbf{T}_i) := [\mathbf{A}_i \mid \mathbf{b}_i]$ /* $\mathbf{T}_i \in \mathbb{F}_q^{m \times (m+1)}$ */
2 **for** $j = 1$ *upto* m **do**
3   ## Try to make pivot $(\mathbf{T}_{[j,j]})$ non-zero
4   **for** $k = j + 1$ *upto* m **do**
5     $(z_i) :=$ SecNonzero($(\mathbf{T}_{[j,j]_i})$)
6     $(z_i) =$ SecNOT((z_i))
7     $(\mathbf{T}_{[j,j:m+1]_i}) =$ SecCondAdd($(\mathbf{T}_{[j,j:m+1]_i}), (\mathbf{T}_{[k,j:m+1]_i}), (z_i)$)
8   ## Check if pivot is non-zero
9   $(t_i) :=$ SecNonzero($(\mathbf{T}_{[j,j]_i})$)
10   $\mathbf{c}_{[j]} :=$ FullAdd((t_i))
11   **if** $\mathbf{c}_{[j]} \neq 0$ **then**
12   ## Multiply row j with the inverse of its pivot
13     $(p_i) :=$ B2Minv($(\mathbf{T}_{[j,j]_i})$)
14     $(\mathbf{T}_{[j,j:m+1]_i}) =$ SecScalarMult($(\mathbf{T}_{[j,j:m+1]_i}), (p_i)$)
15   ## Subtract scalar multiple of row j from the rows below
16   **for** $k = j + 1$ *upto* m **do**
17       $(s_i) :=$ StrongRefresh($(\mathbf{T}_{[k,j]_i})$)
18       $(\mathbf{T}_{[k,j:m+1]_i}) =$ SecMultSub($(\mathbf{T}_{[j,j:m+1]_i}), (\mathbf{T}_{[k,j:m+1]_i}), (s_i)$)
19   **else return** $\perp$
20 **return** $((\mathbf{A}_i), (\mathbf{b}_i))$

This value is securely unmasked (`FullAdd`) and made public in Line 10: if the pivot is still zero the computation is terminated ($c_j == 0$).

Step 3: make pivot $\mathbf{T}_{[j,j]} = 1$. If the pivot element is non-zero, all elements of its row $(\mathbf{T}_{[j,:]_i})$ are multiplied with the inverse of the pivot in a masked fashion. We rely on the `B2Minv` gadget: the pivot element is first converted from its Boolean shared form to a multiplicative sharing, which allows us to compute its multiplicative inverse easily (Line 13). As a result, the `SecScalarMult` gadget operates on a Boolean shared variable and multiplicative shared scalar (Line 14). We note that we do not need to represent a zero coefficient in the multiplicative domain (zero-problem, see [21,27]) as the computation is aborted before in that case.

Step 4: make elements below pivot $\mathbf{T}_{[j,j]}$ zero. Finally, for each of the $k = m - j$ rows below the 'pivot-row' (Line 16–18), the element below the pivot is made zero (column j). Using the `SecMultSub` gadget in Line 18, the pivot-row j is subtracted $\mathbf{T}_{[k,j]}$ times from each row k below the pivot, in the masked domain.

3.6.1 Complexity

The run-time and randomness complexity of `SecRowEch` are:

$$
\begin{aligned}
T_{\texttt{SecRowEch}}(n,m) =& \frac{m^2-m}{2} \cdot (((5n^2+2n-1) + \lceil \log(w+1) \rceil \cdot (5n^2-n+2)) + 1) \\
&+ \frac{2m^3+3m^2+m}{6} \cdot (5n^2-3n) + m \cdot ((5n^2+2n-1) \\
&+ \lceil \log(w+1) \rceil \cdot (5n^2-n+2)) + m \cdot \frac{3n^2-n-2}{2} + m \\
&+ m \cdot \frac{5n^2-5n+4}{2} + \frac{m^2+3m}{2} \cdot (5n^2-3n) + \frac{m^2-m}{2} \cdot \\
&\frac{3n^2-3n}{2} + \frac{2m^3+3m^2+m}{6} \cdot \frac{7n^2-3n}{2}, \\
R_{\texttt{SecRowEch}}(n,m,w) =& \frac{m^2-m}{2} \cdot \frac{\lceil \log(w+1) \rceil^2 - \lceil \log(w+1) \rceil}{2} \cdot (n^2-n) \\
&+ \frac{2m^3+3m^2+m}{6} \cdot (n^2-n)w + m \cdot \frac{\lceil \log(w+1) \rceil^2 - \lceil \log(w+1) \rceil}{2} \cdot \\
&(n^2-n) + m \cdot \frac{(n^2-n)w}{2} + m \cdot \frac{n^2-n}{2} \cdot w + \frac{m^2+3m}{2} \cdot \\
&(n^2-n)w + \frac{m^2-m}{2} \cdot (\frac{n^2-n}{2} \cdot w) + \frac{2m^3+3m^2+m}{6} \cdot \frac{n^2-n}{2} \cdot w.
\end{aligned}
$$

3.6.2 Security We now argue about the first- and high-order security of Algorithm 6 by proving it to be t-NIo secure with $n = t+1$ shares and public output c. This means it provides resistance against an adversary with t probes and allows the algorithm to be used in larger compositions.

Lemma 5. *The gadget* `SecRowEch` *(Algorithm 6) is t-NIo secure with public output* **c**.

Proof. We first prove the security of Steps 1 through 4 from their composition of smaller gadgets.

***Step 1 (G_1 - G_6, t-SNI, Fig.** 4)*: we first show that a single iteration of the loop (Line 4–7) is t-SNI secure. We model the extraction of rows j and k (and elements within that row) from matrix $\mathbf{T}$ as t-NI gadgets G_1 - G_3. This is trivial to show as selected rows from the matrix pass through and the rest is discarded. The `SecNonzero` and `SecNOT` operations are modeled as t-SNI and t-NI gadgets G_4 and G_5, respectively. The `SecCondAdd` operation is modeled as t-SNI gadget G_6, operating on rows j and k. An adversary can probe each gadget G_i internally t_{G_i} and at the output o_{G_i}. The total number of probes in Step 1 is defined as $t_{S_1} = \sum_{i=1}^{6} t_{G_i} + \sum_{i=1}^{5} o_{G_i}$ and the output shares as $|O| = o_{G_6}$. We now show that the internal and output probes of each gadget in Step 1 can be perfectly simulated with $\leq t_{S_1}$ input shares. To simulate the internal and output probes of G_6, t_{G_6} shares of each of its inputs are required. Gadget G_4 is t-SNI and stops the propagation of probes to the input: only t_{G_4} shares of the output of G_3 are required. The internal probes and output shares of gadgets G_1 and G_2 can be simulated with a corresponding number of shares of the input ($\mathbf{T}_i$), which is a problem as the required input shares is (t_{G_1} +

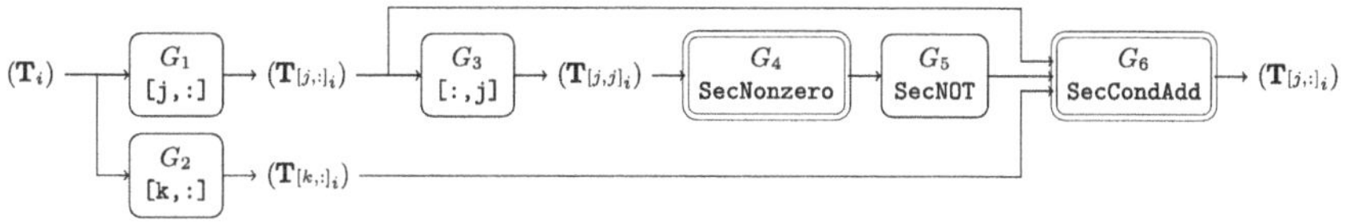

Fig. 4. An abstract diagram of a single iteration k of Step 1 in `SecRowEch` (Algorithm 6). Probes are defined at the row/column and element level (and not matrix-level) to ensure sound simulation.

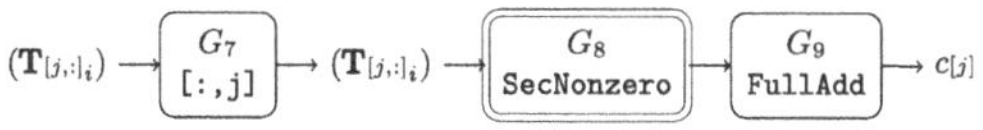

Fig. 5. An abstract diagram of Step 2 in `SecRowEch` (Algorithm 6).

$o_{G_1} + t_{G_2} + o_{G_2} + t_{G_3} + o_{G_3} + t_{G_4} + 2 \cdot t_{G_6})$. It is clear that on a variable-level the probes cannot be perfectly simulated, which is why all gadgets work on a matrix row (or element) level. As such, each of these gadgets only requires the shares of a specific row of the input. And because the rows are independent, t_{G_6} shares of row k and t_{G_6} shares of row j are required, and thus the simulation succeeds. For the entire composition, the required set of shares of the input is $|I| = t_{G_1} + o_{G_1} + t_{G_2} + o_{G_2} + t_{G_3} + o_{G_3} + t_{G_4} + t_{G_6}$, which is independent from $|O|$. As a result, each iteration is t-SNI secure, and as a result, the whole loop (Step 1) is too. □

***Step 2** (G₇ - G₉, t-NIo, **Fig.** 5)*: we model the extraction of element j from a matrix-row as t-NI gadget G_7. As can be seen in the abstract diagram, `SecNonzero` is the t-SNI gadget G_8 and `FullAdd` is t-NI secure G_9. It is clear from its chained structure that the full Step 2 is t-NI secure if $\mathbf{c}[j]$ is given to the simulator. □

***Step 3** (G_{10} - G_{12}, t-SNI, **Fig.** 6)*: initially, the pivot is extracted from row j of matrix $(\mathbf{T}_i)$, which we model as t-NI gadget G_{10}. The t-SNI operations `B2Minv` and `SecScalarMult` are modeled as gadgets G_{11} and G_{12}, respectively. An adversary can probe the intermediate values t_{G_i} and output shares o_{G_i} of each gadget G_i. The total number of possible probes in Step 3 is $t_{S_3} = \sum_{i=10}^{12} t_{G_i} + \sum_{i=10}^{11} o_{G_i}$ and its output shares as $|O| = o_{G_{12}}$. We now show that the internal and output probes of each gadget in Step 3 can be perfectly simulated with $\leq t_{S_3}$ input shares. To simulate the $t_{G_{12}}$ intermediate values and $o_{G_{12}}$ output shares of G_{12}, only $t_{G_{12}}$ shares of the input $(\mathbf{T}[j,:]_i)$ and the output of G_{11} are required. For G_{11} too, the t-SNI property allows to simulate all probes with only $t_{G_{11}}$ of its input. The simulation of $t_{G_{10}} + o_{G_{10}}$ probes on G_{10} requires the same amount of shares from its input. We now sum the required shares of the input $|I|$ that are required to simulate all probes on the gadgets in Step 3. As $|I| = t_{G_{10}} + o_{G_{10}} + t_{G_{11}} + t_{G_{12}} \leq t_{S_3}$ and independent of $|O|$, Step 3 is t-SNI. □

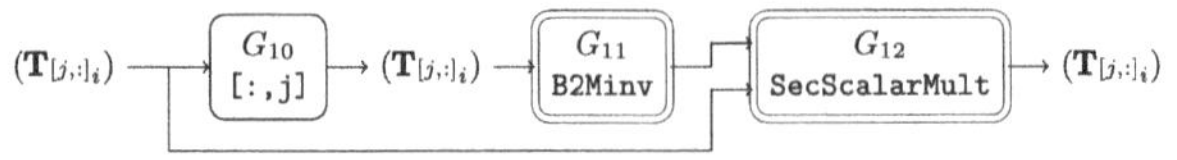

Fig. 6. An abstract diagram of Step 3 in SecRowEch (Algorithm 6).

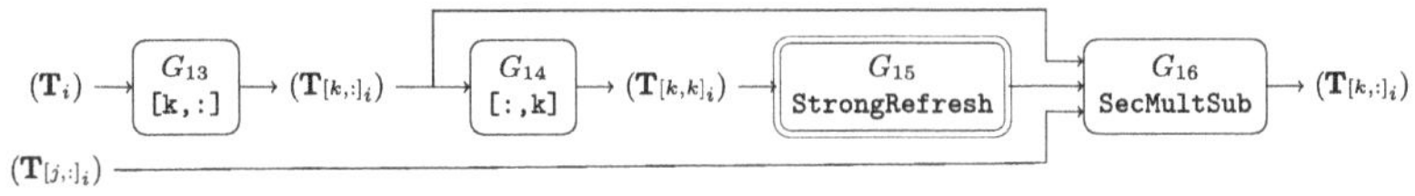

Fig. 7. An abstract diagram of a single iteration k of Step 4 in SecRowEch (Algorithm 6).

***Step 4* (G_{13} - G_{16}, *t-NI, Fig.* 7)**: we first show that a single iteration k of the loop (Line 17–20) is t-NI secure. The extraction of row k and its coefficient j from matrix $(\mathbf{T}_i)$ are modeled as t-NI gadgets G_{13} & G_{14}. We model StrongRefresh as t-SNI gadget G_{15} and the t-NI secure SecMultSub as G_{16}. An adversary can probe both intermediate values t_{G_i} and output shares o_{G_i} of each gadget G_i. The total number of probes in this step is $t_{S_4} = \sum_{i=13}^{16} t_{G_i} + \sum_{i=13}^{15} o_{G_i}$. We now show that all probes on intermediate values and output shares of each gadget in Step 4 can be perfectly simulated with $\leq t_{S_4}$ shares of both inputs. Simulating $t_{G_{16}}$ probes in G_16, requires $t_{G_{16}}$ probes of the output of G_{15}, input $(\mathbf{T}_{[j,:]_i})$ and $(\mathbf{T}_{[k,:]_i})$. Gadget G_{15} stops the propagation of probes from the output to the input, as it is t-SNI. Starting at the output of Step 4 and following the flow through all gadgets towards the input, all probes are summed ($|I|$). As $|I| = t_{G_{13}} + o_{G_{13}} + t_{G_{14}} + o_{G_{14}} + t_{G_{15}} + t_{G_{16}} \leq t_{S_4}$ shares of both inputs are required for simulation of an iteration k in Step 4, it is t-NI secure. As each iteration is independent and computing a single row k, they can be assumed to be executed in parallel. As a result, we can summarize the gadgets in each iteration as single gadgets across all iterations. This means the entire loop is t-NI. □

We now prove the larger composition (Algorithm 6) to be t-NIo. An abstract diagram of an iteration j is shown in Fig. 8, constructed from Step 1–4. We now show that a single (outer) loop is t-NI secure if the value $\mathbf{c}_{[j]}$ is given to the simulator. This is a direct result of each step achieving at least t-NI security and being composed as in Fig. 8 and all public outputs being securely recombined. This means all probes in a single iteration j can be simulated with no more

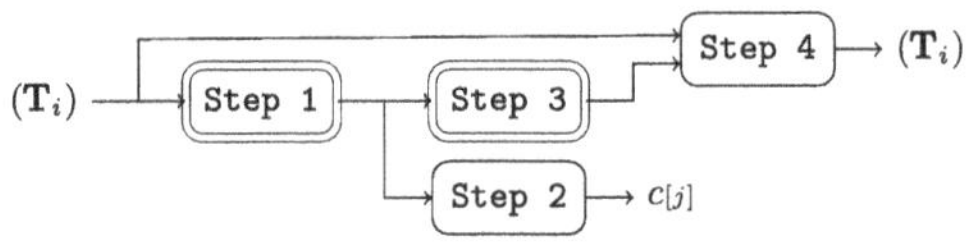

Fig. 8. An abstract diagram of a single iteration j of SecRowEch (Algorithm 6).

number of shares of $(\mathbf{T}_i)$. It is clear that if an adversary can place t probes across different iterations, these can also be simulated with no more number of input shares if $\mathbf{c}$ is given to the simulator. As a result, the entire gadget `SecRowEch` is t-NIo secure when $\mathbf{c}$ is public. □

3.7 Masked Back Substitution with Public Output

The second and final step in solving a system of linear equations ($\mathbf{Ax} = \mathbf{b}$), is performing back substitution on a system (e.g., matrix) in row-echelon form ($[\mathbf{A}_i \mid \mathbf{b}_i]$) and is Boolean shared. We propose to compute the unique solution $\mathbf{x}$ as a public output, with a secure recombination of the shares.

Algorithm 7: `SecBackSub`

Data: 1. A Boolean sharing $(\mathbf{A}_i)$ of matrix $\mathbf{A} \in \mathbb{F}_q^{m \times m}$
2. A Boolean sharing $(\mathbf{b}_i)$ of the vector $\mathbf{b} \in \mathbb{F}_q^m$.
Result: Unique, public solution $\mathbf{x} \in \mathbb{F}_q^m$ such that $\mathbf{Ax} = \mathbf{b}$

for $j = m$ *downto* 2 **do**
  $\mathbf{x}[j] = \texttt{FullAdd}((\mathbf{b}[j]_i))$
  for $k = 1$ *upto* $j - 1$ **do**
    $(\mathbf{b}[k]_i) := (\mathbf{b}[k]_i + \mathbf{x}[j] \cdot \mathbf{A}[k, j]_i)$
$\mathbf{x}[1] = \texttt{FullAdd}((\mathbf{b}[1]_i))$
return $\mathbf{x}$

More precisely, the system is solved by moving from the final row (m) to the first one, as in typical back substitution. Firstly, the solution of the current row $\mathbf{x}[j] = (\mathbf{b}[j]_i)$ is securely unmasked. Secondly, all the elements above in column j of $(\mathbf{A}_i)$ are made zero, by (securely) multiplying all its elements $(\mathbf{A}[1{:}j-1, j]_i)$ with the solution $\mathbf{x}[j]$. As the multiplier is unmasked, the operation can be performed share-wise. For each row, that result is subtracted from the element in vector $\mathbf{b}$, share by share. Finally, this process is repeated for all rows except the first one, which can be directly solved and unmasked.

3.7.1 Complexity The run-time and randomness complexity of `SecBackSub` are:

$$T_{\texttt{SecBackSub}}(n, m) = \frac{3}{2}n^2 m - \frac{3}{2}mn - m + m^2 n, \quad R_{\texttt{SecBackSub}}(n, m, w) = \frac{(n^2 - n)mw}{2}.$$

3.7.2 Security We now argue about the first- and high-order security of Algorithm 7 by proving it to be t-NIo secure with $n = t + 1$ shares and public output $\mathbf{x}$. This means it provides resistance against an adversary with t probes and allows the algorithm to be used in larger compositions.

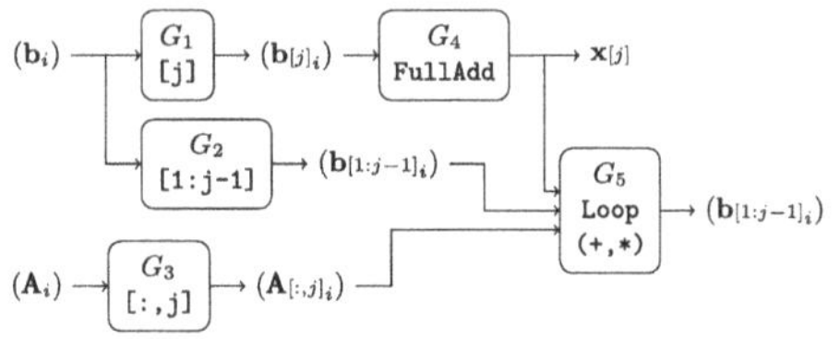

Fig. 9. An abstract diagram of a single iteration j of SecBackSub (Algorithm 7).

Lemma 6. *The gadget* SecBackSub *(Algorithm 7) is t-NIo secure with public output* $\mathbf{x}$.

Proof. We first show that a single iteration j is t-NIo secure with output $\mathbf{x}[j]$, of which an abstract diagram is shown in Fig. 9. We model the extraction of element j and column j from vector $(\mathbf{b}_i)$ and matrix $(\mathbf{A}_i)$ as t-NI gadgets G_1-G_2 and G_3, respectively. We also model the loop of share-wise multiplications and additions in Line 3–4 as a single t-NI gadget. As a result, the iterations are assumed to be executed in parallel, and we summarize them into a single gadget G_5. An adversary can probe the intermediate values t_{G_i} and output shares o_{G_i} of each gadget G_i, except the outputs of the entire gadget. The total number of probes in Algorithm 7 is $t_{A_7} = \sum_{i=1}^{5} t_{G_i} + \sum_{i=1}^{4} o_{G_i}$. To prove Lemma 6, we show that the internal and output probes of each gadget in Alg. 7 can be perfectly simulated with $\leq t_{A_7}$ input shares. As t-NI security implies that the simulation of internal and output probes of a gadget G_i requires a corresponding number of shares of its input. From this, it is clear that on a matrix/vector-level, the probes cannot be perfectly simulated as there are duplicate entries in the sum $(2 \cdot t_{G_5}$ of $(\mathbf{b}_i))$. To overcome this issue, we model gadget G_5 to operate on individual entries in row/column vectors rather than on the complete variables. As a result, to simulate t_{G_5} intermediate values requires t_{G_5} shares of element j and elements $[1 : j-1]$. As the coefficients inside a column/row are independent, the simulation succeeds. Following the flow from the output to the inputs, all probes required for simulation are summed up. We determine the set of shares of the inputs $|I|$, required for simulating the entire algorithm. As $|I| = t_{G_1} + o_{G_1} + t_{G_2} + o_{G_2} + t_{G_3} + o_{G_3} + t_{G_4} + o_{G_4} + t_{G_5} \leq t_{A_7}$, the iteration j is t-NI. We have shown that all t probes placed by an adversary in a single iteration j can be simulated with no more number of shares of inputs $(\mathbf{A}_i)$ and $(\mathbf{b}_i)$. As a result, all probes across different iterations can also be simulated with no more number of input shares. □

4 Application to Different Digital Signature Schemes

This section discusses the operational and randomness cost of the masked Gaussian elimination on multivariate- and code-based digital signatures. In total, we observed that at least the following ten UOV-based digital signatures use some variant of Gaussian elimination: UOV, MAYO, SNOVA, QR-UOV, MQ-Sign, PROV, VOX, TUOV, VDOO, IPRainbow, and WAVE. In between these

Table 2. Cost estimation of masked Gaussian elimination to different digital signature schemes. Here, m represents the dimension of the matrix $\mathbf{A}$, q represents the modulus, and n represents the number of masking shares.

Scheme	NIST Security Level	Scheme Parameters		Operations (x1000)			Randomness (KB)		
		q	m	$n=2$	$n=3$	$n=4$	$n=2$	$n=3$	$n=4$
UOV [7]	I	256	44	105	260	482	742	2226	4452
		16	64	300	747	1392	1112	3336	6671
	III	256	72	428	1065	1986	3146	9437	18873
	V	256	96	985	2459	4590	7360	22079	44158
MAYO [6]	I	16	64	300	747	1392	1112	3336	6671
	III	16	96	973	2434	4546	3680	11040	22079
	V	16	128	2263	5670	10597	8638	25914	51827
QR-UOV [19]	I	7	100	1084	2717	5076	3102	9306	18612
		31	60	249	619	1155	1147	3441	6881
		31	70	388	968	1806	1806	5417	10834
		127	54	184	457	852	1175	3524	7048
	III	7	140	2922	7333	13712	8431	25292	50584
		31	87	730	1825	3407	3432	10295	20590
		31	100	1097	2744	5125	5184	15550	31100
		127	78	531	1327	2476	3472	10415	20829
	V	7	190	7217	18131	33918	20942	62825	125650
		31	114	1610	4032	7533	7646	22937	45873
		31	120	1872	4689	8761	8904	26710	53419
		127	105	1265	3166	5914	8373	25119	50237
SNOVA [35]	I	16	68	357	890	1660	1329	3987	7974
		16	72	421	1051	1961	1573	4719	9437
		16	80	572	1428	2666	2147	6439	12877
	III	16	100	1097	2744	5125	2147	6439	12877
		16	99	1065	2664	4976	4031	12093	24186
		16	128	2263	5670	10597	8638	25914	51827
	V	16	132	2477	6209	11604	9465	28395	56789
		16	135	2647	6634	12400	10119	30356	60712
		16	160	4369	10959	20489	16773	50317	100634
MQ-Sign [33]	I	256	46	119	294	547	845	2534	5068
	III	256	72	428	1065	1986	3146	9437	18873
	V	256	96	985	2459	4590	7360	22079	44158

schemes, UOV, MAYO, SNOVA, and QR-UOV have advanced to the second round of the NIST additional digital signature standardization procedure [29], and MQ-Sign is a second-round candidate for the Korean PQC standardization procedure [31]. Therefore, we have restricted our cost analysis to these five multivariate-based digital signature candidates in this work. As seen from the complexity analysis in Sect. 3, the cost of the masked Gaussian elimination mainly depends on the dimension of the matrix $\mathbf{A}$ (m), the width of the modulus q (w), and the number of shares (n).

We present a cost analysis of the five selected schemes in Table 2. We have used the parameters of the corresponding scheme in the run-time and randomness complexity equations to calculate the expected arithmetic operational and randomness cost of the masked Gaussian elimination for each scheme, respectively. It can be seen from the table that the effect of the matrix dimension m and the share count n is much more potent in operation and randomness costs than the width of the modulus q. For instance, in the two versions of UOV for the NIST security level I, the operational cost of masked GE in UOV-Ip ($m = 44$ & $q = 256$) is 2.9× less compared to UOV-Is ($m = 64$ & $q = 16$) for first-, second-, and third-order masking. The randomness cost of GE in UOV-Ip is 1.5× less compared to UOV-Is for first, second, and third-order masking. Due to similar reasons, the operational cost of first-, second-, and third-order masked GE is 2.3× higher, and the randomness cost is 1.2× higher in MAYO compared to UOV for III and V, both security levels.

As the modulus q in QR-UOV is prime, we considered the next closest power-of-two integer as the modulus during the complexity cost analysis of masked Gaussian elimination on QR-UOV. However, the actual cost is likely to be higher because a masked prime modulus reduction is often more expensive than a masked power-of-two modulus reduction. We can also observe from Table 2 that the operational and randomness costs of masked GE in QR-UOV and SNOVA even vary hugely for the same security level. In fact, two NIST security level III variants ((i) $m = 87$ & $q = 31$, and (ii) $m = 78$ & $q = 127$) of QR-UOV are cheaper to protect than a NIST security level I variant ($m = 100$ & $q = 7$) of QR-UOV. We conclude that the main contributors to operational and randomness cost in masked GE with back substitution are matrix dimension m and masking order $t = n - 1$.

5 Implementation Results

In this section, we discuss our software (C, M4) implementation of the gadgets introduced in Sect. 3 and evaluate their performance for different UOV parameter sets and sharing degrees. The performance results are obtained from running our code[3], which we make publicly available, on the STM32Discovery board, containing an STM32 Arm Cortex-M4 microcontroller. We use the on-chip TRNG for on-the-fly randomness generation, which is included in the total cycle count. Below, we discuss and show results for practically relevant security orders ($n = 2, 3, 4$), but our implementation could be scaled up to arbitrary order. We emphasize that our implementation is only a proof-of-concept. Mitigation of micro-architectural leakages and optimized masked implementations are beyond the scope of this work and left as future work.

Table 3. Detailed performance overview (cycle counts ×1000) of masked Gaussian Elimination ($n = 2, 3, 4$) for UOV-I, -III, -V on Arm Cortex-M4.

Scheme	Operation	Umasked	Masked		
			1st-order	2nd-order	3rd-order
UOV-I (m=44 q=256)	GE (Total)	1034	**15649 (15.1×)**	**39587 (38.3×)**	**69186 (66.9×)**
	SecRowEch	999	15575 (15.6×)	39469 (39.5×)	69021 (69.1×)
	Step 1	80	1998 (25×)	5642 (70.5×)	9901 (123.8×)
	Step 2		39	108	193
	Step 3		598	1335	2426
	Step 4		12938	32383	56498
	SecBackSub	32	74 (2.3×)	118 (3.7×)	164 (5.1×)
UOV-III	GE (Total)	4117	**62680 (15.2×)**	**157901 (38.4×)**	**275768 (67×)**
UOV-V	GE (Total)	9336	**143361 (15.4×)**	**360590 (38.6×)**	**1025942 (109.9×)**

[3] arm-none-eabi-gcc v10.3.1.

5.1 Case Study: UOV

Table 3 shows the performance results (clock cycles) of our masked implementation for all three UOV security levels and scaled to first-, second- and third-masking order. We include the performance numbers of the unmasked UOV reference code [7], of the supported parameter sets. We repeat that the randomness generation overhead is included in the benchmarking results. The full masked GE operation results in about 15.1/15.2/15.4× overhead for 2 shares at NIST security level I/III/V. As expected, the performance overhead increases significantly for higher-order protected implementations. Our second-order masked implementation has overhead factor 38.3/38.4/38.6× for UOV-I, -III and -V, respectively. The third-order implementation has an overhead of 66.9–109.9× for different NIST security levels. The main contributor to the cycle count is the conversion to row-echelon form, more specifically, Steps 1 and 4 ($\sim$ 95%). At all protection orders, the repeated execution of `SecMultSub` and `SecCondAdd` are the main bottlenecks and good targets for future optimizations.

We observe that the masked implementation of Step 1, which makes the pivot element non-zero, has an overhead of $\sim$ 25/70/124× for 2/3/4 shares. The authors of UOV propose an optimization for the iteration of conditional additions (Algorithm 1), which we also implemented. Instead of iterating over all rows below the current pivot row (up to m), the UOV submission describes iterating over (and conditionally adding) only a few rows below the pivot row. The exact amount depends on the parameter selection but ensures a sufficiently low probability of the pivot element being non-zero. We encourage other UOV-like candidates to explore similar optimizations, which will lead to more efficient (masked) implementations of GE with back substitution.

6 Conclusions

In this work, we presented first- and higher-order masked algorithms for Gaussian elimination with back substitution: `SecRowEch` & `SecBackSub`. We analyze several novel multivariate- and code-based PQC schemes and show that GE is a critical operation for solving a system of linear equations and requires side-channel protection. For the same masking order, the matrix dimension m is the main contributor to operation and randomness cost in masked GE. The MAYO scheme has a larger m compared to UOV, and as a result, the GE is 2.3× and 1.2× more expensive to mask. Future work includes analysis of reduced iteration counts in the GE, as proposed in the UOV specification, for other PQC DS candidates. We implement our algorithms in C for arbitrary protection orders and parameter sets of different PQC schemes. We also evaluate its performance on Arm Cortex-M4 platforms. In future work, a complete masking and hardening against physical attacks for all mentioned schemes can be constructed using the methods proposed in this work.

Acknowledgements. This work was partially supported by Horizon 2020 ERC Advanced Grant (101020005 Belfort), Horizon Europe (101070008 ORSHIN), Cyber-Security Research Flanders with reference number VOEWICS02, BE QCI: Belgian-QCI (3E230370) (see beqci.eu), and Intel Corporation. Anindya Ganguly is supported by TCS research fellowship. The work of Angshuman Karmakar is supported by the Research-I foundation from Infosys, the Initiation grant from IIT Kanpur, and the Google India research fellowship.

References

1. Aulbach, T., Campos, F., Krämer, J., Samardjiska, S., Stöttinger, M.: Separating oil and vinegar with a single trace side-channel assisted Kipnis-Shamir attack on UOV. IACR Trans. Cryptogr. Hardw. Embed. Syst. **2023**(3), 221–245 (2023). https://doi.org/10.46586/TCHES.V2023.I3.221-245
2. Banegas, G., et al.: Wave specification document (2023). https://csrc.nist.gov/csrc/media/Projects/pqc-dig-sig/documents/round-1/spec-files/wave-spec-web.pdf
3. Barthe, G., et al.: Strong non-interference and type-directed higher-order masking. In: Weippl, E.R., Katzenbeisser, S., Kruegel, C., Myers, A.C., Halevi, S. (eds.) ACM CCS 2016, pp. 116–129. ACM Press (2016). https://doi.org/10.1145/2976749.2978427
4. Barthe, G., et al.: Masking the GLP lattice-based signature scheme at any order. In: Nielsen, J.B., Rijmen, V. (eds.) EUROCRYPT 2018. LNCS, vol. 10821, pp. 354–384. Springer, Cham (2018). https://doi.org/10.1007/978-3-319-78375-8_12
5. Bettale, L., Coron, J.S., Zeitoun, R.: Improved high-order conversion from Boolean to arithmetic masking. IACR Trans. Cryptogr. Hardw. Embed. Syst. 22–45 (2018). https://doi.org/10.46586/tches.v2018.i2.22-45
6. Beullens, W., Campos, F., Celi, S., Hess, B., Kannwischer, M.J.: Mayo specification document (2023). https://csrc.nist.gov/csrc/media/Projects/pqc-dig-sig/documents/round-1/spec-files/mayo-spec-web.pdf
7. Beullens, W., et al.: UOV: unbalanced oil and vinegar algorithm specifications and supporting documentation version 1.0 (2023). https://csrc.nist.gov/csrc/media/Projects/pqc-dig-sig/documents/round-1/spec-files/UOV-spec-web.pdf
8. Cartor, R., Cartor, M., Lewis, M., Smith-Tone, D.: IPRainbow. In: Cheon, J.H., Johansson, T. (eds.) PQCrypto 2022. LNCS, vol. 13512, pp. 170–184. Springer, Cham (2022). https://doi.org/10.1007/978-3-031-17234-2_9
9. Chari, S., Jutla, C.S., Rao, J.R., Rohatgi, P.: Towards sound approaches to counteract power-analysis attacks. In: Wiener, M. (ed.) CRYPTO 1999. LNCS, vol. 1666, pp. 398–412. Springer, Heidelberg (1999). https://doi.org/10.1007/3-540-48405-1_26
10. Chen, K.Y., Chen, J.P.: Masking floating-point number multiplication and addition of falcon: first-and higher-order implementations and evaluations. IACR Trans. Cryptogr. Hardw. Embed. Syst. **2024**(2), 276–303 (2024)
11. Chou, T., Kannwischer, M.J., Yang, B.: Rainbow on cortex-M4. IACR Trans. Cryptogr. Hardw. Embed. Syst. **2021**(4), 650–675 (2021). https://doi.org/10.46586/TCHES.V2021.I4.650-675
12. Cogliati, B., et al.: Vox specification document (2023). https://csrc.nist.gov/csrc/media/Projects/pqc-dig-sig/documents/round-1/spec-files/vox-spec-web.pdf

13. Coron, J.-S.: High-order conversion from Boolean to arithmetic masking. In: Fischer, W., Homma, N. (eds.) CHES 2017. LNCS, vol. 10529, pp. 93–114. Springer, Cham (2017). https://doi.org/10.1007/978-3-319-66787-4_5
14. Coron, J.S., Großschädl, J., Vadnala, P.K.: Secure conversion between Boolean and arithmetic masking of any order. In: International Workshop on Cryptographic Hardware and Embedded Systems, pp. 188–205. Springer (2014)
15. Coron, J.-S., Spignoli, L.: Secure wire shuffling in the probing model. In: Malkin, T., Peikert, C. (eds.) CRYPTO 2021. LNCS, vol. 12827, pp. 215–244. Springer, Cham (2021). https://doi.org/10.1007/978-3-030-84252-9_8
16. Coron, J.S., Gérard, F., Montoya, S., Zeitoun, R.: High-order polynomial comparison and masking lattice-based encryption. IACR Trans. Cryptogr. Hardw. Embed. Syst. 153–192 (2022). https://doi.org/10.46586/tches.v2023.i1.153-192
17. Coron, J.S., Gérard, F., Trannoy, M., Zeitoun, R.: Improved gadgets for the high-order masking of dilithium. IACR Trans. Cryptogr. Hardw. Embed. Syst. **2023**(4), 110–145 (2023). https://doi.org/10.46586/tches.v2023.i4.110-145
18. Ding, J., et al.: TUOV: specification document v1.0 (2023). https://csrc.nist.gov/csrc/media/Projects/pqc-dig-sig/documents/round-1/spec-files/TUOV-spec-web.pdf
19. Furue, H., et al.: QR-UOV specification document (2023). https://csrc.nist.gov/csrc/media/Projects/pqc-dig-sig/documents/round-1/spec-files/qruov-spec-web.pdf
20. Ganguly, A., Karmakar, A., Saxena, N.: VDOO: a short, fast, post-quantum multivariate digital signature scheme. In: Chattopadhyay, A., Bhasin, S., Picek, S., Rebeiro, C. (eds.) INDOCRYPT 2023, Part II. LNCS, vol. 14460, pp. 197–222. Springer, Cham (2023). https://doi.org/10.1007/978-3-031-56235-8_10
21. Genelle, L., Prouff, E., Quisquater, M.: Thwarting higher-order side channel analysis with additive and multiplicative maskings. In: Preneel, B., Takagi, T. (eds.) CHES 2011. LNCS, vol. 6917, pp. 240–255. Springer, Heidelberg (2011). https://doi.org/10.1007/978-3-642-23951-9_16
22. Goubin, L., et al.: PROV specification document (2023). https://csrc.nist.gov/csrc/media/Projects/pqc-dig-sig/documents/round-1/spec-files/prov-spec-web.pdf
23. Guerreau, M., Martinelli, A., Ricosset, T., Rossi, M.: The hidden parallelepiped is back again: power analysis attacks on falcon. IACR Trans. Cryptogr. Hardw. Embed. Syst. **2022**(3), 141–164 (2022). https://doi.org/10.46586/tches.v2022.i3.141-164
24. Ishai, Y., Sahai, A., Wagner, D.: Private circuits: securing hardware against probing attacks. In: Boneh, D. (ed.) CRYPTO 2003. LNCS, vol. 2729, pp. 463–481. Springer, Heidelberg (2003). https://doi.org/10.1007/978-3-540-45146-4_27
25. Ito, A., Ueno, R., Homma, N.: On the success rate of side-channel attacks on masked implementations: information-theoretical bounds and their practical usage. In: Proceedings of the 2022 ACM SIGSAC Conference on Computer and Communications Security, CCS '22, pp. 1521–1535. Association for Computing Machinery, New York (2022). https://doi.org/10.1145/3548606.3560579
26. Kundu, S., D'Anvers, J., Beirendonck, M.V., Karmakar, A., Verbauwhede, I.: Higher-order masked saber. In: Galdi, C., Jarecki, S. (eds.) SCN 2022. LNCS, vol. 13409, pp. 93–116. Springer, Cham (2022). https://doi.org/10.1007/978-3-031-14791-3_5
27. Mathieu-Mahias, A., Quisquater, M.: Mixing additive and multiplicative masking for probing secure polynomial evaluation methods. IACR Trans. Cryptogr. Hardw.

Embed. Syst. **2018**(1), 175–208 (2018). https://doi.org/10.13154/tches.v2018.i1.175-208
28. NIST: Call for additional digital signature schemes for the post-quantum cryptography standardization process (2022). https://csrc.nist.gov/csrc/media/Projects/pqc-dig-sig/documents/call-for-proposals-dig-sig-sept-2022.pdf. Accessed 30 Oct 2024
29. NIST: IR 8528: Status report on the first round of the additional digital signature schemes for the NIST post-quantum cryptography standardization process. Technical report, U.S. Department of Commerce, Washington, D.C. (2024). https://doi.org/10.6028/NIST.IR.8528
30. Park, A., Shim, K.A., Koo, N., Han, D.G.: Side-channel attacks on post-quantum signature schemes based on multivariate quadratic equations. IACR Trans. Cryptogr. Hardw. Embed. Syst. **2018**(3), 500–523 (2018). https://doi.org/10.13154/tches.v2018.i3.500-523
31. Quantum-Resistant Cryptography Research Group: KPQC competition round 2 (2024). https://www.kpqc.or.kr/competition_02.html. Accessed 30 Oct 2024
32. Schneider, T., Paglialonga, C., Oder, T., Güneysu, T.: Efficiently masking binomial sampling at arbitrary orders for lattice-based crypto. In: Lin, D., Sako, K. (eds.) PKC 2019. LNCS, vol. 11443, pp. 534–564. Springer, Cham (2019). https://doi.org/10.1007/978-3-030-17259-6_18
33. Shim, K.A., Kim, J., An, Y.: MQ-Sign: a new post-quantum signature scheme based on multivariate quadratic equations: shorter and faster (2023). https://www.kpqc.or.kr/images/pdf/MQ-Sign.pdf
34. Ulitzsch, V.Q., Marzougui, S., Tibouchi, M., Seifert, J.P.: Profiling side-channel attacks on Dilithium. In: Smith, B., Wu, H. (eds.) Selected Areas in Cryptography, pp. 3–32. Springer, Cham (2024)
35. Wang, L.C., et al.: SNOVA specification document (2023). https://csrc.nist.gov/csrc/media/Projects/pqc-dig-sig/documents/round-1/spec-files/SNOVA-spec-web.pdf
36. Yi, H., Nie, Z.: Side-channel security analysis of UOV signature for cloud-based Internet of Things. Future Gener. Comput. Syst. **86**, 704–708 (2018). https://doi.org/10.1016/J.FUTURE.2018.04.083

Post-quantum Online/Offline Signatures

Martin R. Albrecht, Nicolas Gama, James Howe(✉), and Anand Kumar Narayanan

SandboxAQ, Palo Alto, CA, USA
{martin.albrecht,nicolas.gama,james.howe,anand.narayanan}@sandboxaq.com

Abstract. Post-quantum signatures have high costs compared to RSA and ECDSA, in particular for smart cards. A line of work originating from Even, Goldreich, and Micali (CRYPTO'89) aimed to reduce digital signature latency by splitting up signing into an *online* and *offline* phase. The online/offline paradigm combines an ordinary long-term signature scheme with a fast, generally one-time, signature scheme. We reconsider this paradigm in the context of lattice-based post-quantum signatures in the GPV framework, with an example instantiation based on Falcon.

1 Introduction

In July 2022, NIST [1] announced its first set of post-quantum cryptography schemes intended for standardisation: the key encapsulation mechanism (KEM) Kyber (aka ML-KEM in FIPS 203 [31]), and three digital signature schemes, Dilithium (aka ML-DSA in FIPS 204 [30]), SPHINCS$^+$ (aka SLH-DSA in FIPS 205 [38]), and lastly Falcon (aka FN-DSA) [36]. While Kyber has *computational* costs similar to RSA and elliptic curves, all three signature standards/standardisation candidates compare less favourably.

Online/offline signatures were formally introduced by Even, Goldreich and Micali [13,14] as a way to speed-up the signing process in applications with constrained computing resources or where signature latency is critical, such as in smart cards. The construction relies on (fast) one-time digital signature algorithms as well as standard (slower) digital signature algorithms.

The basic idea is to break-up signature generation into two parts, one of which is a pre-computation (*offline*), independent of any message m to be signed. This pre-computation can be executed during idle time and consists of the generation of a one-time public-key and secret-key pair, where the one-time public-key is signed using the long-term secret-key. This signing operation will be more computationally expensive than the one-time signature scheme. The *online* phase then depends on and signs m, using the one-time signature scheme with the one-time keys as input.

Among the signature schemes selected, Falcon was selected by NIST for its more compact signatures and fast verification: "due to its low bandwidth and fast verification, Falcon may be a superior choice in some constrained protocol scenarios" [1]. However, for general-purpose constrained applications, Falcon does

A. Patra (Ed.): CT-RSA 2025, LNCS 15598, pp. 273–300, 2025.
https://doi.org/10.1007/978-3-031-88661-4_12

not seem the appropriate choice, as the same report notes. This is in addition to its reliance on double-precision floating-point arithmetic for fast implementation, which can potentially cause issues with signature correctness and which adds an additional attack vector [18,21,22,25,40].

Falcon's genealogy dates back to the earliest proposals for lattice-based signatures, including GGH [17] and NTRUSign [20]. The general idea of these signatures is that the verification key consists of a description of a lattice and the signing key consists of a trapdoor, allowing to sample short elements in the lattice. This then allows to find vectors in the span of the lattice that are close to some target vector produced by calling $H(m)$, where $H(\cdot)$ is some hash function, modelled as a Random Oracle. As noted in [32], care must be taken that these close vectors do not leak information about the trapdoor. Indeed, in [32] devastating attacks were presented against both GGH and NTRUSign, recovering the secret trapdoor using statistical methods on the signatures.

With the GPV framework [16], a method was proposed to produce signatures that are statistically close to being independent of the trapdoor, leading to a signature scheme framework with provable guarantees. Later, NTRUSign was improved [39] and also used to build an identity-based encryption scheme [7]. With further improvements [10], the groundwork was laid for a practical and secure hash-and-sign lattice-based signature scheme, producing Falcon. Proposals to improve upon Falcon were subsequently proposed [9,12].

Carefully sampling from a distribution essentially independent of the trapdoor as in [16] requires noticeable computational resources and typically floating-point arithmetic, leading to the "downsides" noted above.

Given that the attacks from [32] mentioned above are statistical, it is natural to ask how many signatures are required to mount them. Put differently, in an online/offline paradigm where we instantiate the one-time signature scheme with (essentially) NTRUSign, how many signatures can be produced before security no longer holds?

To tackle this question, we rely on statistical tools introduced to the area of lattice-based cryptography in [5]: the Rényi divergence.

1.1 Contributions

We revisit the idea of online/offline signatures for the post-quantum era and propose a simple and efficient signature scheme, along the lines of GPV, which is partially interoperable with Falcon.

We provide a security proof for the proposed signature scheme, quantifying the security as a function of the number of online signatures furnished. This means that our scheme guarantees security only if a tiny number of online signatures allowed before refreshing in the offline phase. In particular, this implies that statistical/geometric attacks such as [8,32] that broke NTRUSign will not infer anything significant about the ephemeral secret key from seeing these few online signatures. A key ingredient in our security proof is Rényi divergence analysis as in [5]. En route, we present new bounds for the Rényi divergence of a discrete spherical Gaussian and a discrete spherical Gaussian convolved (of possibly different mean and covariance) with a compact distribution. This is implicit in the proof of Lemma 1 and may be of use in other cryptographic contexts. We derive these new bounds from first principles since the standard Rényi divergence bounds from [5] and its extensions do not quite apply.

We adapt our scheme to the Falcon setting and show that the scheme remains secure, by quantifying the security in terms of the number of online signatures. Design choices such as lattice dimension, modulus, etc. conform to Falcon-512, enabling easy adoption. Further, key generation and signature verification remain unchanged from Falcon, except for an increase in the allowed verification threshold norm of the signatures. This allows the long-term and few-time signature schemes to share modules, reducing footprint and benefiting implementations on constrained or embedded devices. The signature scheme can be used in different environments, ranging from one-time use up to eight uses. We provide performance expectations based on the security needs of the application within these ranges. As expected, our implementation provides good performance in the online phase when considering a floating point implementation. We consider this permissible despite potential side-channel attack concerns because of the low number of signing operations performed per key.

1.2 Organisation

In Sect. 2, we build up the required mathematical notation and briefly describe the cryptographic definitions and primitives used. In Sect. 3, we present the online/offline signature scheme based on GPV signatures and prove its security. Parts of the proof are deferred to Sect. 4.1. In Sect. 4, we tailor our online/offline signature scheme to Falcon and derive concrete security guarantees in terms of the number of online signatures. In Sect. 4.1, we detail the implementation of our Falcon-based online/offline scheme and present benchmarks to highlight its practicality.

2 Preliminaries

Lattices. We write vectors as columns vectors and use boldface latin alphabets, such as $\mathbf{u}$ or $\mathbf{v}$. The i-th coordinate of a vector $\mathbf{u}$ will be denote as u_i. Matrices will be written with boldface capital latin alphabets such as $\mathbf{A}, \mathbf{B}$. We write $\mathbb{I}_n$ for the identity matrix in dimension n. In our context, a lattice is a discrete free $\mathbb{Z}$-submodule of a finite dimensional real vector space, endowed with the Euclidean metric. The dimension of a lattice is its rank as a $\mathbb{Z}$-module. Lattices we encounter will be explicitly presented in one of the following two ways. In ambient dimension d, an ordered basis $\mathbf{B} := (\mathbf{b}_1, \mathbf{b}_2, \ldots, \mathbf{b}_n) \subset \mathbb{R}^d$ of $\mathbb{R}$-linearly independent vectors defines the rank n lattice $\mathcal{L}(\mathbf{B}) := \{\sum_{i=1}^{n} z_i \cdot \mathbf{b}_i \mid \mathbf{z} \in \mathbb{Z}^n\} \subset \mathbb{R}^d$. The basis $\mathbf{B}$ will also be thought of as the matrix $\mathbf{B}$ consisting of $(\mathbf{b}_1, \mathbf{b}_2, \ldots, \mathbf{b}_n)$ as its sequence of columns, and vice versa. Therefore, $\mathcal{L}(\mathbf{B})$ is the $\mathbb{Z}$-module generated by the columns of $\mathbf{B}$. The second way lattices are presented as sets. For example, the dual of a lattice $\Lambda \subset \mathbb{R}^d$ is defined as $\Lambda^* := \left\{\mathbf{u} \in \mathbb{R}^d \mid \langle \mathbf{u}, \mathbf{x} \rangle \in \mathbb{Z}, \forall \mathbf{x} \in \Lambda\right\} \subset$

$\mathbb{R}^d$ where $\langle , \rangle$ is the inner product in $\mathbb{R}^d$. In either case, lattices are embedded in some real space $\mathbb{R}^d$, which endows them with the Euclidean metric.

For a positive odd integer q, let $\mathbb{Z}_q$ denote the ring $\mathbb{Z}/q\mathbb{Z}$ of residues modulo q and we choose $\{-\lfloor \frac{q}{2} \rfloor, \ldots, 0, \ldots, \lfloor \frac{q}{2} \rfloor\} \subset \mathbb{Z}$ as a preferred set of representatives. For a vector $\mathbf{x} \in \mathbb{Z}^d$ with integer coordinates, let $\mathbf{x} \bmod q \in \mathbb{Z}_q^d$ denote the reduction of each coordinate modulo q.

Babai's Rounding. Babai's rounding algorithm [4] is an algorithm to find a lattice point close to a given target point. This is efficient to compute given a "good" basis $\mathbf{G}$ for a lattice and a target vector $\mathbf{c}$, where $\mathbf{c}$ is in the column $\mathbb{R}$-span of $\mathbf{G}$. The algorithm proceeds by computing $\mathbf{G} \cdot \lfloor \mathbf{G}^{-1} \cdot \mathbf{c} \rceil$. In essence, writing the target $\mathbf{c} = \sum_{i=1}^{d} \alpha_i \cdot \mathbf{g}_i$ as a real linear combination of the columns of $\mathbf{G}$, the Babai rounding $\mathbf{G} \cdot \lfloor \mathbf{G}^{-1} \cdot \mathbf{c} \rceil = \sum_{i=1}^{d} \lfloor \alpha_i \rceil \cdot \mathbf{g}_i$ is the lattice vector obtained by rounding the real coordinates to the nearest integers $\lfloor \alpha_i \rceil$.

Babai's Nearest Plane. As before, consider a good basis $\mathbf{G}$ and a target vector $\mathbf{c} \in \mathbb{R}^d$ in the column $\mathbb{R}$-span of $\mathbf{G}$. Babai's nearest plane algorithm [4] starts at the d-th dimension and asks for a lattice vector $\mathbf{v}_d$, which by addition shifts the real hyperplane $H_{\mathbf{G}}^{d-1}$ generated by first $d-1$ columns of $\mathbf{G}$ closest to $\mathbf{c}$. To find $\mathbf{v}_d$, write the target $\mathbf{c} = \sum_{i=1}^{d} \alpha_i \cdot \mathbf{g}_i^*$ as a real linear combination of the Gram-Schmidt orthogonalisation vectors $\mathbf{g}_i^*$ of the columns of $\mathbf{G}$ and set $\mathbf{v}_d \leftarrow \lfloor \alpha_d \rceil \cdot \mathbf{g}_d$, where $\lfloor \alpha_d \rceil$ is the nearest integer to α_d. The solution for the nearest plane algorithm is $\sum_{i=1}^{d} \mathbf{v}_i$, where one solves for $\mathbf{v}_{d-1}$ recursively, as follows. Forget the last column of $\mathbf{G}$ and consider the same problem, now in one fewer dimension with the new target $\sum_{i=1}^{d-1} \alpha_i \cdot \mathbf{g}_i^* + \lfloor \alpha_d \rceil \cdot \mathbf{g}_d^* - \lfloor \alpha_d \rceil \cdot \mathbf{g}_d$. Here, $\sum_{i=1}^{d-1} \alpha_i \cdot \mathbf{g}_i^* + \lfloor \alpha_d \rceil \cdot \mathbf{g}_d^*$ is the orthogonal projection of $\mathbf{c}$ onto $\lfloor \alpha_d \rceil \cdot \mathbf{g}_d + H_{\mathbf{G}}^{d-1}$. The closeness guarantee of the output to the target is better for the nearest planes compared to rounding. There are also randomised versions of the nearest plane algorithm, including fast versions applicable to special lattices [10]. But rounding is much faster, in comparison with both the plain and the specialised randomised versions.

NTRU Lattices. Let $n = 2^a$ denote a positive power of 2. The NTRU lattices underlying Falcon are certain rank 2 modules over the ring of integers $\mathcal{O}_n \cong \mathbb{Z}(X)/\langle X^n + 1 \rangle$ of the 2n-th cyclotomic field $\mathbb{Q}(X)/\langle X^n + 1 \rangle$, embedded in an inner product space over $\mathbb{R}(X)/\langle X^n + 1 \rangle$, generated as follows. Let q be a prime number that splits in the extension $\mathcal{O}_n/\mathbb{Z}$. That is, $q = 1 \bmod \varphi(n)$, where $\varphi(n) = 2^a - 2^{a-1}$ is the Euler's totient. Start with a secret key consisting of $f, g, F, G \in \mathcal{O}_N$ such that $f \cdot G - g \cdot F = q$, f modulo $q\mathcal{O}_n$ is a unit and integer vectors corresponding to the representations of f, g, F, G are short. Short enough means that the matrix $\mathbf{B} := \begin{bmatrix} g & -f \\ G & -F \end{bmatrix}^t$ has Gram-Schmidt norm at most a constant times $\sqrt{q}$, and is the secret trapdoor basis. When instantiating using Falcon parameters, this constant will be 1.17. The NTRU lattice associated with the secret key f, g, F, G is the rank 2 $\mathcal{O}_n$-module generated by $\mathbf{B}$. The public key is then set as the unique $h \in \mathcal{O}_n$ satisfying $h = g \cdot f^{-1} \mod q\mathcal{O}_n$. Then the same NTRU lattice is also generated by $\left[\begin{smallmatrix} 1 & h \\ 0 & q \end{smallmatrix}\right]^t$, except, this public basis of the same lattice is not short by design. The public and private bases can both be represented succinctly as elements in the ring $\mathcal{O}_n$, which can be thought of as polynomials. In fact, Falcon represents the trapdoor in the Fourier basis as detailed Sect. 2.5, facilitating fast signing times. We will build our signature scheme in the language of lattices over $\mathbb{Z}$, and then specialize to NTRU lattices. Therefore, it is conceptually helpful to also think of the NTRU lattices, which are $\mathcal{O}_n$-modules as lattices over $\mathbb{Z}$. To this end, associate with $-f$, the $n \times n$ integer matrix whose i-th row is the integer vector corresponding to $-f \cdot X^i \mod X^n + 1$. Likewise, for the other elements $g, -F, G$ and h. Under this correspondence, the NTRU lattice may also be viewed as a rank $2n$-lattice over $\mathbb{Z}$.

Distributions. For $\mathbf{c} \in \mathbb{R}^d$ and a positive $s \in \mathbb{R}$, let $\rho_{\mathbf{c},s} : \mathbb{R}^d \longrightarrow \mathbb{R}$ taking $\mathbf{x} \longmapsto \exp\left(-\pi\|\mathbf{x} - \mathbf{c}\|^2/s^2\right)$ denote the Gaussian function with parameter s and centred at $\mathbf{c}$. For a lattice $\Lambda \subset \mathbb{R}^d$, positive $s \in \mathbb{R}$ and vector $\mathbf{c} \in \mathbb{R}^d$, let $D_{\Lambda,s,\mathbf{c}}$ denote the spherical discrete Gaussian probability mass function with support Λ and mass proportional to $D_{\Lambda,s,\mathbf{c}}(\mathbf{x}) \sim \rho(\mathbf{c}, s), \forall\, \mathbf{x} \in \Lambda$. That is,

$$D_{\Lambda,s,\mathbf{c}}(\mathbf{x}) = \frac{\rho_{\mathbf{c},s}(\mathbf{s})}{\sum_{\mathbf{x}\in\Lambda} \rho_{\mathbf{c},s}(\mathbf{x})}, \forall\, \mathbf{x} \in \Lambda.$$

When the discrete Gaussian is centered at the origin, we sometimes suppress the last subscript, that is, $\mathcal{D}_{\Lambda,s} := \mathcal{D}_{\Lambda,s,\mathbf{0}}$. For a lattice Λ and a positive real ϵ, the smoothing parameter $\eta_\epsilon(\Lambda)$ is the smallest positive real number s such that $\sum_{\mathbf{s}\in\Lambda\setminus\mathbf{0}} \rho(\mathbf{s}, 1/s) \geq \epsilon$ [29].

Rényi Divergence. Following [5], the order $a \in (1, \infty]$ Rényi divergence of a pair $(\mathcal{P}, \mathcal{Q})$ of discrete distributions with $\mathrm{Supp}(\mathcal{P}) \subseteq \mathrm{Supp}(\mathcal{Q})$ is defined as

$$R_a(\mathcal{P}||\mathcal{Q}) := \left(\sum_{x\in\mathrm{Supp}(\mathcal{P})} \frac{\mathcal{P}(x)^a}{\mathcal{Q}(x)^{a-1}}\right)^{\frac{1}{a-1}}. \tag{1}$$

We use the following two properties of Rényi divergence in our security proofs.

- Probability preservation: For every event $E \subseteq \mathrm{Supp}(\mathcal{P})$ and $a \in (1, \infty]$

$$\mathcal{Q}(E) \geq \frac{\mathcal{P}(E)^{\frac{a}{a-1}}}{R_a\left(\mathcal{P}||\mathcal{Q}\right)}. \tag{2}$$

- Multiplicativity: The Rényi divergence of a pair of product distributions is the product of the Rényi divergences, that is,

$$R_a\left(\prod_i \mathcal{P}_i || \prod_i \mathcal{Q}_i\right) = \prod_i R_a(\mathcal{P}_i||\mathcal{Q}_i). \tag{3}$$

2.1 Digital Signatures

Definition 1 (Signature Scheme). *A signature scheme* Σ *consists of three PPT algorithms* $(\mathsf{KeyGen}, \mathsf{Sign}, \mathsf{Verify})$ *such that:*

KeyGen *The key generation algorithm is a randomised algorithm that takes as input a security parameter* 1^λ *and outputs a pair* $(\mathsf{vk}, \mathsf{sk})$, *the* verification key *and* signing key, *respectively. We write* $(\mathsf{vk}, \mathsf{sk}) \leftarrow \mathsf{KeyGen}(1^\lambda)$.

Sign *The signing algorithm takes as input a signing key* sk *and a message* μ *and outputs a signature* σ. *We write this as* $\sigma \leftarrow \mathsf{Sign}(\mathsf{sk}, \mu)$. *The signing algorithm may be randomised or deterministic. We may write* $\sigma \leftarrow \mathsf{Sign}(\mathsf{sk}, \mu; r)$ *to unearth the used randomness explicitly.*

Verify *The verification algorithm takes as input a verification key* vk, *a signature* σ *and a message* μ *and outputs a bit* b, *with* $b = 1$ *meaning the signature is valid and* $b = 0$ *meaning the signature is invalid.* Verify *is a deterministic algorithm. We write* $b \leftarrow \mathsf{Verify}(\mathsf{vk}, \sigma, \mu)$.

We require that except with negligible probability over $(\mathsf{vk}, \mathsf{sk}) \leftarrow \mathsf{KeyGen}(1^\lambda)$, *it holds that* $\mathsf{Verify}(\mathsf{vk}, \mathsf{Sign}(\mathsf{sk}, \mu), \mu) = 1$ *for all* μ.

We rely on the standard notion of existential unforgeability under chosen message attacks:

Definition 2 (EUF-CMA). *We define*

$$\mathsf{Adv}^{\text{euf-cma}}_{\mathcal{A},\Sigma}(\lambda) := \Pr[\text{EUF-CMA}^{\mathcal{A}}_{\Sigma}(\lambda) \Rightarrow 1]$$

for $\text{EUF-CMA}^{\mathcal{A}}_{\Sigma}(\lambda)$ *as in Fig. 1 (with* $Q > \mathsf{poly}(\lambda)$*) and say a signature scheme* Σ *is EUF-CMA secure if no PPT/BQP adversary* $\mathcal{A}$ *has non-negligible advantage* $\mathsf{Adv}^{\text{euf-cma}}_{\mathcal{A},\Sigma}(\lambda)$.

2.2 Few-Times Signatures

We will rely on "few-times signature" schemes, which are signature schemes that promise unforgeability in the presence of a signing oracle supporting up to Q signatures.

Definition 3 (EUF-CMA$_Q$). *We define*

$$\mathsf{Adv}^{\text{euf-cma}}_{\mathcal{A},\Sigma,Q}(\lambda) := \Pr[\text{EUF-CMA}^{\mathcal{A}}_{\Sigma,Q}(\lambda) \Rightarrow 1]$$

for $\text{EUF-CMA}^{\mathcal{A}}_{\Sigma,Q}(\lambda)$ *as in Fig. 1 and say a signature scheme* Σ *is EUF-CMA secure for* Q *queries if no PPT/BQP adversary* $\mathcal{A}$ *has non-negligible advantage* $\mathsf{Adv}^{\text{euf-cma}}_{\mathcal{A},\Sigma,Q}(\lambda)$.

$\text{EUF-CMA}_{\Sigma,Q}^{\mathcal{A}}(\lambda)$	$\mathsf{SIGN}(\mu)$
$\mathcal{Q}, c \leftarrow \emptyset, 0$	**if** $c \geq Q$ **then abort**
$\mathsf{vk}, \mathsf{sk} \leftarrow \Sigma.\mathsf{KeyGen}(1^\lambda)$	$\sigma \leftarrow \Sigma.\mathsf{Sign}(\mathsf{sk}, \mu)$
$(\mu^\star, \sigma^\star) \leftarrow \mathcal{A}^{\mathsf{SIGN}}(\mathsf{vk})$	$c \leftarrow c + 1$
return $(\mu^\star, \cdot) \notin \mathcal{Q} \wedge \mathsf{Verify}(\mathsf{vk}, \sigma^\star, \mu^\star)$	$\mathcal{Q} \leftarrow \mathcal{Q} \cup \{(\mu, \sigma)\}$
	return σ

Fig. 1. Existential Unforgeability under Chosen Message Attacks Few Times Signature Schemes (EUF-CMA$_Q$). EUF-CMA is recovered by setting $Q > \mathsf{poly}(\lambda)$.

2.3 Online/Offline Signatures

The notion of online/offline signatures was first proposed by Even, Goldreich, and Micali in [13,27], and improved upon in later works [14,37]. The online/offline paradigm aims to offload significant amounts of computation to a precomputation (or offline) phase that does not depend on the message and can thus be precomputed.

Definition 4 (Online/Offline Signature Scheme). *An online-offline signature scheme* Σ *consists of four PPT algorithms* (KeyGen, PreSign, Sign, Verify) *such that:*

KeyGen *The key generation algorithm is a randomised algorithm that takes as input a security parameter* 1^λ *and outputs a pair* (vk, sk)*, the* verification key *and* signing key*, respectively. We write* $(\mathsf{vk}, \mathsf{sk}) \leftarrow \mathsf{KeyGen}(1^\lambda)$.

PreSign *The pre-signing algorithm takes as input the signing key* sk *and outputs a pre-signing state* ρ*. The presigning algorithm is randomised. We write this as* $\rho \leftarrow \mathsf{PreSign}(\mathsf{sk})$*. The signing algorithm may be randomised or deterministic. We may write* $\rho \leftarrow \mathsf{PreSign}(\mathsf{sk}; r)$ *to unearth the used randomness explicitly.*

Sign *The signing algorithm takes as input a signing key* sk*, a pre-signing stage* ρ *and a message* μ *and outputs a signature* σ*. We write this as* $\sigma \leftarrow \mathsf{Sign}(\mathsf{sk}, \rho, \mu)$*. The signing algorithm may be randomised or deterministic. We may write* $\sigma \leftarrow \mathsf{Sign}(\mathsf{sk}, \rho, \mu; r)$ *to unearth the used randomness explicitly.*

Verify *The verification algorithm takes as input a verification key* vk*, a signature* σ *and a message* μ *and outputs a bit* b*, with* $b = 1$ *meaning the signature is valid and* $b = 0$ *meaning the signature is invalid.* Verify *is a deterministic algorithm. We write* $b \leftarrow \mathsf{Verify}(\mathsf{vk}, \sigma, \mu)$.

We require that except with negligible probability over $(\mathsf{vk}, \mathsf{sk}) \leftarrow \mathsf{KeyGen}(1^\lambda)$ *and over* $\rho \leftarrow \mathsf{PreSign}(\mathsf{sk})$*, it holds that* $\mathsf{Verify}(\mathsf{vk}, \mathsf{Sign}(\mathsf{sk}, \rho, \mu), \mu) = 1$ *for all* μ.

Online-offline signature schemes can be constructed generically by composing two signature schemes. A regular long-term signature scheme, for the offline phase, and a one-time or few-time signature scheme, for both online and offline

$\mathsf{KeyGen}(1^\lambda)$	$\mathsf{PreSign}(\mathsf{sk})$	$\mathsf{Sign}(\mathsf{sk}, \rho, \mu)$
$\mathsf{vk}, \mathsf{sk} \leftarrow \Sigma.\mathsf{KeyGen}(1^\lambda)$	$\mathsf{vk}_Q, \mathsf{sk}_Q \leftarrow \Sigma_Q.\mathsf{KeyGen}(1^\lambda)$	**assert** $\rho.c < Q$
return vk, sk	$\sigma \leftarrow \Sigma.\mathsf{Sign}(\mathsf{sk}, \mathsf{vk}_Q)$	$\sigma_Q \leftarrow \Sigma_Q.\mathsf{Sign}(\rho.\mathsf{sk}_Q, \mu)$
	$c \leftarrow 0$	$\rho.c \leftarrow \rho.c + 1$
	return $\rho := (\mathsf{vk}_Q, \mathsf{sk}_Q, \sigma, c)$	**return** $\sigma := (\rho.\mathsf{vk}_Q, \rho.\sigma, \sigma_Q)$

$\mathsf{Verify}(\mathsf{vk}, \sigma, \mu)$
return $\Sigma.\mathsf{Verify}(\mathsf{vk}, \sigma, \mathsf{vk}_Q) \wedge \Sigma_Q.\mathsf{Verify}(\mathsf{vk}_Q, \sigma_Q, \mu)$

Fig. 2. A generic online/offline signature scheme construction.

phases. We will denote the former by Σ and the latter by Σ_Q. We give the generic construction in Fig. 2.

The security notion for online-offline signature schemes is identical to the EUF-CMA notion for general signature schemes except for semantic changes. In particular, the adversary has oracle access to both Sign and PreSign and its advantage is bounded as follows.

Proposition 1. *Let Σ' be the online-offline construction in Fig. 2. Then for any PPT $\mathcal{A}$, we have $2 \cdot \mathsf{Adv}^{\text{euf-cma}}_{\mathcal{A},\Sigma'}(\lambda) \leq \mathsf{Adv}^{\text{euf-cma}}_{\mathcal{B},\Sigma}(\lambda) + Q' \cdot \mathsf{Adv}^{\text{euf-cma}}_{\mathcal{C},\Sigma_Q,Q}(\lambda)$, where $\mathcal{B}$ and $\mathcal{C}$ are PPT adversaries against Σ and Σ_Q respectively and where Q' is the total number of queries made by $\mathcal{A}$.*

Proof (Sketch). The verification algorithm checks $\Sigma.\mathsf{Verify}(\mathsf{vk}, \sigma, \mathsf{vk}_Q)$ and also $\Sigma_Q.\mathsf{Verify}(\mathsf{vk}_Q, \sigma_Q, \mu)$, so to win an adversary either produced a forgery for Σ or for some Σ_Q. The factor Q' is an artefact of the reduction guessing which instance of Σ_Q the adversary will produces a forgery on; there are at most Q' many of these.

Performance. As discussed above, the appeal of the online-offline approach and the generic construction given in Fig. 2 is to reduce latency when signing messages by pre-computing expensive steps. This comes at a cost of bandwidth (one verification key and two signatures are output by the signing algorithm) and at a cost for verification (two signatures need to be checked). We note that the bandwidth cost can be amortised in some settings.

2.4 GPV Signatures

The framework proposed by Gentry, Peikert, and Vaikuntanathan [16], commonly known as the GPV framework, provides a generic and provably secure hash-and-sign framework based on trapdoor sampling and the Random Oracle Model, see Fig. 3. It can be seen as a provable "fix" for the GGH signature scheme. The key ingredient here is a sampling algorithm that outputs signatures $\mathbf{s}$ whose distribution is statistically close to being independent of the trapdoor td. Let (TrapGen, SampD, SampPre) be PPT algorithms with the following syntax and properties [15,16,28]:

- $(\mathbf{A}, \mathsf{td}) \leftarrow \mathsf{TrapGen}(1^n, 1^m, q)$ takes dimensions $n, m \in \mathbb{N}$, a modulus $q \in \mathbb{N}$. It generates a matrix $\mathbf{A} \in \mathbb{Z}_q^{n\times m}$ and a trapdoor td. For any $n \in \mathsf{poly}(\lambda)$ and $m \geq 5\, n \log q$, the distribution of $\mathbf{A}$ is within $\mathsf{negl}(\lambda)$ statistical distance to the uniform distribution on $\mathbb{Z}_q^{n\times m}$.
- $\mathbf{u} \leftarrow \mathsf{SampD}(1^n, 1^m, s)$ with $m \geq 5\, n \log q$ outputs an element in $\mathbf{u} \leftarrow_{\$} D_{\mathbb{Z}^m, s}$. We have that $\mathbf{v} := \mathbf{A} \cdot \mathbf{u} \bmod q$ is within $\mathsf{negl}(\lambda)$ statistical distance to the uniform distribution on $\mathbb{Z}_q^n$ if $s \geq \eta_\varepsilon(\Lambda_q^\perp(\mathbf{A}))$ for some $\varepsilon \in \mathsf{negl}(\lambda)$.
- $\mathbf{u}' \leftarrow \mathsf{SampPre}(\mathsf{td}, \mathbf{v}, s)$ with $m \geq 5\, n \log q$ takes a trapdoor td, a vector $\mathbf{v} \in \mathbb{Z}_q^n$ and a parameter s. It samples $\mathbf{u}' \in \mathbb{Z}^m$ satisfying $\mathbf{A} \cdot \mathbf{u}' \equiv \mathbf{v} \bmod q$. Furthermore, $\mathbf{u}'$ is within $\mathsf{negl}(\lambda)$ statistical distance to $\mathbf{u} \leftarrow \mathsf{SampD}(1^n, 1^m, s)$ conditioned on $\mathbf{v} \equiv \mathbf{A} \cdot \mathbf{u} \bmod q$.

$\mathsf{KeyGen}(1^\lambda)$	$\mathsf{Sign}(\mu, \mathsf{sk})$
$\mathbf{A}, \mathsf{td} \leftarrow \mathsf{TrapGen}(1^n, 1^m, q)$	$\mathbf{r} \leftarrow_{\$} \{0,1\}^\lambda$; $\mathbf{y} \leftarrow \mathsf{SampPre}(\mathsf{td}, H(\mu, \mathbf{r}), s)$
return $\mathsf{vk} = \mathbf{A}, \mathsf{sk} = \mathsf{td}$	**return** $(\mathbf{y}, \mathbf{r})$

$\mathsf{Verify}(\mathsf{vk}, \sigma, \mu)$
return $\|\mathbf{y}\| \stackrel{?}{\leq} \beta' \wedge H(\mu, \mathbf{r}) \stackrel{?}{\equiv} \mathbf{A} \cdot \mathbf{y}$

Fig. 3. GPV Signatures

2.5 The Falcon Signature Scheme

Falcon [36] is a signature scheme based on the GPV framework and essentially makes two optimisations, these being the use of NTRU lattices [39] and the use of fast Fourier sampling [10]. Specialization to NTRU lattices necessitates assuming the hardness of lattice problems restricted to NTRU lattices. Since NTRU lattices are modules over cyclotomic rings, cryptanalysts have algebraic structure to try and exploit. A vulnerability resulting from the restriction to NTRU lattices is known in the "overstretched" regime, where the modulus q is large in comparison to the dimension n. These regimes are well studied [2,11,23] and are to be avoided. Despite the apparent structure, lattice problems over NTRU lattices have persevered and there is reason to believe they remain hard [24]. Fast Fourier sampling on the other hand is an algorithmic speed up that does not affect the security assumptions. Recall NTRU lattice notation from Sect. 2. In particular, n is a power of 2, q is a prime number such that $q = 1 \bmod \varphi(n)$, and $\mathcal{O}_n \cong \mathbb{Z}(X)/\langle X^n + 1\rangle$ is the ring of integers of the 2n-th cyclotomic field $\mathbb{Q}(X)/\langle X^n + 1\rangle$. Falcon key generation, signature generation, and signature verification are shown in Fig. 4. We note that for consistency with [36], we present Falcon in Fig. 4 such that vectors are row vectors instead of column vectors in contrast to the rest of this work. Throughout, we let $\odot$ denote multiplication in the Fourier domain which extends coordinate-wise to vectors and matrices.

Key Generation. The KeyGen procedure of Falcon consists of two main steps:

- **Solving an NTRU equation** involves generating polynomials for the secret-key f and g with small integer coefficients, as well as generating of $F, G \in \mathcal{O}_n$ such that $f \cdot G - g \cdot F = q$, using NTRUGen.
- **Trapdoor generation** is roughly equivalent to the TrapGen procedure in GPV. It uses the generated polynomials, $f, g, F, G \in \mathbb{Z}[X]/(X^n + 1)$, and with some processing, makes them more compact. The matrix formed of these negacyclic coefficient blocks, $\mathbf{B} \leftarrow \begin{bmatrix} g & -f \\ G & -F \end{bmatrix}^t$, is expressed in FFT domain as $\hat{B}$, and is then used to create $\hat{\mathbf{G}} \leftarrow \hat{\mathbf{B}}^* \cdot \hat{\mathbf{B}}$, which we then use to finally generate a compact trapdoor $\mathsf{T} \leftarrow \mathsf{ffLDL}^*(\hat{\mathbf{G}})$. Superscripts $\hat{}$ and * refer to FFT and complex conjugation, respectively. The procedure then returns $\mathsf{sk} := (\hat{\mathbf{B}}, \mathsf{T})$ and $\mathsf{vk} = h$, where $h \leftarrow g \cdot f^{-1} \mod q$.

Signature Generation. The Sign procedure of Falcon contains three main components:

- **Hashing the message** returns a random vector in $\mathbb{Z}_q^n$ (in the Random Oracle Model). Using SHAKE, some random salt and the message are hashed to produce a polynomial $c \in \mathbb{Z}_q[X]$ of degree n.
- **Trapdoor sampling** computes the signature without leaking the secret key. Falcon employs a fast Fourier sampler called ffSampling, which takes as input $\mathbf{t}$, which is a preimage of c, and T, which is a Falcon tree apart of the secret key and is pre-processed in key generation. The resulting vector $\mathbf{z}$ is an element of the kernel lattice close to $\mathbf{t}$. The uncompressed signature becomes $\mathbf{s} = \hat{\mathbf{B}} \odot (\mathbf{t} - \mathbf{z})$.
- **Compression** takes the inverse FFT of $\mathbf{s}$, denoted (s_0, s_1), satisfying $s_0 + s_1 \cdot h = c \mod q$ and returns s_1, encoded as a bitstring.

Signature Verification. The Verify procedure of Falcon mainly contains reconstructions and bound checks:

- **Reconstructions**. The target c is computed from the message and salt, as is s_1 using the Decompress procedure. There also exists sufficient information to reconstruct $s_0 = c - s_1 \cdot h \mod q$.
- **Bound checks.** The reconstructed signature pair (s_0, s_1) are finally accepted so long as they are small enough, i.e. $||(s_0, s_1)||^2 \leq \lfloor \beta^2 \rfloor$.

3 GPV-Like Few-Time Signatures

The online/offline paradigm relies on a one-time signature scheme for the online signing part. In previous iterations of the paradigm this has been achieved via a Merkle one-time signatures [13,14] or by utilising trapdoor hash functions [37].

In our construction, we base our one-time signature scheme on GGH signatures in "GPV-style", by which we mean instantiating GPV signatures without

KeyGen(ϕ, q)	Sign$(\mathsf{sk}, \mu, \lfloor\beta^2\rfloor)$
$f, g, F, G \leftarrow \mathsf{NTRUGen}(\phi, q)$	$\mathbf{r} \leftarrow\$ \{0,1\}^{320}$
$\mathbf{B} \leftarrow [g, -f; G, -F]$	$c \leftarrow \mathsf{HashToPoint}(\mathbf{r}\\|\mu, q, n)$
$\hat{\mathbf{B}} \leftarrow \mathsf{FFT}(\mathbf{B})$	$\mathbf{t} \leftarrow (-\frac{1}{q}\mathsf{FFT}(c) \odot \mathsf{FFT}(F), -\frac{1}{q}\mathsf{FFT}(c) \odot \mathsf{FFT}(f))$
$\hat{\mathbf{G}} \leftarrow \hat{\mathbf{B}}^* \cdot \hat{\mathbf{B}}$	**do**
$\mathsf{T} \leftarrow \mathsf{ffLDL}^*(\hat{\mathbf{G}})$	**do**
for each leaf of T	$\mathbf{z} \leftarrow \mathsf{ffSampling}_n(\mathbf{t}, \mathsf{T})$; $\mathbf{s} = (\mathbf{t} - \mathbf{z}) \odot \hat{\mathbf{B}}$
$\mathsf{leaf.value} \leftarrow \sigma/\sqrt{\mathsf{leaf.value}}$	**while** $\\|\mathbf{s}\\|^2 > \lfloor\beta^2\rfloor$
$h \leftarrow g \cdot f^{-1} \mod q$	$(s_0, s_1) \leftarrow \mathsf{invFFT}(\mathbf{s})$
return $(\mathsf{sk} := (\hat{\mathbf{B}}, \mathsf{T}), \mathsf{vk} := h)$	$s \leftarrow \mathsf{Compress}(s_1, 8 \cdot \mathsf{sbytelen} - 328)$
	while $s = \bot$
	return $\sigma := (\mathbf{r}, s)$

Verify$(\mathsf{vk}, \sigma, \mu)$
$c \leftarrow \mathsf{HashToPoint}(\mathbf{r}\\|\mu, q, n)$; $s_1 \leftarrow \mathsf{Decompress}(s, 8 \cdot \mathsf{sbytelen} - 328)$
if $(s_1 = \bot)$ **then** 0
$s_0 \leftarrow c - s_1 \cdot h \bmod q$; **if** $\\|(s_0, s_1)\\|^2 \leq \lfloor\beta^2\rfloor$ **then** 1 **else** 0

Fig. 4. The Falcon signature scheme [36].

trapdoor sampling that ensures the outputs are independent of the trapdoor td. Since we are only using the trapdoor a few times, we can bound the leakage and thus security loss. We give our construction in Fig. 5. The only difference is that we precompute Q preimages $\mathbf{x}_{\mathrm{pre},i}$ in key generation, that we "mix in" these preimages during signing that we call $\mathsf{SampPre}_{\gg}$ instead of SampPre when signing.

Unlike SampPre, which is used in Falcon, we can be instead instantiate a more efficient procedure, $\mathsf{SampPre}_{\gg}$, that is indifferent to the output distribution, beyond that the outputs are short. This grants us the freedom to instantiate $\mathsf{SampPre}_{\gg}$ with fast pre-image generating algorithms, without any randomness requirements. We give an example in Fig. 7 based on Babai rounding. By "mix in" we mean taking the sum of $x_{pre,c}$ and x in Sign, which masks $x_{pre,c}$. We use the homomorphic properties on the images and pre-images to assure the mixing works.

Two natural candidates for $\mathsf{SampPre}_{\gg}$ are Babai's rounding and Nearest plane algorithms. The latter, while slower should allow for more online signatures without refreshing the key. We chose the former in our implementation for its speed, facilitating for rapid online signatures.

$\mathsf{KeyGen}(1^\lambda, Q)$	$\mathsf{Sign}(\mu, \mathsf{sk})$
$\mathbf{A}, \mathsf{td} \leftarrow \mathsf{TrapGen}(1^n, 1^m, q)$; $c \leftarrow 0$	$\mathbf{r} \leftarrow\$ \{0,1\}^\lambda$
for $0 \leq i < Q$: $\mathbf{x}_{\text{pre},i} \leftarrow \mathsf{SampD}(1^n, 1^m, s)$	$\mathbf{t}' \leftarrow \mathbf{A} \cdot \mathsf{sk}.\mathbf{x}_{\text{pre},c}$; $\mathbf{t} \leftarrow H(\mu, \mathbf{r})$
return $\mathsf{vk} = \mathbf{A}, \mathsf{sk} = (\mathsf{td}, \{\mathbf{x}_{\text{pre},i}\}_{0 \leq i < Q}, c)$	$\mathbf{x} \leftarrow \mathsf{SampPre}_{\gg}(\mathsf{sk}.\mathsf{td}, \mathbf{t} - \mathbf{t}')$
	$\mathbf{y} \leftarrow \mathbf{x}_{\text{pre},c} + \mathbf{x}$
$\mathsf{Verify}(\mathsf{vk}, \sigma, \mu)$	$\mathsf{sk}.c \leftarrow \mathsf{sk}.c + 1$
return $\|\mathbf{y}\| \stackrel{?}{\leq} \beta' \wedge H(\mu, \mathbf{r}) \stackrel{?}{\equiv} \mathbf{A} \cdot \mathbf{y}$	**return** $(\mathbf{y}, \mathbf{r})$

Fig. 5. Few-Times GPV-style Signatures

3.1 Unforgeability in the ROM

We prove the following theorem to establish the EUF-CMA$_Q$ security of our few time signatures construction in the ROM.

Theorem 1 (Unforgeability). *The advantage* $\mathsf{Adv}^{\text{euf-cma}}_{\mathcal{A},\Sigma,Q}(\lambda)$ *of any Q-query bounded adversary $\mathcal{A}$ playing the* EUF-CMA$_Q$ *security in the ROM game pictured in Fig. 6 successfully forges is bounded as*

$$\mathsf{Adv}^{\text{euf-cma}}_{\mathcal{A},\Sigma,Q}(\lambda) \leq Q \cdot \mathsf{negl}(\lambda) \cdot 2^{Q \cdot \left(\log_2\left(1 + \frac{2\pi \|\mathbf{x}\|^2_{\max}}{s^2}\right) + \frac{\log_2 e}{2}\right)} \cdot \mathsf{Adv}^{\text{sis}}_{\sqrt{2\,m} \cdot s}(\lambda)$$

when $\frac{s^2_{\mathsf{sim}}}{2\pi} = \frac{s^2}{2\pi} + \mathbb{E}_{\mathbf{x}}\left(\|\mathbf{x}\|^2\right)$ *and*

$$\mathsf{Adv}^{\text{euf-cma}}_{\mathcal{A},\Sigma,Q}(\lambda) \leq Q \cdot \mathsf{negl}(\lambda) \cdot 2^{Q \cdot \left(\log_2\left(1 + \frac{2\pi \mathbb{E}_{\mathbf{x}}\left(\|\mathbf{x}\|^2\right)}{s^2}\right) + \frac{\|\mathbf{x}\|^2_{\max} \log_2 e}{2\mathbb{E}_{\mathbf{x}}\left(\|\mathbf{x}\|^2\right)}\right)} \cdot \mathsf{Adv}^{\text{sis}}_{\sqrt{2\,m} \cdot s}(\lambda)$$

when $\frac{s^2_{\mathsf{sim}}}{2\pi} := \frac{s^2}{2\pi} + \|\mathbf{x}\|^2_{\max}$ *and where,*

- $\mathsf{Adv}^{\text{sis}}_{\sqrt{2\,m} \cdot s}(\lambda)$ *is advantage of any PPT adversary against the Short Integer Solutions problem with norm bound* $\sqrt{2\,m} \cdot s$.
- *s is the parameter of the spherical discrete Gaussian* $\mathbf{x}_{pre}$,
- s_{sim} *is the parameter of a simulated spherical discrete Gaussian, and*
- $\|\mathbf{x}\|^2_{\max}$ *is the maximum* $\|\mathbf{x}\|^2$ *over* $\mathbf{x} \sim \mathsf{SampPre}_{\gg}(\mathsf{td}, \mathcal{U}(\mathbb{Z}^n_q))$, *and*
- *λ is the security parameter.*

We prove Theorem 1 using a series of game hops in Appendix A, following the standard GPV proof pattern. We next outline the hops, deferring the details to Appendix A. Game_1 programs the random oracle to answer hash queries as the syndrome of a discrete Gaussian sampler with a possibly larger parameter. Game_2 ensures message-salt pairs are not repeated. Game_3 simulates signatures as pre-images of targets obtained from calling the random oracle on salted messages. Justifying the hop from Game_2 to Game_3 is the non-trivial part of the proof, captured by the following Lemma 1. Game_4 forgets the trapdoor basis matrix and in its place draws one at random. The proof is completed by transforming an adversary that wins Game_4 into an SIS solver.

$\text{EUF-CMA}^{\mathcal{A}}_{\Sigma,Q}(\lambda)$	$\mathsf{SIGN}(\mu)$	$\mathsf{RO}(x)$
$\mathcal{Q}, c \leftarrow \emptyset, 0$	**if** $c \geq Q$ **then abort**	**if** $x \notin \mathcal{H}$ **then**
$\mathsf{vk}, \mathsf{sk} \leftarrow \Sigma.\mathsf{KeyGen}(1^\lambda)$	$\sigma \leftarrow \Sigma.\mathsf{Sign}(\mathsf{sk}, \rho_c, \mu)$	$\mathcal{H}[x] \leftarrow\!\$\ \mathbb{Z}_q^n$
$\{\rho_i \leftarrow \Sigma.\mathsf{PreSign}(\mathsf{sk})\}_{1 \leq i \leq Q}$	$c \leftarrow c+1$	**return** $\mathcal{H}[x]$
$(\mu^\star, \sigma^\star) \leftarrow \mathcal{A}^{\mathsf{SIGN}}(\mathsf{vk})$	$\mathcal{Q} \leftarrow \mathcal{Q} \cup \{(\mu, \sigma)\}$	
return $(\mu^\star, \cdot) \notin \mathcal{Q} \wedge \mathsf{Verify}(\mathsf{vk}, \sigma^\star, \mu^\star)$	**return** σ	

Fig. 6. EUF-CMA$_Q$ in the ROM.

Lemma 1 (Query bounded advantage playing Game_3 **over** Game_2**).** *For every adversary* $\mathcal{A}_Q$ *playing* Game_2 *or* Game_3*, making at most* Q *signature queries before presenting the forgery, and every* $a \in (1, \infty)$*,*

$$\frac{\Pr\left[\mathcal{A}_Q^{\mathsf{Game}_2}(\mathsf{vk}) = 1\right]}{\Pr\left[\mathcal{A}_Q^{\mathsf{Game}_3}(\mathsf{vk}) = 1\right]^{\frac{a-1}{a}}} \leq \left(\frac{s_{\mathsf{sim}}^2}{s^2}\right)^Q \cdot (1+\epsilon)^Q \cdot \exp\left(\frac{(a-1) \cdot \pi \cdot \|\mathbf{x}\|_{\max}^2 Q}{\left(a \cdot (\frac{s_{\mathsf{sim}}^2}{s^2} - 1) + 1\right) \cdot s^2}\right) \tag{4}$$

where,

- *s is the parameter of the spherical discrete Gaussian in* Game_2 $\mathbf{x}_{pre}$*,*
- *s_{sim} is the parameter of the simulator spherical discrete Gaussian in* Game_3*,*
- *$\|\mathbf{x}\|_{\max}^2$ is the maximum $\|\mathbf{x}\|^2$ over* $\mathbf{x} \sim \mathsf{SampPre}_{\gg}(\mathsf{td}, \mathcal{U}(\mathbb{Z}_q^n))$*.*
- *and ϵ is a negligible function in the security parameter with $s_{\mathsf{sim}} \geq s$ and $s_{\mathsf{sim}} \geq \sqrt{\ln(2m(1+1/\epsilon)/\pi)} \cdot \sqrt{(a((s_{\mathsf{sim}}^2/s^2) - 1) + 1)}$.*

Proof. Consider an adversary $\mathcal{A}_Q$ playing Game_2 (Fig. 9) or Game_3 (Fig. 10). Without loss of generality, assume that the adversary $\mathcal{A}_Q$ makes exactly Q signature queries before presenting the forgery. Let $(\mathbf{y}_1, \mathbf{y}_2, \ldots, \mathbf{y}_Q)$ denote the signatures seen by $\mathcal{A}_Q$ while playing Game 2, that is, if the queries were answered by the signing algorithm. Let $\mathcal{D}_1$ denote the join distribution of such a sequence $(\mathbf{y}_1, \mathbf{y}_2, \ldots, \mathbf{y}_Q)$. Let $(\mathbf{y}_1^{\mathsf{sim}}, \mathbf{y}_2^{\mathsf{sim}}, \ldots, \mathbf{y}_Q^{\mathsf{sim}})$ denote the sequence of signature query answers seen by $\mathcal{A}_Q$ while playing Game 3, that is, if the simulator Sim answers the signature queries. Let $\mathcal{D}_2$ denote the joint distribution of such a sequence $(\mathbf{y}_1^{\mathsf{sim}}, \mathbf{y}_2^{\mathsf{sim}}, \ldots, \mathbf{y}_Q^{\mathsf{sim}})$. Let E be the event of a successful adversary forgery at the end. Then $\mathcal{D}_1(E) = \Pr\left[\mathcal{A}_Q^{\mathrm{Game}_2}(\mathsf{vk}) = 1\right]$ and $\mathcal{D}_2(E) = \Pr\left[\mathcal{A}_Q^{\mathrm{Game}_3}(\mathsf{vk}) = 1\right]$ are the probability that the adversary succeeds in Game 2 and Game 3 respectively. From the probability preservation of Rényi entropy (Eq. (2)), for $a \in (1, \infty)$

$$\mathcal{D}_1(E) \leq \left[\mathcal{D}_2(E) R_a\left(\mathcal{D}_1 \| \mathcal{D}_2\right)\right]^{\frac{a-1}{a}}. \tag{5}$$

Therefore, to claim the bound in the lemma, it suffices to bound $R_a(\mathcal{D}_1 \| \mathcal{D}_2)$. We begin by decomposing $\mathcal{D}_1$ and $\mathcal{D}_2$ into distributions indexed by the signature queries. Regardless of the if Game 2 or Game 3 is played, the signatures generated are mutually independent across queries. Therefore, both distributions factor into products $\mathcal{D}_1 = \prod_{j=1}^{Q} \mathcal{D}_{1,j}$ and $\mathcal{D}_2 = \prod_{j=1}^{Q} \mathcal{D}_{2,j}$, where $\mathcal{D}_{1,j}$ and $\mathcal{D}_{2,j}$ are respectively the distributions followed by $\mathbf{y}_j$ and $\mathbf{y}_j^{\mathsf{sim}}$. By the multiplicativity of Rényi divergence, for $a \in [1, \infty]$,

$$R_a\left(\prod_{j=1}^{Q} \mathcal{D}_{1,j} \middle\| \prod_{j=1}^{Q} \mathcal{D}_{2,j}\right) = \prod_{j=1}^{Q} R_a(\mathcal{D}_{1,j} \| \mathcal{D}_{2,j}). \tag{6}$$

Further, $\mathcal{D}_{1,j}, 1 \leq j \leq Q$ are all identical, whose distribution we next determine. Since the signature vector $\mathbf{y} \leftarrow \mathbf{x} + \mathbf{x}_{\text{pre}}$ in Game_2 is the sum of independent vectors $\mathbf{x}$ and $\mathbf{x}_{\text{pre}}$, its distribution is the convolution

$$\mathcal{D}_{\mathbb{Z}^m,s} \circ \mathsf{SampPre}_{\gg}(\mathsf{td}, \mathcal{U}(\mathbb{Z}_q^n)),$$

of the distributions of $\mathbf{x}$ and $\mathbf{x}_{\text{pre}}$. Written explicitly, the signature $\mathbf{y}$ follows the distribution $\mathbf{w} \in \mathbb{Z}^m \longmapsto \Pr[\mathbf{y} = \mathbf{w}]$ mapping

$$\mathbf{w} \longmapsto \frac{\mathbb{E}_{\mathbf{x}}\left[\exp(-\pi\|\mathbf{w} - \mathbf{x}\|^2/s^2)\right]}{\sum_{\mathbf{w}\in\mathbb{Z}^m} \mathbb{E}_{\mathbf{x}} \exp(-\pi\|\mathbf{w} - \mathbf{x}\|^2/s^2)},$$

where the expectation is taken over the pre-images $\mathbf{x} \sim \mathsf{SampPre}_{\gg}(\mathsf{td}, \mathcal{U}(\mathbb{Z}_q^n))$ induced by uniform images $\mathcal{U}(\mathbb{Z}_q^n)$. We denote this distribution as $\mathbb{E}_{\mathbf{x}}\left(\mathcal{D}_{\mathbb{Z}^m,s,-\mathbf{x}}\right)$. In particular, $\mathbb{E}_{\mathbf{x}}\left(\mathcal{D}_{\mathbb{Z}^m,s,-\mathbf{x}}\right)$ has mean zero vector and covariance $s^2 \cdot \mathbb{I}_n + \mathrm{Var}(\mathbf{x})$.

Likewise, $\mathcal{D}_{1,j}, 1 \leq j \leq Q$ are all identical, being $\mathcal{D}_{\mathbb{Z}^m,s_{\mathsf{sim}}}$ by construction. Substituting for $\mathcal{D}_{1,j}$ and $\mathcal{D}_{2,j}$ in Eq. (6), for $a \in [1, \infty]$,

$$R_a\left(\prod_{j=1}^{Q} \mathcal{D}_{1,j} \middle\| \prod_{j=1}^{Q} \mathcal{D}_{2,j}\right) = R_a(\mathbb{E}_{\mathbf{x}}\left(\mathcal{D}_{\mathbb{Z}^m,s,-\mathbf{x}}\right) \| \mathcal{D}_{\mathbb{Z}^m,s_{\mathsf{sim}}})^Q. \tag{7}$$

Therefore, it suffices to upper bound $R_a(\mathbb{E}_{\mathbf{x}}\left(\mathcal{D}_{\mathbb{Z}^m,s,-\mathbf{x}}\right) \| \mathcal{D}_{\mathbb{Z}^m,s_{\mathsf{sim}}})$. From the definition of Rényi divergence (Eq. (1)),

$$\begin{aligned} &R_a(\mathbb{E}_{\mathbf{x}}\left(\mathcal{D}_{\mathbb{Z}^m,s,-\mathbf{x}}\right) \| \mathcal{D}_{\mathbb{Z}^m,s_{\mathsf{sim}}})^{a-1} \\ &= \frac{\left[\sum_{\mathbf{w}\in\mathbb{Z}^m} \exp(-\pi\|\mathbf{w}\|^2/s_{\mathsf{sim}}^2)\right]^{a-1}}{\left[\sum_{\mathbf{w}\in\mathbb{Z}^m} \mathbb{E}_{\mathbf{x}} \exp(-\pi\|\mathbf{w} - \mathbf{x}\|^2/s^2)\right]^a} \sum_{\mathbf{w}\in\mathbb{Z}^m} \frac{\left[\mathbb{E}_{\mathbf{x}} \exp(-\pi\|\mathbf{w} - \mathbf{x}\|^2/s^2)\right]^a}{\exp(-\pi(a-1)\|\mathbf{w}\|^2/s_{\mathsf{sim}}^2)}. \end{aligned}$$

For each $\mathbf{w} \in \mathbb{Z}^m$, by Jensen's inequality

$$\left[\mathbb{E}_{\mathbf{x}} \exp(-\pi\|\mathbf{w} - \mathbf{x}\|^2/s^2)\right]^a \leq \mathbb{E}_{\mathbf{x}} \exp(-a \cdot \pi\|\mathbf{w} - \mathbf{x}\|^2/s^2),$$

since raising the positive random variable $\exp(-\pi \cdot \|\mathbf{w} - \mathbf{x}\|^2/s^2)$ to the a-th power is convex for $a \geq 1$. Therefore,

$$\begin{aligned} &R_a(\mathbb{E}_{\mathbf{x}}\left(\mathcal{D}_{\mathbb{Z}^m,s,-\mathbf{x}}\right) \| \mathcal{D}_{\mathbb{Z}^m,s_{\mathsf{sim}}})^{a-1} \\ &\leq \frac{\left[\sum_{\mathbf{w}\in\mathbb{Z}^m} \exp(-\pi \cdot \|\mathbf{w}\|^2/s_{\mathsf{sim}}^2)\right]^{a-1}}{\left[\sum_{\mathbf{w}\in\mathbb{Z}^m} \mathbb{E}_{\mathbf{x}} \exp(-\pi \cdot \|\mathbf{w} - \mathbf{x}\|^2/s^2)\right]^a} \sum_{\mathbf{w}\in\mathbb{Z}^m} \frac{\mathbb{E}_{\mathbf{x}} \exp(-a \cdot \pi \cdot \|\mathbf{w} - \mathbf{x}\|^2/s^2)}{\exp(-\pi \cdot (a-1) \cdot \|\mathbf{w}\|^2/s_{\mathsf{sim}}^2)}. \end{aligned}$$

First, let us estimate the normalisation factor. Since $\mathbb{Z}^m$ has m $\mathbb{R}-$linearly independent vectors of length one, by [29, Lemma 3.3] the smoothing parameter $\eta_\epsilon(\mathbb{Z}^m) \leq \sqrt{\ln(2m(1+1/\epsilon)/\pi)}$ and for $s_{\mathsf{sim}} \geq \sqrt{\ln(2m(1+1/\epsilon)/\pi)}$ we have,

$$\sum_{\mathbf{w}\in\mathbb{Z}^m} \exp(-\pi\cdot\|\mathbf{w}\|^2/s_{\mathsf{sim}}^2) \leq s_{\mathsf{sim}}(1+\epsilon).$$

By the linearity of expectation:[1]

$$\sum_{\mathbf{w}\in\mathbb{Z}^m} \mathbb{E}_{\mathbf{x}} \exp(-\pi\cdot\|\mathbf{w}-\mathbf{x}\|^2/s^2) = \mathbb{E}_{\mathbf{x}} \sum_{\mathbf{w}\in\mathbb{Z}^m} \exp(-\pi\cdot\|\mathbf{w}-\mathbf{x}\|^2/s^2) \geq s.$$

Therefore,

$$R_a(\mathbb{E}_{\mathbf{x}}\left(\mathcal{D}_{\mathbb{Z}^m,s,-\mathbf{x}}\right)\|\mathcal{D}_{\mathbb{Z}^m,s_{\mathsf{sim}}})^{a-1} \leq \frac{s_{\mathsf{sim}}^{a-1}(1+\epsilon)^{a-1}}{s^a} \sum_{\mathbf{w}\in\mathbb{Z}^m} \frac{\left[\mathbb{E}_{\mathbf{x}} \exp(-a\cdot\pi\cdot\|\mathbf{w}-\mathbf{x}\|^2/s^2)\right]}{\exp(-\pi\cdot(a-1)\cdot\|\mathbf{w}\|^2/s_{\mathsf{sim}}^2)}.$$

By the linearity of expectation, the right hand side equals

$$\begin{aligned}&\frac{s_{\mathsf{sim}}^{a-1}(1+\epsilon)^{a-1}}{s^a} \sum_{\mathbf{w}\in\mathbb{Z}^m} \mathbb{E}_{\mathbf{x}}\left[\frac{\exp(-a\cdot\pi\cdot\|\mathbf{w}-\mathbf{x}\|^2/s^2)}{\exp(-\pi\cdot(a-1)\cdot\|\mathbf{w}\|^2/s_{\mathsf{sim}}^2)}\right]\\ =&\frac{s_{\mathsf{sim}}^{a-1}(1+\epsilon)^{a-1}}{s^a} \sum_{\mathbf{w}\in\mathbb{Z}^m} \mathbb{E}_{\mathbf{x}} \exp\left(-\pi\cdot\left(\frac{a\cdot\|\mathbf{w}-\mathbf{x}\|^2}{s^2} - \frac{(a-1)\cdot\|\mathbf{w}\|^2}{s_{\mathsf{sim}}^2}\right)\right).\end{aligned}$$

Setting $r := s_{\mathsf{sim}}^2/s^2$ and completing the squares in the exponent, we get,

$$\begin{aligned}\frac{r^{a-1}(1+\epsilon)^{a-1}}{s} \sum_{\mathbf{w}\in\mathbb{Z}^m} \mathbb{E}_{\mathbf{x}} \exp\left(\frac{-\pi}{s_{\mathsf{sim}}^2}\cdot\left\{(a\cdot(r-1)+1)\cdot\|\mathbf{w}-\frac{a\cdot r}{a\cdot(r-1)+1}\mathbf{x}\|^2\right.\right.\\ \left.\left. -a\cdot r\left(\frac{a\cdot r}{a\cdot(r-1)+1}-1\right)\|\mathbf{x}\|^2\right\}\right),\end{aligned}$$

which by the linearity of expectation,

$$\begin{aligned}=\frac{r^{a-1}(1+\epsilon)^{a-1}}{s}\cdot\mathbb{E}_{\mathbf{x}}\Bigg[&\exp\left(\frac{\pi\cdot a}{s^2}\left(\frac{a\cdot r}{a\cdot(r-1)+1}-1\right)\|\mathbf{x}\|^2\right)\\ &\cdot\sum_{\mathbf{w}\in\mathbb{Z}^m}\exp\left(\frac{-\pi(a(r-1)+1)}{s_{\mathsf{sim}}^2}\|\mathbf{w}-\frac{a\cdot r}{a\cdot(r-1)+1}\mathbf{x}\|^2\right)\Bigg].\end{aligned}$$

As before, by [29, Lemma 3.3],

$$\sum_{\mathbf{w}\in\mathbb{Z}^m}\exp\left(\frac{-\pi(a(r-1)+1)}{s_{\mathsf{sim}}^2}\|\mathbf{w}-\frac{ar}{a(r-1)+1}\mathbf{x}\|^2\right) \leq \frac{s_{\mathsf{sim}}(1+\epsilon)}{\sqrt{(a(r-1)+1)}},$$

[1] There are no convergence issues here, or later in the proof, when we exchange infinite summations by claiming linearity of expectation, as the summands are not negative.

since $s_{\mathsf{sim}} \geq \sqrt{\ln(2\,m(1+1/\epsilon)/\pi)} \cdot \sqrt{(a((s_{\mathsf{sim}}^2/s^2)-1)+1)}$. In summary,

$$\begin{aligned} & R_a(\mathbb{E}_{\mathbf{x}}\,(\mathcal{D}_{\mathbb{Z}^m,s,-\mathbf{x}})\,\|\mathcal{D}_{\mathbb{Z}^m,s_{\mathsf{sim}}})^{a-1} \\ & \leq \frac{r^a(1+\epsilon)^a}{\sqrt{(a\cdot(r-1)+1)}}\mathbb{E}_{\mathbf{x}}\left[\exp\left(\frac{\pi a}{s^2}\left(\frac{a-1}{a\cdot(r-1)+1}\right)\|\mathbf{x}\|^2\right)\right] \\ & \leq \frac{r^a(1+\epsilon)^a}{\sqrt{(a\cdot(r-1)+1)}}\cdot\exp\left(\frac{\pi\cdot a}{s^2}\left(\frac{a-1}{a(r-1)+1}\right)\|\mathbf{x}\|^2_{max}\right). \end{aligned}$$

Therefore,

$$\begin{aligned} & R_a(\mathbb{E}_{\mathbf{x}}\,(\mathcal{D}_{\mathbb{Z}^m,s,-\mathbf{x}})\,\|\mathcal{D}_{\mathbb{Z}^m,s_{\mathsf{sim}}})^{\frac{a-1}{a}} \\ \leq & \left(\frac{r^a(1+\epsilon)^a}{\sqrt{(a\cdot(r-1)+1)}}\right)^{\frac{1}{a}}\cdot\exp\left(\frac{\pi\beta}{s^2}\left(\frac{a-1}{a\cdot(r-1)+1}\right)\cdot\|\mathbf{x}\|^2_{\max}\right) \\ \leq & r\cdot(1+\epsilon)\cdot\exp\left(\frac{\pi\cdot(a-1)\cdot\|\mathbf{x}\|^2_{\max}}{(a\cdot(r-1)+1)\cdot s^2}\right). \end{aligned}$$

By the probability preservation (Eq. (5)) and multiplicativity (Eq. (7)) of Rényi entropy,

$$\frac{\Pr\left[\mathcal{A}_Q^{Game_2}(\mathsf{vk})=1\right]}{\Pr\left[\mathcal{A}_Q^{Game_3}(\mathsf{vk})=1\right]^{\frac{a-1}{a}}} \leq \left(\frac{s_{\mathsf{sim}}^2}{s^2}\right)^Q\cdot(1+\epsilon)^Q\cdot\exp\left(\frac{(a-1)\cdot\pi\cdot\|\mathbf{x}\|^2_{\max}Q}{\left(a\cdot(\frac{s_{\mathsf{sim}}^2}{s^2}-1)+1\right)\cdot s^2}\right) \tag{8}$$

which is exactly as claimed in the lemma. □

We restrict the Renyi divergence parameter a in the lemma to $a > 1$, allowing calculations with $a-1$ in denominators. While applying the lemma in security arguments, we may optimise over a. Therefore, excluding $a = 1$ is not an issue.

The constraint $s_{\mathsf{sim}} \geq \sqrt{\ln(2\,m(1+1/\epsilon)/\pi)} \cdot \sqrt{(a((s_{\mathsf{sim}}^2/s^2)-1)+1)}$ in the lemma appears too restrictive to apply for large a. This is pessimistic and an artifact of our proof where we used the same ϵ in both applications of the smoothing parameter argument [29][Lemma 3.3]. The second application only contributes a multiplicative factor $(1+\epsilon)^{Q/a}$ to the bound. A more refined analysis with two ϵ parameters is possible, which we exclude for ease of exposition. For many choices of a, the constraint $s_{\mathsf{sim}} \geq \sqrt{\ln(2\,m(1+1/\epsilon)/\pi)}$ might suffice.

Remark 1. As a sanity check, we may consider the parallelepiped attack [32] on NTRU signatures (and its extensions [8]). These attack may try to learn the ephemeral trapdoor basis from the online signatures. Lemma 1 implies that (for well chosen parameters) from only a few online signatures Q this will fail. As the number of signatures Q increases, our bound becomes meaningless, but this does not immediately imply an attack, i.e. it is not a priori clear our bound is tight. We leave to future work to establish tighter bounds, allowing potentially larger Q.

PreSign(sk)

$\mathbf{B} \leftarrow [g, -f; G, -F]$
$\hat{\mathbf{B}} \leftarrow \mathsf{FFT}(\mathbf{B})$
$u_0, u_1 \leftarrow \mathcal{D}_\sigma^2$
$c_{\text{pre}} \leftarrow \mathsf{ComputeTarget}(h, u_0, u_1)$
return $(\rho := u_0, u_1, c_{\text{pre}})$

Sign(sk, ρ, μ)

$\mathbf{r} \leftarrow\$ \{0,1\}^{320}$
$c' \leftarrow \mathsf{HashToPoint}(\mathbf{r}\|\mu, q, n)$
$c \leftarrow c' + c_{\text{pre}}$
$s_0', s_1' \leftarrow \mathsf{SampPre}_{\gg}(c, \hat{\mathbf{B}})$
$s_0 \leftarrow s_0' - u_0$
$s_1 \leftarrow s_1' - u_1$
$s \leftarrow \mathsf{Compress}(s_1)$
return $\sigma := (\mathbf{r}, s)$

ComputeTarget(h, u_0, u_1)

$\hat{u_1} \leftarrow \mathsf{NTT}(u_1)$
$\hat{t} \leftarrow h \odot \hat{u_1}$
$t \leftarrow \mathsf{invNTT}(\hat{t}) + u_0$
return t

SampPre$_{\gg}$($c, \hat{\mathbf{B}}$)

$\hat{c} \leftarrow \mathsf{FFT}(c)$
// $\hat{\mathbf{t}} = (\mathsf{FFT}(c), \mathsf{FFT}(0)) \cdot \hat{\mathbf{B}}^{-1}$
$\hat{\mathbf{t}} \leftarrow \left(-\frac{1}{q} \cdot \hat{c} \odot \mathsf{FFT}(F), -\frac{1}{q} \cdot \hat{c} \odot \mathsf{FFT}(f)\right)$
$\mathbf{t} \leftarrow \mathsf{invFFT}(\hat{\mathbf{t}})$; $\mathbf{t} \leftarrow \mathsf{round}(\mathbf{t})$; $\hat{\mathbf{t}} \leftarrow \mathsf{FFT}(\mathbf{t})$
$\hat{\mathbf{s}} \leftarrow (\mathsf{FFT}(c), \mathsf{FFT}(0)) - \hat{\mathbf{t}} \odot \hat{\mathbf{B}}$
$\mathbf{s} \leftarrow \mathsf{invFFT}(\hat{\mathbf{s}})$
return s

Fig. 7. Few-Times Falcon-style signature generation.

4 A Falcon-Based Online-Offline Signature Scheme

In this section we specialise and analyse the few-times signatures from GPV developed in Sect. 3 to the Falcon-512 setting, by restricting to the NTRU lattice underlying Falcon-512 with lattice dimension $m = 2 \cdot 512$, image space dimension $n = 512$ and modulus $q = 12,289$. Our Falcon-inspired few-times signature scheme is presented in Fig. 7, again following the notation in Falcon (as described in Sect. 2.5), as opposed to GPV.

Remark 2. Many of the elements in Fig. 7 are similar or the same as in Falcon, with a few exceptions. PreSign offloads some of the FFT conversions on the secret key needed during Falcon's signature generation procedure. In this part we also add the offline generation of two Gaussian vectors. ComputeTarget reuses operations required in Falcon's verification procedure. Sign reuses the initial salting and hashing from Falcon, as well as the final compression. However the remaining operations are bespoke, including a faster algorithm for sampling pre-images, SampPre$_{\gg}$, and the algebra used to mask these pre-images. In Fig. 7, SampPre$_{\gg}$ is instantiated with the Babai method, using rounding. PreSign is computed offline, with ComputeTarget, and the remaining operations are computed online.

In our implementation, the short pre-image function SampPre$_{\gg}$ is implemented using Babai rounding. We observed empirically that pre-image lengths have expectation $\mathbb{E}_{\mathbf{x}}\|\mathbf{x}\|_2 = 5584.61$ and standard deviation $= 303.67$. Further, the pre-image lengths appear to be sub-Gaussian in practice, suggesting that except for a probability of 0.03%, the pre-image lengths do not exceed length $5584.61 + 3 \cdot 303.67 = 6495.62$. Guided by this empirical observation, we assume in the analysis that the maximum allowed pre-image length $\|\mathbf{x}\|_{\max} := 6495.62$. In one desires the analysis to strictly conform to the implementation, it is easy to add a rejection sampling step to $\mathsf{SampPre}_{\gg}$, rejecting pre-images larger than $\|\mathbf{x}\|_{\max}$.

We note that GPV security proof does not apply to Falcon, because it assumes $n = \Theta(\lambda)$, $q = \lambda^{\mathcal{O}(1)}$, and $m = \Theta(n \log q)$ whereas Falcon has $m = \Theta(n)$. Thus, like Falcon our scheme has no formal proof of security that reduces some known problem to forgeries. As is standard, we establish parameters using cost estimates for known cryptanalytic attacks. In our case, we rely on the "lattice estimator" from [3].

By matching the simulator and signature variance, we tabulate the security guarantee from Eq. (11). The column "Zero" signature bit security is the bit security assured by the lattice estimator associated with solving SIS with length $\sqrt{(m \cdot s_{\mathsf{sim}}^2)/(2\pi)}$. The choice of parameters we implemented is highlighted in the table as "Implemented".

4.1 Practical Performance

Our implementation is publicly available[2] and reuses parts of the publicly available implementation of Falcon [35]. Our main changes, as shown in Fig. 7, are the way in which the target is computed and the calculation of the short pre-image are reworked. At the same time, many of the typical modules, such as the FFT multiplications, hash functions, and pseudorandomness generation remain as in Falcon. We also adopt the same parameters from the latest version of Falcon except for those which we use for discrete Gaussian sampling.

The discrete Gaussian sampler we require has significantly larger standard deviation than those used in Falcon. In Table 1 we describe security levels for different standard deviation values, which also defines the value we use in our proof-of-concept implementation, $\sigma = 215$. Since the standard deviation we use is larger, adapting the same naïve table-based sampler used in Falcon would be too slow, consume too much memory, and overall be too inefficient. Previous research [6,19] dealt with this issue by adopting Peikert's convolution lemma [33], which meant two Gaussian samplers from much smaller standard deviations could be combined to produce one Gaussian sample from a much larger distribution. This technique was also used in GALACTICS [6], which provides a secure, constant-time design for their Gaussian sampler. Overall, this ensures the clock cycle consumption remains low, which is important despite this being apart of the offline phase.

We give benchmarks in Table 3. All these benchmarks were run using a Raspberry Pi 3 Model B, Revision 1.2, equipped with an ARM Cortex-A53 CPU. The system is configured for AArch32 (32-bit), using the latest version of the

[2] https://github.com/jameshoweee/online-offline-sigs/.

Table 1. Falcon-inspired few-times signature scheme security levels, with security level deterioration by key reuse, for a variety of pre-image and noise parameters.

Pre-image length, Noise std. dev.*	Simulator length†	"Zero" sig bit security‡	Bit security deficit per sig§	4 sig bit security	8 sig bit security
Small noise 1 (5 584.61, 16)	5 608.03	148.3	17.87	76.82	5.34
Small noise 2 (5 584.61, 32)	5 677.71	147.7	15.87	84.22	20.74
Small noise 3 (5 584.61, 64)	5 948.29	145.8	13.87	90.32	34.84
Small noise 4 (5 584.61, 128)	6 925.68	139.7	11.87	92.22	44.74
Matching lengths¶ (5 584.61, 174.51)	7 897.62	135.1	10.97	91.22	47.34
Implemented‖ (5 584.61, 215)	8 861.28	130.9	10.38	89.38	47.86
Small noise 4 (5 584.61, 256)	9 914.47	127.4	9.87	87.92	48.44
Medium noise# (5 584.61, 987.23)	32 081.14	98.0	6.02	73.94	49.84
High noise** (5 584.61, 5 584.61)	178 794.00	71.8	1.98	63.89	55.99

$*$ Describing the (length, noise) as $(\mathbb{E}_{\mathbf{x}}\|\mathbf{x}\|, \frac{s}{\sqrt{2\pi}})$,

† Using $\sqrt{\frac{ms_{\mathsf{sim}}^2}{2\pi}} := \sqrt{\frac{ms^2}{2\pi} + (\mathbb{E}_{\mathbf{x}}\|\mathbf{x}\|)^2}$

‡ Using the lattice estimator with length $\sqrt{(ms_{\mathsf{sim}}^2)/(2\pi)}$,

§ Using Eq. (11)

‖ The parameters used in the implementation in Sect. 4.1,

¶ Where $\mathbb{E}_{\mathbf{x}}\|\mathbf{x}\| = \frac{s\sqrt{m}}{\sqrt{2\pi}}$

\# Where $\mathbb{E}_{\mathbf{x}}\|\mathbf{x}\| = \frac{sm^{1/4}}{\sqrt{2\pi}}$,

$**$ Where $\mathbb{E}_{\mathbf{x}}\|\mathbf{x}\| = \frac{s}{\sqrt{2\pi}}$

Raspberry Pi OS (Bullseye), which is based on Debian 11. We employed GCC version 10.2.1-6+rpi1 for compilation, targeting the ARMv7l (AArch32) architecture. We run the benchmarks on the slowest possible clock speed and only use a single core. The benchmarks are run over 25,000 repetitions and incorporate sleep states where necessary. Overall, these settings all ensure the most fair and accurate results on the embedded device.

For Falcon and our construction we also present benchmarks for both single-precision and double-precision floating-point operations, the former emulates the 53 bits of floating-point precision required, and the latter does this natively by utilising the double precision FPU. One of the particular reasons we chose the ARM Cortex A53 was to observe the contrast between native and emulated floating-point operations. Since previous research on similar low-cost devices like the ARM Cortex M7 have shown non-constant runtimes for Falcon [21], thus we decided to run on the ARM Cortex A53 instead.

Table 2. Key and signature sizes (in bytes) of our Falcon-based online-offline signature scheme alongside Dilithium and Ed25519.

Signature Scheme	Public Key	Secret Key	Signature
Falcon-512	897	7,553	666
This work, uncompressed	897	$15,106 + \tau \cdot 1,024$	897+666+1,024
This work, orig. compressed	897	$15,106 + \tau \cdot 845$	897+666+845
This work, alt. compressed	897	$15,106 + \tau \cdot 780$	897+666+780
Dilithium2	1,312	2,528	2,420
Ed25519	32	32	64

We are assuming an online τ-times signature scheme. Orig. compression uses the same format at Falcon, alt. compression uses different parameters that optimise for our larger parameters.

Table 3. Benchmark results of comparable signature schemes on an ARM Cortex A53.

Signature Scheme	Clock Cycles			Runtime (ms)		
	KeyGen	Sign	Verify	KeyGen	Sign	Verify
Falcon-512-EMU [36]	153M	35M	172K	255.09	58.65	0.28
This work (EMU, offline)	153M	6M	–	255.09	9.45	–
This work (EMU, online)	–	10M	172K	–	16.16	0.28
Falcon-512-FPU [36]	87M	3M	171K	144.93	4.73	0.28
This work (FPU, offline)	87M	1M	–	144.93	1.59	–
This work (FPU, online)	–	0.8M	171K	–	1.29	0.28
Dilithium2 [26]	1.6M	12.5M	1.7M	2.67	20.87	2.82
Ed25519 [34]	0.5M	0.5M	1.4M	0.81	0.84	2.36

In order to fairly compare benchmarks, we also include performance results for Dilithium and Falcon (both using the latest version of their reference implementations) as well as Ed25519 (taken from [34]) (Table 2).

We present our benchmarks using cycle counts as well as runtime (in milliseconds). In Table 3 we present the benchmarks for each of the signature primitives and in Table 4, we present these results using the offline and online separations, all of these are presented for our construction alongside Dilithium2, Falcon-512, and Ed25519, for comparison.

The overall design of this work aims to improve the online cost in comparison to current PQC signature schemes and potentially classical schemes in use today. With respect to offline costs, our construction uses the same key generation procedure and offloads 5.6 m cycles from its signature generation to the offline part, thus increasing the clock cycles required offline by less than 1–4%[3]. These extra offline costs mainly contain FFT transformations of four polynomials, discrete Gaussian sampling of two polynomials, and an NTT calculation of a target polynomial. Thus, there is only a small performance difference between Falcon and our offline costs. When compared to Dilithium and Ed25519 it is orders of magnitude slower, but this is likely going to be the case on every platform and thus is due to the algorithms themselves.

[3] Depending on whether the floating-point arithmetic is emulated or uses the FPU.

Table 4. Categorising ARM Cortex A53 benchmarks for offline/online computations.

Signature Scheme	Clock Cycles		Runtime (ms)	
	Offline	Online	Offline	Online
Falcon-512-EMU [36]	153 048 368	35 362 439	255.09	58.94
This work, EMU	158 718 728	10 042 709	264.53	16.73
Falcon-512-FPU [36]	86 957 688	2 991 232	144.93	5.01
This work, FPU	87 916 636	1 118 903	146.53	1.86
Dilithium2 [26]	1 604 583	14 216 595	2.67	23.69
Ed25519 [34]	483 962	1 920 361	0.81	3.20

Our online costs still consist of FFT conversions, in particular those needed when computing the short preimage, but the module overall is significantly less involved than the preimage computation in Falcon. The remaining operations required in Sign-Online are some randomness generation, hashing of the message, and the compression of the signature. These remaining operations utilise the same functions used in Falcon.

Considering that this proof-of-concept implementation is not highly optimised, the results are promising in comparison to the NIST PQC standards and to current classical standards like Ed25519.

When comparing the online versions of these signature schemes, the reader is reminded that for our scheme (and any scheme that utilises the online/offline paradigm [13,14]) it requires one few-time signature generation and two verifications (one of the long-term signature and one of the few-time signature); the regular signature schemes' costs are simply the cost of one signature generation and one signature verification.

In comparison to the signature generation costs, our construction requires 3.6x less clock cycles compared to Falcon, which reduces to 3.5x when the full online costs are considered with the additional signature verification. We also see that our construction requires fewer clock cycles than Dilithium2, using both native and emulated floating-point arithmetic, and even competes with Ed25519 when using native floats.

When compared to Ed25519 for overall online costs, Falcon's fast verification means we gain advantages when considering total signature and verification costs with Ed25519 requiring just under 2 m clock cycles and our construction requiring just over 1 m cycles, overall reducing cycles needed by 58%.

A Appendix: Proof of Theorem 1

Proof. We start the game hop proof with the EUF-CMA game specialised to the GPV-Online/Offline signatures in the ROM as Game 0, illustrated in Fig. 9. To ease notation, we leave the bookkeeping of the number of queries implicit in the games that follow, i.e. we restrict to adversaries that only submit up to Q queries (Fig. 8).

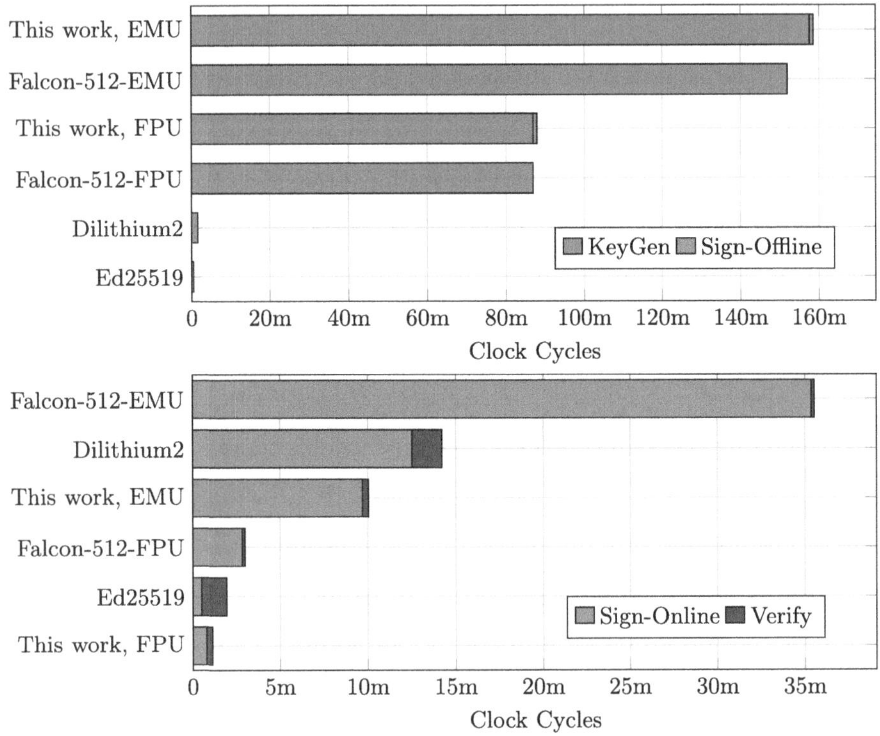

Fig. 8. Key generation, signature generation (offline and online), and verify benchmarks on ARM Cortex A53. Top graph consists of total offline cost, key generation + sign offline cycles. Bottom graph consists of total online cost, signature generation and verification cycles.

Game_1*: Programming the Random Oracle.* In the first hop, we program the random oracle to answer hash queries as follows. Given a $(\mu, \mathbf{r})$ hash query, look up if $(\mu, \mathbf{r})$ was previously queried. If so, answer as before. Otherwise, sample $\mathbf{y} \sim \mathcal{D}_{\mathbb{Z}^m, s_{\mathsf{sim}}}$, using a discrete Gaussian sampler $\mathsf{SampD}(1^n, 1^m, s_{\mathsf{sim}})$ where $s_{\mathsf{sim}}^2 = r \cdot s^2$, for some positive real parameter $r \geq 1$, store $\mathbf{y}^{(s)}$ in a preimage list as $\mathcal{P}(\mu, \mathbf{r}) \leftarrow \mathbf{y}$, and programme the random oracle RO at $(\mu, \mathbf{r})$ as $\mathsf{RO}(\mu, \mathbf{r}) \leftarrow \mathbf{A} \cdot \mathbf{y} \bmod q$. For s_{sim} exceeding the smoothing parameter $\eta_\epsilon(\Lambda^*(\mathbf{A}))$, by [16, Lem 5.2], the syndrome $\mathbf{A} \cdot \mathbf{y} \bmod q$ is within statistical distance 2ϵ of the uniform distribution in $\mathbb{Z}_q^n$. Therefore, Game_0 and Game_1 distributions are statistically close and hence indistinguishable. Therefore the adversary's success probability may only increase by a negligible amount, accounted for in the $Q \cdot \mathsf{negl}(\lambda)$ term in the statement of the theorem.

Game_2*: Checking Message-Salt Pair Repeated Queries.* The next game hop incorporates a check to ensure that during a signature query, the salt drawn by the signing algorithm is not a repetition of a salt that was queried before along with the same message. We justify this hop from Game_1 to Game_2 by invoking the

Game_0	$\mathsf{SIGN}(\mu)$	$\mathsf{RO}(\mu, \mathbf{r})$
$\mathcal{Q}, \mathcal{H}, c \leftarrow \emptyset, \emptyset, 0$	**if** $c \geq Q$ **then abort**	**if** $(\mu, \mathbf{r}) \notin \mathcal{H}$ **then**
$(\mathbf{A}, \mathsf{td}) \leftarrow \mathsf{TrapGen}(1^n, 1^m, q)$	$\mathbf{r} \leftarrow\!\!\$\ \{0,1\}^\lambda$	$\quad \mathcal{H}[\mu, \mathbf{r}] \leftarrow\!\!\$\ \mathbb{Z}_q^n$
$\{(\mathbf{x}^i_{\mathrm{pre}}, \mathbf{t}^i_{\mathrm{pre}}) \leftarrow \Sigma.\mathsf{PreSign}(\mathsf{td})\}_{1 \leq i \leq Q}$	$\mathbf{t} \leftarrow \mathsf{RO}(\mu, \mathbf{r})$	**return** $\mathcal{H}[\mu, \mathbf{r}]$
$(\mu^\star, (\mathbf{y}^\star, \mathbf{r}^\star)) \leftarrow \mathcal{A}_Q^{\mathsf{SIGN},\mathsf{RO}}(\mathbf{A})$	$\mathbf{x} \leftarrow \mathsf{SampPre}_{\gg}(\mathsf{td}, \mathbf{t} - \mathbf{t}^c_{\mathrm{pre}})$	
$b_0 := (\mu^\star, \cdot) \notin \mathcal{Q}$	$\mathbf{y} \leftarrow \mathbf{x} + \mathbf{x}^c_{\mathrm{pre}}$	
$b_1 := \lVert \mathbf{y}^\star \rVert \leq \beta$	$\sigma \leftarrow (\mathbf{y}, \mathbf{r})$	
$b_2 := \mathcal{H}[\mu, \mathbf{r}] = \mathbf{A} \cdot \mathbf{y}^\star$	$c \leftarrow c + 1$	
return $b_0 \wedge b_1 \wedge b_2$	$\mathcal{Q} \leftarrow \mathcal{Q} \cup \{(\mu, \sigma)\}$	
	return σ	

Game_1	$\mathsf{SIGN}(\mu)$	$\mathsf{RO}(\mu, \mathbf{r})$
$\mathcal{Q}, \mathcal{H}, \mathcal{P}, c \leftarrow \emptyset, \emptyset, \emptyset, 0$	**if** $c \geq Q$ **then abort**	**if** $(\mu, \mathbf{r}) \notin \mathcal{H}$ **then**
$(\mathbf{A}, \mathsf{td}) \leftarrow \mathsf{TrapGen}(1^n, 1^m, q)$	$\mathbf{r} \leftarrow\!\!\$\ \{0,1\}^\lambda$	$\quad \mathbf{y} \leftarrow\!\!\$\ \mathsf{SampD}(1^n, 1^m, s_{\mathsf{sim}})$
$\{(\mathbf{x}^i_{\mathrm{pre}}, \mathbf{t}^i_{\mathrm{pre}}) \leftarrow \Sigma.\mathsf{PreSign}(\mathsf{td})\}_{1 \leq i \leq Q}$	$\mathbf{t} \leftarrow \mathsf{RO}(\mu, \mathbf{r})$	$\quad \mathbf{t} := \mathbf{A} \cdot \mathbf{y} \bmod q$
$(\mu^\star, (\mathbf{y}^\star, \mathbf{r}^\star)) \leftarrow \mathcal{A}_Q^{\mathsf{SIGN},\mathsf{RO}}(\mathbf{A})$	$\mathbf{x} \leftarrow \mathsf{SampPre}_{\gg}(\mathsf{td}, \mathbf{t} - \mathbf{t}^c_{\mathrm{pre}})$	$\quad \mathcal{H}(\mu, \mathbf{r}) \leftarrow \mathbf{t}$
$b_0 := (\mu^\star, \cdot) \notin \mathcal{Q}$	$\mathbf{y} \leftarrow \mathbf{x} + \mathbf{x}^c_{\mathrm{pre}}$	$\quad \mathcal{P}(\mu, \mathbf{r}) \leftarrow \mathbf{y}$
$b_1 := \lVert \mathbf{y}^\star \rVert \leq \beta$	$\sigma \leftarrow (\mathbf{y}, \mathbf{r})$	**return** $\mathcal{H}[\mu, \mathbf{r}]$
$b_2 := \mathcal{H}[\mu, \mathbf{r}] = \mathbf{A} \cdot \mathbf{y}^\star$	$c \leftarrow c + 1$	
return $b_0 \wedge b_1 \wedge b_2$	$\mathcal{Q} \leftarrow \mathcal{Q} \cup \{(\mu, \sigma)\}$	
	return σ	

Game_2	$\mathsf{SIGN}(\mu)$	$\mathsf{RO}(\mu, \mathbf{r})$
$\mathcal{Q}, \mathcal{H}, \mathcal{P}, c \leftarrow \emptyset, \emptyset, \emptyset, 0$	**if** $c \geq Q$ **then abort**	**if** $(\mu, \mathbf{r}) \notin \mathcal{H}$ **then**
$\mathit{repeat} \leftarrow \mathsf{false}$	$\mathbf{r} \leftarrow\!\!\$\ \{0,1\}^\lambda$	$\quad \mathbf{y} \leftarrow\!\!\$\ \mathsf{SampD}(1^n, 1^m, s_{\mathsf{sim}})$
$(\mathbf{A}, \mathsf{td}) \leftarrow \mathsf{TrapGen}(1^n, 1^m, q)$	**if** $(\mu, \mathbf{r}) \in \mathcal{H}$	$\quad \mathbf{t} := \mathbf{A} \cdot \mathbf{y} \bmod q$
$\{(\mathbf{x}^i_{\mathrm{pre}}, \mathbf{t}^i_{\mathrm{pre}}) \leftarrow \Sigma.\mathsf{PreSign}(\mathsf{td})\}_{1 \leq i \leq Q}$	$\quad \mathit{repeat} \leftarrow \mathsf{true}$	$\quad \mathcal{H}(\mu, \mathbf{r}) \leftarrow \mathbf{t}$
$(\mu^\star, (\mathbf{y}^\star, \mathbf{r}^\star)) \leftarrow \mathcal{A}_Q^{\mathsf{SIGN},\mathsf{RO}}(\mathbf{A})$	$\quad$ **abort**	$\quad \mathcal{P}(\mu, \mathbf{r}) \leftarrow \mathbf{y}$
$b_0 := (\mu^\star, \cdot) \notin \mathcal{Q}$	$\mathbf{t} \leftarrow \mathsf{RO}(\mu, \mathbf{r})$	**return** $\mathcal{H}[\mu, \mathbf{r}]$
$b_1 := \lVert \mathbf{y}^\star \rVert \leq \beta$	$\mathbf{x} \leftarrow \mathsf{SampPre}_{\gg}(\mathsf{td}, \mathbf{t} - \mathbf{t}^c_{\mathrm{pre}})$	
$b_2 := \mathcal{H}[\mu, \mathbf{r}] = \mathbf{A} \cdot \mathbf{y}^\star$	$\mathbf{y} \leftarrow \mathbf{x} + \mathbf{x}^c_{\mathrm{pre}}$	
return $b_0 \wedge b_1 \wedge b_2$	$\sigma \leftarrow (\mathbf{y}, \mathbf{r})$	
	$c \leftarrow c + 1$	
	$\mathcal{Q} \leftarrow \mathcal{Q} \cup \{(\mu, \sigma)\}$	
	return σ	

Fig. 9. Game_0 to Game_2

fundamental lemma of game playing, which assures that $\Pr[\mathit{repeat}] \leq |Q|/2^{\lambda/2}$, so the distance in this hop is again accounted for in the $Q \cdot \mathsf{negl}(\lambda)$ term.

Game_3	$\mathsf{SIGN}(\mu)$	$\mathsf{RO}(\mu, \mathbf{r})$
$\mathcal{Q}, \mathcal{H}, \mathcal{P}, c \leftarrow \emptyset, \emptyset, \emptyset, 0$	**if** $c \geq Q$ **then abort**	**if** $(\mu, \mathbf{r}) \notin \mathcal{H}$ **then**
repeat $\leftarrow$ false	$\mathbf{r} \leftarrow\!\!\$ \{0,1\}^\lambda$	$\quad \mathbf{y} \leftarrow\!\!\$ \mathsf{SampD}(1^n, 1^m, s_{\mathsf{sim}})$
$(\mathbf{A}, \mathsf{td}) \leftarrow \mathsf{TrapGen}(1^n, 1^m, q)$	**if** $(\mu, \mathbf{r}) \in \mathcal{H}$	$\quad \mathbf{t} := \mathbf{A} \cdot \mathbf{y} \bmod q$
$\{(\mathbf{x}^i_{\mathrm{pre}}, \mathbf{t}^i_{\mathrm{pre}}) \leftarrow \Sigma.\mathsf{PreSign}(\mathsf{td})\}_{1 \leq i \leq Q}$	$\quad$ *repeat* $\leftarrow$ true	$\quad \mathcal{H}(\mu, \mathbf{r}) \leftarrow \mathbf{t}$
$(\mu^\star, (\mathbf{y}^\star, \mathbf{r}^\star)) \leftarrow \mathcal{A}_Q^{\mathsf{SIGN},\mathsf{RO}}(\mathbf{A})$	$\quad$ **abort**	$\quad \mathcal{P}(\mu, \mathbf{r}) \leftarrow \mathbf{y}$
$b_0 := (\mu^\star, \cdot) \notin \mathcal{Q}$	$\mathsf{RO}(\mu, \mathbf{r})$	**return** $\mathcal{H}[\mu, \mathbf{r}]$
$b_1 := \lVert \mathbf{y}^\star \rVert \leq \beta$	$\mathbf{y} \leftarrow \mathcal{P}[\mu, \mathbf{r}]$	
$b_2 := \mathcal{H}[\mu, \mathbf{r}] = \mathbf{A} \cdot \mathbf{y}^\star$	$\sigma \leftarrow (\mathbf{y}, \mathbf{r})$	
return $b_0 \wedge b_1 \wedge b_2$	$c \leftarrow c + 1$	
	$\mathcal{Q} \leftarrow \mathcal{Q} \cup \{(\mu, \sigma)\}$	
	return σ	

Game_4	$\mathsf{SIGN}(\mu)$	$\mathsf{RO}(\mu, \mathbf{r})$
$\mathcal{Q}, \mathcal{H}, \mathcal{P}, c \leftarrow \emptyset, \emptyset, \emptyset, 0$	**if** $c \geq Q$ **then abort**	**if** $(\mu, \mathbf{r}) \notin \mathcal{H}$ **then**
repeated $\leftarrow$ false	$\mathbf{r} \leftarrow\!\!\$ \{0,1\}^\lambda$	$\quad \mathbf{y} \leftarrow\!\!\$ \mathsf{SampD}(1^n, 1^m, s_{\mathsf{sim}})$
$\mathbf{A} \leftarrow\!\!\$ \mathbb{Z}_q^{n \times m}$	**if** $(\mu, \mathbf{r}) \in \mathcal{H}$	$\quad \mathbf{t} := \mathbf{A} \cdot \mathbf{y} \bmod q$
$(\mu^\star, (\mathbf{y}^\star, \mathbf{r}^\star)) \leftarrow \mathcal{A}_Q^{\mathsf{SIGN},\mathsf{RO}}(\mathbf{A})$	$\quad$ *repeat* $\leftarrow$ true	$\quad \mathcal{H}(\mu, \mathbf{r}) \leftarrow \mathbf{t}$
$\{(\mathbf{x}^i_{\mathrm{pre}}, \mathbf{t}^i_{\mathrm{pre}}) \leftarrow \Sigma.\mathsf{PreSign}(\mathsf{td})\}_{1 \leq i \leq Q}$	$\quad$ **abort**	$\quad \mathcal{P}(\mu, \mathbf{r}) \leftarrow \mathbf{y}$
$b_0 := (\mu^\star, \cdot) \notin \mathcal{Q}$	$\mathsf{RO}(\mu, \mathbf{r})$	**return** $\mathcal{H}[\mu, \mathbf{r}]$
$b_1 := \lVert \mathbf{y}^\star \rVert \leq \beta$	$\mathbf{y} \leftarrow \mathcal{P}[\mu, \mathbf{r}]$	
$b_2 := \mathcal{H}[\mu, \mathbf{r}] = \mathbf{A} \cdot \mathbf{y}^\star$	$\sigma \leftarrow (\mathbf{y}, \mathbf{r})$	
return $b_0 \wedge b_1 \wedge b_2$	$c \leftarrow c + 1$	
	$\mathcal{Q} \leftarrow \mathcal{Q} \cup \{(\mu, \sigma)\}$	
	return σ	

Fig. 10. Game_3 and Game_4

Game_3*: Simulating Signatures.* We answer the signature query as depicted in Fig. 10. In particular, the random oracle is called on the input message and the randomly drawn salt, and the returned pre-image y is appended with the salt and set as the signature. We prove that the probability that a Q-query adversary wins Game_2 is at most the probability of winning Game_3, up to the multiplicative factor on the right side of Lemma 1.

Game_4*: Forget the Trapdoor.* The final game hop forgets the trapdoor and in place of the matrix A associated with the trapdoor, draws a random $\mathbf{A} \leftarrow_\$ \mathbb{Z}_q^{n \times m}$. Since the trapdoor generation algorithm generates $\mathbf{A}$ which are pseudorandom, the distribution of Game_3 and Game_4 are indistinguishable.

Constructing a SIS Adversary. An adversary that wins Game_4 can be translated into one that solves the SIS problem as follows. To win Game_4, the adversary has to output a $(\mu^\star, (\mathbf{y}^\star, \mathbf{r}^\star))$ such that $H(\mu^\star, \mathbf{r}^\star) = \mathbf{A} \cdot \mathbf{y}$ and $\|\mathbf{y}^\star\|_2 \leq \beta$. Without querying for $H(\mu^\star, \mathbf{r}^\star)$, the adversary does not know the nearly uniformly random target, and therefore can succeed in guessing with a negligible probability $1/q^n$. Therefore, we may assume that adversary indeed queried for $t := H(\mu^\star, \mathbf{r}^\star)$. The randomness of y from the pre-image sampling algorithm ensures that with high probability $\mathbf{y} \neq \mathbf{y}^\star$. Therefore, the non-zero short vector $\mathbf{y} - \mathbf{y}^\star$ is in the dual of the lattice generated by $\mathbf{A}$, since $\mathbf{A} \cdot \mathbf{y} = \mathbf{A} \cdot \mathbf{y}^\star = H(\mu^\star, \mathbf{r}^\star) \bmod q \Rightarrow \mathbf{A} \cdot (\mathbf{y} - \mathbf{y}^\star) = 0 \mod q$. Further, it is a short lattice vector, since $\|\mathbf{y} - \mathbf{y}^\star\|_2 \leq 2\beta$.

The only hop that contributes non negligibly to the bit security claimed in the theorem is the jump from Game_2 to Game_3, which Lemma 1 bounds as

$$\frac{\Pr\left[\mathcal{A}_Q^{\mathsf{Game}_2}(\mathsf{vk}) = 1\right]}{\Pr\left[\mathcal{A}_Q^{\mathsf{Game}_3}(\mathsf{vk}) = 1\right]^{\frac{a-1}{a}}} \leq 2^{\left(\log_2\left(\frac{s_{\mathsf{sim}}^2}{s^2}\right) + \frac{(a-1)\pi\|\mathbf{x}\|_{\max}^2 \log_2 e}{\left(a(\frac{s_{\mathsf{sim}}^2}{s^2} - 1) + 1\right)s^2}\right)Q}. \tag{9}$$

Here, we ignored the $(1+\epsilon)^Q$ by choosing a small enough parameter $\epsilon = 2^{-128}$. We have the two parameters a and r to optimize this bound. We will pick a to be big enough to ensure $(a-1)/a$ is close to one. By choosing the largest a satisfying the constraint $s_{\mathsf{sim}} \geq \sqrt{\ln(2m(1+1/\epsilon)/\pi)} \cdot \sqrt{(a((s_{\mathsf{sim}}^2/s^2) - 1) + 1)}$ of Lemma 1, we may approximate $(a-1)/a \approx 1$ and $(a-1)/(a(s_{\mathsf{sim}}^2/s^2 - 1)) + 1) \approx 1/(s_{\mathsf{sim}}^2/s^2 - 1)$. Hence, Eq. (9) simplifies to

$$\begin{aligned} &-\log_2\left(\Pr\left[\mathcal{A}_Q^{\mathsf{Game}_2}(\mathsf{vk}) = 1\right]\right) \leq \\ &\quad -\log_2\left(\Pr\left[\mathcal{A}_Q^{\mathsf{Game}_3}(\mathsf{vk}) = 1\right]\right) - \left(\log_2\left(\frac{s_{\mathsf{sim}}^2}{s^2}\right) + \frac{\pi\|\mathbf{x}\|_{\max}^2 \log_2 e}{\left(\frac{s_{\mathsf{sim}}^2}{s^2} - 1\right)s^2}\right)Q. \end{aligned} \tag{10}$$

We bound $\log_2\left(\Pr\left[\mathcal{A}_Q^{\mathsf{Game}_4}(\mathsf{vk}) = 1\right]\right)$ empirically using the lattice estimator [3], which considers the best known cryptanalytic algorithms for forgery by solving SIS. This estimate depends on the choice of the simulator Gaussian parameter s_{sim}. We can choose the s_{sim}^2/s^2 to balance the two terms on Eq. (10). One simple choice (which may not be asymptotically optimal) is to match the simulator and signature variances by setting $\frac{s_{\mathsf{sim}}^2}{2\pi} = \frac{s^2}{2\pi} + \mathbb{E}_{\mathbf{x}}\left(\|\mathbf{x}\|^2\right)$, resulting in the right-most term in Eq. (10) being

$$\left(\log_2\left(1 + \frac{2\pi\mathbb{E}_{\mathbf{x}}\left(\|\mathbf{x}\|^2\right)}{s^2}\right) + \frac{\|\mathbf{x}\|_{\max}^2 \log_2 e}{2\mathbb{E}_{\mathbf{x}}\left(\|\mathbf{x}\|^2\right)}\right) \cdot Q. \tag{11}$$

Another choice is the higher value $\frac{s_{\mathsf{sim}}^2}{2\pi} := \frac{s^2}{2\pi} + \|\mathbf{x}\|_{\max}^2$, resulting in the right-most term in Eq. (10) being

$$\left(\log_2\left(1 + \frac{2\pi\|\mathbf{x}\|_{\max}^2}{s^2}\right) + \frac{\log_2 e}{2}\right) \cdot Q, \tag{12}$$

which is smaller than Eq. (11). Substituting, Eq. (11) and Eq. (12) into Eq. (10), proves the bound. □

References

1. Alagic, G., et al.: NIST IR 8413: Status report on the third round of the NIST post-quantum cryptography standardization process. US Department of Commerce, NIST (2022)
2. Albrecht, M., Bai, S., Ducas, L.: A subfield lattice attack on overstretched NTRU assumptions. In: Robshaw, M., Katz, J. (eds.) CRYPTO 2016, Part I. LNCS, vol. 9814, pp. 153–178. Springer, Heidelberg (2016). https://doi.org/10.1007/978-3-662-53018-4_6
3. Albrecht, M.R., Player, R., Scott, S.: On the concrete hardness of learning with errors. J. Math. Cryptol. **9**(3), 169–203 (2015)
4. Babai, L.: On lovász' lattice reduction and the nearest lattice point problem. Combinatorica **6**, 1–13 (1986)
5. Bai, S., Lepoint, T., Roux-Langlois, A., Sakzad, A., Stehlé, D., Steinfeld, R.: Improved security proofs in lattice-based cryptography: using the Rényi divergence rather than the statistical distance. J. Cryptol. **31**(2), 610–640 (2018)
6. Barthe, G., Belaïd, S., Espitau, T., Fouque, P.-A., Rossi, M., Tibouchi, M.: GALACTICS: Gaussian sampling for lattice-based constant- time implementation of cryptographic signatures, revisited. In: Cavallaro, L., Kinder, J., Wang, X., Katz, J. (eds.) ACM CCS 2019, pp. 2147–2164. ACM Press (2019)
7. Ducas, L., Lyubashevsky, V., Prest, T.: Efficient identity-based encryption over NTRU lattices. In: Sarkar, P., Iwata, T. (eds.) ASIACRYPT 2014, Part II. LNCS, vol. 8874, pp. 22–41. Springer, Heidelberg (2014). https://doi.org/10.1007/978-3-662-45608-8_2
8. Ducas, L., Nguyen, P.Q.: Learning a zonotope and more: cryptanalysis of NTRUSign countermeasures. In: Wang, X., Sako, K. (eds.) ASIACRYPT 2012. LNCS, vol. 7658, pp. 433–450. Springer, Heidelberg (2012). https://doi.org/10.1007/978-3-642-34961-4_27
9. Ducas, L., Postlethwaite, E.W., Pulles, L.N., Woerden, W.: HAWK: module LIP makes lattice signatures fast, compact and simple. In: Agrawal, S., Lin, D. (eds.) ASIACRYPT 2022, Part IV. LNCS, vol. 13794, pp. 65–94. Springer, Cham (2022). https://doi.org/10.1007/978-3-031-22972-5_3
10. Ducas, L., Prest, T.: Fast Fourier orthogonalization. In: Proceedings of the ACM on International Symposium on Symbolic and Algebraic Computation, pp. 191–198 (2016)

11. Ducas, L., van Woerden, W.: NTRU fatigue: how stretched is overstretched? In: Tibouchi, M., Wang, H. (eds.) ASIACRYPT 2021, Part IV. LNCS, vol. 13093, pp. 3–32. Springer, Cham (2021). https://doi.org/10.1007/978-3-030-92068-5_1
12. Espitau, T., et al.: MITAKA: a simpler, parallelizable, maskable variant of falcon. In: Dunkelman, O., Dziembowski, S. (eds.) EUROCRYPT 2022, Part III. Lecture Notes in Computer Science, vol. 13277, pp. 222–253. Springer, Cham (2022). https://doi.org/10.1007/978-3-031-07082-2_9
13. Even, S., Goldreich, O., Micali, S.: On-line/off-line digital signatures. In: Brassard, G. (ed.) CRYPTO 1989. LNCS, vol. 435, pp. 263–275. Springer, New York (1990). https://doi.org/10.1007/0-387-34805-0_24
14. Even, S., Goldreich, O., Micali, S.: On-line/off-line digital signatures. J. Cryptol. **9**(1), 35–67 (1996)
15. Genise, N., Micciancio, D.: Faster Gaussian sampling for trapdoor lattices with arbitrary modulus. In: Nielsen, J.B., Rijmen, V. (eds.) EUROCRYPT 2018, Part I. LNCS, vol. 10820, pp. 174–203. Springer, Cham (2018). https://doi.org/10.1007/978-3-319-78381-9_7
16. Gentry, C., Peikert, C., Vaikuntanathan, V.: Trapdoors for hard lattices and new cryptographic constructions. In: Ladner, R.E., Dwork, C. (eds.) 40th ACM STOC, pp. 197–206. ACM Press (2008)
17. Goldreich, O., Goldwasser, S., Halevi, S.: Public-key cryptosystems from lattice reduction problems. In: Kaliski, B.S. (ed.) CRYPTO 1997. LNCS, vol. 1294, pp. 112–131. Springer, Heidelberg (1997). https://doi.org/10.1007/BFb0052231
18. Guerreau, M., Martinelli, A., Ricosset, T., Rossi, M.: The hidden parallelepiped is back again: power analysis attacks on falcon. IACR TCHES **2022**(3), 141–164 (2022)
19. Güneysu, T., Lyubashevsky, V., Pöppelmann, T.: Practical lattice-based cryptography: a signature scheme for embedded systems. In: Prouff, E., Schaumont, P. (eds.) CHES 2012. LNCS, vol. 7428, pp. 530–547. Springer, Heidelberg (2012). https://doi.org/10.1007/978-3-642-33027-8_31
20. Hoffstein, J., Howgrave-Graham, N., Pipher, J., Silverman, J.H., Whyte, W.: NTRUSign: digital signatures using the NTRU lattice. In: Joye, M. (ed.) CT-RSA 2003. LNCS, vol. 2612, pp. 122–140. Springer, Heidelberg (2003). https://doi.org/10.1007/3-540-36563-X_9
21. Howe, J., Westerbaan, B.: Benchmarking and analysing the NIST PQC lattice-based signature schemes standards on the ARM cortex M7. In: El Mrabet, N., De Feo, L., Duquesne, S. (eds.) AFRICACRYPT 2023. LNCS, vol. 14064, pp. 442–462. Springer, Cham (2023). https://doi.org/10.1007/978-3-031-37679-5_19
22. Karabulut, E., Aysu, A.: FALCON down: breaking FALCON post-quantum signature scheme through side-channel attacks. In: 58th ACM/IEEE Design Automation Conference, DAC 2021, San Francisco, CA, USA, 5–9 December 2021, pp. 691–696. IEEE (2021)
23. Kirchner, P., Fouque, P.-A.: Revisiting lattice attacks on overstretched NTRU parameters. In: Coron, J.-S., Nielsen, J.B. (eds.) EUROCRYPT 2017, Part I. LNCS, vol. 10210, pp. 3–26. Springer, Cham (2017). https://doi.org/10.1007/978-3-319-56620-7_1
24. Langlois, A., Stehlé, D.: Worst-case to average-case reductions for module lattices. DCC **75**(3), 565–599 (2015)
25. Lin, X., Tibouchi, M., Yu, Y., Zhang, S.: Do not disturb a sleeping falcon: Floating-point error sensitivity of the falcon sampler and its consequences. Cryptology ePrint Archive, Paper 2024/1709 (2024)

26. Lyubashevsky, V., et al.: CRYSTALS-DILITHIUM. Technical report, National Institute of Standards and Technology (2022). https://csrc.nist.gov/Projects/post-quantum-cryptography/selected-algorithms-2022
27. Micali, S., Goldreich, O., Even, S.: On-line/off-line digital signing. U.S. Patent #5,016,274 (1991). https://patents.google.com/patent/US5016274A/en
28. Micciancio, D., Peikert, C.: Trapdoors for lattices: simpler, tighter, faster, smaller. In: Pointcheval, D., Johansson, T. (eds.) EUROCRYPT 2012. LNCS, vol. 7237, pp. 700–718. Springer, Heidelberg (2012). https://doi.org/10.1007/978-3-642-29011-4_41
29. Micciancio, D., Regev, O.: Worst-case to average-case reductions based on Gaussian measures. In: 45th FOCS, pp. 372–381. IEEE Computer Society Press (2004)
30. FIPS 204 (Initial Public Draft): Module-Lattice-Based Digital Signature Standard. National Institute of Standards and Technology, NIST FIPS PUB 204, U.S. Department of Commerce (2023)
31. FIPS 203 (Initial Public Draft): Module-Lattice-Based Key-Encapsulation Mechanism Standard. National Institute of Standards and Technology, NIST FIPS PUB 203, U.S. Department of Commerce (2023)
32. Nguyen, P.Q., Regev, O.: Learning a parallelepiped: cryptanalysis of GGH and NTRU signatures. In: Vaudenay, S. (ed.) EUROCRYPT 2006. LNCS, vol. 4004, pp. 271–288. Springer, Heidelberg (2006). https://doi.org/10.1007/11761679_17
33. Peikert, C.: An efficient and parallel gaussian sampler for lattices. In: Rabin, T. (ed.) CRYPTO 2010. LNCS, vol. 6223, pp. 80–97. Springer, Heidelberg (2010). https://doi.org/10.1007/978-3-642-14623-7_5
34. Orson Peters. Ed25519 (2017). https://github.com/orlp/ed25519. Commit: `b1f19fab4aebe607805620d25a5e42566ce46a0e`
35. Pornin, T.: New efficient, constant-time implementations of Falcon. Cryptology ePrint Archive, Report 2019/893 (2019)
36. Prest, T., et al.: FALCON. Technical report, National Institute of Standards and Technology (2022). https://csrc.nist.gov/Projects/post-quantum-cryptography/selected-algorithms-2022
37. Shamir, A., Tauman, Y.: Improved online/offline signature schemes. In: Kilian, J. (ed.) CRYPTO 2001. LNCS, vol. 2139, pp. 355–367. Springer, Heidelberg (2001). https://doi.org/10.1007/3-540-44647-8_21
38. FIPS 205 (Initial Public Draft): Stateless Hash-Based Digital Signature Standard. National Institute of Standards and Technology, NIST FIPS PUB 205, U.S. Department of Commerce (2023)
39. Stehlé, D., Steinfeld, R.: Making `NTRU` as secure as worst-case problems over ideal lattices. In: Paterson, K.G. (ed.) EUROCRYPT 2011. LNCS, vol. 6632, pp. 27–47. Springer, Heidelberg (2011). https://doi.org/10.1007/978-3-642-20465-4_4
40. Zhang, S., Lin, X., Yu, Y., Wang, W.: Improved power analysis attacks on falcon. In: Hazay, C., Stam, M. (eds.) EUROCRYPT 2023, Part IV. LNCS, vol. 14007, pp. 565–595. Springer, Cham (2023). https://doi.org/10.1007/978-3-031-30634-1_19

Symmetric-Key Cryptography

How (Not) to Hash into Class Groups of Imaginary Quadratic Fields?

István András Seres[1(✉)], Péter Burcsi[1], and Péter Kutas[1,2]

[1] Eötvös Loránd University, Budapest, Hungary
seresistvanandras@gmail.com
[2] University of Birmingham, Birmingham, UK

Abstract. Class groups of imaginary quadratic fields (class groups for short) have seen a resurgence in cryptography as transparent groups of unknown order. They are a prime candidate for being a trustless alternative to RSA groups because class groups do not need a (distributed) trusted setup to sample a cryptographically secure group of unknown order. Class groups have recently found many applications in verifiable secret sharing, secure multiparty computation, transparent polynomial commitments, and perhaps most importantly, in time-based cryptography, i.e., verifiable delay functions, (homomorphic) time-lock puzzles, timed commitments, etc. However, there are various roadblocks to making class groups widespread in practical cryptographic deployments. We initiate the rigorous study of hashing into class groups. Specifically, we want to sample a uniformly distributed group element in a class group such that nobody knows its discrete logarithm with respect to any public parameter. We point out several flawed algorithms in numerous publicly available class group libraries. We further illustrate the insecurity of these hash functions by showing concrete attacks against cryptographic protocols, i.e., verifiable delay functions, if they were deployed with one of those broken hash-to-class group functions. We propose two families of cryptographically secure hash functions into class groups. We implement these constructions and evaluate their performance. We release our implementation as an open-source library.

1 Introduction

Sampling a uniformly random group element is a fundamental cryptographic primitive in numerous protocols. It is applied in various algorithms to sample public parameters or map messages to group elements in encryption [10] or signature schemes [13]. In some groups of interest, such as $\mathbb{Z}_p^*$ or $\mathbb{Z}_N^*$ (for a prime p and a semiprime N with unknown factorization) this is a simple task assuming a cryptographically secure hash function $H : \{0,1\}^* \rightarrow \{0,1\}^{2\lambda}$ for some security parameter λ, see efficient constructions in [41]. For other cryptographically interesting groups, such as r-th roots of unity of $\mathbb{Z}_p^*$ or elliptic curve groups, this is a non-trivial task that spurred a long line of research initiated mainly by Icart [40] and refined by Farashahi, Shparlinski, and Voloch [31] and extended to

A. Patra (Ed.): CT-RSA 2025, LNCS 15598, pp. 303–326, 2025.
https://doi.org/10.1007/978-3-031-88661-4_13

pairing-friendly curves (and is already being standardized [33]) by Wahby and Boneh [58] among others [32,35,51].

Buchmann and Williams first proposed cryptography based on class groups of imaginary quadratic fields (class groups for short) in 1988 [18]. Recently, class groups have seen a revived interest in the cryptographic community as class groups offer a transparent instantiation for groups of unknown order, i.e., without a trusted third party or threshold trust assumption in case of a distributed setup. While it is cumbersome to establish an RSA group $\mathbb{Z}_N^*$ in a trustless manner, one either conducts a secure multi-party computation protocol among many peers to create a semiprime without unknown factorization [11,20,25,39] or samples a gigantic modulus that will be guaranteed to have large enough prime factors. On the other hand, class groups allow one to sample a group of unknown order *transparently and efficiently*, i.e., by choosing the discriminant $\Delta = -p$ to be a large enough prime, as there is no efficient algorithm to compute the order of $\mathsf{Cl}(\Delta)$. Class groups were used to build numerous novel cryptographic protocols such as dynamic accumulators [43], linearly homomorphic encryption scheme [22], polynomial commitments [2,19,52] and a plethora of protocols in time-based cryptography, for instance, verifiable delay functions [7,48,59], (homomorphic) time-lock puzzles [45,49], timed commitments [14,57], etc. Even though class groups are a promising candidate to instantiate cryptographic protocols, they are less studied from a theoretical point of view regarding groups of unknown order assumptions [4], e.g., low order, adaptive root assumptions [9], or the inherent sequentiality of repeated squaring. Compared to, e.g., elliptic curve groups or RSA groups, they are also less developed from a practical (lack of more high-quality implementations [16] and developer tooling) point of view.

In this paper, we study cryptographically secure hash functions onto the elements of a class group of imaginary quadratic fields. To our knowledge, this is the first time one has built a surjective, cryptographically secure hash function for class groups of imaginary quadratic fields. Previous constructions either lack security proofs or do not provide implementation and evaluation of their performance [59]. Moreover, we improve and extend the aforementioned solution.

1.1 Applications of Hashing Into Class Groups

We detail four cryptographic applications whose security rely on a cryptographically secure hash-to-class-group function.

Verifiable Delay Functions [7]. In a verifiable delay function (VDF) $g : \{0,1\}^* \rightarrow \mathbb{G}$ for a group of unknown order $\mathbb{G}$ [50], one computes $g(x) := H(x)^{2^T}$ for some time (or delay) parameter T, which is typically $T \approx 2^{35} \cdots 2^{45}$, and hash function $H(\cdot)$ that maps into $\mathbb{G}$ [48,59]. As Wesolowski noted in [59], applying a hash function $H(\cdot)$ in the VDF $g(\cdot)$ is paramount. To see this, let us consider the variant of $g(\cdot)$, where there was no application of $H(\cdot)$ on the input x. Then observe that the adversary by computing $g(x) = x^{2^T} \in \mathbb{G}$ could obtain $g(x^\alpha)$ from $g(x)$ with a single exponentiation, that is, $g(x^\alpha) = g(x)^\alpha$, since $x \rightarrow x^{2^T}$ is a group homomorphism. This contradicts the sequentiality requirement of VDFs, as we require that computing $g(x)$ should take T sequential steps on *any input* x as opposed to the $\mathcal{O}(\log alpha)$ step to compute a single exponentiation.

At the time of writing, the only deployed class group VDF is run by the Chia network [27]. They obviate the problem of hashing into a fixed class group by selecting a new class group $\mathsf{Cl}(\Delta)$ for each epoch by generating a random prime discriminant Δ such that $\Delta \equiv 7 \mod 8$. For every freshly generated $\mathsf{Cl}(\Delta)$, they start the VDF from the fixed form $(2, 1, \frac{\Delta+1}{8})$ which is a canonical ideal of norm 2. Interestingly, one of the isogeny-based VDFs over $\mathbb{F}_p$ from [34] is analogous to this construction in the following sense. Namely, computing powers of an ideal of norm 2 translates to a chain of 2-isogenies on the elliptic curve side. In [34], they need a trusted setup to avoid certain shortcut attacks exactly because it is believed to be hard to hash onto the set of supersingular elliptic curves over $\mathbb{F}_p$ (or even to the full supersingular isogeny graph in general, for that matter [15]).

Contrary to the approach of Chia, we anticipate that future deployments of class group VDFs in programmable blockchains will likely use a fixed class group $\mathsf{Cl}(\Delta)$ for a *transparently and carefully* chosen Δ, i.e., such that it does not contain backdoors [4]. The use of a fixed, standardized class group is also motivated by prospective applications such as distributed randomness beacons [26], time-stamping services [42], consensus algorithms [44], contract signing [14], or lotteries [37]. We envision that using a fixed $\mathsf{Cl}(\Delta)$ in a programmable blockchain will ease these applications' interoperability, programmability, and extendability.

A very recent follow-up work implemented[1] and deployed a fast, non-surjective hash-to-class group function as part of the Sui blockchain's VDF suite [24].

Timed Commitments from Class Groups [57]. Thyagarajan et al. built an efficient CCA timed commitment in class groups. One of the key ingredients of their construction relies on sampling a well-formed, uniformly random public key $\mathsf{pk} \in \mathbb{G}$ that is a class group element. Their construction faces numerous technical challenges due to the lack of a secure hash function with the codomain of the applied class group $\mathbb{G}$. With such a cryptographic tool, their entire construction could be simplified and made more efficient.

Zero-Knowledge Proofs (of Knowledge) in Groups of Unknown Order. Σ-protocols in generic groups of unknown order can achieve soundness error of $\frac{1}{2}$ at best per challenge. This impossibility result was overcome, achieving negligible soundness error using a short unstructured common-reference string containing two fresh random generic group generators [8]. In practice, one must sample these group elements via a cryptographically secure hash-to-class group function.

Transparent Polynomial Commitment Schemes [2,19,52]. Recently, several transparent polynomial commitment schemes have been instantiated in class groups. These protocols often need an unstructured common reference string of many uniformly random class group elements. These group elements could be generated via a cryptographically secure hash-to-class group function.

[1] See: https://github.com/MystenLabs/fastcrypto/blob/main/fastcrypto-vdf/src/class_group/hash.rs.

1.2 Desiderata for a Hash Function Into Class Groups

We call a hash function $\mathsf{H}_{\mathsf{BQForm}} : \{0,1\}^* \rightarrow \mathbb{G}$ mapping to a class group $\mathbb{G}$, cryptographically secure if it satisfies the following four essential properties.

- **Deterministic, and efficient.** Evaluating the function $\mathsf{H}_{\mathsf{BQForm}}(\cdot)$ should be deterministic and efficient. This is non-trivial already in the case of hashing to elliptic curve functions [40].
- **Collision resistance**. It must be hard for any probabilistic polynomial time (PPT) adversary to find two messages $m_1 \neq m_2$ such that $\mathsf{H}_{\mathsf{BQForm}}(m_1) = \mathsf{H}_{\mathsf{BQForm}}(m_2)$.
- **One-way function.** For any image $\mathsf{H}_{\mathsf{BQForm}}(m)$ of the hash function, no PPT adversary should be able to output the pre-image m with non-negligible probability $1/\mathsf{poly}(\lambda)$, where λ is the security parameter.
- **Uniformly distributed.** The function's $\mathsf{H}_{\mathsf{BQForm}}(\cdot)$ codomain must be uniformly distributed in $\mathbb{G}$, i.e., among all reduced binary quadratic forms with a given discriminant Δ. This requirement eliminates many attempts implemented and used in various libraries implementing class group arithmetics.

Lessons Learnt from Cryptographically Insecure Hash Functions. In order to avoid pitfalls when designing cryptographically secure hash functions onto class groups of imaginary quadratic fields, it is worth studying previously proposed hash constructions. Even though some of these proposals were not designed with cryptographic applications in mind, we believe there are valuable lessons that can benefit the future designers of cryptographic hash functions. In particular, to ensure the codomain's uniform distribution of $H(\cdot)$, we analyze the asymptotic distribution properties of coefficients of class group elements $(a, b) \in \mathsf{Cl}(\Delta)$, see Sect. 3.2. These theoretical results on the coefficients' distributions might be of independent interest. A deeper understanding of these discrete probability distributions could inspire novel sampling-based hash algorithms.

Our Contributions. In this work, we make the following contributions.

Flawed hash functions. We review two hash functions onto class groups implemented in various open-source libraries, e.g., SageMath. We demonstrate that both fall short of being an efficient and secure hash function thanks to various vulnerabilities, e.g., the codomain of the hash function is nonuniform or highly skewed. Furthermore, we show concrete attacks against cryptographic protocols, i.e., verifiable delay functions, if they were deployed with one of these insecure hash-to-class group functions.

Provably secure hash constructions. We propose two families of secure and efficient hash functions with class group codomains. The first construction family is inspired by the key generation algorithm of CSIDH [23]. Meanwhile, the second family of hash functions extends and improves the hash function of Wesolowski [59]. We prove both of our constructions' security by only relying on standard cryptographic assumptions, i.e., only assuming cryptographically secure hash functions to $\{0,1\}^{2\lambda}$.

Open-source implementation. We build efficient algorithms that hash securely into class groups of imaginary quadratic fields. Additionally, we provide a publicly available implementation of our proposed hash functions.[2]

This paper is organized as follows. In Sect. 2, we provide the necessary background on (reduced) binary quadratic forms and class groups. In Sect. 3, we show several insecure but used methods to hash into class groups. In Sect. 4, we provide algorithms that are cryptographically secure hash functions and their codomain is a class group of imaginary quadratic fields. We detail our performance evaluation of the three proposed hash functions in Sect. 5. Our paper concludes with open research problems and future directions in Sect. 6.

2 Preliminaries

2.1 Notations and Definitions

The security parameter is denoted as λ. We assume a cryptographically secure hash function $\mathsf{H} : \{0,1\}^* \rightarrow \{0,1\}^{2\lambda}$ of λ bits of security. Furthermore, we assume a deterministic hash function $\mathsf{H}_{\mathsf{Primes}} : \{0,1\}^* \rightarrow \mathsf{Primes}(\lambda)$ with codomain of prime numbers with λ bitlength. This primitive was first discussed and built by Cachin et al. [21]. The divisor function $d(n) : \mathbb{N} \rightarrow \mathbb{N};\ d(n) := \sum_{d|n} 1$ assigns the number of divisors to n. Let $\mathsf{factors}(n)$ denote the multiset of the prime factors of n, i.e., with multiplicity. Whenever we sample x from a set S uniformly at random, we write $x \in_R S$ or sometimes $x \overset{\$}{\leftarrow} S$. $U(c, d)$ denotes the uniform probability distribution on the $[c, d]$ interval. We denote by $b = \mathsf{SqrtModP(a, p)}$ the algorithm which returns b (the smallest positive) such that $b^2 \equiv a \mod p$ iff. $\left(\frac{a}{p}\right) = 1$, otherwise it returns $\perp$. Most of the following definitions, lemmas, and theorems can be found in the excellent textbook of Buchmann and Vollmer on binary quadratic forms [17]. In the rest of this paper, we work with class groups of binary quadratic forms rather than the (isomorphic) ideal class group. This is because the class groups of binary quadratic forms are more efficient and simpler from a computational point of view. We refer to a binary quadratic form $f(x, y) = ax^2 + bxy + cy^2$ by the triple of its coefficients, i.e., $f = (a, b, c)$. In this work, we solely work with integral quadratic forms, i.e., $(a, b, c) \in \mathbb{Z}^3$.

Definition 1 (Discriminant of a form). *The discriminant* Δ *of a form* $f = (a, b, c)$ *is the integer* $\Delta := b^2 - 4ac$.

We work with (the equivalence classes of (cf. Definition 2)) forms with the same discriminant Δ in class group cryptography. When representing a form, we usually drop the last coefficient c and refer to a form as the pair (a, b) since the fixed discriminant will be evident from the context. Note $\Delta \equiv 0 \mod 4 \vee \Delta \equiv 1 \mod 4$, though in our applications $\Delta < 0$ and prime. Sometimes we denote the discriminant of a form f as $\Delta(f)$. The matrix of a form is defined as $M(f) := \begin{pmatrix} \mathrm{a} & \mathrm{b}/2 \\ \mathrm{b}/2 & \mathrm{c} \end{pmatrix}$.

[2] See: https://www.github.com/seresistvanandras/hashingToClassGroups.

Thus, the form $f(x, y)$ can be rewritten as $f(x, y) = (x, y)M(f)(x, y)^T$. We are interested in the transformations of a form f by linear transformations

$$U = \begin{pmatrix} \mathrm{s} & \mathrm{t} \\ \mathrm{u} & \mathrm{v} \end{pmatrix} \in \mathbb{Z}^{2\times 2}, \tag{1}$$

such that $det(U) = 1$, i.e., $U \in SL(2, \mathbb{Z})$. We define $U(x, y) := (sx+ty, ux+vy)$. Then $(fU)(x, y) = (det(U))f(U(x, y))$. We define forms as equivalents that can be transformed into each other with linear transformations.

Definition 2 (Equivalent forms). *Two binary quadratic forms f_1, f_2 are (properly) equivalent if $\exists U \in GL(2, \mathbb{Z}) : f_1 = f_2U$ ($U \in (SL(2, \mathbb{Z})$ in case of proper equivalence). The $GL(2, \mathbb{Z})$-orbit ($SL(2, \mathbb{Z})$-orbit) of a form is called the (proper) equivalence class of that form.*

It is easy to see that equivalent forms have invariants, such as minimum, discriminant, and content. An important infinite subgroup of $SL(2, \mathbb{Z})$ is generated by the matrix $T := \begin{pmatrix} 1 & 1 \\ 0 & 1 \end{pmatrix}$ and we denote the generated subgroup as

$$\Gamma = \left\{ T^s = \begin{pmatrix} 1 & s \\ 0 & 1 \end{pmatrix} : s \in \mathbb{Z} \right\}. \tag{2}$$

The cyclic group Γ acts on the set of positive definite forms. A small computation shows that the elements in the Γ-orbit of f can be given by

$$fT^s = (a, b + 2sa, f(s, 1)). \qquad (s \in \mathbb{Z}) \tag{3}$$

2.2 A Primer on Reduction Theory and Class Groups

This paper focuses solely on forms with *negative discriminant* Δ, which are the most relevant to cryptography [18]. Moreover, we will only focus on *positive definite* binary quadratic forms as we define next.

Definition 3 (Positive definite forms). *A form f is positive definite if $\forall (x, y) \neq (0, 0), (x, y) \in \mathbb{R}^2 : f(x, y) > 0$.*

It is easy to show that a form $f = (a, b)$ is positive definite if and only if $\Delta(f) < 0 \wedge a > 0$.

Definition 4 (Normal binary quadratic form). *A form f is said to be* normal *if $-a < b \leq a$.*

Definition 5 (Reduced binary quadratic form). *We say that a positive definite form $f = (a, b, c)$ is reduced if it is* normal*, $a \leq c$, and if $b \geq 0$ for $a = c$.*

Given a non-reduced form, we can obtain a reduced form by the repeated application of the following two efficient operations.

Definition 6 (Normalization operation). *The normalization operation on the form* (a,b,c) *is given by* $\eta(a,b,c) := (a, b+2ra, ar^2+br+c)$, *where* $r = \lfloor \frac{a-b}{2a} \rfloor$.

Definition 7 (Reduction operation). *The reduction operation on the form* (a,b,c) *is defined as* $\rho(a,b,c) := (c, -b+2sc, cs^2-bs+a)$, *where* $s = \lfloor \frac{c+b}{2c} \rfloor$. *It also outputs a* 2×2 *matrix* T *such that* $M(a,b,c)T = M(\rho(a,b,c))$.

Unlike the normalization operation η, the reduction operation may need multiple iterations before reducing a form. To reduce a form f, one computes $f \leftarrow \eta(f)$ then repeatedly compute $f \leftarrow \rho(f)$ until f is reduced. It can be shown that the number of reduction steps performed by the reduction algorithm $\rho(\cdot)$ when applied to a positive definite form $f = (a,b,c)$ is at most $\lfloor \log_2(a/\sqrt{|\Delta|}) \rfloor + 2$.

For a reduced binary quadratic form (a,b,c), we have that $|b| \leq a \leq \sqrt{\frac{|\Delta|}{3}}$. This is because we have $|\Delta| = 4ac - b^2 \geq 4a^2 - a^2 = 3a^2$. A reduced form with a given discriminant Δ is typically represented as the pair (a,b), i.e., this representation has a size $\approx \log_2(|\Delta|)$. Dobson, Galbraith, and Smith showed how to compress a reduced form to a representation that only has $\frac{3}{4}\log_2(|\Delta|)$ bits [30]. However, in this paper, we denote reduced binary quadratic forms simply with their uncompressed representation, i.e., (a,b). Sometimes, we explicitly spell out the full representation (a,b,c) of a (reduced) binary quadratic form. One can introduce an Abelian group operation and create a group of unknown order from (the equivalence classes of) reduced binary quadratic forms with a given discriminant Δ. This is the famous class group already known to Gauss in 1801 [36]. In the rest of this paper, we use the notations $\mathsf{Cl}(\Delta)$ and $\mathbb{G}$ interchangeably to mean a class group of the imaginary quadratic field with discriminant Δ. By a slight abuse of notation, we also denote the set of *reduced* binary quadratic forms with discriminant Δ by $\mathsf{Cl}(\Delta)$. Recall the class group $\mathsf{Cl}(\Delta)$ is isomorphic to the usual class group of fractional ideals modulo principal ideals [17, Chapter 9].

Complexity of Computing $|\mathsf{Cl}(\Delta)|$. There is no known efficient polynomial-time algorithm to compute the order of $\mathsf{Cl}(\Delta)$. Sutherland's algorithm has exponential worst-case complexity, i.e., $\mathcal{O}(\sqrt{|\mathsf{Cl}(\Delta)|/\log\log|\mathsf{Cl}(\Delta)|})$ [56]. However, Sutherland's algorithm can exploit the structure of $\mathsf{Cl}(\Delta)$ and runs significantly faster when $|\mathsf{Cl}(\Delta)|$ is smooth. The security implications of Sutherland's algorithm in the context of class group cryptography are extensively studied in [30]. Currently, the asymptotically fastest algorithm (often beaten by Sutherland's algorithm in practice) to compute the order of the class group $\mathsf{Cl}(\Delta)$ runs in subexponential time that is $L_{|\Delta|}(1/2)$ and is due to Hafner and McCurley [38]. Moreover, Buchmann's algorithm can additionally compute the structure of $\mathsf{Cl}(\Delta)$. We refer the reader to Biasse et al. [6] for a modern treatment of the security of class group cryptography. We mention the current computational record for computing the order of a class group held by Beullens, Kleinjung, and Vercauteren, whereby the authors calculated $|\mathsf{Cl}(\Delta)|$ using the Hafner-McCurley algorithm for a discriminant Δ of 512-bits running in 52 core years [5].

We denote the set of integral binary quadratic forms with a given discriminant and a coefficient as $\mathcal{F}(\Delta, a) := \{(a,b,c)\Gamma : b, c \in \mathbb{Z}, \Delta(a,b,c) = \Delta\}$. The number of such forms is denoted as $\mathcal{R}(\Delta, a) = |\mathcal{F}(\Delta, a)|$. Note the forms in $\mathcal{F}(\Delta, a)$ are not necessarily reduced, though by definition they belong to different Γ-orbits. It can be shown that the function $\mathcal{R}(\Delta, \cdot)$ is a multiplicative function, i.e., for coprime positive integers a_1, a_2 we have $\mathcal{R}(\Delta, a_1 a_2) = \mathcal{R}(\Delta, a_1)\mathcal{R}(\Delta, a_2)$. Therefore, we need to establish this function's values at prime powers p^e. Next, we recall this result in the following theorem whose proof can be found in [17].

Theorem 1 ($\mathcal{R}(\Delta, a)$ for a prime $a = p$ and prime power $a = p^e$). *Let p be a prime:*

- *If $a = p$, then $\mathcal{R}(\Delta, p) = \left(\frac{\Delta}{p}\right) + 1$.*
- *If $a = p^e$, and $e \geq 1$ then we have the following cases:*
  - *If $\left(\frac{\Delta}{p}\right) = -1$, then $\mathcal{R}(\Delta, p^e) = 0$.*
  - *If $\left(\frac{\Delta}{p}\right) = 0, e \geq 2, p \nmid f(\Delta)$, then $\mathcal{R}(\Delta, p^e) = 0$.*
  - *If $\left(\frac{\Delta}{p}\right) = 1$, then $\mathcal{R}(\Delta, p^e) = 2$.*

Theorem 2 (Establishing $\mathcal{F}(\Delta, p)$ for a prime p). *If $\mathcal{R}(\Delta, p) \geq 1$, then we can compute the corresponding prime forms (p, b, c) as follows.*

- *If $p = 2$, if Δ is odd, then $b = 1$, else $b = 2(\Delta/4 \mod 2)$. Return: $(p, b, (b^2 - \Delta)/(4p))$.*
- *If $p \geq 3$, then let $b \leftarrow \mathsf{SqrtModP}(\Delta, p)$. Return: $(p, \pm b, (b^2 - \Delta)/(4p))$.*

Remark 1. By multiplicativity of $\mathcal{R}(\Delta, \cdot)$ and by Theorem 1, $\mathcal{R}(\Delta, \cdot)$ is always a power of two when positive. Note if $a \leq \sqrt{\frac{|\Delta|}{4}}$, then all the forms in $\mathcal{R}(\Delta, a)$ are reduced since necessarily $|b| \leq a$, cf. Theorem 2, because $b^2 \leq a^2 \leq \frac{|\Delta|}{4}$. Therefore, the resulting form's c coefficient will be at least $c \geq \sqrt{\frac{|\Delta|}{4}}$, meaning that the form is reduced as $a \leq c$ holds as well. In other words, if $\sqrt{\frac{|\Delta|}{4}} \leq a \leq \sqrt{\frac{|\Delta|}{3}}$, then it might be the case that not all forms are reduced in $\mathcal{F}(\Delta, a)$. This phenomenon is clearly displayed in Fig. 1a.

Theorem 3 (Dirichlet's class number formula (1839) [28]). *When $\Delta \leq -5$, Dirichlet's class number formula asserts that*

$$|\mathsf{Cl}(\Delta)| = \frac{\sqrt{|\Delta|} L(1, \chi_\Delta)}{\pi}, \tag{4}$$

where $L(1, \chi_\Delta)$ is the Dirichlet L-function of the character χ_Δ.

Remark 2. Typically $L(1, \chi_\Delta)$ is in the interval $[0.1, 10]$ [55].

3 How *not* to Hash into Class Groups of Imaginary Quadratic Fields?

This section reviews cryptographically insecure hash functions developed and used in various open-source libraries, e.g., the SageMath mathematical software library. We argue why these simple solutions do not meet our requirements, i.e., the image's uniform distribution in $\mathsf{Cl}(\Delta)$, and should not be used in security-critical applications. In the following, we mainly focus on the security aspects of these broken hash functions, even if computing them may be computationally inefficient. We denote the insecure hash functions in the sequel as $h^*(\cdot)$.

3.1 Group Elements with Known Discrete Logarithm

In some applications, it is necessary to sample group elements whose discrete logarithm is unknown to any other element from the set of public parameters. For instance, this is the case in the timed commitment application of class groups as proposed by [57]. Additionally, for certain zero-knowledge proofs of knowledge in groups of unknown order, if the adversary knows the discrete logarithm of the public parameters, they can break the soundness of the proof system [8]. Therefore, in these applications, such a simple hash function as $h_1^* : \{0,1\}^* \rightarrow \mathbb{G} : h_1^*(m) := g^{h(m)}$ for a class group element $g \in \mathbb{G}$ and a cryptographically secure hash function h, is insecure.

3.2 Uniformly Random b

A natural idea for choosing a random reduced quadratic form $(a, b, c) \in \mathsf{Cl}(\Delta)$ would be to first choose a uniformly random value $b \in [0, \sqrt{\frac{|\Delta|}{3}}]$ and compute a, c such that $\Delta = b^2 - 4ac$ holds. We investigate this approach by analyzing the distribution of coefficient b of reduced forms in $\mathsf{Cl}(\Delta)$. A similar strategy is employed by a popular class group cryptography package on GitHub written in Rust.[3] This strategy's implicit assumption is that the distribution of the reduced form's b coefficient in $\mathsf{Cl}(\Delta)$ follows a discrete uniform distribution in $[-\sqrt{\frac{|\Delta|}{3}}, \sqrt{\frac{|\Delta|}{3}}]$. As we show in the full version of this work [53], this does not hold for random Δ: there is a bias in the distribution of b proportional to $\approx \frac{1}{2}\log\Delta - \log b$. This indicates that this natural idea fails to sample a uniform class group element from $\mathsf{Cl}(\Delta)$, hence, contradicting our desiderata. Due to space constraints, we provide the analysis in the full version of this paper [53].

3.3 Random Form and Reduce

Another naïve approach might be to sample uniformly random a binary quadratic form $(a, b) \xleftarrow{R} [0, \sqrt{\frac{|\Delta|}{3}}]^2$ or from some other simple interval $[a, b]^2$. This

[3] See ZenGo-X Class group implementation: https://github.com/ZenGo-X/class.

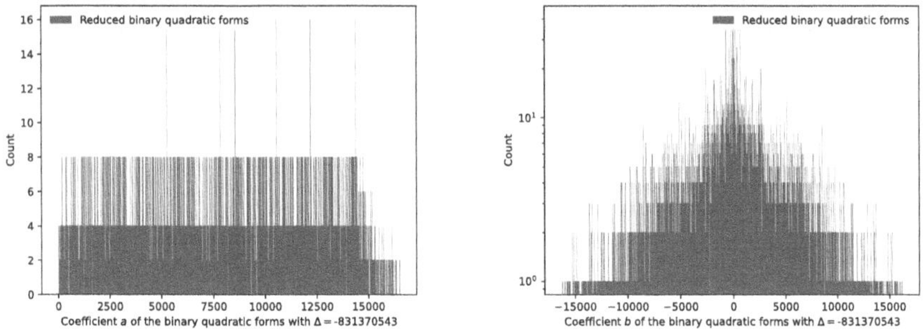

(a) Coefficient a. (b) Coefficient b

Fig. 1. Illustrating the distribution of the coefficient a and b of reduced binary quadratic forms in the class group $\mathsf{Cl}(\Delta)$ with the medium-sized discriminant $\Delta = -831,370,543$. The distribution of coefficient a is partially characterized in Theorem 1. Note the heights of the bars in the left figure are powers of two, except when $\sqrt{\frac{|\Delta|}{4}} \leq a \leq \sqrt{\frac{|\Delta|}{3}}$, i.e., towards the far right end of the figure, cf. Remark 1. We investigate the distribution of coefficient b in the full version [53]. Note the left figure is lin-lin, while the right is log-lin. We provide an example distribution for coefficient c as well, in the full version of this work [53].

approach is implemented by the Sage Quadratic Forms package[4]. It is well documented[5]. The problem of these approaches is that the resulting *reduced* binary quadratic forms, i.e., the class group elements, are not uniformly distributed in those intervals. In particular, as we show next, this would result in a highly skewed non-uniform distribution of reduced binary quadratic forms. Therefore, this approach is also insecure for cryptographic purposes, cf. Sect. 3.4. The next theorem formally characterizes the probability distribution of class group elements output by the function above. For an empirical measurement, see Fig. 3a.

Theorem 4 (Distribution of random forms). *Let* $h_3^*(\cdot) : \{0,1\}^* \rightarrow \mathbb{G}$ *denote the insecure hash function described above, cf. Fig. 2. The output distribution of* $h_3^*(\cdot)$ *follows a power-law distribution in the class group* $\mathbb{G}$. *More formally,* $\forall a \in [1, \sqrt{|\Delta|/3}]$ *we have*

$$\Pr_s[h_3^*(s) = (a', b') | (a,b) \in \mathsf{Cl}(\Delta) \wedge \rho(a', b') = (a,b)] = \mathcal{O}\left(\frac{1}{a}\right). \quad (5)$$

Proof. Let $f = (a,b) \in \mathsf{Cl}(\Delta)$ be a reduced binary quadratic form, and we assume that f was sampled from $[0, \sqrt{\frac{|\Delta|}{3}}]^2$. An easy calculation shows that the

[4] See SageMath random quadratic form function implementation: https://github.com/sagemath/sage/blob/develop/src/sage/quadratic_forms/random_quadraticform.py.

[5] See SageMath random quadratic form function documentation: https://doc.sagemath.org/html/en/reference/quadratic_forms/sage/quadratic_forms/random_quadraticform.html.

How *not* to hash into class groups? vol. #3.

Public parameters: $\mathbb{G} \xleftarrow{R} GGen(\lambda), \mathsf{H} : \{0,1\}^* \rightarrow \{0,1\}^{2\lambda}$ a cryptographically secure hash function.
Public inputs: $x \in \{0,1\}^*$.

1. $cnt = 0$.
2. $h \leftarrow \mathsf{H}(x||cnt)$. Let $(a,b) := (h[0:\lambda], h[\lambda:2\lambda])$. //Note the form (a,b) is most likely a non-reduced form.
3. If $(a,b) \in \mathsf{Cl}(\Delta)$ then: Return $\rho(a,b)$.
   - else $cnt = cnt + 1$, and goto 2.

Fig. 2. This hash-to-class group function is implemented and used by the SageMath open-source mathematical software system. The application of this hash function in certain cryptographic protocols, e.g., in verifiable delay functions, makes the cryptosystem's deployment completely insecure, cf. Sect. 3.4.

Γ-orbit of f contains forms $fT^s = (a, b+2sa, f(s,1))$ for $s \in \mathbb{Z}$, cf. Eq. (3). We observe that the generated Γ-orbit's cardinality in the considered interval $[0, \sqrt{\frac{|\Delta|}{3}}]^2$ is $\mathcal{R}_{f\Gamma} := \left|\left\{fT^s | s \in \mathbb{Z} \wedge fT^s \in [0, \sqrt{\frac{|\Delta|}{3}}]^2\right\}\right| = \left\lfloor \frac{\sqrt{\frac{|\Delta|}{3}} - b}{2a} \right\rfloor$. Denoting the set of all quadratic forms in $[0, \sqrt{\frac{|\Delta|}{3}}]^2$ with discriminant Δ by $\mathsf{A}(\Delta)$, we get the desired $\frac{\mathcal{R}_{f\Gamma}}{|\mathsf{A}(\Delta)|} = \mathcal{O}(\frac{1}{a})$ probability stated in Eq. (5). We remark that it is enough to consider only the Γ-orbit of a form f (the subgroup of $SL(2,\mathbb{Z})$ generated by the matrix T, cf. Eq. (3)), as transformations by other matrices would result in forms f' such that $f' = (a,b) \notin [0, \sqrt{\frac{|\Delta|}{3}}]^2$.

3.4 Breaking Cryptographic Protocols Instantiated with Flawed Hash-to-Class Group Functions

Next, we show that certain cryptographic protocols become insecure when instantiated with insecure hash-to-class group functions described in this section. As an illustrative example, we consider a VDF protocol instantiated with the hash function described in Sect. 3.3. More formally, we consider the VDF function $g^*(x) : \{0,1\}^* \rightarrow \mathbb{G}; x \rightarrow (h_3^*(x))^{2^T} \in \mathbb{G}$, where T is the delay parameter and $h_3^*(\cdot)$ is the insecure hash function presented in Sect. 3.3. We show that an adversary who precomputes all the VDF values z^{2^T} for $\forall z : z = (a,b) \in \mathsf{Cl}(\Delta) \wedge a \in [0, \mathsf{poly}(\lambda)]$ will be able to compute the VDF output with non-negligible probability in λ without computing T sequential squarings in $\mathbb{G}$. In other words, a VDF adversary can exploit the skewed power law distribution of the insecure hash function $h_3^*(\cdot)$ on the class group $\mathsf{Cl}(\Delta)$ by anticipating that the hash output will likely produce forms (a,b) with small norms $a \in [0, \mathsf{poly}(\lambda)]$.

We say that a precomputing adversary $\mathcal{A}_{g^*}^{h_3^*}(\lambda)$ outputs 1 and breaks the VDF $g^*(\cdot)$ iff. $h_3^*(s) = (a,b)$ such that $a \leq \mathsf{poly}(\lambda)$. Next, we compute the probability

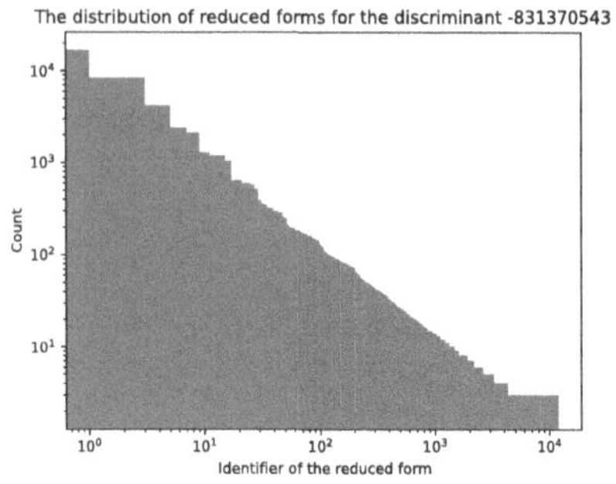

(a) The skewed power-law distribution of reduced binary quadratic forms among all forms in $[0, \sqrt{|\Delta|/3}]^2$ for the medium-sized discriminant $\Delta = -831,370,543$.

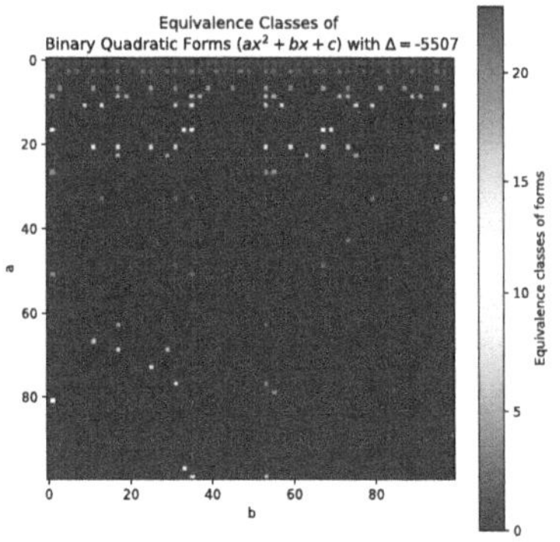

(b) The distribution of equivalent binary quadratic forms in $[0, \sqrt{|\Delta|/3}]^2$ for a small-sized discriminant $\Delta = -5,507$.

Fig. 3. A family of insecure hash functions chooses uniformly random forms (a, b) from the square $[0, \sqrt{|\Delta|/3}]^2$ and subsequently reduces it. In these two figures, we analyze the distribution of the output of this hashing strategy induced on the reduced forms, i.e., group elements in $\mathsf{Cl}(\Delta)$. The deployment of this broken hash function would lead to attacks in certain cryptographic applications, e.g., verifiable delay functions, cf. Sect. 3.4.

that the adversary breaks the (sequentiality of the) VDF. Let $\mathcal{B} \in \mathsf{poly}(\lambda)$.

$$\Pr[\mathcal{A}_{g^*}^{h_3^*}(\lambda) = 1] \approx \frac{\int_1^{\mathcal{B}} \frac{1}{x} dx}{\int_1^{\sqrt{|\Delta|/3}} \frac{1}{x} dx} = \frac{[\ln x]_1^{\mathcal{B}}}{[\ln x]_1^{\sqrt{|\Delta|/3}}} = \frac{\ln(\mathcal{B})}{\ln(\sqrt{|\Delta|/3})} = \log_{\sqrt{|\Delta|/3}}(\mathcal{B}). \tag{6}$$

By choosing $\mathcal{B} := \sqrt{|\Delta|/3}^{1/\lambda}$, we ensure that $\Pr[\mathcal{A}_{g^*}^{h_3^*}(\lambda) = 1] \approx \frac{1}{\lambda}$, i.e., non-negligible in λ, while $\mathcal{B} \in \mathsf{poly}(\lambda)$. We consider the following concrete parameters. For $\lambda = 85$-bit security, we need a discriminant Δ with 3400 bits [30]. Thus, if one chooses $\mathcal{B} := \sqrt{|\Delta|/3}^{1/\lambda} \approx 2^{20}$, then they need to precompute roughly $\mathcal{B}$ VDF evaluations on binary quadratic forms (a, b) such that $a \in \mathcal{B}$. This computation could be done in parallel time T using $\mathcal{B}$ processors. The success probability of this preprocessing attack is roughly $\approx \frac{20}{1700} = 1.17\%$, i.e., non-negligible in λ.

4 How to Hash into Class Groups of Imaginary Quadratic Fields?

In this section, we show how to hash securely and efficiently into class groups. Additionally, we prove the security of our constructions, investigate their friendliness to zero-knowledge proofs, and secure multiparty computation applications.

4.1 Construction #1: Using a Generating Set of Small Norm Ideals

The idea of the following construction is reminiscent of the secret key generation algorithm of CSIDH [23]. In a pre-computation phase, we sample $f_1, \ldots, f_d$ binary quadratic forms with small prime norms (the a coefficient of the form is a small prime $p \in \mathcal{O}(\log|\Delta|)$) in $\mathsf{Cl}(\Delta)$). In [29], it is observed that these group elements are well-distributed and approximately generate the whole group $\mathsf{Cl}(\Delta)$ if the number of generating ideals d is chosen properly. We hash the input x with the hash function $\mathsf{H}_0(\cdot)$ to obtain random bits $b = (b_1, \ldots, b_d)$ and output the approximately equidistributed group element $\prod_{i=1}^{d} f_i^{b_i}$. Next, we prove the security of this hash construction.

How to hash into class groups? Construction #1.

Public parameters: $\mathbb{G} \xleftarrow{R} GGen(\lambda), \mathsf{H}_0 : \{0,1\}^* \to \{0,1\}^d$ a secure hash function. A precomputation outputs $\{f_i\}_{i=1}^{d} \in \mathsf{Cl}(\Delta)^d$ forms with small prime norms, i.e., $\forall i \in [1,d] : f_i = (p_i, b_i) \in \mathsf{Cl}(\Delta)$ for some "small" prime $p_i \in [2, \mathcal{O}(\log|\Delta|)]$.
Inputs: $x \in \{0,1\}^*$.

1. Let $b := \mathsf{H}_0(x)$ and b_i be the ith bit of b.
2. Return: $H(x) := \prod_{i=1}^{d} f_i^{b_i} (\in \mathsf{Cl}(\Delta))$.

Fig. 4. This hash function to class groups of imaginary quadratic fields is reminiscent of the key generation algorithm of CSIDH [23]. The number of the generating ideals d to achieve 2^{-k} statistical uniformity of the codomain is precisely defined in Theorem 5.

Theorem 5 (Construction #1. is secure). *The hash function described in Sect. 4.1 is a cryptographically secure hash function with the codomain of a class group* $\mathsf{Cl}(\Delta)$ *assuming a cryptographically secure hash function* $\mathsf{H}(\cdot)$ *onto* $\{0,1\}^d$ *whenever* $d \geq 2\log|\mathsf{Cl}(\Delta)| + h + 2k$ *yielding a* 2^{-k}*-uniform distribution in* $\mathsf{Cl}(\Delta)$ *with probability at least* $1 - 2^{-h}$.

Proof. We show that Construction #1. satisfies our desiderata.

Collision-resistance Any collision in $H(\cdot)$ results from one of two causes. First, there may be a collision in Step 1. in Fig. 4, i.e., there exists a collision in $\mathsf{H}_0(\cdot)$ which by assumption occurs with negligible probability. Second, if there is a collision in Step 2. in Fig. 4, then $\exists b, b' : \prod_{i=1}^{d} f_i^{b_i} = \prod_{i=1}^{d} f_i^{b'_i}$ for $b = \mathsf{H}_0(x) \wedge b' = \mathsf{H}_0(x') \wedge b \neq b'$. However, this occurs with negligible probability, assuming the order assumption. This is because if a sufficient number of these collisions are found, then there is a simple way of computing the order of the class group. Let

$f_1, \ldots, f_n$ be a fixed set of prime forms. Integer vectors of the form $(k_1, \ldots, k_n)$ for which $\prod_{i=1}^{n} f_i^{k_i}$ corresponds to a principal ideal, forms a lattice (this is often called the relation lattice). If one can find n linearly independent vectors in this lattice (thus a lattice basis), then one can compute the determinant of the lattice in polynomial time, which is known to be equal to the class number. For further details, we refer to [5].

One-Wayness. Assume the adversary $\mathcal{A}$ given $y \in \mathsf{Cl}(\Delta)$, outputs x s.t. $H(x) = y$ with non-negligible probability. Then we create an adversary $\mathcal{A}'$ that breaks the one-wayness of $\mathsf{H}_0(\cdot)$ as follows. $\mathcal{A}'$ is given a challenge $b \in \{0,1\}^d$ computes $y = \prod_{i=1}^{n} f_i^{b_i}$ and forwards it to $\mathcal{A}$. The output x produced by $\mathcal{A}$ satisfies $H(x) = y$. This either means $\mathsf{H}_0(x) = b$ contradicting the one-wayness of H_0 or produces a collision for y which was shown to be computationally infeasible above.

Uniform Distribution. Now, we look at the uniform distribution property. Since the construction has the same image as the Naor-Reingold type PRF from [12, Theorem 23], the same theorem applies in this context as well. Similar constructions also appear in [47] and [1]. The group theoretic statement with regards to the codomain's statistical uniformity was proved in [29, Theorem 3.]. ■

Even though this construction in Section 4.1 has just been proven secure, note that it is not well-suited to VDF applications. Specifically, it is susceptible to the same precomputation attack as described in Sect. 3.4. Formally, $\mathcal{A}$ can precompute for all d prime-norm bases the VDF output $f_i^{2^T} \in \mathsf{Cl}(\Delta)$. In the online phase of the attack, given the hash output $g := \prod_{i=1}^{d} f_i^{b_i}$, $\mathcal{A}$ can compute the VDF output with maximum d group operations as $g^{2^T} = \prod_{i=1}^{d} (f_i^{2^T})^{b_i}$. To counter these attacks, we propose a new family of hash-to-class group functions.

4.2 Construction #2: Wesolowski's Construction

A folklore approach was proposed by Wesolowski in the conference version's appendix of [59] and implemented by Pope[6]. The construction's idea is to generate a uniformly random prime $p \in [0, \sqrt{\frac{|\Delta|}{4}}]$, and if $\left(\frac{\Delta}{p}\right) = 1$ (which should happen on average with probability $\approx 1/2$), we can choose from two binary quadratic forms (p, b) and $(p, -b)$, where b is obtained as $b := (\sqrt{\Delta} \bmod p)$.

Theorem 6 (Construction #2. is secure). *The hash function in Fig. 5 is a cryptographically secure hash function of λ-bit security with the codomain of a class group of imaginary quadratic fields assuming that a $\mathsf{H}_{\mathsf{Primes}}(\cdot)$ hash function with prime number codomain and λ-bit security exists.*

[6] See: https://github.com/GiacomoPope/ClassGroups/blob/main/classgroup.py.

How to hash into class groups? Construction #2.

Public parameters: $\mathbb{G} \overset{R}{\leftarrow} GGen(\lambda), \mathsf{H}_{\mathsf{Primes}} : \{0,1\}^* \to \mathsf{Primes}(\lambda)$ a cryptographically secure hash function. Let Δ be the discriminant corresponding to the generated group $\mathbb{G}$.
Inputs: $x \in \{0,1\}^*$.

1. $i = 0$.
2. Compute $p := \mathsf{H}_{\mathsf{Primes}}(x||i)$. // For the sake of uniform distribution p must be large, i.e., $p \overset{\$}{\leftarrow} [0, \sqrt{|\Delta|/4}]$. We also need to ensure the reducedness of the form.
3. If $\left(\frac{\Delta}{p}\right) = 1$ then let $b := (\sqrt{\Delta} \bmod p)$.
   - else $i = i + 1$, and *goto* 2. //There is no prime form $(p, \cdot) \in \mathsf{Cl}(\Delta)$, cf. Theorem 1.
4. Let $s := (p \mod 3)$. // If $\left(\frac{\Delta}{p}\right) = 1$, then there are two modular square roots: b and $-b$. We need to choose one of them deterministically.
   - If $s == 0 \vee s == 1$: Return $H(x) := (p, b)$.
   - elif $s == 2$: Return $H(x) := (p, -b)$.

Fig. 5. Wesolowski's hash-to-class group construction had been implicitly introduced (though without security proofs, implementation, and performance evaluation) in the conference version of [59]. We improve this construction in Fig. 6.

Proof. We show that Construction #2. satisfies our desiderata. It is easy to see, as we show next, that all the desired properties (i.e., collision resistance, one-wayness, and uniform distribution of the codomain) can be reduced straightforwardly to the corresponding property of the underlying hash function $\mathsf{H}_{\mathsf{Primes}}(\cdot)$.

Collision Resistance. Assume there exists a collision in $H(\cdot)$, i.e., $\exists x, x' \in \{0,1\}^*$ such that $x \neq x'$, with $(p, b) = H(x) = H(x')$. Due to Step 2 of Fig. 5 this means that $p = \mathsf{H}_{\mathsf{Primes}}(x||i) = \mathsf{H}_{\mathsf{Primes}}(x'||i')$ contradicting the collision resistance property of $\mathsf{H}_{\mathsf{Primes}}(\cdot)$.

One-Wayness. Assume the reduction is given a prime p on which it must invert $\mathsf{H}_{\mathsf{Primes}}(\cdot)$. The reduction computes b using Theorem 2 s.t. $(p, b) \in \mathsf{Cl}(\Delta)$ and forwards it to the adversary $\mathcal{A}$. If given $(p, b) \in \mathsf{Cl}(\Delta)$, $\mathcal{A}$ can output a pre-image $x \in \{0,1\}^*$ with non-negligible probability, then simply recompute Step 2 of the hash function in Fig 5, $\mathsf{H}_{\mathsf{Primes}}(x||\cdot)$ until p is obtained for some $i \in \mathbb{Z}$ such that $p = \mathsf{H}_{\mathsf{Primes}}(x||i)$. Such an i is expected to be found in constant number of steps. This (x, i) is a pre-image of p contradicting the one-wayness of $\mathsf{H}_{\mathsf{Primes}}(\cdot)$.

Uniform Distribution of the Codomain. Assuming $\mathsf{H}_{\mathsf{Primes}}(\cdot)$ is uniformly distributed on its codomain $\mathsf{Primes}(\lambda)$, the hash function $H(\cdot)$ codomain's uniformity will be still preserved after the rejection sampling of Step 2 and 3. ∎

Improving Wesolowski's Construction. We want to highlight two major rooms for improvement in the hash function's original version as proposed in the appendix of the conference version of [59], cf. Fig. 5.

- **Inefficiency.** Wesolowski's construction is rather inefficient compared to the first proposed construction, as we show empirically in Sect. 5.2. This is due to the algorithm's costly primality checks in Step 2. Another computational bottleneck is the modular square root function calculation in the Step 3., as it is computed modulo a large prime p ($\gg 2^{1024}$), cf. Sect. 5.1 and Fig. 8a.
- **Lack of surjectivity.** Even though the codomain of this hash function is uniformly distributed in $\mathsf{Cl}(\Delta)$, it might be desirable to produce not only prime forms as the output of a hash-to-class group function.

How to hash into class groups? Construction #2. (Improved version)

Public parameters: $\mathbb{G} \xleftarrow{R} GGen(\lambda)$, $\mathsf{H}_{\mathsf{Primes}} : \{0,1\}^* \rightarrow \mathsf{Primes}(\lambda)$ a cryptographically secure hash function.
Inputs: $x \in \mathbb{Z}, \mathsf{Cl}(\Delta), N$.

1. $(a, \mathcal{P}) \xleftarrow{\$}$ **Bach**WithBias(N, Δ).// $\mathcal{P} = \mathsf{factors}(a)$. See Figure 7.
2. Apply Chinese Remainder Theorem to compute $[B] := (\sqrt{\Delta} \bmod a)$. // We know the factors of a. Note $[B]$ is a list.
3. Let l denote the length of the list B (it is always a power of two). Let $b := B[a \bmod l]$. //We deterministically select one of the modular square roots using the generated factored random a.
   - If $\rho(a,b,c) \neq (a,b,c)$ go to step 1. // Discard unreduced forms.
   - *Return:* (a, b).

Fig. 6. An improved version of Wesolowski's hash function.

We can kill these two birds with one stone. The high-level idea of our improved version of Wesolowski's construction in Fig. 6 is as follows. Instead of just generating prime forms $(p, b) \in \mathsf{Cl}(\Delta)$, for some large prime p, we allow the first step of the algorithm to sample any composite integer $a \in_R [0, \sqrt{|\Delta|/3}]$. However, we need to sample the coefficient a carefully, as we need its factorization as well to compute the corresponding coefficient b. For computing the coefficient b, we must be able to compute modular square roots modulo a as $b = \sqrt{\Delta} \bmod a$, cf. Theorem 2. However, if one does not know the factorization of a, then this is a hard problem. In fact, for a semiprime N, the ability to compute modular square roots is equivalent to factoring. Therefore, we need to sample a random coefficient a along with its factorization. Efficient algorithms to generate a random factored number are available due to Bach [3]. We recall that in our specific application, we need to generate these factored random numbers with a bias toward integers having multiple prime factors. This is due to the theorem

Generating factored random numbers [3] with prime factor multiplicity bias

Public parameters: Δ discriminant, $N_0 \in \mathbb{Z}^+$ small integer, $y = 1$, $\mathcal{P} = \{\emptyset\}$ the multiset of prime factors.

BachWithBias(N, Δ):

1. If $N \leq N_0$. Sample $x \in_R (N/2, N]$ with bias $\mathcal{R}(\Delta, a)$. Factor x. *Return:* $(x, \text{factors}(x))$.
2. While: True.
   (a) $q, \mathcal{P} :=$ genFactorWithBias(N,Δ) // $q = p^\alpha \wedge 2 \leq q \leq N$.
   (b) $N' := N/q$.
   (c) $(z, \mathcal{P}') \xleftarrow{\$} \textbf{BachWithBias}(N', \Delta)$.
   (d) $y := q \cdot z, \mathcal{P} := \mathcal{P} \cup \mathcal{P}'$. Sample $\mu \in_R U(0, 1)$.
   (e) if $\gcd(q, z) = 1$, then $\mu := \mu/\mathcal{R}(\Delta, q)$.
   (f) If $\mu \leq \frac{\log N/2}{\log y}$ then *Return:* $(y, \mathcal{P})$.

Subroutine: genFactorWithBias(N,Δ):

1. Sample an integer $j \in_R [1, \log_2(N)]$. Let $q := 2^j + r$, where the integer r is such that $r \in_R [0, 2^j]$.
2. Sample $\nu \in_R U(0, 1)$.
   (a) If q is a prime power $q = p^\alpha \wedge q \leq N \wedge \nu \leq \delta_N(q) \cdot 2^{\log_2(q)} \wedge \left(\frac{\Delta}{p}\right) = 1$ then *Return:* $(q, \text{factors}(q))$. //We define $\delta_N(q)$ in Section 4.2.
   (b) else goto 1.

Fig. 7. A modified version of Bach's factored random number generation algorithm [3]. In our hash-to-class group application, we need to sample factored random numbers proportional to 2^k, where k is the number of their different prime factors. Moreover, any prime factor p must also satisfy $\left(\frac{\Delta}{p}\right) = 1$. Modifications are written in red.

that characterizes the coefficient a in reduced forms, cf. Theorem 1. Therefore, we slightly need to modify Bach's algorithm, cf. Fig. 7.

We remark that in Step (2a) in Fig. 7 of the genFactorWithBias(N, Δ) subroutine, one can efficiently decide whether q is a prime power. Generating random numbers with the appropriate bias is achieved through the adjustment in Step (2e) $\mu := \mu/\mathcal{R}(\Delta, q)$ which multiplies the overall bias of the returned x by $\mathcal{R}(\Delta, q)$ for each prime power factor q, resulting in the correct bias by the multiplicative property of $\mathcal{R}(\Delta, \cdot)$, cf. Theorem 1. The function $\delta_N(q)$ for a prime power $q = p^\alpha$ is defined as $\frac{\log p}{\log N} \cdot \frac{\text{RF}(N/2q, N/q)}{N}$, where $\text{RF}(K, L)$ is the number of integers x in the interval $(K, L]$ counted with multiplicity $\mathcal{R}(\Delta, x)$. The proof that the generated random numbers have the desired distribution is essentially identical to that of Theorem 1 in [3]. For efficiency, $\text{RF}(\cdot, \cdot)$ should be approximated for large N. Heuristically, a number a with k distinct prime factors has a $1/2^k$ probability of having positive bias $\mathcal{R}(\Delta, x)$, and then the bias is 2^k (with slight adjustments when 2 is one of the prime factors). Therefore, $\mathrm{RF}(K, L)$ is expected to be around $L - K$. Based on empirical observations, we recommend using the approximation $\mathrm{RF}(K, L) \approx c_\Delta \cdot (L - K)$, where c_Δ can be estimated by looking at values of L and K where an exact computation of $\mathrm{RF}(K, L)$ is feasible.

5 Implementation and Performance Evaluation

We report our open-source implementation and evaluate the performance of the cryptographically secure hash function constructions described in Sect. 4.

5.1 Theoretical Performance Evaluation

Next, we evaluate the computational complexity of the suggested hash functions. The performance of the proposed hash functions depends on the public parameters, namely, the size of the chosen discriminant Δ, the number d of forms with small prime norms, and the function $\mathsf{H}_{\mathsf{Primes}}(\cdot)$.

Prime–norm basis hash (cf. Sect. 4.1). This function only computes $\mathcal{O}(d)$ compositions of reduced binary quadratic forms. The fastest algorithm to compute the class group composition is NUCOMP [54]. NUCOMP has a complexity $\mathcal{O}(\mu(n) \cdot n)$ on n-bit discriminants ($n = \log_2(|\Delta|)$), where $\mu(\cdot)$ denotes the complexity of the applied integer multiplication algorithm. Using an FFT-based multiplication algorithm NUCOMP and thus, this hash function achieves the asymptotic complexity $\mathcal{O}(d \log^2|\Delta| \log\log|\Delta|)$. However, we expect concretely better performance from the Prime–norm basis hash than the Wesolowski hash, cf. Fig. 8. Multiplying two small norm elements is significantly more efficient than multiplying two random elements. Thus, a natural optimization is to apply a memory-runtime tradeoff, whereby one precomputes all 2^k products of small norm prime forms for a sliding window of length $k \approx 4 \cdots 8$. Afterwards, these precomputed products could be stored in a lookup table. In the online evaluation phase, the precomputed values are read from the lookup table and multiplied together. Alternatively, one may consider not only binary exponents in Step 2 of Fig. 4 but longer ones to shorten the necessary number of generating ideals. We did not explore these optimizations in our implementation. We leave these promising optimization techniques for future work.

Wesolowski hash (cf. Sect. 4.2). This hash function's two main steps are hashing to primes and the Tonelli–Shanks (TS) algorithm for computing modular square roots. All hashing algorithms with prime number images apply a primality testing algorithm. We hash into primes by repeatedly hashing into the positive integers until we hit a prime. The cost of this approach based on the state-of-the-art Miller–Rabin primality testing [46] implemented with an FFT-based multiplication algorithm is $\mathcal{O}((k + \frac{4}{3}\log p)\log^2 p \log\log p)$, where k is the number of rounds performed to achieve 2^{-2k} soundness error. We expect to test $\mathcal{O}(\log p)$ composite number, and for all composite numbers, the overall expected running time of Miller–Rabin is $\mathcal{O}(\frac{4}{3}\log^3 p \log\log p)$. While for the eventually obtained prime, the complexity is $\mathcal{O}(k \log^2 p \log\log p)$. The TS algorithm has a $\mathcal{O}(\log^2 p)$ expected complexity. Since the randomly sampled prime $p \approx \sqrt{|\Delta|}$, therefore the Wesolowski hash has an overall $\mathcal{O}(\log^3|\Delta|\log\log|\Delta|)$ asymptotic complexity.

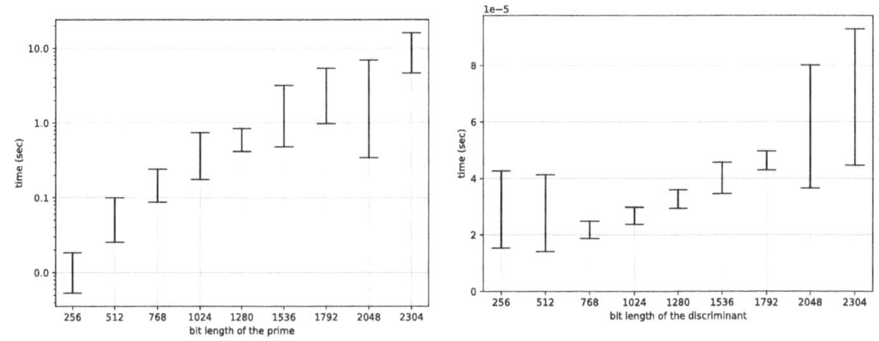

(a) Time to sample a pseudoprime with the Miller–Rabin probabilistic primality testing method ($k = 30$ iteration).

(b) Time to calculate the class group operation in $\mathsf{Cl}(\Delta)$, with the discriminant Δ of given bit size, i.e., from 256 bits to 2304 bits.

Fig. 8. We compare the running times of generating a pseudoprime p (soundness error $\approx 2^{-60}$) and calculate the class group operation in $\mathsf{Cl}(\Delta)$ for various cryptographically relevant parameters p and Δ. These two operations are the main bottlenecks of our proposed hash-to-class group functions.

5.2 Empirical Performance Evaluation

We implemented the hash functions in Python3. Our source code is open-sourced at https://www.github.com/seresistvanandras/hashingToClassGroups. We note that our proof of concept code is *highly unoptimized*. Therefore, we suggest the reader consider solely the ratios (when we compare different hash functions) of the following running times and not their absolute values. We ran all our evaluations on a consumer laptop, a MacBook Air (2017), on a 1,8 GHz Dual-Core Intel Core i5 processor. We note that our implementations are not constant time. We leave it to future work to make our implementations constant time or secret independent for fixed-length inputs.

Our Benchmarks. In our first benchmark, we randomly generated discriminants with bit sizes of 32 bits up to 128 bits to evaluate the hash functions, cf. Fig. 9. We hashed 1,000 random messages for each randomly generated discriminant,

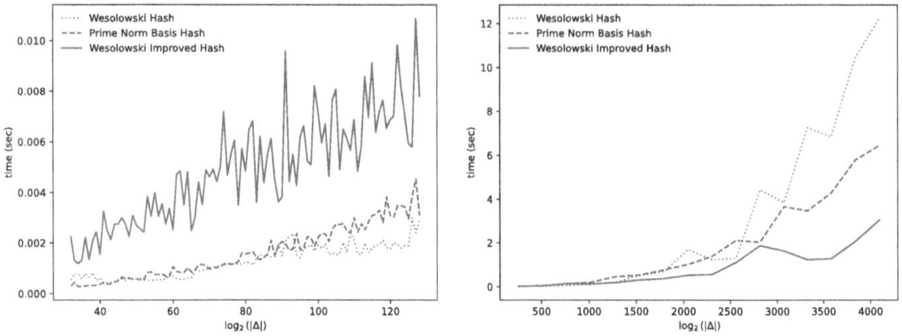

Fig. 9. We evaluate our proposed hash functions' running times. We average the running time of 1000 hashing operations for all three hash functions from 32 bits up to 128 bits discriminants (left). We average the running time of 100 hashing operations for all three hash functions up to 4096 bits discriminants (right).

cf. Sect. 5.2. For all discriminants, we applied the Miller–Rabin primality testing [46] in Wesolowski's hash function with 30 iterations corresponding to $\approx 2^{-60}$ soundness error, i.e., that we erroneously generate a composite integer deemed prime. In our second benchmark, we evaluate our hash to class group functions for cryptographically sized discriminants, i.e., discriminants Δ with at least 1000 bits. Specifically, we randomly sampled discriminants of 256-bit length up to 4096-bit length with a step size of 256 bits. For each discriminant, we hashed 100 random messages and reported the average running time of these hash evaluations, cf. Fig. 9. Naturally, in the case of the Prime–norm basis hash function, we did not count the one-time preprocessing step's running time. Specifically, in the preprocessing step, we generated $2\log|\Delta|$ small prime-norm ideals satisfying the requirement of Theorem 5.

For small parameters, the Wesolowski hash is faster than the Prime–norm basis hash, cf. Sect. 5.2. However, we observe in the experimental running times for *cryptographically secure parameters* that Wesolowski's hash-to-class group function is significantly slower than the one inspired by [23]. We attribute this to the cost of primality testing dominating the running times for larger discriminants. Nevertheless, in cryptographically relevant parameters, both constructions are unbearably slow. In particular, in a class group with 4096-bit discriminant, the Wesolowski hash would take ≈ 10 seconds on average. Interestingly, our improved version of Wesolowski's hash function, cf. Fig. 6, outperforms both previous folklore hash functions for all cryptographically secure discriminants (1024 bits and more), see Section 5.2. We leave it to future work as an exciting research direction to improve the efficiency of these proposed hash functions that will be necessary for real-world cryptographic deployments.

6 Conclusion and Future Directions

This work studied the problem of cryptographically securely hashing into class groups of imaginary quadratic fields. We have shown that several widely used open-source libraries apply insecure hashing algorithms that might affect the security of cryptographic protocols that use those libraries. We proposed three secure hashing algorithms, proved their security, and extensively evaluated their performance on real-world parameters. Despite our over-arching analysis, we leave several directions for future work open. On the practical side, designing more performant and secure hash functions into class groups is an interesting open problem. We also left a constant-time implementation of our proposed hash functions as future work. From a theoretical point of view, it is interesting to characterize in full generality the discrete probability distributions of the coefficients b or c of reduced forms in $\mathsf{Cl}(\Delta)$. Such a piece of information could help design novel hash functions into class groups of imaginary quadratic fields.

Acknowledgements. We are grateful to the CT-RSA reviewers for their helpful and constructive comments that helped significantly improve this manuscript. We thank Antonio Sanso for introducing us to the VDF deployment design of the Chia network. We thank Michael Zhu for inspiring this work. We thank Sanne van de Ven and Berry Schoenmakers for pointing out an error in the original formulation of Theorem 4. We are grateful to Steven Galbraith for pointing out that Construction #1, cf. Fig. 4, is not suitable for VDF applications due to pre-computation attacks. This research was supported by the Ministry of Culture and Innovation and the National Research, Development, and Innovation Office within the Quantum Information National Laboratory of Hungary (Grant No. 2022-2.1.1-NL-2022-00004). Péter Kutas is supported by the János Bolyai Research Scholarship of the Hungarian Academy of Sciences and by the UNKP-23-5 New National Excellence Program. Péter Kutas is also partly supported by EPSRC through grant number EP/V011324/1.

References

1. Alamati, N., De Feo, L., Montgomery, H., Patranabis, S.: Cryptographic group actions and applications. In: Moriai, S., Wang, H. (eds.) ASIACRYPT 2020. LNCS, vol. 12492, pp. 411–439. Springer, Cham (2020). https://doi.org/10.1007/978-3-030-64834-3_14
2. Arun, A., Ganesh, C., Lokam, S.V., Mopuri, T., Sridhar, S.: Dew: a transparent constant-sized polynomial commitment scheme. In: Boldyreva, A., Kolesnikov, V. (eds.) PKC 2023. LNCS, vol. 13941, pp. 542–571. Springer, Cham (2023). https://doi.org/10.1007/978-3-031-31371-4_19
3. Bach, E.: How to generate factored random numbers. SIAM J. Comput. **17**(2), 179–193 (1988)
4. Belabas, K., Kleinjung, T., Sanso, A., Wesolowski, B.: A note on the low order assumption in class group of an imaginary quadratic number fields. Cryptology ePrint Archive (2020)
5. Beullens, W., Kleinjung, T., Vercauteren, F.: CSI-FiSh: efficient isogeny based signatures through class group computations. In: Galbraith, S.D., Moriai, S. (eds.) ASIACRYPT 2019. LNCS, vol. 11921, pp. 227–247. Springer, Cham (2019). https://doi.org/10.1007/978-3-030-34578-5_9

6. Biasse, J.-F., Jacobson, M.J., Silvester, A.K.: Security estimates for quadratic field based cryptosystems. In: Steinfeld, R., Hawkes, P. (eds.) ACISP 2010. LNCS, vol. 6168, pp. 233–247. Springer, Heidelberg (2010). https://doi.org/10.1007/978-3-642-14081-5_15
7. Boneh, D., Bonneau, J., Bünz, B., Fisch, B.: Verifiable delay functions. In: Shacham, H., Boldyreva, A. (eds.) CRYPTO 2018. LNCS, vol. 10991, pp. 757–788. Springer, Cham (2018). https://doi.org/10.1007/978-3-319-96884-1_25
8. Boneh, D., Bünz, B., Fisch, B.: Batching techniques for accumulators with applications to IOPs and stateless blockchains. In: Boldyreva, A., Micciancio, D. (eds.) CRYPTO 2019. LNCS, vol. 11692, pp. 561–586. Springer, Cham (2019). https://doi.org/10.1007/978-3-030-26948-7_20
9. Boneh, D., Bünz, B., Fisch, B.: A survey of two verifiable delay functions using proof of exponentiation. IACR Commun. Cryptol. **1**(1) (2024)
10. Boneh, D., Franklin, M.: Identity-based encryption from the weil pairing. In: Kilian, J. (ed.) CRYPTO 2001. LNCS, vol. 2139, pp. 213–229. Springer, Heidelberg (2001). https://doi.org/10.1007/3-540-44647-8_13
11. Boneh, D., Franklin, M.K.: Efficient generation of shared RSA keys. J. ACM **48**(4), 702–722 (2001)
12. Boneh, D., Kogan, D., Woo, K.: Oblivious pseudorandom functions from isogenies. In: Moriai, S., Wang, H. (eds.) ASIACRYPT 2020. LNCS, vol. 12492, pp. 520–550. Springer, Cham (2020). https://doi.org/10.1007/978-3-030-64834-3_18
13. Boneh, D., Lynn, B., Shacham, H.: Short signatures from the weil pairing. In: Boyd, C. (ed.) ASIACRYPT 2001. LNCS, vol. 2248, pp. 514–532. Springer, Heidelberg (2001). https://doi.org/10.1007/3-540-45682-1_30
14. Boneh, D., Naor, M.: Timed commitments. In: Bellare, M. (ed.) CRYPTO 2000. LNCS, vol. 1880, pp. 236–254. Springer, Heidelberg (2000). https://doi.org/10.1007/3-540-44598-6_15
15. Booher, J., et al.: Failing to hash into supersingular isogeny graphs. Comput. J. bxae038 (2024)
16. Bouvier, C., Castagnos, G., Imbert, L., Laguillaumie, F.: I want to ride my BICYCL: BICYCL implements cryptography in class groups. J. Cryptol. **36**(3), 17 (2023)
17. Buchmann, J., Vollmer, U.: Binary Quadratic Forms. Springer, Heidelberg (2007)
18. Buchmann, J., Williams, H.C.: A key-exchange system based on imaginary quadratic fields. J. Cryptol. **1**(2), 107–118 (1988). https://doi.org/10.1007/BF02351719
19. Bünz, B., Fisch, B., Szepieniec, A.: Transparent SNARKs from DARK compilers. In: Canteaut, A., Ishai, Y. (eds.) EUROCRYPT 2020. LNCS, vol. 12105, pp. 677–706. Springer, Cham (2020). https://doi.org/10.1007/978-3-030-45721-1_24
20. Burkhardt, J., Damgård, I., Frederiksen, T.K., Ghosh, S., Orlandi, C.: Improved distributed RSA key generation using the miller-rabin test. In: CCS. pp. 2501–2515. ACM (2023)
21. Cachin, C., Micali, S., Stadler, M.: Computationally private information retrieval with polylogarithmic communication. In: Stern, J. (ed.) EUROCRYPT 1999. LNCS, vol. 1592, pp. 402–414. Springer, Heidelberg (1999). https://doi.org/10.1007/3-540-48910-X_28
22. Castagnos, G., Laguillaumie, F.: Linearly homomorphic encryption from DDH. In: Nyberg, K. (ed.) CT-RSA 2015. LNCS, vol. 9048, pp. 487–505. Springer, Cham (2015). https://doi.org/10.1007/978-3-319-16715-2_26

23. Castryck, W., Lange, T., Martindale, C., Panny, L., Renes, J.: CSIDH: an efficient post-quantum commutative group action. In: Peyrin, T., Galbraith, S. (eds.) ASIACRYPT 2018. LNCS, vol. 11274, pp. 395–427. Springer, Cham (2018). https://doi.org/10.1007/978-3-030-03332-3_15
24. Chalkias, K.K., Lindstrøm, J., Roy, A.: An efficient hash function for imaginary class groups. Cryptology ePrint Archive (2024)
25. Chen, M., et al.: Diogenes: lightweight scalable RSA modulus generation with a dishonest majority. In: SP, pp. 590–607. IEEE (2021)
26. Choi, K., Manoj, A., Bonneau, J.: SoK: distributed randomness beacons. In: SP, pp. 75–92. IEEE (2023)
27. Cohen, B., Pietrzak, K.: The chia network blockchain. White Paper, Chia. net **9** (2019). https://cdn.bitturk.com/whitepaper/xch.pdf
28. Davenport, H.: Multiplicative Number Theory, vol. 74. Springer, Cham (2013)
29. Dixon, J.D.: Generating random elements in finite groups. Electron. J. Combin. R94–R94 (2008)
30. Dobson, S., Galbraith, S.D.: Trustless groups of unknown order with hyperelliptic curves. IACR Cryptol. ePrint Arch. 196 (2020)
31. Farashahi, R.R., Shparlinski, I.E., Voloch, J.F.: On hashing into elliptic curves. J. Math. Cryptol. **3**(4), 353–360 (2009)
32. Farashahi, R.R., Fouque, P., Shparlinski, I.E., Tibouchi, M., Voloch, J.F.: Indifferentiable deterministic hashing to elliptic and hyperelliptic curves. Math. Comput. **82**(281), 491–512 (2013)
33. Faz-Hernandez, A., Scott, S., Sullivan, N., Wahby, R.S., Wood, C.A.: Hashing to elliptic curves. RFC 9380 (2023). https://doi.org/10.17487/RFC9380, https://www.rfc-editor.org/info/rfc9380
34. De Feo, L., Masson, S., Petit, C., Sanso, A.: Verifiable delay functions from supersingular isogenies and pairings. In: Galbraith, S.D., Moriai, S. (eds.) ASIACRYPT 2019. LNCS, vol. 11921, pp. 248–277. Springer, Cham (2019). https://doi.org/10.1007/978-3-030-34578-5_10
35. Fouque, P.-A., Tibouchi, M.: Indifferentiable hashing to Barreto–Naehrig curves. In: Hevia, A., Neven, G. (eds.) LATINCRYPT 2012. LNCS, vol. 7533, pp. 1–17. Springer, Heidelberg (2012). https://doi.org/10.1007/978-3-642-33481-8_1
36. Gauss, C.F.: Disquisitiones arithmeticae auctore d. Carolo Friderico Gauss. in commissis apud Gerh. Fleischer (1801)
37. Goldschlag, D.M., Stubblebine, S.G.: Publicly verifiable lotteries: applications of delaying functions. In: Hirchfeld, R. (ed.) FC 1998. LNCS, vol. 1465, pp. 214–226. Springer, Heidelberg (1998). https://doi.org/10.1007/bfb0055485
38. Hafner, J.L., McCurley, K.S.: A rigorous subexponential algorithm for computation of class groups. J. Am. Math. Soc. **2**(4), 837–850 (1989)
39. Hazay, C., Mikkelsen, G.L., Rabin, T., Toft, T.: Efficient RSA key generation and threshold paillier in the two-party setting. In: Dunkelman, O. (ed.) CT-RSA 2012. LNCS, vol. 7178, pp. 313–331. Springer, Heidelberg (2012). https://doi.org/10.1007/978-3-642-27954-6_20
40. Icart, T.: How to hash into elliptic curves. In: Halevi, S. (ed.) CRYPTO 2009. LNCS, vol. 5677, pp. 303–316. Springer, Heidelberg (2009). https://doi.org/10.1007/978-3-642-03356-8_18
41. Katz, J., Lindell, Y.: Introduction to Modern Cryptography: Principles and Protocols. Chapman and Hall/CRC (2007)
42. Landerreche, E., Stevens, M., Schaffner, C.: Non-interactive cryptographic timestamping based on verifiable delay functions. In: Bonneau, J., Heninger, N. (eds.)

FC 2020. LNCS, vol. 12059, pp. 541–558. Springer, Cham (2020). https://doi.org/10.1007/978-3-030-51280-4_29
43. Lipmaa, H.: Secure accumulators from Euclidean rings without trusted setup. In: Bao, F., Samarati, P., Zhou, J. (eds.) ACNS 2012. LNCS, vol. 7341, pp. 224–240. Springer, Heidelberg (2012). https://doi.org/10.1007/978-3-642-31284-7_14
44. Long, J.: Nakamoto consensus with verifiable delay puzzle. arXiv preprint arXiv:1908.06394 (2019)
45. Malavolta, G., Thyagarajan, S.: Homomorphic time-lock puzzles and applications. In: Boldyreva, A., Micciancio, D. (eds.) CRYPTO 2019. LNCS, vol. 11692, pp. 620–649. Springer, Cham (2019). https://doi.org/10.1007/978-3-030-26948-7_22
46. Miller, G.L.: Riemann's hypothesis and tests for primality. In: Proceedings of the Seventh Annual ACM Symposium on Theory of Computing, pp. 234–239 (1975)
47. Moriya, T., Onuki, H., Takagi, T.: SiGamal: a supersingular isogeny-based PKE and its application to a PRF. In: Moriai, S., Wang, H. (eds.) ASIACRYPT 2020. LNCS, vol. 12492, pp. 551–580. Springer, Cham (2020). https://doi.org/10.1007/978-3-030-64834-3_19
48. Pietrzak, K.: Simple verifiable delay functions. In: ITCS. LIPIcs, vol. 124, pp. 60:1–60:15. Schloss Dagstuhl - Leibniz-Zentrum für Informatik (2019)
49. Rivest, R.L., Shamir, A., Wagner, D.A.: Time-lock puzzles and timed-release crypto (1996)
50. Rotem, L., Segev, G., Shahaf, I.: Generic-group delay functions require hidden-order groups. In: Canteaut, A., Ishai, Y. (eds.) EUROCRYPT 2020. LNCS, vol. 12107, pp. 155–180. Springer, Cham (2020). https://doi.org/10.1007/978-3-030-45727-3_6
51. Scott, M., Benger, N., Charlemagne, M., Dominguez Perez, L.J., Kachisa, E.J.: Fast hashing to G_2 on pairing-friendly curves. In: Shacham, H., Waters, B. (eds.) Pairing 2009. LNCS, vol. 5671, pp. 102–113. Springer, Heidelberg (2009). https://doi.org/10.1007/978-3-642-03298-1_8
52. Seres, I.A., Burcsi, P.: Behemoth: transparent polynomial commitment scheme with constant opening proof size and verifier time. IACR Cryptol. ePrint Arch. 670 (2023)
53. Seres, I.A., Burcsi, P., Kutas, P.: How (not) to hash into class groups of imaginary quadratic fields? Cryptology ePrint Archive (2024)
54. Shanks, D.: On gauss and composition I, II. In: Proceedings of the NATO ASI on Number Theory and Applications, pp. 163–179. Kluwer Academic Press, Dordrecht (1989)
55. Soundararajan, K.: The number of imaginary quadratic fields with a given class number. Hardy-Ramanujan J. **30** (2007)
56. Sutherland, A.V.: Order computations in generic groups. Ph.D. thesis, Massachusetts Institute of Technology (2007)
57. Thyagarajan, S.A.K., Castagnos, G., Laguillaumie, F., Malavolta, G.: Efficient CCA timed commitments in class groups. In: CCS, pp. 2663–2684. ACM (2021)
58. Wahby, R.S., Boneh, D.: Fast and simple constant-time hashing to the BLS12-381 elliptic curve. Cryptology ePrint Archive (2019)
59. Wesolowski, B.: Efficient verifiable delay functions. In: Ishai, Y., Rijmen, V. (eds.) EUROCRYPT 2019. LNCS, vol. 11478, pp. 379–407. Springer, Cham (2019). https://doi.org/10.1007/978-3-030-17659-4_13

Sequential Indifferentiability of 7-Round Misty Structures

Jiayi Ai[1,2] and Chun Guo[1,3,4](✉)

[1] School of Cyber Science and Technology, Shandong University, Qingdao, China
chun.guo.sc@gmail.com
[2] The State Key Laboratory of Blockchain and Data Security, Zhejiang University, Hangzhou, China
[3] Key Laboratory of Cryptologic Technology and Information Security of Ministry of Education, Shandong University, Qingdao 266237, Shandong, China
[4] Shandong Research Institute of Industrial Technology, Jinan 250102, Shandong, China

Abstract. We investigate the Misty structure with respect to the security notion of sequential indifferentiability of Mandal et al. (TCC 2012). As our main result, we prove sequential indifferentiability for 7-round Misty structures using seven independent random permutations in the rounds. We also prove insecurity for 5 rounds by exhibiting an attack. Our main result implies known-key security of 7 rounds in the sense of correlation intractability, providing the first known-key security results on Misty structures to our knowledge.

1 Introduction

Misty Structures. Blockciphers typically follow two types of structures, namely Feistel networks and substitution-permutation networks (or key-alternating ciphers). Recent developments in blockciphers have pushed revisiting "non-classical" structures. One of them is the Misty network used in Misty [26], Kasumi [11] and the NIST LWC submission TGIF [18]. Compared to the Feistel structure, it is quicker and more resistant to linear and differential cryptanalysis. The Misty structure comes with two flavors, which is now known as Misty-L and Misty-R. Both define $2n$-bit permutations upon n-bit round permutations. In detail, a Misty-L round is described as $\text{Misty-L}^P(L, R) := \big(R, P(L) \oplus R\big)$, while a Misty-R round is described as $\text{Misty-R}^P(L, R) := \big(P(L) \oplus R, P(L)\big)$, as shown in Fig. 1. The t-round Misty-L, resp. Misty-R, construction is simply the composition of t Misty-L, resp. Misty-R, rounds. Though, as noticed [19,20], Misty-L is basically the inverse of Misty-R. This means when the adversary can choose both plaintexts and ciphertexts, the two flavors Misty-L and Misty-R are equivalent modulo some simple non-cryptographic operations.[1]

The provable security analysis of Misty constructions has garnered significant scholarly attention within the Luby and Rackoff framework, wherein the

[1] Misty-R is indeed stronger than Misty-L in CPA settings.

A. Patra (Ed.): CT-RSA 2025, LNCS 15598, pp. 327–348, 2025.
https://doi.org/10.1007/978-3-031-88661-4_14

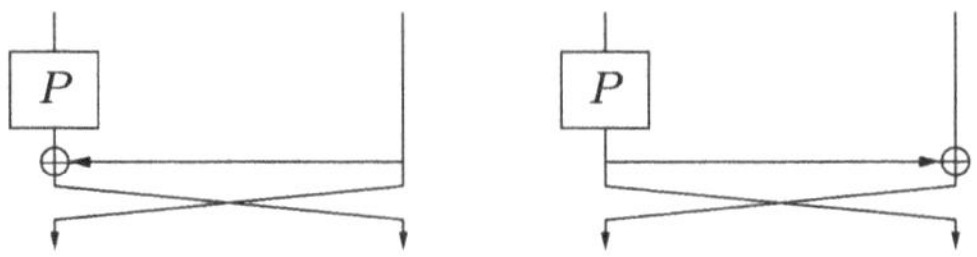

Fig. 1. (Left) One round of the Misty-L construction; (Right) One round of the Misty-R construction.

confidentiality of each round permutation is posited as an inherent attribute, exhibiting true randomness [19,20,23,26,28,30]. In particular, 5 rounds of Misty using n-bit random permutations are necessary and sufficient [28,29] for CCA security up to $2^{\frac{n}{2}}$ adversarial queries (the well-known birthday bound). For better bounds, Lee [23] proved asymptotically optimal security for a large enough number of rounds. Besides, generic distinguishing attacks and quantum attacks against this structure have been investigated in [29] and [12,24] respectively.

Indifferentiability. A blockcipher's traditional security definition is that it *cannot be distinguished from a (secret) random permutation.* Since 2005, several scholarly articles [1,5] have suggested that the concept of *indifferentiability from ideal ciphers* serves as a significantly more robust criterion for assessing the effectiveness of ideal function-based blockciphers. Briefly speaking, for a blockcipher $E^{\mathbf{P}}$ built upon random permutations $\mathbf{P} = (P_1, P_2, ...)$, if there exists an efficient simulator S^E that queries an ideal cipher E to mimic its (non-existent) underlying permutations such that (E, S^E) is indistinguishable from $(E^{\mathbf{P}}, \mathbf{P})$, then $E^{\mathbf{P}}$ is indifferentiable from E [27]. This property implies that the cipher $E^{\mathbf{P}}$ inherits all ideal cipher-properties defined by single-stage games, including security against various forms of related-key and chosen-key attacks.

To establish the equivalence between the random oracle model and ideal cipher model, Coron et al. [5] was the first to prove indifferentiability for blockcipher constructions. Concretely, they proved indifferentiability for a type of 14-round Feistel ciphers. Popularized by this, a number of follow-up works improved Coron et al.'s result [7,9], extended the treatments to other blockcipher constructions such as the key-alternating ciphers [1,8,13–15,22] and substitution-permutation networks (SPNs) [10], and established lower bounds recently [17].

Sequential Indifferentiability and Correlation Intractability. Known-key and chosen-key attacks typically tried to find tuples of inputs/outputs of the blockcipher that satisfy certain *evasive relations* [2]. For example, the first known-key distinguisher against 7-round Feistel-2 cipher [21] distinguishes by finding a pair of inputs/outputs Feistel-$2_7(u) = v$ and Feistel-$2_7(u') = v'$ such that the xor of the right halves of u, v, u' and v' is 0. To formalize this type of security, Knudsen and Rijmen [21] discussed using *Correlation Intractability (CI)*, which was defined by Canetti et al. [2] to formalize a "random oracle-like" property. Though, positive results on CI can only be established in the ideal model [3,4,25]. Concretely, to establish CI, Mandal et al. [25] introduced a weaker variant of indifferentiability termed *sequential-indifferentiability* (*seq-indifferentiability*).

This variant concentrates on distinguishers that follow a strict restriction on the order of queries. Mandal et al. [25] showed that seq-indifferentiability implies CI, and further established seq-indifferentiability and CI for Feistel-based blockciphers. Follow-up works extended such treatments to the aforementioned key-alternating ciphers [3,4,6,16,32] and SPNs [31].

Our Results. We remark that the Misty structures have never been analyzed with respect to (weaker) indifferentiability nor CI. Since a Misty structure transforms an n-bit permutation to a $2n$-bit permutation, such positive results may shed more lights on domain extension of random permutations (which has been studied by Dodis et al. [10]).

We bridge this gap and investigate sequential indifferentiability of Misty structures that use independent n-bit random permutations in each round. For such Misty structure, we first exhibit an attack breaking both sequential indifferentiability and correlation intractability of 5 rounds. We then prove that 7 rounds (see Fig. 2) achieve sequential indifferentiability up to $2^{n/4}$ adversarial queries, where the simulator has complexity q^2. The 7-round Misty thus also achieves CI, with concrete security comparable with 6-round Feistel [25] and 4-round single-key Even-Mansour scheme [3].

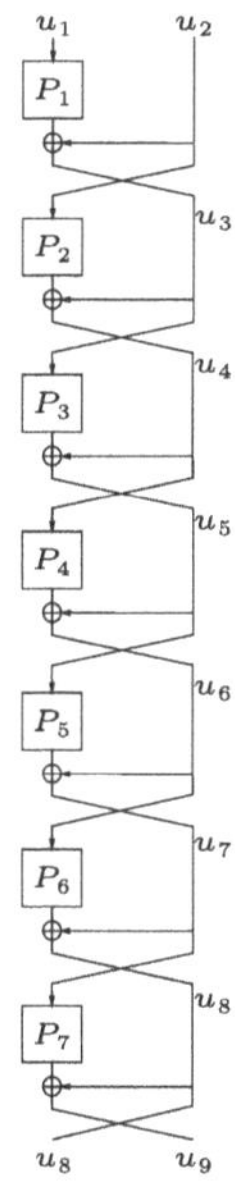

Fig. 2. The 7-round Misty-L construction using seven independent permutations $P_1, ..., P_7$, with notations used in our proof.

The design of our simulator closely follows existing simulators for 6-round Feistel [25] and 4-round single-key Even-Mansour [3], i.e., we "detect" chains in the middle 3rd and 4th rounds, and "adapt" chains in the first and last two rounds. The main difference is that due to the slower diffusion in Misty, our simulator needs an additional round (i.e., the 5th round) to avoid certain collisions. It thus needs 7 rounds in total.

Organization. We supply necessary notations and definitions in Sect. 2. We then describe our attack against 5 rounds and proof for 7 rounds in Sect. 3 and 4 respectively. We finally conclude in Sect. 5.

2 Preliminaries

Notions. We will fix an integer n for the size of the round permutations in Misty structures, and write $N = 2^n$. Denote by $\mathcal{P}(m)$ the set of all permutations on $\{0,1\}^m$. An n-bit random permutation $P : \{0,1\}^n \to \{0,1\}^n$ is a permutation that is uniformly chosen from the set $\mathcal{P}(n)$. Similarly, a $2n$-bit random permutation $\mathbf{\Pi} : \{0,1\}^{2n} \to \{0,1\}^{2n}$ is uniformly chosen from $\mathcal{P}(2n)$.

Misty Constructions. Given a permutation $P : \{0,1\}^n \to \{0,1\}^n$, the 1-round Misty-L construction is the permutation on $\{0,1\}^{2n}$ defined as

$$\text{Misty-L}^P(L,R) := \big(R, P(L) \oplus R\big). \tag{1}$$

See Fig. 1 (left). Its inverse is computed by $(\text{Misty-L}^{-1})^P(L,R) = \big(P^{-1}(L \oplus R), L\big)$. The t-round Misty-L construction associated to t independent random permutations $\mathbf{P} = (P_1, ..., P_t)$ takes inputs $(L,R) \in \{0,1\}^n \times \{0,1\}^n$ and is defined by

$$\text{Misty-L}_t^{\mathbf{P}}(L,R) = \text{Misty-L}^{P_t} \circ ... \circ \text{Misty-L}^{P_1}(L,R).$$

On the other hand, given $P : \{0,1\}^n \to \{0,1\}^n$, the 1-round Misty-R construction is the permutation on $\{0,1\}^{2n}$ defined as

$$\text{Misty-R}^P(L,R) := \big(P(L) \oplus R, P(L)\big), \tag{2}$$

as shown in Fig. 1 (right). As noticed in several papers [19,20,30], Misty-R is stronger than Misty-L in CPA settings. Though, Misty-L is basically the inverse of Misty-R. In fact, if we remove the XOR and the swap operations in the last round, then the obtained Misty-L and Misty-R variants are inverses of each other. This means in CCA security and indifferentiability settings where the adversary can choose both plaintexts and ciphertexts, we can without loss of generality focus on Misty-L constructions.

Sequential Indifferentiability. The notion of sequential indifferentiability (seq-indifferentiability), introduced by Mandal et al. [25], is a weakened variant of (full) indifferentiability of Maurer et al. [27] tailored to a class of restricted distinguishers named *sequential distinguishers*. For concreteness, our formalism concentrates on blockciphers. Consider the blockcipher construction $C^{\mathbf{P}}$ built upon several random permutations $\mathbf{P} = (P_1, P_2, ...)$. A distinguisher $D^{C^{\mathbf{P}},\mathbf{P}}$ with oracle access to both the cipher and the underlying permutations is trying to distinguish $C^{\mathbf{P}}$ from the random invertible permutation $\mathbf{\Pi}$. If D proceeds through the following steps in a strict order, it can be considered as sequential: (1) queries the underlying permutation $\mathbf{P}$ in arbitrary; (2) queries the cipher $C^{\mathbf{P}}$ in arbitrary; (3) outputs the result, and cannot query $\mathbf{P}$ again in this phase. This order of queries is illustrated by the numbers in Fig. 3.

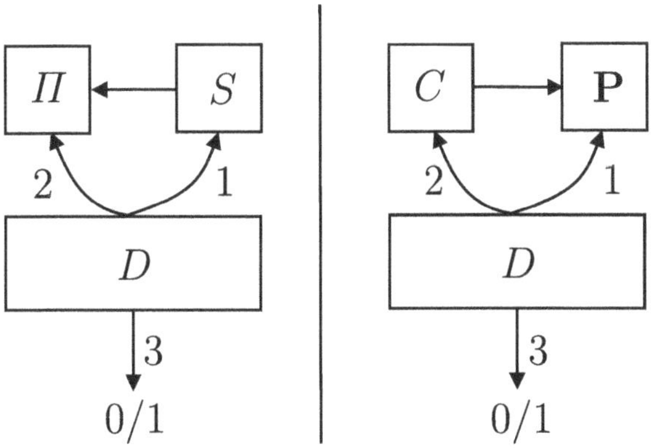

Fig. 3. The concept of sequential indifferentiability involves a scenario where a distinguisher engages with two oracles by making queries in a predetermined sequence. The numbers next to the query arrows denote the precise order in which these queries are made.

In this context, assuming the existence of a simulator $S^{\mathbf{\Pi}}$ that possesses the access to $\mathbf{\Pi}$ and has the capability to emulate $\mathbf{P}$ in such a manner that, from the perspective of any sequential distinguisher D, the system $(\mathbf{\Pi}, S^{\mathbf{\Pi}})$ is indistinguishable from $(C^{\mathbf{P}}, \mathbf{P})$, it follows that $C^{\mathbf{P}}$ can be considered *sequentially indifferentiable* (seq-indifferentiable) from $\mathbf{\Pi}$.

To characterize the adversarial power, we define a notion *total oracle query cost* of D, which refers to the total number of queries received by $\mathbf{P}$ (from D or $C^{\mathbf{P}}$) when D interacts with $(C^{\mathbf{P}}, \mathbf{P})$ [25]. Then, seq-indifferentiability [3,25] is defined as follows.

Definition 1. *A permutation C^{P} with oracle access to t random permutations $\boldsymbol{P} = (P_1, ..., P_t)$ is statistically and strongly $(q, \sigma, \tau, \varepsilon)$-seq-indifferentiable from a random invertible permutation $\mathbf{\Pi}$, if there exists a simulator $S^{\mathbf{\Pi}}$ such that for any sequential distinguisher D of total oracle queries cost q, $S^{\mathbf{\Pi}}$ issues at most σ queries to $\mathbf{\Pi}$ and runs in time at most τ, and*

$$\left|\Pr\left[\boldsymbol{P} \xleftarrow{\$} (\mathcal{P}(n))^t : D^{C^{P},\boldsymbol{P}} \Rightarrow 1\right] - \Pr\left[\mathbf{\Pi} \xleftarrow{\$} \mathcal{P}(2n) : D^{\mathbf{\Pi},S^{\mathbf{\Pi}}} \Rightarrow 1\right]\right| \leq \varepsilon.$$

If D makes q queries, then its total oracle query cost is poly(q). As a concrete example, the t-round Misty construction $\text{Misty}_t^{\mathbf{P}}$ makes t queries to $\mathbf{P}$ to answer any query it receives, and if D makes q_c queries to $\text{Misty}_t^{\mathbf{P}}$ and q_p queries to $\mathbf{P}$, then the total oracle query cost of D is $q_p + tq_c = \text{poly}(q_p + q_c) = \text{poly}(q)$.

Albeit weaker than "full" indifferentiability [27] (which can be viewed as seq-indifferentiability without restricting distinguishers to be sequential), seq-indifferentiability already implies *correlation intractability* in the ideal model [3, 25]. The notion of correlation intractability was introduced by Canetti et al. [2] and adapted to ideal models by Mandal et al. [25]. To formalize, we first define *evasive relations*, i.e., relations such that it is hard for an algorithm with oracle access to a random permutation $\mathbf{\Pi}$ to come with a tuple of inputs $(\alpha_1, \ldots, \alpha_m)$ such that $((\alpha_1, \ldots, \alpha_m), (\mathbf{\Pi}(\alpha_1), \ldots, \mathbf{\Pi}(\alpha_m)))$ satisfies this relation.

Definition 2 (Evasive Relation). *An m-ary relation $\mathcal{R}$ is said (q, ε)-evasive (with respect to a random permutation) if for any oracle Turing machine M making at most q oracle queries, one has*

$$\Pr\Big[\mathbf{\Pi} \xleftarrow{\$} \mathcal{P}(2n), (\alpha_1, \ldots, \alpha_m) \leftarrow M^{\mathbf{\Pi}} : \\ ((\alpha_1, \ldots, \alpha_m), (\mathbf{\Pi}(\alpha_1), \ldots, \mathbf{\Pi}(\alpha_m))) \in \mathcal{R}\Big] \le \varepsilon,$$

where the probability is taken over the random draw of $\mathbf{\Pi}$ and the random coins of M.

To see the usefulness of evasive relations, consider the permutation-based Davies-Meyer construction $\text{DM}^P(m) := m \oplus P(m)$. As shown by Cogliati and Seurin [3], finding the preimage of 0 can be reduced to solving the unary evasive relation "$(x, y) \in \mathcal{R}_{pre}$ iff. $x = y$", while finding a collision of DM^P can be reduced to solving the binary evasive relation "$((x, y), (x', y')) \in \mathcal{R}_{coll}$ iff. $x \oplus y = x' \oplus y'$".

Definition 3 (Correlation Intractable Permutation). *Let C be a permutation construction using (in a black-box way) an underlying primitive P, and let $\mathcal{R}$ be an m-ary relation. $C^{\mathbf{P}}$ is said to be (q, ε)-correlation intractable with respect to $\mathcal{R}$ if for any oracle Turing machine M making at most q oracle queries, one has*

$$\Pr\left[(\alpha_1, \ldots, \alpha_m) \leftarrow M^{\mathbf{P}} : \left((\alpha_1, \ldots, \alpha_m), \left(C^{\mathbf{P}}(\alpha_1), \ldots, C^{\mathbf{P}}(\alpha_m)\right)\right) \in \mathcal{R}\right] \le \varepsilon,$$

where the probability is taken over the random draw of F (in some well-understood set) and the random coins of M.

With the above, we can then formally state that sequential indifferentiability implies correlation intractability (in the ideal model). This was first proven by Mandal et al. [25]. Below we state the improved lemma of Cogliati and Seurin [3, Theorem 2] with concrete bounds.

Lemma 1 (Seq-indifferentiability ⇒ CI). *Let C be a permutation construction using (in a black-box way) an underlying primitive $\boldsymbol{P}$ such that C makes at most t queries to $\boldsymbol{P}$ on any input. Assume that $C^{\boldsymbol{P}}$ is $(q + tm, \sigma, t, \varepsilon)$-seq-indifferentiable from a random permutation. Then for any m-ary relation $\mathcal{R}$, if $\mathcal{R}$ is $(\sigma + m, \varepsilon_{\mathcal{R}})$-evasive with respect to a random permutation, then $C^{\boldsymbol{P}}$ is $(q, \varepsilon + \varepsilon_{\mathcal{R}})$-correlation intractable with respect to $\mathcal{R}$.*

3 Attack Against 5-Round Misty

In this section we exhibit our attack against 5-round Misty. We first show how to break its correlation intractability: by Lemma 1, this would enable breaking correlation intractability.

Concretely, consider a relation $R_{4\text{xor}}$ over 4-tuples such that

$$(((u_1, u_2), (u_6, u_7)), ((u_1', u_2'), (u_6', u_7')), ((u_1'', u_2''), (u_6'', u_7'')), ((u_1''', u_2'''), (u_6''', u_7'''))) \in R_{4\text{xor}}$$

if and only if $u_2 \oplus u_2' \oplus u_2'' \oplus u_2''' = 0$ and $u_6 \oplus u_6' \oplus u_6'' \oplus u_6''' = 0$. Coron et al. [5] proved that this relation is $(q, q^4/N)$-evasive with respect to $2n$-bit random permutations $\mathbf{\Pi}$.

Lemma 2 (Lemma 2.2 [5]). *Let $\mathbf{\Pi} : \{0,1\}^{2n} \to \{0,1\}^{2n}$ be a random permutation, and consider a system issuing at most q queries to $\mathbf{\Pi}$. Denote generically $\left(u_1^i, u_2^i\right), \left(u_6^i, u_7^i\right)$ the inputs/outputs of $\mathbf{\Pi}$ corresponding to the i-th query (independently of whether this is a query to $\mathbf{\Pi}(+,\cdot)$ or $\mathbf{\Pi}(-,\cdot)$. Then, assuming $q \le 2^{2n-1}$, the probability that there exist four queries i_1, i_2, i_3 and i_4 with pairwise different input values such that*

$$u_2^{i_1} \oplus u_2^{i_2} \oplus u_2^{i_3} \oplus u_2^{i_4} = 0 \text{ and } u_6^{i_1} \oplus u_6^{i_2} \oplus u_6^{i_3} \oplus u_6^{i_4} = 0$$

is less than q^4/N.

On the other hand, by querying $\mathbf{P}$, one can easily find four pairs of inputs/outputs of the 5-round $\text{Misty}^{\mathbf{P}}$ satisfying $R_{4\text{xor}}$. By this, 5-round $\text{Misty}^{\mathbf{P}}$ is *not* correlation intractable.

Theorem 1. *The 5-round $\mathit{Misty}^{\boldsymbol{P}}$ using five independent n-bit random permutations $\boldsymbol{P} = (P_1, ..., P_5)$ is not correlation intractable. In particular, there exists an oracle algorithm $M^{\boldsymbol{P}}$ finding distinct inputs $(u_1, u_2), (u_1', u_2'), (u_1'', u_2''), (u_1''', u_2''')$ such that*

$$(((u_1, u_2), (u_6, u_7)), ((u_1', u_2'), (u_6', u_7')), ((u_1'', u_2''), (u_6'', u_7'')), ((u_1''', u_2'''), (u_6''', u_7'''))) \in R_{4\text{xor}}$$

for the outputs $(u_6, u_7) = \mathit{Misty}^{\boldsymbol{P}}(+, (u_1, u_2)), (u_6', u_7') = \mathit{Misty}^{\boldsymbol{P}}(+, (u_1', u_2'))$, $(u_6'', u_7'') = \mathit{Misty}^{\boldsymbol{P}}(+, (u_1'', u_2''))$ and $(u_6''', u_7''') = \mathit{Misty}^{\boldsymbol{P}}(+, (u_1''', u_2'''))$. Moreover, $M^{\boldsymbol{P}}$ makes at most 10 queries and succeeds with probability at least $1 - 1/(N-1)$.

Proof. The algorithm $M^{\mathbf{P}}$ (which gains inspirations from Coron et al.'s [5] attack against 5-round Feistel construction) proceeds as follows (the involved query structure is depicted in Fig. 4):

1. Choose arbitrary values $u_3, u'_3, u_4, u'_4 \in \{0,1\}^n$ such that $u_3 \neq u'_3, u_4 \neq u'_4$ and $u_3 \oplus u_4 = u'_3 \oplus u'_4$, and compute $v_2 \leftarrow u_3 \oplus u_4$ and $v'_2 \leftarrow u_3 \oplus u'_4$.
2. Compute

$$\begin{cases} u_2 \leftarrow P_2(-, v_2), & u'_2 \leftarrow P_2(-, v'_2), \\ v_3 \leftarrow P_3(+, u_3), & v'_3 \leftarrow P_3(+, u'_3), \\ v_4 \leftarrow P_4(+, u_4), & v'_4 \leftarrow P_4(+, u'_4), \\ v_1 \leftarrow u_2 \oplus u_3, & v'_1 \leftarrow u_2 \oplus u'_3, \\ v''_1 \leftarrow u'_2 \oplus u_3, & v'''_1 \leftarrow u'_2 \oplus u'_3, \\ u_1 \leftarrow P_1(-, v_1), & u'_1 \leftarrow P_1(-, v'_1), \\ u''_1 \leftarrow P_1(-, v''_1), & u'''_1 \leftarrow P_1(-, v'''_1). \end{cases}$$

3. If u_1, u'_1, u''_1 and u'''_1 are not pairwise distinct, then output $\perp$.
4. Outputs $(u_1, u_2), (u'_1, u'_2), (u''_1, u''_2), (u'''_1, u'''_2)$.

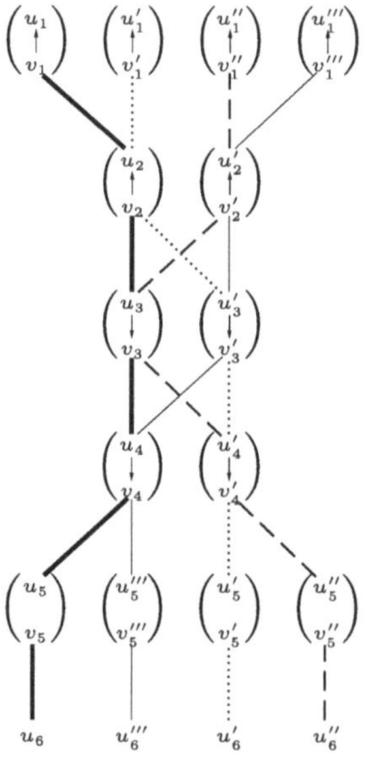

Fig. 4. Values and structures involved in the 5-round attack. Each line in the diagram represents one of the four computation paths within the Misty construction. These paths are distinguished by distinct patterns such as bold, dashed, dotted, and slim. The attack considers inputs/outputs corresponding to $((u_1, u_2), (u_6, u_7)), ((u'_1, u_2), (u'_6, u'_7)), ((u''_1, u'_2), (u''_6, u''_7))$ and $((u'''_1, u'_2), (u'''_6, u'''_7))$. Arrows within the diagram indicate the directions of permutation queries. Note that the values u_5, u'_5, u''_5, and u'''_5 do not explicitly appear in our attack.

Since $u_4 \neq u'_4$ by definition, it holds $v_2 = u_3 \oplus u_4 \neq u_3 \oplus u'_4 = v'_2$. Conditioned on the value $u_2 = P_2^{-1}(v_2)$, $u'_2 \leftarrow P_2^{-1}(v'_2)$ is uniformly sampled from $N - 1$

possibilities. By this, the probability to have $v_1 = u_2 \oplus u_3 = u_2' \oplus u_3' = v_1'''$ cannot exceed $1/(N-1)$. As long as $v_1 \neq v_1''$, it can be seen $v_1' \neq v_1''$ as well. Thus, with probability at least $1 - 1/(N-1)$, we have that v_1, v_1', v_1'' and v_1''' are pairwise distinct at step 3.

Importantly, it can be seen $(u_1, u_2, u_3, u_4), (u_1', u_2, u_3', u_4'), (u_1'', u_2', u_3, u_4')$ and $(u_1''', u_2', u_3', u_4)$ are the intermediate values/$\mathbf{P}$-calls involved in four distinct Misty computations. Computing the Misty structure forward:

- $(u_6, u_7) \leftarrow \text{Misty}^{\mathbf{P}}(+, (u_1, u_2)), (u_6', u_7') \leftarrow \text{Misty}^{\mathbf{P}}(+, (u_1', u_2'))$
- $(u_6'', u_7'') \leftarrow \text{Misty}^{\mathbf{P}}(+, (u_1'', u_2'')), (u_6''', u_7''') \leftarrow \text{Misty}^{\mathbf{P}}(+, (u_1''', u_2'''))$,

the left halves of the four ciphertexts have:

$$u_6 = u_3 \oplus v_2 \oplus v_3 \oplus v_4, \qquad u_6' = u_3' \oplus v_2 \oplus v_3' \oplus v_4',$$
$$u_6'' = u_3 \oplus v_2' \oplus v_3 \oplus v_4', \qquad u_6''' = u_3' \oplus v_2' \oplus v_3' \oplus v_4.$$

Hence, they always have $u_2 \oplus u_2' \oplus u_2'' \oplus u_2''' = 0$ and $u_6 \oplus u_6' \oplus u_6'' \oplus u_6''' = 0$. This completes the proof. □

Using the above oracle algorithm $M^{\mathbf{P}}$, we can easily break the sequential indifferentiability of the 5-round $\text{Misty}^{\mathbf{P}}$.

Theorem 2. *Consider the 5-round* $\text{Misty}^{\mathbf{P}}$ *using five independent* n*-bit random permutations* $\mathbf{P} = (P_1, ..., P_5)$*. Then, there exists a sequential distinguisher* D *that has attack advantage at least* $1 - \frac{1}{N-1} - \frac{(q_S+4)^4}{N}$ *against any simulator* $S^{\mathbf{\Pi}}$ *making at most* q_S *queries to* $\mathbf{\Pi}$.

Proof. We first describe the distinguisher D. The distinguisher D interacts with a system $\Sigma = (\mathbf{\Pi}, \mathbf{P})$ which is either $(\mathbf{\Pi}, S^{\mathbf{\Pi}})$ or $(\text{Misty}^{\mathbf{P}}, \mathbf{P})$. We assume that the interface of $\mathbf{\Pi}$ and $\text{Misty}^{\mathbf{P}}$ is of the form $\text{Perm}(\delta, Z)$, where $\delta \in \{+, -\}$ indicates if the $2n$-bit permutation is queried on the forward or inverse direction and $Z \in \{0,1\}^{2n}$ indicates the actual query. We further assume that the interface of $S^{\mathbf{\Pi}}$ or $\mathbf{P}$ is of the unified form $\text{Query}(i, \delta, w)$ with $i \in \{1, ..., t\}$, $\delta \in \{+, -\}$ and $w \in \{0,1\}^n$. Concretely, when $\delta = +$, the query $\text{Query}(i, \delta, w)$ indicates querying the i-th permutation $P_i(w)$ (which is either "real" or simulated by $S^{\mathbf{\Pi}}$) on the forward; when $\delta = -$, the query $\text{Query}(i, \delta, w)$ indicates querying the inverse $P_i^{-1}(w)$.

With the above notations, D proceeds as follows:

1. Use $\text{Query}(i, \cdot, \cdot)$ to answer M's query to $P_i(\cdot, \cdot)$ to run the oracle algorithm M described in the proof of Theorem 1.
2. If M outputs $\perp$ then output 0. Else, collect M's outputs $(u_1, u_2), (u_1', u_2')$, (u_1'', u_2'') and (u_1''', u_2''').
3. Query $(u_6, u_7) \leftarrow \text{Perm}(+, (u_1, u_2)), (u_6', u_7') \leftarrow \text{Perm}(+, (u_1', u_2)), (u_6'', u_7'') \leftarrow \text{Perm}(+, (u_1'', u_2'))$ and $(u_6''', u_7''') \leftarrow \text{Perm}(+, (u_1''', u_2'))$.
4. If $u_6 \oplus u_6' \oplus u_6'' \oplus u_6''' = 0$ then output 1, else output 0.

Since M only queries the underlying permutations, D is sequential. By Theorem 1, when $\Sigma = (\text{Misty}^{\mathbf{P}}, \mathbf{P})$, one has $\Pr\left[D^{\text{Misty}^{\mathbf{P}},\mathbf{P}} \Rightarrow 1\right] \geq 1 - \frac{1}{N-q}$.

When $\Sigma = (\mathbf{\Pi}, S^{\mathbf{\Pi}})$, $\Pr\left[D^{\mathbf{\Pi},S^{\mathbf{\Pi}}} \Rightarrow 1\right]$ is bounded by the probability that the union of D and S succeeds in finding four random permutation inputs/outputs $\mathbf{\Pi}(+,(u_1,u_2)) = (u_6,u_7)$, $\mathbf{\Pi}(+,(u_1',u_2')) = (u_6',u_7')$, $\mathbf{\Pi}(+,(u_1'',u_2'')) = (u_6'',u_7'')$ and $\mathbf{\Pi}(+,(u_1''',u_2''')) = (u_6''',u_7''')$ satisfies the relation $R_{4\text{xor}}$. Since D and S make at most q_S+4 queries to $\mathbf{\Pi}$ in total, the probability is at most $(q_S+4)^4/N$ by Lemma 2. Gathering the above yields the lower bound $1 - \frac{1}{N-1} - \frac{(q_S+4)^4}{N}$ on the attack advantage. □

4 Sequential Indifferentiability of 7-Round Misty

This section proves seq-indifferentiability for the 7-round Misty, as shown in Fig. 2.

Theorem 3. *Assume that $P_1, ..., P_7$ are seven independent random permutations. Let $N = 2^n$ and $q^2 \leq N/4$. Then, the 7-round Misty scheme is strongly and statistically $(q,\sigma,\tau,\varepsilon)$-seq-indifferentiable from a random invertible permutation, where*

$$\sigma = q^2,\ \tau = O(q^2),\ \varepsilon = \frac{185q^4}{N}.$$

By Lemma 1, Theorem 3 implies that for any (q^2,ε)-evasive relation $\mathcal{R}$, the 7-round Misty construction is $\left(q, \varepsilon + \mathcal{O}\left(q^4/2^n\right)\right)$-correlation intractable with respect to $\mathcal{R}$. The bounds resemble [3].

To prove Theorem 3, we first describe our simulator in Sect. 4.1. With the simulator, we then establish indistinguishability of the real and the ideal or simulated worlds in Sect. 4.2.

4.1 Simulator of Misty

Simulator Notions. The simulator maintains an internal table Π_i that establishes a mapping of entries $(\delta, w) \in \{+,-\} \times \{0,1\}^n$ to values $w' \in \{0,1\}^n$ for each i = 1,...,7, initially undefined for all entries. We introduce the notation Π_i^+, resp. Π_i^-, which denote the sets of strings $w \in \{0,1\}^n$, for which $\Pi_i(+,w)$ and $\Pi_i(-,w)$ are defined.

The simulator provides the distinguisher with an interface $\text{Query}(i,\delta,w)$ which enables querying of the internal permutations, where $i \in \{1,...,7\}$ represents the permutation, $\delta \in \{+,-\}$ denotes whether the query is direct or inverse, and $w \in \{0,1\}^n$ indicates the value being queried.

Following [3,5], we render the randomness employed by the simulator explicit through a tuple of random permutations $\mathbf{P} = (P_1, ..., P_7)$, where each P_i is assigned a single interface denoted by $P_i := \{+,-\} \times \{0,1\}^n \rightarrow \{0,1\}^n$. Moreover, for any $u, v \in \{0,1\}^n, P_i(+,u) = v \Leftrightarrow P_i(-,v) = u$. As argued [1], the use of such explicit randomness is actually equivalent with lazy sampling.

If a value is already in the table and a new assignment occurs, the previous value is overwritten. We define the size of each table Π_i as $|\Pi_i| = \max\{|\Pi_i^+|, |\Pi_i^-|\}$. It is easy to see $|\Pi_i^+| = |\Pi_i^-|$ as long as no value is overwritten.

Simulation Strategy. Upon receipt of a Query(i, δ, w), the simulator searches table Π_i to ascertain whether the corresponding answer $\Pi_i(\delta, w)$ is already defined. If so, the simulator outputs the answer and remains in a state of readiness for the next query. Otherwise, it queries the explicit randomness source $w' := P_i(\delta, w)$ to have a random answer, and defines both $\Pi_i(\delta, w)$ and $\Pi_i(\overline{\delta}, w')$ as w' and w, respectively.

The simulator then runs a chain completion mechanism to ensure consistency with the random invertible permutation $\mathbf{\Pi}$ after selecting the answer w' at random and before returning it to the distinguisher. Namely, in the scenario where the distinguisher initiates Query(i, δ, w) with i being either 3 or 4, the simulator completes all newly created chains (v_3, u_4), where $v_3 \in \Pi_3^-$ and $u_4 \in \Pi_4^+$ by executing the procedure $Complete^+(v_3, u_4)$ or $Complete^-(v_3, u_4)$.

For instance, suppose that the distinguisher queries Query$(3, +, u_3)$, where u_3 has not been previously queried. The simulator then queries $\mathbf{P}$ for the random response $v_3 := P_3(+, u_3)$. Then for each $u_4 \in \Pi_4^+$, the simulator evaluates the Misty construction forward, letting $v_4 := \Pi_4(+, u_4)$, $u_5 := v_3 \oplus u_4$ and $v_5 :=$ Query$(5, +, u_5)$, then $u_6 := v_4 \oplus u_5$ and $u_7 := v_5 \oplus u_6$, and backward, letting $u_3 := \Pi_3(-, v_3)$, $v_2 := u_3 \oplus u_4$, $u_2 :=$ Query$(2, -, v_2)$, $v_1 := u_2 \oplus u_3$, $u_1 :=$ Query$(1, -, v_1)$ and $(u_8, u_9) := \mathbf{\Pi}(+, (u_1, u_2))$ (thus issuing a query to $\mathbf{\Pi}$ to perform a"wrap around"), then $v_6 := u_7 \oplus u_8$, $v_7 := u_8 \oplus u_9$, until the corresponding input/output values (u_6, v_6) for the sixth permutation and (u_7, v_7) for the seventh permutation are defined. In order to ensure consistency of the simulated Misty construction with $\mathbf{\Pi}$, the simulator then "adapts" (rather than setting randomly) table Π_6 and Π_7 by setting $\Pi_6(+, u_6) := v_6$, $\Pi_6(-, v_6) := u_6$, $\Pi_7(+, u_7) := v_7$ and $\Pi_7(-, v_7) := u_7$.

We will subsequently demonstrate that such an adaptation does not result in overwriting, i.e., the four values are undefined prior to the occurrence of adaptation. If the query is made to Query$(3, -, \cdot)$, the adaptation process pertains to tables Π_1 and Π_2. Moreover, the situation with Query$(4, \cdot, \cdot)$ is in line with that of Query$(3, \cdot, \cdot)$.

Simulator in Pseudocode. Our simulator is formally described in pseudocode as follows.

```
Simulator S^{Π,P}
Variables: tables Π_1,...,Π_7, all initially empty
public procedure Query(i, δ, w)
  if (δ, w) ∉ Π_i then
    w' := P_i(δ, w)
    Π_i(δ, w) := w'
    Π_i(δ̄, w') := w
    if i = 3 then
```

```
        if δ = + then
            v3 = w'
            forall u4 ∈ Π4^+ do
                Complete^+(v3, u4)
        else if δ = − then
            v3 = w
            forall u4 ∈ Π4^+ do
                Complete^-(v3, u4)
    else if i = 4 then
        if δ = + then
            u4 = w
            forall v3 ∈ Π3^- do
                Complete^+(v3, u4)
        else if δ = − then
            u4 = w'
            forall v3 ∈ Π3^- do
                Complete^-(v3, u4)
```

```
private procedure Complete^+(v3, u4)
    v4 := Π4(+, u4)
    u5 := v3 ⊕ u4
    v5 := Query(5, +, u5)
    u6 := v4 ⊕ u5
    u7 := v5 ⊕ u6
    u3 := Π3(−, v3)
    v2 := u3 ⊕ u4
    u2 := Query(2, −, v2)
    v1 := u2 ⊕ u3
    u1 := Query(1, −, v1)
    (u8, u9) := 𝚷(+, (u1, u2))
    v6 := u7 ⊕ u8
    v7 := u8 ⊕ u9
    // Adapt: may overwrite
    Π6(+, u6) := v6
    Π6(−, v6) := u6
    Π7(+, u7) := v7
    Π7(−, v7) := u7
```

```
private procedure Complete^-(v3, u4)
    u3 := Π3(−, v3)
    v2 := u3 ⊕ u4
    v4 := Π4(+, u4)
    u5 := v3 ⊕ u4
    v5 := Query(5, +, u5)
    u6 := v4 ⊕ u5
    v6 := Query(6, +, u6)
    u7 := v5 ⊕ u6
    v7 := Query(7, +, u7)
    u8 := v6 ⊕ u7
    u9 := v7 ⊕ u8
    (u1, u2) := 𝚷(−, (u8, u9))
    v1 := u2 ⊕ u3
    // Adapt: may overwrite
    Π1(+, u1) := v1
    Π1(−, v1) := u1
    Π2(+, u2) := v2
    Π2(−, v2) := u2
```

4.2 The Indistinguishability Proof

It remains to establish two claims for any distinguisher D: (a) the simulator $S^{\mathbf{\Pi},\mathbf{P}}$ possesses a bounded complexity; (b) the real world is indistinguishable from the ideal (or simulated) world. To this end, we introduce a helper intermediate system in the next paragraph. Then, subsequent paragraphs establish claims (a) and (b) in turn.

Intermediate System. We use three systems for the proof, as shown in Fig. 5. In detail, we denote $S^{\mathbf{\Pi},\mathbf{P}}$ the simulator with oracle access to the random invertible permutation $\mathbf{\Pi}$ and using random permutations $\mathbf{P}$ as source of randomness. Let $\Sigma_1(\mathbf{\Pi}, S^{\mathbf{\Pi},\mathbf{P}})$ be the system capturing the ideal (or simulated) world, where $\mathbf{\Pi}$ is a random invertible permutation, and $\mathbf{P} = (P_1, ..., P_7)$ are independent random permutations. All sources of randomness in system Σ_1 are captured by the pair $(\mathbf{\Pi}, \mathbf{P})$. Let $\Sigma_3(\text{Misty}^{\mathbf{P}}, \mathbf{P})$ be the real world, and all the randomness of system Σ_3 is captured by $\mathbf{P}$. We follow [3,25] and introduce $\Sigma_2(\text{Misty}^{S^{\mathbf{\Pi},\mathbf{P}}}, S^{\mathbf{\Pi},\mathbf{P}})$ as an intermediate system, which is derived from Σ_1 by substituting the left oracle $\mathbf{\Pi}$ with an Misty instance that queries the simulator to evaluate and the rest remains unchanged, so all the randomness of system Σ_2 is captured by $(\mathbf{\Pi}, \mathbf{P})$.

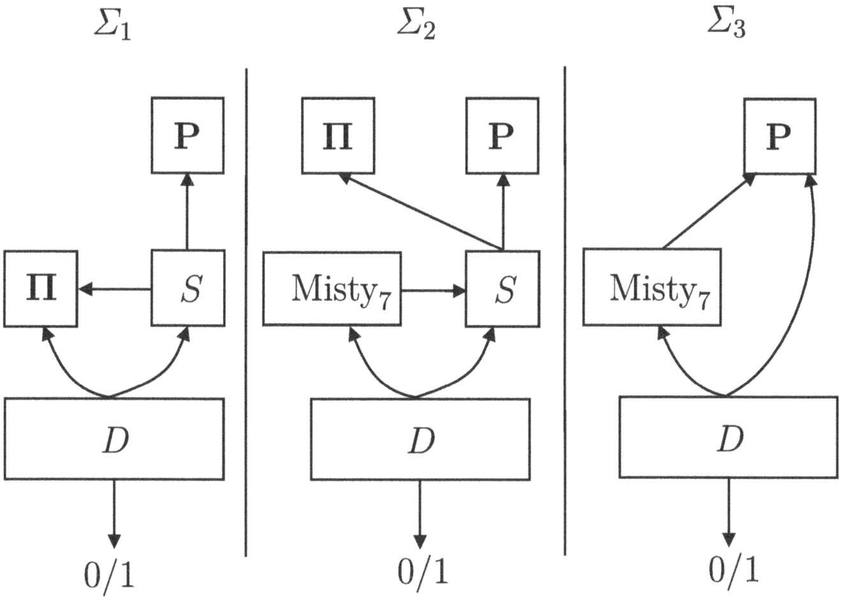

Fig. 5. Systems used in the seq-indifferentiability proof.

We consider a deterministic, fixed sequential distinguisher D, which has a maximum total oracle query cost of q. The remaining key points are as follows.

Complexity of $S^{\mathbf{\Pi},\mathbf{P}}$

Lemma 3. *Consider an execution of the simulator $S^{\mathbf{\Pi}}$ where the simulator receives at most q queries in total. Then:*

(*i*) *the size of* Π_3,Π_4 *is at most* q, *and the size of* Π_1, Π_2, Π_5, Π_6, Π_7 *is at most* $q^2 + q$;
(*ii*) *the simulator executes Complete*$^+$ *and Complete*$^-$ *at most* q^2 *times, makes at most* q^2 *queries to* $\mathbf{\Pi}$, *and runs in time* $O(q^2)$.

Proof. $S^{\mathbf{\Pi},\mathbf{P}}$ adds records to Π_3 or Π_4 only when a corresponding query to Query(i, δ, w) is made by the distinguisher, where $i = 3, 4$. Thus, the size of Π_3 and Π_4 increases by 1 each query, and cannot be greater than q. Procedure *Complete*$^+$ and *Complete*$^-$ are called once for each pair $(v_3, u_4) \in \Pi_3^- \times \Pi_4^+$, hence at most q^2 times in total. Moreover, since the simulator performs precisely one query to $\mathbf{\Pi}$ for each execution of *Complete*$^+$ or *Complete*$^-$, so the total number of queries made by the simulator to $\mathbf{\Pi}$ is at most q^2. Elements are added to Π_1, Π_2, Π_5, Π_6 or Π_7 only when a corresponding Query (i,δ, w) is made to the simulator where $i = 1, 2, 5, 6, 7$ and when *Complete*$^+$ or *Complete*$^-$ is called. As a result, the size of Π_1, Π_2, Π_5, Π_6 and Π_7 cannot be greater than $q^2 + q$. Since the simulator running time is dominated by the executions of *Complete*$^+$ and *Complete*$^-$, so is thus $O(q^2)$.

Overwrite Probability of $S^{\mathbf{\Pi},\mathbf{P}}$. Built upon the bounds given in Sect. 4.2, we analyze each of the overwriting possibilities in turn.

Definition 4. *A pair* $(\mathbf{\Pi}, \boldsymbol{P})$ *is said bad if the simulator overwrites the entry of its tables* Π_i *during an execution of* $D^{\Sigma_2(\mathbf{\Pi},\boldsymbol{P})}$. *Otherwise the pair is said good.*

Overwriting may happen either during a random assignment at line 7 or when adapting a chain at lines 41, 42, 43 and 44 in the procedure *Complete*$^+$ and lines 60, 61, 62 and 63 in the procedure *Complete*$^-$.

Firstly, we analyze the probability of overwrite during a random assignment.

Lemma 4. *The probability that* $S^{\mathbf{\Pi},\boldsymbol{P}}$ *overwrite at line 7 is at most* $\frac{16q^4}{N}$.

Proof. To begin, let BadRandom represent the occurrence of an overwrite during a random assignment, namely, the overwrite occurs at line 7. Note that the total number of queries received by the simulator in Σ_2 is exactly the total oracle query cost q of the distinguisher. All that has to be taken into account is the probability of an overwrite in Π_1, Π_2, Π_6 or Π_7, since entries in Π_3, Π_4 and Π_5 are never adapted, they can never be overwritten either. When a random assignment occurs at Π_i for $i = 1, 2, 6, 7$ that w' is randomly defined as $w' := P_i(\delta, w)$, it can only overwrite a value that was added when adapting the chain, but not the value that previously added during a random assignment. By Lemma 3 (i), there are at most $q^2 + q$ random assignments in Π_1, Π_2, Π_6 and Π_7, so that w' is uniformly random in a set of size at least $N - (q^2 + q)$. Moreover, by Lemma 3 (ii), there are at most q^2 values have gone through the adaptation chain. So the probability that w' is equivalent to one of the at most q^2 values previously added in table Π_i when adapting the chain is at most $\frac{q^2}{N-(q^2+q)}$. Summing over the at most $q^2 + q$ random assignments in Π_1, Π_2, Π_6 or Π_7, we have

$$\Pr[\mathsf{BadRandom}] \leq 4(q^2 + q) \times \frac{q^2}{N - (q^2 + q)} \leq \frac{16q^4}{N},$$

assuming $q^2 + q \leq N/2$. □

Next, we analyze the probability of overwrite when adapting a chain. Let BadAdapt represent the occurrence of an overwrite when adapting a chain (v_3, u_4), namely, the overwrite occurs at lines 41, 42, 43, 44 in the procedure *Complete*$^+$ and lines 60, 61, 62, 63 in the procedure *Complete*$^-$. Consider the i-th execution of *Complete*$^+$ (v_3, u_4), resp. *Complete*$^-$ (v_3, u_4), with the assumption that BadRandom and $\mathsf{BadAdapt_j}$ do not occur for $1 \leq j \leq i-1$. This indicates that before the i-th call to the procedure *Complete*$^+$ (v_3, u_4), resp. *Complete*$^-$ (v_3, u_4), no value was overwritten.

To upper bound the probability of BadAdapt, we need a helper lemma as follows.

Lemma 5. *Inside every call to Complete*$^+$*, resp. Complete*$^-$*, the random invertible permutation query* $\mathbf{\Pi}(+, (u_1, u_2))$*, resp.* $\mathbf{\Pi}(-, (u_8, u_9))$*, is fresh. Namely, the simulator* $S^{\mathbf{\Pi},P}$ *never made this query* $\mathbf{\Pi}(+, (u_1, u_2))$*, resp.* $\mathbf{\Pi}(-, (u_8, u_9))$*, before.*

Proof. Take the query $\mathbf{\Pi}(+, (u_1, u_2))$ as an example and the proof of $\mathbf{\Pi}(-, (u_8, u_9))$ is similar to this. The query $\mathbf{\Pi}(+, (u_1, u_2))$ made by the simulator during the evaluation of the Misty construction forward is fresh, meaning that it has not been made before and that (u_1, u_2) has not been received as an answer to a previous query $\mathbf{\Pi}(-, (u_8, u_9))$. To demonstrate this, we assume that it is not the case, which implies that the query had already been executed when another chain, denoted by (v'_3, u'_4), was being completed. However, we have assumed that no value was overwritten in the tables before the call to *Complete*$^+$ (v_3, u_4). Consequently, it can be easily observed that (v'_3, u'_4) must be equal to (v_3, u_4), which is impossible since the simulator complete any chain at most once by construction. Therefore, the random invertible permutation must be fresh. □

Now we can upper bound the probability of BadAdapt.

Lemma 6. *The probability that* $S^{\mathbf{\Pi},P}$ *overwrite at lines 41, 42, 43 and 44 in the procedure Complete*$^+$ *and lines 60, 61, 62 and 63 in the procedure Complete*$^-$ *is at most* $\frac{16q^4}{N}$.

Proof. We first consider the case D querying Query$(3, +, u_3)$ which triggers an execution of the procedure *Complete*$^+$. Our goal is to show that the values $\Pi_6(+, u_6) := v_6$, $\Pi_6(-, v_6) := u_6$, $\Pi_7(+, u_7) := v_7$ and $\Pi_7(-, v_7) := u_7$ are undefined previously with high probability.

- Recall that $u_6 := v_4 \oplus u_5$ and $u_5 := v_3 \oplus u_4$, which implies that $u_6 := v_4 \oplus v_3 \oplus u_4$. Moreover, the distinguisher called Query$(3, +, u_3)$, which means v_3 is a newly obtained random value. Since there are at most q random assignments in Π_6, the value of v_3 is selected randomly from a set of size that is at least $N - q$. So the probability of u_6 being equal to one of the at most $q^2 + q$ values already in Π_6 is at most $\frac{q^2+q}{N-q}$.

- We next consider the case of u_7. Since $u_7 := v_5 \oplus u_6$ and we have previously discussed the randomness of u_6, so the probability that u_7 is equal to one of the at most $q^2 + q$ values already in Π_7 is at most $\frac{q^2+q}{N-q}$.
- As for $v_6 := u_7 \oplus u_8$ and $v_7 := u_8 \oplus u_9$, by Lemma 5 the query $\mathbf{\Pi}(+, (u_1, u_2))$ made by the simulator during the evaluation of the Misty construction forward is fresh, meaning that it has not been made before and that (u_1, u_2) has not been received as an answer to a previous query $\mathbf{\Pi}(-, (u_8, u_9))$. This indicates that the value of u_8, resp. u_9, returned by $\mathbf{\Pi}$ are randomly selected from a set with a size of at least $N - q^2$, based on the fact that the simulator makes at most q^2 queries to $\mathbf{\Pi}$ as specified in Lemma 3. As a result, considering the randomness of u_8, it follows that $v_6 := u_7 \oplus u_8$ is equal to one of the at most $q^2 + q$ values that already exist in the table Π_6 with a probability of at most $\frac{q^2+q}{N-q^2}$. Similarly, $v_7 := u_8 \oplus u_9$ is equal to one of the at most $q^2 + q$ values that already exist in the table Π_7 with a probability of at most $\frac{q^2+q}{N-q^2}$.

The case where D querying Query$(4, +, u_4)$ triggering *Complete*$^+$ is similar: the call to Query$(4, +, u_4)$ will "download" the response v_4 from $\mathbf{P}$, meaning that v_4 is uniform in at least $N - q$ possibilities, and further:

- The probability that $u_6 = v_4 \oplus v_3 \oplus u_4$ equals one of the at most $q^2 + q$ values in Π_6 is at most $\frac{q^2+q}{N-q}$;
- The probability that $u_7 = v_5 \oplus u_6$ equals one of the at most $q^2 + q$ values in Π_7 is at most $\frac{q^2+q}{N-q}$.

On the other hand, $v_6 = u_7 \oplus u_8$ and $v_7 = u_8 \oplus u_9$ still get randomness from $\mathbf{\Pi}(+, (u_1, u_2))$, and thus the probability that either of them equal values in Π_6 or Π_7 respectively is at most $\frac{2(q^2+q)}{N-q^2}$.

Now we consider the case D querying Query$(3, -, v_3)$ which triggers an excution of the procedure *Complete*$^-$. Our goal becomes to show that the values $\Pi_1(+, u_1) := v_1$, $\Pi_1(-, v_1) := u_1$, $\Pi_2(+, u_2) := v_2$ and $\Pi_2(-, v_2) := u_2$ are undefined previously with high probability.

- Recall that $v_2 := u_3 \oplus u_4$, since the distinguisher called Query$(3, -, v_3)$, which means u_3 is a newly obtained random value. As discussed above, since there are at most q random assignments in Π_3, the value of u_3 is selected randomly from a set of size that is at least $N - q$. So the probability of v_2 being equal to one of the at most $q^2 + q$ values already in Π_2 is at most $\frac{q^2+q}{N-q}$.
- As $(u_1, u_2) := \mathbf{\Pi}(-, (u_8, u_9))$, by Lemma 5 we have the query $\mathbf{\Pi}(-, (u_8, u_9))$ made by the simulator during the evaluation of the Misty construction forward is fresh, so the value of u_1, resp. u_2, returned by $\mathbf{\Pi}$ are randomly selected from a set with a size of at least $N - q^2$, so u_1, resp. u_2, is equal to one of the at most $q^2 + q$ values that already exist in the table Π_1, resp. Π_2, with a probability of at most $\frac{q^2+q}{N-q^2}$.
- Since $v_1 := u_2 \oplus u_3$, considering the randomness of u_3, then the probability of v_1 being equal to one of the at most $q^2 + q$ values already in Π_1 is at most $\frac{q^2+q}{N-q}$.

The case where D querying Query$(4, -, v_4)$ triggering $Complete^-$ is similar: the call to Query$(4, -, v_4)$ will "download" the response u_4 from $\mathbf{P}$, meaning that u_4 is uniform in at least $N - q$ possibilities, and further:

- The probability that $v_2 := u_3 \oplus u_4$ equals one of the at most $q^2 + q$ values in Π_2 is at most $\frac{q^2+q}{N-q}$;
- The probability that $v_1 := u_2 \oplus u_3$ equals one of the at most $q^2 + q$ values in Π_1 is at most $\frac{q^2+q}{N-q}$.

On the other hand, u_1 and u_2 still get randomness from $\mathbf{\Pi}(-, (u_8, u_9))$, and thus the probability that either of them equal values in Π_1 or Π_2 respectively is at most $\frac{2(q^2+q)}{N-q^2}$.

Considering the procedure $Complete^+$, resp. $Complete^-$, which has a maximum of q^2 calls, hence, by summing over all that calls, we have,

$$\begin{aligned}
&\Pr[\mathsf{BadAdapt}|\overline{\mathsf{BadRandom}}] \\
\leq &\sum_{i=1}^{q^2} \Pr[\mathsf{BadAdapt_i}|\overline{\mathsf{BadRandom}} \wedge \overline{\mathsf{BadAdapt_j}}, j = 1, ..., i-1] \\
\leq &\, q^2\Big(\frac{2(q^2+q)}{N-q} + \frac{2(q^2+q)}{N-q^2}\Big) \leq \frac{16q^4}{N},
\end{aligned}$$

as claimed. □

We have already discussed the two cases of overwrite, namely $\mathsf{BadRandom}$ and $\mathsf{BadAdapt}$. Now we upper bound the probability that a random pair $(\mathbf{\Pi}, \mathbf{P})$ is bad.

Lemma 7. *Consider a distinguisher D of total oracle query cost at most q, with $q^2 \leq N/4$. Then a uniformly random pair $(\mathbf{\Pi}, \boldsymbol{P})$, where $\mathbf{\Pi} \leftarrow \mathcal{P}(2n)$ and $\boldsymbol{P} \xleftarrow{\$} (\mathcal{P}(n))^7$, is bad with probability at most $\frac{32q^4}{N}$.*

Proof. Gathering Lemmas 4 and 6 yields the bound. □

Indistinguishability of Σ_1 and Σ_3. A random tuple $(\mathbf{\Pi}, \mathbf{P})$ is *good*, if $S^{\mathbf{\Pi},\mathbf{P}}$ does not overwrite in $D^{\Sigma_2(\mathbf{\Pi},\mathbf{P})}$. It can be proved that, for any good tuple $(\mathbf{\Pi}, \mathbf{P})$, the transcript of the interaction of D with $\Sigma_1(\mathbf{\Pi}, \mathbf{P})$ and $\Sigma_2(\mathbf{\Pi}, \mathbf{P})$ is exactly the same. This means the gap between Σ_1 and Σ_2 is the overwrite probability.

Σ_1 to Σ_2. The proof for this step simply follows [3,25].

Lemma 8. *For any distinguisher D of total oracle query cost at most q, it holds*

$$\Big|\Pr[D^{\Sigma_1(\mathbf{\Pi},S^{\mathbf{\Pi},P})} = 1] - \Pr[D^{\Sigma_2(Misty^{S^{\mathbf{\Pi},P}},S^{\mathbf{\Pi},P})} = 1]\Big| \leq \frac{32q^4}{N}.$$

Proof. Note that in Σ_1 and Σ_2, the sequential distinguisher D necessarily first queries $\mathcal{S}$ and then $\mathbf{\Pi}$ (in Σ_1) or Misty (in Σ_2) only. Thus, the transcript of the first phase of the interaction (i.e., for the queries of D to $S^{\mathbf{\Pi},\mathbf{P}}$) is clearly the same, since in both cases they are answered by $\mathcal{S}$ using the same randomness $(\mathbf{\Pi}, \mathbf{P})$. For the second phase of the interaction (i.e., queries of D to its left oracle), it directly follows from the adaptation mechanism. Hence, the transcripts of the interaction of D with $\Sigma_1(\mathbf{\Pi}, \mathbf{P})$ and $\Sigma_2(\mathbf{\Pi}, \mathbf{P})$ are the same for any good tuple $(\mathbf{\Pi}, \mathbf{P})$. Further using Lemma 7 yields

$$\begin{aligned}&\left|\Pr[D^{\Sigma_1(\mathbf{\Pi}, S^{\mathbf{\Pi},\mathbf{P}})} = 1] - \Pr[D^{\Sigma_2(\text{Misty}^{S^{\mathbf{\Pi},\mathbf{P}}}, S^{\mathbf{\Pi},\mathbf{P}})} = 1]\right| \\ \leq\ & \Pr[(\mathbf{\Pi}, \mathbf{P})\ \textit{is bad}] \leq \frac{32q^4}{N},\end{aligned}$$

as claimed. □

Σ_2 to Σ_3: Randomness Mapping. We now bound the gap between Σ_2 and Σ_3. Following [3,5], the technique is the randomness mapping argument.

We define a map Λ mapping pairs $(\mathbf{\Pi}, \mathbf{P})$ either to the special symbol $\perp$ when $(\mathbf{\Pi}, \mathbf{P})$ is bad, or to a pair of *partial permutations* $\mathbf{P}' = (P_1', ..., P_7')$ when $(\mathbf{\Pi}, \mathbf{P})$ is good. A partial permutation is a function P_i': $\{+, -\} \times \{0, 1\}^n \to \{0, 1\}^n \cup \{*\}$, such that for all $x, y \in \{0, 1\}^n$, $P_i'(+, x) = y \neq * \Leftrightarrow P_i'(-, y) = x \neq *$.

Then map Λ is defined for good pairs $(\mathbf{\Pi}, \mathbf{P})$ as follows: run $D^{\Sigma_2(\mathbf{\Pi},\mathbf{P})}$, and consider the tables Π_i of the simulator at the end of the execution: then fill all undefined entries of the Π_i's with the special symbol $*$. The result is exactly $\Lambda(\mathbf{\Pi}, \mathbf{P})$. Since for a good pair $(\mathbf{\Pi}, \mathbf{P})$, the simulator never overwrite an entry in its tables, it follows that $\Lambda(\mathbf{\Pi}, \mathbf{P})$ is a pair of partial permutations as just defined above. We say that a pair of partial permutations $\mathbf{P}' = (P_1', ..., P_7')$ is good if it has a good preimage by Λ. Then, we say that a pair of permutations $\mathbf{P}$ extends a pair of partial permutations $\mathbf{P}' = (P_1', ..., P_7')$, denoted $\mathbf{P} \vdash \mathbf{P}'$, if for each $i = 1, ..., 7$, P_i and P_i' agree on all entries such that $P_i'(\delta, x) \neq *$.

By definition of the randomness mapping, for any good tuple of partial permutations $\mathbf{P}'$, the outputs of $D^{\Sigma_2(\mathbf{\Pi},\mathbf{P})}$ and $D^{\Sigma_3(\mathbf{P})}$ are equal for any pair $(\mathbf{\Pi}, \mathbf{P})$ such that $\Lambda(\mathbf{\Pi}, \mathbf{P}) = \mathbf{P}'$ and any tuple of permutations $\mathbf{P}$ such that $\mathbf{P} \vdash \mathbf{P}'$. Let Ω_1 be the set of partial permutations $\mathbf{P}'$ such that $D^{\Sigma_2(\mathbf{\Pi},\mathbf{P})}$ output 1 for any pair $(\mathbf{\Pi}, \mathbf{P})$ such that $\Lambda(\mathbf{\Pi}, \mathbf{P}) = \mathbf{P}'$. Then, we have the following ratio.

Lemma 9. *Consider a fixed distinguisher D with total oracle query cost at most q. Then, for any $\boldsymbol{P}' = (P_1', ..., P_7') \in \Omega_1$, it holds*

$$\frac{\Pr\left[\boldsymbol{P} \vdash \boldsymbol{P}'\right]}{\Pr\left[\Lambda(\mathbf{\Pi}, \boldsymbol{P}) = \boldsymbol{P}'\right]} \geq 1 - \frac{121q^4}{N}.$$

Proof. Since the number of "non-empty" entries $P_i'(x) \neq *$ is $|\Pi_i|$ for $i = 1, ..., 7$, fix a good tuple of partial permutations $\mathbf{P}' = (P_1', ..., P_7')$, we have

$$\Pr\left[\mathbf{P} \vdash \mathbf{P}'\right] = \prod_{i=1}^{7} \prod_{j=0}^{|\Pi_i|-1} \frac{1}{N - j}.$$

Fix any good preimage $(\widetilde{\Pi}, \widetilde{\mathbf{P}})$ of $\mathbf{P}'$. Then for any tuple $(\mathbf{\Pi}, \mathbf{P})$, $\Lambda(\mathbf{\Pi}, \mathbf{P}) = \mathbf{P}'$ *iff* the transcript of the interaction of $\mathcal{S}$ with $(\mathbf{\Pi}, \mathbf{P})$ in $D^{\Sigma_2(\mathbf{\Pi},\mathbf{P})}$ is the same as the transcript of the interaction of $\mathcal{S}$ with $(\widetilde{\mathbf{\Pi}}, \widetilde{\mathbf{P}})$ in $D^{\Sigma_2(\widetilde{\mathbf{\Pi}},\widetilde{\mathbf{P}})}$.

Assume that during the Σ_2 execution $D^{\Sigma_2(\widetilde{\mathbf{\Pi}},\widetilde{\mathbf{P}})}$, $\mathcal{S}$ makes $q_{\mathbf{\Pi}}$ and q_i ($1 \leq i \leq 7$) queries to $\widetilde{\mathbf{\Pi}}$ and $\widetilde{P}_i$. Then,

$$\Pr\big[\Lambda(\mathbf{\Pi}, \mathbf{P}) = \mathbf{P}'\big] \leq \Bigg(\prod_{j=0}^{q_{\mathbf{\Pi}}-1} \frac{1}{N^2 - j}\Bigg)\Bigg(\prod_{i=1}^{7}\prod_{j=0}^{q_i-1} \frac{1}{N - j}\Bigg).$$

We can see that $2q_{\mathbf{\Pi}} + \sum_{i=1}^{7} q_i = \sum_{i=1}^{7} |\Pi_i| \leq 4q^2 + 7q$: since $\sum_{i=1}^{7} q_i$ equal the number of sampled records in Π_i, while $2q_{\mathbf{\Pi}}$ equal the number of adapted records in Π_1, Π_2, Π_6 and Π_7. It thus holds

$$\begin{aligned}
\frac{\Pr\big[\mathbf{P} \vdash \mathbf{P}'\big]}{\Pr\big[\Lambda(\mathbf{\Pi}, \mathbf{P}) = \mathbf{P}'\big]} &\geq \frac{\prod_{i=1}^{7}\prod_{j=0}^{|\Pi_i|-1} \frac{1}{N-j}}{\Big(\prod_{j=0}^{q_{\mathbf{\Pi}}-1} \frac{1}{N^2-j}\Big)\Big(\prod_{i=1}^{7}\prod_{j=0}^{q_i-1} \frac{1}{N-j}\Big)} \\
&\geq \prod_{j=0}^{q_{\mathbf{\Pi}}-1}\left(1 - \frac{j}{N^2}\right)\prod_{i=1}^{7}\prod_{j=0}^{q_i-1}\left(1 - \frac{j}{N}\right) \\
&\geq 1 - \frac{2q_{\mathbf{\Pi}}^2 + \sum_{i=1}^{7} q_i^2}{N} \\
&\geq 1 - \frac{(4q^2 + 7q)^2}{N} \\
&\geq 1 - \frac{121q^4}{N},
\end{aligned}$$

as claimed. □

Lemma 10. *For any distinguisher D with total oracle query cost at most q, it holds*

$$\left|\Pr\big[D^{\Sigma_2(Misty^{S^{\mathbf{\Pi},P}}, S^{\mathbf{\Pi},P})} = 1\big] - \Pr\big[D^{\Sigma_3(Misty^{P}, \boldsymbol{P})} = 1\big]\right| \leq \frac{153q^4}{N}.$$

Proof. Gathering Lemmas 7 and 9 yields

$$\begin{aligned}
&\left|\Pr\big[D^{\Sigma_2(\mathrm{Misty}^{S^{\mathbf{\Pi},\mathbf{P}}}, S^{\mathbf{\Pi},\mathbf{P}})} = 1\big] - \Pr\big[D^{\Sigma_3(\mathrm{Misty}^{\mathbf{P}},\mathbf{P})} = 1\big]\right| \\
\leq& \Pr\big[(\mathbf{\Pi}, \mathbf{P}) \textit{ is bad}\big] + \sum_{\mathbf{P}' \in \Omega_1} \Pr\big[\Lambda(\mathbf{\Pi}, \mathbf{P}) = \mathbf{P}'\big] - \sum_{\mathbf{P}' \in \Omega_1} \Pr\big[\mathbf{P} \vdash \mathbf{P}'\big] \\
\leq& \Pr\big[(\mathbf{\Pi}, \mathbf{P}) \textit{ is bad}\big] + \sum_{\mathbf{P}' \in \Omega_1} \Pr\big[\Lambda(\mathbf{\Pi}, \mathbf{P}) = \mathbf{P}'\big]\left(1 - \frac{\Pr\big[\mathbf{P} \vdash \mathbf{P}'\big]}{\Pr\big[\Lambda(\mathbf{\Pi}, \mathbf{P}) = \mathbf{P}'\big]}\right) \\
\leq& \frac{32q^4}{N} + \frac{121q^4}{N} \sum_{\mathbf{P}' \in \Omega_1} \Pr\big[\Lambda(\mathbf{\Pi}, \mathbf{P}) = \mathbf{P}'\big] \\
\leq& \frac{153q^4}{N},
\end{aligned}$$

as claimed. □

Gathering Lemmas 8 and 10 yields the bound in Theorem 3.

5 Conclusion

We provide the first known-key security analysis of the Misty structure, which has been used in several blockcipher standards. We focus on the security notion of sequential indifferentiability, and prove negative and positive results at 5 and 7 rounds respectively.

We note that there is a gap of 1 round between our negative and positive results. Closing this gap as well as extending our treatments to other Misty variants (e.g., using correlated round permutations, or using random involutions) would be interesting future works.

Acknowledgements. We thank Chenyu Xiao for discussions at the early stage. The authors were supported by the National Key Research and Development Program of China (Grant 2023YFA1011200) and the National Natural Science Foundation of China (Grant 62372274).

References

1. Andreeva, E., Bogdanov, A., Dodis, Y., Mennink, B., Steinberger, J.P.: On the indifferentiability of key-alternating ciphers. In: Canetti, R., Garay, J.A. (eds.) CRYPTO 2013, Part I. LNCS, vol. 8042, pp. 531–550. Springer, Heidelberg (2013)
2. Canetti, R., Goldreich, O., Halevi, S.: The random oracle methodology, revisited. J. ACM **51**(4), 557–594 (2004)
3. Cogliati, B., Seurin, Y.: On the provable security of the iterated Even-Mansour cipher against related-key and chosen-key attacks. In: Oswald, E., Fischlin, M. (eds.) EUROCRYPT 2015, Part I. LNCS, vol. 9056, pp. 584–613. Springer, Heidelberg (2015)
4. Cogliati, B., Seurin, Y.: Strengthening the known-key security notion for block ciphers. In: Peyrin, T. (ed.) FSE 2016. LNCS, vol. 9783, pp. 494–513. Springer, Heidelberg (2016)
5. Coron, J.-S., Holenstein, T., Künzler, R., Patarin, J., Seurin, Y., Tessaro, S.: How to build an ideal cipher: the indifferentiability of the Feistel construction. J. Cryptol. **29**(1), 61–114 (2016)
6. Da, Q., Xu, S., Guo, C.: Sequential indifferentiability of confusion-diffusion networks. In: Adhikari, A., Küsters, R., Preneel, B. (eds.) INDOCRYPT 2021. LNCS, vol. 13143, pp. 93–113. Springer, Cham (2021)
7. Dachman-Soled, D., Katz, J., Thiruvengadam, A.: 10-round Feistel is indifferentiable from an ideal cipher. In: Fischlin, M., Coron, J.-S. (eds.) EUROCRYPT 2016, Part II. LNCS, vol. 9666, pp. 649–678. Springer, Heidelberg (2016)
8. Dai, Y., Seurin, Y., Steinberger, J.P., Thiruvengadam, A.: Indifferentiability of iterated Even-Mansour ciphers with non-idealized key-schedules: five rounds are necessary and sufficient. In: Katz, J., Shacham, H. (eds.) CRYPTO 2017, Part III. LNCS, vol. 10403, pp. 524–555. Springer, Heidelberg (2017)

9. Dai, Y., Steinberger, J.P.: Indifferentiability of 8-round Feistel networks. In: Robshaw, M., Katz, J. (eds.) CRYPTO 2016, Part I. LNCS, vol. 9814, pp. 95–120. Springer, Heidelberg (2016)
10. Dodis, Y., Stam, M., Steinberger, J.P., Liu, T.: Indifferentiability of confusion-diffusion networks. In: Fischlin, M., Coron, J.-S. (eds.) EUROCRYPT 2016, Part II. LNCS, vol. 9666, pp. 679–704. Springer, Heidelberg (2016)
11. ETSI. Universal mobile telecommunications system (UMTS); specification of the 3GPP confidentiality and integrity algorithms. Document 2: Kasumi algorithm specification. (3GPP TS 35.202 version 3.1.2 Release 1999)
12. Gouget, A., Patarin, J., Toulemonde, A.: (Quantum) cryptanalysis of misty schemes. In: Hong, D. (ed.) ICISC 20. LNCS, vol. 12593, pp. 43–57. Springer, Heidelberg (2020)
13. Guo, C., Lin, D.: On the indifferentiability of key-alternating Feistel ciphers with no key derivation. In: Dodis, Y., Nielsen, J.B. (eds.) TCC 2015. LNCS, vol. 9014, pp. 110–133. Springer, Heidelberg (2015)
14. Guo, C., Lin, D.: A synthetic indifferentiability analysis of interleaved double-key Even-Mansour ciphers. In: Iwata, T., Cheon, J.H. (eds.) ASIACRYPT 2015, Part II. LNCS, vol. 9453, pp. 389–410. Springer, Heidelberg (2015)
15. Guo, C., Lin, D.: Indifferentiability of 3-round even-mansour with random oracle key derivation. IACR Cryptology ePrint Archive, p. 894 (2016)
16. Guo, C., Lin, D.: Separating invertible key derivations from non-invertible ones: sequential indifferentiability of 3-round even-mansour. Des. Codes Cryptogr. **81**(1), 109–129 (2016)
17. Guo, C., Wang, L., Lin, D.: Impossibility of indifferentiable iterated blockciphers from 3 or less primitive calls. IACR Cryptology ePrint Archive, p. 226 (2023). To appear at EUROCRYPT 2023
18. Iwata, T., et al.: Thank goodness it's friday (TGIF). Submission to Round **1**, 157 (2019)
19. Iwata, T., Yoshino, T., Kurosawa, K.: Non-cryptographic primitive for pseudorandom permutation. In: Daemen, J., Rijmen, V. (eds.) FSE 2002. LNCS, vol. 2365, pp. 149–163. Springer, Heidelberg (2002)
20. Iwata, T., Yoshino, T., Yuasa, T., Kurosawa, K.: Round security and super-pseudorandomness of MISTY type structure. In: Matsui, M. (ed.) FSE 2001. LNCS, vol. 2355, pp. 233–247. Springer, Heidelberg (2002)
21. Lars, R.: Knudsen and Vincent Rijmen. Known-key distinguishers for some block ciphers. In: Kurosawa, K. (ed.) ASIACRYPT 2007. LNCS, vol. 4833, pp. 315–324. Springer, Heidelberg (2007)
22. Lampe, R., Seurin, Y.: How to construct an ideal cipher from a small set of public permutations. In: Sako, K., Sarkar, P. (eds.) ASIACRYPT 2013, Part I. LNCS, vol. 8269, pp. 444–463. Springer, Heidelberg (2013)
23. Lee, J., Koo, B.: Security of the misty structure using involutions as round functions. IEICE Trans. Fundam. Electron. Commun. Comput. Sci. **93-A**(9), 1612–1619 (2010)
24. Luo, Y.Y., Yan, H.L., Wang, L., Hu, H.G., Lai, X.J.: Study on block cipher structures against Simon's quantum algorithm. J. Cryptol. Res. **6**(5), 561–573 (2019)
25. Mandal, A., Patarin, J., Seurin, Y.: On the public indifferentiability and correlation intractability of the 6-round Feistel construction. In: Cramer, R. (ed.) TCC 2012. LNCS, vol. 7194, pp. 285–302. Springer, Heidelberg (2012)
26. Matsui, M.: New block encryption algorithm MISTY. In: Biham, E. (ed.) FSE'97. LNCS, vol. 1267, pp. 54–68. Springer, Heidelberg (1997)

27. Ueli, M.: Maurer, Renato Renner, and Clemens Holenstein. Indifferentiability, impossibility results on reductions, and applications to the random oracle methodology. In: Naor, M. (ed.) TCC 2004. LNCS, vol. 2951, pp. 21–39. Springer, Heidelberg (2004)
28. Minier, M., Gilbert, H.: Stochastic cryptanalysis of Crypton. In: Schneier, B. (ed.) FSE 2000. LNCS, vol. 1978, pp. 121–133. Springer, Heidelberg (2001)
29. Nachef, V., Patarin, J., Treger, J.: Generic attacks on misty schemes. In: Abdalla, M., Barreto, P. (eds.) LATINCRYPT 2010. LNCS, vol. 6212, pp. 222–240. Springer, Heidelberg (2010). https://doi.org/10.1007/978-3-642-14712-8_14
30. Piret, G., Quisquater, J.-J.: Security of the MISTY structure in the Luby-Rackoff model: improved results. In: Handschuh, H., Hasan, A. (eds.) SAC 2004. LNCS, vol. 3357, pp. 100–113. Springer, Heidelberg (2004)
31. Xu, S., Da, Q., Guo, C.: Minimizing even-mansour ciphers for sequential indifferentiability (without key schedules). In: Isobe, T., Sarkar, S. (eds.) INDOCRYPT 2022. LNCS, vol. 13774, pp. 125–145. Springer, Cham (2022)
32. Shanjie, X., Da, Q., Guo, C.: Chosen-key secure even-mansour cipher from a single permutation. IACR Trans. Symmetric Cryptol. **2023**(1), 244–287 (2023)

Multiparty Computation and Zero-Knowledge

Secure Computation with Penalties, Revisited: How to Handle Coins with Various Colors

Takeshi Nakai(✉)

Toyohashi University of Technology, Toyohashi, Aichi, Japan
nakai@cs.tut.ac.jp

Abstract. Secure computation with penalties aims to achieve fairness in secure computation protocols by imposing monetary penalties on adversarial parties. A fundamental problem to constructing a protocol that involves monetary entities is how to formalize them in the computational model. Bentov and Kumaresan (Crypto 2014) introduced a new computational model with special atomic entities called coins that capture currency and showed a protocol for secure computation with penalties in the model. Their model, secure computation with coins, assumes coins have several properties that are natural in the sense of expressing currency. However, on the other hand, it also requires the unnatural assumption "all coins are indistinguishable from each other" for a technical reason to accomplish the security proof. The motivation of this work is to remove the assumption from the coins to make the model a more general. We propose a new model, secure computation with color coins, such that coins have identifiable colors and do not hold the indistinguishability property. Furthermore, our model allows us to set different prices for each color. We show that secure computation with penalties can be realized in our model. To do this, we make some modifications to the ideal functionality of secure computation with penalties to adapt it to our model without losing the essence, i.e., fairness with penalties.

1 Introduction

1.1 Backgrounds

Secure computation is a cryptographic protocol that enables mutually distrustful parties to evaluate an arbitrary function without revealing their private inputs [32]. Fairness is a security notion for secure computation, and it guarantees that the protocol always terminates with either all parties learning the output or no parties learning it. In a fair protocol, it is impossible for any adversary that received the output to abort the protocol without disclosing the output to honest parties. Cleve [13] shows that any protocol for the coin-flipping functionality cannot fulfill fairness in the two-party setting. Unfortunately, the result implies that fairness is impossible to achieve when a majority of parties are not honest, except in certain functions [3,4,19].

A. Patra (Ed.): CT-RSA 2025, LNCS 15598, pp. 351–374, 2025.
https://doi.org/10.1007/978-3-031-88661-4_15

There is a line of work achieving fairness by imposing monetary penalties on adversaries, e.g., [1,2,7,9,10,22,24,26,27,29,30]. In this approach, an adversarial party that aborts the protocol after receiving the output is forced to pay honest parties a predetermined amount of money. If we can determine the penalty amount appropriately, adversaries will refrain from aborting to avoid losing money, and the protocol will achieve fairness. Such a mechanism, for instance, can be implemented by using a trusted bank [27,30] or a cryptocurrency [2,9,24,26].

A fundamental problem in constructing cryptographic protocols involving monetary entities is how to formalize them in the computational model. An approach is to treat money as just integer quantities recorded on a public ledger. The public ledger is formalized as an ideal functionality, which is intended to capture blockchain-based cryptocurrencies [6,14,15,22]. In such frameworks, parties can realize money transfer by sending a message specifying the sender, recipient, and amount to the ideal functionality. Note that the money transfer is expressed in the ideal functionality implicitly. Hence, this approach has the advantage of being able to handle money without deviating from the standard computational model, e.g., the Universal Composability (UC) model [11].

Another approach is to treat money as special entities called *coins*. In this approach, parties carry out the protocol by passing coins between them, like communication of messages, but the coins are clearly distinguished from the standard messages. The coins are defined as atomic entities that hold the following properties: (**P1**) Parties can transfer their own coins to the other parties freely, (**P2**) Multiple parties cannot hold the same coin simultaneously, (**P3**) Coins cannot be neither forged nor duplicated, and (**P4**) All coins are perfectly indistinguishable from each other. Bentov and Kumaresan [9] proposed a new computational model, called *secure computation with coins* (SCC), based on the coins. We note that parties are formalized as specialized Interactive Turing Machines (ITMs) that can handle the coins in the SCC model. Compared to the above-mentioned formalization based on the public ledger, the SCC model aims to capture monetary entities more generally. While, as far as we know, all existing protocols based on the SCC model are supposed to be implemented with blockchain-based cryptocurrencies [9,10,24–26,29], the definition of coins is intended to capture not only such digital currency but also overall currency, including physical one.

Related Works. A number of works have been dedicated to developing techniques to circumvent the impossibility result of fairness. The major approaches are the gradual release [8,18] and the optimistic model [5,28]. In the gradual release approach, parties gradually disclose the output using multiple rounds instead of revealing it at once. As a result, the adversary cannot learn much more about the output than honest parties, even if it aborts during the protocol. However, this solution has the drawback of requiring many rounds. The optimistic model supposes the existence of a Trusted Third Party (TTP). If all parties behave honestly, they do not need to communicate with the TTP. The TTP works to restore fairness only if there is an adversarial party. This solution is more efficient than the gradual release; however, it has the drawback of relying on the honesty of the third party. Another approach to achieving fairness is using blockchain as a public bulletin board [12].

1.2 Our Motivation and Contribution

Reviewing the definition of coins, we can see that properties **P1**–**P3** are natural to capture currency. On the other hand, property **P4** is somewhat unnatural and seems to be introduced only for the technical reason of security proofs. Indeed, it plays an essential role in the security proof for Bentov–Kumaresan's protocol for secure computation with penalties, as we will explain later. Imposing property **P4** on coins is unpreferable in terms of the generality of the model. Because of property **P4**, the model cannot deal with *multiple monetary entities that are distinguishable from each other or have mutually distinct prices*. Our motivation comes from the goal of modifying the SCC model to a more general one by removing property **P4** from the definition of coins. The model we are aiming to build allows the existence of the above-mentioned monetary entities that the SCC model cannot deal with.

To accomplish the goal, we follow the SCC model but with some modifications. Our model, *secure computation with color coins*, supposes that coins have identifiable colors. Since coins of different colors are distinguishable from each other, property **P4** clearly does not hold. Note that properties **P1**–**P3** are assumed also in our model. The prices of coins are determined depending on colors; thus, our model allows monetary entities with mutually distinct prices. Our definition of coins is intended to capture not only currency but also overall physical/digital entities having asset values. A question arising from eliminating property **P4** is whether or not the protocol constructed in the SCC model can be realized in our model. To provide a positive answer to this question, we show that Bentov–Kumaresan's protocol for secure computation with penalties can be realized in our model with almost no changes to the procedure. Since their security proof of the protocol relies heavily on property **P4**, a workaround is necessary to prove the security in our model. We modify the ideal functionality of secure computation with penalties as the workaround.

Overview of the Workaround. The secure computation with penalties formalized in the SCC model requires that honest parties input their coins as deposit to the ideal functionality. This functionality ensures that the deposit coins are returned to the honest parties *without ever sending them to the adversary*, which implies that honest parties never lose coins. In the security proof, which follows the real/ideal simulation paradigm, the ideal-world simulator needs to simulate the real-world adversary's view regarding the communications of coins in addition to standard messages. That is, it must complete the simulation using only the coins given to corrupted parties. Property **P4** plays an essential role for which the simulator succeeds in its simulation with this limitation.

In our formalization, the ideal functionality of secure computation with penalties allows the simulator to swap its own color coins with a subset of deposits. We require that the swap is *equivalent*. Hence, the functionality ensures that honest parties get back their deposit coins at the same price as the input, although the content may change by the swaps. Moreover, the swap allows the simulator to accomplish the simulation even while the adversary can distinguish coins, i.e., without property **P4**.

1.3 Basic Notations and Settings

Let $|X|$ denote the number of elements in a set X. Let $\mathbb{N} := \{0, 1, 2, \dots\}$. For any positive integer i, $[i]$ represents the set of integers $\{1, \dots, i\}$. Let n be the overall number of parties in a protocol. We denote by $H \subseteq [n]$ (resp. $C \subseteq [n]$) the set of honest (resp. corrupted) parties, where $H \cap C = \emptyset$, $|H| + |C| = n$, and $|C| < n$ hold. We consider security against only static adversaries, which determine the set of corrupted parties at the onset of the protocol. Let λ denote the security parameter. All parties are assumed to be non-uniform Probabilistic Polynomial-Time (PPT) algorithms in λ. We suppose that all parties are connected with pairwise secure channels over synchronous network.

Organization. The remaining part of this paper is organized as follows: In Sect. 2, we describe Bentov–Kumaresan's model [9], secure computation with coins, to clarify the difference from one we will propose. Section 3 shows our model, secure computation with color coins. Furthermore, we introduce an ideal functionality for secure computation with penalties adapted to our model. Section 4 shows a multiparty protocol realizing secure computation with penalties in our introduced model. Section 5 presents a security proof for the protocol. To demonstrate a technique of security proof briefly, we focus on the three-party case in this section. We conclude this paper in Sect. 6.

2 Overview of the SCC Model

2.1 Secure Computation with Coins (SCC)

In secure computation with coins, parties can deal with a non-standard entity called *coins*. A coin is defined as an atomic entity representing money, and is assumed to be having the following properties.

P1. Any party can transfer his/her coins to another party freely.
P2. No multiple parties hold the same coin simultaneously.
P3. Coins cannot be duplicated and forged. (All parties can verify the validity of every coin).
P4. Each coin is perfectly indistinguishable from one another.

The notation $\mathsf{coins}(\cdot)$ is used to express coins. For positive integers x, y, if a party having $\mathsf{coins}(x)$ receives $\mathsf{coins}(y)$ from another party, then the party holds $\mathsf{coins}(x+y)$ as a result. If a party having $\mathsf{coins}(x)$ sends $\mathsf{coins}(y)$ to another party, then the party holds $\mathsf{coins}(x - y)$ as a result.

The security of the SCC model follows the real/ideal simulation paradigm in the UC framework [11]. The only difference from the standard model is that parties are formalized as specialized ITMs that can handle (i.e., hold, send, and receive) coins. To hold coins, each party has a *wallet* and a *safe*. Parties can move coins freely between their own wallets and safes. In addition to being able to communicate with an adversary freely, an environment can modify all parties' wallets arbitrarily at the onset and during the execution of the protocol. On the other hand, the safes are out of the environment's control. As an important remark, only the environment can manufacture coins, and thus all coins used in the protocol are given by the environment to the parties' wallets. Suppose that every honest party moves coins, of which amount is sufficient to carry out the protocol, into his/her safe before the beginning of the protocol. Also, the honest parties store coins received from other parties during the protocol directly in their own safes. The assumptions ensure that honest parties do not lack coins during the protocol execution.

2.2 Secure Computation with Penalties in the SCC Model

Some ideal functionalities can handle coins in the SCC model. Secure computation with penalties $\mathcal{F}_f^*$ is one of such functionalities [9]. Roughly speaking, it guarantees the following two properties.

(**a**) For any honest party, his/her wealth at the end of protocol is never less than at the beginning (i.e., no honest party loses money).
(**b**) If an adversary learns the output, but an honest party cannot, then the honest party is compensated with a predetermined amount of coins.

Here, a party's wealth is referred to the amount of coins in his/her safe. See Functionality 1 for its formal description. The public parameters q and d specify the amount of compensation and deposit, respectively. The deposit refers to the coins that honest parties must input to the functionality. In addition to corrupted parties' input values, an adversary inputs H' ($\subseteq H$), which corresponds to the set of honest parties who are compensated. Only if $H' = H$, the adversary can learn the output before the honest parties do. The adversary can choose whether to tell the output to honest parties or abort without revealing it by responding "continue" or "abort". If the adversary chooses "continue", all honest parties learn the output and get no compensation. Otherwise, every honest party can obtain $\mathsf{coins}(q)$ as compensation instead of not learning the output.[1] Remark that deposit coins, i.e., $\mathsf{coins}(d)$, are always returned to the honest parties, never once in the hands of the adversary. By this feature, we can easily see that $\mathcal{F}_f^*$ guarantees property (**a**).

Bentov and Kumaresan [9] use *claim-or-refund functionality* to realize a protocol for secure computation with penalties. The functionality involves two parties, a sender and a receiver, and consists of three phases: deposit, claim, and

[1] In the case of "continue", the set H'' is used to treat the particular cases where all honest parties learn the output, but some honest parties are compensated. See [9] for the further details.

refund. In the deposit phase, a sender sends $\mathsf{coins}(c)$, a predicate ϕ, and round number τ to the functionality. In the claim phase, the receiver sends a witness w to the functionality. Only if both $\phi(w) = 1$ holds and the message is sent within τ, the functionality sends $\mathsf{coins}(c)$ to the receiver. In the refund phase, if the receiver did not claim within τ, then the functionality refunds $\mathsf{coins}(c)$ to the sender at round $\tau + 1$.

A Technique of Security Proof. In the SCC model, an ideal-world simulator needs to simulate a real-world adversary's view regarding communications of coins in addition to standard messages. Since the simulator cannot create coins, it must perform the simulation using only coins provided by an environment. Reviewing Functionality 1 in light of this, we can see that the simulator must complete the simulation using only the coins given to corrupted parties in the security proof of a protocol intended to realize $\mathcal{F}_f^*$. Nevertheless, Bentov–Kumaresan's protocol realizing $\mathcal{F}_f^*$ involves procedures where honest parties send their coins to corrupted parties. In their security proof, the simulator generates the adversary's view using deposit coins sent by corrupted parties towards claim-or-refund functionalities as a substitute for honest parties' coins. That is, the view that an adversary receives coins from honest parties in the real world is generated by using the coins of corrupted parties in the ideal world. It is important to note that property **P4** of coins is essential here. If the adversary can distinguish between the honest parties' coins and the corrupted parties' ones, this simulation technique does not work well.

3 Basic Model: Secure Computation with Color Coins

Recall that our goal is to extend the SCC model to a more general one by removing property **P4** from the definition of coins. To accomplish the goal, we follow the SCC model, but redefine the coins to capture monetary entities that are distinguishable from each other or have mutually distinct prices.

3.1 Model and Definition

As the main difference from the SCC model, our model uses new atomic entities, *color coins*, instead of the coins. Each color coin has an identifiable color, and thus, the coins are distinguishable from each other. Furthermore, we allow coins with different colors to have mutually distinct prices. We present the definitions of color coins, the model of protocol execution, and security below.

Color Coins. As in the SCC model [9], we define a coin as an atomic entity, and suppose that each party has a wallet and a safe. The difference from [9] is that each coin has an identifiable color, which is formalized as a non-negative integer, readable from each coin. That is, color coins do not hold property **P4**. In addition to properties **P1**–**P3**, color coins hold the following properties:

Functionality 1 Secure computation with penalties $\mathcal{F}_f^*$

Setup: The session identifier is sid. Running with parties $P_1, \ldots, P_n$, and a simulator $\mathcal{S}$ that corrupts parties $\{P_i\}_{i \in C}$. Let d denote the deposit amount for honest parties, and let q denote the penalty amount.

Input phase: Wait to receive the following messages.
- (input, $sid, ssid, i, x_i, \mathsf{coins}(d)$) from P_i for all $i \in H$.
- (input, $sid, ssid, \{x_i\}_{i \in C}, H', \mathsf{coins}(h'q)$) from $\mathcal{S}$, where $H' \subseteq H$ and $h' = |H'|$.

Output phase: Perform the following process.
1. Send (return, $sid, ssid, \mathsf{coins}(d)$) to P_i for $i \in H$.
2. Compute $(y_1, \ldots, y_n) \leftarrow f(x_1, \ldots, x_n)$.
   - If $h' = 0$, then send message (output, $sid, ssid, y_i$) to P_i for $i \in [n]$, and terminate.
   - If $0 < h' < h$, then send (extra, $sid, ssid, \mathsf{coins}(q)$) to P_i for each $i \in H'$, and terminate, where $h := |H|$.
   - If $h' = h$, then send message (output, $sid, ssid, \{y_i\}_{i \in C}$) to $\mathcal{S}$.
3. In the case of $h' = h$, continue the processes below. $\mathcal{S}$ returns (continue, $sid, ssid, H''$), where $H'' \subseteq H$, then perform the following process:
   i. Send (output, $sid, ssid, y_i$) to P_i for all $i \in H$.
   ii. Send (payback, $sid, ssid, \mathsf{coins}((h - h'')q)$) to $\mathcal{S}$, where $h'' = |H''|$.
   iii. Send (extrapay, $sid, ssid, \mathsf{coins}(q)$) to P_i for each $i \in H''$.

   Else if $\mathcal{S}$ returns (abort, $sid, ssid$), send (penalty, $sid, ssid, \mathsf{coins}(q)$) to P_i for all $i \in H$.

P5. Each coin is perfectly indistinguishable from other coins of the same color.
P6. Any party cannot change the colors of coins.

Note that our model does not prohibit that multiple coins have the same color. By property **P5**, we can see that cases of using only one color is equivalent to Bentov–Kumaresan's coins. The price is determined for each color; thus, coins of different colors can have different asset values. The prices are determined by a price function, shown later.

Notations and Definitions. Let $\mathsf{CLR} = \{\mathrm{clr}_1, \ldots, \mathrm{clr}_m\} \subset \mathbb{N}$ denote the set of overall colors, and let $\mathsf{price} : \mathsf{CLR} \to \mathbb{N} \backslash \{0\}$ be a function, called a price function, to specify a price of each color coin. We suppose $i < j \Rightarrow \mathrm{clr}_i < \mathrm{clr}_j$ holds. We call $\mathsf{numclr} = \{(n_1, \mathrm{clr}_1), \ldots, (n_m, \mathrm{clr}_m)\}$ a set of numbered colors, where $n_i \in \mathbb{N}$ for all $i \in [m]$. Describing a set of numbered colors, we often omit writing the entries of which number is zero. We denote by $\mathsf{CC}(\mathsf{numclr})$ a set of color coins that consists of n_i coins whose color is clr_i for $i \in [m]$. Given $\mathsf{CC}(\mathsf{numclr})$, any party can learn numclr from it.

Define $\mathsf{Sum}^{\mathsf{cc}}_{\mathsf{price}}(\mathsf{CC}(\mathsf{numclr})) := \sum_{i \in [m]} n_i \cdot \mathsf{price}(\mathrm{clr}_i)$, which means the total price of $\mathsf{CC}(\mathsf{numclr})$. Let $\mathsf{Sum}^{\mathsf{clr}}_{\mathsf{price}}(\mathsf{numclr}) := \sum_{i \in [m]} n_i \cdot \mathsf{price}(\mathrm{clr}_i)$. For $\mathsf{coins} = \mathsf{CC}(\mathsf{numclr})$, let $\mathsf{Map}_{\mathrm{num}}(\mathsf{coins}) := \mathsf{numclr}$, and $\mathsf{Map}_{\mathrm{clr}}(\mathsf{coins})$ denote the set of colors coins hold, i.e., it is the set of colors of which corresponding number is non-zero. For two sets of numbered colors, $\mathsf{numclr}_1 = \{(n_1, \mathrm{clr}_1), \ldots, (n_m, \mathrm{clr}_m)\}$ and

$\mathsf{numclr}_2 = \{(n'_1, \mathrm{clr}_1), \ldots, (n'_m, \mathrm{clr}_m)\}$, $\mathsf{numclr}_1 \subset_{\mathsf{clr}} \mathsf{numclr}_2$ means that $n_i \leq n'_i$ holds for all $i \in [m]$. To send $\mathsf{CC}(\mathsf{numclr}')$ from a party holding $\mathsf{CC}(\mathsf{numclr})$ to another party, it must fulfill $\mathsf{numclr}' \subset_{\mathsf{clr}} \mathsf{numclr}$.

Suppose P_1 holds $\mathsf{CC}(\mathsf{numclr}_1)$ now. If P_1 receives $\mathsf{CC}(\mathsf{numclr}_2)$ from another party, then we consider that P_1 holds $\mathsf{CC}(\{(n_1 + n'_1, \mathrm{clr}_1), \ldots, (n_m + n'_m, \mathrm{clr}_m)\})$ as a result. Similarly, if P_1 sends $\mathsf{CC}(\mathsf{numclr}_2)$ to another party, then we consider that P_1 holds $\mathsf{CC}(\{(n_1 - n'_1, \mathrm{clr}_1), \ldots, (n_m - n'_m, \mathrm{clr}_m)\})$ as a result.

We call $\mathsf{numprc} = \{(n_1, p_1), \ldots, (n_\ell, p_\ell)\}$ a set of numbered prices, where $n_i, p_i \in \mathbb{N} \setminus \{0\}$ for all $i \in [\ell]$, $i \neq j \Rightarrow p_i \neq p_j$, and $\ell \leq m$. Let $\mathsf{Map}_{\mathsf{price}}(\mathsf{numclr})$ denote a set of numbered prices derived by the following process:

1. Compute multiset $Q = \{(n_1, \mathsf{price}(\mathrm{clr}_1)), \ldots, (n_m, \mathsf{price}(\mathrm{clr}_m))\}$, and remove all elements whose number is zero, i.e., $n_i = 0$, from Q.
2. Repeat the following steps.
   - If there exist i, j such that $i \neq j$ and $\mathsf{price}(\mathrm{clr}_i) = \mathsf{price}(\mathrm{clr}_j)$ in Q, then add new element $(n_i + n_j, \mathsf{price}(\mathrm{clr}_i))$ into Q, and remove two elements $(n_i, \mathsf{price}(\mathrm{clr}_i))$ and $(n_j, \mathsf{price}(\mathrm{clr}_j))$ from Q.
   - Otherwise, return Q as the output of $\mathsf{Map}_{\mathsf{price}}(\mathsf{numclr})$.

Intuitively, $\mathsf{Map}_{\mathsf{price}}(\mathsf{numclr}) = \{(n_1, p_1), \ldots, (n_\ell, p_\ell)\}$ means that $\mathsf{CC}(\mathsf{numclr})$ consists of n_i color coins whose price is p_i for $i \in [\ell]$.

Model of Protocol Execution. Our model follows the UC framework [11], except that the involved entities, an environment, an adversary, parties, and special ideal functionalities, deal with color coins. Suppose that only the environment can manufacture color coins. We assume that all parties' wallets and safes are empty at the beginning of the process.

We describe real and ideal processes in our model, secure computation with color coins, below: An environment $\mathcal{Z}$ is activated first. At the activation, in addition to choose parties' inputs, it initializes each party's wallet, i.e., $\mathcal{Z}$ can insert any number of color coins into every wallet. Furthermore, $\mathcal{Z}$ gives each party P_i a price function price_i. We here note that our model does not prohibit the environment from choosing distinct price functions, i.e., there can be exist $i, j \in [n]$ such that $\mathsf{price}_i \neq \mathsf{price}_j$ for $i \neq j$.[2] If an honest party does not receive enough color coins to carry out the protocol from $\mathcal{Z}$, he/she denies participation in the protocol. Otherwise, every honest party moves color coins of which amount is sufficient to carry out the protocol into his/her safe. At the beginning of the protocol execution, $\mathcal{Z}$ activates an adversary (resp. a simulator) that controls corrupted parties in the real (resp. ideal) process. Afterwards, $\mathcal{Z}$ can interact with the adversary or the simulator, and can read and modify every party's wallet arbitrarily throughout the protocol execution. We suppose that honest parties move all coins in their safes into their wallets after completing the protocol execution. Thus, in addition to read the local outputs of honest parties,

[2] This allows the model to involve the settings where the price of each color differs depending on each party, such as the value of a painting may vary from person to person. However, this paper does not deal with such situations to simplify discussion.

$\mathcal{Z}$ can see the distribution of all color coins finally. $\mathcal{Z}$ serves as the interactive distinguisher between the real and ideal processes, and outputs a bit after the protocol execution.

Security. Consider a real process to carry out a protocol π with an ideal functionality $\mathcal{G}$ is intended to realize an ideal functionality $\mathcal{F}$. Note that $\mathcal{G}$ and $\mathcal{F}$ may handle color coins. Let $\text{HYBRID}^{\mathcal{G}}_{\pi,\mathcal{A},\mathcal{Z}}(\lambda, z)$ denote the output of environment $\mathcal{Z}$, given an auxiliary input z, in the real process to carry out π with $\mathcal{G}$, where $\mathcal{Z}$ interacts with an adversary $\mathcal{A}$. Let $\text{IDEAL}_{\mathcal{F},\mathcal{S},\mathcal{Z}}(\lambda, z)$ denote the output of an environment $\mathcal{Z}$ in the ideal process of $\mathcal{F}$, where $\mathcal{Z}$ interacts with a simulator $\mathcal{S}$.

Definition 1. *We say that a protocol* π CC-*realizes* $\mathcal{F}$ *with abort in the* $\mathcal{G}$-*hybrid model if for every non-uniform PPT adversary* $\mathcal{A}$, *there exists a non-uniform PPT simulator* $\mathcal{S}$ *such that for any non-uniform PPT environment* $\mathcal{Z}$, *two families of probability distributions* $\{\text{HYBRID}^{\mathcal{G}}_{\pi,\mathcal{A},\mathcal{Z}}(\lambda, z)\}_{\lambda\in\mathbb{N},z\in\{0,1\}^*}$ *and* $\{\text{IDEAL}_{\mathcal{F},\mathcal{S},\mathcal{Z}}(\lambda, z)\}_{\lambda\in\mathbb{N},z\in\{0,1\}^*}$ *are computationally indistinguishable for* λ.

3.2 Special Ideal Functionalities

In our model, some ideal functionalities handle color coins. To differentiate them from the standard ideal functionalities, we call such functionalities "special ideal functionalities," described with superscript cc, e.g., $\mathcal{F}^{\text{cc}}_{\text{xxx}}$. (The term follows Bentov-Kumaresan's work [9], and they use superscript $*$ like $\mathcal{F}^*_f$).

In the next section, we will show a protocol for secure computation with penalties based on the claim-or-refund functionality. In preparation for that, we introduce special ideal functionalities for the secure computation with penalties and the claim-or-refund, which are adapted to our model.

Secure Computation with Penalties. In adapting the secure computation with penalties to our model, we should pay attention to the fact that property **P4** plays an essential role in a security proof in the SCC model. Since color coins do not hold the property, the similar proof technique cannot be used in our model. We address this issue by modifying the ideal functionality of secure computation with penalties. It must be careful not to lose the essence of the functionality by modifications. The essence is, in other words, the two properties shown in Sect. 2.2, i.e., (**a**) no honest party loses money and (**b**) if an adversary steals the output, honest parties are compensated with coins.

Functionality 2 shows the modified ideal functionality for secure computation with penalties $\mathcal{F}^{\text{cc}}_f$. It starts with the price phase for which makes price functions to be the same for all parties. (This phase is to simplify discussion by prohibiting the existence of distinct price functions). As the main difference from Functionality 1, we split the input phase into two phases, one for the honest parties (the first input phase) and one for corrupted parties (the second input phase). Moreover, we add a phase that allows a simulator to *swap* corrupted parties' color

Functionality 2 Secure computation with penalties $\mathcal{F}_f^{\mathsf{cc}}$

Setup: The session identifier is sid. Running with parties $P_1, \ldots, P_n$, and a simulator $\mathcal{S}$ that corrupts parties $\{P_j\}_{j \in C}$. Let $\{D_i\}_{i \in H}$ be the sets of numbered prices, which are the parameters of deposits. Let q denote the penalty amount. Initialize an empty set W_i for $i \in H$. (Below, we regard W_i as a set of color coins).

Price phase: Wait to receive a message $(\text{price}, sid, ssid, \mathsf{price}_i)$ from P_i for all $i \in [n]$. If there exist $i, j \in [n]$ such that $i \neq j$ and $\mathsf{price}_i \neq \mathsf{price}_j$ hold, then terminate. Otherwise, set $\mathsf{price} := \mathsf{price}_i$, and proceed to the next phase.

First Input phase: Wait to receive a message $(\text{1st\_input}, sid, ssid, i, x_i, \mathsf{coins}_i)$ from P_i for all $i \in H$, where coins_i is a set of color coins such that $D_i = \mathsf{Map}_{\mathsf{price}}(\mathsf{Map}_{\mathrm{num}}(\mathsf{coins}_i))$. Each coins_i is put into W_i. Given the messages for all $i \in H$, send $(\text{1st\_input}, sid, ssid, \{\mathsf{Map}_{\mathrm{num}}(\mathsf{coins}_i)\}_{i \in H})$ to $\mathcal{S}$, and proceed to the next phase.

Swap Phase: Wait to receive the following messages from $\mathcal{S}$.

- Receiving $(\text{swap}, sid, ssid, i, \mathsf{coins}'_{\mathcal{S}}, \mathsf{numclr})$, check if $\mathsf{numclr} \subset_{\mathsf{clr}} \mathsf{Map}_{\mathrm{num}}(W_i)$ and $\mathsf{Sum}^{\mathsf{cc}}_{\mathsf{price}}(\mathsf{coins}'_{\mathcal{S}}) = \mathsf{Sum}^{\mathsf{clr}}_{\mathsf{price}}(\mathsf{numclr})$ hold. If both went ok, take $\mathsf{CC}(\mathsf{numclr})$ from W_i and send it to $\mathcal{S}$, and put $\mathsf{coins}'_{\mathcal{S}}$ into W_i.
- Receiving $(\text{swap}, sid, ssid, i, j, \mathsf{numclr}_i, \mathsf{numclr}_j)$, check if $\mathsf{numclr}_i \subset_{\mathsf{clr}} \mathsf{Map}_{\mathrm{num}}(W_i)$, $\mathsf{numclr}_j \subset_{\mathsf{clr}} \mathsf{Map}_{\mathrm{num}}(W_j)$, and $\mathsf{Sum}^{\mathsf{clr}}_{\mathsf{price}}(\mathsf{numclr}_i) = \mathsf{Sum}^{\mathsf{clr}}_{\mathsf{price}}(\mathsf{numclr}_j)$ hold. If all went ok, take $\mathsf{CC}(\mathsf{numclr}_i)$ from W_i and put it into W_j, and take $\mathsf{CC}(\mathsf{numclr}_j)$ from W_j and put it into W_i.
- Receiving $(\text{complete}, sid, ssid)$, proceed to the next phase.
- Receiving $(\text{halt}, sid, ssid)$, send $(\text{return}, sid, ssid, W_i)$ to P_i for $i \in H$, and terminate.

Second Input phase: Wait to receive a message $(\text{2nd\_input}, sid, ssid, \{x_j\}_{j \in C}, H', \{\mathsf{coins}'_i\}_{i \in H'})$ from $\mathcal{S}$, where $H' \subseteq H$, $h' = |H'|$, and coins'_i is a set of color coins such that $\mathsf{Sum}^{\mathsf{cc}}_{\mathsf{price}}(\mathsf{coins}'_i) = q$. Given the message, proceed to the next phase.

Output phase: Perform the following process.

1. Send $(\text{return}, sid, ssid, W_i)$ to P_i for $i \in H$.
2. Compute $(y_1, \ldots, y_n) \leftarrow f(x_1, \ldots, x_n)$.
   - If $h' = 0$, then send message $(\text{output}, sid, ssid, y_i)$ to P_i for $i \in [n]$, and terminate.
   - If $0 < h' < h$, then send $(\text{extra}, sid, ssid, \mathsf{coins}'_i)$ to P_i for each $i \in H'$, and terminate, where $h := |H|$.
   - If $h' = h$, then send message $(\text{output}, sid, ssid, \{y_i\}_{i \in C})$ to $\mathcal{S}$.
3. In the case of $h' = h$, continue the processes below. $\mathcal{S}$ returns $(\text{continue}, sid, ssid, H'')$, where $H'' \subseteq H$, then perform the following process:
   i. Send $(\text{output}, sid, ssid, y_i)$ to P_i for all $i \in H$.
   ii. Send $(\text{payback}, sid, ssid, \mathsf{coins}'_j)$ to $\mathcal{S}$ for $j \in H \setminus H''$.
   iii. Send $(\text{extrapay}, sid, ssid, \mathsf{coins}'_i)$ to P_i for each $i \in H''$.

   Else if $\mathcal{S}$ returns $(\text{abort}, sid, ssid)$, send $(\text{penalty}, sid, ssid, \mathsf{coins}'_i)$ to P_i for all $i \in H$.

coins with honest parties' ones between the two phases. This phase is the key ingredient to resolve the above-mentioned issue. To request a swap, a simulator sends a message that consists of an identifier of honest party i, corrupted par-

Functionality 3 Claim-or-refund functionality $\mathcal{F}_{\mathrm{CR}}^{\mathsf{cc}}$

Setup: The session identifier is sid. Running with parties $P_1, \ldots, P_n$ and a simulator $\mathcal{S}$.

Deposit phase: Receiving (deposit, $sid, ssid, s, r, \phi_{s,r}, \tau,$ coins) from P_s, perform the following process, where coins is a set of color coins.

1. If $|\mathsf{Map}_{\mathrm{clr}}(\mathsf{coins})| \geq 2$, then returns coins to P_s, and terminate the process. Otherwise, record the message (deposit, $sid, ssid, s, r, \phi_{s,r}, \tau, \mathsf{Map}_{\mathrm{num}}(\mathsf{coins})$).
2. Send all parties (deposit, $sid, ssid, s, r, \phi_{s,r}, \tau, \mathsf{Map}_{\mathrm{num}}(\mathsf{coins})$).
   - Ignore any future messages with the same $ssid$ from P_s to P_r.

Claim phase: Receiving (claim, $sid, ssid, s, r, \phi_{s,r}, \tau, \mathsf{numclr}, w$) from P_r within round τ, perform the following process.

1. Check the two conditions:
   - (deposit, $sid, ssid, s, r, \phi_{s,r}, \tau, \mathsf{numclr}$) was recorded,
   - $\phi_{s,r}(w) = 1$.
2. If both checks are passed, perform the following process:
   i. send (claim, $sid, ssid, s, r, \phi_{s,r}, \tau, \mathsf{numclr}, w$) to all parties,
   ii. send (claim, $sid, ssid, s, r, \phi_{s,r}, \tau, \mathsf{CC}(\mathsf{numclr})$) to P_r,
   iii. delete the record (deposit, $sid, ssid, s, r, \phi_{s,r}, \tau, \mathsf{numclr}$).

Refund phase: In $\tau + 1$, if the record (deposit, $sid, ssid, s, r, \phi_{s,r}, \tau, \mathsf{numclr}$) was not deleted, then perform the following process:

1. send (refund, $sid, ssid, s, r, \phi_{s,r}, \tau,$ coins) to P_s,
2. delete the record (deposit, $sid, ssid, s, r, \phi_{s,r}, \tau, \mathsf{numclr}$).

ties' coins $\mathsf{coins}'_{\mathcal{S}}$, and a set of numbered colors numclr. The message means that the simulator is requesting to swap $\mathsf{coins}'_{\mathcal{S}}$ with $\mathsf{CC}(\mathsf{numclr})$ that $\mathcal{F}_f^{\mathsf{cc}}$ holds as P_i's deposit. To achieve the requested swap, $\mathsf{Sum}^{\mathsf{cc}}_{\mathsf{price}}(\mathsf{coins}'_{\mathcal{S}}) = \mathsf{Sum}^{\mathsf{clr}}_{\mathsf{price}}(\mathsf{numclr})$ must hold, i.e., it needs to be an exchange between two sets of color coins being equivalent. (For a technical reason, we allow the simulator to also swap two sets of color coins, which are equivalent, between two honest parties' deposits). Intuitively, the swap feature in the ideal world allows real-world adversaries to exchange two sets of color coins, which are equivalent but may be different kinds, with honest parties. The ideal functionality ensures that every honest party gets back his/her deposit at the same price as the input, although the content may change by the swaps.

As the second main difference, $\mathcal{F}_f^{\mathsf{cc}}$ specifies the contents of honest parties' deposits by sets of numbered prices $\{D_i\}_{i \in H}$ instead of specifying the amount by d. We require this change to bridge the following gap between real and ideal worlds: Consider a protocol that involves procedures that honest P_1 sends a color coin whose price is p_i to P_i and another color coin whose price is p_j to P_j. By the existence of these procedures, we require an environment $\mathcal{Z}$ to give P_1 the two color coins to execute the protocol in the real world. However, if we make the condition of deposit by just amount, e.g., $d = p_i + p_j$, an environment may give P_1 a *single* color coin whose price is $p_i + p_j$. In such cases, honest P_1 should deny participation in the protocol in the real world since he/she cannot complete the procedure. On the other hand, in the ideal world, P_1 can complete the first input phase using the single color coin, and thus, a simulator can proceed to the output phase.

Claim-Or-Refund Functionality. Functionality 3 shows the modified ideal functionality for claim-or-refund $\mathcal{F}_{\mathrm{CR}}^{\mathrm{cc}}$. As already mentioned in Sect. 2.2, it involves two parties, a sender P_s and a receiver P_r, and consists of three phases: deposit, claim, and refund. We call the message sent in the deposit phase a deposit transaction. A deposit transaction is available to only one color, as shown in the deposit phase. This is because we envisage that the implementation depends on the color, such as Bitcoin [31], Ethereum [16], banks, or couriers. That is, it seems too strong assumption that a single deposit transaction can handle an arbitrary set of colors, in practice.

For the sake of clarity, we assume that every deposit transaction deals with a single color coin in our protocol. For instance, suppose a party want to send color coins of which total price is two. Then, there are two possible ways: it sends two color coins each of which price is one, or a single color coin whose price is two. Our protocol always adapts the later way. Based on this assumption, we use the following arrow notation to denote a deposit transaction.

$$P_s \xrightarrow[p,\ \tau]{w} P_r$$

After which P_s makes the above deposit transaction, P_r can claim to receive the *single* color coin whose price is p only if he/she publishes witness w within round τ. The color coin is refunded back to the original holder P_s in round $\tau+1$ if P_r does not claim within τ. Note that the above arrow notation does not state the color explicitly. Hence, even if there are two arrows with the same description, the underlying colors may differ. Hereafter, we use a notation $\mathsf{cc}(p)$ for a positive integer p to represent a single color coin whose price is p.

4 Protocol for Secure Computation with Penalties

Suppose parties $P_1, \ldots, P_n$ hold their inputs $x_1, \ldots, x_n$, respectively. Hereafter, we assume that functionality f delivers the same output to all parties, without loss of generality. It should be mentioned that our protocol mostly follows Bentov-Kumaresan's one [9]. In particular, the procedure of our protocol is almost the same as theirs. The main difference that arises from the introduction of color coins appears in the security proof.

4.1 Protocol Overview

We note that fair secure computation can be reduced to fair reconstruction of a secret [20]. Our protocol consists of two phases, the share generation and the fair reconstruction. First, in the share generation phase, the parties run a protocol that securely computes n shares of $f(x_1, \ldots, x_n)$ *with abort*. This phase does not guarantee fairness and uses no color coins. In the fair reconstruction phase, the parties run a fair reconstruction protocol to reconstruct the secret and learn $f(x_1, \ldots, x_n)$ with penalties. We assume that all parties agree on the price function at the beginning of the protocol.

The Share Generation Phase. The underlying secret sharing scheme in this phase is the *non-malleable secret sharing with publicly verifiability and publicly reconstructibility* (pubNMSS). Taking a secret s as input, the pubNMSS generates tag-token pairs $(\mathsf{tag}_i, T_i)_{i\in[n]}$, and outputs token T_i and $\mathsf{Tags} = (\mathsf{tag}_1, \ldots, \mathsf{tag}_n)$ to each party P_i. The parties can reconstruct s only if they learn all tokens. In a reconstruction process, parties can verify the validity of token T_i using tag_i for all $i \in [n]$. Informally, the tag-token pairs have the following properties.

- For any $S \subsetneq \{T_1, \ldots, T_n\}$, S and Tags leak no information about secret s.
- For any $i \in [n]$, any PPT adversary cannot generate $T'_i\,(\neq T_i)$ such that (tag_i, T'_i) is a valid tag-token pair.

The tags are generated using the *honest-binding commitment*. The honest binding commitment has two properties: *honest-binding* and *equivocation*. Loosely speaking, it ensures that a commitment generated honestly always holds the binding property (i.e., the honest-binding), but one generated maliciously can be de-committed to any value (i.e., the equivocation). An honest-binding commitment can be constructed from one-way functions. (See the details in [17]).

In the share generation phase, the parties run a secure computation protocol such that, taking x_i as P_i's input, it delivers (T_i, Tags) to P_i as the output for $i \in [n]$. The tokens $T_1, \ldots, T_n$ are n-out-of-n secret shares for the secret $f(x_1, \ldots, x_n)$. It is known that the existence of ideal oblivious transfer $\mathcal{F}_{\mathrm{OT}}$ is sufficient to achieve secure computation for any standard functionality with constant rounds [21,23]. Hence, the first phase can be realized with constant rounds in the $\mathcal{F}_{\mathrm{OT}}$-hybrid model.

The Fair Reconstruction Phase. Fair reconstruction ensures that parties who each hold a secret share reconstruct the secret in a fair manner. More precisely, fair reconstruction used in this paper guarantees that if an adversary learns the secret but an honest party does not, then the honest party obtains compensation. Also, it ensures that no honest parties lose money. Namely, the fair reconstruction fulfills properties (**a**) and (**b**), shown in Sect. 2.2.

Each party P_i holds (T_i, Tags) at the beginning of this phase. The parties execute a fair reconstruction protocol in the $\mathcal{F}_{\mathrm{CR}}^{\mathrm{cc}}$-hybrid model to reconstruct the secret $f(x_1, \ldots, x_n)$. To achieve properties (**a**) and (**b**), the protocol prevents corrupted parties from aborting without revealing their tokens by using monetary penalties and compensations. We show the details of our fair reconstruction protocol in the next subsection.

4.2 Fair Reconstruction Protocol

Our fair reconstruction protocol consists of two phases: deposit and claim. In the deposit phase, parties make deposit transactions of which conditions are verification predicates of tokens. Once the parties confirm that all transactions have been created, they proceed to the claim phase. In the claim phase, parties claim the transactions by revealing their tokens and receive color coins. (We note again that the protocol is almost the same as Bentov-Kumaresan's work [9]).

Below, to make clear the idea of fair reconstruction, we follow the discussion shown in [9]: We first describe a naïve approach to the two-party case, and show how to solve the problem of the naïve approach. After that, we present our fair reconstruction protocol for the n-party setting.

Naïve Approach. Suppose that the number of parties is two. A naïve approach is to make a deposit transaction from P_1 to P_2 and a deposit transaction of the reverse direction as follows:

$$P_1 \xrightarrow[q,\ \tau]{T_2} P_2 \tag{1}$$

$$P_2 \xrightarrow[q,\ \tau]{T_1} P_1 \tag{2}$$

The above arrow means that "P_2 can receive $\mathsf{cc}(q)$ only if P_2 reveals T_2 within round τ, otherwise $\mathsf{cc}(q)$ is refunded back to P_1." The bottom arrow is similar. At first glance, the above approach seems to achieve a fair reconstruction since if only one party publishes his/her token, then the party can receive $\mathsf{cc}(q)$ from the other party as compensation. However, it is not true. For instance, when P_2 is corrupted, P_2 can steal $\mathsf{cc}(q)$ from honest P_1 as follows: after making transaction (1), P_2 claims the transaction to receive $\mathsf{cc}(q)$ without making transaction (2). As a result, honest P_1 loses $\mathsf{cc}(q)$, which violates condition (**a**).

Solution to the Two-Party Setting. Our two-party protocol is as follows:

$$P_1 \xrightarrow[q,\ \tau_2]{T_1 \wedge T_2} P_2 \tag{1}$$

$$P_2 \xrightarrow[q,\ \tau_1]{T_1} P_1 \tag{2}$$

where the rounds satisfy $\tau_1 < \tau_2$. Hereafter, we assume $\tau_i < \tau_{i+1}$ for any positive integer i, and the intervals are sufficient to complete the procedures. We note that transaction (1) means that P_2 can receive $\mathsf{cc}(q)$ only if P_2 publishes both T_1 and T_2 within round τ_2. In this approach, P_1 first makes transaction (1). After that, P_2 makes transaction (2). In the claim phase, P_1 first claims transaction (2) by publishing T_1. Afterwards, P_2 claims transaction (1), and reveal T_2.

This protocol circumvents the attack shown in the naïve approach, and realizes fair reconstruction. As a result of making transaction (1) first, P_2 cannot claim this transaction without making transaction (2) since P_2 does not know T_1 yet. Also, if P_2 aborts after P_1 claims, then P_1 obtains $\mathsf{cc}(q)$ as compensation. Thus, P_2 needs to publish T_2 in order not to lose $\mathsf{cc}(q)$. Also, it is trivial that if both parties behave honestly, they does not lose coins. Hence, the above protocol guarantees properties (**a**) and (**b**).

Solution to the n-Party Setting. We can construct an n-party fair reconstruction by extending the above two-party one. We show the protocol in Protocol 4.

In the deposit phase, the deposit transactions are created from top to bottom, i.e., (1) to $(2n-2)$. In the claim phase, the deposit transactions are claimed in the reverse direction, i.e., $(2n-2)$ to (1). The horizontal lines separate each round, i.e., deposit transactions belonging to the same section can be created (or claimed) in one round. Hence, the protocol requires n rounds in each of deposit and claim phases. We give an intuitive understanding about the security of the n-party protocol, below. It is trivial that no parties lose coins if all parties behave honestly. Thus, we consider only the cases where there are adversarial parties.

Suppose a corrupted party aborts in the deposit phase. Since no honest party publishes his/her token and pay coins yet, the adversary does not learn the secret nor receives any coins from honest parties. The protocol satisfies the properties (**a**) and (**b**) in this case. Note that an adversary may claim a transaction before the deposit phase completes. Suppose an adversary corrupts $P_1, \ldots, P_{i-1}$. After making the transaction by P_i, the adversary can claim it without making the remaining transactions. In this case, $P_i, \ldots, P_n$ claim the transactions as the procedure. As a result, all party learn the output, and every honest party does not lose money. Hence, this case fulfills the properties too.

Next, let us consider the case where a corrupted party aborts in the claim phase. Suppose P_i aborts in the claim phase. $P_1, \ldots, P_{i-1}$ have already claimed, and each of them holds $\mathsf{cc}(q)$. Since the adversary must corrupt every $P_i, \ldots, P_n$ to learn the secret, we can see that the protocol fulfills condition (**b**). Note that the protocol does not ensure every honest party to receive compensation if an adversary aborts without learning the secret. We can check that the protocol guarantees (**a**) easily, and this case also satisfies the two properties.

Remark 1. The above discussion about the protocol does not mention the colors of the coins. This is because the colors involved in the protocol depend on the initialization by the environment, i.e., color coins and price functions distributed at the beginning of the protocol. Hence, the colors used in the protocol cannot be predetermined. That said, for a technical reason, it is necessary to set a rule so that the colors used in each step are uniquely determined according to the initialization by the environment. To determine the rule, we prioritize colors based on the values. (Recall that colors are defined as non-negative integers). We assume that honest parties use colors with lower values as a priority. Let $\mathsf{CLR}_{i,p}$ denote a set of colors whose price is p and that P_i receives from the environment. For instance, suppose P_1 is given coins with several colors each of which price is q from the environment. We assume that P_1 uses $\min(\mathsf{CLR}_{1,q})$ for deposit transaction (1). The same is true for the other parties. In other words, for $i \in [n] \setminus \{1, 2\}$, P_i uses $\min(\mathsf{CLR}_{i,q})$ and $\min(\mathsf{CLR}_{i,(i-1)q})$ for his/her deposit transactions. For P_2, there are two transactions to send the same price q, i.e., (2) and $(2n-2)$. In this case, we assume that the smallest color is used for transaction (2) and the second smallest color is used for transaction $(2n-2)$. Note that corrupted parties do not necessarily follow this rule.

In summary, we can derive the following theorem.

Protocol 4 Fair Reconstruction Protocol

$$P_1 \xrightarrow[q,\ \tau_n]{T_1 \wedge \cdots \wedge T_n} P_n \tag{1}$$

$$P_2 \xrightarrow[q,\ \tau_n]{T_1 \wedge \cdots \wedge T_n} P_n \tag{2}$$

$$\vdots$$

$$P_{n-1} \xrightarrow[q,\ \tau_n]{T_1 \wedge \cdots \wedge T_n} P_n \tag{$n-1$}$$

$$P_n \xrightarrow[(n-1)q,\ \tau_{n-1}]{T_1 \wedge \cdots \wedge T_{n-1}} P_{n-1} \tag{n}$$

$$P_{n-1} \xrightarrow[(n-2)q,\ \tau_{n-2}]{T_1 \wedge \cdots \wedge T_{n-2}} P_{n-2} \tag{$n+1$}$$

$$\vdots$$

$$P_4 \xrightarrow[3q,\ \tau_3]{T_1 \wedge T_2 \wedge T_3} P_3 \tag{$2n-4$}$$

$$P_3 \xrightarrow[2q,\ \tau_2]{T_1 \wedge T_2} P_2 \tag{$2n-3$}$$

$$P_2 \xrightarrow[q,\ \tau_1]{T_1} P_1 \tag{$2n-2$}$$

Theorem 1. *Assuming the existence of one-way function, for every n-party functionality f there exists a protocol that* CC*-realizes* $\mathcal{F}_f^{\mathsf{cc}}$ *in the* $(\mathcal{F}_{\mathrm{OT}}, \mathcal{F}_{\mathrm{CR}}^{\mathsf{cc}})$*-hybrid model. The protocol requires* $O(n)$ *rounds and* $O(n)$ *calls of* $\mathcal{F}_{\mathrm{CR}}^{\mathsf{cc}}$.

5 Security Proof

In secure computation with color coins, a simulator needs to simulate two kinds of view: one regarding standard messages and another regarding color coins. The simulation for the former is the same as the proof of Bentov-Kumaresan's protocol [9]. Hence, we focus only on the simulation for the latter. Recall that the simulator needs to simulate the distribution of color coins to honest parties in addition to the adversary's view.

5.1 Proof for the Three-Party Case

To demonstrate a technique of the simulation briefly, we present a proof of Theorem 1 for the case of $n = 3$. Our reconstruction protocol in the three-party case is described as follows:

$$P_1 \xrightarrow[q,\ \tau_3]{T_1 \wedge T_2 \wedge T_3} P_3 \tag{1}$$

$$P_2 \xrightarrow[q,\ \tau_3]{T_1 \wedge T_2 \wedge T_3} P_3 \tag{2}$$

$$P_3 \xrightarrow[2q,\ \tau_2]{T_1 \wedge T_2} P_2 \tag{3}$$

$$P_2 \xrightarrow[q,\ \tau_1]{T_1} P_1 \tag{4}$$

Note that transactions (1) and (2) can be created (claimed) in a single round, and the protocol requires three rounds in each of deposit and claim phases. Let ϕ_i denote the verification algorithm for tokens used in transaction (i) for $i \in [4]$. The parameters of the honest parties' deposits are as follows: $D_1 := \{(1, q)\}$, $D_2 := \{(2, q)\}$, and $D_3 := \{(1, 2q)\}$. Hence, if honest P_1 is not given $\mathsf{cc}(q)$ from an environment $\mathcal{Z}$, then he/she refuses to participate in the protocol. (The similar is true for the other two parties). Below, $\mathcal{Z}$ is supposed to provide each party with the minimum amount of coins necessary to carry out the protocol. For the sake of clarity, suppose that colors of all coins used in the protocol are distinct. Let $\mathrm{clr}_1, \ldots, \mathrm{clr}_4$ be colors used in deposit transactions (1),...,(4), respectively, where $\mathsf{price}(\mathrm{clr}_i) = q$ for $i \in \{1, 2, 4\}$ and $\mathsf{price}(\mathrm{clr}_3) = 2q$. Hereafter, we denote by coin_i the coin whose color is clr_i for $i \in [4]$. $\mathsf{SimWallet}$ is the set of color coins the simulator holds.

We begin to make up a simulator. A simulator $\mathcal{S}$ starts by invoking an adversary $\mathcal{A}$ internally, and gives all coins received from $\mathcal{Z}$ to $\mathcal{A}$. Hence, $\mathsf{SimWallet}$ is empty at the beginning of the simulation. Suppose that $\mathcal{S}$ succeeds to extract corrupted parties' inputs from $\mathcal{A}$ in the simulation process for the share generation phase. Let x'_i denote the input of corrupted P_i. If $\mathcal{A}$ sends a coin intended for $\mathcal{F}^{\mathsf{cc}}_{\mathrm{CR}}$, $\mathcal{S}$ receives the coin and adds it into $\mathsf{SimWallet}$.

We first consider the cases where $\mathcal{A}$ aborts in the deposit phase. For instance, let us consider the case where $C = \{2\}$ and corrupted P_2 does not create transaction (4). Suppose that transaction (2) has already been created by the adversary. Hence, $\mathsf{SimWallet} = \{\mathsf{coin}_2\}$ holds now. Also, $W_1 = \{\mathsf{coin}_1\}$, and $W_3 = \{\mathsf{coin}_3\}$. In this case, $\mathcal{S}$ works as follows.

1. Send (halt, $sid, ssid$) to $\mathcal{F}_f^{\mathsf{cc}}$ without ever requesting the swap. As a result, P_1 and P_3 receive $\{\mathsf{coin}_1\}$ and $\{\mathsf{coin}_3\}$ from $\mathcal{F}_f^{\mathsf{cc}}$, respectively.
2. Send (refund, $sid, ssid, 2, 3, \phi_2, \tau_3, \mathsf{coin}_2$) to $\mathcal{A}$ at round $\tau_3 + 1$.

Finally, $\mathcal{S}$ outputs whatever $\mathcal{A}$ outputs. By the above process, the color coins are distributed to honest parties as the corresponding real process. Furthermore, the adversary's view regarding color coins is also identical to one's view in the real process. We can simulate the other cases where the adversary aborts in the deposit phase in a similar way. (Here, we omit cases where an adversary refuses to create its transaction and further claims a transaction created by an honest party. These cases can be simulated by similarly using the swap feature, as shown in the following discussions). Hereafter, we assume that the deposit phase completes as in the procedure. We show how to simulate the distribution of color coins depending on the set of corrupted parties. Below, $\mathcal{S}$ is supposed to output whatever $\mathcal{A}$ outputs when the simulation terminates.

Case of $C = \{1\}$. In this case, $\mathsf{SimWallet} = \{\mathsf{coin}_1\}$, $W_2 = \{\mathsf{coin}_2, \mathsf{coin}_4\}$, and $W_3 = \{\mathsf{coin}_3\}$ at the beginning of the claim phase. If $\mathcal{A}$ aborts, i.e., P_1 does not claim transaction (4) within τ_1, then $\mathcal{S}$ sends (refund, $sid, ssid, 2, 1, \phi_4, \tau_1, \mathsf{coin}_1$) to $\mathcal{A}$ at round $\tau_1 + 1$. Moreover, it sends ($sid, ssid$, halt) to $\mathcal{F}_f^{\mathsf{cc}}$ without ever requesting the swap, and $\mathcal{F}_f^{\mathsf{cc}}$ terminates. Otherwise, if $\mathcal{A}$ claims transaction (4), i.e., it sends (claim, $sid, ssid, 2, 1, \phi_4, \tau_1, \{\mathrm{clr}_4\}, T_1$) intended for $\mathcal{F}_{\mathrm{CR}}^{\mathsf{cc}}$ within τ_1, $\mathcal{S}$ checks the validity of token T_1. If it is invalid, $\mathcal{S}$ ignores the message.[3] Otherwise, $\mathcal{S}$ performs the following process.

1. Send (swap, $sid, ssid, 2, \{\mathsf{coin}_1\}, \{(1, \mathrm{clr}_4)\}$) to $\mathcal{F}_f^{\mathsf{cc}}$, and receive $\{\mathsf{coin}_4\}$ from $\mathcal{F}_f^{\mathsf{cc}}$. Then, $\mathsf{SimWallet} = \{\mathsf{coin}_4\}$, $W_2 = \{\mathsf{coin}_1, \mathsf{coin}_2\}$, and $W_3 = \{\mathsf{coin}_3\}$.
2. Send (claim, $sid, ssid, 2, 1, \phi_4, \tau_1, \mathsf{coin}_4$) to $\mathcal{A}$.[4] As a result, $\mathsf{SimWallet}$ becomes empty.
3. Send (swap, $sid, ssid, 2, 3, \{(1, \mathrm{clr}_1), (1, \mathrm{clr}_2)\}, \{(1, \mathrm{clr}_3)\}$) to $\mathcal{F}_f^{\mathsf{cc}}$. Then, $W_2 = \{\mathsf{coin}_3\}$ and $W_3 = \{\mathsf{coin}_1, \mathsf{coin}_2\}$.
4. Send (complete, $sid, ssid$) to $\mathcal{F}_f^{\mathsf{cc}}$.
5. Send (2nd_input, $sid, ssid, x_1', \emptyset, \emptyset$) to $\mathcal{F}_f^{\mathsf{cc}}$.

Since this case corresponds to $h' = 0$, $\mathcal{F}_f^{\mathsf{cc}}$ delivers the output to all parties and terminates. Also, P_2 and P_3 receive $\{\mathsf{coin}_3\}$ and $\{\mathsf{coin}_1, \mathsf{coin}_2\}$ from $\mathcal{F}_f^{\mathsf{cc}}$, respectively.

Case of $C = \{2\}$. In this case, $\mathsf{SimWallet} = \{\mathsf{coin}_2, \mathsf{coin}_4\}$, $W_1 = \{\mathsf{coin}_1\}$, and $W_3 = \{\mathsf{coin}_3\}$ at the beginning of the claim phase. First, let us consider the case where $\mathcal{A}$ aborts, i.e., P_2 does not claim transaction (3) within τ_2. In this case, $\mathcal{S}$ performs the following process. Note that honest P_1 has already claimed transaction (4).

[3] If $\mathcal{A}$ sends a message containing an invalid token, the simulator always ignore the message. We omit such cases in the following discussions.

[4] We omit the simulation for the message broadcast by $\mathcal{F}_{\mathrm{CR}}^{\mathsf{cc}}$, which corresponds to step 2-i in the claim phase of Functionality 3.

1. Send $(\text{complete}, sid, ssid)$ to $\mathcal{F}_f^{\mathsf{cc}}$.
2. Send $(\text{2nd\_input}, sid, ssid, x_2', \{1\}, \{\mathsf{coin}_4\})$ to $\mathcal{F}_f^{\mathsf{cc}}$.
3. Send $(\text{refund}, sid, ssid, 2, 3, \phi_2, \tau_3, \mathsf{coin}_2)$ to $\mathcal{A}$ at round $\tau_3 + 1$. As a result, $\mathsf{SimWallet}$ becomes empty.

Since this case corresponds to $0 < h' < h$, $\mathcal{F}_f^{\mathsf{cc}}$ does not deliver the output to any party, and terminates. P_1 and P_3 receive $\{\mathsf{coin}_1, \mathsf{coin}_4\}$ and $\{\mathsf{coin}_2\}$ from $\mathcal{F}_f^{\mathsf{cc}}$, respectively.

Next, let us consider the case where $\mathcal{A}$ claims transaction (3). In this case, $\mathcal{S}$ performs the following process.

1. Send $(\text{swap}, sid, ssid, 3, \{\mathsf{coin}_2, \mathsf{coin}_4\}, \{(1, \text{clr}_3)\})$ to $\mathcal{F}_f^{\mathsf{cc}}$, and receive $\{\mathsf{coin}_3\}$ from $\mathcal{F}_f^{\mathsf{cc}}$. Then, $\mathsf{SimWallet} = \{\mathsf{coin}_3\}$, $W_1 = \{\mathsf{coin}_1\}$, and $W_3 = \{\mathsf{coin}_2, \mathsf{coin}_4\}$.
2. Send $(\text{claim}, sid, ssid, 3, 2, \phi_3, \tau_2, \mathsf{coin}_3)$ to $\mathcal{A}$. As a result, $\mathsf{SimWallet}$ becomes empty.
3. Send $(\text{swap}, sid, ssid, 1, 3, \{(1, \text{clr}_1)\}, \{(1, \text{clr}_4)\})$ to $\mathcal{F}_f^{\mathsf{cc}}$. Then, $W_1 = \{\mathsf{coin}_4\}$ and $W_3 = \{\mathsf{coin}_1, \mathsf{coin}_2\}$.
4. Send $(\text{complete}, sid, ssid)$ to $\mathcal{F}_f^{\mathsf{cc}}$.
5. Send $(\text{2nd\_input}, sid, ssid, x_2', \emptyset, \emptyset)$ to $\mathcal{F}_f^{\mathsf{cc}}$.

Since this case corresponds to $h' = 0$, $\mathcal{F}_f^{\mathsf{cc}}$ delivers the output to all parties, and terminates. Also, P_1 and P_3 receive $\{\mathsf{coin}_4\}$ and $\{\mathsf{coin}_1, \mathsf{coin}_2\}$ from $\mathcal{F}_f^{\mathsf{cc}}$, respectively.

Remark 2. In the case of $C = \{2\}$, $\mathcal{A}$ may create deposit transactions using clr_2 and clr_4 in reverse. In other words, it may use clr_2 for transaction (4), and clr_4 for transaction (2). Note that $\mathcal{S}$ can see the colors used in the transactions from the messages sent by $\mathcal{A}$ intended for $\mathcal{F}_{\text{CR}}^{\mathsf{cc}}$. Hence, this case can be simulated by simply swapping the two colors in the above procedure.

Case of $C = \{3\}$. In this case, $\mathsf{SimWallet} = \{\mathsf{coin}_3\}$, $W_1 = \{\mathsf{coin}_1\}$, and $W_2 = \{\mathsf{coin}_2, \mathsf{coin}_4\}$ at the beginning of the claim phase. Note that honest parties have already claimed transactions (4) and (3), and the adversary learns the output before honest parties do. $\mathcal{S}$ works as follows.

1. Send $(\text{swap}, sid, ssid, 2, \{\mathsf{coin}_3\}, \{(1, \text{clr}_2), (1, \text{clr}_4)\})$ to $\mathcal{F}_f^{\mathsf{cc}}$, and receive $\{\mathsf{coin}_2, \mathsf{coin}_4\}$ from $\mathcal{F}_f^{\mathsf{cc}}$. Then, $\mathsf{SimWallet} = \{\mathsf{coin}_2, \mathsf{coin}_4\}$, $W_1 = \{\mathsf{coin}_1\}$, and $W_2 = \{\mathsf{coin}_3\}$.
2. Send $(\text{swap}, sid, ssid, 1, \{\mathsf{coin}_4\}, \{(1, \text{clr}_1)\})$ to $\mathcal{F}_f^{\mathsf{cc}}$, and receive $\{\mathsf{coin}_1\}$ from $\mathcal{F}_f^{\mathsf{cc}}$. Then, $\mathsf{SimWallet} = \{\mathsf{coin}_1, \mathsf{coin}_2\}$, $W_1 = \{\mathsf{coin}_4\}$, and $W_2 = \{\mathsf{coin}_3\}$.
3. Send $(\text{complete}, sid, ssid)$ to $\mathcal{F}_f^{\mathsf{cc}}$.
4. Send $(\text{2nd\_input}, sid, ssid, x_3', \{1, 2\}, \{\mathsf{coin}_i\}_{i \in \{1,2\}})$ to $\mathcal{F}_f^{\mathsf{cc}}$. As a result, $\mathsf{SimWallet}$ becomes empty.

Since this case corresponds to $h' = h$, $\mathcal{F}_f^{\mathsf{cc}}$ delivers the output to $\mathcal{S}$. Also, P_1 and P_2 receive $\{\mathsf{coin}_4\}$ and $\{\mathsf{coin}_3\}$ from $\mathcal{F}_f^{\mathsf{cc}}$, respectively. There are four possible behaviours that $\mathcal{A}$ can perform: **(I)** $\mathcal{A}$ does not claim neither transaction (1) nor (2), **(II)** $\mathcal{A}$ claims only transaction (1), **(III)** $\mathcal{A}$ claims only transaction (2), **(I V)** $\mathcal{A}$ claims both transactions (1) and (2).

Case I. $\mathcal{S}$ sends (abort, sid, $ssid$) to $\mathcal{F}_f^{\mathsf{cc}}$. Then, P_1 and P_2 receive $\{\mathsf{coin}_1\}$ and $\{\mathsf{coin}_2\}$ from $\mathcal{F}_f^{\mathsf{cc}}$, respectively.

Case II. $\mathcal{S}$ sends (continue, sid, $ssid$, $\{2\}$) to $\mathcal{F}_f^{\mathsf{cc}}$. Then, P_2 and $\mathcal{S}$ receive $\{\mathsf{coin}_2\}$ and $\{\mathsf{coin}_1\}$ from $\mathcal{F}_f^{\mathsf{cc}}$, respectively. Afterwards, $\mathcal{S}$ sends (claim, $sid, ssid, 1, 3, \phi_1, \tau_3, \mathsf{coin}_1$) to $\mathcal{A}$.

Case III. $\mathcal{S}$ sends (continue, sid, $ssid$, $\{1\}$) to $\mathcal{F}_f^{\mathsf{cc}}$. Then, P_1 and $\mathcal{S}$ receive $\{\mathsf{coin}_1\}$ and $\{\mathsf{coin}_2\}$ from $\mathcal{F}_f^{\mathsf{cc}}$, respectively. Afterwards, $\mathcal{S}$ sends (claim, $sid, ssid, 2, 3, \phi_2, \tau_3, \mathsf{coin}_2$) to $\mathcal{A}$.

Case IV. $\mathcal{S}$ sends (continue, sid, $ssid$, $\emptyset$) to $\mathcal{F}_f^{\mathsf{cc}}$. Then, $\mathcal{S}$ receives $\{\mathsf{coin}_1, \mathsf{coin}_2\}$ from $\mathcal{F}_f^{\mathsf{cc}}$, and sends (claim, $sid, ssid, 1, 3, \phi_1, \tau_3, \mathsf{coin}_1$) and (claim, $sid, ssid, 2, 3, \phi_2, \tau_3, \mathsf{coin}_2$) to $\mathcal{A}$.

Case of $C = \{1, 2\}$. In this case, $\mathsf{SimWallet} = \{\mathsf{coin}_1, \mathsf{coin}_2, \mathsf{coin}_4\}$ and $W_3 = \{\mathsf{coin}_3\}$ at the beginning of the claim phase. The simulation way for the case where $\mathcal{A}$ does not claim transaction (4) is almost the same as the case of $C = \{1\}$. Hence, we suppose $\mathcal{A}$ claims transaction (4) within τ_1. $\mathcal{S}$ sends (claim, $sid, ssid, 2, 1, \phi_4, \tau_1, \mathsf{coin}_4$) to $\mathcal{A}$. Afterwards, if $\mathcal{A}$ does not claim transaction (3) within τ_2, then $\mathcal{S}$ sends (refund, $sid, ssid, 1, 3, \phi_1, \tau_3, \mathsf{coin}_1$) and (refund, $sid, ssid, 2, 3, \phi_2, \tau_3, \mathsf{coin}_2$) to $\mathcal{A}$ at round $\tau_3 + 1$. Moreover, it sends (sid, $ssid$, halt) to $\mathcal{F}_f^{\mathsf{cc}}$ without ever requesting the swap, and $\mathcal{F}_f^{\mathsf{cc}}$ terminates. Otherwise, if $\mathcal{A}$ claims transaction (3), $\mathcal{S}$ performs the following process.

1. Send (swap, $sid, ssid, 3, \{\mathsf{coin}_1, \mathsf{coin}_2\}, \{(1, \mathrm{clr}_3)\}$) to $\mathcal{F}_f^{\mathsf{cc}}$, and receive $\{\mathsf{coin}_3\}$ from $\mathcal{F}_f^{\mathsf{cc}}$. Then, $\mathsf{SimWallet} = \{\mathsf{coin}_3\}$ and $W_3 = \{\mathsf{coin}_1, \mathsf{coin}_2\}$.
2. Send (claim, $sid, ssid, 3, 2, \phi_3, \tau_2, \mathsf{coin}_3$) to $\mathcal{A}$. As a result, $\mathsf{SimWallet}$ becomes empty.
3. Send (complete, sid, $ssid$) to $\mathcal{F}_f^{\mathsf{cc}}$.
4. Send (2nd_input, $sid, ssid, \{x'_i\}_{i \in \{1,2\}}, \emptyset, \emptyset$) to $\mathcal{F}_f^{\mathsf{cc}}$.

Since this case corresponds to $h' = 0$, $\mathcal{F}_f^{\mathsf{cc}}$ delivers the output to all parties, and terminates. Also, P_3 receives $\{\mathsf{coin}_1, \mathsf{coin}_2\}$ from $\mathcal{F}_f^{\mathsf{cc}}$.

Case of $C = \{1, 3\}$. In this case, $\mathsf{SimWallet} = \{\mathsf{coin}_1, \mathsf{coin}_3\}$ and $W_2 = \{\mathsf{coin}_2, \mathsf{coin}_4\}$ at the beginning of the claim phase. The simulation way for the case where $\mathcal{A}$ does not claim transaction (4) is almost the same as the case of $C = \{1\}$. Hence, we suppose $\mathcal{A}$ claims transaction (4) within τ_1. Then, $\mathcal{S}$ performs the following process.

1. Send (swap, $sid, ssid, 2, \{\mathsf{coin}_3\}, \{(1, \mathrm{clr}_2), (1, \mathrm{clr}_4)\}$) to $\mathcal{F}_f^{\mathsf{cc}}$, and receive $\{\mathsf{coin}_2, \mathsf{coin}_4\}$ from $\mathcal{F}_f^{\mathsf{cc}}$.
2. Send (claim, $sid, ssid, 2, 1, \phi_4, \tau_1, \mathsf{coin}_4$) to $\mathcal{A}$. Then, $\mathsf{SimWallet} = \{\mathsf{coin}_1, \mathsf{coin}_2\}$ and $W_2 = \{\mathsf{coin}_3\}$.
3. Send (complete, sid, $ssid$) to $\mathcal{F}_f^{\mathsf{cc}}$.
4. Send (2nd_input, $sid, ssid, \{x'_i\}_{i \in \{1,3\}}, \{2\}, \{\mathsf{coin}_2\}$) to $\mathcal{F}_f^{\mathsf{cc}}$.

Since this case corresponds to $h' = h$, $\mathcal{F}_f^{\mathsf{cc}}$ delivers the output to $\mathcal{S}$. Also, P_2 receive $\{\mathsf{coin}_3\}$ from $\mathcal{F}_f^{\mathsf{cc}}$. As in the case of $C = \{3\}$, there are four possible behaviours that $\mathcal{A}$ can perform: **(I)** $\mathcal{A}$ does not claim neither transaction (1) nor

(2), **(II)** $\mathcal{A}$ claims only transaction (1), **(III)** $\mathcal{A}$ claims only transaction (2), **(IV)** $\mathcal{A}$ claims both transactions (1) and (2). Note that $\mathsf{SimWallet} = \{\mathsf{coin}_1\}$, here.

Case I. $\mathcal{S}$ sends $(\text{abort}, sid, ssid)$ to $\mathcal{F}_f^{\mathsf{cc}}$. Then, P_2 receives $\{\mathsf{coin}_2\}$ from $\mathcal{F}_f^{\mathsf{cc}}$. Also, $\mathcal{S}$ sends $(\text{refund}, sid, ssid, 1, 3, \phi_1, \tau_3, \mathsf{coin}_1)$ to $\mathcal{A}$ at round $\tau_3 + 1$.
Case II. $\mathcal{S}$ sends $(\text{continue}, sid, ssid, \{2\})$ to $\mathcal{F}_f^{\mathsf{cc}}$. Then, P_2 receives $\{\mathsf{coin}_2\}$ from $\mathcal{F}_f^{\mathsf{cc}}$. Afterwards, $\mathcal{S}$ sends $(\text{claim}, sid, ssid, 1, 3, \phi_1, \tau_3, \mathsf{coin}_1)$ to $\mathcal{A}$.
Case III. $\mathcal{S}$ sends $(\text{continue}, sid, ssid, \emptyset)$ to $\mathcal{F}_f^{\mathsf{cc}}$. Then, $\mathcal{S}$ receives $\{\mathsf{coin}_2\}$ from $\mathcal{F}_f^{\mathsf{cc}}$. Afterwards, $\mathcal{S}$ sends $(\text{claim}, sid, ssid, 2, 3, \phi_2, \tau_3, \mathsf{coin}_2)$. Also, it sends $(\text{refund}, sid, ssid, 1, 3, \phi_3, \tau_3, \mathsf{coin}_1)$ to $\mathcal{A}$ at round $\tau_3 + 1$.
Case IV. $\mathcal{S}$ sends $(\text{continue}, sid, ssid, \emptyset)$ to $\mathcal{F}_f^{\mathsf{cc}}$. Then, $\mathcal{S}$ receives $\{\mathsf{coin}_2\}$ from $\mathcal{F}_f^{\mathsf{cc}}$, and sends $(\text{claim}, sid, ssid, 1, 3, \phi_1, \tau_3, \mathsf{coin}_1)$ and $(\text{claim}, sid, ssid, 2, 3, \phi_2, \tau_3, \mathsf{coin}_2)$ to $\mathcal{A}$.

Case of $C = \{2, 3\}$. In this case, $\mathsf{SimWallet} = \{\mathsf{coin}_2, \mathsf{coin}_3, \mathsf{coin}_4\}$, $W_1 = \{\mathsf{coin}_1\}$ at the beginning of the claim phase. Note that honest P_1 has already claimed transactions (4), and the adversary learns the output before the honest party does. $\mathcal{S}$ performs the following process.

1. Send $(\text{swap}, sid, ssid, 1, \{\mathsf{coin}_4\}, \{(1, \text{clr}_1)\})$ to $\mathcal{F}_f^{\mathsf{cc}}$, and receive $\{\mathsf{coin}_1\}$ from $\mathcal{F}_f^{\mathsf{cc}}$. Then, $\mathsf{SimWallet} = \{\mathsf{coin}_1, \mathsf{coin}_2, \mathsf{coin}_3\}$, $W_1 = \{\mathsf{coin}_4\}$.
2. Send $(\text{complete}, sid, ssid)$ to $\mathcal{F}_f^{\mathsf{cc}}$.
3. Send $(\text{2nd\_input}, sid, ssid, x_2', \{1\}, \{\mathsf{coin}_1\})$ to $\mathcal{F}_f^{\mathsf{cc}}$.

This case corresponds to $h' = h$, and $\mathcal{F}_f^{\mathsf{cc}}$ delivers the output to $\mathcal{S}$. Also, P_1 receives $\{\mathsf{coin}_4\}$ from $\mathcal{F}_f^{\mathsf{cc}}$. Since the $\mathcal{A}$ can choose whether or not to claim for each of the transactions (1)–(3), there are eight possible behaviours that $\mathcal{A}$ can perform. We here describe only the five cases: **(I)** $\mathcal{A}$ does not claim all of the three transaction, **(II)** $\mathcal{A}$ claims all of the three transactions, **(III)** $\mathcal{A}$ claims only transaction (1), **(IV)** $\mathcal{A}$ claims only transaction (2), and **(V)** $\mathcal{A}$ claims only transaction (3). (The remaining cases can be simulated in a similar way). Note that $\mathsf{SimWallet} = \{\mathsf{coin}_2, \mathsf{coin}_3\}$.

Case I. $\mathcal{S}$ sends $(\text{abort}, sid, ssid)$ to $\mathcal{F}_f^{\mathsf{cc}}$. Then, P_1 receives $\{\mathsf{coin}_1\}$ from $\mathcal{F}_f^{\mathsf{cc}}$. Also, $\mathcal{S}$ sends $(\text{refund}, sid, ssid, 3, 2, \phi_3, \tau_2, \mathsf{coin}_3)$ at round $\tau_2 + 1$, and $(\text{refund}, sid, ssid, 2, 3, \phi_2, \tau_3, \mathsf{coin}_2)$ at round $\tau_3 + 1$ to $\mathcal{A}$.
Case II. $\mathcal{S}$ sends $(\text{continue}, sid, ssid, \emptyset)$ to $\mathcal{F}_f^{\mathsf{cc}}$, and receives $\{\mathsf{coin}_1\}$ from $\mathcal{F}_f^{\mathsf{cc}}$. $\mathcal{S}$ sends $(\text{claim}, sid, ssid, 3, 2, \phi_3, \tau_2, \mathsf{coin}_3)$ to $\mathcal{A}$. Afterwards, it also sends $(\text{claim}, sid, ssid, 1, 3, \phi_1, \tau_3, \mathsf{coin}_1)$ and $(\text{claim}, sid, ssid, 2, 3, \phi_2, \tau_3, \mathsf{coin}_2)$ to $\mathcal{A}$.
Case III. $\mathcal{S}$ sends $(\text{continue}, sid, ssid, \emptyset)$ to $\mathcal{F}_f^{\mathsf{cc}}$, and receives $\{\mathsf{coin}_1\}$ from $\mathcal{F}_f^{\mathsf{cc}}$. $\mathcal{S}$ sends $(\text{claim}, sid, ssid, 1, 3, \phi_1, \tau_3, \mathsf{coin}_1)$ to $\mathcal{A}$. It also sends $(\text{refund}, sid, ssid, 3, 2, \phi_3, \tau_2, \mathsf{coin}_3)$ at round $\tau_2 + 1$ and $(\text{refund}, sid, ssid, 2, 3, \phi_2, \tau_3, \mathsf{coin}_2)$ at round $\tau_3 + 1$ to $\mathcal{A}$.
Case IV. $\mathcal{S}$ sends $(\text{continue}, sid, ssid, \{1\})$ to $\mathcal{F}_f^{\mathsf{cc}}$. Then, P_1 receives $\{\mathsf{coin}_1\}$ from $\mathcal{F}_f^{\mathsf{cc}}$. $\mathcal{S}$ sends $(\text{claim}, sid, ssid, 2, 3, \phi_2, \tau_3, \mathsf{coin}_2)$ to $\mathcal{A}$. It also sends $(\text{refund}, sid, ssid, 3, 2, \phi_3, \tau_2, \mathsf{coin}_3)$ to $\mathcal{A}$ at round $\tau_2 + 1$.

Case V. $\mathcal{S}$ sends (abort, $sid, ssid$) to $\mathcal{F}_f^{\mathsf{cc}}$. Then, P_1 receives $\{\mathsf{coin}_1\}$ from $\mathcal{F}_f^{\mathsf{cc}}$. $\mathcal{S}$ sends (claim, $sid, ssid, 3, 2, \phi_3, \tau_2, \mathsf{coin}_3$) to $\mathcal{A}$. It also sends (refund, $sid, ssid$, $2, 3, \phi_2, \tau_3, \mathsf{coin}_2$) to $\mathcal{A}$ at round $\tau_3 + 1$.

We complete making up the simulation. In each case, the adversary's view and the distribution of color coins are identical to the real process.

5.2 Proof for the n-Party Case

We can construct a simulator for the n-party case in a similar way to the three-party case. It is important to note that the ideal-world simulator can learn the colors used in the corresponding real process that the simulator needs to simulate. Specifically, the simulator can determine the colors used by the corrupted parties from the messages sent by the adversary intended for $\mathcal{F}_{\mathrm{CR}}^{\mathsf{cc}}$, and the ones used by the honest parties from the messages sent by $\mathcal{F}_f^{\mathsf{cc}}$ in the first input phase. Note that we set the priority of colors that honest parties use in Remark 1. Namely, these messages determine the color used for each transaction in the real process uniquely. We defer the full proof of Theorem 1 to the full version.

6 Conclusion

To make the SCC model more general, we proposed a new model: secure computation with color coins. Our model does not assume that coins are indistinguishable from one another, which is the main difference from the SCC model. We showed that a protocol for secure computation with penalties, which was originally designed in the SCC model, can be realized in our model with almost no changes to the procedure. (Precisely, the procedure of our protocol is the same as Bentov-Kumaresan's one [9] except for the following three points: The agreement of the price function is required among all parties, the claim-or-refund functionality is modified to adapt to our model, and parties need to determine the color coins used in the protocol according to the initialization by an environment). This implies that a mixture of various kinds of monetary entities can be used as color coins in the protocol.

In the SCC model, several protocols for other functionalities have been proposed, such as the secure lottery [9] and the secure cash distribution [10,25]. We leave an open question of whether these protocols can be realized in our model as with the secure computation with penalties.

Acknowledgment. This work was supported by JSPS KAKENHI Grant Number JP23K16880, JST CREST Japan Grant Number JPMJCR22M1, and JST CRONOS Japan Grant Number JPMJCS24K2.

References

1. Alper, H.K., Küpçü, A.: Optimally efficient multi-party fair exchange and fair secure multi-party computation. ACM Trans. Priv. Secur. **25**(1) (2021)
2. Andrychowicz, M., Dziembowski, S., Malinowski, D., Mazurek, Ł.: Fair two-party computations via bitcoin deposits. In: Financial Cryptography and Data Security, pp. 105–121. Springer, Heidelberg (2014)
3. Asharov, G., Beimel, A., Makriyannis, N., Omri, E.: Complete characterization of fairness in secure two-party computation of Boolean functions. In: Theory of Cryptography, pp. 199–228. Springer, Heidelberg (2015)
4. Asharov, G., Lindell, Y., Rabin, T.: A full characterization of functions that imply fair coin tossing and ramifications to fairness. In: Theory of Cryptography, pp. 243–262. Springer, Heidelberg (2013)
5. Asokan, N., Schunter, M., Waidner, M.: Optimistic protocols for fair exchange. In: Proceedings of the 4th ACM Conference on Computer and Communications Security, CCS 1997, pp. 7–17. ACM (1997)
6. Avizheh, S., Safavi-Naini, R.: Fair private set intersection using smart contracts. In: Applied Cryptography and Network Security, pp. 74–104. Springer (2024)
7. Baum, C., David, B., Dowsley, R.: Insured MPC: efficient secure computation with financial penalties. In: Financial Cryptography and Data Security: 24th International Conference, FC 2020, pp. 404–420. Springer (2020)
8. Beaver, D., Goldwasser, S.: Multiparty computation with faulty majority. In: 30th Annual Symposium on Foundations of Computer Science, pp. 468–473 (1989)
9. Bentov, I., Kumaresan, R.: How to use bitcoin to design fair protocols. In: Advances in Cryptology – CRYPTO 2014, pp. 421–439. Springer, Heidelberg (2014)
10. Bentov, I., Kumaresan, R., Miller, A.: Instantaneous decentralized poker. In: Advances in Cryptology – ASIACRYPT 2017, pp. 410–440. Springer (2017)
11. Canetti, R.: Universally composable security. J. ACM **67**(5) (2020)
12. Choudhuri, A.R., Green, M., Jain, A., Kaptchuk, G., Miers, I.: Fairness in an unfair world: fair multiparty computation from public bulletin boards. In: Proceedings of the 2017 ACM SIGSAC Conference on Computer and Communications Security, CCS 2017, pp. 719–728. ACM (2017)
13. Cleve, R.: Limits on the security of coin flips when half the processors are faulty. In: Proceedings of the Eighteenth Annual ACM Symposium on Theory of Computing, STOC 1986, pp. 364–369. ACM (1986)
14. Dziembowski, S., Eckey, L., Faust, S.: FairSwap: how to fairly exchange digital goods. In: Proceedings of the 2018 ACM SIGSAC Conference on Computer and Communications Security, CCS 2018, pp. 967–984. ACM (2018)
15. Dziembowski, S., Eckey, L., Faust, S., Malinowski, D.: Perun: virtual payment hubs over cryptocurrencies. In: 2019 IEEE Symposium on Security and Privacy (SP), pp. 106–123 (2019)
16. Wood, G., et al.: Ethereum: a secure decentralised generalised transaction ledger. Ethereum project yellow paper (2019)
17. Garay, J.A., Katz, J., Kumaresan, R., Zhou, H.-S.: Adaptively secure broadcast, revisited. In: Proceedings of the 30th Annual ACM SIGACT-SIGOPS Symposium on Principles of Distributed Computing, PODC 2011, pp. 179–186. ACM (2011)
18. Goldwasser, S., Levin, L.: Fair computation of general functions in presence of immoral majority. In: Advances in Cryptology-CRYPTO 1990, pp. 77–93. Springer, Heidelberg (1991)

19. Gordon, S.D., Hazay, C., Katz, J., Lindell, Y.: Complete fairness in secure two-party computation. J. ACM **58**(6) (2011)
20. Gordon, S.D., Ishai, Y., Moran, T., Ostrovsky, R., Sahai, A.: On complete primitives for fairness. In: Theory of Cryptography, pp. 91–108. Springer, Heidelberg (2010)
21. Ishai, Y., Prabhakaran, M., Sahai, A.: Founding cryptography on oblivious transfer – efficiently. In: Advances in Cryptology – CRYPTO 2008, pp. 572–591. Springer, Heidelberg (2008)
22. Kiayias, A., Zhou, H.-S., Zikas, V.: Fair and robust multi-party computation using a global transaction ledger. In: Proceedings of the 35th Annual International Conference on Advances in Cryptology, EUROCRYPT 2016, vol. 9666, pp. 705–734. Springer (2016)
23. Kilian, J.: Founding crytpography on oblivious transfer. In: Proceedings of the Twentieth Annual ACM Symposium on Theory of Computing, STOC 1988, pp. 20–31. ACM (1988)
24. Kumaresan, R., Bentov, I.: Amortizing secure computation with penalties. In: Proceedings of the 2016 ACM SIGSAC Conference on Computer and Communications Security, CCS 2016, pp. 418–429. ACM (2016)
25. Kumaresan, R., Moran, T., Bentov, I.: How to use bitcoin to play decentralized poker. In: Proceedings of the 22nd ACM SIGSAC Conference on Computer and Communications Security, CCS 2015, pp. 195–206. ACM (2015)
26. Kumaresan, R., Vaikuntanathan, V., Vasudevan, P.N.: Improvements to secure computation with penalties. In: Proceedings of the 2016 ACM SIGSAC Conference on Computer and Communications Security, CCS 2016, pp. 406–417. ACM (2016)
27. Lindell, A.Y.: Legally-enforceable fairness in secure two-party computation. In: Topics in Cryptology – CT-RSA 2008, pp. 121–137. Springer, Heidelberg (2008)
28. Micali, S.: Secure protocols with invisible trusted parties. In: Workshop for Multi-Party Secure Protocols. Weizmann Institute of Science (1998)
29. Nakai, T., Shinagawa, K.: Constant-round linear-broadcast secure computation with penalties. Theoret. Comput. Sci. **959**, 113874 (2023)
30. Nakai, T., Shinagawa, K.: Secure multi-party computation with legally-enforceable fairness. Int. J. Inf. Secur. **23**, 3609–3623 (2024)
31. Nakamoto, S.: Bitcoin: a peer-to-peer electronic cash system. Decentralized business review (2008)
32. Yao, A.C.: Protocols for secure computations. In: Proceedings of the 23rd Annual Symposium on Foundations of Computer Science, pp. 160–164 (1982)

Universal Adaptor Signatures from Blackbox Multi-party Computation

Michele Ciampi[1], Xiangyu Liu[2,3](✉), Ioannis Tzannetos[2,4], and Vassilis Zikas[3]

[1] University of Edinburgh, Edinburgh, UK
michele.ciampi@ed.ac.uk
[2] Purdue University, West Lafayette, USA
{liu3894,itzannet}@purdue.edu
[3] Georgia Institute of Technology, Atlanta, USA
vzikas@gatech.edu
[4] National Technical University of Athens, Athens, Greece

Abstract. Adaptor signatures (AS) extend the functionality of traditional digital signatures by enabling the generation of a *pre-signature* tied to an instance of a hard NP relation, which can later be turned (adapted) into a full signature upon revealing a corresponding witness. The recent work by Liu et al. [ASIACRYPT 2024] devised a generic AS scheme that can be used for any NP relation—which here we will refer to as *universal adaptor signatures* scheme, in short UAS—from any one-way function. However, this generic construction depends on the Karp reduction to the Hamiltonian cycle problem, which adds significant overhead and hinders practical applicability.

In this work, we present an alternative approach to construct universal adaptor signature schemes relying on the *multi-party computation in the head* (MPCitH) paradigm. This overcomes the reliance on the costly Karp reduction, while inheriting the core property of the MPCitH—which makes it an invaluable tool in efficient cryptographic protocols—namely, that the construction is black-box with respect to the underlying cryptographic primitive (while it remains non-black-box in the relation being proven). Our framework simplifies the design of UAS and enhances their applicability across a wide range of decentralized applications, such as blockchain and privacy-preserving systems. Our results demonstrate that MPCitH-based UAS schemes offer strong security guarantees while making them a promising tool in the design of real-world cryptographic protocols.

1 Introduction

Blockchain technology was born out of a need for secure, transparent, and decentralized systems, with Bitcoin [18] serving as the first major application. Initially, blockchain's primary purpose was to enable peer-to-peer digital transactions without relying on a centralized authority. Over time, this innovation laid the foundation for decentralized finance (DeFi), a financial ecosystem built on

A. Patra (Ed.): CT-RSA 2025, LNCS 15598, pp. 375–398, 2025.
https://doi.org/10.1007/978-3-031-88661-4_16

blockchain, offering an alternative to traditional financial intermediaries. DeFi enables lending, borrowing, trading, and other financial services through smart contracts, allowing users to maintain control over their assets without depending on centralized entities.

As DeFi rapidly grew, it gained significant adoption within and beyond the cryptocurrency space, attracting users, developers, and institutional players. The promise of financial inclusion, coupled with the potential to earn yields and participate in decentralized governance, spurred widespread interest. However, with this increase in adoption came notable challenges, particularly in terms of scalability. Popular blockchains like Ethereum struggled with network congestion, leading to high transaction fees and slower processing times. These limitations emphasized the critical need for blockchain systems to handle the growing demand efficiently. Scalability remains a central focus for the continued growth of DeFi and blockchain applications, with efforts directed toward reducing bottlenecks, increasing transaction throughput, and lowering fees to ensure that blockchain networks can support a global user base.

A method that has been proposed to address such scalability challenges is the use of adaptor signatures (AS) [2,19]. Adaptor signatures enable more efficient transaction processing by reducing the amount of data that needs to be stored and validated on-chain. This cryptographic technique allows participants to conditionally reveal certain information, such as secrets, only when specific conditions are met. By minimizing the need for complex scripts and offloading much of the computation, adaptor signatures help streamline transactions and reduce associated fees.

Adaptor signatures (AS) were introduced by Poelstra [19,20]. A first formal definition was given by Aumayr et al. [1,2]. It defined AS as an extended version of digital signatures which incorporates a cryptographic relation between a so-called *pre-signature* and a witness for an NP statement. In more detail, in an AS scheme, the signer produces a pre-signature tied to a hard relation R, and any party who knows the witness y to Y (where $(Y, y) \in R$) can transform (i.e., adapt) this pre-signature into a valid signature. Once the full signature is made public, the signer can extract the witness y from both the pre-signature and the full signature. Due to these features adaptor signatures can introduce a layer of fairness and trust between participants, which makes them particularly useful in scenarios like fair exchanges and cross-chain swaps.

The notion of AS also has the natural requirement that the adapted signature does not leak information about the witness. This guarantees that only those who generated the pre-signature will get access to the witness. Such a feature becomes particularly relevant in the blockchain context, in which for example an entity wants to sell the witness for Y, conditioned on being paid in some cryptocurrency. AS can be used to perform exactly this task atomically, by letting the buyer of y issue a pre-signature for a transaction that pays the seller. The seller, to get the money simply needs to complete the signature by adapting it. Upon generating the adapted signature, the seller will be rewarded, and the extraction property of the AS scheme guarantees that the buyer will learn the witness y. It is easy to see that in such a scenario, it would be preferable that the adapted signature (that will be posted on the blockchain) does not leak information about y, as this would allow anyone participating in the blockchain protocol to learn y for free. This property was formalized as *witness hiding* in [17].

AS schemes can be applied in blockchain systems to reduce on-chain computation while maintaining security. Key applications include:

Atomic Swaps. Atomic swaps [8,20] allow two parties to exchange assets from different cryptocurrencies (e.g., Bitcoin and Ethereum) without intermediaries. Both parties lock their funds on-chain and exchange pre-signatures tied to a shared hard relation instance. Once the pre-signature is adapted by one party using their witness, the other party can extract the witness and adapt the second pre-signature, ensuring a fair exchange of assets without one party holding an unfair advantage.

Cross-Chain Atomic Swaps. Similar to atomic swaps, cross-chain swaps [7,13] involve two different blockchains, where assets from different chains are exchanged securely. Alice and Bob lock funds on their respective blockchains and exchange pre-signatures for transactions. The same instance Y and witness y are used across both chains, allowing each party to adapt their pre-signatures once they observe the other party's adapted signature, ensuring secure asset transfer across both blockchains.

Multi-Hop Payments. Multi-hop payments [8] enable multiple parties to route payments among themselves via a common intermediary, assuming they share a payment channel. While the original protocol [8] has each party sample a new instance-witness pair for every transaction, we simplify it by allowing all parties to use the same instance, provided that intermediate parties do not collude. Consider three parties: Alice, Bob, and Charlie where Alice wishes to pay cryptocurrency (say c) to Charlie. First, Alice and Bob lock funds on the blockchain within a payment channel as collateral, followed by Bob and Charlie. Charlie then randomly samples an instance-witness pair (Y, y) and forwards the instance Y to Alice and Bob. Alice initiates the transaction by creating a pre-signature $\tilde{\sigma}_A$ and sending it to Bob. Bob, in turn, generates his own pre-signature $\tilde{\sigma}_B$ and forwards it to Charlie. Once Charlie receives $\tilde{\sigma}_B$, he can convert it into a full signature σ_B by using the witness y, allowing him to finalize the transaction on the blockchain and receive the amount c. Simultaneously, Bob can derive the witness y from $\tilde{\sigma}_B$ and σ_B, adapt his pre-signature $\tilde{\sigma}_A$ into a full signature σ_A, and complete his transaction to obtain c.

Universal AS (UAS). While most previous works [2,8,16,21,23,24] focus on constructing AS schemes based on specific signatures schemes (such as ECDSA [2] and Schnorr [2,24]) and for script-related relations (like the public/secret key relation in signatures), only two works [5,17] have explored AS schemes for generic NP relations, which we refer to as *universal adaptor signature schemes (in short, UAS)*. Dai et al. [5] gave a generic construction of universal AS. However, their scheme does not provide witness hiding as the witness is fully exposed in the adapted signature itself. To address this issue, Liu et al. [17] proposed a construction that leverages the NP-completeness of the Hamiltonian cycle problem. In particular, they creates an AS scheme which can be used for the case of Hamiltonian cycles. Since any NP relation can be reduced to that problem, this provides a universal AS scheme. However, when the target NP language we need for our application is not the language of Hamiltonian cycles—which will be the case in most, if not all, applications of universal AS—then before using the scheme of [17] a Karp reduction [15] needs to be used to reduce the statement at hand to an instance of the Hamilton cycle problem. This makes the above result of purely theoretical value, because the Karp reductions (in particular to Hamilton cycle) is a computationally expensive operation. Thus an question left open by [17] is whether we can avoid relying on the expensive Karp reduction, which takes us closer to a practical system.

In fact, Liu et al. suggested that a possible way to get such a result could be by using the multi-party computation in the head (MPCitH)paradigm [14] which has proven invaluable in the design of practical (zero-knowledge) proofs. However, as observed there, the techniques of [17] appear to be incompatible with MPCitH. The reason is that the scheme of [17] requires the existence of a sigma protocol in which the first round is independent of the witness (a property satisfied by the sigma-protocol for Hamiltonian cycles proposed in [3]). This feature is not satisfied by the sigma-protocol obtained via the MPCitH approach. Indeed, in this, the first round consists of the commitments of the parties' views that executed an MPC protocol to check the membership of an instance-witness pair in an NP relation. In particular the input of these parties corresponds to a share of the witness. Hence, the views depend on the witness itself, and as such the first round of the obtained sigma-protocol is not witness-independent. As such [17] left the following natural question remained open:

Question: *How to construct more efficient UAS schemes from the MPCitH paradigm?*

In this work, we solve this open problem by proposing a new approach to construct universal adaptor signatures from the MPCitH paradigm.

1.1 Our Contributions

In this work, we present a novel approach to construct universal adaptor signatures (UAS) from the *multi-party computation in the head* (MPCitH) paradigm [14]. Furthermore, we enhance the applicability across a wide range of decentralized applications, such as blockchain and privacy-preserving systems. Our results demonstrate that MPCitH-based AS schemes lead to more efficient protocols, making them a promising candidates for real-world cryptographic protocols.

1.2 Technical Overview

In this section we take a brief overview of our approach.

Generic Construction for NP Relations [17]**.** We start by recalling the generic construction proposed in [17]. The key insight is that the process used to extract the witness of universal adaptor signatures (UAS) shares some similarities with the notion of *special soundness* of sigma protocols. Special soundness requires that a witness can be extracted from two valid transcripts (that refer to the same NP instance) with the same first-round message but different challenges (we refer to Sect. 2.5 for a formal definition of sigma protocols). In Liu et al.'s generic construction, a pre-signature for a message m with respect to an instance Y (a Hamiltonian graph) is of the form

$$\tilde{\sigma} = (\bar{\sigma}, cmt, ch = m_{\mathbf{0}}, rsp),$$

where $\bar{\sigma}$ is a regular signature on message (m, Y, cmt), and (cmt, ch, rsp) is a simulated transcript of Blum's sigma protocol w.r.t. instance Y for the Hamiltonian cycle problem [3,10], with $m_{\mathbf{0}}$ being an all-zero string. Moreover, Blum's sigma protocol has the property that one can simulate a transcript with the challenge 0^λ, and then use the same first-round message to reply to a different challenge if the witness for the statement being proven is known. Hence, with the knowledge of a witness y, the pre-signature can be adapted into a full signature

$$\sigma = (\bar{\sigma}, cmt, ch' = m, rsp'),$$

where (cmt, ch', rsp') is another valid transcript with challenge being the message m to be signed. By the special soundness of the sigma protocol, a witness y for the instance Y can be extracted from both the pre-signature $\tilde{\sigma}$ and the adapted signature σ.

MPC-in-the-Head Paradigm. Now we recall the multi-party computation in the head (MPCitH) paradigm [14], which transforms a secure n-party MPC protocol Π into a sigma protocol. Let R be an NP relation with Y an instance and y a corresponding witness such that $(Y, y) \in R$. Let f_R be the functionality such that

$$f_R(Y, y_1, ..., y_n) = 1 \text{ if and only if } (Y, \bigoplus_{i \in [n]} y_i) \in R.$$

Let Π be an MPC protocol securely realizing f_R. The high-level idea of the MPCitH paradigm is that, the prover, with public input Y and private input y, first shares y into n pieces of secrets $y_1, ..., y_n$, and then simulates "in the head" the running of Π with party P_i taking y_i as the local private input. The prover then commits the views of all parties, where the view View_i consists of the input and output of P_i, the randomness used for P_i, and the transcripts sent to/from P_i. Upon receiving commitments of all views, the verifier randomly samples two distinct indexes i, j, and asks the prover to open the corresponding views of P_i and P_j. The verifier then checks whether View_i and View_j are well-formed and consistent with each other. In this informal part of the paper, we will refer to this protocol with Π^{MPCitH}. Unfortunately, this protocol cannot be used in the approach of [17] we have just recalled due to the first round being dependent on the witness. For this reason, we will follow a different approach.

Our New Approach. The high-level idea is as follows. Let (pk, sk) be a public-secret-key pair of a standard unforgeable signature scheme. The public-secret key of our adaptor signature corresponds exactly to (pk, sk).

To issue a pre-signature for an NP statement Y and message m, the signer generates a public-secret-key pair for a public-key encryption scheme (pk^e, sk^e), and sign (using the standard signature scheme) (m, Y, pk^e) thus obtaining $\bar{\sigma}$. The pre-signature is represented by the tuple

$$\tilde{\sigma} = (pk^e, sk^e, \bar{\sigma}).$$

To adapt the signature (i.e., to complete the signature) we require the adaptor to execute Π^{MPCitH} proving the knowledge of a witness for y, but with the following difference. In the first round the views of the MPC protocol are not committed but encrypted using the public-key pk^e. In summary, the adapted signature simply consists of Π^{MPCitH}, where the views in the first round are computed using a public-key encryption scheme instead of a commitment scheme. What we have just described would make the generation of the adapted signature an interactive protocol (given that Π^{MPCitH} is interactive). To make it non-interactive, we apply the Fiat-Shamir transform [9] thus obtaining a proof π, which represents our adapted signature

$$\sigma = (Y, pk^e, \bar{\sigma}, \pi).$$

We now argue that our scheme satisfies the most relevant properties required by a secure adaptor signature scheme.

- **Unforgeability.** This is inherited from the underlying signature scheme. Indeed, generating a standard signature requires generating a pre-signature and adapting the signature. This is clearly impossible unless sk is known, or the adversary breaks the unforgeability property of the standard signature scheme we use.
- **Witness extractability.** The extractabiltiy property requires that having the pre-signature $\tilde{\sigma}$ and the adapted signature σ with respect to a statement Y, it must be possible to extract the witness for Y. Note that the pre-signature contains the secret key sk^e of the encryption scheme used to generate the first round of Π^{MPCitH}. The extractor can use sk^e to decrypt the first round message of Π^{MPCitH} and extract all the shares contained in the view of the MPC parties, and finally reconstruct the witness. Arguing that the extraction is successful even when the adapted signature is generated by a malicious adversary, requires some care, and we refer the reader to the technical section of the paper for more details.
- **Witness hiding.** Witness hiding requires that by looking at the adapted signature σ (without the knowledge of the pre-signature $\tilde{\sigma}$), no adversary should be able to infer something about the witness for Y. We recall that the adapted signature σ simply corresponds to an application of the Fiat-Shamir transform on the protocol Π^{MPCitH}. This in a nutshell corresponds to a non-interactive zero-knowledge proof, which by definition hides the witness for the statement proven.

1.3 Roadmap

This paper is organized as follows. In Sect. 2, we present the preliminaries, including extractable commitments, the MPCitH paradigm, and the syntax and security notions of adaptor signatures. In Sect. 3 we show our main contribution: the generic construction of UAS from the MPCitH paradigm, along with its security proof. In Sect. 4 we discuss several issues related to the application of UAS on blockchains.

2 Preliminaries

We use $\lambda \in \mathbb{N}$ to denote the security parameter throughout this paper. For $\mu \in \mathbb{N}$, define $[\mu] := \{1, 2, ..., \mu\}$. Denote by $x := y$ the operation of assigning y to x. Denote by $x \stackrel{\$}{\leftarrow} \mathcal{S}$ the operation of sampling x uniformly at random from a set $\mathcal{S}$. For a distribution $\mathcal{D}$, denote by $x \leftarrow \mathcal{D}$ the operation of sampling x according to $\mathcal{D}$. For an algorithm $\mathcal{A}$, denote by $y \leftarrow \mathcal{A}(x; r)$, or simply $y \leftarrow \mathcal{A}(x)$, the operation of running $\mathcal{A}$ with input x and randomness r and assigning the output to y. For deterministic algorithms $\mathcal{A}$, we also write as $y := \mathcal{A}(x)$ or $y := \mathcal{A}(x; r)$. "PPT" is short for probabilistic polynomial-time.

Min-entropy. Let X a random variable (distribution) defined over $\mathcal{S}$. The min-entropy of X is defined as $\mathbf{H}_\infty(X) := -\log(\max_{s \in \mathcal{S}} \Pr[X = s])$.

2.1 Extractable Commitments

We recall the definition of extractable commitments in [22].

Definition 1 (Extractable Commitments). *An extractable commitment scheme* $\mathsf{eCOM} = (\mathsf{TdGen}, \mathsf{Com}, \mathsf{Ver}, \mathsf{Ext})$ *consists of the following four algorithms.*

- $(ck, td) \leftarrow \mathsf{TdGen}(1^\lambda)$. *The trapdoor key generation algorithm takes as input the security parameter* λ, *and outputs a commitment key* ck *and a trapdoor* td.
  We denote as $(ck, td) := \mathsf{TdGen}(1^\lambda; r)$ *if the randomness* r *is specified during trapdoor key generation.*
- $(c, d) \leftarrow \mathsf{Com}(ck, m)$. *The commitment algorithm takes as input* ck *and a message* m, *and outputs a commitment* c *and an opening* d.
- $0/1 \leftarrow \mathsf{Ver}(ck, c, m, d)$. *The verification algorithm takes as input* ck, c, m *and* d, *and outputs a bit.*
- $m' \leftarrow \mathsf{Ext}(td, c)$. *The extraction algorithm takes as input* td *and* c, *and outputs a message* m'.

Correctness. *For any* $(ck, td) \leftarrow \mathsf{Gen}(1^\lambda)$, *any message* m *and* $(c, d) \leftarrow \mathsf{Com}(ck, m)$, *it holds that* $\mathsf{Ver}(ck, c, m, d) = 1$.

If the trapdoor td is set to be empty, then we define a regular commitment scheme $\mathsf{Com} = (\mathsf{Gen}, \mathsf{Com}, \mathsf{Ver})$, where TdGen is replaced with the key generation algorithm $ck \leftarrow \mathsf{Gen}(1^\lambda)$.

Definition 2 (Extractability). *An extractable commitment scheme* eCOM *has extractability, if for any unbounded adversary* $\mathcal{A}$*, the advantage*

$$\mathsf{Adv}^{ext}_{\mathsf{eCOM},\mathcal{A}}(\lambda) := \left| \Pr\left[\begin{array}{c} (ck, td) \leftarrow \mathsf{TdGen}(1^\lambda) \\ (c, m, d) \leftarrow \mathcal{A}(ck); m' \leftarrow \mathsf{Ext}(td, c) \end{array} : \begin{array}{c} \mathsf{Ver}(ck, c, m, d) = 1 \\ \wedge\ m \neq m' \end{array} \right] \right|$$

is negligible over λ.

We say eCOM *has perfect extractability if* $\mathsf{Adv}^{ext}_{\mathsf{eCOM},\mathcal{A}}(\lambda) = 0$.

In our construction of adaptor signatures in Sect. 3, we require honest extractability, which guarantees perfect extractability against honest committers.

Definition 3 (Statistical Binding). *An extractable commitment scheme* eCOM *has statistical binding, if for any unbounded adversary* $\mathcal{A}$*, the advantage*

$$\mathsf{Adv}^{binding}_{\mathsf{eCOM},\mathcal{A}}(\lambda) := \left| \Pr\left[\begin{array}{c} (ck, td) \leftarrow \mathsf{TdGen}(1^\lambda) \\ (c, m_0, m_1, d_0, d_1) \leftarrow \mathcal{A}(ck) \end{array} : \begin{array}{c} m_0 \neq m_1 \\ \wedge\ \mathsf{Ver}(ck, c, m_0, d_0) = 1 \\ \wedge\ \mathsf{Ver}(ck, c, m_1, d_1) = 1 \end{array} \right] \right|$$

is negligible over λ.

We say eCOM *has perfect binding if* $\mathsf{Adv}^{binding}_{\mathsf{eCOM},\mathcal{A}}(\lambda) = 0$.

Definition 4 (Hiding of Extractable Commitments). *An extractable commitment scheme* eCOM *has hiding, if for any stateful PPT adversary* $\mathcal{A}$*, the advantage*

$$\begin{aligned} \mathsf{Adv}^{hiding}_{\mathsf{eCOM},\mathcal{A}}(\lambda) := \Bigg| &\Pr\left[\begin{array}{c} (ck, td) \leftarrow \mathsf{TdGen}(1^\lambda); (m_0, m_1, st) \leftarrow \mathcal{A}(ck) \\ (c, d) \leftarrow \mathsf{Com}(ck, m_0) \end{array} : \mathcal{A}(st, c) = 1 \right] \\ &- \Pr\left[\begin{array}{c} (ck, td) \leftarrow \mathsf{TdGen}(1^\lambda); (m_0, m_1, st) \leftarrow \mathcal{A}(ck) \\ (c, d) \leftarrow \mathsf{Com}(ck, m_1) \end{array} : \mathcal{A}(st, c) = 1 \right] \Bigg| \end{aligned}$$

is negligible over λ.

The properties of statistical binding and (computational) hiding for a regular commitment scheme COM can be defined similarly.

Definition 5 (κ-Min-Entropy of Commitments). *An extractable commitment scheme* eCOM *has* κ*-min-entropy, if for any* $(ck, td) \leftarrow \mathsf{TdGen}(1^\lambda)$*, any message* m*, we have* $\mathbf{H}_\infty(c) \geq \kappa$*, where* c *is computed as* $(c, d) \leftarrow \mathsf{Com}(ck, m)$.

Extractable commitments can be constructed from public-key encryption (PKE) schemes, where the public key serves as the commitment key, the secret key serves as the trapdoor, and the commitment is a ciphertext of a message with r—the randomness used in the encryption—being the opening. We refer to the full version [4] for the definition of PKE and the transform we have just highlighted.

2.2 Signatures

Definition 6 (Signatures). *A signature scheme* $\mathsf{SIG} = (\mathsf{Gen}, \mathsf{Sign}, \mathsf{Ver})$ *consists of the following three algorithms.*

- $(pk, sk) \leftarrow \mathsf{Gen}(1^\lambda)$. *The key generation algorithm takes as input the security parameter* λ, *and outputs a public key* pk *and a secret key* sk.
- $\sigma \leftarrow \mathsf{Sign}(sk, m)$. *The signing algorithm takes as input* sk *and a message* m, *and outputs a signature* σ.
- $0/1 \leftarrow \mathsf{Ver}(pk, m, \sigma)$. *The verification algorithm takes as input* pk, m, *and* σ, *and outputs a bit* b *indicating the validity of* σ *(w.r.t.* m*).*

Correctness. *For any* $(pk, sk) \leftarrow \mathsf{Gen}(1^\lambda)$, *any message* m *and* $\sigma \leftarrow \mathsf{Sign}(sk, m)$, *it holds that* $\mathsf{Ver}(pk, m, \sigma) = 1$.

Definition 7 (Unforgeability of Signatures). *A signature scheme* SIG *is unforgeable under chosen message attacks (UF-CMA secure), if for any PPT adversary* $\mathcal{A}$, *the advantage*

$$\mathsf{Adv}^{uf}_{\mathsf{SIG},\mathcal{A}}(\lambda) := \Pr[\mathsf{Exp}^{uf}_{\mathsf{SIG},\mathcal{A}}(\lambda) = 1]$$

is negligible over λ, *where the experiment* $\mathsf{Exp}^{uf}_{\mathsf{SIG},\mathcal{A}}(\lambda)$ *is defined in Fig. 1.*

$\mathsf{Exp}^{uf}_{\mathsf{SIG},\mathcal{A}}(\lambda)$:	$\textsc{Sign}(m)$:
$(pk, sk) \leftarrow \mathsf{Gen}(1^\lambda)$; $\mathcal{S} := \varnothing$	$\sigma \leftarrow \mathsf{Sign}(sk, m)$
$(m^*, \sigma^*) \leftarrow \mathcal{A}^{\textsc{Sign}(\cdot)}(pk)$	$\mathcal{S} := \mathcal{S} \cup \{m\}$
	Return σ
Return $((m^* \notin \mathcal{S}) \wedge (\mathsf{Ver}(pk, m^*, \sigma^*)))$	

Fig. 1. The UF-CMA security experiment of signature scheme SIG.

2.3 NP Languages

Let $\{R_\lambda\} \subseteq (\{0,1\}^* \times \{0,1\}^*)_\lambda$ be a series of binary relations indexed by parameter λ. If λ is fixed then we simply denote R_λ as R. We call R an NP relation if there is an efficient algorithm to check whether $(Y, y) \in R$. The relation R defines an NP language $\mathcal{L}_R := \{Y \in \{0,1\}^* \mid \exists y \in \{0,1\}^* \ s.t.\ (Y, y) \in R\}$. We call Y the instance (not necessarily in $\mathcal{L}_R$), and y a witness of Y if $(Y, y) \in R$. Usually, there is an efficient sample algorithm that returns an instance-witness pair. Formally, $(Y, y) \leftarrow \mathsf{Sample}(R)$.

Definition 8 (Hard Relations). *A binary relation* R *is hard (one-way), if for any PPT adversary* $\mathcal{A}$, *the advantage*

$$\mathsf{Adv}^{ow}_{R,\mathcal{A}}(\lambda) := \Pr[(Y, y) \leftarrow \mathsf{Sample}(R); y' \leftarrow \mathcal{A}(R, Y) \ : \ (Y, y') \in R]$$

is negligible over λ.

2.4 (Universal) Adaptor Signatures

Definition 9 ((Universal) Adaptor Signatures [2,17]). *An adaptor signature scheme w.r.t. a relation R consists of seven algorithms* $\mathsf{AS} = (\mathsf{Gen}, \mathsf{Sign}, \mathsf{Ver}, \mathsf{pSign}, \mathsf{pVer}, \mathsf{Adapt}, \mathsf{Ext})$, *where the first three algorithms are defined as regular signatures (cf. Definition 6), and the last four are defined as follows.*

- $\tilde{\sigma} \leftarrow \mathsf{pSign}(sk, m, Y)$. *The pre-sign algorithm takes as input sk, m and an instance Y, and outputs a pre-signature $\tilde{\sigma}$.*
- $b \leftarrow \mathsf{pVer}(pk, m, Y, \tilde{\sigma})$. *The pre-verification algorithm takes as input pk, m, Y and $\tilde{\sigma}$, and outputs a bit indicating the validity of $\tilde{\sigma}$.*
- $\sigma \leftarrow \mathsf{Adapt}(pk, m, \tilde{\sigma}, y)$. *The adaption algorithm takes as input pk, m, $\tilde{\sigma}$ and a witness y as input, and outputs an adapted signature σ.*
- $y/\perp \leftarrow \mathsf{Ext}(pk, m, Y, \tilde{\sigma}, \sigma)$. *The extraction algorithm takes as input pk, m, Y, $\tilde{\sigma}$ and σ, and outputs a witness y, or a failure symbol $\perp$.*

Except for the correctness as defined in Definition 6, we additionally require the pre-signature correctness, the adaption correctness, and the extraction correctness.

For any $(pk, sk) \leftarrow \mathsf{Gen}(1^\lambda)$, *any message m, any $(Y, y) \in \mathcal{R}$, any* $\tilde{\sigma} \leftarrow \mathsf{pSign}(sk, m, Y)$, $\sigma \leftarrow \mathsf{Adapt}(pk, m, \tilde{\sigma}, y)$, *and* $y' \leftarrow \mathsf{Ext}(pk, m, Y, \tilde{\sigma}, \sigma)$, *it holds that*

1. *(Pre-signature correctness)* $\mathsf{pVer}(pk, m, Y, \tilde{\sigma}) = 1$, *and*
2. *(Adaption correctness)* $\mathsf{Ver}(pk, m, \sigma) = 1$.
3. *(Extraction correctness)* $(Y, y') \in R$.

We call an AS scheme a universal adaptor signature (UAS) scheme (denoted as UAS*), if the scheme is defined for generic NP relations.*

We require unforgeability, witness extractability, pre-signature adaptability, and witness hiding for the security of adaptor signatures.

Unforgeability. The adversary cannot generate a valid pre-signature or a regular signature on a fresh message.
Witness extractability. The signer can extract a witness from the pre-signature and the adapted signature.
Pre-signature adaptability. The receiver can adapt a valid pre-signature into a valid (full) signature with the knowledge of a witness.
Witness hiding The adapted signature leaks no additional information about the witness.

We formally define these security notions, following the works by Dai et al. [5] and Liu et al. [17].

Definition 10 (Unforgeability of Adaptor Signatures). *An adaptor signature scheme* AS *w.r.t. binary relation R is unforgeable under chosen message attacks (UF-CMA secure), if for any PPT adversary $\mathcal{A}$,* $\mathsf{Adv}^{uf}_{\mathsf{AS},\mathcal{A}}(\lambda) := \Pr[\mathsf{Exp}^{uf}_{\mathsf{AS},\mathcal{A}}(\lambda) = 1]$ *is negligible over λ, where the experiment* $\mathsf{Exp}^{uf}_{\mathsf{AS},\mathcal{A}}(\lambda)$ *is defined in Fig. 2.*

$\underline{\mathsf{Exp}^{uf}_{\mathsf{AS},\mathcal{A}}(\lambda)}$: $(pk, sk) \leftarrow \mathsf{Gen}(1^\lambda)$; $\mathcal{S} := \varnothing$; $\mathcal{T}[m] := \varnothing$ $(m^*, \sigma^*) \leftarrow \mathcal{A}^{\text{SIGN}(\cdot),\text{PSIGN}(\cdot,\cdot),\text{NEWY}()}(pk)$ Return $(b_1 \wedge (b_{2,1} \vee b_{2,2}))$, where b_1: $\mathsf{Ver}(pk, m^*, \sigma^*) = 1 \ \wedge \ m^* \notin \mathcal{S}$ $b_{2,1}$: $\mathcal{T}[m^*] = \varnothing$ $b_{2,2}$: $\forall (Y, \tilde{\sigma}) \in \mathcal{T}[m^*] : Y \in \mathcal{Y}$	$\underline{\text{SIGN}(m)}$: $\sigma \leftarrow \mathsf{Sign}(sk, m)$ $\mathcal{S} := \mathcal{S} \cup \{m\}$ Return σ $\underline{\text{PSIGN}(m, Y)}$: $\tilde{\sigma} \leftarrow \mathsf{pSign}(sk, m, Y)$ $\mathcal{T}[m] := \mathcal{T} \cup \{(Y, \tilde{\sigma})\}$ Return $\tilde{\sigma}$	$\underline{\text{NEWY}()}$: $(Y, y) \leftarrow \mathsf{Sample}(R)$ $\mathcal{Y} := \mathcal{Y} \cup \{Y\}$ Return Y

Fig. 2. The UF-CMA security experiment of adaptor signature scheme AS.

Definition 11 (Witness Extractability of Adaptor Signatures). *An adaptor signature scheme* AS *w.r.t. relation* R *is witness extractable, if for any PPT adversary* $\mathcal{A}$, $\mathsf{Adv}^{we}_{\mathsf{AS},\mathcal{A}}(\lambda) := \Pr[\mathsf{Exp}^{we}_{\mathsf{AS},\mathcal{A}}(\lambda) = 1]$ *is negligible over* λ, *where the experiment* $\mathsf{Exp}^{we}_{\mathsf{AS},\mathcal{A}}(\lambda)$ *is defined in Fig. 3.*

$\underline{\mathsf{Exp}^{we}_{\mathsf{AS},\mathcal{A}}(\lambda)}$: $(pk, sk) \leftarrow \mathsf{Gen}(1^\lambda)$; $\mathcal{S} := \varnothing$; $\mathcal{T}[m] := \varnothing$ $(m^*, \sigma^*) \leftarrow \mathcal{A}^{\text{SIGN}(\cdot),\text{PSIGN}(\cdot,\cdot)}(pk)$ Return $(b_1 \wedge b_2)$, where b_1: $\mathsf{Ver}(pk, m^*, \sigma^*) = 1 \ \wedge \ m^* \notin \mathcal{S}$ b_2: $\forall (Y, \tilde{\sigma}) \in \mathcal{T}[m^*] : (Y, \mathsf{Ext}(pk, m^*, Y, \tilde{\sigma}, \sigma^*)) \notin R$ // all $(Y, \tilde{\sigma})$ in the pre-sign list lead to a failed extraction	$\underline{\text{SIGN}(m)}$: $\sigma \leftarrow \mathsf{Sign}(sk, m)$ $\mathcal{S} := \mathcal{S} \cup \{m\}$ Return σ $\underline{\text{PSIGN}(m, Y)}$: $\tilde{\sigma} \leftarrow \mathsf{pSign}(sk, m, Y)$ $\mathcal{T}[m] := \mathcal{T} \cup \{(Y, \tilde{\sigma})\}$ Return $\tilde{\sigma}$

Fig. 3. The witness extractability experiment of adaptor signature scheme AS.

Definition 12 (Pre-signature Adaptability of Adaptor Signatures). *An adaptor signature scheme* AS *w.r.t. relation* R *has pre-signature adaptability, if for any public key* pk, *any message* m, *any* $(Y, y) \in R$ *and pre-signature* $\tilde{\sigma}$ *s.t.* $\mathsf{pVer}(pk, m, Y, \tilde{\sigma}) = 1$, *it holds that* $\mathsf{Ver}(pk, m, \mathsf{Adapt}(pk, m, \tilde{\sigma}, y)) = 1$.

Definition 13 (Witness Hiding of Adaptor Signatures). *An adaptor signature scheme* AS *w.r.t. relation* R *is witness hiding, if there exists a simulator* Sim *such that, for any PPT adversary* $\mathcal{A}$,

$$\mathsf{Adv}^{wh}_{\mathsf{AS},\mathsf{Sim}\mathcal{A}}(\lambda) := |\Pr[\mathsf{Exp}^{wh}_{\mathsf{AS},\mathsf{Sim},\mathcal{A},0}(\lambda) = 1] - \Pr[\mathsf{Exp}^{wh}_{\mathsf{AS},\mathsf{Sim},\mathcal{A},1}(\lambda) = 1]|$$

is negligible over λ, *where the experiments* $\mathsf{Exp}^{wh}_{\mathsf{AS},\mathsf{Sim},\mathcal{A},b}(\lambda)$ $(b \in \{0, 1\})$ *are defined in Fig. 4.*

$\mathsf{Exp}^{wh}_{\mathsf{AS},\mathsf{Sim},\mathcal{A},b}(\lambda)$:	$\text{CHALL}_0(pk, sk, m)$	$\text{CHALL}_1(pk, sk, m)$
$(Y, y) \leftarrow \mathsf{Sample}(R)$	If $f_{\mathsf{AS}}(pk, sk) \neq 1$: Return $\perp$	If $f_{\mathsf{AS}}(pk, sk) \neq 1$: Return $\perp$
Return $\mathcal{A}^{\text{CHALL}_b(\cdot,\cdot,\cdot)}(Y)$	// check the validity of (pk, sk)	// check the validity of (pk, sk)
	$\tilde{\sigma} \leftarrow \mathsf{pSign}(sk, m, Y)$	$\sigma \leftarrow \mathsf{Sim}(pk, sk, m, Y)$
	$\sigma \leftarrow \mathsf{Adapt}(pk, m, \tilde{\sigma}, y)$	Return σ
	Return σ	

Fig. 4. The witness hiding experiments of adaptor signature scheme AS.

2.5 Sigma Protocols

Definition 14 (Sigma Protocols [6]). *A sigma protocol Σ for an NP relation R is a three-move interactive protocol between a prover $\mathcal{P}$ and a verifier $\mathcal{V}$ working as follows.*

- $0/1 \leftarrow \langle \mathcal{P}(y), \mathcal{V}\rangle(Y)$. *Both the prover $\mathcal{P}$ and the verifier $\mathcal{V}$ share the common input Y, and $\mathcal{P}$ additionally takes y as a private input. After the interaction, $\mathcal{V}$ outputs a bit b for accept/reject, based on the transcript and Y.*
- *The transcript consists of three moves: the first move is a commitment cmt sending from $\mathcal{P}$ to $\mathcal{V}$. The second move is a challenge ch sending from $\mathcal{V}$ to $\mathcal{P}$, where ch is sampled from some finite set $\mathcal{CH}$. The third move is a response rsp sending from $\mathcal{P}$ to $\mathcal{V}$.*

We require the following properties for Σ.

- ***Completeness.*** *For all $(Y, y) \in R$, the verifier $\mathcal{V}$ outputs 1 after an honest running of the protocol, i.e., $1 \leftarrow \langle \mathcal{P}(y), \mathcal{V}\rangle(Y)$.*
- ***Special Soundness*** *There is a polynomial time extractor $\mathcal{E}$ such that given any pair of accepted transcripts (cmt, ch, rsp) and (cmt, ch', rsp') for any instance Y such that $ch \neq ch'$, the extractor $\mathcal{E}$ can extract a witness y such that $(Y, y) \in R$ except for a negligible probability.*
- ***Honest-Verifier Zero-Knowledge.*** *There is a PPT simulator* Sim *such that for all $(Y, y) \in R$, the output of* $\mathsf{Sim}(Y)$ *is distributed computationally close to the distribution of the transcript by an honest execution $\langle \mathcal{P}(y), \mathcal{V}\rangle(Y)$.*

Definition 15 (Public-Coin Sigma Protocols). *A sigma protocol Σ is public-coin if the challenge ch sent by the verifier $\mathcal{V}$ is uniformly sampled from the challenge space $\mathcal{CH}$.*

The well-known Fiat-Shamir transform [9] can be used to compile a public-coin sigma protocol into a non-interactive zero-knowledge argument (NIZK) scheme in the random oracle model (ROM), by setting the challenge as $ch := \mathsf{H}(aux, cmt)$ and outputting $\pi = (cmt, rsp)$, where aux is some public information (e.g., the message to be signed when compiling a sigma protocol into a signature scheme in the ROM), and rsp is the response (the third move) of the sigma protocol. We omit the detailed description of the Fiat-Shamir transform here.

2.6 Multi-party Computation

We recall the definition and security properties of MPC in [14].

Let $P_1, ..., P_n$ be n parties. All parties share a global input Y and each party P_i privately holds a share of secret y_i. We basically consider n-party functionality f_R w.r.t. an NP relation R which maps the input $(Y, y_1, ..., y_n)$ to an n-tuple of outputs.

The n-party protocol Π is specified via its next message function. More precisely, $\Pi(i, Y, y_i, r_i, (m_1, ..., m_r))$ returns the set of n messages sent by P_i in round $r+1$, given the global input Y, its local secret share y_i, its random coins r_i, and the messages $m_1, ..., m_r$ it received in the first r rounds. The output of Π also indicates that the protocol should terminate and return the final output of Π.

We use View_i to denote the view of P_i in the running of Π, which consists of y_i, r_i, and the messages P_i received. Note that if P_i is honest, then the messages P_i sent out and the final output of P_i are totally determined by View_i.

Definition 16 (Consistent Views). *A pair of views* $\mathsf{View}_i, \mathsf{View}_j$ *from parties* P_i, P_j *are consistent (w.r.t. the protocol* Π *and the global input* Y*), if the outgoing messages implicit in* View_i *are identical to the incoming messages reported in* View_j *and vice versa.*

Lemma 1 (Local v.s. Global Consistency [14]). *Let* Π *be an* n*-party protocol and* Y *be a global input. Let* $\mathsf{View}_1, ..., \mathsf{View}_n$ *be* n *views. All pairs of views* $\mathsf{View}_i, \mathsf{View}_j$ *are consistent (w.r.t.* Π *and* Y*) if and only if there exists an honest execution of* Π *with global input* Y *in which* View_i *is the view of* P_i *for all* $i \in [n]$.

Definition 17 (Correctness of Π). *We say* Π *realizes a deterministic* n*-party functionality* $f(Y, y_1, ..., y_n)$ *with perfect (resp., statistical) correctness if for all inputs* $Y, y_1, ..., y_n$*, the probability that the output of some player is different from the output of* f *is 0 (resp., negligible over* λ*), where the probability is over the independent choice of random coins* $r_1, ..., r_n$.

Definition 18 (t-Privacy of Π). *Let* $1 \leq t < n$. *We say that* Π *realizes* f *with prefect* t*-privacy if there exists a simulator* Sim *such that for any inputs* $Y, y_1, ..., y_n$ *and every set of corrupted parties* $T \subset [n]$ *s.t.* $|T| \leq t$*, the joint view* $\mathsf{View}_T(Y, y_1, ..., y_n)$ *of parties in* T *is distributed identically to the output of* $\mathsf{Sim}(T, Y, (y_i)_{i \in T}, f_T(Y, y_1, ..., y_n))$. *This definition can be relaxed to statistical or computational privacy defined similarly.*

2.7 MPC in the Head Paradigm

In this subsection we present the MPCitHead paradigm [14] that transfers an n-party MPC protocol Π into a public-coin sigma protocol Σ.

Let R be an NP relation, and f_R is a functionality corresponding to R such that

$$f_R(Y, y_1, ..., y_n) = 1 \text{ if and only if } (Y, \bigoplus_{i \in [n]} y_i) \in R.$$

Let COM be a commitment scheme with statistical binding and computational hiding, and $ck \leftarrow \mathsf{COM.Gen}(1^\lambda)$ be a commitment key known to both the prover $\mathcal{P}$ and the verifier $\mathcal{V}$.[1] Let Π be an $(n-1)$-private-n-party MPC protocol realizing f_R. We construct a sigma protocol $\Sigma^{\mathsf{COM}}_{\Pi,R,\ell} = \langle \mathcal{P}, \mathcal{V} \rangle$ for the NP relation R as follows. Note that we run $\ell = \Omega(\lambda)$ executions of Π in parallel to reduce the soundness error.

1. The setup algorithm returns $ck \leftarrow \mathsf{COM.Gen}(1^\lambda)$ as the common reference string.
2. For $j \in [\ell]$, $\mathcal{P}$ proceeds as follows:
   (a) Randomly sample $y_1^{(j)}, ..., y_{n-1}^{(j)}$, and set $y_n^{(j)} := y \bigoplus_{i\in[n-1]} y_i^{(j)}$.
   (b) Emulate "in their head" the execution of Π with inputs $(Y, y_1^{(j)}, ..., y_n^{(j)})$ and obtain views $\mathsf{View}_1^{(j)}, ..., \mathsf{View}_n^{(j)}$.
   (c) For $i \in [n]$, $(c_i^{(j)}, d_i^{(j)}) \leftarrow \mathsf{COM.Com}(ck, \mathsf{View}_i^{(j)})$.
3. $\mathcal{P}$ sends $(c_i^{(j)})_{i\in[n],j\in[\ell]}$ to $\mathcal{V}$.
4. $\mathcal{V}$ sends $(u^{(j)})_{j\in[\ell]}$ as the challenge to $\mathcal{P}$, where $u^{(j)} \in [n]$ is independently sampled at random for all $j \in [\ell]$.
5. $\mathcal{P}$ sends $(\mathsf{View}^{(j)}_{i\neq u^{(j)}}, d^{(j)}_{i\neq u^{(j)}})_{i\in[n],j\in[\ell]}$ to $\mathcal{V}$.
6. $\mathcal{V}$ accepts if and only if the followings hold for all $j \in [\ell]$.
   (a) For all $i \in [n]\backslash\{u^{(j)}\}$, $(\mathsf{View}_i^{(j)}, d_i^{(j)})$ is the correct opening of commitment $c_i^{(j)}$.
   (b) For all $i \in [n] \setminus \{u^{(j)}\}$, P_i finally output 1 (in the j-th execution).
   (c) For all distinct $i, i' \in [n] \setminus \{u^{(j)}\}$, $\mathsf{View}_i^{(j)}$ and $\mathsf{View}_{i'}^{(j)}$ are consistent with each other.

Theorem 1. *Assume $n \geq 3$ be a constant. If Π realizes f_R with perfect correctness and either perfect, statistical, or computational $(n-1)$-privacy, and* COM *be a commitment protocol with statistical binding and computational hiding, then $\Sigma^{\mathsf{COM}}_{\Pi,R,\ell}$ described above is a public-coin sigma protocol for R.*

We refer to the full version [4] for the proof of Theorem 1.

The 2-private 3-party GMW protocol [11,12] is prehaps the simplest instance that is appliable for the above MPCitH transformation. We refer to [14] for more MPC protocols in the literature.

The above described sigma protocol Σ (from the MPCitH paradigm) can further be transferred into a non-interactive zero-knowledge (NIZK) argument scheme via the Fiat-Shamir transform [9] in the random oracle model (ROM). We omit the formal proof here.

---

[1] In our construction of universal adaptor signatures, the commitment scheme of the MPCitH paradigm is replaced with an extractable commitment scheme where the commitment key and the trapdoor are generated by the signer. Here we present the core construction of the MPCitH protocol as a warm-up of our construction in Sect. 3, and omit the generation of the commitment key.

3 Universal Adaptor Signatures from the MPCitH Paradigm

In this section we present our generic construction of universal adaptor signatures (UAS) from the MPCitH paradigm. Let R be a hard relation, and f is a functionality corresponding to R such that

$$f_R(Y, y_1, ..., y_n) = 1 \text{ if and only if } (Y, \bigoplus_{i \in [n]} y_i) \in R.$$

Let SIG be a signature scheme, eCOM be an extractable commitment scheme as defined in Sect. 2.1, Π be an n-party MPC protocol securly realizing the functionality f_R, $\ell = \Omega(\lambda)$, and $\mathsf{H} : \{0,1\}^* \to [n]^\ell$ be a random oracle. Our universal adaptor signature scheme UAS is constructed as follows.

- $\mathsf{Gen}(1^\lambda)$. The key generation algorithm returns $(pk, sk) \leftarrow \mathsf{SIG.Gen}(1^\lambda)$.
- $\mathsf{pSign}(sk, m, Y)$. On inputs sk, m and instance Y, the pre-signing algorithm does the following.
  1. $(ck, td) \leftarrow \mathsf{eCOM.TdGen}(1^\lambda; r)$, where r is the randomness uniformly sampled according to the specification of the tradpoor key generation algorithm of eCOM.
  2. $\bar{\sigma} \leftarrow \mathsf{SIG.Sign}(sk, (m, Y, ck))$.
  3. Return $\tilde{\sigma} := (r, \bar{\sigma})$.
- $\mathsf{pVer}(pk, m, Y, \tilde{\sigma})$. On inputs pk, m, Y, and $\tilde{\sigma} = (r, \bar{\sigma})$, the pre-verification algorithm does as follows.
  1. Compute $(ck, td) := \mathsf{eCOM.TdGen}(1^\lambda; r)$.
  2. Return $\mathsf{SIG.Ver}(pk, (m, Y, ck), \bar{\sigma})$.
- $\mathsf{Adapt}(pk, m, \tilde{\sigma}, y)$. On inputs pk, m, $\tilde{\sigma} = (r, \bar{\sigma})$ and witness y, the adaption algorithm does the following.
  - Compute $(ck, td) := \mathsf{eCOM.TdGen}(1^\lambda; r)$.
  - Generate a zero-knowledge proof $\pi = (cmt, rsp)$ for instance Y through the MPCitH paradigm and the Fiat-Shamir transform. In more detail, π is computed as follows:
    1. For $j \in [\ell]$, randomly sample $y_1^{(j)}, ..., y_{n-1}^{(j)}$, and set $y_n^{(j)} := y \bigoplus_{i \in [n-1]} y_i^{(j)}$.
    2. For $j \in [\ell]$, emulate the execution of Π with inputs $(Y, y_1^{(j)}, ..., y_n^{(j)})$ and obtain views $\mathsf{View}_1^{(j)}, ..., \mathsf{View}_n^{(j)}$.
    3. Set $cmt := (c_i^{(j)})_{i \in [n], j \in [\ell]}$, where $(c_i^{(j)}, d_i^{(j)}) \leftarrow \mathsf{eCOM.Com}(ck, \mathsf{View}_i^{(j)})$ for $i \in [n]$ and $j \in [\ell]$.
    4. Compute $\mathsf{H}(m, Y, ck, \bar{\sigma}, cmt) = (u^{(1)}, ..., u^{(\ell)})$.
    5. Set $rsp := (\mathsf{View}_{i \neq u^{(j)}}^{(j)}, d_{i \neq u^{(j)}}^{(j)})_{j \in [\ell]}$.
  - Return $\sigma := (Y, ck, \bar{\sigma}, \pi := (cmt, rsp))$.
- $\mathsf{Sign}(sk, m)$. On inputs sk and message m, the signing algorithm does the following.

1. Sample a fresh instance-witness pair via $(Y, y) \leftarrow \mathsf{Sample}(R)$.
2. $\tilde{\sigma} \leftarrow \mathsf{pSign}(sk, m, Y)$.
3. Return $\sigma \leftarrow \mathsf{Adapt}(pk, m, \tilde{\sigma}, y)$.

- $\mathsf{Ver}(pk, m, \sigma)$. On inputs pk, m, and $\sigma = (Y, ck, \bar{\sigma}, \pi)$, the verification algorithm returns 1 if the followings hold and 0 otherwise.
  1. $\mathsf{SIG.Ver}(pk, (m, Y, ck), \bar{\sigma}) = 1$.
  2. π is a valid zero-knowledge proof, where the verification in proceeds as follows.
     (a) Parse $\pi = (cmt, rsp) = \left((c_i^{(j)})_{i\in[n],j\in[\ell]}, (\mathsf{View}_i^{(j)}, d_i^{(j)})_{i\in G^{(j)},j\in[\ell]}\right)$ with $G^{(j)} \subset [n]$ and $|G^{(j)}| = n-1$.
     (b) Compute $\mathsf{H}(m, Y, ck, \bar{\sigma}, cmt) = (u^{(1)}, ..., u^{(\ell)})$.
     (c) Output 1 if and only if the following hold for all $j \in [\ell]$:
        i. $G^{(j)} = [n] \setminus \{u^{(j)}\}$;
        ii. $\mathsf{eCOM.Ver}(ck, c_i^{(j)}, \mathsf{View}_i^{(j)}, d_i^{(j)}) = 1$ for $i \in G^{(j)}$ (all openings of the commitments are correct).
        iii. For $i \in G^{(j)}$, party P_i finally outputs 1 (in the j-th execution).
        iv. Every pair of distinct views in $(\mathsf{View}_i^{(j)})_{i\in G^{(j)}}$ are consistent.
- $\mathsf{Ext}(pk, m, Y, \tilde{\sigma}, \sigma)$. On inputs pk, m, Y, $\tilde{\sigma} = (r, \bar{\sigma})$ and $\sigma = (Y', ck', \bar{\sigma}', \pi)$, the adaption algorithm proceeds as follows.
  1. Compute $\mathsf{eCOM.TdGen}(1^\lambda; r) = (ck, td)$ and $\mathsf{H}(m, Y, ck, \bar{\sigma}, cmt) = (u^{(1)}, ..., u^{(\ell)})$.
  2. If $(Y' \neq Y) \vee (ck' \neq ck)$, return $\perp$.
  3. If $\mathsf{Ver}(pk, m, \sigma) = 0$, return $\perp$.
  4. Parse $\pi = (cmt, rsp)$ and $cmt = (c_i^{(j)})_{i\in[n],j\in[\ell]}$. For $j \in [\ell]$ and $i \in [n]$, $\mathsf{View}_i^{(j)} \leftarrow \mathsf{eCOM.Ext}(td, c_i^{(j)})$.
  5. Let $y_i^{(j)}$ be the private input of $\mathsf{View}_i^{(j)}$. If there exist $j^* \in [\ell]$ such that $(Y, \bigoplus_{i\in[n]} y_i^{(j^*)}) \in R$, return $y := \bigoplus_{i\in[n]} y_i^{(j^*)}$. Otherwise, return $\perp$.

Theorem 2. *If* SIG *is an UF-CMA-secure signature scheme,* eCOM *is an extractable commitment scheme with extractability, statistical binding, computational hiding, and κ-min-entropy ($\kappa = \Omega(\lambda)$), R is a hard relation, Π is an n-party MPC protocol realizing f_R with $(n-1)$-privacy, and* H *works as a (programmable) random oracle, then* UAS *constructed above is a universal adaptor signature scheme with UF-CMA security, witness extractability, pre-signature adaptability, and witness hiding.*

Proof. The correctness of UAS is guaranteed by the correctness of SIG, the verification correctness and extractability of eCOM, and the correctness of Π.

Now we prove the security of UAS.

Witness Extractability. Let $\mathcal{A}$ be an adversary against the witness extractability of UAS, and (m^*, σ^*) be $\mathcal{A}$'s final output, where $\sigma^* = (Y^*, ck^*, \bar{\sigma}^*, \pi^*)$. Recall that for $\mathcal{A}$ to win in the witness extractability experiment (cf. Definition 11), it must hold that

1. $\mathsf{SIG.Ver}(pk, (m^*, Y^*, ck^*), \bar{\sigma}^*) = 1$, π^* is a zero-knowledge proof for instance Y^* that the verifier accepts, and $\mathcal{A}$ never asks $\textsc{Sign}(m^*)$.
2. The witness extraction fails for all $(Y, \tilde{\sigma} = (r, \bar{\sigma}) \in \mathcal{T}[m^*])$.

We analyze $\mathcal{A}$'s advantage in two cases.

- **Case 1.** There exists no item $(Y, \tilde{\sigma} = (r, \bar{\sigma})) \in \mathcal{T}[m^*]$ with $\mathsf{eCOM.TdGen}(1^\lambda; r) = (ck, td)$ such that, $Y = Y^*$ and $ck = ck^*$.
- **Case 2.** There exist an item $(Y, \tilde{\sigma} = (r, \bar{\sigma})) \in \mathcal{T}[m^*]$ with $\mathsf{eCOM.TdGen}(1^\lambda; r) = (ck, td)$ such that, $Y = Y^*$ and $ck = ck^*$.

Recall that $\mathcal{A}$ never queries $\textsc{Sign}(m^*)$, and $\bar{\sigma}^*$ is a valid signature w.r.t. (m^*, Y^*, ck^*). If Case 1 happens, then we can construct a reduction algorithm $\mathcal{A}'$ that breaks the UF-CMA security of the underlying signature scheme SIG. We omit the details of the reduction here.

Now consider $\mathcal{A}$'s advantage in Case 2. Let Q_{H} be the total number of hash queries by $\mathcal{A}$. We first analyze the subcase where $\mathcal{A}$ has queried $\mathsf{H}(q^*) = \mathsf{H}(m^*, Y^*, ck^*, \bar{\sigma}^*, (c_i^{(j)})_{i\in[n], j\in[\ell]})$ before outputting $(m^*, \sigma^* = (Y^*, ck^*, \bar{\sigma}^*, \pi^*))$, where $\pi^* = \Big((c_i^{(j)})_{i\in[n], j\in[\ell]}, (\mathsf{View}_i^{(j)}, d_i^{(j)})_{i\in G^{(j)}, j\in[\ell]}\Big)$.

We call $q = (m, Y, ck, \bar{\sigma}, cmt = (c_i^{(j)})_{i\in[n], j\in[\ell]})$ a *good* query, if there exists an item $(Y, \tilde{\sigma} = (r, \bar{\sigma})) \in \mathcal{T}[m]$ such that $\mathsf{eCOM.TdGen}(1^\lambda; r) = (ck, td)$. It is easy to see that in Case 2, the query q^* that related to $\mathcal{A}$'s final forgery is a good query.

For good query $q = (m, Y, ck, \bar{\sigma}, cmt = (c_i^{(j)})_{i\in[n], j\in[\ell]})$, define the following two events:

- Fail: the event that there exists no $j \in [\ell]$ such that $(Y, \bigoplus_{i\in n} y_i^{(j)}) \in R$, where $\overline{\mathsf{View}_i^{(j)}} \leftarrow \mathsf{eCOM.Ext}(td, c_i^{(j)})$, and $y_i^{(j)}$ is the private input of $\overline{\mathsf{View}_i^{(j)}}$ for $i \in [n]$ and $j \in [\ell]$. If Fail happens to a good query q, we also denote as $\mathsf{Fail}(q) = 1$.
- Pass: the event that there exists $\bar{\sigma}'$ and $rsp = (\mathsf{View}_i^{(j)}, d_i^{(j)})_{i\in G^{(j)}, j\in[\ell]}$ such that $(m, \sigma = (Y, ck, \bar{\sigma}', cmt, rsp))$ passes the verification of UAS. If Pass happens to a good query q, we also denote as $\mathsf{Pass}(q) = 1$.

Given a good query $q = (m, Y, ck, \bar{\sigma}, cmt = (c_i^{(j)})_{i\in[n], j\in[\ell]})$, we analyze the probability that $\mathsf{Fail}(q) = 1$ and $\mathsf{Pass}(q) = 1$ in Case 2. Let $(Y, \tilde{\sigma} = (r, \bar{\sigma})) \in \mathcal{T}[m]$ and $\mathsf{eCOM.TdGen}(1^\lambda; r) = (ck, td)$. Recall that eCOM has extractability and statistical binding. Therefore, for $i \in [n]$ and $j \in [\ell]$, except for a negligible binding error, the commitment $c_i^{(j)}$ can only be opened to $\overline{\mathsf{View}_i^{(j)}} \leftarrow \mathsf{eCOM.Ext}(td, c_i^{(j)})$. By Lemma 1, if Fail happens, then there exist a group of indexes $(\hat{i}^{(1)}, ..., \hat{i}^{(\ell)}) \in [n]^\ell$ such that for any $j \in [\ell]$, either $\overline{\mathsf{View}_{\hat{i}^{(j)}}^{(j)}}$ exposes an output of 0 for party $P_{\hat{i}^{(j)}}$, or $\overline{\mathsf{View}_{\hat{i}^{(j)}}^{(j)}}$ is inconsistent with some other view $\overline{\mathsf{View}_{i\neq\hat{i}^{(j)}}^{(j)}}$.

Let $\mathsf{H}(q) = (u^{(1)}, ..., u^{(\ell)}) \in [n]^\ell$, and let $(\hat{i}^{(1)}, ..., \hat{i}^{(\ell)}) \in [n]^\ell$ be defined as above. For a message-signature pair $(m, \sigma = (Y, ck, \bar{\sigma}', cmt =$

$(c_i^{(j)})_{i\in[n],j\in[\ell]}, rsp = (\mathsf{View}_i^{(j)}, d_i^{(j)})_{i\in G^{(j)},j\in[\ell]}))$ that passes the verification, it must hold that

1. $G^{(j)} = [n] \setminus \{u^{(j)}\}$;
2. For $i \in G^{(j)}$: $\mathsf{eCOM.Ver}(ck, c_i^{(j)}, \mathsf{View}_i^{(j)}, d_i^{(j)}) = 1$, and $\mathsf{View}_i^{(j)} = \overline{\mathsf{View}}_i^{(j)}$.
3. For $i \in G^{(j)}$, party P_i finally outputs 1 (in the j-th execution).
4. Every pair of distinct views in $(\mathsf{View}_i^{(j)})_{i\in G^{(j)}}$ are consistent.

Therefore, for a good query q, if Fail happens, then Pass happens only if $(u^{(1)}, ..., u^{(\ell)}) = (\hat{i}^{(1)}, ..., \hat{i}^{(\ell)})$. Since H is a random oracle and $\mathsf{H}(q)$ remains undefined until $\mathsf{H}(q)$ is invoked by $\mathcal{A}$, we have that

$$\Pr[\mathsf{Pass}(q) \wedge \mathsf{Fail}(q) \wedge \text{Case } 2] \leq \Pr[\mathsf{Pass}(q) \mid (\mathsf{Fail}(q) \wedge \text{Case } 2)] \leq 1/n^{\ell}.$$

Let $(m^*, \sigma^* = (Y^*, ck^*, \bar{\sigma}^*, \pi^*))$ be $\mathcal{A}$'s final forgery. If $\mathcal{A}$ successes in Case 2, then there must exist a related good query $\mathsf{H}(q^*) = \mathsf{H}(m^*, Y^*, ck^*, \bar{\sigma}^*, cmt = c_i^{(j)})_{i\in[n],j\in[\ell]})$ such that $\mathsf{Pass}(q^*) = 1$ and $\mathsf{Fail}(q^*) = 1$. There are in total Q_{H} random oracle queries by $\mathcal{A}$. Therefore, the probability that $\mathcal{A}$ successes is bounded by Q_{H}/n^{ℓ}.

Then we consider the subcase of Case 2 where $\mathcal{A}$ has never queried $\mathsf{H}(q^*) = \mathsf{H}(m^*, Y^*, ck^*, \bar{\sigma}^*, (c_i^{(j)})_{i\in[n],j\in[\ell]})$. Similar to the analysis above, it is easy to see that $(\mathsf{Fail}(q^*) = 1 \wedge \mathsf{Pass}(q^*) = 1)$ cannot happen unless $\mathcal{A}$ successfully guess the output of $\mathsf{H}(q^*)$, which happens with probability $1/n^{\ell}$.

In summary, there exist an PPT adversary $\mathcal{A}'$ and a negligible function $negl(\cdot)$ such that

$$\mathsf{Adv}^{we}_{\mathsf{UAS},\mathcal{A}}(\lambda) \leq \mathsf{Adv}^{uf}_{\mathsf{SIG},\mathcal{A}'}(\lambda) + \frac{Q_{\mathsf{H}} + 1}{n^{\ell}} + negl(\lambda),$$

where Q_{H} is the total number of random oracle queries by $\mathcal{A}$. This concludes the proof of witness extractability.

UF-CMA Security. Let $\mathcal{A}$ be an adversary against the UF-CMA security of UAS, and $(m^*, \sigma^* = (Y^*, ck^*, \bar{\sigma}^*, \pi^*))$ be $\mathcal{A}$'s final forgery in the unforgeability experiment (cf. Definition 10). Recall that for $\mathcal{A}$ to win, it must hold that

1. $\mathsf{SIG.Ver}(pk, (m^*, ck^*, Y^*), \bar{\sigma}^*) = 1$, and π^* is a valid zero-knowledge proof for instance Y^*.
2. $\mathcal{A}$ never queries $\textsc{Sign}(m^*)$, and
3. (a) either $\mathcal{T}[m^*] = \varnothing$ (i.e., $\mathcal{A}$ never asks $\textsc{pSign}(m^*, Y)$ for any Y), or
   (b) for all $(Y, \tilde{\sigma} = (r, \bar{\sigma})) \in \mathcal{T}[m^*]$, it holds that $Y \in \mathcal{Y}$ (i.e., $\mathcal{A}$ only queries $\textsc{pSign}(m^*, Y)$ for Y whose witness is unknown to it).

We first analyze the case $1 \wedge 2 \wedge (a)$. It is easy to see that in this case, $\mathcal{A}$ does not get any signature on message $(m^*, \cdot, \cdot)$ during either pre-signing queries or signing queries. Therefore, we can construct a reduction algorithm $\mathcal{A}_1$ that breaks the UF-CMA security of SIG.

Then we analyze the case $1 \wedge 2 \wedge (b)$. We further divide it into the following two subcases.

(i) For all $(Y, \tilde{\sigma} = (r, \bar{\sigma})) \in \mathcal{T}[m^*]$ and $\mathsf{eCOM.TdGen}(1^\lambda; r) = (ck, td)$, it holds that $(Y, ck) \neq (Y^*, ck^*)$.
This means that $\mathcal{A}$ does not obtain a signature on message (m^*, Y^*, ck^*) during either pre-signing queries or signing queries. Consequently, $\mathcal{A}$ breaks the UF-CMA security of the underlying SIG.

(ii) There exists $(Y, \tilde{\sigma} = (r, \bar{\sigma}))) \in \mathcal{T}[m^*]$ and $\mathsf{eCOM.TdGen}(1^\lambda; r) = (ck, td)$, such that $(Y, ck) = (Y^*, ck^*)$.
This means that $\mathcal{A}$ adapts some pre-signature to a valid full signature without knowing a witness. We analyze this case by showing an algorithm $\mathcal{A}_2$ such that, once the event $(1 \wedge 2 \wedge (b) \wedge (ii))$ happens, $\mathcal{A}_2$ is able to break the one-wayness of R.

$\mathcal{A}_2$ first receives an instance $\hat{Y}$ from its own challenger, and then simulates the experiment to $\mathcal{A}$ as follows.

1. $\mathcal{A}_2$ randomly selects $\eta \leftarrow [Q]$ with Q the number of queries to $\textsc{NewY}()$ by $\mathcal{A}$. Then $\mathcal{A}_2$ generates $(pk, sk) \leftarrow \mathsf{SIG.Gen}(1^\lambda)$ and sends pk to $\mathcal{A}$.
2. $\mathcal{A}_2$ simulates the signing oracle $\textsc{Sign}$ and the pre-signing oracle $\textsc{pSign}$ as normal.
3. $\mathcal{A}_2$ simulates the new instance oracle $\textsc{NewY}()$ as normal, except that $\mathcal{A}_2$ returns $\hat{Y}$ upon receiving the η-th query to $\textsc{NewY}()$.
4. $\mathcal{A}_2$ simulates the random oracle H as normal. In more details, $\mathcal{A}_2$ maintains a table $\mathcal{H}$ which is initialized to be empty. Upon receiving a query $\mathsf{H}(q)$, if $\mathcal{H}[q]$ has not been defined, then $\mathcal{A}_2$ randomly samples $ch \leftarrow [n]^\ell$ and define $\mathcal{H}[q] := ch$. Finally $\mathcal{A}_2$ returns $\mathcal{H}[q]$.
5. At last $\mathcal{A}$ outputs $(m^*, \sigma^* = (Y^*, ck^*, \bar{\sigma}^*, \pi^* = (cmt^*, rsp^*)))$. If $Y^* \neq \hat{Y}$ then $\mathcal{A}_2$ aborts immediately. Otherwise, $\mathcal{A}_2$ checks if $(1 \wedge 2 \wedge (b) \wedge (ii))$ holds. If so, $\mathcal{A}_2$ retrieves $(Y^*, \tilde{\sigma} = (r, \bar{\sigma})) \in \mathcal{T}[m^*]$ such that $\mathsf{eCOM.TdGen}(1^\lambda; r) = (\tilde{ck}^*, td^*)$. Let $cmt^* = (c_i^{(j)})_{i \in [n], j \in [\ell]}$. For $j \in [\ell]$ and $i \in [n]$, $\mathcal{A}_2$ extracts the views $\mathsf{View}_i^{(j)} \leftarrow \mathsf{eCOM.Ext}(td^*, c_i^{(j)})$ and hence the private inputs $y_i^{(j)}$. If there exists $j^* \in [\ell]$ such that $(Y^*, \bigoplus_{i \in [n]} y_i^{(j^*)}) \in R$, then $\mathcal{A}_2$ outputs $y := \bigoplus_{i \in [n]} y_i^{(j^*)}$. Otherwise, $\mathcal{A}_2$ outputs $\perp$.

Similar to the analysis of Case 2 in the proof of witness extractability above, we know that for every good query $q = (m, Y, ck, \bar{\sigma}, cmt = (c_i^{(j)})_{i \in [n], j \in [\ell]})$, $\mathcal{A}_2$ successes in extracting a witness for Y except for a negligible probability $1/n^\ell$. Let Q_H be the total number of queries to the random oracle $\mathsf{H}(\cdot)$. Since the query q^* related to $\mathcal{A}$'s final forgery is good in case $(1 \wedge 2 \wedge (b) \wedge (ii))$, $\mathcal{A}_2$ is able to extract a witness of Y^* except for a probability $(Q_\mathsf{H} + 1)/n^\ell$.

In $\mathcal{A}_2$'s simulation, the challenge instance $\hat{Y}$ is randomly embedded into one query during the simulation of $\textsc{NewY}()$, and hence $Y^* = \hat{Y}$ holds with probability $1/Q$, where Q is the number of queries to $\textsc{NewY}()$. Therefore, if $\mathcal{A}$ breaks the unforgeability of UAS in case $(1 \wedge 2 \wedge (b) \wedge (ii))$ with probability ϵ, then $\mathcal{A}_2$ is able to break the one-wayness of the hard relation R with probability at least $\frac{\epsilon - (Q_\mathsf{H}+1)/n^\ell}{Q}$.

In summary, there exist PPT adversaries $\mathcal{A}_1, \mathcal{A}_2$, and a negligible function $negl(\cdot)$ such that

$$\mathsf{Adv}^{uf}_{\mathsf{UAS},\mathcal{A}}(\lambda) \leq \mathsf{Adv}^{uf}_{\mathsf{SIG},\mathcal{A}_1}(\lambda) + Q \cdot \mathsf{Adv}^{ow}_{R,\mathcal{A}_2}(\lambda) + \frac{Q_{\mathsf{H}}+1}{n^{\ell}} + negl(\lambda),$$

which finishes the proof of unforgeability.

Pre-signature Adaptability. Recall that a pre-signature is of the form $\tilde{\sigma} = (r, \bar{\sigma})$, where $\mathsf{eCOM.TdGen}(1^{\lambda}; r) = (ck, td)$ and $\bar{\sigma} \leftarrow \mathsf{SIG.Sign}(sk, (m, Y, ck))$. To adapt it to a full signature, it is only required to attach a zero-knowledge proof π^* for instance Y^*, using ck as the commitment key. The pre-signature adaptability is directly implied by the correctness of Π and the correctness of eCOM.

Witness Hiding. To prove the witness hiding property of UAS, we need to design a simulator Sim which can simulate an adapted signature given (m, Y), which is indistinguishable from a signature generated by the pre-sign-and-adaption paradigm with the knowledge of y.

We design Sim similarly to the signing algorithm, with the only difference being that Sim generates a zero-knowledge proof π for instance Y without knowing a witness y as follows (which, is similar to the zero-knowledge simulator in the proof of Theorem 1 but works in the random oracle model).

In more details, Sim works as follows.

1. $(ck, td) \leftarrow \mathsf{eCOM.TdGen}(1^{\lambda}; r)$, where r is the randomness uniformly sampled according to the specification of eCOM.
2. $\bar{\sigma} \leftarrow \mathsf{SIG.Sign}(sk, (m, Y, ck))$.
3. For all $j \in [\ell]$, independently sample $u^{(j)} \leftarrow [n]$ at random.
4. For all $j \in [\ell]$, randomly sample $y_i^{(j)}$ for $i \in [n] \setminus \{u^{(j)}\}$, and invoke the simulator of the MPC protocol Π to obtain views $(\mathsf{View}_i^{(j)})_{i \in [n] \setminus \{u^{(j)}\}}$.
5. For all $j \in [\ell]$ and $i \in [n] \setminus \{u^{(j)}\}$, $(c_i^{(j)}, d_i^{(j)}) \leftarrow \mathsf{eCOM.Com}(ck, \mathsf{View}_i^{(j)})$.
6. For all $j \in [\ell]$, $(c_{u^{(j)}}^{(j)}, d_{u^{(j)}}^{(j)}) \leftarrow \mathsf{eCOM.Com}(ck, \mathbf{0})$ (where $\mathbf{0}$ denotes an all-zero bit string).
7. Let $cmt := (c_i^{(j)})_{i \in [n], j \in [\ell]}$. Reprogram H such that $\mathsf{H}(m, Y, ck, \bar{\sigma}, cmt) = (u^1, ..., u^{(\ell)})$. If the item already exists in $\mathcal{H}$, then abort and return $\perp$.
8. Finally, return the simulated signature $\sigma := (Y, ck, \bar{\sigma}, \pi := (cmt, rsp))$, where $rsp := \left((\mathsf{View}_i^{(j)})_{i \neq u^{(j)}}, (d_i^{(j)})_{i \neq u^{(j)}}\right)_{j \in [\ell]}$.

We first argue that the simulated transcript distributes computationally close to the transcript by an honest execution, if the reprogramming does not fail.

- The challenge $(u^{(1)}, ..., u^{(\ell)})$ simulated by Sim distributes identically to the honestly generated one since it is uniformly sampled.
- The private inputs in the response rsp simulated by Sim distribute identically to the honestly generated ones, since they are all independent and random strings.

- For every $j \in [\ell]$, the $n-1$ views revealed in the response distribute identically (resp., statistically/computationally close) to the honestly generate ones, due to the $(n-1)$-privacy of the MPC protocol Π.
- For every $j \in [\ell]$, all commitments $c_i^{(j)}$ for $i \in [n] \setminus \{u^{(j)}\}$ are distributed identically. Moreover, the commitment $c_{u^{(j)}}^{(j)}$ will not be revealed in the transcript, and hence $c_{u^{(j)}}^{(j)}$ in the simulation distributes computationally close to the one honestly generated, due to the hiding of eCOM.

Therefore, the simulated signature is distributed computationally close to the honestly generate one.

It is left to prove that the reprogramming fails with a negligible probability $Q_{\mathsf{H}}/2^{\kappa n \ell}$ with Q_{H} the number of hash queries by $\mathcal{A}$, which is guaranteed by the κ-min-entropy of eCOM. As a result, the witness hiding of UAS holds. □

4 Adaptor Signatures on Blockchains

While adaptor signatures (AS) offer an innovative approach to secure transactions and privacy-preserving protocols in decentralized applications, several technical challenges must be addressed during their deployment. These challenges primarily relate to security, efficiency, and the coordination of protocol components. Additionally, shifting some computations to off-chain approaches inherently raises valid concerns that need to be carefully managed.

4.1 Secure Transmission of Pre-Signatures

In the deployment of adaptor signatures, pre-signatures must be exchanged between participants (e.g., Alice and Bob in a cross-chain swap). Ensuring the secure transmission of these pre-signatures is crucial, as any interception could expose sensitive data. Pre-signatures contain critical cryptographic information and must be transmitted over secure channels, such as encrypted communication protocols (e.g., TLS), to prevent man-in-the-middle attacks. If we further assume a public key infrastrcture, the presignature should be encrypted under the public key of the witness holder, prior to transmission.

In the context of AS, if a malicious actor intercepts the message containing the pre-signature, even if they alter the data, no asset loss will occur. This is because the pre-signature verification algorithm will detect any modification, causing the procedure to abort. The worst-case scenario arises when a malicious actor learns the witness by possessing both the pre-signature and the adapted signature. In this case, without paying for the information, an adversary could exploit an insecure transmission channel to deduce the witness. Therefore, ensuring secure communication channels is paramount to protecting sensitive information and maintaining the integrity of the AS process.

4.2 Integrity of Pre-Signature Adaptation

A core component of adaptor signatures (AS) involves adapting pre-signatures into full signatures upon revealing a witness (e.g., a private key or secret). Ensuring the integrity of this adaptation process is essential. Any vulnerability in the adaptation could allow an adversary to forge signatures. Careful implementation of cryptographic primitives and validation of the adaptation is required to avoid security breaches. The associated risks of forgery become greater if the AS algorithm necessitates a trusted setup, as this creates additional dependencies on the trustworthiness of the setup phase. If the setup is compromised or if the trusted entity that performed the setup, behaves maliciously, it could lead to significant security vulnerabilities, allowing unauthorized parties to forge signatures or otherwise undermine the integrity of the AS framework. Therefore, in cases involving a trusted setup, it is crucial that the inputs used during the setup are destroyed after their purpose has been fulfilled to mitigate the risk of exploitation.

4.3 Collusion and Replay Attacks

In scenarios where multiple parties are involved, the potential for collusion exists. An adversary may attempt to collaborate with one or more parties to exploit the adaptor signature mechanism, leading to unauthorized access to assets or information. Additionally, replay attacks may occur if a pre-signature is intercepted and reused in a different context. To mitigate these risks, it is imperative to implement robust protocols for nonce generation and transaction identifiers to ensure that each signature operation is unique and cannot be replayed.

The risk of replay attacks is heightened in account-based models, such as Ethereum, compared to the UTXO (Unspent Transaction Output) model, where transactions are directly tied to input UTXOs. In Ethereum's account-based model, smart contracts can be invoked multiple times, even if it was not the original intention, leading to unintended consequences based on the protocol's design. This vulnerability has made Ethereum susceptible to replay attacks, where a transaction could be executed again, potentially allowing adversaries to exploit the system and access assets without authorization. However, replay attacks can be mitigated if the smart contract implementing the protocol incorporates mechanisms to identify and prevent such invocations, ensuring that each transaction is processed uniquely and as intended.

4.4 Computational Complexity

The computational overhead associated with generating and adapting adaptor signatures can pose challenges, particularly in high-frequency trading environments or scenarios requiring rapid transaction throughput. As the number of participants increases, the complexity of managing the pre-signature and adaptation processes can lead to performance bottlenecks. Optimizing these processes while maintaining security is critical to achieving practical implementations of adaptor signatures (AS) in real-world applications.

To effectively scale up the use of AS, it is essential to identify every aspect of the framework that can be further optimized. Examining the algorithms and protocols used for signature generation and adaptation can reveal opportunities for efficiency improvements. In our specific case, the owner of the witness (e.g., the secret in an AS) can precompute the MPC-in-the-Head while the sender is transmitting the pre-signature to them. This concurrent precomputation could further enhance the system's efficiency by overlapping processes that would typically be sequential, thus reducing the time needed for signature adaptation and overall transaction finalization. By streamlining these processes and minimizing computational requirements, the AS framework can be better suited for high-demand applications and broader adoption in various sectors.

Acknowledgments. Michele Ciampi and Xiangyu Liu were partially funded by Sunday Group, Inc. Ioannis Tzannetos was funded by AnalytiXIN. Vassilis Zikas was funded in part by NSF grant No. 2055599 and Sunday Group, Inc.

References

1. Aumayr, L., et al.: Generalized bitcoin-compatible channels. IACR Cryptology ePrint Archive, p. 476 (2020)
2. Aumayr, L., et al.: Generalized channels from limited blockchain scripts and adaptor signatures. In: Tibouchi, M., Wang, H. (eds.) ASIACRYPT 2021. LNCS, vol. 13091, pp. 635–664. Springer, Cham (2021). https://doi.org/10.1007/978-3-030-92075-3_22
3. Blum, M.: How to prove a theorem so no one else can claim it. In: Proceedings of the International Congress of Mathematicians, vol. 1, p. 2. Citeseer (1986)
4. Ciampi, M., Liu, X., Tzannetos, I., Zikas, V.: Universal adaptor signatures from blackbox multi-party computation. Cryptology ePrint Archive (2024)
5. Dai, W., Okamoto, T., Yamamoto, G.: Stronger security and generic constructions for adaptor signatures. In: INDOCRYPT 2022, Kolkata, India, 11–14 December 2022, Proceedings, vol. 13774, pp. 52–77. Springer, Cham (2022)
6. Dao, Q., Grubbs, P.: Spartan and bulletproofs are simulation-extractable (for free!). In: Advances in Cryptology - EUROCRYPT 2023, Lyon, France, 23–27 April 2023, Proceedings, Part II, vol. 14005, pp. 531–562. Springer, Cham (2023)
7. Deshpande, A., Herlihy, M.: Privacy-preserving cross-chain atomic swaps. In: International Conference on Financial Cryptography and Data Security, pp. 540–549. Springer, Cham (2020)
8. Esgin, M.F., Ersoy, O., Erkin, Z.: Post-quantum adaptor signatures and payment channel networks. In: Chen, L., Li, N., Liang, K., Schneider, S. (eds.) ESORICS 2020. LNCS, vol. 12309, pp. 378–397. Springer, Cham (2020). https://doi.org/10.1007/978-3-030-59013-0_19
9. Fiat, A., Shamir, A.: How to prove yourself: practical solutions to identification and signature problems. In: Advances in Cryptology - CRYPTO 1986, Santa Barbara, California, USA, 1986, Proceedings, vol. 263, pp. 186–194. Springer, Cham (1986)
10. Goldreich, O.: The Foundations of Cryptography - Volume 1: Basic Techniques. Cambridge University Press (2001)

11. Goldreich, O.: The Foundations of Cryptography - Volume 2: Basic Applications. Cambridge University Press (2004)
12. Goldreich, O., Micali, S., Wigderson, A.: How to play any mental game or A completeness theorem for protocols with honest majority. In: Proceedings of the 19th Annual ACM Symposium on Theory of Computing, pp. 218–229. ACM, New York (1987)
13. Gugger, J.: Bitcoin-monero cross-chain atomic swap. Cryptology ePrint Archive (2020)
14. Ishai, Y., Kushilevitz, E., Ostrovsky, R., Sahai, A.: Zero-knowledge from secure multiparty computation. In: Proceedings of the 39th Annual ACM Symposium on Theory of Computing, San Diego, California, USA, 11–13 June 2007, pp. 21–30. ACM (2007)
15. Karp, R.M.: Reducibility among combinatorial problems. In: Proceedings of a symposium on the Complexity of Computer Computations. The IBM Research Symposia Series, pp. 85–103. Plenum Press, New York (1972)
16. Klamti, J.B., Hasan, M.A.: Post-quantum two-party adaptor signature based on coding theory. Cryptography **6**(1), 6 (2022)
17. Liu, X., Ioannis, T., Zikas, V.: Adaptor signatures: new security definition and A generic construction for NP relations. IACR Cryptology ePrint Archive, p. 1051 (2024)
18. Nakamoto, S.: Bitcoin: a peer-to-peer electronic cash system. Satoshi Nakamoto (2008)
19. Poelstra, A.: Scriptless scripts. Presentation Slides (2017). https://download.wpsoftware.net/bitcoin/wizardry/mw-slides/2017-03-mit-bitcoin-expo/slides.pdf. Accessed May 2024
20. Poelstra, A.: Mimblewimble and scriptless scripts. Presentation Slides (2018). https://download.wpsoftware.net/bitcoin/wizardry/mw-slides/2018-01-10-rwc/slides.pdf. Accessed May 2024
21. Renan, F., Kutas, P.: Sqiasignhd: Sqisignhd adaptor signature. IACR Cryptology ePrint Archive, p. 561 (2024)
22. Santis, A.D., Crescenzo, G.D., Persiano, G.: Necessary and sufficient assumptions for non-iterative zero-knowledge proofs of knowledge for all NP relations. In: ICALP 2000, vol. 1853, pp. 451–462. Springer, Cham (2000)
23. Tairi, E., Moreno-Sanchez, P., Maffei, M.: Post-quantum adaptor signature for privacy-preserving off-chain payments. In: Borisov, N., Diaz, C. (eds.) FC 2021. LNCS, vol. 12675, pp. 131–150. Springer, Heidelberg (2021). https://doi.org/10.1007/978-3-662-64331-0_7
24. Tu, B., Zhang, M., Yu, C.: Efficient ECDSA-based adaptor signature for batched atomic swaps. In: ISC 2022, Bali, Indonesia, 18–22 December 2022, Proceedings, vol. 13640, pp. 175–193. Springer, Cham (2022)

White-box Crypto

Affine Equivalence-Based Key-Recovery Attacks on White-Box Implementations of the SM4 Block Cipher

Zexuan Chen[1] and Jiqiang Lu[1,2](✉)

[1] School of Cyber Science and Technology, Beihang University, Beijing 100083, China
{czxyeah,lvjiqiang}@buaa.edu.cn
[2] HangZhou Innovation Institute, Beihang University, Hangzhou 310051, China

Abstract. The SM4 block cipher has a generalised Feistel structure with four 32-bit branches and a 128-bit user key, which is a Chinese national standard and an ISO international standard. Following Chow et al.'s seminal work of white-box cryptography in 2002, a few white-box SM4 implementations with external encodings have been proposed since 2009, among which, except the one using linear internal encodings, all the others (i.e. the ones using affine internal encodings) are regarded as (practically) secure against key-recovery attack so far, partially because secret constant parts from affine encodings hinder some attack methods under Feistel structure, like algebraic and affine equivalence attacks, though several published attacks recovered a masked key with such constants, while by contrast all published white-box AES implementations have been practically broken mainly with such attack methods. As a consequence, one may think that Feistel structure is better than SPN structure in terms of their security on white-box cryptography. In this paper, we apply Derbez et al.'s affine equivalence algorithm to the generalised Feistel cipher SM4, and give an affine equivalence-based attack framework to recover the original user key of these white-box SM4 implementations with a very practical complexity of about $t^2 \cdot 2^{32}$ for affine encodings or $t \cdot 2^{27}$ for linear encodings (with t being a small integer 1 or 2), by exploring implementation particulars and exploiting a differential meet-in-the-middle approach and the SM4 key expansion formula to filter out a few secret parameters. Finally, as examples, we apply this framework to recover the original user key of Xiao and Lai's and Bai and Wu's white-box SM4 implementations for the first time, with a time complexity of 2^{32} and 2^{34} respectively, and to recover the original user key of Shi et al.'s white-box SM4 implementation with a time complexity of 2^{27}, significantly lower than the previous attack complexity of 2^{49}. Our work shows how to apply Derbez et al.'s affine equivalence algorithm to a Feistel cipher and all such white-box SM4 implementations are not practically secure like white-box AES, and designers of white-box implementations of Feistel ciphers should pay attention to this framework.

Keywords: White-box cryptography · SM4 block cipher · Affine equivalence · Self-equivalence

A. Patra (Ed.): CT-RSA 2025, LNCS 15598, pp. 401–425, 2025.
https://doi.org/10.1007/978-3-031-88661-4_17

1 Introduction

In 2002, Chow et al. [9] introduced white-box cryptography, which is concerned with security in so-called white-box security model: an attacker has full control over the execution environment and execution details of a software implementation, and Chow et al. constructed a white-box AES implementation with a series of sequential networked white-box tables, where each white-box table hides the original input or output with one or more secret linear or/and non-linear encodings (called external encoding(s) when the original input or output is plaintext or ciphertext, and internal encoding(s) otherwise), and the input encoding(s) of a white-box table is the inverse of the output encoding(s) of the previous white-box table (protected plaintext if no), so that the original data can be protected and preserved. Since then, other white-box AES implementations with external encodings like [1,3,13,18,24] have been proposed, but all have been practically broken mainly with algebraic attack, affine equivalence attack and collision attack [3,5,10,11,14,17].

The affine equivalence problem [6] studies whether two non-linear bijections are affine equivalent: given two (non-linear) $n \times n$-bit bijections $\mathcal{F}$ and $\mathcal{S}$, find two invertible $n \times n$-bit affine mappings $\mathcal{A}$ and $\mathcal{B}$ such that $\mathcal{F}(\cdot) = \mathcal{B}(\mathcal{S}(\mathcal{A}(\cdot)))$ (note that it degenerates into the self-equivalence problem $\mathcal{S}(\cdot) = \mathcal{B}(\mathcal{S}(\mathcal{A}(\cdot)))$ when $\mathcal{F} = \mathcal{S}$ and into the linear equivalence problem when $\mathcal{A}$ and $\mathcal{B}$ are linear mappings [6]). It has wide applicability in cryptanalysis nowadays, for example, $\mathcal{S}$ can represent the S-box layer of a round of some block cipher and $\mathcal{F}$ can represent a white-box implementation of this round with secret input and output affine encodings. In 2003, Biryukov et al. [6] gave a solution algorithm with a time complexity of $O(n^3 \cdot 2^{2n})$. In 2018, Dinur [12] gave a solution algorithm with a time complexity of $O(n^3 \cdot 2^n)$; and Derbez et al. [11] gave a refined algorithm for the cases that $\mathcal{S}$ consists of several parallel identical or distinct S-boxes under whether the S-box is self-equivalent, which targets for an Substitution-Permutation Network (SPN) block cipher and works on two consecutive rounds when attacking Baek et al.'s white-box AES implementation [1].

Different from AES, the SM4 [22] block cipher, formerly known as SMS4 [21], has a generalised Feistel structure, which became a Chinese national standard [22] in 2016 and an ISO international standard [23] in 2021. The main research results on white-box SM4 implementation with external encodings are as follows. In 2009, under Chow et al.'s white-box framework, Xiao and Lai [25] proposed a white-box SM4 implementation using affine internal encodings (and general XOR operations), following their white-box AES implementation [24]. In 2015, Shi et al. [20] proposed a lightweight white-box SM4 implementation using linear internal encodings and random numbers under the dual cipher concept [4]. In 2016, Bai and Wu [2] proposed a white-box SM4 implementation by expressing an original data byte as two or more shares protected with different affine encodings. In 2018, Lin et al. [15] applied Biryukov et al.'s affine equivalence result [6] to give a key-recovery attack on Shi et al.'s white-box SM4 implementation with a time complexity of 2^{49}, Pan et al. [19] showed that the security of Xiao and Lai's and Bai and Wu's white-box SM4 implementations is mainly based on the constants of affine encodings, which have an equivalent space of approximately 2^{48} and 2^{144}, respectively. In 2020, Yao and Chen [26] proposed a white-box SM4 implementation based on dummy states and affine encodings. Recently, Lu et al. [16] concluded that the collision-based attacks of [14,17] are not applicable to white-box SM4 implementations due to the linear transformation of SM4, because the rank of the relevant linear system is much smaller than the number of involved unknowns. (Notice that several other published attacks are not mentioned here, for they have been shown to be incorrect [16,19].) In short, except Lin et al.'s attack on Shi et al.'s white-box SM4 implementation with a time complexity of 2^{49}, there is no whatsoever key-recovery attack on the white-box SM4 implementations, particularly those with affine encodings. This is partially because for Feistel structure, a round key is mixed with the secret constants of the input affine encodings of this round function, and the XOR value of a branch with the output of this round function is an input to the next round function, so the next round key is mixed additionally with the secret constants from the affine encodings of this branch, which are different from round to round. This is why Derbez et al. [11] claimed the applicability of their affine equivalence algorithm only for attacking SPN ciphers.

In this paper, we apply Derbez et al.'s affine equivalence algorithm to SM4. First, we give a specific expression of the 2040 pairs of affine mappings for the self-equivalence property of the SM4 S-box under Biryukov et al.'s self-equivalence algorithm, and verify its correctness both theoretically and experimentally, which is a primary foundation for our attacks. Then, we make an affine equivalence-based key-recovery attack framework on the white-box SM4 implementations, consisting of three phases: (1) use Derbez et al.'s affine equivalence algorithm and the above-mentioned specific expression for SM4 S-box self-equivalence to obtain all possible 2040 pairs of candidate input and output affine encodings for each of the four S-boxes in white-box implementation of a round function, where input encoding includes the corresponding round key byte; (2) use a differential meet-in-the-middle approach on two consecutive rounds to cancel the effect of the secret constant from the affine encoding of the branch XORing with the output of the round function of the former round, and identify the correct input affine encodings of the two round functions from all candidates; (3) repeat the above phases for subsequent more rounds to recover more secret white-box parameters, so that an expression with only one secret 32-bit unknown can be constructed by SM4's key expansion formula, solving which with exhaustive search leads to the recovery of a round key and the original user key. As examples, we apply this attack framework to Xiao and Lai's, Bai and Wu's and Shi et al.'s white-box SM4 implementations with a time complexity of 2^{32}, 2^{34} and 2^{27}, respectively, recovering their original user key very practically for the first time.

Our work shows how to apply Derbez et al.'s affine equivalence algorithm from SPN ciphers to a generalised Feistel cipher, and suggests that all such white-box SM4 implementations are not practically secure and new white-box SM4 design should be explored even for a semi-practical security level under external encodings, like white-box AES. We would like to explicitly express that our work is concerned with white-box implementations with external encodings. There are white-box implementations without external encodings on plaintext or/and ciphertext, concerned by the newly Differential Computation Analysis [7] research direction for addressing pure software white-box implementation. Anyway, white-box implementation with external encodings represents a conservative bottom line: if there is no way for a secure white-box implementation with external encodings, there is no way for a secure white-box implementation without external encodings.

The remainder of the paper is organized as follows. We briefly describe the notation, the SM4 block cipher and Derbez et al.'s affine equivalence result in Sect. 2, describe our attack framework in Sect. 3, and apply the attack framework to Xiao and Lai's, Bai and Wu's, and Shi et al.'s white-box SM4 implementations in Sects. 4 to 6, respectively. Section 7 concludes this paper.

2 Preliminaries

In this section, we give the notation and briefly describe the SM4 block cipher and Derbez et al.'s affine equivalence result.

2.1 Notation

We use the following notation throughout this paper.

$\|\|$	bit string concatenation
$\oplus$	bitwise logical exclusive XOR
$\lll$	left rotation of a bit string
$\circ$	functional composition. Let f and g be two functions, $f \circ g(\cdot) = f(g(\cdot))$
Δ	difference with respect to the $\oplus$ operation

2.2 The SM4 Block Cipher

SM4 has a generalised Feistel structure with a 128-bit block size and four 32-bit branches, a 128-bit user key and a total of 32 rounds [23]. Denote by $\mathcal{F}$ the round encryption function, by $(X_r, X_{r+1}, X_{r+2}, X_{r+3})$ the 128-bit input to the r-th round, and by rk_r the 32-bit r-th round key, where $X_r \in GF(2)^{32}$ and $0 \leq r \leq 31$. As depicted in Fig. 1, the r-th round encryption of SM4 is given by

$$X_{r+4} = \mathcal{F}(X_r, X_{r+1}, X_{r+2}, X_{r+3}, rk_r) = X_r \oplus \mathcal{T}(X_{r+1}, X_{r+2}, X_{r+3}, rk_r),$$

where $\mathcal{T} : GF(2)^{32} \rightarrow GF(2)^{32}$ is composed of a non-linear transformation τ and a linear transformation $\mathcal{L}$, that is, $\mathcal{T}(x) = \mathcal{L}(\tau(x))$.

The non-linear transformation $\tau : GF(2)^{32} \rightarrow GF(2)^{32}$ is composed of four parallel S-boxes and is defined as $\tau(x) = (S(x_0)||S(x_1)||S(x_2)||S(x_3))$, where $x = (x_0, x_1, x_2, x_3) \in (GF(2)^8)^4$, and S is the S-Box of SM4. The linear transformation $\mathcal{L} : GF(2)^{32} \rightarrow GF(2)^{32}$ is defined as $\mathcal{L}(x) = x \oplus (x \lll 2) \oplus (x \lll$

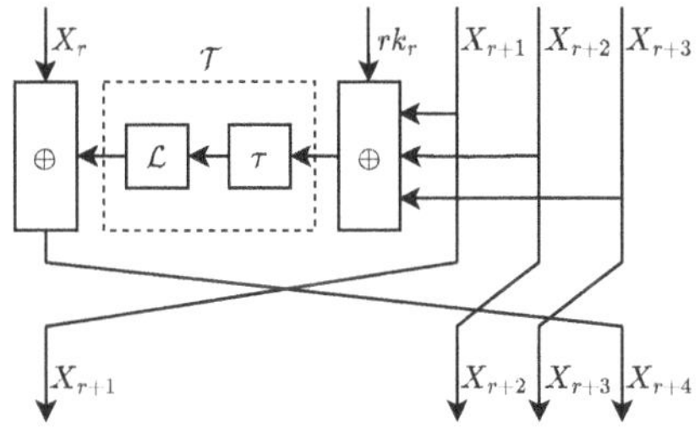

Fig. 1. An encryption round of SM4

10) $\oplus (x \lll 18) \oplus (x \lll 24)$. In particular, as described in [2], the linear transformation $\mathcal{L}$ of SM4 can also be represented as a 32×32-bit non-singular matrix

$$\begin{bmatrix} B_1 & B_2 & B_2 & B_3 \\ B_3 & B_1 & B_2 & B_2 \\ B_2 & B_3 & B_1 & B_2 \\ B_2 & B_2 & B_3 & B_1 \end{bmatrix},$$

where B_1, B_2 and B_3 are all 8×8-bit non-singular matrix. Represent $\mathcal{L}$ as four 32×8-bit matrices $\mathcal{L} = \begin{bmatrix} \mathcal{L}_0 & \mathcal{L}_1 & \mathcal{L}_2 & \mathcal{L}_3 \end{bmatrix}$, let x_0, x_1, x_2, x_3 be four byte variables, and define

$$\mathcal{L}_0(x_0) = \begin{bmatrix} B_1 & B_3 & B_2 & B_2 \end{bmatrix}^T \cdot x_0, \ \mathcal{L}_1(x_1) = \begin{bmatrix} B_2 & B_1 & B_3 & B_2 \end{bmatrix}^T \cdot x_1,$$
$$\mathcal{L}_2(x_2) = \begin{bmatrix} B_2 & B_2 & B_1 & B_3 \end{bmatrix}^T \cdot x_2, \ \mathcal{L}_3(x_3) = \begin{bmatrix} B_3 & B_2 & B_2 & B_1 \end{bmatrix}^T \cdot x_3,$$

then $\mathcal{L}(x_0||x_1||x_2||x_3) = \mathcal{L}_0(x_0) \oplus \mathcal{L}_1(x_1) \oplus \mathcal{L}_2(x_2) \oplus \mathcal{L}_3(x_3)$.

Ciphertext (Y_0, Y_1, Y_2, Y_3) is resulted from 32 iterations of the round encryption function $\mathcal{F}$ and finally a reverse transformation $\mathcal{R} : GF(2)^{128} \rightarrow GF(2)^{128}$, that is $(Y_0, Y_1, Y_2, Y_3) = \mathcal{R}(X_{32}, X_{33}, X_{34}, X_{35}) = (X_{35}, X_{34}, X_{33}, X_{32})$.

Key Schedule. For $0 \leq r \leq 31$, the round keys are generated from a 128-bit user key $MK = (MK_0, MK_1, MK_2, MK_3) \in (GF(2)^{32})^4$ in the following way:

$$(K_0, K_1, K_2, K_3) = (MK_0 \oplus FK_0, MK_1 \oplus FK_1, MK_2 \oplus FK_2, MK_3 \oplus FK_3),$$
$$rk_r = K_{r+4} = K_r \oplus \widehat{\mathcal{T}}(K_{r+1} \oplus K_{r+2} \oplus K_{r+3} \oplus CK_r), \quad (1)$$

where FK_j $(j = 0, 1, 2, 3)$ and CK_r are 32-bit public constants, and $\widehat{\mathcal{T}}$ is the linear transformation of $\mathcal{T}$ with $\mathcal{L}$ being replaced by the linear transformation $\widehat{\mathcal{L}} = x \oplus (x \lll 13) \oplus (x \lll 23)$.

2.3 Derbez et al.'s Affine Equivalence Result

Definition 1 (Affine Equivalence [6]). *Two known n-bit non-linear bijections $\mathcal{F}$ and $\mathcal{S}$ are defined to be affine equivalent if there exist two n-bit affine mappings $\mathcal{A}$ and $\mathcal{B}$ such that $\mathcal{F} = \mathcal{B} \circ \mathcal{S} \circ \mathcal{A}$.*

Solving the affine equivalence problem is to find two affine mappings $\mathcal{A}$ and $\mathcal{B}$. If $\mathcal{F}$ and $\mathcal{S}$ are identical, this is defined to be self-equivalent.

Definition 2 (Self-Equivalence [6]**).** *An n-bit non-linear bijection $\mathcal{S}$ is defined to be self-equivalent if there exists a pair of n-bit affine mappings $(\mathcal{A}, \mathcal{B})$ such that $\mathcal{S} = \mathcal{B} \circ \mathcal{S} \circ \mathcal{A}$.*

In 2018, Derbez et al. [11] proposed a refined affine equivalence algorithm that treats $\mathcal{S}$ as a parallel of several S-boxes of the same size, which is exactly the scenario of the S-box layer of a block cipher. Their main idea is to first isolate the input and output subspaces of the S-boxes by finding input difference space for each S-box, then apply Dinur's or Biryukov et al.'s equivalence algorithm [6,12] to each S-box individually according to different cases of the S-boxes. Derbez et al. claimed the applicability of their algorithm for recovering affine encodings only on white-box implementation of an SPN cipher (based on Chow et al.'s framework). Here we summarise their affine equivalence result as Theorem 1, and we refer the reader to [11] for more details.

Theorem 1 (from [11]**).** *Let $(\mathcal{S}_0, \cdots, \mathcal{S}_{k-1})$ is a parallel application of k m-bit S-boxes $\mathcal{S}_i$ $(0 \le i \le k-1, n = k \cdot m)$, $\mathcal{A}$ and $\mathcal{B}$ be n-bit affine mappings and $\mathcal{F}$ be an n-bit non-linear bijection such that $\mathcal{F} = \mathcal{B} \circ (\mathcal{S}_0, \cdots, \mathcal{S}_{k-1}) \circ \mathcal{A}$. Knowing $\mathcal{S}_i$ and given oracle access to $\mathcal{F}$ (but not $\mathcal{F}^{-1}$), Derbez et al.'s affine equivalence algorithm can find two affine mappings $\mathcal{A}'$ and $\mathcal{B}'$ such that $\mathcal{F} = \mathcal{B}' \circ (\mathcal{S}_1, \cdots, \mathcal{S}_k) \circ \mathcal{A}'$ with a time complexity of $O(2^m \cdot n^3 + l \cdot 2^m \cdot n^3 + k \cdot n^3 + k \cdot m^3 \cdot 2^m)$ if the k S-boxes are identical and each S-box is not self-equivalent, or $O(2^m \cdot n^3 + l \cdot 2^m \cdot n^3 + k \cdot n^3 + k \cdot m^3 \cdot 2^{2m})$ if the k S-boxes are identical and each S-box is self-equivalent, or $O(l \cdot 2^m \cdot n^3 + k \cdot n^3 + m \cdot n^2 \cdot 2^m)$ if the k S-boxes are different one another and each S-box is not self-equivalent, or $O(l \cdot 2^m \cdot n^3 + k \cdot n^3 + m \cdot n^2 \cdot 2^{2m})$ otherwise, where l is the number of test values.*

3 Affine Equivalence-Based Key-Recovery Attack Framework on White-Box SM4 Implementations

In this section, we give the expression for the 2040 pairs of affine mappings for SM4 S-box self-equivalence and present the affine equivalence-based attack framework on white-box SM4 implementations. We extend the applicability of Derbez et al.'s affine equivalence algorithm from SPN ciphers to a generalised Feistel cipher by exploiting a differential meet-in-the-middle approach and an observation dedicated to the generalised Feistel structure at a high level.

3.1 Expression of the 2040 Pairs of Affine Mappings for SM4 S-Box Self-Equivalence

In 2003, Biryukov et al. [6] gave an algorithm for finding self-equivalence relations of an S-box. It is easy to get that there are 2040 self-equivalence relations for the SM4 S-box by using Canright's approach [8]. Considering the SM4 S-box is defined as $S(x) = \mathcal{M}((\mathcal{M} \cdot x)^{-1})$ with $\mathcal{M}(\cdot)$ being a fixed affine mapping over a finite field and $x \in GF(2^8)$, we obtain the following Theorem 2 on the specific expression of the 2040 pairs of affine mappings for SM4 S-box self-equivalence, which is a foundation for our attacks.

Theorem 2. *Let $[a]$ be the 8×8-bit matrix that corresponds to a multiplication by a in $GF(2^8)$ and $\mathcal{H}$ be the 8×8-bit matrix that performs the squaring operation in $GF(2^8)$. A general expression for 2040 pairs of affine mapping $\mathcal{A}$ and $\mathcal{B}$ that satisfy $S = \mathcal{B} \circ S \circ \mathcal{A}$ can be derive:*

$$\mathcal{A}(x) = \mathcal{M}^{-1}\left([a] \cdot \mathcal{H}^i \cdot \mathcal{M} \cdot x\right), \ \mathcal{B}(x) = \mathcal{M}\left(\mathcal{H}^{-i} \cdot [a] \cdot \mathcal{M}^{-1} \cdot x\right),$$

where $0 \leq i \leq 7$ and $a \in GF(2^8) \backslash \{0\}$.

Proof. $\mathcal{H}$ can be easily computed using the method from [4]. Since $|\mathcal{H}| = 1$, the inverse matrix of $\mathcal{H}$ exists and is unique:

$$\mathcal{H} = \begin{bmatrix} 1&0&0&0&1&0&0&0 \\ 0&0&0&0&0&1&0&1 \\ 0&1&0&0&1&1&0&0 \\ 0&0&0&0&0&1&1&1 \\ 0&0&1&0&1&1&1&0 \\ 0&0&0&0&1&1&1&0 \\ 0&0&0&1&1&0&1&0 \\ 0&0&0&0&1&0&1&0 \end{bmatrix}, \quad \mathcal{H}^{-1} = \begin{bmatrix} 1&1&0&1&0&0&0&1 \\ 0&1&1&1&0&1&0&0 \\ 0&0&0&0&1&1&0&0 \\ 0&0&0&0&0&0&1&1 \\ 0&1&0&1&0&0&0&1 \\ 0&0&0&0&0&1&0&1 \\ 0&1&0&1&0&0&0&0 \\ 0&1&0&0&0&1&0&1 \end{bmatrix}.$$

Furthermore, one can easily check that $\mathcal{H}^8 = I$ and thus $\mathcal{H}^{-i} = \mathcal{H}^{8-i}$. By the definition of $\mathcal{H}$, $\mathcal{H}^i \cdot x = x^{2^i}$ implies $(\mathcal{H}^i \cdot x)^{-1} = \mathcal{H}^i \cdot x^{-1}$. Bringing the formulas in Theorem 1 into Definition 1 for verification, we have

$$\begin{aligned} S(x) = \mathcal{B} \circ S \circ \mathcal{A}(x) &= \mathcal{M}\left(H^{-i} \cdot [a] \cdot \left([a] \cdot H^i \cdot \mathcal{M} \cdot x\right)^{-1}\right) \\ &= \mathcal{M}\left(H^{-i} \cdot [a] \cdot ([a]^{-1} \cdot H^i \cdot (\mathcal{M} \cdot x)^{-1})\right) \\ &= \mathcal{M}((\mathcal{M} \cdot x)^{-1}). \end{aligned}$$

Since a has 255 different values for each i, we can find exactly $8 \times 255 = 2040$ different pairs of affine mappings $(\mathcal{A}, \mathcal{B})$.

3.2 Affine Equivalence-Based Key-Recovery Attack Framework

Below we assume that the concerned white-box SM4 implementation uses affine encodings (including the special case linear encodings when the constants of the affine encodings are zero) to protect the original four branches and round function, generates k $m \times n$-bit white-box tables for a round function, and uses a diagonal affine encoding $\mathcal{I}_r$ (of k $m \times m$-bit affine encodings $\mathcal{I}_{r,i}$ $(0 \leq i \leq k-1)$) for the input of white-box tables and a general $n \times n$-bit affine encoding $\mathcal{O}''_{r+4}$ for its output. The process of generating k $m \times n$-bit white-box tables for the

r-th round can be represented as an $n \times n$-bit bijection $F_r = \mathcal{U}_r \circ (S, \cdots, S) \circ \mathcal{V}_r$, where $\mathcal{V}_r = \oplus_{rk_r} \circ \mathcal{I}_r$ and $\mathcal{U}_r = \mathcal{O}''_{r+4} \circ \mathcal{L}$ are n-bit affine transformations, with $\mathcal{I}_r$ and $\mathcal{O}''_{r+4}$ being n-bit input and output encodings, respectively, and rk_r being the r-th round key.

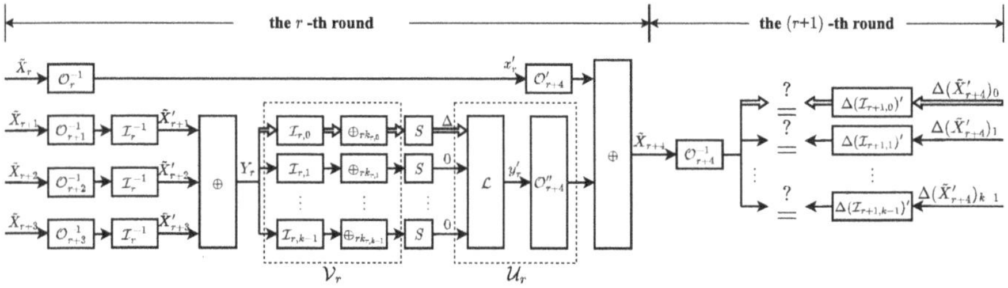

Fig. 2. Our affine equivalence-based attack framework

Here, $n = m \cdot k$ (specifically, $n = 32$, $m = 8$ and $k = 4$ for the white-box SM4 implementation, since the SM4 S-box is 8-bit, and there are $k = 4$ parallel S-boxes in a round function). All the afore-mentioned white-box SM4 implementations can be expressed eventually in this format. Our attack framework consists of the following three phases, as illustrated in Fig. 2.

1. **Obtaining all the equivalent affine encodings on a round function.** This phase is to obtain all the pairs of equivalent affine mappings $\mathcal{V}'_r$ and $\mathcal{U}'_r$ such that $F_r = \mathcal{U}'_r \circ (S, \cdots, S) \circ \mathcal{V}'_r$. To achieve this, we employ Derbez et al.'s affine equivalence algorithm [11], which enables us to find all input difference space $I_{r,i}$ that activates the i-th S-box ($0 \leq i \leq k-1$). Eventually, k input difference spaces can be computed by Theorem 2, and we have $I_r = diag(I_{r,0}, \cdots, I_{r,k-1})$. Due to S-box's self-equivalence property, the computed I_r may not equal $\mathcal{V}_r$; and there are 2040 equivalent representations for $\mathcal{V}'_{r,i}$ that correspond to the correct affine mapping $\mathcal{V}_{r,i}$ (that makes the i-th S-box active). Thus, we have $\mathcal{V}'_r = diag(\mathcal{V}'_{r,0}, \cdots, \mathcal{V}'_{r,k-1})$. Given a $\mathcal{V}'_r$, the corresponding $\mathcal{U}'_r$ can be determined. Since all the four S-boxes are identical in a round of SM4 and the S-box S is self-equivalent, when the input affine encoding is diagonal, the time complexity of this phase is only $O(k \cdot m^3 \cdot 2^{2m})$ by Theorem 1 under the case of identical and self-equivalent S-boxes (Note that Derbez et al.'s affine equivalence result is for general $n \times n$-bit input and output affine mappings, but some of the executions are not required for a diagonal affine encoding here).
2. **Identifying the correct affine encodings.** This phase is to find the correct affine encodings $\mathcal{V}_r$ and $\mathcal{U}_r$. As depicted in Fig. 2, the output encodings $\mathcal{O}'_{r+4}$ and $\mathcal{O}''_{r+4}$ of the two 32-bit branches x'_r and y'_r are different but are linearly related to the encoding $\mathcal{O}_{r+4} = \mathcal{O}'_{r+4} \oplus \mathcal{O}''_{r+4}$ of the branch $\tilde{X}'_{r+4}$. This feature of Feistel structure is the main reason for the failure of applying some existing attack methods to SM4, including Derbez et al.'s affine equivalence attack on

white-box AES [11], for there is a secret constant from the affine encoding $\mathcal{O}'_{r+4}$ of x'_r. To overcome this, we employ a differential meet-in-the-middle approach to identify the correct encodings by considering two consecutive rounds. First, we set different Y_r's so that only the i-th S-box of the r-th round has an non-zero output difference, Δ say, so we have the difference $\mathcal{L}\cdot(0,...,0,\Delta,0,...,0)$ after the $\mathcal{L}$ operation. Then, we set $\tilde{X}_r = 0$, and use the same Y_r's to get k m-bit differences $\Delta(\tilde{X}'_{r+4})_i$ in the $(r+1)$-th round. Since the encoding $\mathcal{O}_{r+4}$ will be canceled, applying the linear part (denoted by $\Delta(\mathcal{I}_{r+1,i})$) of the correct one out of the 2040 candidates $\mathcal{V}'_{r+1,i}$ to $\Delta(\tilde{X}'_{r+4})_i$ will equal $(\mathcal{L}\cdot(0,...,0,\Delta,0,...,0))_i$. We assume one $\mathcal{V}_{r,i}$ corresponds to t $\mathcal{V}_{r+1,i}$ (here t is a small integer, specifically, t is 1 in Xiao and Lai's implementation and is 2 in Bai and Wu's implementation), and just need to build and search the hash table for a pair of blocks $(\mathcal{V}'_{r,i}, \mathcal{V}'_{r+1,i})$, so the time complexity of this phase is $O(2k \cdot 2040^t)$.
3. **Recovering a round key as well as the user key.** This phase is to recover a round key and the user key. If the input encoding $\mathcal{I}_r$ is linear, the vector of $\mathcal{V}_r = \oplus_{rk_r} \circ \mathcal{I}_r$ is the round key, and we can extract it as $\mathcal{V}_r(0)$. If the input encoding $\mathcal{I}_r$ is affine, the vector of $\mathcal{V}_r$ is a linear relationship between the round key and the $t \cdot k$ unknown vectors in $\mathcal{I}_r$, and this linear relationship can be recovered as $\mathcal{V}_r(0)$. Consider subsequent three more rounds, which form three new series of two consecutive rounds (together with the last second round), and we repeat the above phases to each of the three series to recover more secret white-box parameters. In the case of linear encodings, the recovered four round keys lead to the user key. In the case of affine encodings, depending on specific implementation designs, by SM4's key expansion formula Eq. (1) we use a few recovered white-box parameters to construct an expression with only one secret 32-bit unknown, solving which with exhaustive search leads to a round key and the user key. (This secret 32-bit unknown is a round key in Xiao and Lai's implementation, while it is a white-box parameter in Bai and Wu's implementation.) The time complexity of this phase is $O(t^2 \cdot 2^{32})$ for the case of affine encodings.

The attack framework has a total time complexity of $O(t \cdot k \cdot m^3 \cdot 2^{2m} + 2k \cdot 2040^t + t^2 \cdot 2^{32}) \approx O(t \cdot k \cdot m^3 \cdot 2^{2m} + 2k \cdot 2^{11t} + t^2 \cdot 2^{32})$ for the case of affine encodings, and $O(t \cdot k \cdot m^3 \cdot 2^{2m} + 2k \cdot 2040^t) \approx O(t \cdot k \cdot m^3 \cdot 2^{2m} + 2k \cdot 2^{11t})$ for the case of linear encodings. We would like to remark that the white-box SM4 implementations do not use non-linear encodings, however, if there were non-linear encodings, one could peel off them first by some means, as mentioned previously by others [1,5].

4 Key-Recovery Attack on Xiao and Lai's White-Box SM4 Implementation

In this section, we apply our attack framework to recover the original user key of Xiao and Lai's white-box SM4 implementation for the first time.

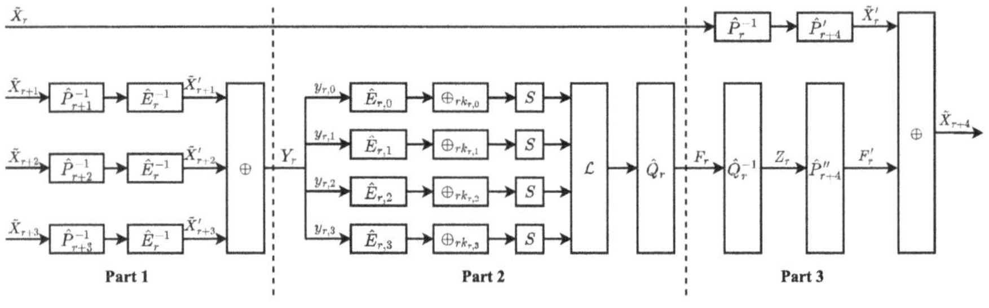

Fig. 3. An encryption round of Xiao and Lai's white-box SM4 implementation

4.1 Xiao and Lai's White-Box SM4 Implementation

In 2009, Xiao and Lai [25] proposed a white-box implementation of SM4 for the first time, with external encodings. To hide each internal state of SM4, their implementation uses affine mapping and encodes the inputs and outputs of the transformation function $\mathcal{T}$ containing the key information to generate lookup tables. The implementation of an encryption round consists of the following three parts depicted in Fig. 3.

Part 1 - Implementation of $\tilde{X}_{r+1} \oplus \tilde{X}_{r+2} \oplus \tilde{X}_{r+3}$. Define a 32-bit invertible affine encoding $\hat{P}_{r+j}(\cdot) = P_{r+j}(\cdot) \oplus p_{r+j}$, where the linear part P_{r+j} is a 32×32-bit matrix and p_{r+j} is a 32-bit vector. For $0 \leq r \leq 31$, cancel the three output encodings $\hat{P}_{r+1}, \hat{P}_{r+2}$ and $\hat{P}_{r+3}$ from the last round to recover the original values of $\tilde{X}_{r+1}, \tilde{X}_{r+2}$ and $\tilde{X}_{r+3}$, and immediately apply the inverse $\hat{E}_r^{-1}$ of a 32-bit block diagonal affine encoding $\hat{E}_r$ with 8-bit blocks $\hat{E}_{r,k}(\cdot) = E_{r,k}(\cdot) \oplus e_{r,k}$, where $E_{r,k}$ is an invertible 8×8-bit matrix and $e_{r,k}$ is an 8-bit vector ($k = 0, 1, 2, 3$). This part can be summarised as

$$\tilde{X}'_{r+j} = \hat{E}_r^{-1} \circ \hat{P}_{r+j}^{-1}(\tilde{X}_{r+j}) = \hat{M}_{r+j}^r(\tilde{X}_{r+j}), \quad Y_r = \tilde{X}'_{r+1} \oplus \tilde{X}'_{r+2} \oplus \tilde{X}'_{r+3},$$

where Y_r is a 32-bit variable and $1 \leq j \leq 3$.

Part 2 - Implementation of $\mathcal{T}(Y_r \oplus rk_r)$. In order to avoid generating some impractical lookup tables, Xiao and Lai proposed to build four 8-bit to 32-bit lookup tables. Define $\hat{Q}_r(\cdot) = Q_r(\cdot) \oplus q_r$ as a 32-bit affine encoding, where Q_r is an invertible 32×32-bit matrix, and q_r is a 32-bit vector. The input Y of Part 2 is represented as 4 bytes $Y_r = (y_{r,0}, y_{r,1}, y_{r,2}, y_{r,3})$, which are inputs for the four 8-bit to 32-bit lookup tables $Table_{r,j}$ ($0 \leq r \leq 31, 0 \leq j \leq 3$), constructed as follows:

$$Table_{r,0}(y_{r,0}) = Q_r \circ \mathcal{L}_0 \circ S \circ \oplus_{rk_{r,0}} \circ \hat{E}_{r,0}(y_{r,0}),$$
$$Table_{r,1}(y_{r,1}) = Q_r \circ \mathcal{L}_1 \circ S \circ \oplus_{rk_{r,1}} \circ \hat{E}_{r,1}(y_{r,1}),$$
$$Table_{r,2}(y_{r,2}) = Q_r \circ \mathcal{L}_2 \circ S \circ \oplus_{rk_{r,2}} \circ \hat{E}_{r,2}(y_{r,2}),$$
$$Table_{r,3}(y_{r,3}) = \hat{Q}_r \circ \mathcal{L}_3 \circ S \circ \oplus_{rk_{r,3}} \circ \hat{E}_{r,3}(y_{r,3}),$$

where the round key rk_i is represented as four bytes $rk_r = (rk_{r,0}, rk_{r,1}, rk_{r,2}, rk_{r,3})$. The final output of this part is the XOR of the four 32-bit outputs of the four lookup tables, which is denoted by $F_r = \oplus_{j=0}^{3} Table_{r,j}$. If we drop the exponent notation for the round and merge the key addition with affine encoding, F_r can be represented in the following form:

$$F_r = \mathcal{U}_r \circ (S, \cdots, S) \circ \mathcal{V}_r,$$

where $\mathcal{U}_r$ is a 32-bit affine mapping of the form $\mathcal{U}_r(\cdot) = U_r(\cdot) \oplus u_r = Q_r \circ \mathcal{L}(\cdot) \oplus q_r$, $\mathcal{V}_r$ is a 32-bit affine mapping of the form $\mathcal{V}_r(\cdot) = V_r(\cdot) \oplus v_r = E_r(\cdot) \oplus (e_r \oplus rk_r)$, $E_r = diag(E_{r,0}, E_{r,1}, E_{r,2}, E_{r,3})$, and $e_r = (e_{r,0}, e_{r,1}, e_{r,2}, e_{r,3})$.

Part 3 - Implementation of $\tilde{X}_{r+4}$. This part uses the output F_r of Part 2 and the protected form $\tilde{X}_r$ to calculate $\tilde{X}_{r+4}$, as follows:

$$\tilde{X}'_r = \hat{P}'_{r+4} \circ \hat{P}_r^{-1}(\tilde{X}_r), \quad F'_r = \hat{P}''_{r+4} \circ \hat{Q}_r^{-1}(F_r), \quad \tilde{X}_{r+4} = \tilde{X}'_r \oplus F'_r,$$

where $\hat{P}'_{r+4}$ and $\hat{P}''_{r+4}$ are 32-bit to 32-bit affine mappings of the forms $\hat{P}'_{r+4}(\cdot) = \hat{P}_{r+4}(\cdot) \oplus a'_{r+4}$ and $\hat{P}''_{r+4}(\cdot) = \hat{P}_{r+4}(\cdot) \oplus a''_{r+4}$, respectively, with a'_{r+4} and a''_{r+4} being two 32-bit vectors meeting $a'_{r+4} \oplus a''_{r+4} = p_{r+4}$.

External Encodings. The external encoding is divided into external input encoding $\mathcal{Z}^{in}$ and external output encoding $\mathcal{Z}^{out}$, both of which are 32-bit affine mappings. Let X_l be the original value without output encoding protection, the external input encoding is defined by $X_l = \mathcal{Z}_l^{in}(\tilde{X}_l) = P_l(\tilde{X}_l) \oplus p_l$ with $0 \le l \le 3$, and the external output encoding is defined by $X_l = \mathcal{Z}_{l-31}^{out}(\tilde{X}_l) = P_l^{-1}(\tilde{X}_l) \oplus P_l^{-1} \cdot p_l$ with $31 \le l \le 34$.

4.2 Attacking Xiao and Lai's White-Box SM4 Implementation

In this subsection, we apply our attack framework to Xiao and Lai's white-box SM4 implementation. Recall that each lookup table of a round function can be represented as $F_r = \mathcal{U}_r \circ (S, \cdots, S) \circ \mathcal{V}_r$, where $\mathcal{U}_r$ and $\mathcal{V}_r$ are affine mappings, and we can recover the correct blocks $\mathcal{U}_r$ and $\mathcal{V}_r$ by solving the affine equivalence problem and using specific attacks. Next, the specific structure of the encodings within the implementation is utilized to get the value of an XOR operation performed between any two consecutive round keys. Finally, the key expansion algorithm of SM4 is used to recover a round key with a complexity of $O(2^{32})$.

An Equivalent Representation of Lookup Tables. Recall that the output of Part 2 is of the form $F_r = \oplus_{j=0}^{3} Table_{r,j} = \mathcal{U}_r \circ (S, \cdots, S) \circ \mathcal{V}_r$ for one round, where $\mathcal{U}_r$ and $\mathcal{V}_r$ are unknown affine mappings. Since the problem is identical for each round, we drop the subscripts r that represent the number of rounds without any loss of generality in this subsection. Since $\hat{E} = diag(\hat{E}_0, \hat{E}_1, \hat{E}_2, \hat{E}_3)$ is a block diagonal affine mapping where each block is 8-bit, so we have $\mathcal{V} = diag(\mathcal{V}_0, \mathcal{V}_1, \mathcal{V}_2, \mathcal{V}_3)$ where $\mathcal{V}_i$ is an 8-bit affine mapping. In that case, we want to find an equivalent representation of the two affine mappings $\mathcal{U}'$ and $\mathcal{V}'$ such that $F = \mathcal{U}' \circ (S, \cdots, S) \circ \mathcal{V}'$.

Computing $\mathcal{V}'$. We aim to recover four equivalent affine mappings $\mathcal{V}'_i$ ($i = 0, 1, 2, 3$) to build $\mathcal{V}$. Let $y_j \in GF(2)^8$, since we can evaluate F by summing over the lookup tables $Table_i$, consider the following form of input:

$$\oplus_{i=0}^{3} Table_i(0, \cdots, 0, y_j, 0, \cdots, 0).$$

Recall that $\mathcal{V}$ is a block diagonal affine mapping, thus only one S is active at this input. We now have an 8-bit to 32-bit mapping, that is $G \circ S \circ \mathcal{V}_i$, where G is an 8×32-bit affine function. Noting that G, S and $\mathcal{V}_i$ are all injections (at least) by the construction, we can calculate an affine projection P such that $P \circ G \circ S \circ \mathcal{V}_i$ is a bijection over $GF(2)^8$, and the bijection is affine equivalent to the S-box of SM4. The basic idea is to calculate a unique mapping to construct a bijection. Afterward, we can use the affine equivalence algorithm from [6] to recover $\mathcal{V}_i$ with a complexity of about $O(8^3 \cdot 2^{2\times 8}) = O(2^{25})$.

It has been verified that there are 2040 self-equivalence relations for the S-box of SM4. This means there are 2040 pairs of 8-bit affine transformations $(\mathcal{A}, \mathcal{B})$ such that $S = \mathcal{B} \circ S \circ \mathcal{A}$. Therefore, the affine equivalence algorithm will not exactly recover $\mathcal{V}_i$, but there exists the relation $\mathcal{V}'_i = \mathcal{A} \circ \mathcal{V}_i$, where $\mathcal{A}$ has 2040 possible values, so we recover the 2040 candidates $\mathcal{V}'_i$ for $\mathcal{V}_i$. Repeating the same method as described above four times, and all $\mathcal{V}'_i$ ($i = 0, 1, 2, 3$) can be computed.

Recovering $\mathcal{U}'$. Recall our function $F = \mathcal{U}' \circ (S, \cdots, S) \circ \mathcal{V}'$, where $\mathcal{V}'$ is known, and our goal is to find $\mathcal{U}'$. Once we have determined $\mathcal{V}'$, we can easily recover the corresponding $\mathcal{U}'$. We split the linear part U' of $\mathcal{U}'$ into components, such that $U' = (U'_0, \cdots, U'_3)$, where U'_i is a 32×8-bit matrix. Algorithm 1 can use any candidate for each $\mathcal{V}'_i$ to calculate the corresponding U'_i by computing the image of each vector of the canonical basis through U'.

After calculating U', to recover the vector u' of $\mathcal{U}'$, for one $y \in GF(2)^{32}$, we only need to compute the following equations:

$$z' = U' \circ (S, \cdots, S) \circ \mathcal{V}'(y), \quad z = \oplus_{i=0}^{3} Table_i((y)_i), \quad u' = z \oplus z'.$$

Now we have a computationally easy function $F = \mathcal{U}' \circ (S, \cdots, S) \circ \mathcal{V}'$. The complexity of recovering $\mathcal{U}'$ and $\mathcal{V}'$ is dominated by computing four 8-bit affine transformations $\mathcal{V}'_i$, which lead to a complexity of about $O(4 \times 8^3 \times 2^{2\times 8}) = O(2^{27})$.

Identifying the Correct Encodings. By using the method of the previous subsection, we can obtain an equivalent representation of the lookup table of 32 rounds $F_r = \mathcal{U}'_r \circ (S, \cdots, S) \circ \mathcal{V}'_r$. In this subsection, we can choose any two consecutive rounds to recover the correct encodings $\mathcal{U}_r$ and $\mathcal{V}_r$. The overall strategy is depicted in Fig. 4 and detailed below.

Combining Part 2 and Part 3 such that the affine encoding $\hat{Q}_r$ is canceled out, we have $\bar{F}_r(Y_r) = \hat{P}''_{r+4} \circ \mathcal{L} \circ (S, \cdots, S) \circ \mathcal{V}_r(Y_r)$. Let $\tilde{X}_r = 0$,

Algorithm 1. Computing U'_i

$y_i^0 \leftarrow$ random element in $GF(2)^8$;
$y^0 \leftarrow (0, \cdots, 0, y_i^0, 0, \cdots, 0) \in GF(2^8)^4$;
$z^0 \leftarrow \oplus_{i=0}^{3} Table_i((y^0)_i)$ ▷ $(y^0)_i$ represents the i-th byte of y^0
$g_i^0 \leftarrow S(\mathcal{V}'_i(y_i^0))$;
for each $e_j = (0, \cdots, 0, 1, 0, \cdots, 0) \in GF(2)^8$ **do** ▷ Denotes that the j-th position is 1
    $g_i^j \leftarrow g_i^0 \oplus e_j$; ▷ $1 \leq j \leq 7$
    $y_i^j \leftarrow (\mathcal{V}'_i)^{-1}(S^{-1}(g_i^j)$;
    $y^j \leftarrow (0, \cdots, 0, y_i^j, 0, \cdots, 0)$;
    $z^j \leftarrow \oplus_{i=0}^{3} Table_i((y^j)_i)$;
    $\Delta z^j \leftarrow z^0 \oplus z^j$;
    j-th column of $U'_i \leftarrow \Delta z^j$;
end for

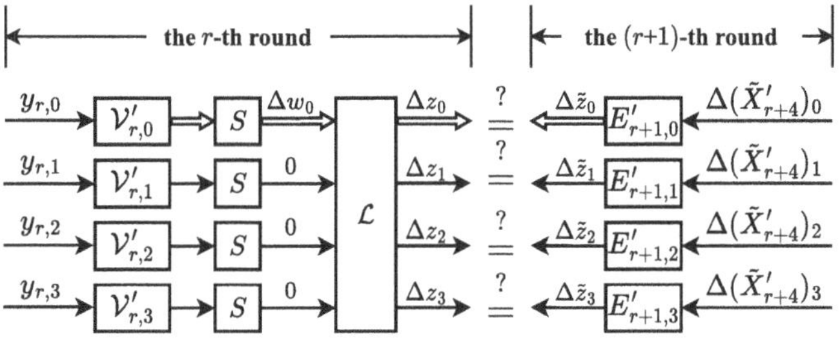

Fig. 4. Identifying correct affine encodings in Xiao and Lai's implementation

combing Part 2 in the r-th round, Part 3 in the r-th round and Part 1 in the $(r+1)$-th round involved by $\tilde{X}_{r+4}$, $\tilde{X}'_{r+4}$ is computed as: $\tilde{X}'_{r+4} = E_{r+1}^{-1} \circ \left(\mathcal{L} \circ (S, \cdots, S) \circ V_r(Y_r) \oplus P_r^{-1} \cdot p_r \oplus e_{r+1}\right)$. Recall that $\hat{P}_r(\cdot) = P_r(\cdot) \oplus p_r$ and $\hat{E}_{r+1}(\cdot) = E_{r+1}(\cdot) \oplus e_{r+1}$, if $E_{r+1}(\tilde{X}'_{r+4})$ is computed, the result is the value of an XOR operation between the variable $\mathcal{L} \circ (S, \cdots, S) \circ V_r(Y_r)$ and the fixed vector $P_r^{-1} \cdot p_r \oplus e_{r+1}$.

Algorithm 2. Identifying the encodings in Xiao and Lai's implementation

$y^0, \cdots, y^m \leftarrow$ messages with byte y_0^l taking different values and byte $y_i^l = 0$ if $i \neq 0$;
for each candidate $\mathcal{V}'_{r,0}$ for $\mathcal{V}_{r,0}$ **do**
    $\Delta w_0^l \leftarrow S(\mathcal{V}'_{r,0}(y_0^0)) \oplus S(\mathcal{V}'_{r,0}(y_0^l))$;
    $(\Delta z_0^l, \Delta z_1^l, \Delta z_2^l, \Delta z_3^l) \leftarrow \mathcal{L} \cdot (\Delta w_0^l, 0, 0, 0)$;
    Store $\mathcal{V}'_{r,0}$ in a hash table $\mathcal{T}_z$ indexed by $(\Delta z_0^1, \cdots, \Delta z_0^m)$;
end for

$(\tilde{X}'_{r+4})^l \leftarrow \hat{M}^{r+1}_{r+4} \circ (\bar{F}_r(y^l) \oplus \hat{P}'_{r+4} \circ \hat{P}_r^{-1}(0))$; $\triangleright$ $\hat{M}^{r+1}_{r+4} = \hat{E}_r^{-1} \circ \hat{P}_{r+j}^{-1}$
$\Delta(\tilde{X}'_{r+4})^l_0 \leftarrow (\tilde{X}'_{r+4})^0_0 \oplus (\tilde{X}'_{r+4})^l_0$;
for each candidate $\mathcal{V}'_{r+1,0}$ for $\mathcal{V}_{r+1,0}$ **do**
  $\Delta \tilde{z}^l_0 \leftarrow E'_{r+1,0} \cdot \Delta(\tilde{X}'_{r+4})^l_0$; $\triangleright$ $E'_{r+1}$is denoted as 2040 candidates for E_{r+1}
  if $(\Delta \tilde{z}^1_0, \cdots, \Delta \tilde{z}^m_0) \in \mathcal{T}_z$ **then**
    We have correct $\mathcal{V}_{r+1,0}$ and $\mathcal{V}_{r,0}$ under $\mathcal{T}_z[\Delta \tilde{z}^1_0, \cdots, \Delta \tilde{z}^m_0]$;
    break;
  end if
end for
for each candidate $\mathcal{V}'_{r+1,j}$ for $\mathcal{V}_{r+1,j}$ $(j = 1, 2, 3)$ **do**
  if $E'_{r+1,j} \cdot \Delta(\tilde{X}'_{r+4})^l_i = \Delta z^l_i$ **then**
    We have the correct $\mathcal{V}_{r+1,j}$;
  end if
end for
Once we have recovered all the correct $\mathcal{V}_{r+1,j}$ $(0 \leq j \leq 3)$, *we can use the same method to recover all the correct remaining* $\mathcal{V}_{r,j}$ $(1 \leq j \leq 3)$.

We will use difference to eliminate the effect of the fixed vector. Recall that we already know that the candidates $\mathcal{V}'_r$ and $\mathcal{V}'_{r+1}$, but identifying the correct blocks $\mathcal{V}_r$ and $\mathcal{V}_{r+1}$ is our goal. To do so, represent $\mathcal{V}_r$ and $\mathcal{V}_{r+1}$ as $\mathcal{V}'_r$ and $\mathcal{V}'_{r+1}$, respectively, and we will use a differential meet-in-the-middle approach. The details of this process are provided in Algorithm 2.

There are a total of 2040^2 candidates for $(\mathcal{V}_{r,0}, \mathcal{V}_{r+1,0})$, we employ the differential meet-in-the-middle approach to identify the correct $(\mathcal{V}_{r,0}, \mathcal{V}_{r+1,0})$. When searching for a match, we use a 32-bit filter by concatenating 8-bit values of $\Delta z^1_0, \cdots, \Delta z^m_0$, taking $m = 4$. This filter is effective in sufficiently identifying the right candidates enough. The time complexity of identifying the correct $\mathcal{V}_{r,j}$ is mainly on building and matching of the hash table for the 2040 candidates for each block, leading to the complexity of about $O(8 \cdot 2040) \approx O(2^{14})$ to recover $\mathcal{V}_r$ and $\mathcal{V}_{r+1}$.

Recovering the User Key. Once $\mathcal{V}_r$ and $\mathcal{V}_{r+1}$ are recovered, we can get two invertible matrices E_r and E_{r+1}, and two vectors $v_r = e_r \oplus rk_r$ and $v_{r+1} = e_{r+1} \oplus rk_{r+1}$ by setting $\mathcal{V}_r(0)$ and $\mathcal{V}_{r+1}(0)$. In the white-box attack context, the composite affine mappings $\hat{M}^r_{r+3}$ and $\hat{M}^{r+1}_{r+3}$ are publicly visible in Xiao and Lai's implementation. This means that the values of $m^r_{r+3} = E_r^{-1} \cdot P_{r+3}^{-1} \cdot p_{r+3} \oplus E_r^{-1} \cdot e_r$ and $m^{r+1}_{r+3} = E_{r+1}^{-1} \cdot P_{r+3}^{-1} \cdot p_{r+3} \oplus E_{r+1}^{-1} \cdot e_{r+1}$ are known, after setting $\hat{M}^r_{r+3}(0)$ and $\hat{M}^{r+1}_{r+3}(0)$. We only need to compute the following two equations to obtain the value of an XOR operation performed between two consecutive rounds of round keys:

$$E_r \cdot m^r_{r+3} \oplus E_{r+1} \cdot m^{r+1}_{r+3} = e_r \oplus e_{r+1} = t, \; t \oplus v_r \oplus v_{r+1} = rk_r \oplus rk_{r+1} = \alpha_{r+1}.$$

Repeating all the previous steps of the attack for a few subsequent rounds, the value of an XOR operation performed between any two round keys can be computed:

$$rk_r \oplus rk_{r+1} = \alpha_{r+1}, \quad rk_r \oplus rk_{r+2} = \alpha_{r+2},$$
$$rk_r \oplus rk_{r+3} = \alpha_{r+3}, \quad rk_r \oplus rk_{r+4} = \alpha_{r+4}.$$

Since the round key in the white-box SM4 implementation is the same as the round key in SM4, we use the key expansion algorithm of SM4 to recover the round key rk_r. We replace all the required round keys in Eq. (1) for generating rk_{r+4} with rk_r:

$$\alpha_{r+4} = \widehat{T}(rk_r \oplus \alpha_{r+1} \oplus \alpha_{r+2} \oplus \alpha_{r+3} \oplus CK_{r+4}).$$

Considering that the round key rk_r is 32-bit, we can search up to 2^{32} times to recover the unique round key rk_r, which leads to a complexity of $O(2^{32})$. Once the round key rk_r is recovered, the vector values of all-round keys and all affine mappings in the implementation can be accessed with complexity $O(1)$. So far, we have recovered the P_k and p_k $(0 \leq k \leq 35)$, so we easily recover the external input and output encodings.

Therefore, we can recover the user key and external encodings. The cost is dominated by exploring all the possibilities of the round key rk_r, which has a time complexity of $O(2^{32})$.

Note that the last key-recovery phase can be summarised as follows. Under the generalised Feistel structure, one branch (i.e. $\tilde{X}_{r+3}$) entering a round function also enters the next round function and the white-box protection form (i.e. P_{r+3}^{-1}) of this branch (i.e. $\tilde{X}_{r+3}$) remains unchanged within the two rounds, so that we can use the recovered white-box operations to get $e_r \oplus e_{r+1}$ and the XOR value of the two round keys, and thus by considering subsequent rounds we can get the XOR value of any two consecutive round keys and use a round key to represent any other round key, forming an expression with only a given round key by SM4's round key expansion formula.

We implemented the attack in `C++` on a desktop computer with a single core (`Intel Core i7-7700 CPU @ 3.60GHz`), and it recovered the 128-bit user key and the external input and output encodings in less than two minutes.

5 Key-Recovery Attack on Bai and Wu's White-Box SM4 Implementation

In this section, we apply our attack framework to recover the original user key of Bai and Wu's white-box SM4 implementation for the first time.

5.1 Bai and Wu's White-Box SM4 Implementation

Bai and Wu.'s implementation [2] uses only affine encodings, and consists of two types of lookup tables, namely 8-bit to 32-bit **TD** tables and 16-bit to 32-bit **TR**

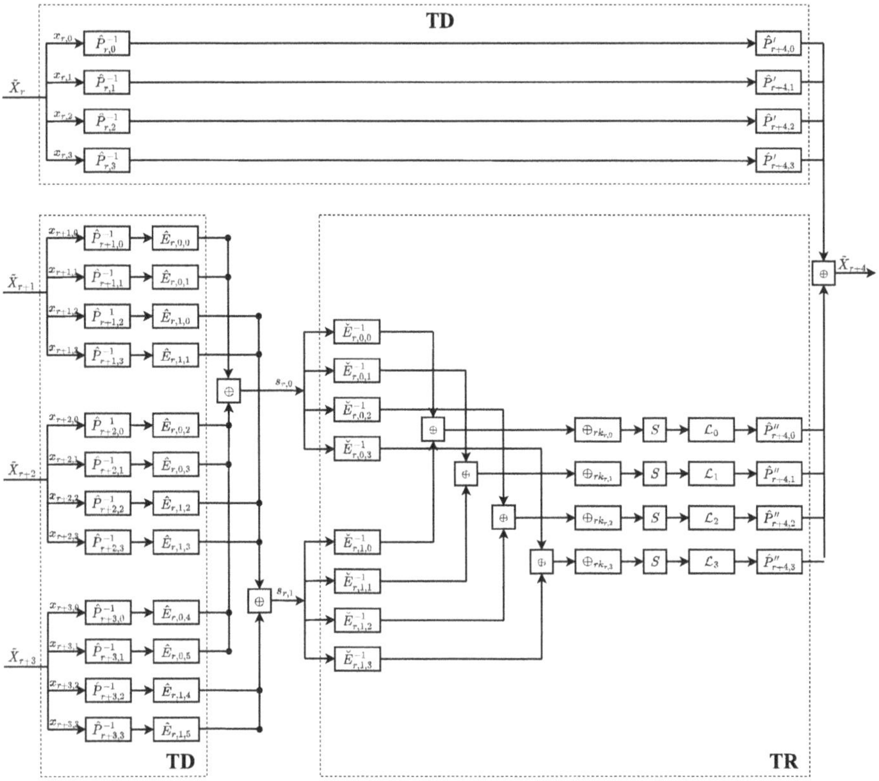

Fig. 5. An encryption round of Bai and Wu's white-box SM4 implementation

tables, plus 32-bit XOR operations. As depicted in Fig. 5, each round involves 16 **TD** tables, 4 **TR** tables and a few XOR operations.

First, a layer of sixteen 8-bit to 32-bit $\mathbf{TD}_{r,i,j}$ tables $(0 \le r \le 31, 0 \le i, j \le 3)$, defined as

$$\mathbf{TD}_{r,i,j}(\cdot) = \begin{cases} \hat{P}'_{r+4,j} \circ \hat{P}^{-1}_{r+i,j}(\cdot), i = 0; \\ \hat{E}_{r,\lfloor j/2 \rfloor,l} \circ \hat{P}^{-1}_{r+i,j}(\cdot), i = 1, 2, 3; \end{cases}$$

where

- $\hat{P}^{-1}_{r+i,j}(\cdot) = P^{-1}_{r+i,j}(\cdot) \oplus P^{-1}_{r+i,j} \cdot p_{r+i,j}$, $P^{-1}_{r+i,j}$ is the j-th 32×8-bit strip of the inverse $P^{-1}_{r+i} = (P^{-1}_{r+i,0}, P^{-1}_{r+i,1}, P^{-1}_{r+i,2}, P^{-1}_{r+i,3})$ of the linear part P_{r+i} of the 32-bit affine encoding $\hat{P}_{r+i}(\cdot) = P_{r+i}(\cdot) \oplus p_{r+i}$ on branch $\tilde{X}_{r+i}$, $p_{r+i,j}$ is a 32-bit vector, and $\oplus_{j=0}^{3} p_{r+i,j} = p_{r+i}$.
- $\hat{P}'_{r+4,j}(\cdot) = P_{r+4}(\cdot) \oplus p'_{r+4,j}$ is a 32-bit affine encoding, $p'_{r+4,j}$ is a 32-bit vector, and $\oplus_{j=0}^{3} p'_{r+4,j} = p'_{r+4}$. Note that $\hat{P}'_{r+4}(\cdot) = P_{r+4}(\cdot) \oplus p'_{r+4}$ is the 32-bit affine encoding to protect the original value of branch $\tilde{X}_r$.

- $\hat{E}_{r,\lfloor j/2 \rfloor,l}(\cdot) = E_{r,\lfloor j/2 \rfloor}(\cdot) \oplus e_{r,\lfloor j/2 \rfloor,l}$ is a 32-bit affine encoding ($l = 2 \times (i-1) + (j \bmod 2)$, $E_{r,\lfloor j/2 \rfloor} = diag(E_{r,\lfloor j/2 \rfloor,0}, E_{r,\lfloor j/2 \rfloor,1}, E_{r,\lfloor j/2 \rfloor,2}, E_{r,\lfloor j/2 \rfloor,3})$ is a 32-bit diagonal matrix with $E_{r,\lfloor j/2 \rfloor,t}$ being an invertible 8×8-bit matrix ($t = 0, 1, 2, 3$), and $e_{r,\lfloor j/2 \rfloor,l}$ is a 32-bit vector, and $\oplus_{l=0}^{5} e_{r,\lfloor j/2 \rfloor,l} = e_{r,\lfloor j/2 \rfloor}$.

Then, a layer of 32-bit XOR operations on twelve **TD** tables, each of which involves six **TD** outputs, producing two 32-bit values $s_{r,0}$ and $s_{r,1}$. Let $\tilde{X}_{r+i} = (x_{r+i,0}, x_{r+i,1}, x_{r+i,2}, x_{r+i,3})$, where $x_{r+i,j}$ represents a byte variable ($0 \le j \le 3$), as follow:

$$s_{r,0} = \oplus_{i=1}^{3} \left(\mathbf{TD}_{r,i,0}(x_{r+i,0}) \oplus \mathbf{TD}_{r,i,1}(x_{r+i,1}) \right),$$
$$s_{r,1} = \oplus_{i=1}^{3} \left(\mathbf{TD}_{r,i,2}(x_{r+i,2}) \oplus \mathbf{TD}_{r,i,3}(x_{r+i,3}) \right).$$

Next, a layer of four 16-bit to 32-bit $\mathbf{TR}_{r,j}$ tables ($0 \le r \le 31, 0 \le j \le 3$). Each $\mathbf{TR}_{r,j}$ is used to perform the transformation $\mathcal{T}$ partially, defined as

$$\mathbf{TR}_{r,j}(\cdot) = \hat{P}''_{r+4,j} \circ \mathcal{L}_j \circ S \circ \oplus_{rk_{r,j}} \circ \left(\breve{E}_{r,0,j}^{-1}(\cdot) \oplus \breve{E}_{r,1,j}^{-1}(\cdot) \right),$$

where $\breve{E}_{r,h,j}^{-1}(\cdot) = E_{r,h,j}^{-1}(\cdot) \oplus E_{r,h,j}^{-1} \cdot \hat{e}_{r,h,j}$ is an 8-bit affine mapping ($h = 0, 1$), $(\hat{e}_{r,h,0}, \hat{e}_{r,h,1}, \hat{e}_{r,h,2}, \hat{e}_{r,h,3}) = e_{r,h}$ is a 32-bit vector, and $\hat{P}''_{r+4,j}(\cdot) = P_{r+4}(\cdot) \oplus p''_{r+4,j}$ is a 32-bit affine encoding, with $p''_{r+4,j}$ being a 32-bit vector such that $\oplus_{j=0}^{3} p''_{r+4,j} = p''_{r+4}$. In addition, $\oplus_{j=0}^{3}(p'_{r+4,j} \oplus p''_{r+4,j}) = p_{r+4}$ is the constant part of the 32-bit affine encoding $\hat{P}_{r+4}(\cdot) = P_{r+4}(\cdot) \oplus p_{r+4}$ on branch $\tilde{X}_{r+4}$.

At last, a layer of 32-bit XOR operations on 4 **TD** tables and 4 **TR** tables to produce the 32-bit output $\tilde{X}_{r+4}$ of the r-th round, define $s_{r,h} = (s_{r,h,0}, s_{r,h,1}, s_{r,h,2}, s_{r,h,3})$ as follow:

$$\tilde{X}_{r+4} = \left(\oplus_{j=0}^{3} \mathbf{TR}_{r,j}(s_{r,0,j}, s_{r,1,j}) \right) \oplus \left(\oplus_{j=0}^{3} \mathbf{TD}_{r,0,j}(x_{r,j}) \right).$$

Exteral encodings. The external encodings of Bai and Wu's implementation are similar to the external encodings in Xiao and Lai's implementation.

5.2 Attacking Bai and Wu's White-Box SM4 Implementation

In this subsection, we apply our attack framework to Bai and Wu's white-box SM4 implementation. Unlike Xiao and Lai's implementation, Bai and Wu's implementation has a complex internal encoding for the entire encryption process. To fully break the implementation, we initially preprocess the lookup tables and subsequently recover the unique round key and external encodings based on specific encoding structures with a complexity of $O(2^{34})$.

An Equivalent Representation of Lookup Tables. Finding the input encoding can easily be done if this encoding can be represented as a block diagonal affine mapping where each block is 8-bit. Knowing that the two byte variables

$(s_{r,0,j}, s_{r,1,j})$ $(0 \le j \le 3)$ are the inputs to each $\mathbf{TR}_{r,j}$, let consider the functions $\mathbf{TR}_{r,j}(\alpha, 0)$ and $\mathbf{TR}_{r,j}(0, \beta)$ with $\alpha, \beta \in GF(2)^8$. Then we have:

$$\mathbf{TR}_{r,j}(\alpha, 0) = \hat{P}''_{r+4,j} \circ \mathcal{L}_j \circ S\left(E^{-1}_{r,0,j}(\alpha) \oplus E^{-1}_{r,0,j} \cdot \hat{e}_{r,0,j} \oplus E^{-1}_{r,1,j} \cdot \hat{e}_{r,1,j} \oplus rk_{r,j}\right),$$
$$\mathbf{TR}_{r,j}(0, \beta) = \hat{P}''_{r+4,j} \circ \mathcal{L}_j \circ S\left(E^{-1}_{r,1,j}(\beta) \oplus E^{-1}_{r,0,j} \cdot \hat{e}_{r,0,j} \oplus E^{-1}_{r,1,j} \cdot \hat{e}_{r,1,j} \oplus rk_{r,j}\right).$$

We define $\mathcal{V}_{r,h,j}(\cdot) = E^{-1}_{r,h,j}(\cdot) \oplus (E^{-1}_{r,0,j} \cdot \hat{e}_{r,0,j} \oplus E^{-1}_{r,1,j} \cdot \hat{e}_{r,1,j} \oplus rk_{r,j})$ $(h = 0, 1)$, which is an 8-bit affine mapping, and define $\mathcal{U}_{r,j}(\cdot) = \hat{P}''_{r+4,j} \circ \mathcal{L}_j(\cdot)$ which is an 32-bit affine mapping. Then the above functions can also be represented as eight 8-bit to 32-bit lookup tables $F_{r,h,j}$:

$$F_{r,h,j} = \mathcal{U}_{r,j} \circ S \circ \mathcal{V}_{r,h,j},$$
$$F_{r,h} = \oplus_{j=0}^{3}(\mathcal{U}_{r,j} \circ S \circ \mathcal{V}_{r,h,j}) = \mathcal{U}_r \circ (S, \cdots, S) \circ \mathcal{V}_{r,h}.$$

For the sake of clarity, we drop all the subscripts representing the round number r subsequently. Since E_h is a diagonal matrix, we can easily define $\breve{E}_h^{-1} = diag(\breve{E}^{-1}_{h,0}, \breve{E}^{-1}_{h,1}, \breve{E}^{-1}_{h,2}, \breve{E}^{-1}_{h,3})$. Then we have $\mathcal{V}_h = diag(\mathcal{V}_{h,0}, \mathcal{V}_{h,1}, \mathcal{V}_{h,2}, \mathcal{V}_{h,3})$ as a diagonal block affine mapping where each block is 8-bit. We want to find an equivalent representation of $\mathcal{U}'$ and $\mathcal{V}'_h$ such that $F_h = \mathcal{U}' \circ (S, \cdots, S) \circ \mathcal{V}'_h$.

Computing $\mathcal{V}'_h$. We aim to recover the eight $\mathcal{V}'_{h,j}$ $(0 \le h \le 1, 0 \le j \le 3)$ affine mappings. Let $y_i \in GF(2)^8$, consider the functions $\oplus_{j=0}^{3} F_{h,j}(0, \cdots, 0, y_i, 0, \cdots, 0)$ with different h. Since $\mathcal{V}_h$ is block diagonal with 8-bit blocks, only one S will be active. By a similar process, we can find 2040 candidates for each block $\mathcal{V}'_{h,j}$, and exploring all the blocks will lead to a complexity of $O(2 \cdot 4 \cdot (8^3 \cdot 2^{2\times 8})) = O(2^{28})$.

Recovering of $\mathcal{U}'$. Once we have determined $\mathcal{V}'_{h,j}$, U'_j can be easily recovered. Recall the function $F_h = \mathcal{U} \circ (S, \cdots, S) \circ \mathcal{V}_h$, and notice that $\mathcal{U}$ is the same in F_0 and F_1, so we need only $\mathcal{V}'_0$ or $\mathcal{V}'_1$ to find the corresponding $\mathcal{U}'$. By using a similar method as in Sect. 4, we can calculate the corresponding $\mathcal{U}'$ for any $\mathcal{V}'_h$. Now we have a computationally easy function $F_h = \mathcal{U}' \circ (S, \cdots, S) \circ \mathcal{V}'_h$.

Identifying the Correct Encodings. Using the above method 32 times, we have the affine mappings $\mathcal{U}'_r$ and $\mathcal{V}'_{r,h}$ such that $F_{r,h} = \mathcal{U}'_r \circ (S, \cdots, S) \circ \mathcal{V}'_{r,h}$. We can exactly recover $\mathcal{U}_r$ and $\mathcal{V}_{r,h}$ by exploiting two consecutive rounds, Algorithm 3 and Fig. 6 give this process.

Let Z_r denote the 32-bit variable immediately after the $\mathcal{L}$ operation under the 16-bit input $(s_{r,0,j}, s_{r,1,j})$ $(0 \le j \le 3)$, if $\tilde{X}_r = 0$, then we have

$$\begin{aligned}\tilde{X}_{r+4} &= (\oplus_{j=0}^{3}\mathbf{TD}_{r,0,j}(0)) \oplus (\oplus_{j=0}^{3}\mathbf{TR}_{r,j}(s_{r,0,j}, s_{r,1,j}))\\ &= (\hat{P}'_{r+4} \circ \hat{P}_r^{-1}(0)) \oplus (\hat{P}''_{r+4}(Z_r)) = P_{r+4} \cdot Z_r \oplus P_{r+4} \cdot P_r^{-1} \cdot p_r \oplus p_{r+4}.\end{aligned}$$

Note that $\tilde{X}_{r+4}$ is affected not only by the variable Z_r but also by the fixed vector $P_r^{-1} \cdot p_r \oplus p_{r+4}$. Since each affine encoding $\breve{E}^{-1}_{r+1,h}$ $(h = 0, 1)$ is associated with three different inputs $\tilde{X}_{r+2}, \tilde{X}_{r+3}$ and $\tilde{X}_{r+4}$, each $\mathbf{TD}_{r,i,j}(1 \le i \le 3)$ is affected by the unknown vector $e_{r,h,l}(0 \le l \le 5)$ before an XOR operation.

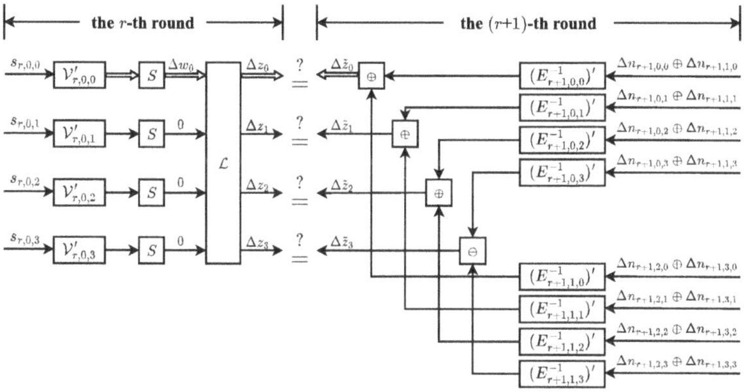

Fig. 6. Identifying correct affine encodings in Bai and Wu's implementation

---

Algorithm 3. Identifying the encodings in Bai and Wu's implementation

---

$s^0_{r,0,0}, \cdots, s^m_{r,0,0} \leftarrow (m+1)$ different values;
$s^0_{r,0,q}, \cdots, s^m_{r,0,q} (q = 1, 2, 3) \leftarrow 0$;
$s^0_{r,1,q}, \cdots, s^m_{r,1,q} (q = 0, 1, 2, 3) \leftarrow 0$;
for each candidate $\mathcal{V}'_{r,0,0}$ for $\mathcal{V}_{r,0,0}$ **do**
    $\Delta w^i_0 \leftarrow S(\mathcal{V}'_{r,0,0}(s^0_{r,0,0})) \oplus S(\mathcal{V}'_{r,0,0}(s^i_{r,0,0}))$;
    $(\Delta z^i_0, \Delta z^i_1, \Delta z^i_2, \Delta z^i_3) \leftarrow \mathcal{L} \cdot (\Delta w^i_0, 0, 0, 0)$;
    Store $\mathcal{V}'_{r,0,0}$ in a hash table $\mathcal{T}_z$ indexed by $(\Delta z^1_0, \cdots, \Delta z^m_0)$;
end for
$\tilde{X}^i_{r+4} \leftarrow \mathbf{TR}_{r,0}(s^i_{r,0,0}, s^i_{r,1,0}) \oplus (\oplus^3_{j=1} \mathbf{TR}_{r,j}(s^i_{r,0,j}, s^i_{r,1,j})) \oplus (\oplus^3_{j=0} \mathbf{TD}_{r,0,j}(0))$;
for $j = 0, ..., 3$ **do**
    $n^i_{r+1,j} \leftarrow \mathbf{TD}_{r+1,3,j}(\tilde{X}^i_{r+4,j})$;
    $\Delta n^i_{r+1,j} \leftarrow n^0_{r+1,j} \oplus n^i_{r+1,j}$;
    $\triangleright\ \Delta n^i_{r+1,j} = (\Delta n^i_{r+1,j,0}, \Delta n^i_{r+1,j,1}, \Delta n^i_{r+1,j,2}, \Delta n^i_{r+1,j,3})$
end for
OUT:
for each candidate $(\mathcal{V}_{r+1,0,0})'$ for $\mathcal{V}_{r+1,0,0}$ **do**
    for each candidate $(\mathcal{V}_{r+1,1,0})'$ for $\mathcal{V}_{r+1,1,0}$ **do**
        $\Delta \tilde{z}^i_0 \leftarrow (E^{-1}_{r+1,0,0})' \cdot (\Delta n^i_{r+1,0,0} \oplus \Delta n^i_{r+1,1,0}) \oplus (E^{-1}_{r+1,1,0})' \cdot (\Delta n^i_{r+1,2,0} \oplus \Delta n^i_{r+1,3,0})$;
        if $(\Delta \tilde{z}^1_0, \cdots, \Delta \tilde{z}^m_0) \in \mathcal{T}_z$ **then**
            We have the correct $\mathcal{V}_{r,0,0}$,$\mathcal{V}_{r+1,0,0}$ and $\mathcal{V}_{r+1,1,0}$ under $\mathcal{T}_z[\Delta \tilde{z}^1_0, \cdots, \Delta \tilde{z}^m_0]$;
            break OUT;
        end if

```
    end for
end for
for each candidate (V_{r+1,0,j})' for V_{r+1,0,j} (j = 1,2,3) do
    for each candidate (V_{r+1,1,j})' for V_{r+1,1,j} (j = 1,2,3) do
        if Δz_j^i = (E^{-1}_{r+1,0,j})'·(Δn^i_{r+1,0,j} ⊕ Δn^i_{r+1,1,j}) ⊕ (E^{-1}_{r+1,1,j})'·(Δn^i_{r+1,2,j} ⊕ Δn^i_{r+1,3,j}) then
            We have the correct V_{r+1,0,j} and V_{r+1,1,j};
        end if
    end for
end for
s^0_{r,1,0}, s^1_{r,1,0} ← messages with byte s^i_{r,1,0} taking 2 different values;
s^0_{r,1,q}, s^1_{r,1,q} (q = 1,2,3) ← 0;
s^0_{r,0,q}, s^1_{r,0,q} (q = 0,1,2,3) ← 0;
for each candidate V'_{r,1,0} for V_{r,1,0} do
    Δt^1_0 ← S(V'_{r,1,0}(s^0_{r,1,0})) ⊕ S(V'_{r,1,0}(s^1_{r,1,0}));
    (Δu^1_0, Δu^1_1, Δu^1_2, Δu^1_3) ← L · (Δt^1_0, 0, 0, 0);
    X̃^i_{r+4} ← TR_{r,0}(s^i_{r,0,0}, s^i_{r,1,0}) ⊕ (⊕^3_{j=1} TR_{r,j}(s^i_{r,0,j}, s^i_{r,1,j})) ⊕ (⊕^3_{j=0} TD_{r,0,j}(0))
    n^i_{r+1,j} ← TD_{r+1,3,j}(X̃^i_{r+4,j});
    Δn^1_{r+1,j} ← n^0_{r+1,j} ⊕ n^1_{r+1,j};
    Δũ^1_0 ← E^{-1}_{r+1,0,0} · (Δn^1_{r+1,0,0} ⊕ Δn^1_{r+1,1,0}) ⊕ E^{-1}_{r+1,1,0} · (Δn^1_{r+1,2,0} ⊕ Δn^1_{r+1,3,0});
    if Δũ^1_0 = Δu^1_0 then
        We have the correct V_{r,1,0};
        break;
    end if
end for
Once we have all the correct V_{r+1,0,j} and V_{r+1,1,j} (j = 0,1,2,3), we can use the same method to identify the correct remaining V_{r,0,l} and V_{r,1,l} with 1 ≤ l ≤ 3.
```

To remove the effect of the fixed vector, we construct the input difference $\Delta x_{r+4,j}$ for each of the four tables $\mathbf{TD}_{r+1,3,j}$ in the $(r+1)$-th round, then:

$$\begin{cases} \Delta\mathbf{TD}_{r+1,3,j} = E_{r+1,0} \cdot P^{-1}_{r+4,j}(\Delta x_{r+4,j}), j = 0, 1; \\ \Delta\mathbf{TD}_{r+1,3,j} = E_{r+1,1} \cdot P^{-1}_{r+4,j}(\Delta x_{r+4,j}), j = 2, 3. \end{cases}$$

Similarly, we also use a differential meet-in-the-middle approach to recover the correct affine encodings $\mathcal{V}_{r,h,j}$ and $\mathcal{V}_{r+1,h,j}$.

The S-box carrying the round key information in the $\mathbf{TR}$ table that generates $\tilde{X}_{r+4}$ receives inputs that are derived from two 8-bit different branches of an XOR operation, which will lead to the $(r+1)$-th round of the $\mathbf{TD}$ table involving

$\tilde{X}_{r+4}$ associating two different affine matrices $E_{r+1,0}$ and $E_{r+1,1}$. As a result, it takes about a time complexity of 2^{22} to build and match the hash table for each block, and then roughly a time complexity of $O(8 \cdot 2040^2) \approx O(2^{25})$ to recover all $\mathcal{V}_{r,h,j}$ and $\mathcal{V}_{r+1,h,j}$.

Recovering the User Key. We have recovered affine encodings $\mathcal{V}_{r,h,j}$ and $\mathcal{V}_{r+1,h,j}$, since $\mathcal{V}_{r,h}$ is a block diagonal affine mapping, we can get four 32×32-bit matrices $E_{r,0}$, $E_{r,1}$, $E_{r+1,0}$ and $E_{r+1,1}$, and two 32-bit vectors $v_r = E_{r,0}^{-1} \cdot e_{r,0} \oplus E_{r,1}^{-1} \cdot e_{r,1} \oplus rk_r$ and $v_{r+1} = E_{r+1,0}^{-1} \cdot e_{r+1,0} \oplus E_{r+1,1}^{-1} \cdot e_{r+1,1} \oplus rk_{r+1}$. In addition, we can get P_{i+4} and p''_{i+4} from the recovered $\mathcal{U}_r$.

We set the inputs of all **TD**'s of the r-th and $(r+1)$-th rounds to zero, and perform the corresponding XOR operations according to a specific structure of encodings, then we can get two pairs of values $(s'_{r,0}, s'_{r,1})$ and $(s'_{r+1,0}, s'_{r+1,1})$, and a fixed vector value $\alpha = P_{r+4} \cdot P_r^{-1} \cdot p_r \oplus p'_{r+4}$. By the above known information, we can compute:

$$P_{r+4}^{-1} \cdot (\alpha \oplus p''_{r+4}) = P_r^{-1} \cdot p_r \oplus P_{r+4}^{-1} \cdot p_{r+4} = \beta,$$

$$E_{r,0}^{-1} \cdot s'_{r,0} \oplus E_{r,1}^{-1} \cdot s'_{r,1} \oplus v_r = P_{r+1}^{-1} \cdot p_{r+1} \oplus P_{r+2}^{-1} \cdot p_{r+2} \oplus P_{r+3}^{-1} \cdot p_{r+3} \oplus rk_r = t_r,$$

$$E_{r+1,0}^{-1} \cdot s'_{r+1,0} \oplus E_{r+1,1}^{-1} \cdot s'_{r+1,1} \oplus v_{r+1} = P_{r+2}^{-1} \cdot p_{r+2} \oplus P_{r+3}^{-1} \cdot p_{r+3} \oplus$$
$$P_{r+4}^{-1} \cdot p_{r+4} \oplus rk_{r+1} = t_{r+1},$$

$$t_r \oplus t_{r+1} \oplus \beta = P_r^{-1} \cdot p_r \oplus P_{r+1}^{-1} \cdot p_{r+1} \oplus rk_r \oplus rk_{r+1} = \gamma_{r,1}.$$

Repeating all the previous steps of the attack, the value of XOR operations performed between any two rounds of the round keys and the corresponding vectors can be computed:

$$P_r^{-1} \cdot p_r \oplus P_{r+i}^{-1} \cdot p_{r+i} \oplus rk_r \oplus rk_{r+i} = \gamma_{r,i}.$$

where $0 \leq r, i \leq 31$. Unlike in Xiao and Lai's white-box SM4 implementation, the input to the S-box in Bai and Wu's implementation is generated through an XOR operation on two 8-bit variables. Specifically, the function $\breve{E}_{r,0,j}^{-1}(s_{r,0}) \oplus \breve{E}_{r,1,j}^{-1}(s_{r,1})$ is a surjection. Below we use the key expansion algorithm of SM4 three times to recover the correct round key.

In Eq. (1) for generating rk_{r+4}, we use different fixed vectors to replace the round keys except rk_r:

$$\gamma_{r,4} \oplus \beta = \widehat{T}(P_r^{-1} \cdot p_r \oplus \gamma_{r,1} \oplus \gamma_{r,2} \oplus \gamma_{r,3} \oplus t_r \oplus CK_{r+4}).$$

Considering that $P_r^{-1} \cdot p_r$ is a 32-bit vector, so search up to 2^{32} times to recover $P_r^{-1} \cdot p_r$. We can compute the values of $P_{r+1}^{-1} \cdot p_{r+1}$ and $P_{r+2}^{-1} \cdot p_{r+2}$ by using a similar method. Since $t_{r-1} = P_r^{-1} \cdot p_r \oplus P_{r+1}^{-1} \cdot p_{r+1} \oplus P_{r+2}^{-1} \cdot p_{r+2} \oplus rk_{r-1}$ can be easily obtained, we can recover the unique correct round key rk_{r-1}. Although we have recovered the correct round key rk_{r-1}, the implementation cannot be completely broken based on current information. Specifically, there is no way to recover the external encoding at this point. To solve this problem, we need to search again up to 2^{32} times to get the value of $P_{r-1}^{-1} \cdot p_{r-1}$. After that, all round keys and unknown affine vectors in this implementation can be computed with complexity $O(1)$, and external encodings can be recovered as well.

Therefore, we can recover all round keys and external encodings, and the attack's time complexity is dominated by searching the space of 32-bit values four times, which is $O(4 \cdot 2^{32}) = O(2^{34})$.

We implemented the attack in `C++` on the desktop computer (a single core `Intel Core i7-7700 CPU @ 3.60 GHz`), and it recovered the 128-bit user key and the external input and output encodings in less than ten minutes.

6 Key-Recovery Attack on Shi et al.'s White-Box SM4 Implementation

In this section, we apply our attack framework to recover the original user key of Shi et al.'s white-box SM4 implementation with a very practical time complexity.

6.1 Shi et al.'s White-Box SM4 Implementation

The main idea of Shi et al.'s white-box SM4 implementation [20] is to generate confusion matrices using dual ciphers and random numbers to construct lookup tables. As described in [4], SM4 is an $EGF(2)^8$ cipher, and we can construct 9360 8×8 matrices of $GF(2)^8$, generating isomorphisms for each other over $GF(2)^8$. The process for an encryption round is depicted in Fig. 7.

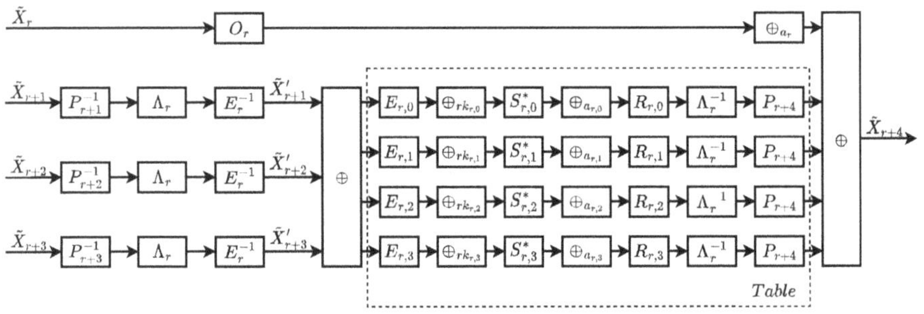

Fig. 7. An encryption round of Shi et al.'s white-box SM4 implementation

Let $M = \{M_0, M_1, \cdots, M_{9359}\}$ be the set of all these 9360 matrices, where M_r is the matrix selected in the r-th round from M. Let $a_{r,j}$ be a random element in $GF(2)^8$, where $0 \leq r \leq 31, 0 \leq j \leq 3$. The definition of linear encodings P_r and E_r is identical to Xiao and Lai's implementation. Define the linear transformation $Q_{r+j} : GF(2)^{32} \rightarrow GF(2)^{32}$ as $\tilde{X}'_{r+j} = Q_{r+j}(\tilde{X}_{r+j}) = E_r^{-1} \circ \Lambda_r \circ P_{r+j}^{-1}(\tilde{X}_{r+j})$, where $1 \leq j \leq 3$ and $\Lambda_r = (M_r||M_r||M_r||M_r)$ denotes four M_r operations in parallel. Then, define the substitution transformation S_r^* :

$GF(2)^8 \to GF(2)^8$ as $S_r^*(x) = M_r \circ S \circ M_r^{-1}(x)$. Let $y_{r,j} \in GF(2)^8 (0 \le j \le 3)$, the function $Table_{r,j} : GF(2)^8 \to GF(2)^{32}$ is defined to be

$$Table_{r,j}(y_{r,j}) = P_{r+4} \circ \Lambda_r^{-1} \circ R_{r,j} \circ \oplus_{a_{r,j}} \circ S_r^* \circ \oplus_{K_{r,j}} \circ E_{r,j}(y_{r,j}),$$

where $R_{r,j}(y_{r,j}) = \Lambda_r \circ \mathcal{L}_j \circ M_r^{-1}(x)$, and $K_{r,j} = M_r(rk_{r,j})$ is defined as a new round key, with $rk_{r,j}$ being the j-th byte of the r-th round key of SM4. In addition, a constant a_r and a linear transformation $O_r : GF(2)^{32} \to GF(2)^{32}$ are defined as:

$$a_r = \oplus_{j=0}^3 (P_{r+4} \circ \Lambda_r^{-1} \circ R_{r,j}(a_{r,j})), \quad O_r(\cdot) = P_{r+4} \circ P_r^{-1}(\cdot).$$

The round function $\mathcal{R}_r : (GF(2)^{32})^4 \to GF(2)^{32}$ of Shi et al.'s implementation can be described by using these definitions and transformations:

$$\begin{aligned}\mathcal{R}_r(\tilde{X}_r, \tilde{X}_{r+1}, \tilde{X}_{r+2}, \tilde{X}_{r+3}) = \; & a_r \oplus O_r(\tilde{X}_r) \oplus \\ & \left(\oplus_{j=0}^3 Table_{r,j}\left(I_j\left(\oplus_{n=1}^3 Q_{r+n}(\tilde{X}_{r+n})\right)\right)\right),\end{aligned}$$

where I_j is the j-th 32×8 strip of a 32×32-bit unit matrix.

By simplifying the above equation, we can easily represent $Table_{r,j}$ as

$$Table_{r,j}(y_{r,j}) = (P_{r+4} \circ \mathcal{L}_j \circ S \circ \oplus_{rk_{r,j}} \circ M_r^{-1} \circ E_{r,j}(x)) \oplus (P_{r+4} \circ \mathcal{L}_j \circ M_r^{-1}(a_{r,j})).$$

Let $F_r = \oplus_{j=0}^3 Table_{r,j}$, then F_r can be represented as $F_r = \mathcal{U}_r \circ (S, \cdots, S) \circ \mathcal{V}_r$, where $\mathcal{V}_r$ and $\mathcal{U}_r$ are 32-bit affine mappings. Let $\theta_{r,j} = M_r^{-1} \cdot E_{r,j}$, then we have $\mathcal{V}_r(\cdot) = V_r(\cdot) \oplus v_r = \theta_r(\cdot) \oplus rk_r$, where $\theta_r = diag(\theta_{r,0}, \theta_{r,1}, \theta_{r,2}, \theta_{r,3})$ is an invertible diagonal matrix. Defining $g_{r,j} = P_{r+4} \circ \mathcal{L}_j \circ M_r^{-1}(a_{r,j})$, it becomes evident that $a_r = \oplus_{j=0}^3 g_{r,j}$, and we express $\mathcal{U}_r(\cdot) = U_r(\cdot) \oplus u_r = P_{r+4} \cdot \mathcal{L}(\cdot) \oplus a_r$.

Exteral Encodings. Let $P_l = \mathcal{Z}_l^{in}$ as external input encoding and $P_{31+l} = \mathcal{Z}_l^{out}$ as external output encoding for $l = 0, 1, 2, 3$. Note that the external encodings of this implementation are linear.

6.2 Attacking Shi et al.'s White-Box SM4 Implementation

Since we have already provided an equivalent representation of the lookup tables, the same method can be used to Shi et al.'s implementation to recover 32-bit affine encodings $\mathcal{V}_r$ and $\mathcal{U}_r$. Note that no further action is required after recovering the affine encoding $\mathcal{V}_r$ since the vector part of $\mathcal{V}_r$ is the key rk_r. At this point, we can recover external encodings with complexity $O(1)$ since the encodings in the implementation are linear.

As a result, we can recover the correct round key and external encodings, and the attack's time complexity is dominated by finding the four affine encodings $\mathcal{V}'_{r,j}$ $(j = 0, 1, 2, 3)$, which is about $O(4 \cdot 2^{25}) = O(2^{27})$.

7 Concluding Remarks

In this paper, we have presented an affine equivalence-based attack framework for practically recovering the original user key of the white-box SM4 implementations with affine (or linear) encodings, and have applied this framework to Xiao and Lai's, Bai and Wu's and Shi et al.'s white-box SM4 implementations with a time complexity of 2^{32}, 2^{34} and 2^{27}, respectively. We can similarly attack Yao and Chen's white-box SM4 implementation with a time complexity of 2^{32}, as it can be simplified to Xiao and Lai's implementation. Our work shows how to apply Derbez et al.'s affine equivalence algorithm from SPN ciphers to a generalised Feistel cipher, and suggests that all such white-box SM4 implementations are not practically secure and new white-box SM4 design should be explored even for a semi-practical security level under external encodings, like white-box AES. Designers of white-box implementation of Feistel ciphers should pay attention to this affine equivalence-based attack framework.

References

1. Baek, C.H., Cheon, J.H., Hong, H.: White-box AES implementation revisited. J. Commun. Netw. **18**(3), 273–287 (2016)
2. Bai, K., Wu, C.: A secure white-box SM4 implementation. Secur. Commun. Netw. **9**(10), 996–1006 (2016)
3. Bai, K., Wu, C., Zhang, Z.: Protect white-box AES to resist table composition attacks. IET Inf. Secur. **12**(4), 305–313 (2018)
4. Barkan, E., Biham, E.: In how many ways can You write Rijndael?. In: ASIACRYPT 2002, LNCS, vol. 2501, pp. 160–175. Springer (2002)
5. Billet, O., Gilbert, H., Ech-Chatbi C.: Cryptanalysis of a white box AES implementation. In: SAC 2004, LNCS, vol. 3357, pp. 227–240. Springer (2004)
6. Biryukov, A., Cannière, C.D., Braeken, A., Preneel, B.: A toolbox for cryptanalysis: linear and affine equivalence algorithms. In: EUROCRYPT 2003, LNCS, vol. 2656, pp. 33–50. Springer (2003)
7. Bos, J. W., Hubain, C., Michiels, W., Teuwen, P.: Differential computation analysis: hiding your white-box designs is not enough. In: CHES 2016, LNCS, vol. 9813, pp. 215–236. Springer (2016)
8. Canright D.: A very compact S-box for AES. In: CHES 2005, LNCS, vol. 3659, pp 441–455. Springer (2005)
9. Chow, S., Eisen, P.A., Johnson, H., van Oorschot, P.C.: White-box cryptography and an AES implementation. In: SAC 2002, LNCS, vol. 2595, pp. 250–270. Springer (2002)
10. De Mulder Y., Roelse P., Preneel B.: Cryptanalysis of the Xiao-Lai white-box AES implementation. In: SAC 2012, LNCS, vol. 7707, pp. 34–49. Springer (2013)
11. Derbez, P., Fouque, P., Lambin, B., Minaud, B.: On recovering affine encodings in white-box implementations. IACR Trans. Cryptograph. Hardware Embed. Syst. **2018**(3), 121–149 (2018)
12. Dinur I.: An improved affine equivalence algorithm for random permutations. In: EUROCRYPT 2018, LNCS, vol. 10820, pp. 413–442. Springer (2018)
13. Karroumi, M.: Protecting white-box AES with dual ciphers. In: ICISC 2010, LNCS, vol. 6829, pp. 278–291. Springer (2011)

14. Lepoint, T., Rivain, M., De Mulder, Y., Roelse, P., Preneel, B.: Two attacks on a white-box AES implementation. In: SAC 2013, LNCS, vol. 8282, pp. 265–285. Springer (2013)
15. Lin, T., Yan, H., Lai, X., Zhong, Y., Jia, Y.: Security evaluation and improvement of a white-box SMS4 implementation based on affine equivalence algorithm. Comput. J. **61**(12), 1783–1790 (2018)
16. Lu, J., Li, J., Chen, Z., Li, Y.: Cryptanalysis of a type of white-box implementations of the SM4 block cipher. Comput. J. **67**(5), 1663–1673 (2024)
17. Lu, J., Wang, M., Wang, C., Yang, C.: Collision-based attacks on white-box implementations of the AES block cipher. In: SAC 2022, LNCS, vol. 13742, pp. 328–352. Springer (2024)
18. Luo R., Lai X., You R.: A new attempt of white-box AES implementation. In: SPAC 2014, pp. 423–429. IEEE (2014)
19. Pan, W., Qin, T., Jia, Y., Zhang, W.: Analysis of two white-box implementations of SM4 algorithm. J. Cryptol. Res. **5**(6), 651–671 (2018). (in Chinese with English abstract)
20. Shi, Y., Wei, W., He, Z.: A lightweight white-box symmetric encryption algorithm against node capture for WSNs. Sensors **15**(5), 11928–11952 (2015)
21. Office of State Commercial Cryptography Administration of China: The SMS4 Block Cipher (2006). (in Chinese)
22. Standardization Administration of China: Information Security Technology - SM4 Block Cipher Algorithm (2016)
23. ISO/IEC 18033-3:2010/AMD 1:2021, Information technology – Security techniques – Encryption algorithms – Part 3: Block ciphers – Amendment 1: SM4. International Organization for Standardization, Switzerland
24. Xiao Y., Lai X.: A secure implementation of white-box AES. In: CSA 2009, pp. 1–6. IEEE (2009)
25. Xiao Y., Lai X.: White-box cryptography and an SMS4 implementation. In: the 2009 Annual Conference of the Chinese Association of Cryptologic Research, pp. 24–34. (2009). (in Chinese with English abstract)
26. Yao, S., Chen, J.: A new method for white-box implementation of SM4 algorithm. J. Cryptol. Res **7**(3), 358–374 (2020). (in Chinese with English abstract)

Author Index

A. Patra (Ed.): CT-RSA 2025, LNCS 15598, pp. 427–428, 2025.
https://doi.org/10.1007/978-3-031-88661-4

The manufacturer's authorised representative in the EU is Springer Nature Customer Service Centre GmbH, Europaplatz 3, 69115 Heidelberg, Germany. If you have any concerns regarding our products, please contact ProductSafety@springernature.com

Printed and bound by CPI Group (UK) Ltd, Croydon, CR0 4YY
01/10/2026
02225908-0013